THE DATA QUALITY BLUEPRINT

A PRACTICAL AND HOLISTIC APPROACH

A COMPREHENSIVE
STEP BY STEP GUIDE
TO AN EFFECTIVE & LONG
LASTING ENTERPRISE-WIDE
DATA QUALITY SOLUTION

JOHN PARKINSON

The UK Copyright Service

Copyright © 2015-2016 John Parkinson. All rights reserved.
This work is registered with the UK Copyright Service:
Registration No: 284693622
Published by Holifast Limited: A UK Limited Company.
Please contact info@holifast.co.uk
ISBN: 978-0-9935843-0-5

No part of this publication may be reproduced or transmitted in any form or by any means, electronic or mechanical, including photocopying, recording, or any information storage or retrieval system, without permission in writing from the author and/or publisher. Details on how to seek permission and further information about the publisher's permissions policies can be found on the website www.dataqualityblueprint.com.

Knowledge and best practice in the field of data quality is constantly changing. As new information becomes available changes to methodologies may be necessary, and in any case no methodology can be applicable without modification to the organisation in question, as every organisation differs. Practitioners must always rely on their own knowledge and experience in evaluating or using any of the methods described in this publication.

To the fullest extent of the law, neither the publishers, the author, contributors nor editors assume any liability for any injury and/or damage to persons, property or information as a matter of this publication's liability, negligence or otherwise, or from any use or operation of any of the methods, products, instructions, or ideas contained in this publication.

Permissions

A significant amount of time was expended in investigation of permissions necessary for the quotations of speech and text that appear in this book. Unfortunately much guidance available is self-contradictory. As a result, whilst not having any association with Wiley-Blackwell, I have used the permissions guidelines provided to Wiley-Blackwell authors (available online) as a guideline. This document is clear, concise, and unambiguous, and references the Publisher's Association guidelines. Where I have quoted larger portions of text, or images clearly subject to copyright, these permissions are noted below and at the relevant point in the text.

I gratefully acknowledge The Open Group for permission to incorporate figure 5-1 of its copyrighted material from TOGAF Version 9.1 in the chapter on architecture remediation. TOGAF and The Open Group are registered trademarks of The Open Group.

Several quotations from the DAMA Data Management Body of Knowledge (*Data Management Body of Knowledge*, DAMA-BOK, Mosely et Al, Data Management Association, 2010) exist in this book, and all are appropriately attributed. The shorthand of DAMA-BOK is also used as opposed to "DAMA Data Management Body of Knowledge". Note that the DAMA Body of Knowledge states:

"All rights reserved. No part of this book may be reproduced or transmitted in any form or by any means, electronic or mechanical, including photocopying or recording, or by any information storage and retrieval systems, without written permission from DAMA International, except for appropriately attributed quotations."

I also gratefully acknowledge the permission from Technics publications to use material from *Data Modeling Made Simple: A Practical Guide for Business and IT Professionals*.

Dedication

This book is dedicated to all the people who have put up with me writing this book for two years.

There is an especial mention to, and forgiveness begged from, those who asked, in all innocence, "How is the book going?"

You know who you are.

Acknowledgements

One does not complete a book like this entirely by oneself. In this case, I would like to thank the following:

Editor:
Gary Smailes, Bubblecow.

Exterior Design:
Bex White, Senior Creative, Blink Design Studios Limited.

Typesetting and Interior Design:
John Parkinson (author) in collaboration with Darren Southworth, Studio2Design.

Beta readers:
Jenny Bowskill & Rebecca Kent.

Most importantly, I need to thank my long-suffering wife Kirsty who has had me spouting data quality at her for years.

John Parkinson, 2016

The Data Quality Blueprint
A PRACTICAL AND HOLISTIC APPROACH

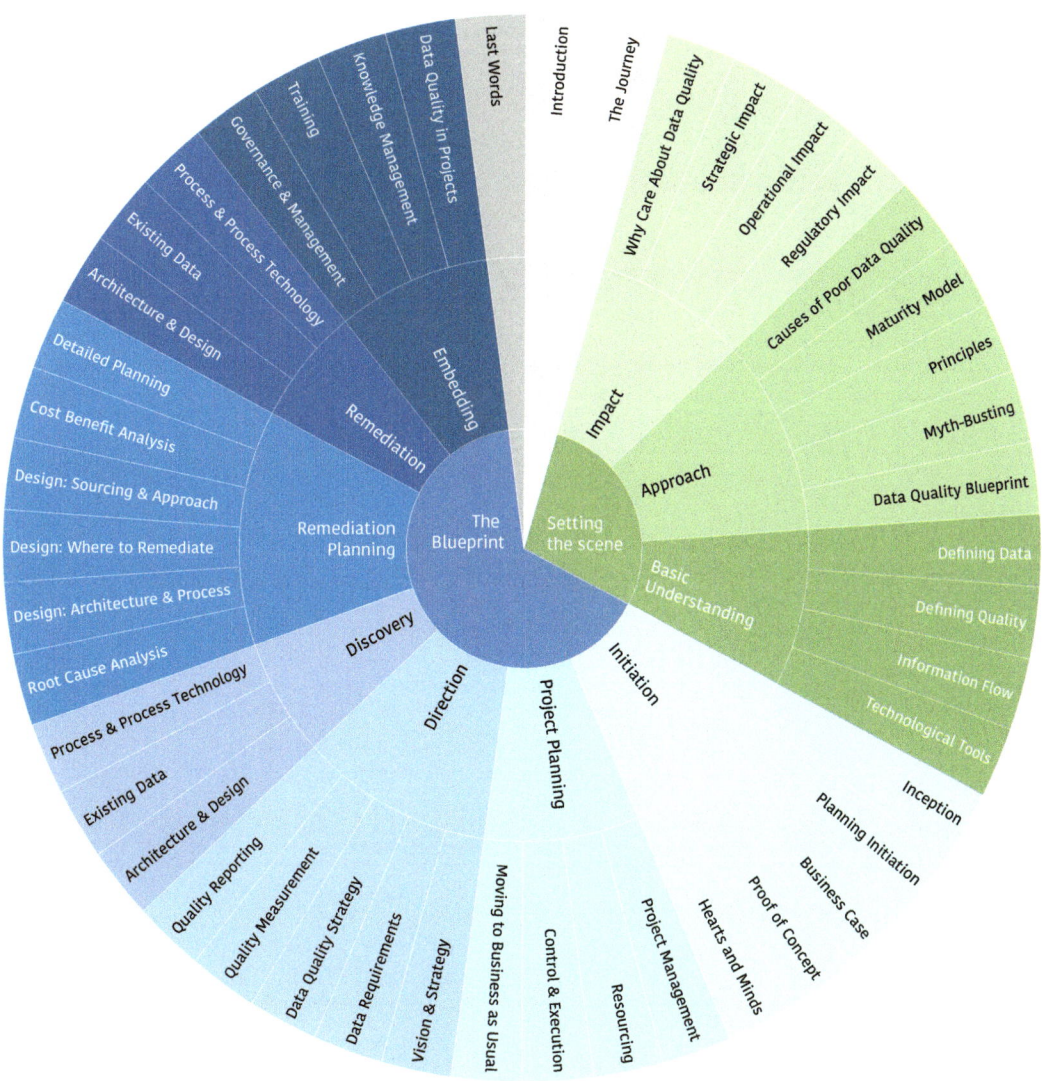

Blueprint:
A design that shows how an objective may be achieved
An original prototype that influences subsequent design or practice
A detailed plan or program of action

About the author

Every day organisations across the globe capture, collate, transform, present and utilise information. Information flows within an organisation from a contact centre through a myriad of information stores towards financial planning and reporting and finally to the executive and potentially a regulator. However, large organisations are typically fragmented, and whilst information specialists exist within islands at each stage, communication failures between these islands are the pain points in information quality today. In many organisations, business and information technology professionals appear incapable of connecting.

Twenty years ago the same applied to architects and civil engineers. One forward-thinking institution ran a "Civil Engineering and Architecture" degree cramming an architecture degree and a civil engineering degree together, with the aim of creating individuals who could talk across both professions. This was my degree. It was a good grounding, as it taught how to reconcile individuals with different agendas and bring both parties together on a journey. In those days the journey was to create a great building. Now my journey is bringing business and IT professionals together to create data quality.

In the last years of the last century the building industry (and the rest of the economy) entered a recession and I changed career to study as an accountant. Three years later a Chartered Accountant started wondering where the information on which my profession relied came from. I then started worrying, wondering, reading, and learning about data.

My company was heavily involved in mergers of building societies, and I spent time working as a consultant scrutineer for the UK regulator. These large data quality engagements involved hundreds of people working to remediate data to meet regulatory expectations and legal requirements. On the way I learnt:

- About project management and how it can be an interesting challenge and a thankless task.
- About data quality and how bad it usually is.
- About data remediation and the problems it faces.
- About data transformation and migration and what are the common problems.
- About data analysis & profiling and how useful it can be.
- About business process, its effect on data, and its transformation and migration and what a difference it can make.
- About data governance (and lack of) and how important that is.
- Many broader skills like stakeholder management.
- A fair bit about technology.

I also worked with many clients across many sectors on data and business process related engagements. This work covered data strategy, data governance and data quality, data and process analysis and design, financial and data modelling as well as finance and risk transformation. Over time I turned into a professional with wide experience and knowledge in the field.

I am still a Chartered Accountant; however over time have also become a PRINCE2 Practitioner, a TOGAF 9.1 Enterprise Architect, and a Certified Information Systems Auditor (CISA). I'm currently using my spare time to work through the MCSE BI (Database Administration) qualifications, ITIL and BPM. I also have first-hand experience of a wide range of technology products across information design, management, discovery and governance.

At the time of writing I hold the position of UK Data Governance lead for a major global consultancy and have also had the honour of being invited to speak at a number of conferences on the subject of data, data governance and data quality. I regularly write articles for publication worldwide.

I am a member of ICAEW (Institute of Chartered Accountants), ISACA (Information Systems and Control Association), AEA (Association of Enterprise Architects), The International Association for Information and Data Quality (IAIDQ), and the Data Management Association (DAMA).

In my spare time I am a keen rock climber and martial artist. I hope you enjoy reading this book as much as I have enjoyed writing it.

John Parkinson, 2016

About the reader

A far more important consideration than any description of the author is their assumptions of the reader. In order to pitch this book at a consistent level, I must make some assumptions about the reader, for if I am going to take a reader on a journey then I need to define a start point. So what have I assumed about you?

I have assumed you have broad brush knowledge of data quality issues resulting from normal, every-day, interaction with the world. This may be because you:

- Run a business or work in a business that is affected by data quality issues.
- Are sick of your name being misspelled on official communication and may have had the kind of argument with a customer services agent that makes you wish organisations valued data quality more than they currently do.
- Are not massively technical, or you are at least open to the idea of approaching data quality from a holistic perspective. If you are business orientated, you are prepared to acquire some technical knowledge if it makes you better able to communicate with technical teams and understand the technical challenges.
- Are intelligent and have a healthy dose of common sense.

In relation to data quality I have assumed that either; you have a data quality problem and want to do something about it; you do not know whether you have a data quality problem but would like to find out; you wish to find out more about data quality and approaches to solve it – whether as a data quality professional, an interested third party or simply because it is a subject area you are interested in – or you have tried a number of times to solve a data quality problem without success.

I have assumed the reader is looking for practical tips and/or a structured approach to a solution. In an attempt to make the book as relevant to as many people as possible, I have started with an overview and then delved further into detail as the book progresses. It follows that some sections of the book are therefore more aimed at the executive (the overview), and other sections at those who are more focused on the detail.

For the executive or business professional

If you are an executive or business manager, it is the first chapters of the book (Chapters 1-15) that are important. These cover why you should care and outline the approach to data quality. If you wish to know more about how to solve a problem within your organisation, for example you may want to know what can be done, how hard it is, and how to best communicate with your managers and IT department, then this book aims to give you what you need.

For the data quality practitioner

You may be a data quality practitioner, or someone who has a role to solve a data quality problem. You may be thinking "this looks like a big job, where do I start?" In this case the whole book is for you.

For the IT professional

You may be an IT developer, who is trying to understand why data quality is important, and why, possibly, just buying a data quality tool isn't the only solution. If so I hope you'll read the whole book.

For the interested party

Finally, you may just be interested in the subject and would like to learn more.

I have tried to make this book useful to you all. If you already have a good grounding or even detailed knowledge about data quality, then there are large parts of this book that will not be strictly necessary for you to read, and may cover knowledge you already possess. However, hopefully you will not know it all, and will find large sections give new information.

Summary: A Common Sense Approach

I am hoping that any sensible reader working their way through The Data Quality Blueprint will think on a regular basis, "but that's common sense." If so, that is because it is. Nothing in this book is rocket science. It takes a common problem – poor data quality – but a problem that many organisations struggle how to approach, and breaks it down into easily digestible chunks.

If you reach the end of the book and think "but that's all sensible, common sense, and there's nothing difficult or technical about it at all" then I would agree with you. If you reach the end of the book thinking "but that's all sensible, common sense, and there's nothing difficult or technical about it at all – *and I was thinking it would be difficult*" then I have done the job I was trying to do.

Contents

SECTION 1: Overview — 1
1. Introduction — 5
2. The Data Quality Blueprint: The Journey — 13

SECTION 2: The Impact of Poor Data Quality — 25
3. Why Care About Data Quality? — 27
4. Strategic Impact of Poor Data Quality — 33
5. Operational Impact of Poor Data Quality — 45
6. Regulatory Impact of Poor Data Quality — 61

SECTION 3: Approach — 77
7. The Causes of Poor Data Quality — 81
8. Data Quality Maturity Model — 91
9. Principles — 99
10. Myth-busting — 105
11. The Data Quality Blueprint — 115

SECTION 4: Basic Understanding — 123
12. Defining Data — 127
13. Defining Quality — 135
14. How does Information Flow? — 143
15. Technological Tools for Data Quality — 155

SECTION 5: The Data Quality Blueprint — 167
16. Methodology Overview — 169

SECTION 5.1: Initiation — 171
17. Laying the foundations: Inception — 175
18. Planning the Initiation Stage — 181
19. Building the Business Case — 187
20. Creating a Proof of Concept — 203
21. Winning Hearts and Minds — 209

SECTION 5.2: Project Planning — 231
22. Project Management — 233
23. Resourcing — 251
24. Control & Execution — 263
25. Moving on to Business As Usual — 271

SECTION 5.3: Direction — 277

26	Vision and Strategy	281
27	Data Requirements	293
28	Data Quality Strategy	303
29	Quality Measurement	313
30	Quality Reporting	323

SECTION 5.4: Discovery — 331

31	Section Overview	333
32	Discovery: Architecture & Design	335
33	Discovery: Existing Data	347
34	Discovery: Process & Process Technology	359

SECTION 5.5: Remediation Planning — 371

35	Section Overview	375
36	Root Cause Analysis	379
37	Remediation design for Architecture and Process	391
38	Remediation design for data: where to remediate	413
39	Remediation design for data: sourcing and approach.	421
40	Cost Benefit Analysis	435
41	Detailed Planning	443

SECTION 5.6: Remediation — 449

42	Section Overview	451
43	Remediation: Architecture & Design	453
44	Remediation: Existing Data	465
45	Remediation: Process and Process Technology	479

SECTION 5.7: Embedding — 491

46	Section Overview	495
47	Data Governance & Management	497
48	Training	515
49	Knowledge Management	527
50	Data Quality in Projects	541

SECTION 6: Last Words — 549

51	Wrap Up	551

SECTION 7: Appendices — 555

52	Bibliography	559
53	Data Quality Artefacts	561
54	Sample Interview Questions	565

55	Sample Data Strategy	573
56	Sample Data Quality Strategy	579
57	Data Governance Terms of Reference	591
58	Sample Project Plan	595

INDEX — 627

| 59 | INDEX | 627 |

SECTION 1 OVERVIEW

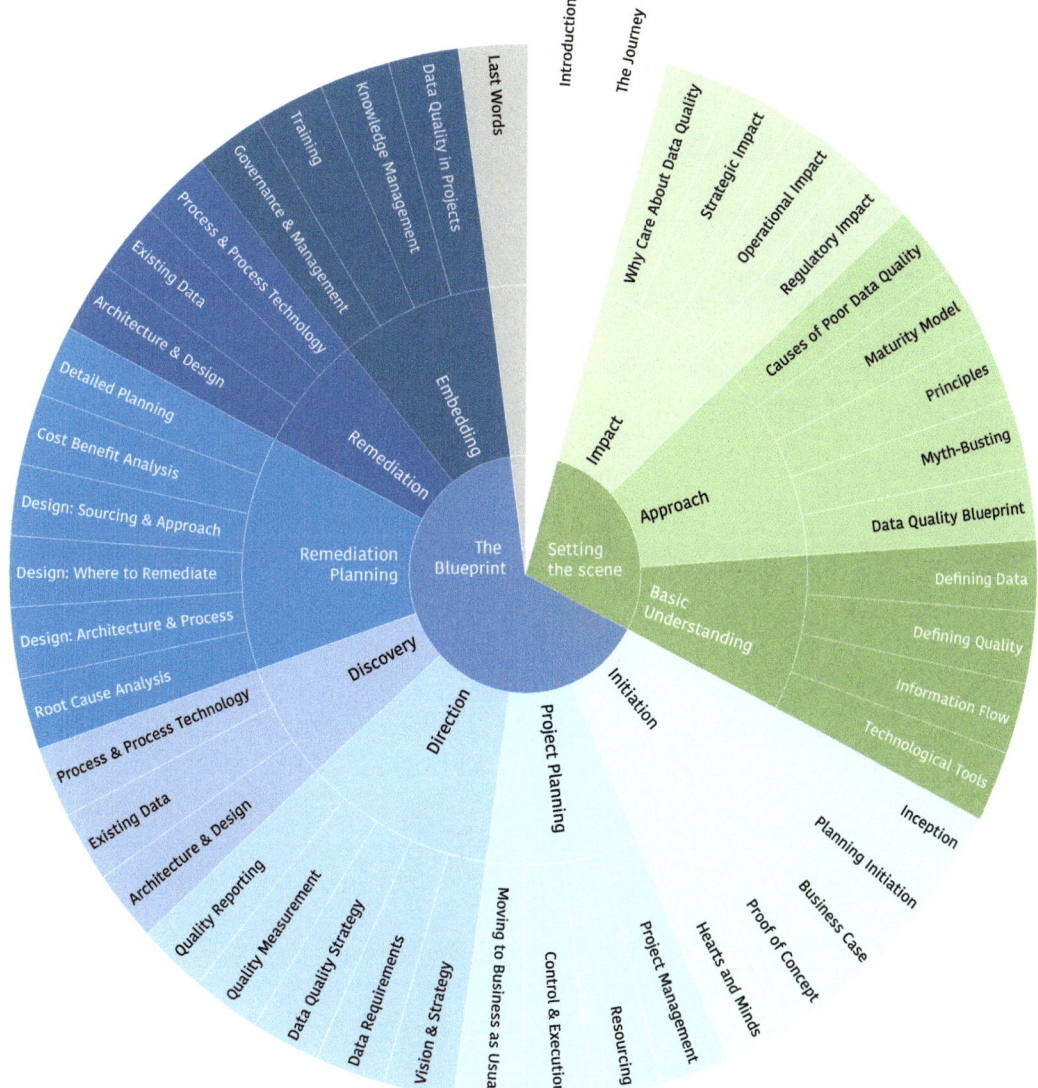

SECTION 1: INDEX

CHAPTER 1: Introduction — 5
1.1	Structure	5
1.2	Why is this Book Required?	5
1.3	Why did Data Quality become such a Major Issue?	6
1.4	Is there a Key Message?	10
1.5	Summary	11

CHAPTER 2: The Data Quality Blueprint — 13
2.1	Visual Map	13
2.2	Section 1: Overview	14
2.3	Section 2: Impact of Data Quality on the Organisation	14
2.4	Section 3: Approach	15
2.5	Section 4: Basic Understanding: Bridging the Business – IT Gap	16
2.6	Section 5: Methodology: The Approach to Data Quality	17
2.7	Section 6: Last Words	23
2.8	Section 7: Appendices	23

The Vimes' "Boots" Theory of Socio-Economic Unfairness

"The reason that the rich were so rich, Vimes reasoned, was because they managed to spend less money.

Take boots, for example. He earned thirty-eight dollars a month plus allowances. A really good pair of leather boots cost fifty dollars. But an affordable pair of boots, which were sort of OK for a season or two and then leaked like hell when the cardboard gave out, cost about ten dollars. Those were the kind of boots Vimes always bought, and wore until the soles were so thin that he could tell where he was in Ankh-Morpork on a foggy night by the feel of the cobbles.

But the thing was that good boots lasted for years and years. A man who could afford fifty dollars had a pair of boots that'd still be keeping his feet dry in ten years' time, while the poor man who could only afford cheap boots would have spent a hundred dollars on boots in the same time and would still have wet feet."

Terry Pratchett, Men at Arms, Corgi, 1993.

Lesson: Doing things cheaply costs you more and results in poorer service all the time.

The Cost of Poor Quality

The influential book "The Cost of Poor Quality" written by H. James Harrington as far back as 1987 details the way in which a poor quality approach will cost businesses money.

His point is that poor quality costs money; in terms of rework, repair, lost sales, customer dissatisfaction, and many other areas. The cost is substantial, and far exceeds the marginal additional cost of doing things right the first time. I quote:

> *"In many companies Poor Quality Cost accounts for 40% of the sale price".*

IBM, for example, reported that their Poor Quality Cost ranged between 20% and 40% of revenue before they started their quality improvement process.......

James E Preston, President of Avon noted that '–the cost of building quality into product is 5% of sales, whilst the cost of non-conformance is 20%'."

Again, the lesson is: It is (much) cheaper to do things right the first time than to do them badly and then fix them later.

SECTION 1 OVERVIEW

CHAPTER 1 INTRODUCTION

1.1   Structure

This introductory chapter looks to set the scene and cover some basics. These are:

- Why is this book required?
- Why data quality became such a major issue?
- What do I consider to be the key messages I would like a reader to take away from this book?

1.2   Why is this Book Required?

> "There is not a company on the planet that does not have a data quality problem"
> **Gartner Research vice president Andreas Bitterer**

This book is all about helping organisations improve their data quality. However why is this particular book required when there are publications covering the same or similar topics?

The reason is that in the last twenty years – whilst dealing with data quality across many organisations and sectors – I have read numerous publications that cover the subject of data quality and have not as yet read a non-technical book that covers the data quality problem in a holistic way. Most deal exclusively with the data that already exists and ignore the data that will be added tomorrow. They also ignore the environment in which that data exists – the design and architecture of the organisation – and also ignore where the organisation is heading – its overall strategy.

To use the analogy of the existing data being a lake that is fed by tributaries (which represent the processes in the organisation), there is no point cleaning up a data lake that is heavily polluted with poor data, to the point where it is pristine and beautiful, and then continuing to feed it sludge on a daily basis. Equally, there is no point in cleaning the tributaries but then emptying this sparkling clean data into a lake polluted with the accumulated rubbish of decades of poor data management. There is no point doing either if the lake is about to be drained and a housing estate built there instead. All elements have to be addressed.

Many data quality publications do not consider the organisation as a holistic unit. They are often jargon-obsessed, deeply technology-focused and badly over-analysed. "Extremely inaccessible" would be a description of many. At the same time organisations implement data quality initiatives, with varying levels of success. There is a chasm between the business and IT, with IT losing touch with the business aims and the business not understanding the language and priorities of IT, and neither understanding that they are in the same ship sailing down the same river and they need to work together. Sometimes data quality is presented as an end in itself, a puzzle box that, when solved, has aesthetic or geometrical perfection, but does not actually have a use, or, beyond the challenge in solving the box, a business reason to exist.

My view is that everything that occurs within an organisation must act to support, directly or indirectly, the bottom line, and demonstrate that it is doing so. This applies whether the bottom line is profit, or positive patient outcomes, or simply reduction in costs passed to taxpayers. This book has tried to combine three perspectives.

- **One**, it attacks the problem from a holistic perspective covering the whole organisation. It then takes this perspective apart into its component parts.
- **Two,** it looks to bridge the gap between the technical and non-technical. It looks to give business leaders a perspective on data quality and why it matters, but also to give IT leaders a perspective on how data quality affects the business so they can build the bridge from their direction as well.
- **Lastly**, it aims to give a practitioner a template from which to approach data quality. A means by which those who have gone before can pass on a way of solving the problem. This is a combination of step by step instructions – but with the explanation that they are to be used as a guide as opposed to the only truth – a plan, and a representation of how the future state should look.

Hence it is called "The Data Quality Blueprint".

1.3 Why did Data Quality become such a Major Issue?

Obtaining quality information is currently one of the greatest challenges facing organisations in an increasingly digital world, and it can be said without exaggeration that those organisations who are best placed to use the information they hold will be in the best position to operate in the future. So how has it come to this, that even five years after the financial crisis a group of senior regulators from around the globe can say:

"Five years after the financial crisis, firms' progress toward consistent, timely, and accurate reporting of top counterparty exposures fails to meet both supervisory expectations and industry self-identified best practices. **The area of greatest concern remains firms' inability to consistently produce high-quality data.**" [1]
[My emphasis]

I will now look at some of the underlying factors that have contributed to the current data quality crisis.

1. Senior Supervisors Group report on counterparty data, 2014.

1.3.1   Disconnect between business and IT

In the beginning there were no computers. Data was held as paper files, and paper moved around offices on spikes. I was at a client office as late as the mid-nineties where this was still the case. Computers, if used, were utilised for the financial accounts and little else. The accountant would create the accounts on a computer with a six inch green screen tucked in the corner of the finance office.

Information technology started with the geek in the office who understood how to operate this box in the corner. It has now evolved to massive departments which have their own language, projects, budget, reporting structure, and sometimes their own "business liaison officers" whose job it is to interpret the world of business into geek-speak.

However, despite the deconstruction of the acronym "IT", "Information" appears to have been lost underneath a quest for "Technology". I often hear complaints that an IT department cannot or will not see how issues affect the business, and do not understand that the business supports the continued existence of IT as a department or as part of the organisation.

So the first reason for the problem is that the business and the technology it relies on became divorced. The custodians of the information and the consumers of the same information are unable to communicate.

1.3.2   Quality is not valued

> "There is nothing in the world that some man cannot make a little worse and sell a little cheaper, and he who considers price only is that man's lawful prey"
> **John Ruskin; English critic, essayist, & reformer (1819-1900)**

A depressing fact about many organisations is that quality is not valued as much as either time or money, even though poor quality will result in more time and money at a later date. Given a choice between poorly performing and cheap, and well performing but expensive, many organisations will choose the former. In many projects cancelling the testing phase to save money has become almost traditional, resulting in many years of frustration for the users.

Quality is considered irrelevant. Time and time again, when looking at data quality issues I see the results from a disregard for quality. I have seen not one but many organisations implement a system that they knew would not meet business requirements because it was cheaper than the one that would. It is of no surprise that when no-one values quality and no-one is rewarded as a result of quality, that quality does not occur. Thus the second reason for poor quality.

1.3.3 Data Quantity

> "Big data is what happened when the cost of storing information became less than the cost of making the decision to throw it away"
> **George O'Reilly**

Data storage was once really expensive. Once it was considered a waste of valuable resources to store dates with four digit years and as a result two digits would have to do – and the Year 2000 problem was born. Now, data storage costs almost nothing. I can go into a local shop and buy enough storage for seventy million pages of text for less than the price of a take-away meal.

The quantity is huge; however extracting meaning from the data is an ever-growing challenge. Organisations are simply swamped by data, and retaining quality has become a daunting task. Business Intelligence, a separate and growing discipline and now big business, has developed out of this need. Data visualisation has likewise flowered into an industry which utilises the inherent ability of humans to comprehend more information if it is presented in a visual form. However, the well-known garbage-in-garbage-out means that little meaning can be derived if the data itself is of poor value. So the third reason for poor data quality is that there is too much data.

Healthcare Network

Mental health trusts' data quality lagging behind, says auditor

Mental health trusts' quality accounts worse than acute trusts, says Audit Commission

1.3.4 Lack of a joined up approach

A barrier to data quality in many organisations is the lack of a joined up approach, a concentration on ungoverned and tactical solutions rather than holistic strategic solutions. This introduces problems of short-termism and a siloed mentality.

To use an analogy of building a bridge, the first stage needs to be that a problem is identified. This problem may be that getting from one side of the river to another currently involves a swim as there is no dry means of travel. It may be that an existing bridge is overloaded or is in poor repair. The organisation needs to define requirements. Examples may be:

- To not get wet when crossing the river.
- To get from one side to another in 5 minutes or less.

The next stage is defining a solution. There will be a number of potential solutions, which may involve building another bridge, or building a landing stage and using boats. It may involve widening an existing bridge, it may involve using a mass transit system and reducing traffic, it may involve looking in detail at why people want to get from one side of the river to another and reducing demand, potentially by creating what they are looking for on both banks.

The eventual solution will then be decided, based on the immediate problem and the overall strategy for the area, set at a national or local government level. A plan for implementation will be drawn up including a specific set of actions. For a new bridge, foundations will have to be created, then the superstructure, then the road itself, and finally street lighting and possibly some planting, before the road is opened to the public.

Most organisational changes – including data quality projects – operate nothing like this. To continue to flog the same analogy, a more real-life description would unfold as below.

No-one will define requirements. Someone will start planting flowers on the old bridge and replacing the lighting. Three other people will half-build a landing stage and buy a rowboat. The local government will state that there is a need for a new bridge, but won't take it further. Someone will start building a bit of roadway on the island in the middle of the river. Someone else builds a bridge a mile downstream (away from the roads) on the assumption that if a bridge exists then people will walk to the bridge to go over it (known as the "build it and they will come" approach).

The end state of many attempts at solving the problem could be likened to the experience of going to a landing stage, being rowed across to the bit of road on the island, walking across this bit of road, and then swimming the rest of the way, possibly carrying a plant. At which point the organisation states that it has achieved its aim.

It will be clear to any reader that the latter solution is a waste of valuable time, money and resources and produces a sub-standard solution. So a fourth reason for poor data quality is fragmented approaches and tactical, short-term thinking.

1.3.5 So why the book?

Data quality problems are endemic in most large organisations, partly due to the above, partly due to other reasons not mentioned. Whilst it is often a concern for executives, it is a concern that has largely remained unaddressed, certainly until recent regulation has forced a spotlight on data quality. The holistic approach recommended by The Data Quality Blueprint is about deciding where you are going, deciding how you will get there, and then orchestrating the whole organisation to get there with the minimum cost and the maximum efficiency.

To do the job once, and well.

This book is not a detailed explanation of everything to do with data quality. Otherwise it would be ten times the size. Data quality is a broad subject, incorporating many other disciplines, from project management, though data and process analysis, business and data architecture, business analysis, business process management and many more. To write in detail on each of these is beyond the scope of this book. This book is necessarily written at a high level. If you wish to discover more detail about any of the elements required then there are many publications to enable you to do so, and where this is relevant I have highlighted this fact. This is also a detailed bibliography contained in the appendices.

1.4 Is there a Key Message?

Within the first section of any book an author wants to set the tone, mention major points he or she wishes to make, and to set the scene. So what are the key messages that I would like the reader to understand from this book? I wanted to get the most important point out of the way first.

To successfully create a lasting solution to data quality you need to look at the organisation as a whole and where it is going.

Information is used by the organisation on a daily basis to inform decisions that affect its future. It goes without saying that the information needs to be of sufficient quality to allow these decisions to be made. The information needs of the organisation must be defined before it can decide whether this is the case. The corporate vision and the data strategy of the organisation and its data requirements need to define the objectives of any data quality initiative. Without an objective, how does the organisation know where to go?

It is also pointless spending time and money correcting historical data and not looking at the way in which data flows into information systems. Every hour, on average, in the UK:

- 684 people change address
- 47 die
- 13 divorce
- 30 companies are dissolved
- 80 people are born
- 30 are married
- 51 business are created

To put it bluntly, if you do not consider process as well as data then you are wasting your time and money. If the processes are broken then poor quality data will be added to the information store daily, and faster than it can be cleaned.

Another way of wasting time is not considering the overall design of information flows within the organisation. There is no point spending time remediating information stores which feed nothing, or are due for replacement, and there may be times when it is better to solve high level design issues before starting on data or process. This brings us to the next key message.

Data quality is not just a technology problem.

Because of the word "data", data quality problems are often assumed to be technological problems to be solved by technological people in a technological way. This is incorrect. However the effect is that the problem is pushed into the IT world and ceases to have any interest to a business stakeholder. This makes the problem unsolvable.

Ideally, I would much prefer the term "Information Quality" to stress the business relevance; however "Data Quality" is an industry standard phrase and I accept that it needs to be used, but I also wish to explain where and why the perception is incorrect.

Whilst processes use technology, and whilst IT are custodians of the data as they have de facto custody of technological assets like databases, the IT department do not create the data, experience the effects of poor data, nor do they have the information to correct poor data. IT can help – they often have the tools and the skills to work with data on a large scale – but they should never be in the driving seat. In this book I have considered technology as an element of process, and as an enabler, but not as a separate subject in itself.

1.5 Summary

In this introductory chapter I have discussed why I believe that this book is required, and how it adds to the existing data quality knowledge base. I have explained how it addresses areas which are not commonly covered in many publications. I have also outlined several reasons why data quality is an endemic problem in many organisations, and also what I consider the key messages that a reader should take away from this book. In the next chapter I will outline the overall structure of this book and walk the reader through the methodology that I will subsequently recommend to address data quality issues in a holistic manner.

A note on this book.

As stated in the introduction, my experience relates mainly to the financial services sector in the United Kingdom, with some experience in public sector (local and national government & health). As would therefore be expected the examples in this book are drawn predominantly from the financial sector in the United Kingdom.

Notwithstanding the above, I have made effort to select such examples as are cross-sector applicable – for example those areas covering customer data quality are directly relevant to every organisation. I would also note that whilst I am aware that there may be an overall financial sector bias in terms of the examples, I believe that this book will be relevant to all organisations in terms of the methodologies and practices.

SECTION 1 OVERVIEW

CHAPTER 2 THE DATA QUALITY BLUEPRINT: THE JOURNEY

2.1 Visual map

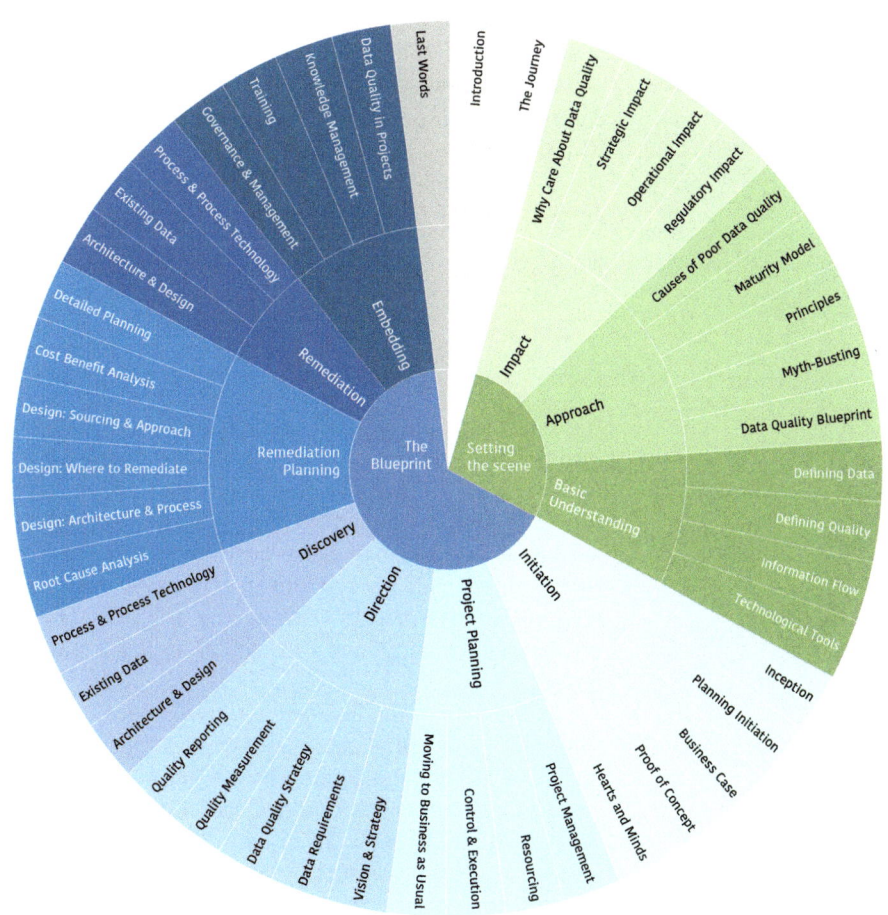

I have on occasion had cause to read a book which appears to have no structure. It is a painful process to orientate yourself within the book, to find relevant chapters quickly, or to construct an information image within your own (mental) filing system. I have tried to avoid placing the reader of this particular book in that situation.

To this end, the above diagram shows the book as a whole in order to enable a reader to locate the part of the book that interests them, and also to see how it relates to the total.

The book divides into four major components with twelve sections. The four components are the introduction; followed by setting the scene, then the methodology itself, and then a final wrap-up. In this chapter I will introduce the various sections of the book and explain the overall structure and how the narrative flows.

2.2   Section 1: Overview

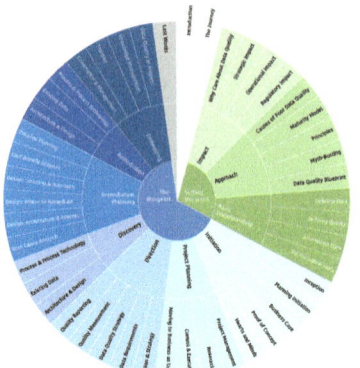

In this book I have tried to take the reader on a data quality journey. This journey covers the identification, definition, assessment and resolution of data quality problems. This journey looks to address data quality not as a one-off, but for the long term.

In the initial section (of which this chapter is a part) I am covering basics. The reasons for writing this book, why data quality problems are so endemic, key messages and the structure of the book and the information it contains. Here I explain what I am going to say, and how I am going to say it.

2.3   Section 2: Impact of Data Quality on the Organisation

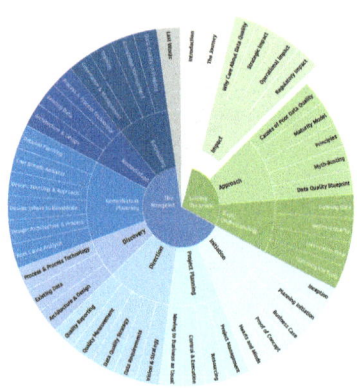

The second section of the book covers the impact of poor data quality. The objective is to show how poor data quality can really make a mess of the aspirations of an organisation. At the least, poor data quality will bar the organisation from fulfilling its potential; at worst it may cause business failure. The impact on the organisation is divided into three chapters, which cover the strategic impact of poor data quality, the operational impact of poor data quality, and the regulatory impact of poor data quality.

In the case of the last chapter, this is necessarily at a high level as it would be impossible to cover all the impacts of data quality in all the regulated sectors in any publication, not least because regulations are changed continuously and any publication would be instantly out of date. I have therefore restricted myself to a general discussion of regulation and how poor data quality can impede regulatory compliance, whilst giving a few examples from selected sectors.

2.4 Section 3: Approach

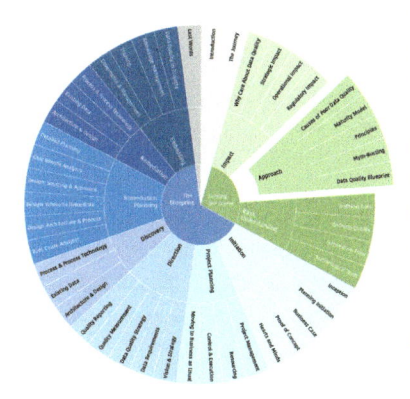

The third section takes the reader through a logical progression ending with a description of the methodology. It picks up from the impact of data quality discussed in the prior chapters and covers a number of subject areas which describe the evolution of the methodology to its current form. The intention is to demonstrate to the reader why looking at an organisation in a holistic way is necessary to truly address data quality, and why it is more efficient and effective to take this approach. The particular areas that are covered in this section are:

■ What causes poor data quality
After considering the impact of poor data quality in the previous section, and hence why an organisation should care, this section starts by covering the causes.

■ Data quality maturity model
To start the journey to good data quality, it is desirable to understand the data quality maturity model. This particular model describes five stages on the path to data quality, and introduces the reader to the ideal end state. A reader should be able to directly relate their own organisation to the maturity model. This is not in any way a prescriptive model, but does demonstrate the ways in which differing organisations can benchmark their data quality.

■ Principles
In order to solve data quality as a problem the organisation needs to first set principles. These principles are the laws by which the organisation will approach data quality. For the Data Quality Blueprint these are defined up front, as they will inform and guide everything else that is done.

■ Myth-busting
There are a lot of myths in existence in relation to data quality. These are the ways in which many organisations may think they can solve data quality, but unfortunately from my own experience do not work in practice. The objective for this section is to take a few of the more common approaches and explain why they do not work, before going on, in the next chapter, to explain what will.

■ Methodology
To provide a foundation for the rest of the book, this chapter outlines the methodology I believe is the best approach to a data quality solution. This section of the book will give any reader a high level understanding of this holistic approach, what is contained in each stage, and why.

2.5 Section 4: Basic Understanding: Bridging the Business – IT Gap

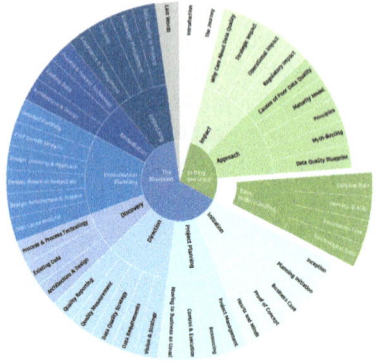

As stated at the start of the book, one of the most basic problems that face the business and IT professional looking to attack a data quality problem together is a lack of mutual understanding. Language that an IT professional commonly uses to describe data will mean little to a business professional – and vice versa. Whilst it is not assumed that both areas are totally ignorant of the other, it helps the reader – whichever side they sit, or indeed if they sit in the middle – if they can establish a baseline where the language from both sides is consistent and mutually understood.

The first chapter in this section is designed to show the IT professional the business way of looking at data – which is largely by the way it is used, and the business professional the IT way of looking at data – which is largely by the way it is exists and behaves.

In the same way, perceptions of quality are often split across the IT/business boundary. A quality characteristic that is considered by the business professional as important may be considered irrelevant by the IT professional. Hence the second chapter covers the definitions and components of quality. The next chapter looks at the way that data flows through an organisation, introduces and describes the major elements of data architecture, and gives a high level view of the way the moving parts fit together.

The last chapter covers technology. Whilst I say a number of times in this book that technology is not the answer, it can certainly help on a data quality journey.

One of the problems with a book is that it is, by its nature, a point in time. It will be created potentially years before the reader picks it up and opens the first page. In that time a software product will be born and die, or be upgraded from an also-ran to a market leader. At the time of writing a number of good products exist which can materially complement a data quality initiative. Whilst I am not going to mention product names due to the aforesaid volatility of the market, I will briefly look at the several types of data quality product and how they can help any remediation.

Despite the name, I have tried to avoid a technological approach in The Data Quality Blueprint. My view is that technology can help you get to your destination, but it cannot tell you where you are going, and it should **never** be the driver.

2.6 Section 5: Methodology: The Approach to Data Quality.

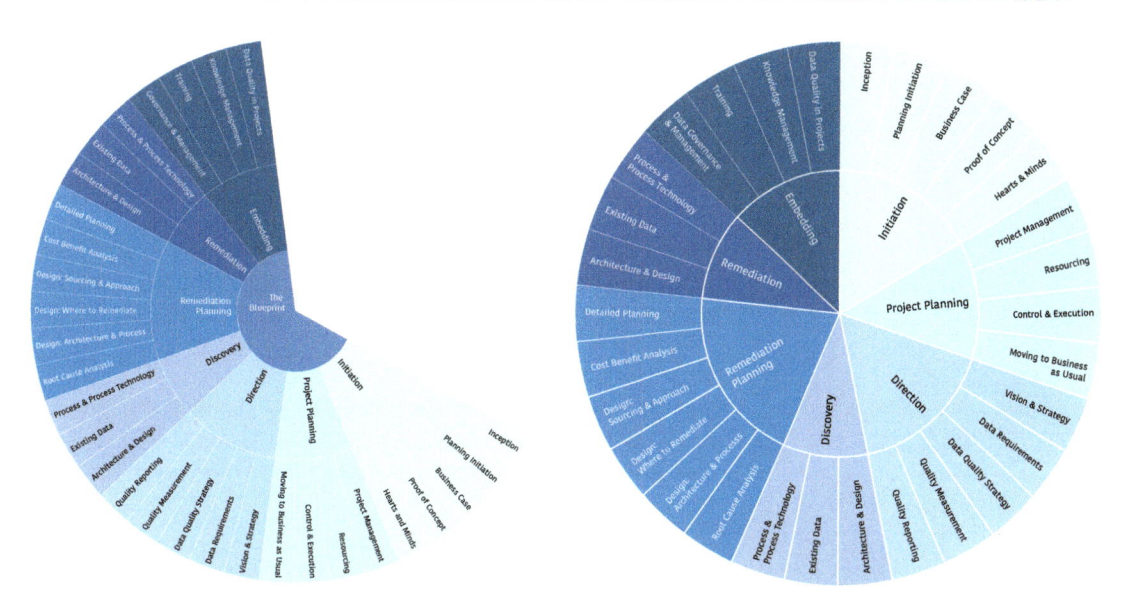

The rest of the book describes The Data Quality Blueprint in detail.

The large graphic we have already introduced is representative of the book as a whole. Within the methodology sections I have used a smaller and simpler graphic to indicate where within the methodology itself the individual chapters reside. This allows the methodology to stand alone, outside the context of the book. It is a break-out of the elements shown above.

There are many data quality methodologies out there. This is not meant to be a replacement though it may be a complement, especially to those methodologies that are focused on technological solutions. However I believe that over-engineering a data quality approach can be a problem in itself, and imposing a strict sequence to tasks can have negative effects. The project management chapter (described later) shows, for example, that many tasks can run in parallel. What I have tried to do is group the tasks involved in a typical data quality project, and put them in a logical order.

I've called it "The Data Quality Blueprint" but please do not think this the only path to nirvana. Many paths exist, and please feel free to take the elements you like out of this methodology and cut and paste with others that work for you or your organisation.

From this point on in the book I have assumed that the organisation wishes to implement a project to address data quality problems using the blueprint as a guide. I will take the reader through the project stage by stage, explaining the inputs to and outputs from each stage and the tasks to be performed. I will explain the planning of the project, the options in the overall approach, the resources required, and how they should be utilised. In short, it is a detailed walkthrough of how to solve data quality within an organisation.

5.1 Project Initiation

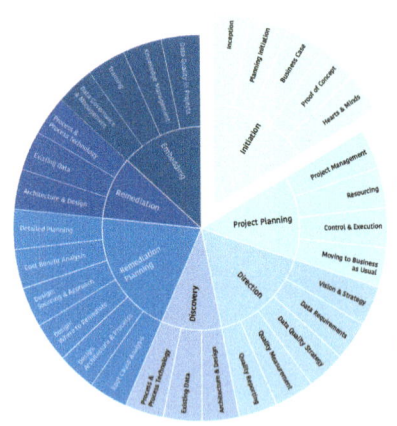

Any project will start with an initiation stage. This stage will start with problem identification and gather information to understand the issues. It will set objectives and a scope, will propose an approach and create a business case. It will then look to gain buy-in from the organisation to move to the next stage.

■ Laying the foundations (Inception)
The first stage in any approach is basic understanding of the organisation and the problems it is facing. This includes meeting key stakeholders and deciding on an overall approach.

■ Planning
From the very start the project needs to be planned. The project needs to understand what it is required to do and in what order. Overall governance needs to be agreed and a plan created.

■ Building the business case
It could be argued that good data quality is part of running a successful organisation, but in reality it will be necessary to prove why a data quality project is a good idea, and this proof needs to be persuasive. Far too many data quality projects fail at this hurdle – everyone will know it is a good idea, but no-one can prove the benefit that it will bring. This section shows how to make a watertight business case.

■ Proof of concept
A business case may look good on paper, but to win the day you have to prove it. This section deals with a seldom approached element of data quality, creating a proof of concept.

■ Hearts and Minds
You are not going to do it on your own. In order to make a data quality project successful others will need to be convinced. This section approaches this problem and suggests ways to solve it.

5.2 Project Planning: How do we get there in one piece and without killing each other?

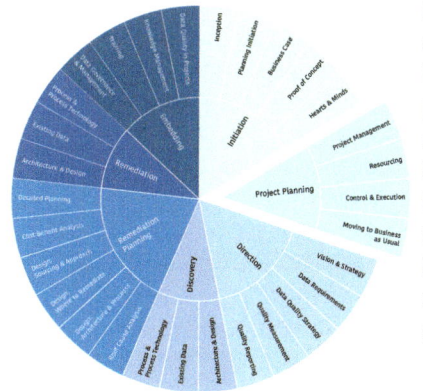

I have been involved with many data quality projects. I have also managed both specific data quality projects and other large information management projects. This chapter includes approaches for splitting up the project into modules, it covers the resources that are needed and the skills these resources need to have. Probably more than any other chapter, this chapter needs to be read with an eye on the appendices, which include a wealth of information on the management of a data quality project, including examples of artefacts and deliverables that could be used to facilitate a data quality project, as well as a full detailed data quality project plan.

5.3 Direction: Where are we going and what do we want to achieve?

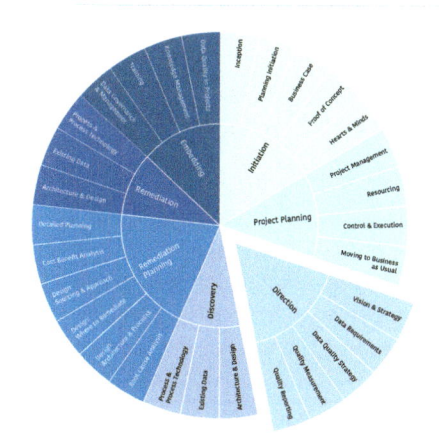

Before an organisation embarks on a data quality journey it needs to decide where it is going. Some organisations have already made this decision, but others are still trying to find the map. The map is necessary, as there is no point jumping in and remediating data without any idea of the information needs of the organisation or the quality that is required from that information.

For those organisations that do not have a map, this section outlines how one can be created. It takes the reader through the creation of a data strategy, data quality strategy, data requirements, data quality requirements and data metrics – key performance indicators specifically for data quality which will be required to both measure the current data quality as-is, and monitor it over the timescale of the project and beyond. It also includes a chapter on the reporting of data quality and dashboarding. If the organisation is truly bought in to the creation of a long term solution then regular reporting of the information quality is essential.

5.4 Discovery: Where are we now?

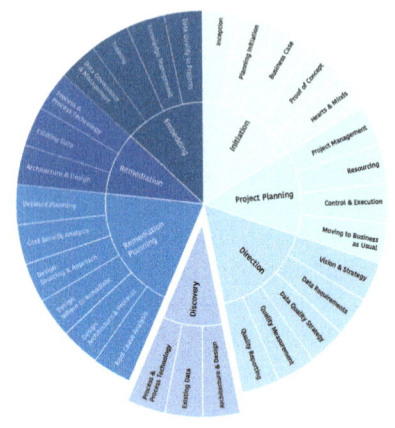

The next stage in our data quality journey is to find out the current situation. This stage covers the analysis and assessment of the overall organisational design and whether the organisation has any high level blockers to achieving data quality. Blockers occur in many organisations and whilst they may not necessarily be addressed within the project, they need to be considered and their effect mitigated. This section will also cover the familiar task of profiling the existing data, and also the less familiar task of business process assessment, where the project looks at how business processes contribute to poor quality data. The reason this stage is placed here is that assessment should be made in full knowledge of the information requirements of the business, otherwise it is likely, if not inevitable, that much time will be wasted.

5.5 Remediation planning

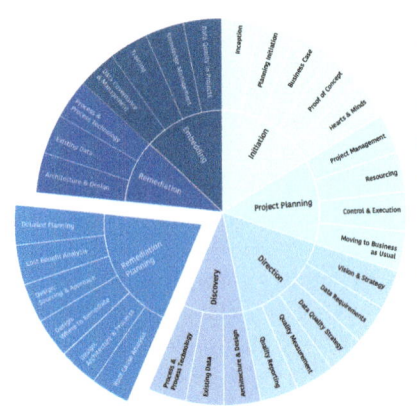

Remediation planning is the pivotal point of the project. This is where everything is drawn together and not only the future state of the organisation is determined, but also the steps that must be taken to transition from here to there. Necessary inputs are the results from the discovery phase which will inform the rest of the project.

The first stage in remediation planning is a root cause analysis. This examines the issues that have come out of the discovery phase and looks at why they have occurred. This stage is critical to the efficiency of the project as a single root cause may result in many data quality issues. There is no point cleaning data if the actual problem is a process issue that remains unaddressed, and will continue to pollute the data. It goes without saying that this part of the project does take time.

The organisation needs to take time to understand exactly what is required, rather than rushing off and remediating the first bit of data it sees. Like many other areas of human experience, a little bit of planning reaps rewards in that the actual work can be done faster, more effectively, and cheaper than would otherwise be the case.

The next chapters cover the remediation design. This is the creation and consideration of options to remediate architecture, data and process. This work creates options for remediation. It also covers where remediation should fit in the overall architecture of the organisation – where is remediation most effectively and efficiently performed? It is surprising how many organisations decide to perform remediation at the point where it is least effective. The next chapter covers cost benefit analysis. The project needs to take the output from the work so far, put a value on the remediation options, and match this with the value generated from the solution. It needs to revisit the business case, identify quick wins – and the other elements that need a bit more thinking about and should be considered later. This is a stage where the organisation needs to do some heavy thinking. Lastly in the chapter on detailed planning I will discuss the blow-by-blow approach to remediation. This covers tasks that need to be performed before launching into the remediation itself.

5.6 Remediation

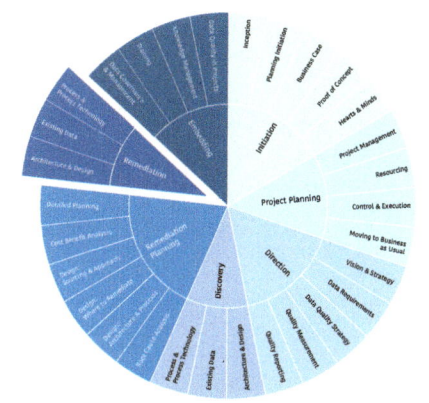

In contrast to many publications on the subject, the actual remediation of data quality issues forms a relatively small part of this book. To use an analogy, replacing an individual component within a car engine may not necessarily take a considerable amount of time. This is in comparison to the overall process that will involve fault-finding, discovery of the actual issue, isolating and removing the faulty component and then – after replacement – trying to make sure that the issue does not recur (which may of course involve driver education). So is the same with remediation. Once all the preparation has been completed the work can proceed rapidly. It is the organisations that try and perform the preparation work at the same time as the work itself that tie themselves in expensive knots. This section contains a relatively high level description of the remediation process, looking at approaches to remediation, tools, techniques, and the task flow of taking poor architecture, data and process and changing it from bad to good.

5.7 Embedding

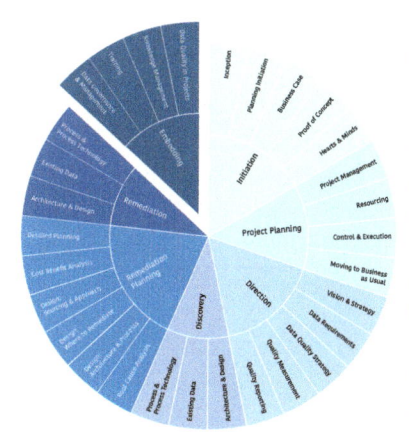

Now that the organisation has achieved good data quality, the challenge is to keep it good. It is a stage of the process that many organisations don't so much do badly, but don't do at all. In order to achieve long lasting data quality, new processes must be embedded into business as usual, a governance framework must be established, knowledge needs to be maintained, and training imparted – otherwise there is a certainty that the organisation will be facing the same problems (and the same effort required to remediate) in a short period of time. Whilst some embedding has already been discussed (for example, remediation of processes so that they are less likely to cause poor data), we need to look at the other components of embedding data quality within an organisation to ensure that the changes made last longer than the next customer request to change their address. The elements that are brought together in this section are:

Governance

Data governance is the organisational function that acts to guide data management and to align data management with the overall governance and risk appetite of the organisation. As data governance is an integral part of ensuring the long term data quality within the organisation, it is placed within the "Embedding" chapter, as a function that acts to keep data quality on the straight and narrow after any remediation project is completed. I have included in this chapter a description of an industry standard data management taxonomy and shown how The Data Quality Blueprint both maps to and supports its requirements.

Training

Many data quality issues stem from poor or non-existent training. Individuals in the organisation need to be aware of why data quality matters and how they can each make a contribution to ensuring the data quality in the organisation starts good and stays good. In this chapter I cover who should be trained, how they should be trained, what the training should consist of, and when the training should occur.

Knowledge management

Over the period of the project a considerable amount of valuable knowledge has been created and the challenge is to ensure that knowledge is not lost. Knowledge management is another area where organisations perform poorly, the most common approach being to place all artefacts in a shared information repository where they can moulder, unused, in peace. This chapter takes another approach and looks at the problem more practically, discussing what people want to know and how they wish to search for it, and how best to ensure that they have access to the information they need. It may be a surprise to know that the most effective means of knowledge management is cheaper and easier than creating a vast knowledge repository. This chapter is applicable across a much wider canvas than merely data quality. However, I have approached the chapter using data quality as a worked example.

Data quality within a project environment

The data quality project that has just been covered in detail over the previous sections will not be the last project that the organisation undertakes. The organisation will be undertaking projects continuously and the challenge is to ensure that these projects do not destroy what the data quality project has achieved. This short chapter – which covers the challenges of data quality within an individual project – is equally applicable to an organisation that has not undertaken a remediation project.

2.7 Section 6: Last Words

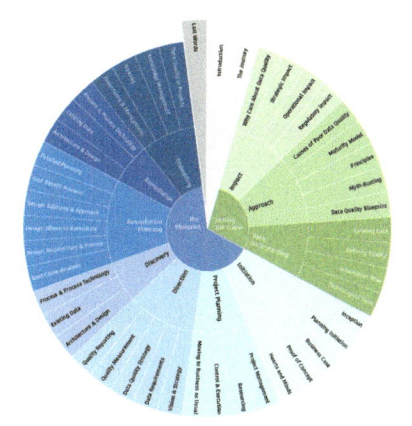

This final section contains a brief consideration of future data. In years to come any organisation will be using types of data that do not exist now. Some data is yet to come. This short chapter discusses the likely characteristics of future data, and how an organisation will have to adapt. Finally, there are few last words to wrap up the book and make some brief comments on the overall journey.

2.8 Section 7: Appendices

I have included within the appendices a large amount of information that is relevant for the data quality professional. The information included should be enough to give a significant head-start to any organisation that is looking to implement a data quality project. This section includes:

- Artefacts relating to a data quality project
- Sample questions that can be used to identify data quality issues
- Data governance terms of reference
- A sample data strategy
- A sample data quality strategy
- A full data quality project plan task list

A note or two...

A note on big data.

A current buzzword that I will briefly mention now is "Big Data" which is defined as data at a volume where the means of storing and analysing becomes too big for traditional relational databases and more innovative solutions have to be employed, of which there are a number on the market. Big data is seen by many as the path to data nirvana, but the truth is that most organisations cannot organise and obtain meaning from the data that they already have. Data quality is often somewhere between appalling and abysmal, and really most businesses are not ready for a challenge that is hundreds of times greater than the challenge they are already failing to address.

This book is not about "big data" as such, it focuses on the quality of any data. Obviously large amounts of data may have data quality issues in the same way as small amounts of data, but in most cases the tasks are similar, just a larger job.

A note on pedantry

Latin scholars may tell you that "data" is plural, the singular being "datum". Practically, in everyday English, "datum" has fallen out of general use, and the use of the word "data" as a collective noun is normal. "The data is poor" is common usage; "The data are poor" may be technically correct but sounds wrong. In this book I'm going to go with the majority and treat the word data as a collective noun taking a singular or plural pronoun depending on context. I know this appears a minor point, but some people do get bothered about these kinds of things.

SECTION 2
THE IMPACT OF POOR DATA QUALITY

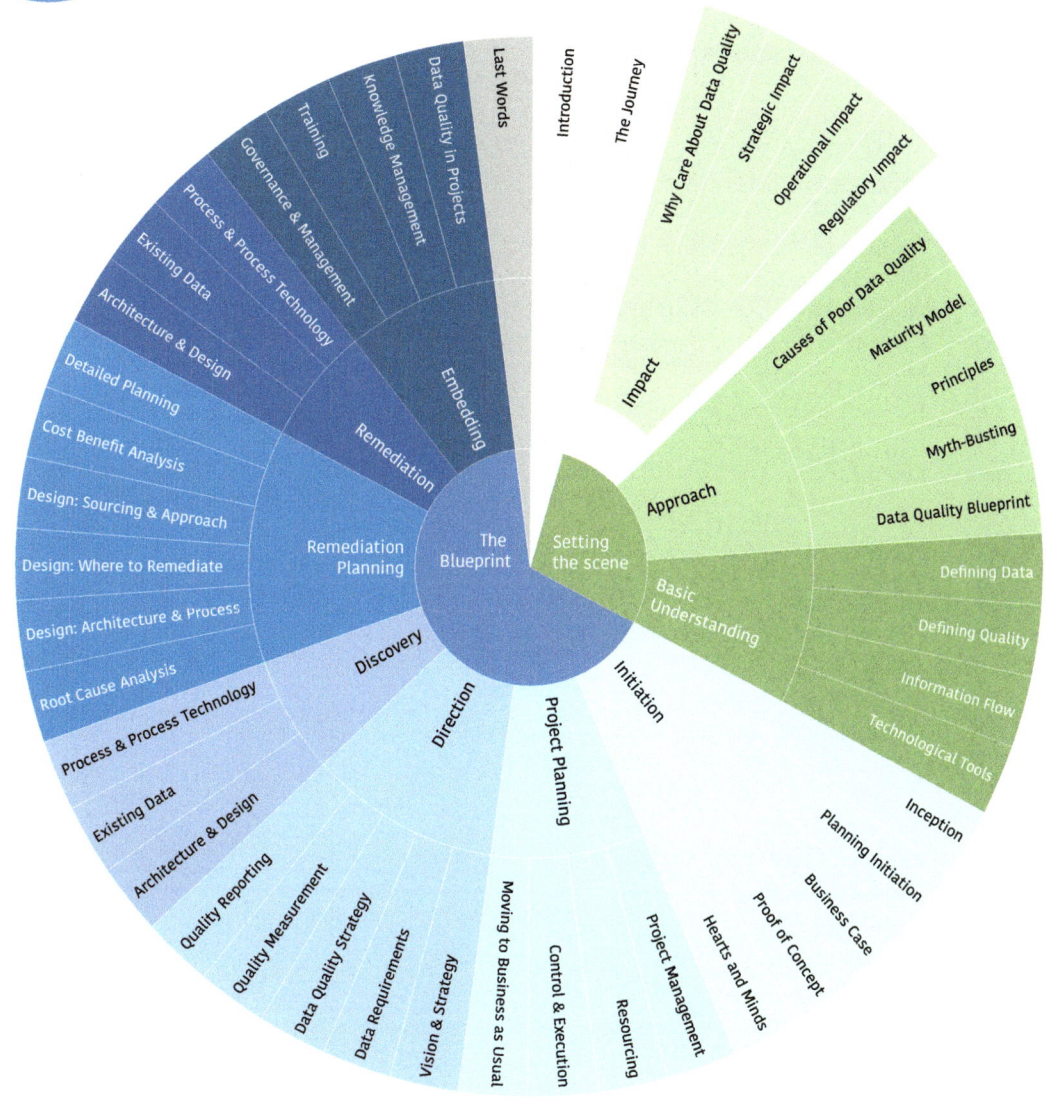

Impact

Why care about Data Quality?
The Impact Poor Data Quality has on the organisation

SECTION 2: INDEX

CHAPTER 3: Why Care About Data Quality? — 27
- 3.1 Structure — 27
- 3.2 Overview — 27
- 3.3 Why is nothing done? — 28
- 3.4 Summary — 31

CHAPTER 4: Strategic Impact of Poor Data Quality — 33
- 4.1 Structure — 33
- 4.2 Overview — 33
- 4.3 The Cost of Poor Decisions (or the cost of a badly informed executive) — 34
- 4.4 Risk and Capital Management — 36
- 4.5 Poor Relations between IT and the Business — 39
- 4.6 Lack of Trust of Data throughout the Organisation — 40
- 4.7 Missed Opportunities — 41
- 4.8 Business Intelligence and Mis-targeted Marketing — 42
- 4.9 Reputational Impact — 43
- 4.10 Summary — 43

CHAPTER 5: Operational Impact of Poor Data Quality — 45
- 5.1 Structure — 45
- 5.2 Introduction — 45
- 5.3 Time Cost of repeatedly reworking of Existing Data — 46
- 5.4 Loss of Efficiency — 47
- 5.5 Cost of Project Failure — 48
- 5.6 Missed Sales Opportunities — 49
- 5.7 Poor Customer Relations & Customer Retention — 51
- 5.8 IT Costs — 52
- 5.9 Mailing Overspend — 53
- 5.10 Crime and Terrorism — 54
- 5.11 Transactional Failures — 56
- 5.12 Data Migration — 57
- 5.13 Profitability — 58
- 5.14 Summary — 58

CHAPTER 6: Regulatory Impact of Poor Data Quality — 61
- 6.1 Structure — 61
- 6.2 Overview — 61
- 6.3 What does the regulator require? — 63
- 6.4 How can Poor Data Quality impede Compliance? — 65
- 6.5 How the Regulator is Enforcing its Wishes — 73
- 6.6 ISO 8000 — 75
- 6.7 Summary — 76

… SECTION 2 — THE IMPACT OF POOR DATA QUALITY

CHAPTER 3: WHY CARE ABOUT DATA QUALITY?

3.1 Structure

This section of the book discusses four topics:

1. High level overview and introduction
2. Strategic impact of poor data quality
3. Operational impact of poor data quality
4. Regulatory impact of poor data quality

This chapter covers the first of these topics.

3.2 Overview

> "Data quality problems plague every department, in every industry, at every level, and for every type of information."
> **Gartner, "Key Trends Driving the Change in Data Quality Technology"**

Why it is necessary to consider data quality? The answer is that poor data quality will cost you a lot of money, and if that wasn't enough, poor data quality will result in adverse regulatory attention, up to and including fines and incarceration. It is therefore, I would submit, worth doing something about it. In this chapter I will briefly outline some of the reasons why data quality is not seen as a major issue before delving deeper into the cost of poor information in following chapters.

3.3 Why is nothing done?

> **Bank of Scotland fined £4.2m for bad mortgage data**
>
> FSA issues £4.2 million penalty to BoS for sending misleading mortgage offers, due to poor integration between mortgage records systems

The most visible sign of a data quality failure is often a large and embarrassingly public regulatory fine, or embarrassingly negative newspaper headlines. Business leaders of my experience often look at such news and realise it could easily be their own organisation, but continue in the same manner without addressing the problem because they don't really know where to start, or which thread to pull to start to unravel the problem and start on the journey to a solution. These same leaders often fail to consider the everyday operational cost of poor data quality, which is costing them money whether the regulator gets involved or not. On an everyday basis poor data quality will lose you money through bad business decisions, loss of revenue and massively increased internal costs. Most business leaders know this, but why is nothing ever done?

3.3.1 Reason 1: We think it's an IT problem

> **Serious Fraud Office launches probe into Tesco accounting scandal**

Part of the trouble is that as soon as the word "data" is mentioned it is seen as an IT problem and therefore not business relevant. However, almost everything that any organisation does, on any day, is based on information. It therefore follows that the quality of this information will affect all parts of the organisation. However, referring to a point I will make and continue to make, data is too often seen as a technical issue. It is often confined to technical discussions, whereas in reality it is the asset upon which all decisions are made and all transactions are based. Data, therefore, should be business led, business specified, and business governed. For if it is not led, specified and governed by the business then the organisation will make incorrect decisions on incorrect information, the adequacy of which has been specified by someone else.

I will come on to principles later, but one of the central principles of The Data Quality Blueprint is that the approach is a partnership between the business and IT.

3.3.2 Reason 2: We think it doesn't cost us much on a daily basis (as long as the regulator doesn't step in)

> "When business leaders make strategic decisions, which are based on bad data, those decisions can result in Financial loss, negatively impact customer relationships and irreparably damage an organization's credibility in the market. In fact, ovum, a global analyst firm, estimated "that poor data quality costs U.S. Businesses at least 30% of revenues – a staggering $700 billion per year"".
> **Pitney Bowes Business Insight, 2013.**

It is difficult to quantify exactly how much a given level of poor data will cost an organisation. Because data is pervasive through an organisation, one issue may affect many departments and a single error can have wide-ranging consequences. However, any organisation with poor data quality – which unfortunately is in my experience the majority – will be paying for that poor data quality. A (non-exhaustive) list of some of the ways in which poor data quality can affect the average organisation is shown below.

- Cost of regulatory failure
- Fraud and loss
- Cost of project failure
- Reputational damage
- Poor customer experience
- Poor customer retention
- The cost of bad decisions made and good decisions not made
- Missed sales opportunities and poor targeting of marketing
- Increased internal costs
- Poor relationships between IT and business
- Lack of trust
- Poor risk management
- Mailing overspend
- Costs of rework
- IT costs
- Remediation costs
- Transactional failures
- Increased data migration efforts

There is no part of the organisation that does not suffer the effects of poor data quality. An area neglected in many articles and books that cover data quality is the cost of poor data quality. A large number of estimates, however, do exist – and the financial numbers are surprisingly large. Collected below are a range of estimates from a number of prominent publications on data quality.

"Three proprietary studies yielded estimates in the 8-12% of revenue range." [2]

"Poor information quality costs organizations 20-35% of operating revenue wasted in recovery from process failure and information scrap and rework." [3]

"The average perceived cost of poor data quality is as high as 10% of organisations' revenues" [4]

In 2002, Tom Redman claimed that *"Poor data quality costs the typical company up to twenty percent of revenue."* [5]

The Data Warehousing Institute estimates that data quality problems cost U.S. businesses more than $600 billion a year. [6]

Capgemini found that poor data cost the UK economy £67 billion per year – £46 billion in the private sector and £21 billion in the public sector [7]

Inaccurate data is affecting the company bottom line. 77 percent of companies believe their bottom line is affected by inaccurate and incomplete contact data and on average, respondents believe 12 percent of revenue is wasted. [8]

Gartner, in 2011, stated [9]:

Poor data quality is a primary reason for 40% of all business initiatives failing to achieve their targeted benefits.

Data quality effects overall labour productivity by as much as a 20%.

As more business processes become automated, data quality becomes the rate limiting factor for overall process quality.

Whilst not every organisation will necessarily show savings at this level, substantial, material savings should be expected from any data quality initiative. Moreover, if approached in the correct way, so the remediation effort is a one off and processes as well as data are addressed, the ongoing benefit will be substantial. Another of the central principles of The Data Quality Blueprint is that the work is performed once and once only.

---

2. *The Impact of Poor Data Quality in the Typical Enterprise*, Tom Redman, ACM Magazine, 1998
3. *Information Quality Applied*, Larry English, Wiley, 2009
4. Information Impact International, 1998
5. *A long, strange trip ahead: Process management and data quality*, Tom Redman, 2002
6. *Data Quality and the Bottom Line*, TDWI, 2002
7. Capgemini, 2008
8. *The state of Data Quality*, Experian, 2014
9. *Measuring the Business value of Data Quality*, Gartner 2011.

3.3.3   Reason 3: We think it's too big a problem to solve.

A third reason nothing is done about data quality is that it is often considered too big a problem to solve. There are too many data sources and too much data, so that trying to approach the problem from any direction appears a daunting – and expensive – task. That is where this book and The Data Quality Blueprint comes in. The objective is to show the reader that a big problem can be approached in small steps, and that effort can be planned so it is spent most effectively and efficiently with the most positive effect for the least amount of money.

It is also worth noting that the objective of The Data Quality Blueprint is to start with the poor data quality that is causing the greatest business impact and can be remediated with the smallest effort. The organisation starts with the work that will make the biggest difference. Following the approach described in this book absolutely does not mean that an organisation will "boil the ocean" and look to remediate all data – that is an entirely unrealistic goal that would waste time and resources. Another of the central principles of The Data Quality Blueprint is to do as little work as possible.

> **Wolverhampton**
>
> # Wrong body was cremated due to spelling mistake and inadequate ID checks
>
> Errors led to body of Phil Bradburn being cremated instead of that of West Midlands MEP Philip Bradbourn

3.4   Summary

At this point we have covered a few of the reasons why nothing is done about data quality. This chapter is largely setting the scene for us to delve a little deeper and really find out where the costs mount up. Within the next three chapters I will cover:

- The strategic impacts of poor data quality – strategic impacts are difficult to measure, but are pervasive through the organisation. The main cost here is the cost of ignorance and the cost of poor decisions.
- The operational impacts of poor data quality – operational impacts are the way in which poor data quality costs you money on a day to day basis in a real, obvious, and measurable way.
- The regulatory effects of poor data quality – the costs of data quality that every business hopes to avoid. How regulators are increasingly focusing on data quality.

SECTION 2: THE IMPACT OF POOR DATA QUALITY

CHAPTER 4: STRATEGIC IMPACT OF POOR DATA QUALITY

4.1 Structure

This section of the book discusses four topics:

1. High level overview and introduction
2. Strategic impact of poor data quality
3. Operational impact of poor data quality
4. Regulatory impact of poor data quality

This chapter covers the second of these topics.

4.2 Overview

> "Because of lack of information, processes, and tools, through 2012, more than 35 percent of the top 5,000 global companies will regularly fail to make insightful decisions about significant changes in their business and markets."
> **Gartner, 2009.**

Within this book I have divided the discussion on the impact of poor data quality into three areas, the first of these being "Strategic". I believe this is the greatest cost of poor data quality in the organisation, but is also the most difficult to measure and understand, as the information to assess the impact is customarily non-existent. Within this chapter I will take you through some of the major impacts within the strategic space and demonstrate why they are so important, and why they are so affected by data quality.

4.3 The Cost of Poor Decisions (or the cost of a badly informed executive)

Probably the largest single cost of poor data quality is the cost of poor decisions. On a daily basis executives make decisions on the future of their organisation, and these decisions will be based on information. It naturally follows that if the information is incorrect then the decisions will be incorrect.

> *"The Data Warehousing Institute estimates that data quality problems cost U.S. businesses more than $600 billion a year.*
>
> *Yet, most executives are oblivious to the data quality lacerations that are slowly bleeding their companies to death.*
>
> *More injurious than the unnecessary printing, postage, and staffing costs is the slow but steady erosion of an organization's credibility among customers and suppliers, as well as its inability to make sound decisions based on accurate information."*[10]

The general response from organisations is that whilst data quality is accepted to be an issue, the view is that information is unlikely to be "materially" incorrect. I would disagree here. Apart from the data quality errors that hit the headlines because an organisation had got their data wrong by an amount measuring into the billions, my experience is that many critical business decisions are finely balanced and the margin between go/no go can be tipped either way based on small changes in underlying information. For example, a small change in margin, extrapolated out 10 years, may be the difference between a buy or not buy acquisition decision.

Tesco

Tesco's profits black hole bigger than expected and runs back several years

Supermarket, which is unable to provide any guidance on full-year profits, also said its under-fire chairman Sir Richard Broadbent is to resign

Media reports regularly will parade the cost of bad decisions across the business pages, and I am constantly surprised that more organisations do not think more about why these bad decisions were taken. Whilst it is of course possible to blame market changes, in many cases I would submit that – given better information – the bad decision would not have occurred in the first place. We often state that we would have done things differently if we knew then what we know now – the 20/20 hindsight rule. I would suggest that in many cases organisations did actually know the critical information before the poor decision, but the data quality was so poor that the organisation was not able to access it, or not in a timely manner.

It is difficult to put a value to the poor decision as because the good decision was not made, it is difficult to determine the effect of not making it. However, I would imagine that most of the players who received large regulatory fines would rather have previously made the decision to invest more in their data quality.

---

10. *Data Quality and the Bottom Line*, Wayne W. Eckerson, 2001

For example:

Data duplication (more than one record per customer) is an endemic problem within many sectors, but especially within the financial sector. Within my experience I have seen up to 15% duplication in any individual organisation and 10% is perfectly normal; let us consider the effect. For an organisation with a relatively modest 10% duplication;

- The customer numbers reported to the regulator are wrong.
- Market share will be 10% incorrect.
- Cash flow and profitability predictions will be wrong.
- Value/customer, earnings/customer and other similar key management metrics are incorrect.

This shows how a relatively small amount of duplication – and one entirely in line with industry norms – can have a significant effect. This, of course, does not touch on the many other reasons why customer data may be wrong (e.g. deceased customers incorrectly treated as live, test customers on the live database). Nor does it touch on the many other forms of data that may be incorrect – for example exchange rates, balances, product types, historical performance information, etc. The organisation will make decisions on a daily basis as a result of what it believes are values for critical metrics, and with poor data quality many (all?) will be wrong, with the resulting impact on what the organisation could have been. The table below summarises a few examples of the effect poor data can have on decision-making

Example of poor data quality	Example of poor decision as a result	Effect
Incorrect profit data	Either divestment of profitable business or retention of an unprofitable business that would have been sold if the true profitability figures were known.	- Loss of group profit - Erosion of shareholder value
Incorrect margin data	Either divestment of profitable business or retention of an unprofitable business that would have been sold if the true profitability figures were known.	- Loss of group profit - Erosion of shareholder value
Incorrect number of customers hence earnings per customer incorrect and market share incorrect.	Profitable customers may be divested or unprofitable customers retained All decisions based on market share will be incorrect.	- Loss of group and organisation profit - Erosion of shareholder value
Cost base information incorrect	Projects to reduce cost base may be poorly targeted, or targeted on cost already at a minimum.	- Wasted resources

Example of poor data quality	Example of poor decision as a result	Effect
Project performance data incorrect	Projects cancelled when on track or allowed to continue when financially unviable.	- Wasted resources - Erosion of value
Business cases incorrect	Projects authorised when unviable	- Wasted resources - Erosion of value
Financial account data incorrect	Dividends paid incorrectly Accounts incorrect Pay and bonus changes undeserved	- Shareholder confidence - Market confidence - Adverse audit report - Regulatory fines
Valuation data incorrect	Incorrect asset values, assets not treated in accordance with their value to the business. Accounts incorrect.	- Regulatory fines - Increased risk

4.4 Risk and Capital Management.

"Risk comes from not knowing what you're doing."
Warren Buffett

Risk management is integral to every modern organisation and critically depends on correct information, whether it be on assets and liabilities, interest rates, product, stock or cash, or any other measure. Unfortunately, in many organisations the data quality is not of a standard that allows the organisation to effectively manage its risks.

Although credit scoring systems are being implemented and used by many banks nowadays, they do face a number of limitations. A first limitation concerns the data that is used to estimate credit scoring models. Since data is the major, and in most cases the only, input to building these models, its quality and predictive ability is key to their success..........The disposal of high-quality data is a very important pre-requisite to build good credit scoring models. [11]

Without accurate information on the factors underlying risk exposure, then the organisation may either be closer to the edge than it thinks, or not making efficient use of its assets and therefore be at a competitive disadvantage. Risk management covers a wide spectrum. Traditionally, in financial sector, a deconstruction of risk is as shown in the hierarchy below. Almost all of these will critically depend on correct information.

---

11. *Credit Risk Management, Basic Concepts,* Gestel and Baesens, 2009

Risk

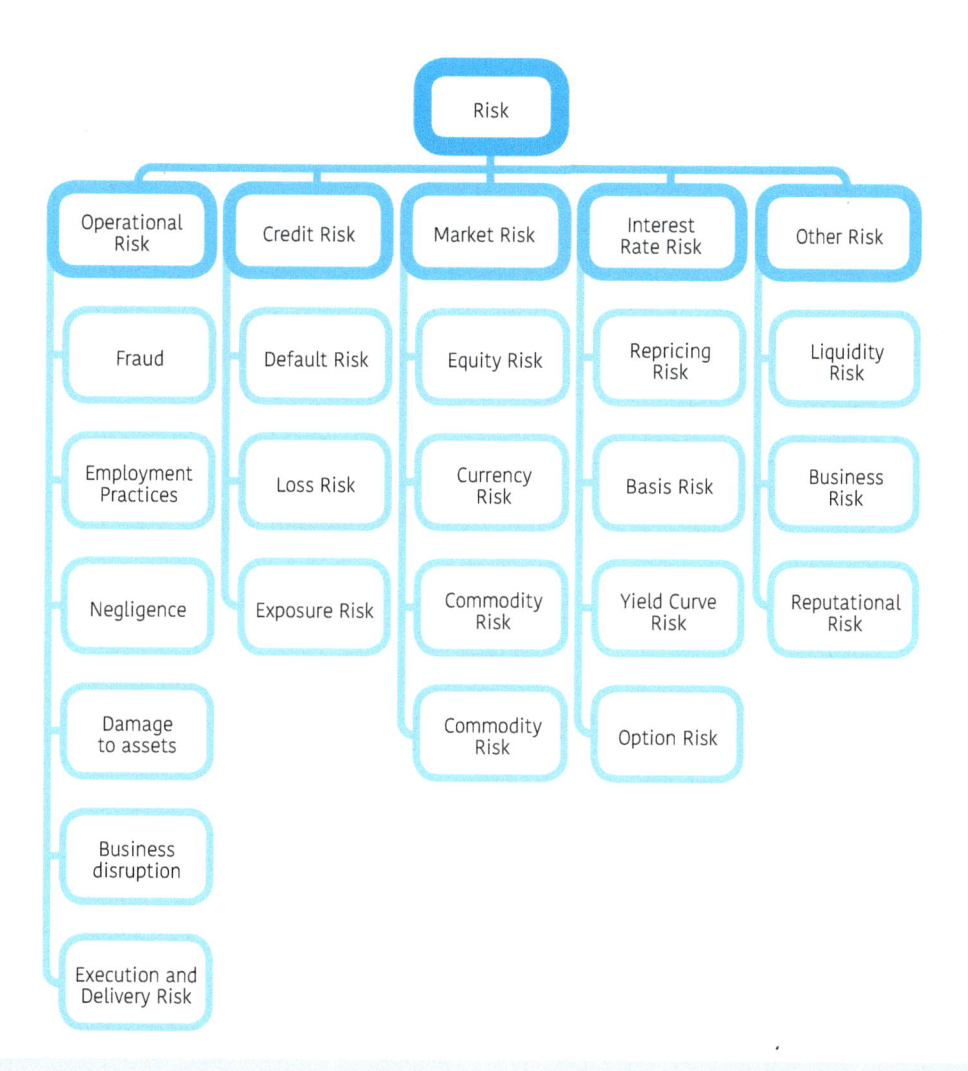

- **Operational Risk**
  - Fraud
  - Employment Practices
  - Negligence
  - Damage to assets
  - Business disruption
  - Execution and Delivery Risk
- **Credit Risk**
  - Default Risk
  - Loss Risk
  - Exposure Risk
- **Market Risk**
  - Equity Risk
  - Currency Risk
  - Commodity Risk
  - Commodity Risk
- **Interest Rate Risk**
  - Repricing Risk
  - Basis Risk
  - Yield Curve Risk
  - Option Risk
- **Other Risk**
  - Liquidity Risk
  - Business Risk
  - Reputational Risk

> "A big New York bank found that the data in its credit-risk management database were only 60 percent complete, necessitating double-checking by anyone using it."
> **Richard Wang and Diane Strong, *Beyond Accuracy, what data means to data consumers*, 1996.**

Risk management is an integral part of capital management, as – within the finance sector at least – the amount of capital that an organisation is required to hold is inextricably linked to its analysis of the risk of either default or valuation (in the case of banks) or of claim (in the case of insurance).

In addition, on a day to day basis most large organisations calculate how much cash they are likely to need to operate their business and this cash comes with a cost attached, being the cost of the money not earned by keeping the funds in a more advantageous location. Clearly the more accurately the capital requirements – operational and strategic – of the organisation can be calculated the better off and more efficiently it can manage its funds. For example, having enough funds to cover the next day operation is critical, and depends on correct data on the current funds and exactly what will be needed the next day. The latter is likely to be calculated on historical trends. All of this is information-driven. Poor data quality will result in poor capital management and loss of opportunity for a better return, or increased capital risk.

The effect of poor data quality on wider risk management can be broadly categorised into the measurement of the validity of the risk models that underpin the business, and the measurement of risk. Measurement of the effect of poor data quality on risk should be a critical KPI of any organisation. Risk is a derived value, and it is derived from data, specifically data on how likely is disaster to occur and what would be the impact if it does. Clearly an organisation with poor data quality is going to fail to adequately measure its exposure to risk. It may either overestimate the safety margin it needs, and run at a level where it is not making the best use of its resources, or, worse, underestimate the same and then be caught short when the worst occurs or when exposed to stress. Equally it may underestimate the frequency of threat, or the degree to which a loss event will affect areas of the organisation.

For example, credit risk depends on default risk, loss risk and exposure risk.

```
                    Credit Risk
         ┌──────────────┼──────────────┐
    Default Risk     Loss Risk    Exposure Risk
```

Default risk is the risk of default, loss risk is the risk relating to the magnitude of the loss, and the exposure risk relates to the ability of financial products to change in size over time (for example, credit card balances). Default risk will be calculated on a basket of customer characteristics (income, age, credit history) and loss risk on the product (value of the property in the case of a mortgage). Any deficiency in data quality will result in an incorrect measure.

Risk modelling uses a variety of techniques to calculate the risk to the organisation from a portfolio of assets or liabilities or similar. The validity of these models is intrinsically linked to the quality of the data that they use. The challenge is to adequately measure the effect of poor quality in the underlying data. For example, it is possible to take a risk model and determine the numerical effect of poor data on the model. Risk models will take an input of – for example – probability of default. This will be calculated on a number of factors, and each will have a data quality element to them. It is possible to estimate the change in risk if the data turned out to be incorrect by running the risk model for different data quality scenarios. For example:

- What if all the "unknown" or unpopulated lines of data were at the highest risk rating possible – or at the lowest?
- What if the data was wrong by 5%, or 10%?

The table below summarises a few examples of the effect poor data can have on risk management.

Example of poor data quality	Result	Effect
Risk weighted assets (from which capital adequacy is derived) is based on a combination of PD, LGD, EAD, etc. If any of these are incorrect then capital calculations will be incorrect.	Capital calculations incorrect Inefficient use of capital resources	- Loss of group profit - Erosion of shareholder value
Threat frequency incorrect	Resources are utilised to mitigate a risk that is unlikely to occur – or resources are not utilised to mitigate a risk that is likely.	- Incorrect use (loss) of capital
Magnitude of potential loss incorrect	The (incorrect) information results in a significant loss to the organisation as no steps have been taken to guard against it.	- Loss of capital - Loss of profitability - Erosion of shareholder value

4.5 Poor Relations between IT and the Business.

"When asked how they address their technical issues at work, 40% of employees said their first choice was IT, however, 40 percent said their first choice was to either look for an answer on the Internet (23%) or turn to a co-worker who doesn't work in IT (17%). For 19% of employees, IT was their third choice."
Gartner vice president Debra Logan

Poor data quality will result in poor relations between IT and the business – two parts of the organisation that should work hand-in-glove, but rarely do. There is often a degree of distrust between IT and the business it supports, as the different departments traditionally do not understand each other well. However, poor data quality makes a bad situation worse.

As data comes from IT systems the data is often seen by the business as "IT-derived" and if data does not meet their expectations then they are likely to blame IT. However, IT will understandably state that the quality of business data is not their problem, and that they are merely custodians of what has been placed in systems by the business, and it is up to the business to solve it. This is a fundamental disconnect that exists throughout organisations where data is poor, and whilst it is difficult to put an exact value on the problem the table below describes a number of effects this can have. Business and IT have to work together to make the organisation a success. Having poor data quality simply breeds distrust and suspicion.

Symptom	Cause	Business effect
IT projects do not deliver expected business benefit	Poor understanding of requirements by IT, poor relationships mean that requirements are simply passed over the fence rather than business and IT working together	■ Project failure cost ■ Project rework cost ■ Loss of capital ■ Loss of changes that could have been made
IT projects do not deliver expected business benefit	Poor specification of the requirements by the business, leaving it to IT to interpret the requirement without guidance	■ Project failure cost ■ Project rework cost ■ Loss of capital ■ Loss of changes that could have been made
IT projects over-run	IT do not see business priorities – either time or cost – as relevant, and hence do not operate in either the most efficient or effective way	■ Project failure cost ■ Project rework cost ■ Loss of capital ■ Loss of changes that could have been made
Delays due to IT "procedures"	IT see the business as "a pain in the neck" and do not see business priorities as important	■ Time-critical business processes fail ■ Personnel time wasted chasing critical changes
Critical projects not implemented	Because the business – which ultimately needs to sign off funding – does not trust IT time is wasted on excessive governance of the sign-off process	■ Critical projects delayed ■ Personnel time wasted ■ Projects over-run
Problems fall between business and IT resulting in no-one taking ownership	Solution delayed Time wasted in argument	■ Personnel time wasted ■ Savings in time and effort from solution not realised
Operation is to the Service Level Agreement, not to what is most efficient, effective, or possible	Service level agreements used to control IT relationship	■ Un-necessary delays ■ Time wasted

4.6 Lack of Trust of Data throughout the Organisation

"Common data errors plague 91 percent of organizations."
Experian, The State of Data Quality, 2014

If data quality is poor, time and effort will be wasted within the organisation due to lack of trust in data. Departments may have different figures for the same metric, each of which is calculated internally as central data is not trusted. This lack of trust may stem from different definitions used in different departments, or, often multiple databases with different information – no "single version of the truth". In fact, lack of trust may cause a problem even when there is little wrong with the data. Relatively minor data quality issues may still cause staff to expend considerable effort to corroborate the system-produced data. Even after a data quality improvement project, staff may continue to undertake extensive checking operations as they do not believe the data as historically it has always been incorrect. Although lack of trust may point to data quality issues it may also point to cultural issues. It will be necessary, if undertaking a data quality project, to ensure staff are part of the dialogue, and that they subsequently gain a trust of what the data is showing them. In terms of quantification of the amount of money to be saved by increasing the somewhat nebulous value "trust", this is dealt with in the "operational impact of data quality" section under "time costs of rework of data". However, the table below describes a number of effects this can have.

Cause	Result	Business effect
Departmental staff rework data to achieve accurate values	Staff time and effort wasted	Loss of group profit Erosion of shareholder value
Even when data accurate repeated checking is in place	Staff time and effort wasted	Personnel time wasted Increased costs
Multiple versions of the golden source	Staff time and effort wasted	Personnel time wasted Increased costs
Departmental staff rework data to achieve accurate values	Significant "shadow IT" where business critical information is held in locations such as local drives, not backed up nor secured	Increased organisational risk
Departmental staff rework data to achieve accurate values	Critical staff vulnerabilities exist throughout the organisation	Increased organisational risk

4.7 Missed Opportunities.

The timeliness of information is important. "The early bird catches the worm" is as true in business as in nature, and the quicker a business is to identify an issue – whether it be falling profitability in a department or on a product line, or a market change that affects sales, the quicker it can react. A common scenario is that management information is substantially out of date. Receipt of the sales data from 1st–31st March at the board meeting towards the end of April is fine if you don't mind looking at statistics that are nearly two months old, but that is (often) the accepted norm. The longer it takes to put together management information the more out of date it will be. The poorer the data quality, the more fragmented the data, the more time it will take to weave a coherent story and the longer it will take to get to decision makers. By this point in time it is likely that any opportunity has long passed, or that the upside has been substantially reduced by faster and more flexible competitors. The table below describes a number of effects this can have.

Issue	Opportunities missed	Business effect
Cannot capitalise on changes in market	Market changes happen overnight, and often the best results are obtained by those who are quickest to react	▪ Loss of group profit ▪ Erosion of shareholder value
Cannot capitalise on actions by competitor	A competitor may make a mistake, or it may change its strategy, or may be subject to adverse publicity. In the same way as the above, the earliest to react is likely to reap the greatest reward.	▪ Loss of profit ▪ Loss of turnover ▪ Loss of market share
Cannot stop things going wrong	If a part of the organisation is losing money then it can be stopped only once the loss is known. A delay of even days may result in large losses that could have been stopped if known about early enough.	▪ Erosion of shareholder value ▪ Loss of capital ▪ Loss of profit ▪ Loss of margin

4.8 Business Intelligence and Mis-targeted Marketing

"81 percent of organizations encounter problems when trying to generate meaningful business intelligence, mainly due to data inaccuracies."
Experian, The State of Data Quality, 2014

In order to gain insight into your current operation, the data that is used to gain that insight needs to be correct. "Garbage in, garbage out" being the most succinct way of putting this. Critical measures such as customer profitability, market penetration, even basic information relating to the number of customers will be incorrect if the data is wrong, and incorrect decisions will be made which are likely to be strategically adverse to the business. Business intelligence that covers subjects such as customer propensity to buy, sell, or default, is pointless if the data you are using is not of a good enough quality for you to rely on the results. The use of big data – with potentially billions of data points – can to a degree get around this problem on the basis that "it cannot all be wrong, can it?" The problem with big data in relation to data quality – discussed elsewhere in this book – is that big data is often "someone else's data" and the quality is unknown. There may be a lot of it but it might all be rubbish.

Unfortunately, in some poor data quality environments, the lack of quality is often made up for by quantity, and the executive is then expected to try and work out a true picture themselves by looking for correlation between hundreds of measures. This is inefficient and those who set strategy and manage the organisation would be better served by being given one, correct, figure rather than hundreds of might-be-rights. Although partially covered by the "missed opportunities" section above, data quality will determine who an organisation thinks are its best and worst customers, and data mining will underpin marketing and, to an extent, product and pricing decisions. The table below describes a number of effects this can have.

Issue	Marketing effect	Business Impact
Cannot identify largest customers	Customers are not valued or treated in any special way, do not feel valued, and take business elsewhere	Lower turnover Lower profit Reduced market share
Cannot identify customers with the most potential up sell or cross-sell	Customers are not targeted in the most productive way	Lower turnover Lower profit Reduced market share
Cannot identify most or least profitable customers	The reason for the profitability (or otherwise) of these customers cannot be determined and hence no action can be taken to either use them as examples or look to improve their profitability	Lower margin Lower profit
Cannot identify most or least profitable products	As above	Lower margin Lower profit

4.9 Reputational Impact

"Getting names wrong can have a significant impact on individuals and companies. Reputations can be damaged, often irreparably. With 2015 still in its infancy, we've already seen two major UK public sector organisations paying a high price for not focusing sufficiently on something as apparently simple as getting a name right."
***What's in a name? How poor Data Quality can lead to catastrophic reputational damage**, IPL, 2015*

Except in rare cases of spectacular organisational failure, well documented and forming a small, select group who have made national news and which no organisation wishes to join, the cost of reputational damage resulting from poor data quality is difficult to determine. Of the organisations that have blazed a trail down the path to oblivion, few have been helpful enough to specifically note that poor data quality was the cause of their demise, but certainly a number would state that "if we knew then what we know now....."

4.10 Summary

In this chapter I have tried to cover the strategic impact of poor data quality. This has covered:

- The cost of poor decisions (or the cost of a badly informed executive).
- Risk and capital management.
- Poor relations between IT and the business.
- Lack of trust of data throughout the organisation.
- Missed opportunities.
- Business intelligence and mis-targeted marketing.
- Reputational impact.

It should be seen that poor data quality is a cancer that infects everything in an organisation and everything that the organisation does. It is not simply an IT problem, or a nice-to-have, it is costing money every day. In the next chapter I will cover the operational impacts of poor data quality in the same way.

SECTION 2: THE IMPACT OF POOR DATA QUALITY

CHAPTER 5: OPERATIONAL IMPACT OF POOR DATA QUALITY

5.1 Structure

This section of the book discusses four topics:

1. High level overview and introduction
2. Strategic impact of poor data quality
3. Operational impact of poor data quality
4. Regulatory impact of poor data quality

This chapter covers the third of these topics.

5.2 Introduction

"Gartner research shows that poor-quality customer data leads to significant costs, such as higher customer turnover, excessive expenses from customer contact processes like mail-outs and missed sales opportunities. But companies are now discovering that data quality has a significant impact on their most strategic business initiatives, not only sales and marketing. Other back-office functions like budgeting, manufacturing and distribution are also affected."
Gartner 2007

Operational costs of poor data quality are more quantifiable in comparison to the strategic costs. Typically data quality publications appear to be reticent on this, and I will confess to wondering why. It may be because the focus is so concentrated on the IT angle that business costs are a secondary element, or simply may be seen as a nebulous measurement it is difficult to firmly grasp. As with strategic impacts of poor data quality, there is an understanding gap to be bridged with many parts of an organisation. Data quality may be seen as being "good enough" for day to day operation, and therefore what is the problem? "After all we make a profit?" "If it ain't broke, don't fix it".

My view here is to use the analogy of an individual taking a long journey in an old and worn-out car. Whilst they may get to the destination, it will not be as fast, or as smooth, or in as much comfort as a more recent model. Of course, the risk of mishap is greater in the older model, the brakes will not work as well, and there is going to come a time where someone is going to have to get out and push. So it is with data quality. Running an organisation with poor data is possible, but hard work. In the same way that the new car will be far more fuel-efficient than the old, running an organisation with poor data quality it costs you money. Organisations operationally haemorrhage funds as a result.

In this chapter, I will take you through some of the more common ways in which organisations lose money due to the poor quality of their data. It is not a complete, exhaustive list, because poor data quality will cost an organisation everywhere. However, this chapter will cover the basics. I would suggest that it is highly likely that some of the contents of this chapter will remind you of similar behaviours and problems in an organisation from your direct experience.

5.3   Time Cost of repeatedly reworking of Existing Data

This is one of the most frustrating causes of high operational business cost, because it is so preventable. This issue occurs when staff at managerial levels spend a large amount of time cleaning data before use – whether this be for critical business decisions, or before incorporating it into reports for the executive or the regulator. This follows on from the comments in the earlier chapter about trust – or lack of it – being a significant strategic and tactical challenge to an organisation. If professional staff do not trust the data they use to make decisions then they will take steps to either or both determine the quality of data, or clean it themselves.

Anecdote
The financial controller of a large organisation once stated to me that his staff were spending 80% of their time cleansing data and 20% of their time using it.

This is a common scenario and is not the best use of the time of expensive staff, who are not by nature or job description, data professionals (though they may well be extremely good indeed due to long-suffering experience). Their time should be better spent managing the business and utilising the data rather than spending time cleaning it in spreadsheets. Unfortunately, this is often not seen as an issue by the board, because they are insulated from the time and trouble needed to meet their requirements. "Get me the sales figures for August" says the CEO to the Head of Finance, who passes the request on to an analyst. The CEO, and sometimes the Head of Finance, have no idea that the seemingly innocent and easy "get me the sales figures for August" means:

- days of work collating the sales figures from various departments (all of who use slightly different month ends or definitions of the word "sales"),
- amalgamating them (probably in spreadsheets),
- cleaning the data
- mashing the whole together to obtain a sales figure which will then be presented to the CEO three days later

– all for a report that should be run in seconds.

Of course, as the CEO will assume that the report will be run in seconds, they will be annoyed that it has taken three days and will probably have a poor view of the Head of Finance. The Head of Finance may understand, but may simply be annoyed and frustrated with the analyst, and the analyst has been set an impossible task as systems do not support the business requirements, due to poor communication between the business, IT and the application vendor some years in the past. Improving the data quality will vastly increase productivity across these staff, and rather than the data being cleaned at every month end the work can be performed once for an immediate and long term benefit. In terms of quantifying the amount of money to be saved it is moderately easy to ask staff about their role and how they use data and calculate the savings if much of the transformational cleansing was not necessary. To create the greatest effect on productivity these staff must be involved in any data quality project, and bring their requirements into the objectives, as otherwise a large amount of work can be undertaken to swap one cleaning activity for another. The table below describes a number of ways in which poor data quality in this area will harm the organisation.

Issue	Cause	Business Impact
Reports not delivered on time	Data has to be reworked as it arrives incorrectly	▪ Wasted personnel time ▪ Higher costs
Reports contain errors	Data has to be amalgamated from many sources as it is not fit for purpose	▪ Poor decisions made
Data is not trusted	Staff spend time checking data when it is actually correct	▪ Wasted personnel time ▪ Higher costs
Staff working long hours	Staff having to spend time reworking data	▪ High staff turnover
Staff working long hours	Staff not appreciated	▪ High staff turnover
Requirement for repeated checking and cross-checking	Complexity means great difficulty in creating information	▪ Wasted personnel time ▪ Higher costs
Critical person vulnerabilities	High end user computing means only one person may know how to provide reporting	▪ Greater risk to the business
Higher end user computing	Most rework is performed locally, on local drives	▪ Greater risk to the business

5.4   Loss of Efficiency

Anecdote
A friend manages an optical practice. When spectacles or contact lenses arrive from the manufacturer the practice rings up the customer to let them know, so the customer can come in and collect them. Many phone numbers are, however, incorrect.

The member of staff responsible then has to find some headed paper, and print out and post a letter to let the customer know their spectacles or contact lenses have arrived. This not only takes far longer than a phone call, so the staff time cost is greater, but postage costs are far higher than the cost of the phone call, the news reaches the customer slower, and the personal contact from a phone call is better customer service than a letter, which can be impersonal.

A very common effect of poor data quality is that the organisation cannot perform tasks as efficiently as it would if the data quality was good. The example used above is typical. Because of the data quality failure a second best approach has to be taken, costing money.

This may appear a trivial example, but multiply by millions of customers in a large enterprise and the cost is substantial. Multiply by every process affected and the cost can be massive. To give a scale, in the example above a 30 second phone call may cost less than £0.05. A letter, in time and postage costs, will be unlikely to cost less than £1.00. This is a twentyfold increase in cost.

The job is still done, but there is a measurable loss in efficiency.

Issue	Cause	Business Impact
Inefficient processes have to be used	Data does not exist that would enable ideal process to be followed	▪ Wasted personnel time ▪ Higher costs

5.5 Cost of Project Failure

"More than 50 percent of data warehouse projects will have limited acceptance, or will be outright failures, as a result of a lack of attention to data quality issues"…"the average time for the construction of a data warehouse is 12 to 36 months and the average cost for its implementation is between $1 million to $1.5 million"
Gartner, 2007

Failed projects cost vast amounts of money. The reasons for project failure vary, but are often due to poor data quality. Of course, any project may fail as a result of data quality issues, but particular emphasis for **IT-related** project failures will be:

- Data Warehousing
- Business Intelligence
- Single Customer View
- Big Data
- Management Information
- Data Migration

Business-related projects that are likely to fail as a result of data quality may include:

- Strategy Development
- Internal Cost Reduction Exercises
- Marketing Initiatives
- Profitability management

With the cost of large projects running into the millions, this is a lot of money to throw away. Going back to a previous comment, it is common, when picking over the corpse of a recently dead project for managers to state that "if only we knew then what we know now". I would submit that in at least 50% of the cases there was the possibility for them to know, but the data quality was not there for them to access the information. The table below describes a number of ways in which data quality in this area will harm the organisation.

Issue	Effect	Business Impact
Project data needs significant cleansing	Project overruns time and/or budget	▪ Higher cost ▪ Excess capital expenditure
Project data needs significant cleansing	Project requires source system experts that was not originally included in budget	▪ Higher costs ▪ Expert cannot perform day job ▪ Higher risk to business
Project performance data incorrect	Unable to determine success of project Unable to make decision to terminate until too late	▪ Wasted resources ▪ Wasted time ▪ Higher costs ▪ Project failure

5.6 Missed Sales Opportunities

"Data is oxygen to the direct marketing community. All the elegant solutions and revenue generating mechanisms – segmentation, personalisation, in- bound/out-bound integration, analytics, profiling, event-triggering and so on – are starved of life without it, and tainted by impurities in it."
Jeremy Bedford

A common scenario is organisations have siloed data. This often occurs when an organisation sells multiple products, has recently acquired another organisation, or is departmentally fragmented. Due to commonality of this scenario it will be used as an example multiple times in the book.

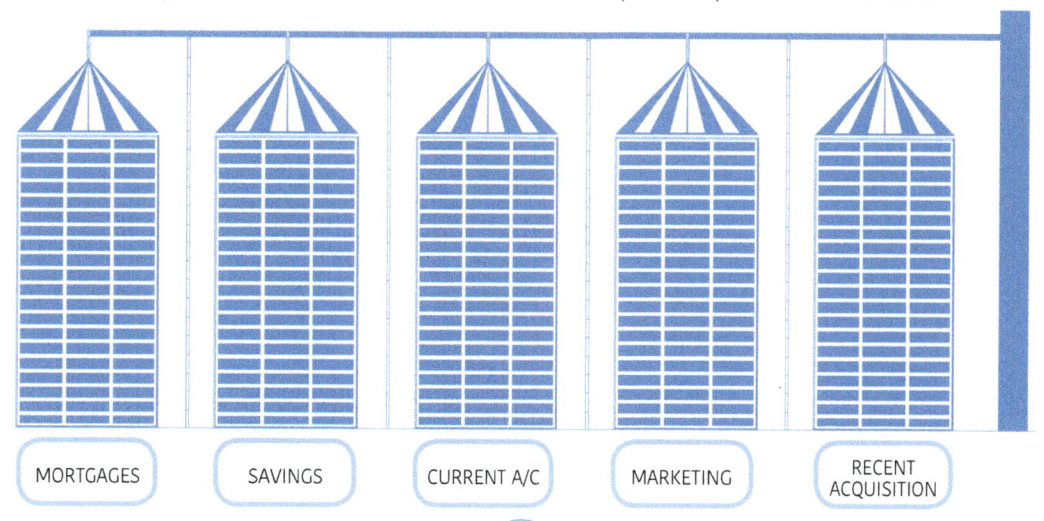

MORTGAGES SAVINGS CURRENT A/C MARKETING RECENT ACQUISITION

In the above diagram, the mortgage, savings, current account, as well as the marketing data are all held in each silo and do not interact. The recently bought organisation stands alone. This creates problems, and many organisations are endeavouring to create a single customer view to enable cross-selling and to facilitate cross-organisation reporting. Poor data quality may make this impossible, and may, as a result, cause reputational damage and customer dissatisfaction. For example, the intention is to try and sell Product A which is already owned by Customer A (your existing computer) to Customer B (a new customer in the organisation you have just bought). With poor data quality you may find:

- Customer B already has Product A – and is now irritated with you.
- Customer B = Customer A – and is now irritated with you.
- Customer C = Customer A = Customer B and is one of your most loyal customers and has all your products, and you've now made yourself look stupid, and made it look to Customer A/B/C that you don't value their custom.

Alternatively, you may find:

- Customer A doesn't actually have Product A. Customer B has Product A.
- So when you try and sell Product A to Customer B they say they already have it, and you've missed the opportunity to sell it to Customer A who would have happily given you the money.

Even after establishing what you think is a single customer view poor data quality means that it is easy to:

- Miss opportunities for revenue
- Inflict reputational damage

The table below describes a number of ways in which data quality in this area will harm the organisation.

Issue	Missed Sales Opportunity	Business Impact
Cannot identify customers who do not have products	Do not sell to customers	- Lower turnover - Lower profit - Reduced market share
Cannot identify customers who do have products	Customers are not targeted in the most productive way	- Lower turnover - Lower profit - Reduced market share
Cannot identify relationships between customers	People who live together may do similar things. If one has insurance for being a climber, and the other party does not, has the company missed a sales opportunity if it cannot recognise this?	- Lower turnover - Lower profit - Reduced market share

Issue	Missed Sales Opportunity	Business Impact
Cannot de-duplicate customers	Customers targeted multiple times causing reputational damage and eventually causing customer loss	- Reduced market share - Lower turnover - Lower profit

5.7   Poor Customer Relations & Customer Retention

Anecdote
One acquaintance of mine with a long African surname told me it took **five years** for her bank to get the name on her current account spelt correctly.

Whilst this is likely to raise a smile with most (potentially due to their own experiences), the degree of frustration for the individual is difficult to appreciate.

It goes without saying that poor data quality is frustrating for customers. Most individuals who have non-standard or easily misspelled names have first-hand experience of ringing up contact centres to be told that they do not exist, or the organisation has no record of a transaction (as it occurred under a different customer ID), or that a letter has not been received (ditto). This may include being refused service as the "ID" is in the wrong name, being unable to pay for items, a long and frustrating argument whenever contacting the bank, or potential problems setting up direct debits and standing orders. Needless to say this is not the way to create happy customers, as they are expected to spend time and money to sort out a problem with data quality that should not have occurred in the first place and was never their fault.

A good way of detecting this kind of data quality issue is customer complaints. A flag can indicate whether data quality issues are causing problems for the organisation's customer experience and the problem queued for remediation. It is also possible via this method to get a feel for costs of the customer experience in terms of customer retention. If a customer repeatedly complains about their name being incorrectly spelt, and then leaves the organisation, then it is reasonable to assume that the persistent inability to correct data quality issues is a factor in their desertion. These metrics are reasonably easily obtainable. However, and this is important, in order to work this out there is often a sea change required in attitude.

"The customer failed security because they got their date of birth wrong" is something I have heard on more than one occasion. Really? A customer got their own date of birth wrong? Is that actually likely? Customers may forget passwords on a daily basis, but date of birth? As soon as a customer gets a key element of information, such as a date of birth or address incorrect, the first assumption should be either fraud or that the data quality on the systems is incorrect – rather than the customer not being able to remember their own date of birth – and, if anti-fraud checks are passed, a flag raised to that effect – "suspected data quality issue on date of birth". The table below describes a number of ways in which data quality in this area will harm the organisation

Issue	Effect	Business Impact
Security data incorrect	Customer cannot access accounts and leaves organisation	■ Wasted personnel time ■ Reduced market share ■ Lower turnover
Customer name incorrect	Customer resentment results in customer leaving organisation	■ Reduced market share ■ Lower turnover ■ Reputational damage
Incorrect address data	Customer private details mailed elsewhere	■ Data protection issues ■ Legal and regulatory fines ■ Reputational damage

Anecdote

Another experience of an individual with one bank was badly marred (and they eventually left) because the bank had managed to record the individual's date of birth wrong. As the date of birth was an integral part of the security questions whenever the customer rang the bank they failed security checks until some helpful operator told the individual which one, of the various security questions, they had got wrong.

However, changing the date of birth meant sending off an original birth certificate, copies were not acceptable. As it turned out the birth certificate the customer had been safely stowing all these years was not, actually, an original – it was a certified copy. This was not enough for this particular bank.

This individual would have had to request another original from the national register office, and then send it to the bank, who then might deem to change the date of birth on the account, and then the individual might be able to get through security.

Except they didn't. That particular individual left the bank.

5.8   IT Costs

Certain types of poor data quality are going to result in increased IT costs, and some of these are measurable. This may not top the league of increased-costs-due-to-poor-data-quality, but are still significant. To take the example used before of 10% duplication:

- All queries that are run by every area of the business will take longer as they have to query more data.
- Data storage costs are greater than they need to be.
- Maintenance costs will be higher than they should be.
- Remaining storage capacity is understated and large projects to upgrade IT infrastructure will be undertaken earlier than strictly required.
- The disaster recovery site is over-specified, and if it has to be used, it is likely to take longer to transfer operations.

With the exception of the latter two, it is relatively easy to measure the overall cost in terms of IT cost per data item. The marginal cost of holding the extra data will be the extra 10% on everything that is involved with servicing the customer data. The earlier statement that the cost of poor data is 20% of revenue now starts to make sense. In a service organisation the cost of sales is primarily that work undertaken to service customers or customer data. However if 10% of those customers are duplicates, then a cost of 20-30% of turnover starts to look plausible. This is especially the case given that quality costs through duplication are only one element of poor data quality cost. Increased IT costs are going to be critical when a business is on the cusp of major change (platform upgrade or similar) as a result of data volume or data performance. A data quality initiative may, in addition to all the other benefits, allow major change/upgrade to be postponed. This, in itself, it unlikely to be a reason for a data quality initiative, but it is certainly an ancillary benefit and should be counted in the business case if relevant. The table below describes a number of ways in which data quality in this area will harm the organisation.

Issue	Effect	Business Impact
Duplication of data	IT storage costs higher Disaster Recovery costs higher	Higher costs
Duplication of data	Queries take longer to run Decision to make capital purchases taken earlier than required	Higher costs Adverse cash flow
Incorrect data	Cleansing required hence higher complexity and specialist skillset	Higher costs
Inconsistent data	Significant time required to ensure data routines cope with every data possibility Higher risk of disaster recovery failure	Higher costs Greater risk

5.9   Mailing Overspend

One of the easiest demonstrations of the cost of poor quality is customer mailing. Most businesses will send documents or packages to a customer address, whether it be statements, invoices, marketing, or deliveries. Even in today's digital world, the amount of individual physical mail is staggering. In 2012-2013 Royal Mail, according to their own information, delivered over 15 billion items, around 58 million items a day.[12] It is relatively trivial to find out for an individual business the cost of poor address data quality.

---

12.   Royal Mail Published Accounts, 2013.

- The carrier will tell you how many items are undeliverable.
- It is reasonably easy to work out a rough level of duplication in the mailing file.

The former is invalid addresses, the latter is duplicate addresses. Royal Mail, according to a Freedom of Information request, shreds 25 million undeliverable items per year. Nearly 300,000 letters or packages a week are sent to the returns centre. However, these are merely undeliverable addresses. Incorrect addresses – in respect of old addresses or simply wrong addresses – are harder to detect.

Anecdote
A colleague of mine recently ended up in a row with his bank after they stopped all his accounts. He had recently moved house, and unfortunately the bank had recorded the new address incorrectly. As far as the bank were concerned they were sending him a number of increasingly red letters requesting that he solve a problem, however he was not receiving these letters.

This ended up in an abject apology from the bank, a large refund, a goodwill refund and a vast amount of wasted time – quite apart from an unhappy customer.

The table below describes a number of ways in which data quality in this area will harm the organisation.

Issue	Effect	Business Impact
Delivery to a non-existent address	Mail returned (hence incurring costs)	- Wasted personnel time - Wasted IT costs - Wasted mailing costs
Delivery to the wrong address	If the householder simply puts the letter in the bin, you may never know	- Wasted personnel time - Wasted IT costs - Wasted mailing costs
Data protection breach	Sending confidential data to the wrong person	- Legal sanction - Regulatory sanction
Reputational damage	Customer leaves	- Reduction in market share - Reduction in turnover - Reduction in profit

5.10 Crime and Terrorism

JUN 29

Insurer calls for FSA to set standards on data quality to help combat fraud

2009

Ecclesiastical Insurance has called for the Financial Services Authority to set standards in governance of insurance claims and on data quality to help combat fraud. Simon Arundel, risk manager, claims and risk services, at Ecclesiastical Insurance, said at the IEA and Marketforce's Claims Forum 2009: "If the FSA says treat customers fairly, we do it. If it said that we must change the quality of data, this would be our priority. I'd like to see the FSA involved in the governance of claims."

Good data quality will mitigate exposure to loss through crime. In the same way it is difficult to find a significant but small item in an untidy room poor data quality makes it more difficult to identify criminal activity. This is not only critical to operational loss, but also critical to relationships with the regulator (of which more in the next chapter), who are understandably very interested in activities to identify and limit criminal activity. In this regard, the following quote is relevant.

> *"Criminals' efforts to distance their money from their crime is greatly aided by access to the financial system. To guard against this, and to allow the authorities to trace suspicious funds, the law imposes a range of obligations on financial services institutions – to know who your clients are and where their money comes from."* [13]

Criminals and terrorists are often known to the authorities, and will go to great lengths to hide their real identities from the organisations with which they do business lest they are identified and reported. For example, without access to the financial system the activity of criminals is severely curtailed, as they need access to normal banking operations to fund their activities and engage with legitimate organisations. Criminals will go to lengths to disguise their identity which includes the use of false names and addresses. The financial system needs to be able to identify them, both to ensure that they are brought to justice but also to protect the innocent users of the financial system from crime.

Equally, money laundering – by which profit from criminal activities is transformed into money that appears to be from legal activities – is critical to enable a criminal to practically profit from their crime. Criminals will attempt to hide their activities through the use of multiple layers of obfuscation between their crime and the eventual use of the money. The financial system goes to some lengths to limit the potential for money laundering and to enable criminals to be brought to justice. These lengths depend on the knowledge of the customer and an understanding of the pattern of transactions expected from both criminal and innocent activity. Finally, terrorists can be identified by the pattern of their transactions through the banking system. Not only by large transfers to and from areas with significant terrorist activity, but also suspicious activity or unusual transactions.

Good quality data enables an organisation to be confident when it discovers criminal activity. By removing the issue of data quality from the possible reasons for a pattern of characteristics that meet criteria indicating crime, the work required to identify crime is reduced – crime can be discovered earlier, and remedial action taken to prevent further loss. In reality, in many cases it is impossible to discover criminal activity as poor data quality creates thousands of false positives or no results at all. Alternatively, the identification of criminal activity takes too long because of the time taken to filter out the real crimes from the background noise. Criminal activity that may have had minimal impact if it was discovered at an early stage is allowed to continue with an increasing loss to the organisation and an increasing impact on its innocent customers. The table below describes a number of ways in which data quality in this area will harm the organisation.

---

13. Tracey McDermott, Director of Enforcement & Financial Crime, the FCA, at the FCA Financial Crime Conference, 2013.

Issue	Effect	Business Impact
Crime not identified	Organisation has to bear loss	■ Higher costs
Crime not identified on a timely basis	Embarrassing admission of system failure	■ Reputational damage ■ Legal and regulatory sanction
Unable to link customer data	Only part of a crime is identified	■ Higher costs ■ Reputational damage ■ Legal and regulatory sanction
Unable to share crime data with authorities in a timely manner	Requests for data records not met	■ Legal and regulatory sanction

5.11 Transactional Failures.

It is the nature of most organisations that transactions depend on data being transferred from one department to another and for data to be matched between one department and another. These processes are generally automated, and poor data quality can cause poor matching between a sending and receiving data set, which can potentially cost large amounts of money.

Anecdote

To give a real world example, one large financial institution used a look-up table to determine the amount of sales within a day and thence the amount of funds that needed to be sourced from the financial markets. Due to a typing error in one of the lookup tables an entire product group was not picked up, resulting in a significant (multi-million) loss overnight due to movement in exchange rate. Yes there are process issues inherent in this example, but there are data quality issues too.

The table below describes a number of ways in which data quality in this area will harm the organisation.

Issue	Effect	Business Impact
Matching of information between systems fails	Incorrect reporting, incorrect decision making	■ Lower profit ■ Loss of revenue ■ Regulatory and legal issues ■ Loss of shareholder value
Transactions occur but not on a timely basis	Rectification of transactional failures mean that the transaction still occurs, but after a delay	■ Wasted personnel time ■ Loss of opportunity

5.12 Data Migration

> "83% of data migration projects either fail or exceed their budgets and schedules."
> **Gartner, 2005**

Any organisation that is looking to implement a data migration, or to implement a new IT system, should absolutely consider data quality before the data migration is undertaken. In fact, implementing a data quality project beforehand will significantly reduce the costs of the migration – and is much more likely to make the project a success. To take the above statement further, many data migration projects fail – often at huge cost – specifically because of the poor data quality in the source systems. It all comes down to the fact that data that is a mess is difficult to move. There are a number of choices at this point for data quality issues affecting migration:

- Ignore and accept that the data will not migrate
- Fix before the migration
- Fix after the migration
- Fix during the migration
- Ignore and persist with the migration with the errors

A data migration will typically create hundreds of data quality related queries for the business if the source of the data is poor. These need to be addressed by business professionals who are experts in the affected areas. These decisions in relation to the data cannot be made by the IT team, or the data migration team. Failure to address data quality issues before starting a migration will result in any one or all of the below:

- A soaring cost of the migration.
- An increase in timescale for the migration (and therefore cost).
- A massive workload for busy individuals within the business areas who had no idea they would have to make hundreds or thousands of data decisions as part of the migration project that they thought was going to be delivered by IT.

The table below describes a number of ways in which data quality in this area will harm the organisation.

Issue	Effect	Business Impact
Data rejected by target	Data most be remediated or transformed in transit to meet target system rules	- Wasted personnel time - Higher costs
Referential integrity lost as some data transfers and some does not	Data most be remediated or transformed in transit to retain referential integrity	- Wasted personnel time - Higher costs

Issue	Effect	Business Impact
Automatic migration impossible	Manual migration used as a stop-gap until data issues solved	■ Wasted personnel time ■ Higher costs
Existing poor data transferred to target system	Target system polluted, migration never delivers results	■ Reputational damage ■ Poor return on investment

5.13 Profitability

Of course, all of the above contribute to profitability. It is difficult to determine in advance how much the profitability of the business will improve in relation to aggregate data quality improvements. In certain cases – like reduction in staff time, or customer complaints – a calculation is possible of the potential reduction in cost that would result from a data quality initiative, and this can be used to create a matrix of data quality costs which can be used to support a business case.

Anecdote
An insurance business once sold approximately 1 million policies per month. These were sold through a combination of brokers, direct sales, re-insurers, etc, and spanned general and life insurance. The profitability of any given policy was a complex mix of the wholesale cost of the insurance, the amount paid by the customer, the method of payment of the customer, the mode of sale (direct, indirect), etc.

Data discovery work mapped the profitability of all products against the combination of factors that made up cost of sales, and found that, unsurprisingly, the data being used to determine profitability was wrong. The organisation made some major changes to their product portfolio and saved within a year an amount 100 times the cost of the project.

Here the improvement in data quality resulted in massive changes to the revenue model within the organisation as the improved data resulted in an understanding that the business model was fundamentally flawed.

5.14 Summary

In this chapter I have outlined the impact that poor data quality has from an operational perspective and how it adversely affects operational costs throughout the organisation. Specific examples given in the text include:

- Time cost of repeatedly reworking existing data
- Poor customer relations & customer retention.
- Loss of efficiency
- Cost of project failure.
- Missed sales opportunities
- Mailing overspend.
- IT Costs

- Transactional failures.
- Fraud and loss
- Profitability
- Data migration

As stated at the end of the previous chapter, it can be seen that poor data quality is a cancer that infects everything in an organisation and everything that the organisation does. Whilst the above chapter – due to the brevity inherent in giving a high level overview – has not touched on all of the potential poor data quality impacts on an organisation, nor delved deep into any one issue, it has hopefully shown that poor data quality costs money on an everyday basis. In the next chapter I will cover the regulatory impacts of poor data quality in the same way.

SECTION 2: THE IMPACT OF POOR DATA QUALITY

CHAPTER 6: REGULATORY IMPACT OF POOR DATA QUALITY

6.1 Structure

This section of the book discusses four topics:

1. High level overview and introduction
2. Strategic impact of poor data quality
3. Operational impact of poor data quality
4. Regulatory impact of poor data quality

This chapter covers the last of these topics.

6.2 Overview

Financial Regulatory Forum
New regulations require cleaner data

Most industries are regulated. The requirements of the regulator may vary from setting principles at a high level but then relying on the existing laws of the land, to a hands-on approach requiring organisations to submit regular reports covering their operations, an approach that will be supported by many specific laws enacted for that purpose. I would submit that in recent years regulators across all sectors are moving towards the "hands-on" approach, and requiring increasingly extensive returns from the organisations within their remit. This also takes advantage of moving towards an increasingly data-driven world, where details of organisations operations are – in theory at least – held in a format that facilitates transfer to a regulatory body.

In this environment the data quality of the organisation becomes critical due to its role in satisfying the regulator that the organisation is meeting its regulatory and legal obligations. Poor data quality can undermine this aim, lose the regulator's trust, and result in severe fines (and worse). This chapter discusses this topic.

However, no book will ever be able to discuss the regulations and laws for every sector in every country. A detailed discussion of the regulations affecting just the financial sector in one jurisdiction would take a book (or books) in itself. It quickly became obvious that the original aim of comparing and contrasting the regulatory effect of data quality across the world was a task beyond the space available in this book. I was also aware that any analysis would be instantly out of date as new regulations are continually released and updated by global bodies, and by the time a reader opened this section it would be of limited relevance except as a historical record of the regulations in force at time of writing. In fact, in the time between my starting this chapter and finishing the book, several major regulatory changes were announced. As a result this chapter, like many others in the book, is necessarily at a high level. In this chapter I will look to cover:

- What does the regulator require from organisations in terms of data quality? This includes the consideration of the regulator's view on data quality, but also what does the regulator consider to be its own data quality requirements? I will draw from the statements from several regulators in disparate sectors to illustrate common themes in regulatory direction.

- How will poor data quality adversely affect the ability of an organisation to be compliant with both the laws of the land, and the wishes of the regulator? Here I feel there are a number of common scenarios which, although not an exhaustive list, show the ways in which compliance will be adversely affected by poor data quality.

- How forceful are the regulators in enforcing their wishes? Is this something that organisations really should worry about? Here I will draw mainly on the finance sector and use this sector as an example of a highly regulated environment where the regulator is very pro-active in both hands-on regulation, but also publically releasing details of issues found and enforcements made.

- Specific regulations where data quality is going to be critical.

Like I said above, this is necessarily at a high level. However, every organisation will have a regulatory officer who will know the regulations affecting that industry and the impact non-compliance is likely to have, and – because it is their job – they will be far more up to date than a book which is by its nature a fixed point in time.

6.3   What does the regulator require?

> # Poor quality data impairing bank regulatory reporting capabilities
>
> Regulatory reporting requirements in the financial services industry are proliferating.

The specific requirements will depend on the regulator; however I am of the view that there are common themes. Rather than considering regulations affected by poor data (which is most of them) I will take the alternative of briefly discussing the approach outlined by several sectors, specifically the financial services regulator in the United Kingdom and the United States, the health and medical sector in the United Kingdom, the water supply regulation and the electricity generation regulator both in the UK. Whilst this is clearly in no way a comprehensive study of the regulations affected by data quality, it does show a broad spectrum of regulatory approach across sectors. Given most sectors in most countries are moving towards more regulation not less, and in certain sectors (notably finance) the trend is towards global regulation in any case, the above should be widely applicable, and applicable to most readers.

The finance industry

In the UK the prime regulators in the finance industry are the Bank of England, the Financial Conduct Authority (FCA) and the Prudential Regulation Authority (PRA), which regulate both wholesale and retail lending, including banks, mutual societies, financial advisors, and also regulate the consumer credit industry as a whole. In September 2013 the FCA released its own data strategy, outlining the principles that it would consider when looking at data. This is a clear insight into the regulator's thoughts in terms of data. This data strategy states:

> "Data and information is a key enabler to our success, supporting our drive to be a forward-looking risk-based regulator that operates efficiently. **Good quality data and information**, handled well and available quickly will give us deeper insight into the markets we regulate and allow us to be more efficient at identifying and tackling risks."[14] [My Emphasis]:

Here the regulator has clearly stated that good quality data and information are critical to its function, and clearly, given that data comes direct from the regulated entities under its responsibility, then the regulator is going to expect that good quality data is what those organisations are going to provide.

The sentiment outlined above by the UK regulator is echoed in the US regulatory system. In the United States, the Board of Governors of the Federal Reserve System outlined their strategic framework in a 25-page document released in February 2013. In this document the board stated that its

---

14.   www.fca.org.uk/news/fca-data-strategy

priorities for the next four years included six themes, one of which was to: "redesign data governance and management processes to enhance the Board's data environment". It goes on to state that:

"Since the onset of the financial crisis, ad hoc data collections have increased; thus, uniformity and guidance are necessary to ensure appropriate data quality" [15]

It is clear that on both sides of the Atlantic Ocean regulators are on the same page. It is a drive towards greater information quality.

The power industry

Looking at other sectors, Ofgem (the UK electricity and gas market regulator) stated in March 2015 that:

Tackling data quality issues effectively requires an appropriate understanding of the harm caused to consumers. While processes can be complex and lead to difficulties in obtaining evidence of harm, this is not an insurmountable barrier to progress, which could include more effective monitoring and enforcement where appropriate. We expect ongoing work undertaken by industry to take these factors into account.

Here the regulator has emphasised the harm to customers created by poor data quality, and expects the industry to work to resolve this.

The health industry

The Health Service in the UK has been particularly active in both the promotion of a good data strategy and also the promotion of data quality. The Health and Social Care Information Centre stated in their third annual report, dated 2014, that:

This report once again emphasises the importance of good quality data to the health and social care sectors. Both the development of the False or Misleading Information (FOMI) offence, enacted in the Care Act 2014, and the United Kingdom Statistics Authority (UKSA) exposure draft report on Quality Assurance and Audit Arrangements for Administrative Data4 lend weight to the importance of such work

Extending the auditing of data quality beyond Payment by Results to other data and services where poor data quality could impact most on direct clinical care has not happened. However, the investigation of possible FOMI offences and the UKSA recommendations regarding audit of administrative data sources should ensure that the extension of data quality auditing is revisited

The two case studies in the report show that improving data quality can bring important benefits to significantly different types of stakeholder

---

15. Strategic Framework 2012-2015, February 2013, Board of Governors of the Federal Reserve System

The health industry, like the finance industry, relies on good quality data to operate. The regulator requires that in order to competently monitor the industry good quality data is supplied by organisations under regulation. In the United States AHIMA (the American Health Information Management Association) stated that:

Quality healthcare depends on the availability of quality data. Poor documentation, inaccurate data, and insufficient communication can result in errors and adverse incidents. Inaccurate data threatens patient safety and can lead to increased costs, inefficiencies, and poor financial performance. Further, inaccurate or insufficient data also inhibits health information exchange (HIE), and hinders clinical research, performance improvement, and quality measurement initiatives[16]

Utility industries

Ofwat, the UK water regulator, stressed the need for data quality in 2013. In that year it undertook an exercise to audit the quality of the data it was receiving from organisations within its sector. The report on this investigation stated:

In total we made 191 individual queries to companies about the quality of the data. About two thirds of our queries resulted in companies making data changes. There were 14,000 changes to individual data items, which represents about 10% of the data that all companies submitted.

In short, whilst it is admittedly no surprise to any reader, regulators and responsible organisations in all sectors are calling out for quality data from the organisations under their responsibility.

6.4   How can Poor Data Quality impede Compliance?

"On average, U.S. companies believe 25 percent of their data is inaccurate."
Experian, The State of Data Quality, 2014

As stated above, there are few regulations existing in any jurisdictions where poor data quality will not cause a regulated organisation to face challenges. Taking this discussion further, I have noted below a few of the ways in which poor data quality can affect compliance.

6.4.1   Out of control

A basic requirement of any company management is that they are in control of their organisation. This is a common tenet of most regulated environments. The presumption of an effective control framework is written into regulations across the globe. The 2002 Sarbaines-Oxley Act, for example, states:

---

16.   AHIMA. "Assessing and Improving EHR Data Quality (Updated)." Journal of AHIMA 84, no.2 (March 2013): 48-53 [expanded online version]

SEC. 404. MANAGEMENT ASSESSMENT OF INTERNAL CONTROLS.

(a) RULES REQUIRED.– The Commission shall prescribe rules requiring each annual report required by section 13(a) or 15(d) of the Securities Exchange Act of 1934 (15 U.S.C. 78m or 78o(d)) to contain an internal control report, which shall – (1) state the responsibility of management for establishing and maintaining an adequate internal control structure and procedures for financial reporting; and (2) contain an assessment, as of the end of the most recent fiscal year of the issuer, of the effectiveness of the internal control structure and procedures of the issuer for financial reporting.

(b) INTERNAL CONTROL EVALUATION AND REPORTING.– With respect to the internal control assessment required by subsection (a), each registered public accounting firm that prepares or issues the audit report for the issuer shall attest to, and report on, the assessment made by the management of the issuer. An attestation made under this subsection shall be made in accordance with standards for attestation engagements issued or adopted by the Board. Any such attestation shall not be the subject of a separate engagement.

To draw out the critical point here, the organisation has to report on the effectiveness of its internal controls and the auditors have to corroborate this report.

The problem, and a problem very much under the radar until something goes wrong – is that because of data quality failings in internal reporting the top of the organisation does not have an accurate view of the organisation as a whole, what it is doing and what risks it is facing. This means that it cannot act to solve problems, and – as mentioned in a previous chapter – will make incorrect decisions. The management is therefore **not** in control as it is **not** receiving correct information. If the management is out of control it is breaching the regulations – such as Sarbaines-Oxley – in place to ensure that it is. A large part of data governance – which I will talk about at length later – is about establishing corporate control over information, and a subset of data governance is ensuring management of data quality.

Another example of this kind of regulation is Solvency II. Solvency II is a directive applicable to insurance companies used to determine the regulatory capital an organisation needs to hold to mitigate the risk of unforeseen losses. This has large implications for the insurance industry. At a high level, Solvency II is divided into three areas. The first covers financial reporting and capital requirements, the second risk management and governance, and the third talks of the required returns to regulators and the role of the regulator. Of particular note to the data quality practitioner is the system of governance, covered under Article 41. This states:

"Member States shall require all insurance and reinsurance undertakings to have in place an effective system of governance which provides for sound and prudent management of the business.

That system shall at least include an adequate transparent organisational structure with a clear allocation and appropriate segregation of responsibilities and an effective system for ensuring the transmission of information. It shall include compliance"[17]

---

17. DIRECTIVE 2009/138/EC OF THE EUROPEAN PARLIAMENT AND OF THE COUNCIL of 25 November 2009

Whilst this is a little vague, clarification was issued in consultation paper 43, subtitled "Technical Provisions – Article 85f Standards for Data Quality". This states:

"Quality of data is crucial in the scope of valuation of technical provisions, mainly, because:

The more complete and correct the data is, the more consistent and accurate final estimates will be;

The application of a wider range of methodologies for calculating the best estimate is made possible, improving the chances of application of adequate and robust methods for each case.

Validation of methods is more reliable and leads to more credible conclusions, once a reasonable level of quality of data is achieved.

Effective comparisons over time and in relation to market data are possible, which leads, for instance, to a better knowledge of the businesses in which the undertaking operates and its performance." [18]

The paper goes into further detail and describes the components of data quality, what is considered good data quality, and the steps an organisation should undertake if it is "data deficient". Again, the regulator has been explicit on its expectations of organisations in respect of data quality.

To conclude, an organisation that does not have good data quality will break regulations due to not having sufficient governance – and hence control – over its own actions.

6.4.2 Simply breaching data quality regulations

Some regulations require that data is accurate per se. For example, the UK 1998 Data Protection Act states, as principle 4, that:

"Personal data shall be accurate and, where necessary, kept up to date." [19]

Here, this non-industry specific law (applicable to all organisations in the UK) has been explicitly clear on government expectations if an organisation holds personal data. I would suggest that there are a large number of organisations that are currently in breach of this particular law.

For another example, BCBS 239, a globally-relevant document released by the BASEL committee for banking supervision, states that:

"A bank's board and senior management should promote the identification, assessment and management of data quality risks as part of its overall risk management framework" (Principle 1)

---

18. Consultation Paper No. 43: Technical Provisions – Article 85 f Standards for Data Quality.
19. Data Protection Act 1998, TSO, 1998.

"Accuracy & Integrity: A bank should be able to generate accurate and reliable risk data to meet normal and stress/crisis reporting accuracy requirements. Data should be aggregated on a largely automated basis so as to minimise the probability of errors." (Principle 3)

"Accuracy: Risk management reports should accurately and precisely convey aggregated risk data and reflect risk in an exact manner. Reports should be reconciled and validated."(Principle 7) [20]

REGULATORY REQUIRED DATA QUALITY AS DECISION-MAKING SUPPORT

Current challenges for banks due to requirements of BCBS #239

The committee has been clear here. In a short (28 page) document it has clearly stated its requirements for the banking sector, and many of those requirements relate directly to data quality. An organisation with poor data quality is breaking the regulations per se.

6.4.3 Unable to identify breaches and in a timely fashion

Of course, critical to regulatory compliance is being able to identify when a breach of regulation occurs. In this regard, any organisation with poor data quality is going to struggle far more than an organisation that can trust its data. Poor data quality is likely to confuse the search for regulatory breach by the creation of many false positives. If none of the data can be trusted, then how is an organisation to identify the anomalies which indicate something bad is going on?

The organisation with poor data quality will not only fail to identify the breach but even if it does it is unlikely to be identified in sufficient time for something to be done about it. Identification on a timely basis will minimise loss to the organisation. Identification of a regulatory breach years after the event will merely result in vastly higher restitution costs, and greater regulatory sanction than if the breach was identified and rectified at the time.

Whilst I will deconstruct the components of data quality in a later chapter, timeliness of data is an oft-ignored component of information. There is no point having the right data way too late to do anything about it.

I have mentioned above that the timeliness of data is critical to minimising the impact of a regulatory breach. I have also mentioned that poor data quality can swamp any system looking to identify regulatory breaches with false positives. A matter to consider is that any legal or regulatory breach is likely to start small. Detecting the initial signs of a regulatory breach is dependent on the organisation being able to trust its data at a detail level, and to correlate between many data fields. These correlations should provide the first signs of trouble but an organisation with poor data quality will be unlikely to ever see them in the first place.

---

20. http://www.bis.org/publ/bcbs239.pdf

6.4.4   Incorrect data

Severn Trent fined £36million for 'lying' about customer data and providing a poor service

Most regulators require that organisations submit data, and the regulator uses this data to help them regulate the industry. The quantity and nature of the data required will vary from industry to industry, but no regulator is going to be satisfied with incorrect submissions. Many regulators – especially in the finance sector – require transaction level data – details of every sale. The product sales data required in the UK from the insurance industry is a case in point. There are any number of organisations that have submitted incorrect information to the regulator as a result of poor data quality. Some have subsequently been the subject of regulatory fines; others have confessed to the regulator and worked with the regulator to achieve compliance.

Of course, quite apart from the information submitted being incorrect, where data fields are used to select the data to be reported to the regulator, and those fields are incorrect, then the organisation is breaching its reporting requirements by not selecting and submitting the right data. For example, if a time field is being used to select relevant data in a particular quarter, but the field is not reliable, then whilst each individual line may be of good quality, it may be incorrectly identified from a time point of view. There are a number of examples where the regulator has fined organisations for submitting incorrect data. Looking back over the last few years, some specific examples from the finance sector are shown below.

Amount	Organisation	Date	Reason
£5,620,300	The Royal Bank of Scotland plc and The Royal Bank of Scotland N.V	16/07/2013	For incorrectly reporting transactions made in the wholesale market
£205,128	Plus500UK Limited	24/10/2012	For failing to provide accurate and timely transaction reports to the FSA.
£49,000	James Sharp and Company	24/10/2012	For failing to provide accurate and timely transaction reports to the FSA

6.4.5   Unable to meet regulatory requests

Most regulators will request ad hoc data from organisations within their area of responsibility. It is therefore obvious that if an organisation is not able to source good quality data from its system then it cannot provide good quality data to the regulator.

Publically available information identifies a number of organisations where a request from the regulator has resulted in data being extracted from information systems and found to be of too poor quality to submit, either untrustworthy or occasionally ambiguous, or where the same data extracted from different source systems has resulted in different answers. The result is the poor quality data being cleansed as a one off exercise – generally by management level staff in evenings and weekends – in order to provide the submission. This is, needless to say, horrendously inefficient. What if the data just came off the systems in a state fit to transmit? Wouldn't that be easier?

"Counterparty reporting for management and supervisors should be the product of standardized, repeatable, and highly automated processes. While some firms have developed their information technology infrastructure further to support improved counterparty reporting, many still rely on time-consuming and error-prone manual processes"
Senior Supervisor's Group report on counterparty data, 2014

I would also mention here (a point that I will come back to later in the book) that it is critical for information quality to be remediated at the lowest level of granularity, which generally means on the source systems.

Particularly relevant to this chapter is that data becomes more aggregated as it moves away from source systems towards board reporting and the regulator. Regulatory reports are most often created from the top layer of the data architecture. If data cleansing is undertaken at this point, or in fact any other point not the source systems, then the aggregated information is no longer a true representation of the underlying systems. As a result when a request for more detail is received then the organisation faces serious problems, as with aggregated information no longer matching granular information that is supposedly based upon, it will look like either the granular or the aggregate information submitted is incorrect. There is no real way out of this for the organisation apart from making extensive apologies and doing what should have occurred in the first place and remediate data on the source systems.

An illustrative example here – reported in February 2014 – relates to the UK government initiative to require organisations to proactively return personal data to consumers. The objective, which was backed by Google, Royal Bank of Scotland, British Gas and Visa, was to allow consumers easy access to their personal data. At least one report [21] suggested that this initiative was dropped because organisations did not wish to advertise to consumers publically exactly how bad their data quality was.

6.4.6 False sense of security

Another scenario is that because of poor quality data an organisation that thinks it is complying with all the rules is actually not doing so. For example, it may be against the law to offer credit to under-18s, but if dates of birth are wrong, how will you ever know, on a daily basis, whether you are breaking the law?

This is another aspect of being out of control, but one could argue is worse. At least an organisation that knows it is out of control can look to put in measures to remediate the situation. An organisation that is blissfully unaware that it is breaching regulations will continue in its path, safe

---

21. http://www.out-law.com/en/articles/2014/february/midata-initiative-may-have-stalled-due-to-poor-data-quality-says-it-consultant/

in the assumed knowledge that it is compliant. As succinctly expressed below:

...the potential exists for incorrect conclusions to be drawn from analytical data. These data, and their subsequent conclusions, often exist in reports for years until the "data time bomb" explodes in a fury of backpedalling, accusation, expense, and reinvestigation. [22]

I have certainly personally witnessed situations where the "fury of backpedalling, accusation, expense and re-investigation" has occurred.

6.4.7   Failure to treat customers fairly

Critical to both regulatory compliance and good business practice is treating customers fairly and protecting them from exploitation. This covers desired outcomes that products and services are appropriate for the customer, that advice is suitable and takes account of circumstances, and that consumers are provided with clear information before, during and after the sale.

Clearly the information held on the customer will be critical to achieving all of the above. In addition, detecting whether the above has been achieved depends on accurate management information. If there is a high drop-off between initial contact and offer does this indicate a high volume of inappropriate products? Does a high volume of sales against expectations indicate that products are being mis-sold? None of this can be picked up without good quality data.

> *"We have identified that firms' MI is often limited to quantitative data, which is sometimes very narrow in scope, and is often not supported with qualitative data. In a number of firms, we have seen MI on the products being sold and the commission received, but minimal information on the quality of the sale made."*
> **"Treating customers fairly – culture", Financial Conduct Authority, 2007.**

6.4.8   Failure to prevent fraud

Fraud impacts regulation in several ways. First, there is the simple fraud that is directly affecting the organisation, where criminals attempt to defraud the organisation of funds. Second, and especially if you are a financial services organisation, there is the protection of your customers against fraudulent behaviour that targets them.

Critical to compliance with AML legislation is knowing your customer, and data quality is critical to that. Basic information such as name and address, if quality is poor, can allow loopholes for criminals to exploit.

In 2014 the Coalition Against Insurance Fraud undertook a study of the challenges facing insurance companies in preventing and detecting fraud. This cited poor data integration and poor data quality as being third in line (behind lack of resources and excessive false positive rates – the latter of which could also be a data quality failing) of the challenges faced. This document stated:

---

22. Quality Control: The Great Myth, Thomas L. Francoeur.

Data is the most valuable commodity for any anti-fraud technology. As such, technology is only as good as the data. [23]

6.4.9 Anti-terrorism and proceeds of crime legislation

Severn Trent fined £36million for 'lying' about customer data and providing a poor service

We unfortunately live at a time when governments throughout the world are finding it necessary to enact increasingly enabling legislation to identify and curtail terrorist activities. In the financial sector especially, compliance with this legislation is strictly enforced, and the ability to comply with orders to freeze customer funds, and identify suspicious activity, whether it be for the purpose of furthering terrorist activities or not, is critical.

In order to comply with this legislation good data quality is required. There have been several instances where organisations, asked to freeze accounts, are unable to do so in a timely manner due to duplication of customer records, or have failed to link customers due to data quality issues. There is no point successfully freezing the accounts for Mr John Smith if the accounts for Mr J Smith are left fully functional.

6.4.10 Missed opportunities for savings

It is occasionally the case that an organisation that can demonstrate that it has a high level of data quality has the opportunity to use that quality data to reduce its regulatory burden. An example here is Basel II. Basel II sets out the amount of capital that organisations are required to hold to buttress themselves against risk, one component of which is credit risk. The regulation introduces the concept of risk weighted assets, where the total value of the asset (for example, a mortgage) is multiplied by its risk weight. These risk weights are set by the regulation for each class of asset.

CRD IV reporting - New validations and data quality
Published: 04/12/2014

The Financial Conduct Authority (FCA) and the Prudential Regulation Authority (PRA) will be activating 317 new validations on 17 December 2014.

However the regulation accepts that if an organisation can prove that its assets are less (or more) risky than the norm – and that it has sufficient data to prove that is the case – then it can opt

---

23. The State of Insurance Fraud Technology, Coalition Against Insurance Fraud, 2014.

to use the internal ratings based approach where it uses its own information to calculate the risk. For a bank with less risky assets this is likely to result in a lower capital requirement.

Here an organisation with good data quality can reduce the regulatory burden by simply proving that it has good data quality – to an extent, at least.

6.4.11 Basic errors

Finally, poor data quality results in basic errors. Analysis conducted by IT Governance of Data Protection Act contraventions in 2014 covering breaches of the data protection act stated:

> *"32% of all incidents were due to personal or sensitive data being inappropriately disclosed or sent to the wrong recipient. Repeated errors – such as sending information to the wrong recipients due to incorrect fax numbers or email addresses – were common."*

6.5 How the Regulator is Enforcing its Wishes

Banks 'pay 60%' of profits in fines and customer payments

A colleague once quipped to me that that the ROI (return on investment) for data governance and data quality projects should be re-acronymed as ROI (Risk of Incarceration) for the directors of the company. As any number of organisations have discovered, especially in the recent past, regulators are unafraid to levy extremely large fines – as of writing date, fines for the LIBOR rigging scandal are well into the billions. Regulators are also more open to the idea of pursuing individuals for their failings – for example, in 2014 the Financial Times stated:

> *"It is still relatively rare in the UK for the former chief executive of a listed company to be jailed but it is becoming more common as regulators attitudes have hardened."* [24]

How much regulatory attention poor data quality is actually likely to cost the average organisation in regulatory fines is difficult to measure. However, according to the FCA's own website, in 2013-2014 a total of over £3 billion in fines has been levied against organisations for a variety of reasons. Looking at this list [25], it is interesting to highlight some specific entries from a data quality point of view.

---

24. http://www.ft.com/cms/s/0/aad326f4-8447-11e4-bae9-00144feabdc0.html
25. http://www.fsa.gov.uk/about/press/facts/fines/2012 and http://www.fca.org.uk/firms/being-regulated/enforcement/fines

The Data Quality Blueprint

Amount	Organisation	Date	Reason
£4,718,800	Deutsche Bank AG	21/08/2014	For failing to accurately report all the CFD Equity Swaps
£7,192,500	Aberdeen Asset Managers Limited and Aberdeen fund management	02/09/2013	For failing to identify, and therefore properly protect, client money placed in Money Market Deposits with third party banks
£4,200,000	Bank of Scotland	19/10/2012	For failing to keep accurate mortgage records
£400,000	James Joseph Corr	28/03/2012	For publishing misleading information to investors about the credit quality of Welcome's loan book
£200,000	Peter Douglas Miller	28/03/2012	For publishing misleading information to investors about the credit quality of Welcome's loan book

The above are those fines from the last two years that specifically mention data quality. There are many fines relating to failures in systems of control which have a quality component. Two selected examples are below.

Amount	Organisation	Date	Reason
£284,432,000	Barclays Bank Plc	20/05/2015	Barclays' controls over its FX business were inadequate and ineffective. It primarily relied on its front office FX business to identify, assess and manage the relevant risks – however, the front office failed to pick up on obvious risks associated with confidentiality, conflicts of interest and trader conduct
£226,800,000	Deutsche Bank AG	23/04/2015	What is more, Deutsche Bank had defective systems to support the audit and investigation of misconduct by traders. For example, the Bank's systems for identifying and recording traders' telephone calls and for tracing trading books to individual traders were inadequate. As a result, Deutsche Bank took over two years to identify and produce all relevant audio recordings requested by the FCA.

The two examples above, and many others in the last few years, highlight a problem where organisations do not produce information from their systems of sufficient quality to enable them to identify when something is going seriously wrong. The problem is as much poor information as anything else. Another recent fine worth highlighting is the below:

Amount	Organisation	Date	Reason
£16,000,000	The Prudential Assurance Company Limited	27/03/2013	For failing to deal with the FSA in an open and cooperative manner

In reality, most regulators are reasonable, and a company making a concerted effort to improve will be looked on more favourably than one with their head in the sand hoping the problem goes away on its own or, worse, actively looking to deceive the regulator. Working with the regulator to demonstrate how you are addressing problems is even better. Potential consequences of non-compliance will clearly include:

- Loss of reputation (affecting customers, suppliers and competitors).
- Increased work dealing with the regulatory body.
- Likely further inspections in the future.
- Actual incarceration of the directors

It may never happen, and if it does the effect is unknowable in advance. Even the average cost is not much use, because it is not meaningful. The issue is risk. How much is an organisation prepared to spend to lower the risk of a calamitous event that could potentially result in huge fines and the incarceration of the directors? My own view is that it would be unwise to spend nothing, and after that it is all down to risk appetite. In a highly regulated industry I would submit it is better to do more than less.

6.6   ISO 8000

Notwithstanding the comment made in the introduction that coverage of all regulations in all environments is outside the scope of this book, there is another regulation/standard that is worth specifically mentioning, and that is ISO 8000. This is a standard for data quality that is currently under development. Some elements have already been published at the time of writing, notably:

- ISO/TS 8000-1:2011, Data quality – Part 1: Overview
- ISO 8000-2:2012, Data quality – Part 2: Vocabulary
- ISO/TS 8000-100:2009, Data quality – Part 100: Master data: Exchange of characteristic data: Overview
- ISO 8000-102:2009, Data quality – Part 102: Master data: Exchange of characteristic data: Vocabulary
- ISO 8000-110:2009, Data quality – Part 110: Master data: Exchange of characteristic data: Syntax, semantic encoding, and conformance to data specification

- ISO/TS 8000-120:2009, Data quality – Part 120: Master data: Exchange of characteristic data: Provenance
- ISO/TS 8000-130:2009, Data quality – Part 130: Master data: Exchange of characteristic data: Accuracy
- ISO/TS 8000-140:2009, Data quality – Part 140: Master data: Exchange of characteristic data: Completeness
- ISO/TS 8000-150:2011, Data quality – Part 150: Master data: Quality management framework

Although the full impact of ISO 8000 is not yet known, it is likely that it will gain the same importance as ISO 27001 where firms will actively seek certification in data quality. In certain industries ISO 8000 is likely to become a de facto requirement.

6.7 Summary

In this chapter I have discussed the impact that poor data quality has on the ability of an organisation to comply with the rules and regulations that govern its existence. There are a multitude of other regulations that I could place in this area of the book, but I did not wish to go into any detail in an area which can – and does – change so regularly as to make a fixed reference point of dubious merit. For each industry and geographical area, I would encourage the reader to investigate the regulations applicable and how it will affect them, and to look at those regulations with a data quality perspective.

I have tried in the above chapter to outline why regulatory compliance is important. I have given several examples of the thinking behind the regulations, and given some examples of the major regulatory standards. In the last three chapters I have looked to define a problem. In the next section I will start looking at how to solve it.

SECTION 3
THE APPROACH TO DATA QUALITY

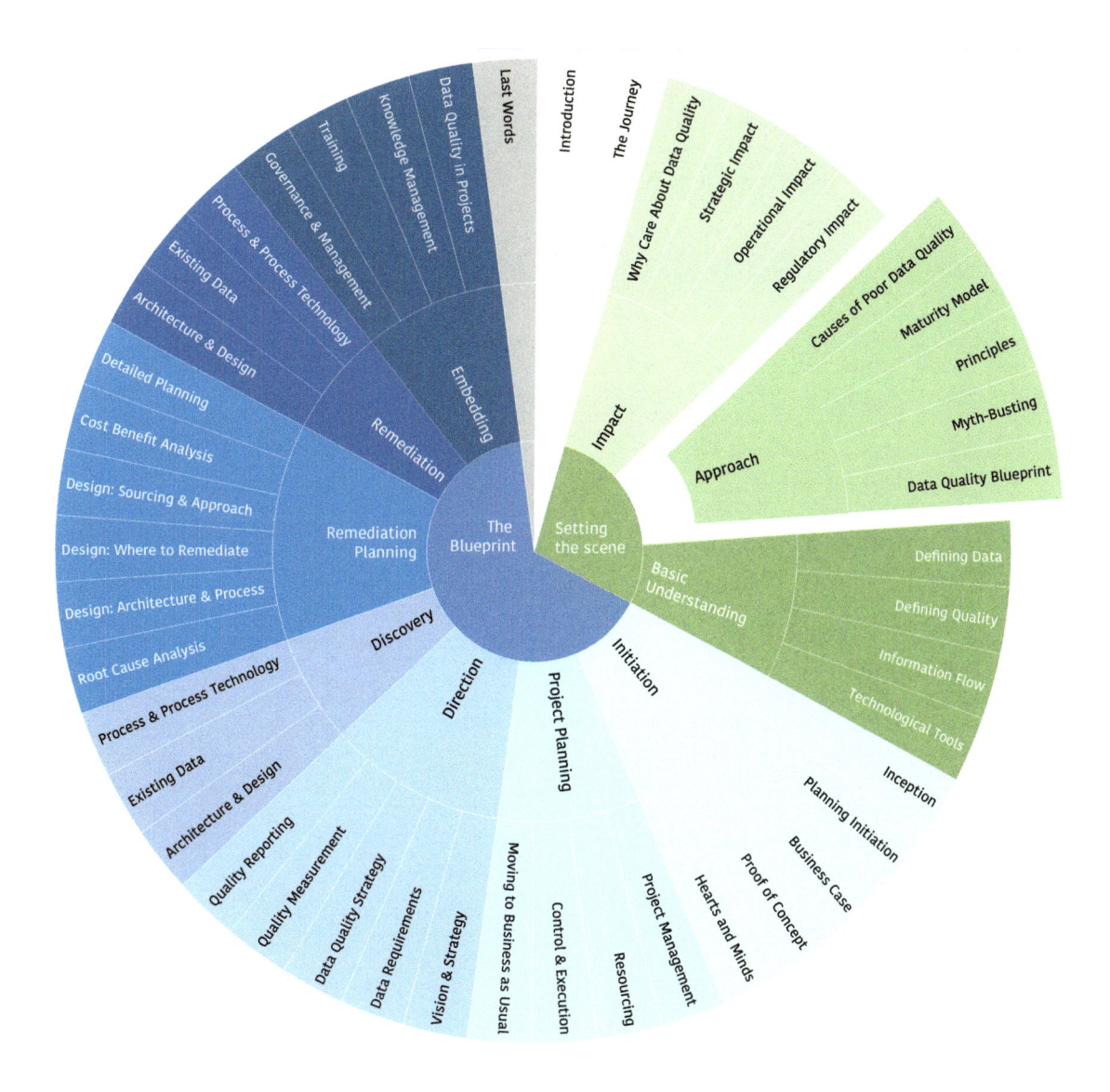

The Blueprint

Setting the scene
- **Impact**
  - Introduction
  - The Journey
  - Why Care About Data Quality
  - Strategic Impact
  - Operational Impact
  - Regulatory Impact
- **Approach**
  - Causes of Poor Data Quality
  - Maturity Model
  - Principles
  - Myth-Busting
  - Data Quality Blueprint

Initiation
- **Basic Understanding**
  - Defining Data
  - Defining Quality
  - Information Flow
  - Technological Tools
- **Project Planning**
  - Inception
  - Planning Initiation
  - Business Case
  - Proof of Concept
  - Hearts and Minds
  - Project Management
  - Resourcing
  - Control & Execution
  - Moving to Business as Usual

Direction
- Vision & Strategy
- Data Requirements
- Data Quality Strategy
- Quality Measurement
- Quality Reporting

Discovery
- Architecture & Design
- Existing Data
- Process & Process Technology
- Root Cause Analysis

Remediation Planning
- Design: Architecture & Process
- Design: Where to Remediate
- Design: Sourcing & Approach
- Cost Benefit Analysis
- Detailed Planning

Remediation
- Architecture & Design
- Existing Data
- Process & Process Technology
- Governance & Management
- Training

Embedding
- Knowledge Management
- Data Quality in Projects

Last Words

77

SECTION 3: INDEX

CHAPTER 7: The Causes of Poor Data Quality — 81
7.1	Structure	81
7.2	Overview	81
7.3	Causes at a High Level	82
7.4	No Defined Direction	84
7.5	No Governance or Management	85
7.6	Poor Architecture	86
7.7	People	89
7.8	Poor Process and resultant Poor Data	89
7.9	Summary	90

CHAPTER 8: Data Quality Maturity Model — 91
8.1	Structure	91
8.2	Overview	91
8.3	Self-Defeating	92
8.4	Aware	93
8.5	Engaged	93
8.6	Managed	94
8.7	Ideal/Optimising	95
8.8	Analysis	96
8.9	Assessment	96
8.10	Summary	97

CHAPTER 9: Principles — 99
9.1	Structure	99
9.2	Overview	99
9.3	Principle 1: The business is in the driving seat	99
9.4	Principle 2: We're all in this together	100
9.5	Principle 3: Do it once, do it well	100
9.6	Principle 4: Treat data as an asset	101
9.7	Principle 5: People are the key	101
9.8	Principle 6: Embed data quality in the organisation	102
9.9	Principle 7: Do as little work as possible	102
9.10	Summary	103

CHAPTER 10: Myth-busting — 105
10.1	Structure	105
10.2	Overview	105
10.3	The Internal Audit Solution	106
10.4	Technology to the Rescue	106

10.5	IT will solve it, it's their data!	107
10.6	Any Data is better than No Data	108
10.7	The Data Quality Department	110
10.8	MDM: Master Data Management	111
10.9	Implement Data Governance (and do it well)	112
10.10	Summary	112

CHAPTER 11: The Data Quality Blueprint — 115

11.1	Structure	115
11.2	Overview	115
11.3	High Level Methodology	116
11.4	Initiate	117
11.5	Project Planning	117
11.6	Direction	118
11.7	Discovery	119
11.8	Remediation Planning	119
11.9	Remediation	120
11.10	Embedding	120
11.11	Bringing it All Together	121
11.12	Summary	122

SECTION 3: THE APPROACH TO DATA QUALITY

CHAPTER 7: THE CAUSES OF POOR DATA QUALITY

7.1 Structure

This section of the book covers the following topics:

1. What affects data quality
2. Data quality maturity model
3. Principles
4. Myth-busting
5. The Data Quality Blueprint

This chapter covers the first of these topics.

7.2 Overview

> *"Information is an asset that is generated through numerous processes, with multiple feeds of raw data that are combined, processed, and fed out to multiple customers both inside and outside your organization"*
>
> **David Loshin, *Evaluating the Business Impacts of Poor Data Quality*, Knowledge Integrity.**

The last section explained why you should care about data quality. It is now time to look at what causes poor data quality. Here we will start to see the evolution of The Data Quality Blueprint, which examines all elements of the organisation from the data quality perspective. This chapter starts the process by deconstructing the causes of poor data quality and creating some high level headings which we can then examine in more detail.

7.3 Causes at a High Level

The short answer as to what causes poor data quality is "process failure". However, this is using "process" in its widest term as relating to "things that are done in the organisation", and "failure" as "failure to create or maintain quality information". After all, everything is a process, from primary data capture to sending a report to a regulator. This is not particularly useful to the data quality practitioner, so we need to expand.

If we take the points mentioned above, a better analysis might be that poor data quality may occur because people are not incentivised towards data quality, people are incorrectly trained, the underlying technology is of poor quality, not suitable for the task, or incorrectly configured, the process is poorly controlled, poorly designed, or is prone to error. Thus, reasons for poor quality can be divided into:

- The people that perform the process
- The technology that supports the process
- The design of the process
- The management of the process

This is not quite complete, because this considers a process in isolation and does not cover interactions between processes. Therefore we also need to consider the way that processes fit together (organisational architecture) and the way that the management of processes fits together (organisational governance).

7.3.1 Step 1

This brings us to a picture that looks a little like the below. I have shown "people" separate to "process" because (except in rare cases) most people will perform more than one process.

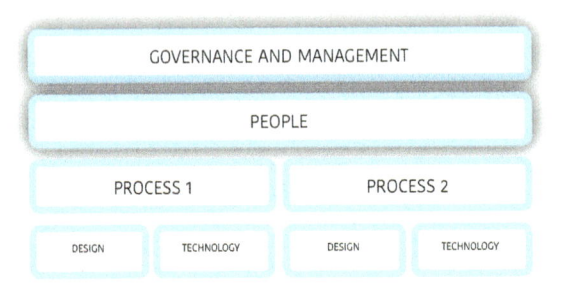

Information quality allows the organisation to achieve good decisions, and through these its own success. Therefore we need to know the key aims of the organisation in order to identify the information that is required to support them. That information would come from the overall organisational strategy and the data strategy, which now need to be incorporated.

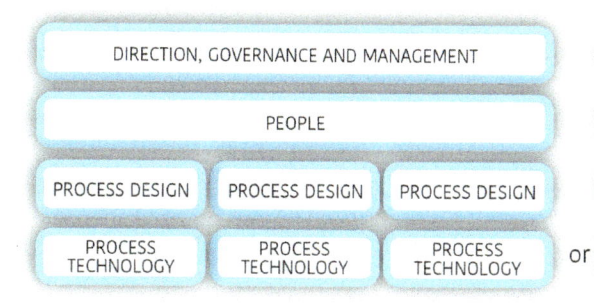

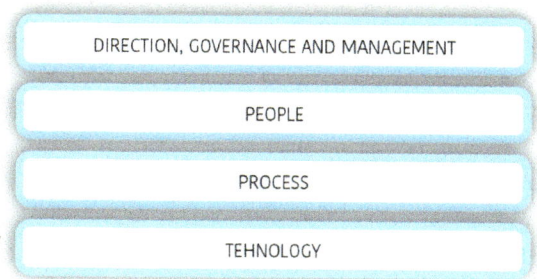

Chapter 7: The Causes of Poor Data Quality

DIRECTION, GOVERNANCE AND MANAGEMENT				DIRECTION, GOVERNANCE AND MANAGEMENT
PEOPLE				PEOPLE
PROCESS DESIGN	PROCESS DESIGN	PROCESS DESIGN	or	PROCESS
PROCESS TECHNOLOGY	PROCESS TECHNOLOGY	PROCESS TECHNOLOGY		TEHNOLOGY

Failure at any one of these points is likely to cause data quality issues.

To summarise, the organisation needs to define its direction and the quality of the information it requires. Without this component it is impossible to determine whether information quality meets business requirements. The organisation also needs to govern and manage the processes to align them with the overall direction and ensure that that the information meets quality requirements. Training should equip individuals so they can perform processes well, and each process needs to be designed to factor in information quality, both in terms of the people that perform the process and the technology they use to perform it. Equally knowledge needs to be managed, so people can support the organisation effectively. The important consideration often missed here is that people, process and technology are not separate. Many consultancies prepare a diagram like the above and then attack each of people, process and technology as separate items that do not inter-relate. In fact, the organisation is supported by people, who perform processes, using technology.

7.3.2 Step 2

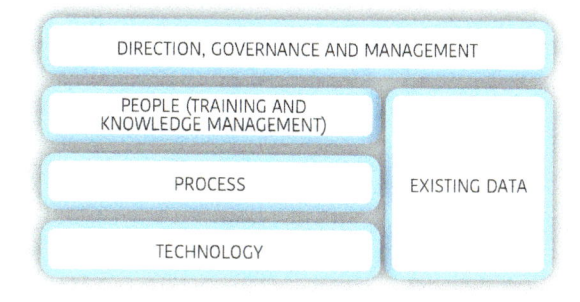

DIRECTION, GOVERNANCE AND MANAGEMENT	
PEOPLE (TRAINING AND KNOWLEDGE MANAGEMENT)	
PROCESS	EXISTING DATA
TECHNOLOGY	

If we consider an organisation with a data quality problem, then we have the people, process and technology, and we also have the millstone of existing data, dragging against the organisation on every step.

7.3.3 Step 3

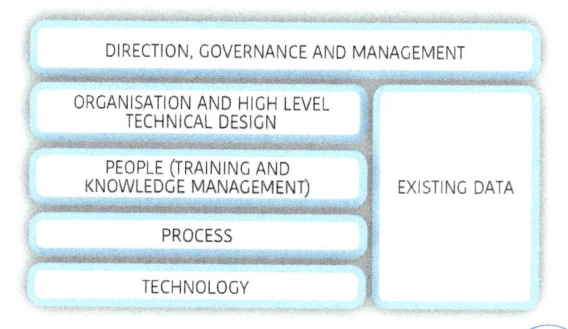

DIRECTION, GOVERNANCE AND MANAGEMENT	
ORGANISATION AND HIGH LEVEL TECHNICAL DESIGN	
PEOPLE (TRAINING AND KNOWLEDGE MANAGEMENT)	EXISTING DATA
PROCESS	
TECHNOLOGY	

In order to move the organisation forward, we need to look at the organisational design at a holistic level where people, process and technology are considered together.

The Data Quality Blueprint

7.3.4 Step 4

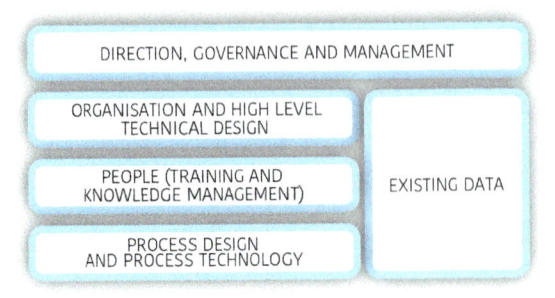

DIRECTION, GOVERNANCE AND MANAGEMENT	
ORGANISATION AND HIGH LEVEL TECHNICAL DESIGN	EXISTING DATA
PEOPLE (TRAINING AND KNOWLEDGE MANAGEMENT)	
PROCESS DESIGN AND PROCESS TECHNOLOGY	

We have already talked about how process and process technology are inextricably linked, which updates our diagram to that shown below.

7.3.5 Step 5

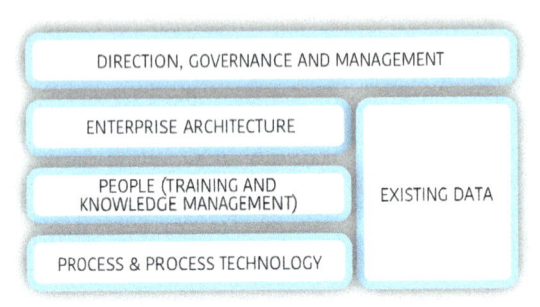

DIRECTION, GOVERNANCE AND MANAGEMENT	
ENTERPRISE ARCHITECTURE	EXISTING DATA
PEOPLE (TRAINING AND KNOWLEDGE MANAGEMENT)	
PROCESS & PROCESS TECHNOLOGY	

Further changes are required to finalise the representation. Organisational design and high level technical design is normally referred to as "enterprise architecture". So we end up with a diagram looking like the one below.

This overview gives a base upon which to proceed. I will refer to this diagram throughout the rest of the book, and examine each element in a little more detail now.

7.4 No Defined Direction

The first element that will affect data quality is the organisation's ability to know what data it needs, what are its requirements for that data, and how it will achieve its aims. This is described in the data strategy, which informs data requirements, data quality requirements and the data quality strategy. This flow is shown in the diagram below. I will examine each of these in the "direction" chapter, but in order to get its data quality "right" an organisation needs to define its information and information quality requirements first.

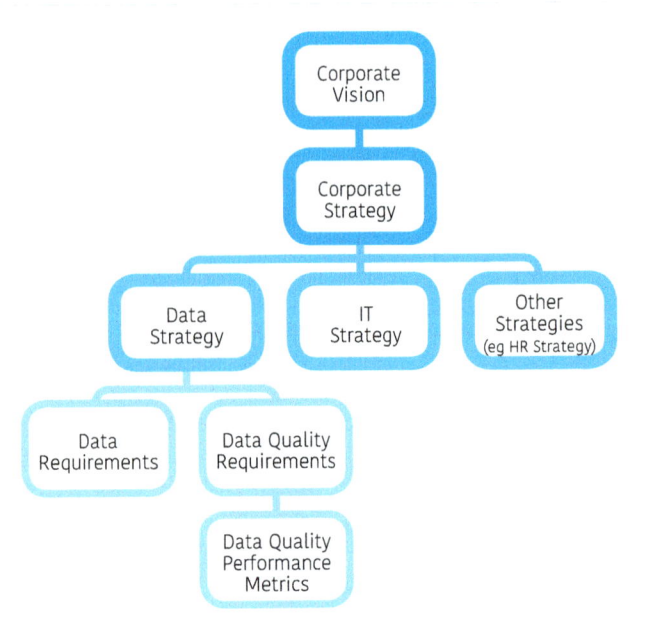

Information requirements will be set by the data strategy as a combination of the information that the organisation needs to report to the regulator, report to the board, manage its operations and operate its business. The information requirements, once defined, can be used to set the data quality that is required to run the organisation. It goes without saying that without any defined data requirements no organisation will ever really possess good data quality – as there is no way of defining "good". To use an analogy, it is a bit like setting a large number of unqualified people the job of building a wall – with no other instructions, such as where, how high, of what materials, etc. The results will be chaotic at best, a shambles at worst. So it is with data quality.

7.5   No Governance or Management

Data governance and data management are critical to data quality. The two terms are often wrongly confused, and the easiest way to explain the difference between the two is that data management represents the tasks that are required for the day to day management of the data in the organisation, and data governance is the manner in which the data management is organised, directed and aligned to the organisation's strategy, corporate governance and risk appetite. Lack of basic governance is a key issue in organisational data quality. For example:

- If new projects are not required to answer basic questions about how they will manage their data quality, then it is highly likely they will not bother to do so.
- If departments are not required to report on their data quality, they will not do so. In which case any data quality problems will go unknown and unresolved (until a report to the regulator is found to be incorrect).
- If there is no organisation-wide forum where data issues can be raised, and decisions made, then when data issues are noticed nothing will occur as there is no way of highlighting them.
- If there is no executive who is taking responsibility for the quality of information in the organisation, then in an environment of competition for scarce resources, issues of poor information quality will always be shouted down by those with louder voices or more authority.
- If information additions to the organisation (for example a new application) are not required to use the same meanings as those that exist within the existing organisation then it is easy to see how inaccuracy and lack of consistency can occur.

Lack of data governance is a basic problem, but one that has far-reaching effects on data quality. It should be emphasised here that the existence of data governance – per se – is not going to solve data quality issues, but it will highlight failings in data management that will enable data quality issues to be corrected.

7.6 Poor Architecture

The way in which the organisation fits together – its architecture – has a considerable effect on data quality. Part of the reason why data quality remediation – and business process remediation for that matter – often appears to be or becomes an overwhelming task is there is no obvious place to start – everything connects to everything else. It is necessary to consider the architecture to see if there is a fundamental problem. Because architecture is an abstract concept I will spend a little time here explaining architecture and how it is relevant.

Architecture is the overall organisational design expressed through differing views. Different people see organisations in different ways, and various architectures are the organisation seen through various filters. If you ask the CEO, the Chief Accountant, an IT developer, the network supplier, and a customer to draw an organisation then their pictures will be very different. The CEO will see profit units, the accountant will see flows of funds, the IT developer may see applications, the network supplier will see cables and servers and the customer will see contact centres and branches, and a head office. These different ways of seeing how the business fits together comprise architectures. Together, they summate to the enterprise architecture.

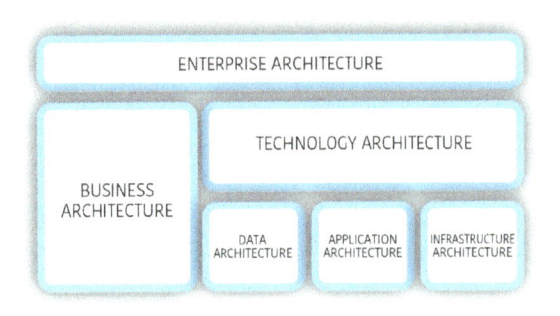

Enterprise Architecture is traditionally split into four components (I'm loosely using The Open Group's TOGAF framework here, but other architectural approaches are perfectly as good, for example the Zachman Framework, the Object Management Group, etc). The design of each of these can make the achievement of data quality aims easy or extremely hard. Architectures are useful as they allow the organisation to be considered as a whole and this facilitates our approach to data quality.

7.6.1 Business architecture

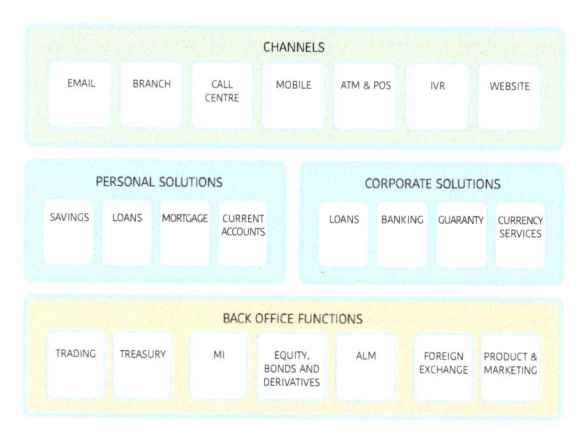

Business architecture is the way in which the business fits together. At a high level it may be nothing more than the overall group diagram, showing the major building blocks of an organisation, but at a lower level it shows the way in which the various business processes interact. This allows the data quality resulting from each process to be linked.

7.6.2 Data architecture

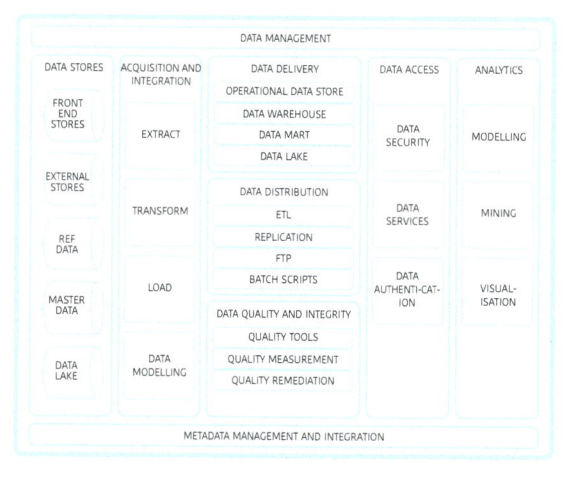

Data Architecture will illustrate the stores of data within an organisation, and the way in which data flows between them.

Data architecture, done well, can significantly improve the ability of the organisation to achieve good data quality, done badly – or, more normally, not done at all – it can make the task significantly harder.

Data architecture is clearly the most relevant to data quality, and after this brief explanation of the various architecture types in this chapter, then will be the data architecture that we mostly consider in the rest of the book.

7.6.3 Application architecture

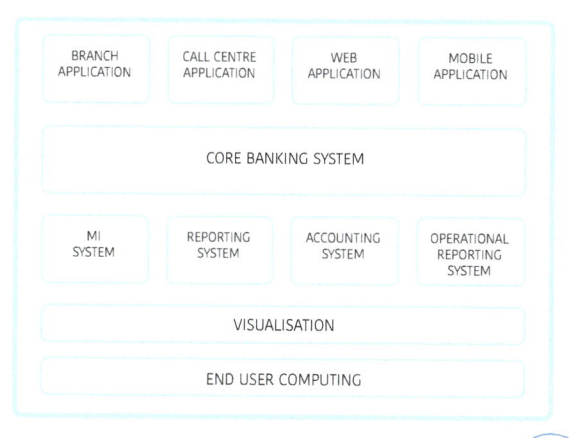

Application architecture defines the way in which applications interact. A modern organisation will consist of hundreds or thousands of separate applications. The overall estate may consist of:

- Core operational systems
- Finance applications
- Planning tools
- Desktop applications
- Specialist applications
- Data-related tools

The interaction of the applications will be relevant to data quality. Some applications talk to eachother effectively, some do not. Some applications can be effectively used for transforming information, some cannot. The choice is of what to plug in and how it will contribute to the successful flow of information.

7.6.4 Technology architecture

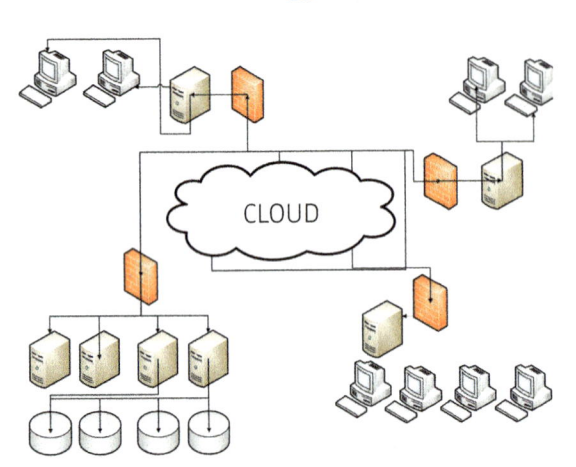

Technology architecture defines the underlying workings of the organisation's IT world, networks, routers, servers, and the wiring that connects them. At its most basic it is a network diagram, however much more information is included within technology architecture than just infrastructure. I would suggest that this element of architecture has limited direct relevance to data quality, as it is the databases and applications that sit on top of the technology that have the primary relevance. As a result I will not be discussing this in any detail. That said the technology architecture is the enabler of all that sits on top of it.

7.6.5 How does this affect data quality?

Poor architecture is commonly one of the reasons why the data quality problem became so out of control in the first place. Architectural governance for new projects is rarely done well. However, it is possible to establish an architectural governance framework to ensure that projects act within the agreed architectural framework of the organisation. Whilst architectural renovation (changing what is already there) is often difficult, the contribution of architecture to the data quality problem should absolutely be considered as there may be potential to significantly reduce the scale of the remediation required if architectural improvements can be made.

For example
In a heavily siloed business with five divisions, the remediation effort may require remediating five copies of the data, one for each silo. Collapsing the architecture so all five divisions operate via one customer database, which is then remediated, may actually be considerably cheaper than remediating five silos, which will then – naturally – get out of sync at a rate of 685 address changes per hour (UK).

If the application architecture is extremely complex, then it is much more likely for data quality problems to occur.

7.7 People

It is unfortunately the case that staff are often incentivised by productivity and productivity is measured in throughput. This may be in terms of calls per hour or average call length, or in terms of number of claims processed per day. The result is that quality, being neither valued nor targeted, will unsurprisingly not occur. Training is also overlooked. For some reason is it often assumed that staff will just "know" where to make the judgement call between speed and accuracy, or somehow magically be able to achieve both, thereby violating one of the fundamental rules of business, in that you can only ever have two out of cheap, fast and good. Much as the stitch in time saves nine, it is much cheaper to stop any problem occurring – data quality as much as any other problem – rather than clean up the mess later. To continue my analogy of building a wall, one could specify a brick wall, in a particular location, to a certain height, but without some training the wall is not going to get very high – or look a mess and then fall over later. Training is fundamental. It is probably the number one defence against data quality in the organisation, and it is rarely done at all, let alone done well.

7.8 Poor Process and resultant Poor Data

"It is very common to find that the data to support many of the business information needs is simply not available at the levels required, or that it is of such bad quality that it is impossible to use. Resolution of these types of issues often requires fundamental changes to business processes."
Alison Newell

Process failures fundamentally cause data quality issues. Whilst a data quality project may look to clean the existing data, there is no point doing this without looking at the processes that created it. Controlling new data will not create organisation-wide data quality if the good data is just being added to a pool of poor quality data – whilst over time the good data will improve the overall situation, it will be a very slow process as old, poor quality data becomes increasingly historical. According to Royal Mail[26], each year in the UK:

- 12% of the population move home
- 75,000 businesses relocate
- 512,000 people die
- 230,000 people get married

Cleaning current data is pointless if new data being added is of poor quality. Equally, data is rarely totally static, and if a rule of thumb says that 2% of data will change on a monthly basis it does not take many months before data is back to poor quality again, even after a major remediation exercise.

---

26. Royal Mail Annual Accounts, 2014

Within process there are several components. These are the people who perform the process (which we have already considered), the technology they use to perform the process, and the way in which it is done – specifically the design of the process.

■ Design

The design of the process needs to consider data quality. It needs to consider the way in which tasks are performed and controlled, and the effect this has on information quality. Every part of every process should consider the risk to information quality, and how that risk should be mitigated. An example here may be a process to capture customer details. It is accepted that people spell their names in an infinite number of ways, and it is also accepted that with the myriad of accents and the quality of phone lines it is possible for contact centre personnel to mis-hear customer names. So how does the process design mitigate this risk?

■ Technology

The consideration of technology is important. In this book I have considered technology as a tool or enabler that helps the organisation to complete tasks, rather than an entity in itself. However, the technology that is used for an individual process should support the goal of information quality. Applications should be configured so that it is difficult to input poor quality data, or automatic checks should be created to highlight failures. It is also possible to utilise reference data sets to constrain the input of, for example, titles, to accepted values. Alternatively, poor implementation of technology can cause data quality issues. For example, automatic routines that transfer data from one system to another can corrupt or lose data.

7.9 Summary

In this chapter I have outlined at a high level the factors that will affect data quality in an organisation. To recap, these are:

- No direction, in terms of strategy or requirements.
- Poor governance and/or management.
- Poor architecture, in terms of the way the organisation fits together.
- Poorly trained and poorly incentivised people.
- Poor process in terms of either design or technology.

This discussion should enable the reader to start to look at organisations and see the way that they waste time and resources through poor data quality. In the next chapter I will describe the data quality maturity model, a way of benchmarking an organisation in relation to the causes of poor data quality, and explain how it can be used to assess the approach to data quality within any organisation.

SECTION 3 — THE APPROACH TO DATA QUALITY

CHAPTER 8: DATA QUALITY MATURITY MODEL

8.1 Structure

This section of the book covers the following topics:

1. What affects data quality
2. Data quality maturity model
3. Principles
4. Myth-busting
5. The Data Quality Blueprint

This chapter covers the second of these topics.

8.2 Overview

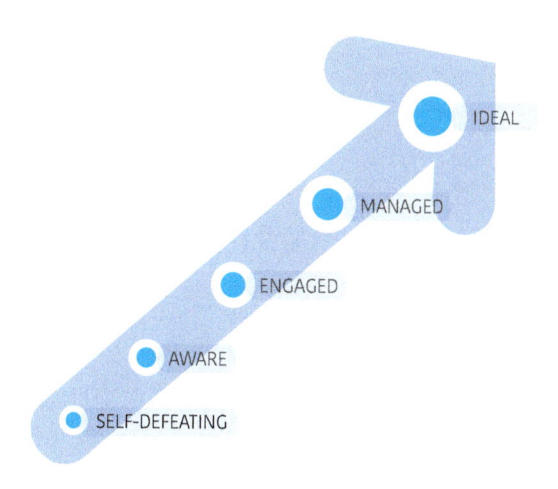

- IDEAL
- MANAGED
- ENGAGED
- AWARE
- SELF-DEFEATING

In the previous chapter we considered the causes of poor data quality in an organisation. A useful tool at this point is a maturity model. This looks at where, for each of these causes, an organisation sits on a continuum from risky to ideal. However, each organisation needs to decide where on the continuum it wishes to aim as "ideal" or "optimising" may not necessarily be appropriate for every organisation due to the investment required to achieve this status, though clearly this will depend on the starting point. Also, organisations may find that certain areas where quality is critical – for example risk or capital management – may require a higher level of data quality maturity than others.

The Data Quality Blueprint

```
┌─────────────────────────────────────────────────┐
│                   ORGANISATION                  │
│  ┌───────────────────────────────────────────┐  │
│  │  DIRECTION, GOVERNANCE AND MANAGEMENT     │  │
│  └───────────────────────────────────────────┘  │
│  ┌─────────────────────────┐  ┌──────────────┐  │
│  │  ENTERPRISE ARCHITECTURE│  │              │  │
│  └─────────────────────────┘  │              │  │
│  ┌─────────────────────────┐  │ EXISTING DATA│  │
│  │  PEOPLE (TRAINING AND   │  │              │  │
│  │  KNOWLEDGE MANAGEMENT)  │  │              │  │
│  └─────────────────────────┘  └──────────────┘  │
│  ┌─────────────────────────┐                    │
│  │ PROCESS & PROCESS TECHNOLOGY │               │
│  └─────────────────────────┘                    │
└─────────────────────────────────────────────────┘
```

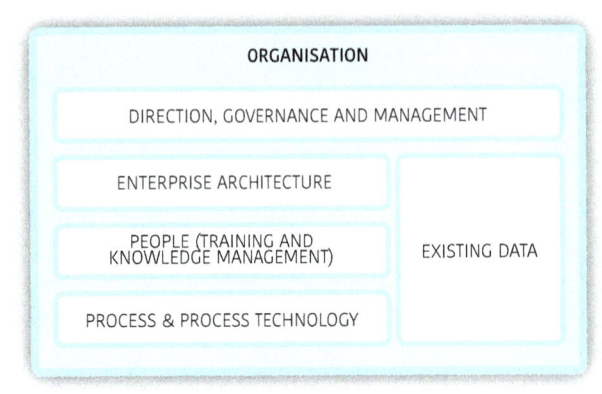

Within this chapter I have outlined the characteristics of the maturity model stages and mapped these onto the causes of poor data quality outlined in the previous chapter.

- Direction
- Governance & Management
- Architecture
- People
- Process
- Existing Data

I have divided the maturity model into five stages: self-defeating, aware, engaged, managed and ideal, which I will now look at in more detail.

8.3   Self-Defeating

The organisation has no interest in data quality or, most likely, in quality at all. The cheapest tactical solution wins every time, strategy is irrelevant. Vast amount of time is wasted re-performing cleansing tasks that should really only ever have to be done once. The excuse given when auditors or interested outsiders ask is that people are never given time or budget to sort matters out properly. I have worked with a worrying number of large organisations who exist at this point.

SELF-DEFEATING	
Direction	We do not have a data vision, strategy or requirements
Governance	We do not have any data governance. Data is not managed. In fact, the concept of data management is not recognised.
Architecture	There is no recognition of the effect that architecture has on data quality. Architectural approaches either do not proceed at all (i.e. there is most likely no architecture function) or feel that data quality is irrelevant. Applications exist in their own silos.
People	People are actively incentivised to reduce quality in the quest for better throughput. Data quality does not form part of any organisational training.
Process	We do not consider data quality in process design or process technology
Existing Data	Existing data is in a poor state, with many data quality problems across the organisation
TAGLINE: We have bigger problems than data quality.	

8.4 Aware

The organisation understands that they have a data quality problem but does not really have any idea how to approach it. The organisation does not know how much poor data quality costs them. They hope it is not a lot but have a nagging worry that it's going to come back and bite them really badly. They hope that it won't hit them reputationally or irritate the regulator. From my experience, this is another common maturity level for an organisation.

AWARE	
Direction	We have created a data strategy and are now looking at how this cascades into data requirements and data quality strategy. Data requirements are in place locally for a few departments.
Governance	A basic governance framework is in the process of being established. We understand that data needs to be managed and are in the process of setting up some data quality reporting.
Architecture	Architecture is defined and initial work has been undertaken to look at the effect on data quality. However, no remediation has taken place. The interaction of applications and the resultant effect on data quality is recognised, however no complete list of applications within the organisation exists, nor does any map of how they interact.
People	Staff are made aware of quality issues and how they affect the enterprise, but such awareness is restricted to a few minutes in an induction programme and the odd news-letter.
Process	We understand that process design and technology will cause data quality issues, but are not really sure where to start.
Existing Data	In a poor state, but some profiling has been undertaken and there is understanding of the quality of the data.

TAGLINE: We know it is a problem but don't know how to fix it.

8.5 Engaged

The organisation is getting there. They have projects in place to examine and rectify data problems, and are aware of and actively addressing data quality. In most sectors, this kind of organisation is about as good as it gets.

ENGAGED	
Direction	We have a data strategy and are working to define data requirements and data quality requirements. Data requirements for most departments exist and are in the process of being compared to create a homogenous data standard throughout the organisation.
Governance	We have a strong governance framework that is acting to identify issues with data management in the organisation. We have a good understanding of the tasks inherent to data management and what they involve. We are working through the data management in the organisation to ensure it conforms to best practice.
Architecture	Architecture is defined and initial work has been undertaken to look at the effect on data quality. Some work has been undertaken to improve architectural elements, and architectural standards have been put in place so that new architectural changes are completed with an understanding of data quality.
People	Staff are aware of quality issues and the importance of data quality in the organisation. Regular refresher courses are mandatory to reinforce the message.
Process	It is accepted that some process designs cause information problems, and initial work has been undertaken to look at data quality pain points and some remediation work has been achieved.
Existing Data	Getting better

TAGLINE: We are fixing our data quality problems. We know where we are going; we've just not got there yet.

8.6 Managed

The organisation has an extensive governance process that oversees information management. Poor quality information is captured and reported. The input of data into the organisation is strictly controlled, and validation checkpoints exist at every point. Board reporting includes the quality of information in the organisation. This kind of organisation is rarely seen.

MANAGED	
Direction	Data vision, data strategy, data quality requirements all exist and have been developed in partnership between business and IT, they are regularly reviewed. Data requirements have been defined at an enterprise level. These include quality expectations for the data within each area of the business.
Governance	We have a formal governance framework that meets regularly. It decides on all issues that relate to data governance. We have a holistic view of data management, including a full taxonomy. We consider each element of data management closely and have a reporting suite that runs monthly which will identify any data quality issues.

MANAGED	
Architecture	Architecture is formally defined. All architectural changes have to be signed off by an architectural standards board that will assess any proposed change against a number of criteria, data quality being one.
People	Every staff member's appraisal is based on the quality of the product they produce and the quality of the data that they own.
Process	All solutions and applications are listed in a directory and all interactions are mapped. New technology is carefully considered on the basis of a number of criteria, one of which is data quality.
Existing Data	Mostly in good shape, a few anomalies slip through.
TAGLINE: Our data quality problem is under firm control	

8.7 Ideal/Optimising

Data quality is embedded in the organisation. There is no data quality department, because data quality is the responsibility of everyone. Each process has quality at its heart, because the organisation knows that doing things twice badly costs more than doing it once well. I have only seen this once, and then only in a subset of an organisation.

IDEAL / OPTIMISING	
Direction	Data vision, data strategy, data quality requirements all exist and have been developed in partnership between business and IT, they are regularly reviewed. Data requirements are enterprise-wide, business defined, and cover all elements of data.
Governance	We have a "light touch" governance framework that meets occasionally when necessary. Most issues are decided at a lower level. Data management is light touch as the processes have been designed to get data right first time.
Architecture	Data quality is embedded in every area of the organisation, including architecture. As a result when architectural changes are proposed the question as to the effect on data quality is an integral part of the assessment.
People	Staff understand the effect of poor quality – not just in respect of data – and act to ensure it does not occur and remove it.
Process	Processes are not implemented if they are going to cause data quality problems.
Existing Data	In good shape
TAGLINE: We not only know that we do not have a data quality problem, we can demonstrate this – at a moment's notice – to anyone who asks. We are proud of our data management and can demonstrate how it improves our business profitability, our people and our customers.	

8.8 Analysis

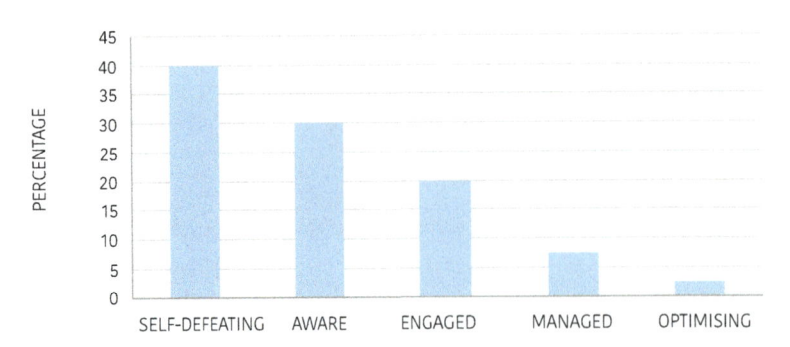

[Bar chart showing percentages across maturity stages: SELF-DEFEATING ~40%, AWARE ~30%, ENGAGED ~20%, MANAGED ~8%, OPTIMISING ~3%]

> "As the practitioners in the organization gain a more thorough understanding of the methods for identifying the sources for data flaws, they become more proactive in identifying and resolving potential issues before negative business impacts occur."
> **David Loshin, *The Practitioners Guide to Data Quality Improvement*, Elsevier, 2011**

The interesting comment about the above maturity model is that the last place –"ideal/optimising" – would actually cost considerably less to operate than "managed". The ideal organisation has a quality-aware mind-set. An organisation at stage "managed" is bludgeoning the problem to death, and has, by dint of huge effort, killed it. In the ideal organisation the problem never got to grow. The actual data quality of "managed" may equal that of "ideal" – but whereas "managed" achieves this through massive effort, "ideal" achieves it through almost no effort at all. Another interesting comment is that the continuum is a continuum of attitude, not effort. Any organisation can enter the continuum at any point, simply by a change in mind-set. It is not necessary to go through all stages before you reach the nirvana, and equally some parts of an organisation may exist in "self-defeating" whilst others are at "ideal".

I have worked with a large number of organisations, and I would estimate that the vast majority sit at the lower end of the scale. This is an unscientific analysis, but is based on my own industry experience. Most data quality projects, publications and strategies try and get an organisation to "managed" and most executives see "managed" as their personal nirvana. In a way, this is doing things the hard way. The Data Quality Blueprint is designed to move organisations towards "Ideal".

8.9 Assessment

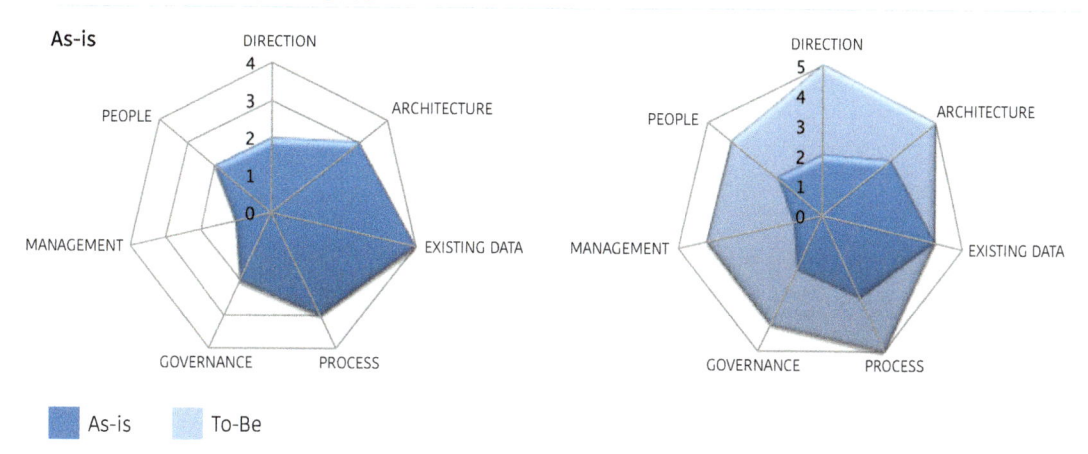

Assessment of an organisation against the maturity model is a useful approach to any data quality project. Here I particularly favour a spider diagram as it enables a rapid and visual assessment of the organisation against where it wants to be in terms of overall data quality. Whilst not in any way a replacement for a detailed investigation (of which more later) it enables a quick assessment.

The other advantage of this form of visual representation is that it is possible to superimpose the "to-be" desired situation. Whilst it may be thought that every organisation would wish to aim for the maximum in every category, this may not be the case. Movement towards "ideal" may not involve significant cost but will involve a culture change for many organisations, and these do not occur overnight. An example of the "as-is" and "to-be" superimposed on the same graph is shown above. It can be seen how this instantly identifies the area where work is required, and, conversely, where the organisation already meets requirements.

8.10 Summary

Within this chapter I have outlined a methodology for the assessment of data quality maturity, and described the characteristics of the organisation at each stage of the maturity model. This maturity model covers direction, governance and management, architecture, people, process and data – specifically the elements of an organisation that we have previously determined to be key factors causing poor data quality. This maturity model enables an organisation to describe where they are, but more importantly where they are going, and is an important tool in defining the scope of a data quality project and its direction. The next chapter looks at principles to be used on this journey.

SECTION 3: THE APPROACH TO DATA QUALITY

CHAPTER 9: PRINCIPLES

9.1 Structure

This section of the book covers the following topics:

1. What affects data quality
2. Data quality maturity model
3. Principles
4. Myth-busting
5. The Data Quality Blueprint

This chapter covers the third of these topics.

9.2 Overview

Before starting on any data quality project it is desirable to determine basic principles that will underpin the approach. These should guide the project from beginning to end.

The rule for principles of any kind is that there should be limited in number, but they set the approach for the whole project, and every major decision within the project can be measured as to whether it supports or undermines them. Within this short chapter I have documented a number of important basic principles I feel are critical to the successful execution of a data quality project. I will use these throughout the remainder of the book to inform the overall approach.

9.3 Principle 1: The business is in the driving seat

> "'Dirty Data' is a Business Problem, Not an IT Problem."
> **Gartner, 2007**

Data quality is a business problem that must be solved by the business. The IT department cannot and should not be running a data quality project. Before any data quality project starts the following basic facts need to be understood by both business and IT:

- The business is responsible for the data.
- The business is responsible for the quality of the data.
- The business is responsible for the remediation of the data.
- The business is responsible for defining the quality of the data needed.

If a data quality project is run by IT then it is most likely to fail – in fact, lack of business involvement has cursed many IT projects to failure many times. However, the business need to work in concert with IT to achieve their aims. A data quality implementation needs to bring together the business and IT professionals to work together for the benefit of a common goal. This brings me to the next principle.

9.4 Principle 2: We're all in this together.

"A critical first step is for the business leader to acknowledge ownership of the organizations data and its data quality issues. Improving the quality of the organization's data must be lead by the business, but the business will not have to go at it alone. Business and IT have a shared ownership of and accountability for protecting and enhancing the organization's data."
Pitney Bowes Business Insight, 2013.

The business cannot do it alone. Data sits on IT systems and IT is normally the only department with direct access.

Data quality remediation work normally divides into that work done manually, and that done either via a bulk update or via a data quality application. If a data quality improvement requires a bulk update of data or if an application needs installation and configuration then IT are the best placed to do the work.

The involvement of IT will absolutely be required for remediation of data. Equally, technology underpins processes, as most processes run on technology systems. If the data quality remediation is also looking to change process then this will most often require the buy-in of IT. Therefore a data quality project should be a healthy partnership between the business and IT.

9.5 Principle 3: Do it once, do it well

"People forget how fast you did a job – but they remember how well you did it"
Howard Newton

A data quality project should only ever be implemented once. A data quality project is often a large endeavour which will draw on resources from all areas of the organisation. It is not something that any organisation should want to – or have to – do twice.

There's no point cleaning up the data for it to get into a poor state again a few months later. This is unfortunately not uncommon in data quality projects, and often the reason why data quality is seen as an insurmountable problem. The reason poor data quality keeps coming back is precisely because organisations and data quality projects fail to think about the problem holistically.

Understanding data quality means understanding that doing things quickly, cheaply and badly costs money. A mantra for any data quality project should be;

> "Do Not Run A Poor Quality Data Quality Project."

Otherwise you'll be running another one in a couple of years, and have wasted a lot of resources in the process.

9.6 Principle 4: Treat data as an asset

> "The underlying message of all these examples is that information is an asset in its own right."
> **Frank Buytendijk, research vice president at Gartner, 2013.**

Data in an organisation should be treated as an asset, but what does this mean for a data quality project?

It means treat every bit of data as if it is a valuable, physical asset. It has taken time and effort for the original customer to tell you their address, it has taken time and effort for the call centre agent or branch staff member to type it into the information systems and this data has then been lovingly preserved for years, religiously backed-up and used many times. It has cost money, probably quite a lot of money. Do not discard it unless you are certain that it will not be valuable now or in the future.

Take the time to update data with care. Look to understand the data and why it is in its present state before deciding on a solution. Even if you have an obvious error, do not rush to remediate as it may be a pointer to process failures or data failures that will affect many thousands of records, and which may not be as obvious. Do not treat your existing data as simply trash to deserve obliteration and replacement with something shiny and new.

9.7 Principle 5: People are the key

> "Data quality tools do not solve data quality problems – people solve data quality problems."
> **David Loshin**

It is unfortunately the case that many organisations treat data quality as a technical problem to be solved by technical people in technical ways. However poor data quality is a people and process problem with technological elements, not a technological problem.

What's more, in order to solve a data quality problem, it will be necessary to win the hearts and minds of the organisation. It is necessary to engage with people, not computers. It is necessary to persuade the executive that data quality is causing them to lose money on a day to day basis, it is necessary to persuade business leaders that despite the word "data" being in the phrase "data quality" that actually solving data quality needs the business leaders to show the way regards what data, and what quality. It is necessary to persuade the IT department that they really do want to help solve the data quality problem as it will make their lives easier. It is about persuading people there is a business case for a data quality project.

It is about training people to recognise poor quality when they see it, it is about empowering people to do something about it, it is about managing the knowledge (generally in people's heads) of the way information flows through an organisation, it is about understanding how people manage, and use, information, and how they make decisions.

A data quality project needs to understand the people in the organisation, what they are doing with information and how they are doing it. People are not technology. They have hopes, fears, and aspirations. They are irrational and cantankerous, and are not always open to change. Their involvement needs to be nurtured.

9.8 Principle 6: Embed data quality in the organisation

"A company with a highly developed culture of quality spends, on average, $350 million less annually fixing mistakes than a company with a poorly developed one"
IBM

I have always advocated that data quality process should become embedded in the organisation. After the initial pain of cleaning historical data is complete, then the organisation needs to embed a good quality mindset, rather than poor-or-irrelevant quality mind-set. At this point the data quality project should disappear. It has now become part of the organisation.

Whilst some degree of monitoring is necessary to gently steer the data quality process onward, what is not needed is a large data quality department. The objective of this approach is to make data quality endemic in the organisation. Quality management needs to be in place so that data quality issues can be identified and addressed, but that is all. Data quality should become just another operational measurement, and only require a brief look at the dials to make sure they are in the green.

9.9 Principle 7: Do as little work as possible

"Diligence is a good thing, but taking things easy is much more restful."
Mark Twain

The objective of a data quality project is not to boil the ocean, nor is the objective to make data quality in the organisation perfect. The objective is to do the minimum possible that allows the organisation to meet its information objectives. This means that the end state of the data should be described as "good enough", not "perfect". It also means that once this state of affairs is reached, a data quality project has completed its objectives.

Fundamentally, the approach should be based around minimum necessary work, and if work is undertaken it needs to be undertaken in as effective and efficient a manner as possible and only ever done once. (Principle 3)

9.10   Summary

Within this chapter I have listed a number of principles that should underpin the approach to the project. The principles should be kept in mind throughout any data quality project. I will, in fact, refer to them throughout the rest of the book. The principles should be applied by the reader at any point where there is something new, as they allow the reader to reach beyond the narrow confines of the book and to apply the principles to any data quality issues, wherever they may be.

The next step is to outline The Data Quality Blueprint; however before I do this I feel it is necessary to examine some of the alternative approaches to data quality and to discuss the reasons that these approaches are not as effective, and how The Data Quality Blueprint brings something new. This is the subject of the next chapter.

SECTION 3: THE APPROACH TO DATA QUALITY

CHAPTER 10: MYTH-BUSTING

10.1 Structure

This section of the book covers the following topics:

1. What affects data quality
2. Data quality maturity model
3. Principles
4. Myth-busting
5. The Data Quality Blueprint

This chapter covers the fourth of these topics.

10.2 Overview

I have spent quite a lot of time explaining what affects data quality. I have explained that in order to effectively address data quality issues a holistic approach should be utilised, which looks at every relevant element of the organisation. Unfortunately this does not mean that many organisations do not try and improve data quality in a faster, cheaper or less effective way. This is often a result of poor understanding of the issues surrounding data quality – which this book was written, in part, to address.

Ironically, this often results in an ineffective project where the data rapidly returns to a poor state. I feel that for this reason it is necessary to look at some of the ways in which data quality is implemented "on the cheap". In this chapter I will discuss some of the approaches I have seen in practice. For each I will show how, whilst they cover elements of the causes of data quality, they do not cover them all.

10.3   The Internal Audit Solution

The business recognises that data quality is a problem, and appreciates, to its credit, that it needs to be a business rather than an IT solution. This is excellent. The way that the project is approached, however, is less than ideal. The stages of the common internal audit solution are as follows:

- Give someone responsibility for data quality. This is usually someone who is already fairly busy, will probably work in internal audit.
- Make them responsible for rolling out data quality within the enterprise.
- If particularly generous, give them some resources to help, say one or two full time equivalents.

The problem with this is approach is:

- There are simply not enough resources.
- There is no executive buy-in. One person in internal audit does not have the authority to initiate the enterprise-wide changes that will be required.
- There is no framework for data quality.

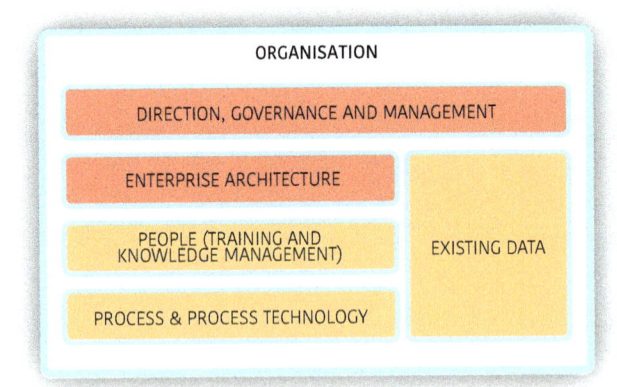

As a result the chance of any meaningful improvement in data quality is low. The person concerned will do their best, but they do not have a realistic chance of making a difference to data quality across the enterprise.

This approach, over a long period of time, may cover process to an extent, may make an effect on existing data, and may touch on people, but will not cover direction, governance or management, or enterprise architecture.

Verdict: 3/10

10.4   Technology to the Rescue

The organisation sees data quality as something that is quickly solvable by an application. They believe that records can be run through a black box that will automatically correct all the data for them. The organisation buys an "Enterprise Data Quality" tool. This approach is astoundingly common. Whilst some data can be corrected, computers are not very good at doing this automatically. Computers are also fairly hopeless at de-duplicating records. To illustrate this by an example, take the four records below.

Title	Forename	Surname	DOB	Address	Postcode
Miss	Elizabeth	Smith	01/01/1980	1 Station Road	S70 1PG
Miss	Liz	Smith	01/01/1980	1 Station Road	S70 1RG
Mrs	Beth	Jones	01/01/1980	15 Park Place	S70 1BG
Mr	Steve	Jones	01/01/1978	15 Park Place	S70 1BG

A human can rapidly see that almost certainly Liz Smith of 1 Station Road married and moved in with Steve Jones of 15 Park Place, and also appears to have a predilection for changing the contraction of her name. A computer is bad at this kind of logic. Applications are good at helping to identify the data issues within a data set. Some applications may also enable you to track other remediation efforts. An application cannot however de-duplicate 100% of data, solve data issues or perform "best source" analysis. Buying an application does not equal solving data quality. It facilitates the ability of humans to solve data quality. An application used as a black box to solve data issues will also break data lineage. It will take an input from source systems, "remediate", and then output to a "cleansed" database. If it has done its job perfectly, you then have good data quality for reporting, however the data now does not match the source systems. All the problems in relation to customer experience, mailing the wrong people, or mailing them twice, or wrong invoicing, and so on, still remain. Worse, it is most likely that the application has done the work "mostly" right, which means that you now have the original problem plus a set of new ones, and – because data lineage is broken – no way of working out what has occurred, how to fix it, or whether your reporting is correct or not. It may look better, but is it? You cannot tell anymore.

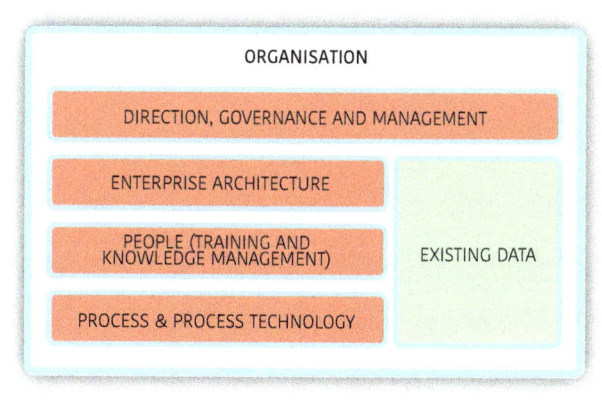

The reason that this approach is so common is that it aligns well with the business propensity to outsource data problems to IT, and also with IT's propensity to see the answer to all problems as being more shiny kit. So both sides of the organisation will willingly push a solution which unfortunately simply does not work as well as either will expect.

This approach can make the existing data set look good, and may well change much of the data for the better. However, it does nothing for direction, governance or management, architecture, people or process. It also may store up future problems for the organisation.

Verdict: 2/10

10.5 IT will solve it, it's their data!

The business recognises that data quality is a problem but sees it as an IT problem. After all, is "data" not an IT word? As a result IT is asked to "solve" the data quality problem. IT may not know the business and often does not understand the business effects of data. It is unlikely to have the time to dedicate to a holistic solution to data quality problems. The view of most IT professionals I speak to is that whilst they understand that they are custodians of the business data, they also clearly understand that is the business who own the data. The most likely outcome is that IT will look at the various data sets and come up with a huge list of questions for the business. Examples may be:

- What is the correct format for an address?
- What is a customer?

- What is a product?
- What are the allowable titles?
- Where do we sell our products (will affect allowable values for many fields)?
- How does the organisation want to format addresses for Scottish flats[27]?

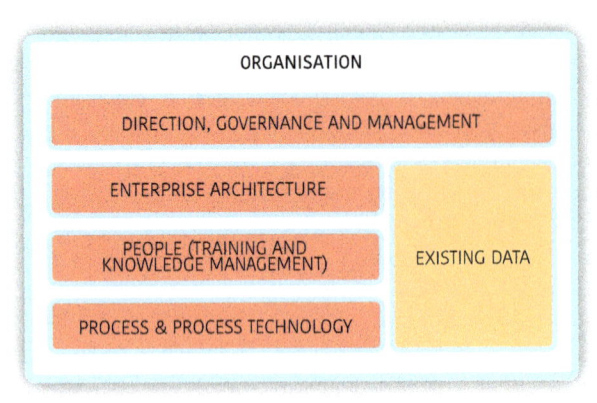

These will be passed back to the business sponsor, who will pass them out to the various departments. The departments will almost certainly have no time to address the issues (after all, isn't this an IT problem?), and the whole process will grind to a halt.

The best that can come of this approach is some easy data cleansing will occur on fields that can be efficiently dealt with by automatic update.

This approach will cover the existing data to a certain extent, but nothing else.

Verdict: 2/10

10.6   Any Data is better than No Data

The business tells IT to solve the data problems, IT recognises that data is a problem, and decides that the reason there is a problem is because everything is the wrong format and there are loads of missing values. The obvious solution to the above problems is to force format the existing data to the required format (often corrupting or destroying thousands of records) and then fill all the missing data with default values (now you don't know what is correct data and what is default data).

This can cause some **major** business problems.

For example, suppose you are reserving against losses in a mortgage portfolio. You are trying to work out the propensity of the mortgage holders to default. You have data on approximately 50% of the mortgage holders and how many months they are in arrears. The rest of the data is blank. For the business it is an easy process to take the propensity to default of the records with data and extrapolate across the rest of the portfolio.

Under this approach to data quality someone who has not really considered the downstream implications will fill in all those blanks with zeros. It is now impossible to work out the propensity to default. How do you tell the "real" zeros from the "default" zeros? Most likely is that all this will occur behind the scenes and the business will not know there are default values in their data. The propensity to default will therefore be calculated too low, and the reserve against the portfolio will

---

27.   A somewhat common problem. Scottish flats are commonly addressed in a number of ways. An example may be the number of the floor followed by the number of the flat. Hence 4/4 4 Station road. Other options can include 4F, 4 Station Road (Fourth Floor Front, 4 Station Road), T/L, 4 Station Road (Top Left, 4 Station Road), 4R (4th Floor, Right Flat), etc. Scottish flat addresses confuse many address systems.

be too low, with the resulting business impact when it all goes wrong. This example, incidentally, is something that has actually occurred in my own experience.

To take another example: It is decided to populate null dates of birth with 1/1/1900. Now assume marketing want to send out a mail with an offer for credit that can legally only go to those over the age of 18 and for business reasons only want to go to people in regular work and are under the age of normal retirement (say, 65).

Suddenly there is a problem, because there are now a lot of centenarians on the customer database who will be marked ineligible due to being over the age of retirement. If marketing then perform investigations and find out this is the default value, then they are no further forward, because they cannot just mail them all, because some might actually be under 18, and suddenly the marketing department is breaking the law. At this point, none of the options are good:

- They could omit mailing anyone with a date of birth of 1/1/1900. This is self-limiting the coverage (and hence success) of the campaign.
- They could add a flag for people who they think are actually under 18 or over 65 (increasing complexity, increasing work, and all because the right thing wasn't done first time).
- Could add a flag to all 1/1/1900 dates of birth to indicate they are actually "unknown" and get the contact centre to ask these people their actual DOB whenever they contact the organisation.

Unfortunately to the average IT person (I've had discussions with many on this subject), default values are "good". This is because:

- They meet technical criteria.
- Are not "null" (null values (i.e. "unpopulated") have an irritating habit of making queries and databases misbehave).
- Are formatted according to the rules of the field.
- Do not break constraints or activate triggers.
- Are nicely predictable.
- Do not cause unexpected errors.

In short, they "behave" and "play nicely with others". To a business person, however, default values are "bad", because:

- They mean that there is no idea what values are actual data and what are default values.
- They mask unknowns.
- The allow huge data quality issues to exist under the radar
- There is a nasty suspicion that they have been used to overwrite actual valid and business-relevant but "awkward" (to IT) data
- They change business outcomes

In short are "dangerous" and "undermine trust and use of the whole data set".

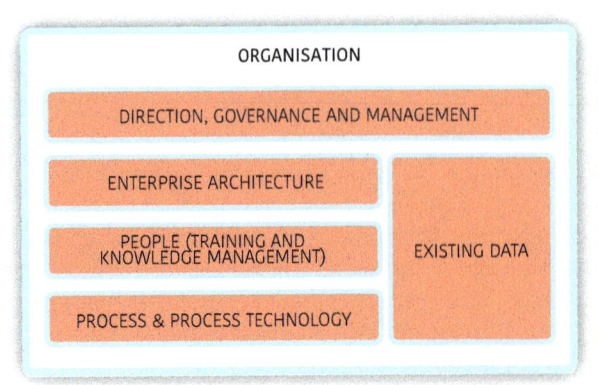

As it is the business that should be driving any data quality work then it can be seen that populating with default values will make the problem a lot worse. Default values are really bad. It is much better to know what you don't know, than move to a position where you don't know what you don't know.

This approach makes matters worse.

Verdict: 0/10

10.7 The Data Quality Department

A slightly logical approach – after all we have an internal audit department, why not a data quality department? Setting up a data quality department and expecting it to solve data quality problems is showing an ignorance of the size of the problem and expecting a small department to solve a huge issue. To give an idea of scale:

- One company I worked with that solved data quality problems to a fixed regulatory deadline ended up throwing 500 people at the problem for 18 months.
- For another – smaller – organisation in the same position the data quality effort occupied 200 people for a year.

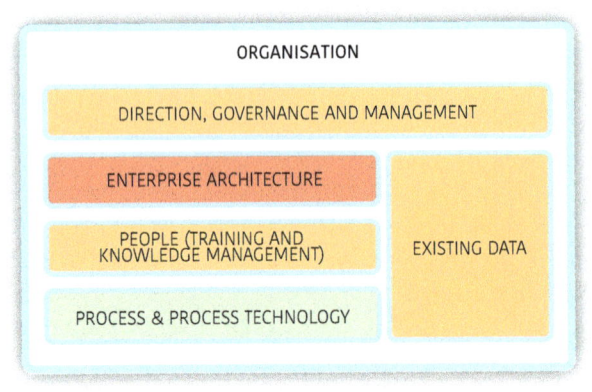

The other problem with a data quality department is that it, by necessity, is working at a high level, looking at management and regulatory reports. I will talk about where in the data landscape it is best to attack a data quality problem in a later chapter; however, if data quality is going to be solved, it has to be done at the coalface, not up on the surface.

This approach, over a long period of time, may cover process to an extent, may make an effect on existing data, and may touch on people, but will not cover direction, though it may cover governance or management. Enterprise architecture is unlikely to be touched.

Verdict: 5/10

10.8 MDM: Master Data Management.

Anecdote
A relatively small organisation I am aware of had 65 copies of the customer database including all customer data. A colleague, in conversation, mentioned that they were aware of an organisation that had 350,000 copies.

No. Not a typo. Three Hundred and Fifty Thousand.

Master Data Management is concerned with implementing controls and (potentially) a single data store for (usually) customer and product data, determining best source or golden source, and implementing processes and procedures to reduce or eliminate duplication. Originally, master data was seen as customer data – customer names, addresses, contact details. The critical characteristic of this data was that it was used by many areas across the organisation, and hence there was value in acting to control this data centrally. It was often out of control, with customer data duplicated throughout the organisational information stores. This corresponded nicely with various initiatives to create a "single customer view" where all customer data was brought together in one place. Further down the road, organisations realised that there were other information sets that would fall nicely into the banner of "Master Data" – product data for example.

I have spoken to many practitioners, and they often talk about their frustration that many organisations that implement master data management – universally acronymed to MDM – are talking about a technological solution, a database with a rules engine. However, really, it should be the case that MDM is as much a business-focused approach as anything else, not un-akin to the mindset that is used for both data governance and data quality, in that the business needs to define the problem and its solution and work with IT to implement it. In practice, it almost never is, so here I will deal with the practical, real, let's-buy-some-kit approach. MDM projects can, however, be a great help by identification of business critical data and then getting all this data in the same place. It will still almost certainly be rubbish data, but it will at least be in one location. The work to correct data quality issues will therefore be better targeted and more effective, though this will, of course, depend on how the MDM solution has been implemented. For example:

- Is it mandated from the top – in which case it may be a shiny new database that no-one uses.
- Is it a departmental initiative – in which case it doesn't hold all the data.
- Is there buy-in from the wider business? – if not the rest of the organisation may keep using their own sources of data.
- Are there multiple MDM solutions? You would be amazed at how many organisations have multiple golden sources of data.

The main problem with MDM is that it is often seen as a solution in itself. "We have solved our data quality, we have implemented MDM." This is straight out of the "We have a data strategy, we are implementing SAP" school of thought, and shows that the person talking:

- Does not know what MDM really is or the benefits it brings to the organisation
- Does not know how it will help data quality
- Probably has swallowed the vendor's sales spiel a bit too wholeheartedly.

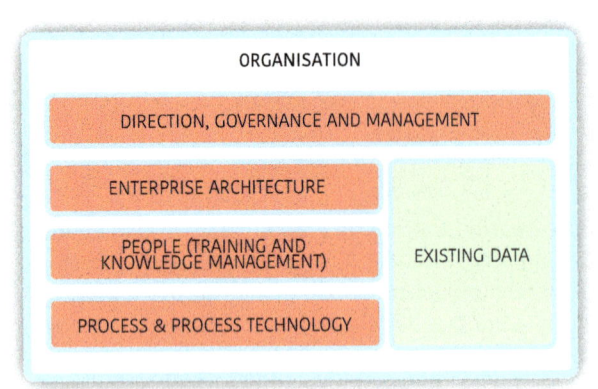

Here, there is the opportunity for some gentle education. Hopefully at this point the listener will look thoughtful and start asking you how to cover the bits they missed.

This approach may be reasonably effective for existing data, but does not touch anything else.

Verdict: 2/10

10.9 Implement Data Governance (and do it well)

As a data governance practitioner as well as a data quality one, I get dispirited when organisations see data governance as a one-stop solution to data quality. Data governance is about alignment and direction of data management, not remediation of data quality.

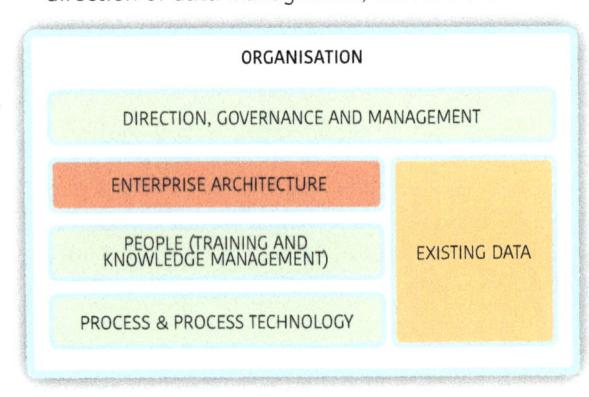

Unfortunately, despite my misgivings, data governance, implemented properly, will act as an instigator and accelerant to data quality, as by highlighting deficiencies in data management, will make data quality problems visible at a high level in the organisation, and hence will promote their resolution.

This approach will cover direction (to an extent), governance, management and probably people and process. It will not cover existing data directly (though may highlight issues) and will not cover architecture at all.

Verdict: 7/10

10.10 Summary

In this chapter I have outlined a number of the common, but unfortunately less effective ways in which data quality is approached in many organisations. To its credit, the industry is changing as the "data quality on the cheap" approach is seen to fail to meet its objectives, or meets its objectives only to see the data quality rapidly degrade as there has been no attempt to address process or to embed the changes.

At this point the reader should be able to see that many of the common approaches to data quality are deficient as they miss out important parts of the problems, and can start to understand that without attacking the problem on all sides, so to speak, long lasting data quality will not be possible. It is this attacking on all sides that The Data Quality Blueprint attempts to do.

In the next chapter I will outline what I consider should be the overall approach to data quality. I will break the various elements of the journey into stages and will define what is incorporated within each stage. This then forms a basis for the step by step implementation described in the second half of the book.

SECTION 3: THE APPROACH TO DATA QUALITY

CHAPTER 11: THE DATA QUALITY BLUEPRINT

11.1 Structure

This section of the book covers the following topics:

1. What affects data quality
2. Data quality maturity model
3. Principles
4. Myth-busting
5. The Data Quality Blueprint

This chapter covers the last of these topics.

11.2 Overview

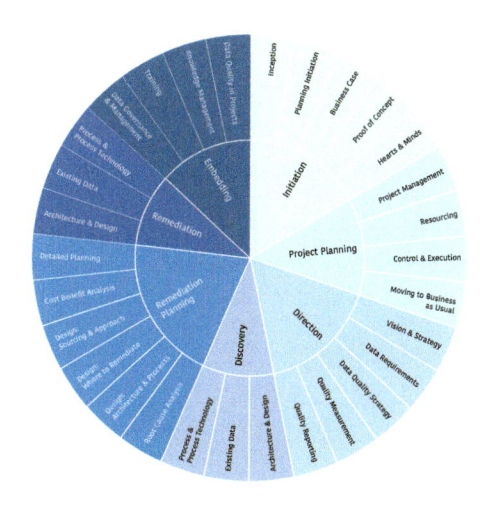

Over the past few chapters I have discussed what affects data quality in an organisation and introduced the data quality maturity model. I have discussed the principles that any data quality approach should follow, and also discussed the reasons why data quality initiatives fail to deliver on expectations. In this chapter I will introduce what I consider to be the most effective approach. Regarding this as "a methodology" is possibly giving it too grand a title, as what I have tried to do here is to group together the tasks that would be involved in a typical data quality assignment that will cover all of the causes of poor quality, and put them in a logical order.

To guide the reader within the methodology I have created a basic graphic which is used within the methodology sections later in the book as a reference point. The main part of the rest of the book steps through a project in detail; however, at this stage I only intend to cover the subject at a high level as there are other subjects (notably "What is Data?" and "What is Quality?") to cover first.

11.3 High Level Methodology

The methodology needs to cover all of the areas that were considered earlier to affect data quality in an organisation, namely:

- Direction
- Existing data
- Governance and management
- Process
- Architecture
- People

ORGANISATION
- DIRECTION, GOVERNANCE AND MANAGEMENT
- ENTERPRISE ARCHITECTURE
- PEOPLE (TRAINING AND KNOWLEDGE MANAGEMENT)
- EXISTING DATA
- PROCESS & PROCESS TECHNOLOGY

We will start with the corporate vision; define where the organisation is going, and what information it requires in order to reach its destination. Clearly in order to start on a journey, you need to define the destination; otherwise much time and effort can be lost hopelessly meandering around back roads. After this, the next step is to work out how to get there. To solve data quality, it needs to be embedded within the organisation, historical problems need to be rectified, and processes amended to make sure they do not recur. Therefore the data quality project will need to specifically include:

- A data strategy, data quality strategy, defined data requirements and data quality requirements and alignment with the organisational vision.
- A data governance framework, defined data owners and data stewards, and board level representation.
- Data quality awareness embedded into data-related functions and processes and the implementation of incentives on data quality.
- A quality management control framework to ensure that, as much as possible, data quality breaches cannot happen, and if they do happen, they are rapidly detected and corrected.
- Business, data and application architecture that are created to make achieving good data quality as easy as possible.
- Remediation of existing data to erase the historical problems.
- Processes redesigned to consider data quality.
- Training and incentivisation of people.
- Knowledge sharing on all of the above.

There clearly needs to be a sequence to the implementation. Unfortunately it is not possible to simply step down (or up) the graphic above. You can if you are creating an organisation from scratch, but this will not work in an existing one. The Data Quality Blueprint wraps what needs to be achieved into a project format, a methodology where you can start at the beginning in a pre-existing organisation, work your way through and reach the end, and every one of the issues that affect data quality will have been covered in a logical and effective way. For example, you cannot (or should not) start remediating historical data until you have defined the data requirements, and equally, you should not do anything unless you have determined that it will support the aims of the organisation. The project will need to be planned. The blueprint takes the reader through the planning stage and, even if you have never been in a project environment before, will outline what is needed and when. There are project products (like a business case) that need to be prepared; otherwise it is likely that the project will never receive signoff. The Data Quality Blueprint is a recipe and blow-by-blow description of how to solve data quality problems.

11.4   Initiate

The initiation stage lays the foundations for the rest of the project. It builds the business case, engages the stakeholders and proves the case for the larger project. It contains a proof of concept which allows business leaders to see why and how data quality is important to the organisation, and estimates how much effort it will take to address current data quality issues. This stage is fundamental to the project and sets the scene for the organisation.

Laying the foundations/ inception	Basic logistical and hygiene tasks required to start the project.
Initiation planning	The initiation stage requires planning as much as the rest of the project. This is the first of three planning phases over the life of the project.
Business case	No project should go anywhere without a business case, and the same applies to a data quality project. The business case defines scope and objectives and the value that the business will gain from the project, and how it will gain that value, and how much the value will exceed the investment necessary to realise that value.
Proof of concept	The proof of concept is a device to prove the business case. It takes a small section of the business and demonstrates how the business case will work in practice.
Hearts and minds	A data quality project will not succeed without the support of the people in the organisation. Their buy-in is critical. Get it in place up front.

11.5   Project Planning

How do we get there in one piece and without killing each other? This stage is the first of two major planning phase in the project (and, with the initiation planning, the third overall). The first planning phase takes the project from initiation to the point where the discovery work is completed. It covers the production of the project plan, resource planning, the definition of artefacts, deliverables and dependencies, and the overall approach to the project. I would note here that I have placed in the appendices examples of artefacts that could potentially be used to facilitate a data quality project, as well as a full data quality project plan.

Project management	Managing a project of any size is a necessary requirement. The project needs to decide its approach, how it will be controlled, and where decision points will exist. It also needs to define what it will deliver and dependencies on other areas of the organisation needed in order to make the project a success.
Resources	Resources need to be defined, identified, and allocated. This may be everything from human resources to desk space or IT equipment.
Project plan	The project plan will order and control everything that comes after it in the project. It is the book by which the project will live, and enables those involved in the project to understand what is required and by when.

11.6 Direction

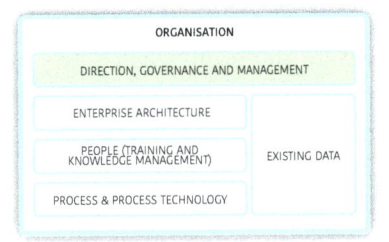

The most important part of a data quality remediation project is to decide direction. There is no point jumping in and remediating data without any idea of the quality that is required or how it supports the organisation. This stage determines what is required in terms of data quality, and sets the requirements for the project.

Corporate vision & strategy	The corporate vision defines everything that the organisation does. Every event within the organisation should support this, no exceptions. The corporate vision is the final destination of the organisation. The corporate strategy defines how the corporate vision will be achieved.
Data vision & data strategy	The corporate vision informs and defines the data vision. The data vision defines the data strategy. The data strategy defines the approach to information in the organisation.
Data requirements and data quality requirements	The data strategy defines the data requirements of the organisation. Data quality requirements define the data quality that the organisation will accept.
Data quality performance metrics and data quality reporting	In order to measure both the quality of the existing data, and also to determine the effectiveness of any remediation work you need to define the metrics you will use.

11.7 Discovery

The next stage is to determine the current situation. This covers analysis and assessment of architecture, process and existing data.

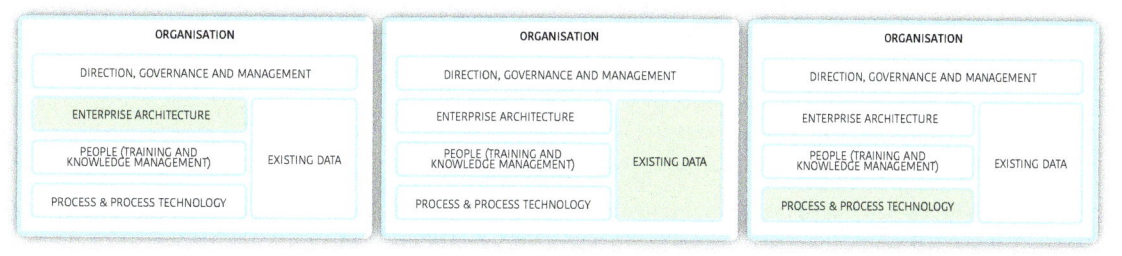

Discovery and assessment of architectural existing state	This phase takes the available information on the overall organisational design, and discovers the information if it is not available. This enables an assessment of the organisational architecture and its effect on data quality.
Discovery and assessment of existing data	This phase covers the discovery of data stores and the profiling of the data, to discover its existing state
Discovery and assessment of existing processes	This phase covers examination of existing processes within the context of data quality. Do the processes support data quality, or do existing processes contribute to the data quality problem?

11.8 Remediation Planning

The remediation planning is the pivotal point of the project. All information is drawn together and the way forward to create the desired future state can be determined. This includes the second big planning phase. With the discovery phase completed the organisation has a lot more information and it can revalidate the business case and plan remediation tasks in detail.

Root cause analysis	The work to determine the underlying cause of the data quality issues
Remediation design	Define how varying architecture, data and process items will be remediated
Cost-benefit analysis	For each root cause and proposed design estimate the cost to fix and the benefit that this will bring
Detailed planning	Divide the data and process into work streams that align with the effort and method of remediation. Define the management process around the remediation effort, how it will be managed and how it will be controlled.

11.9 Remediation

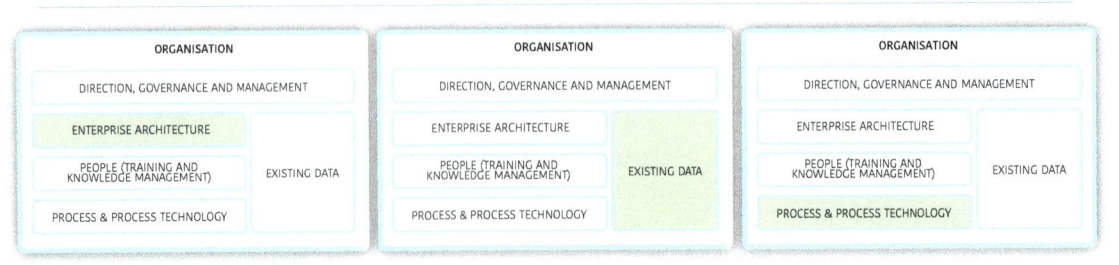

This stage takes the output from the remediation planning and starts the remediation work. This is the transformation of the data, process and architecture of the organisation to one where quality is at the fore.

Remediate architecture	Where possible, removing the blockers to data quality that are as a result of the overall design of the organisation
Remediate data	This phase covers taking the results from the profiling and the remediation planning and remediating the data. This will include replacement of data, rectification of data and, potentially, deletion of data that is no longer required by the organisation.
Remediate processes	This phase covers taking the results from the profiling and the remediation planning and remediating the process. This will include process design, process remediation, process and change management and integration into business as usual.

11.10 Embedding

Embedding is the part of the project where the organisation makes sure that the data and processes stay good. The existing data is remediated once, processes are put in place so that new data retains its quality, and the data quality project fades from view, it having done its job and with data quality now being an embedded part of the organisation. This part of the project deals with the last of these.

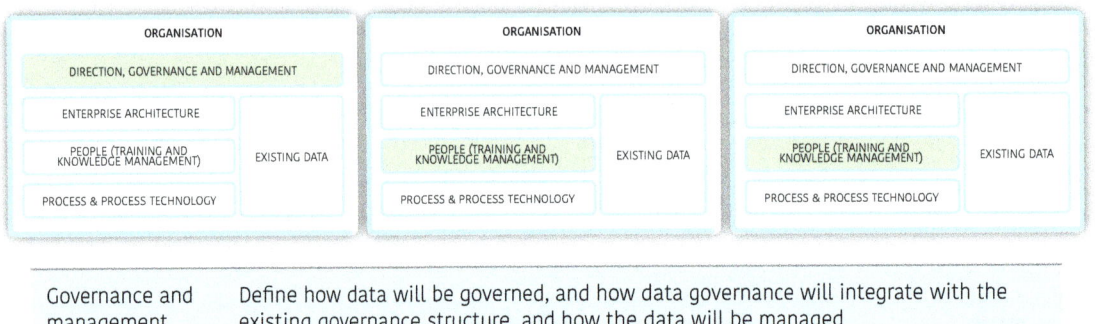

Governance and management	Define how data will be governed, and how data governance will integrate with the existing governance structure, and how the data will be managed
Training	It is important that individuals within the organisation understand and are bought into the principles that support the quality of the data within the organisation. This is the job of training.

Chapter 11: The Data Quality Blueprint

Knowledge management	During the data quality project a vast amount of information will be discovered and created on the organisation and the processes and data within it. It is vital that this information is not lost and is shared in the appropriate way with the elements of the organisation that need it.

11.11 Bringing it All Together

The diagram below brings all of the above together into one coherent whole.

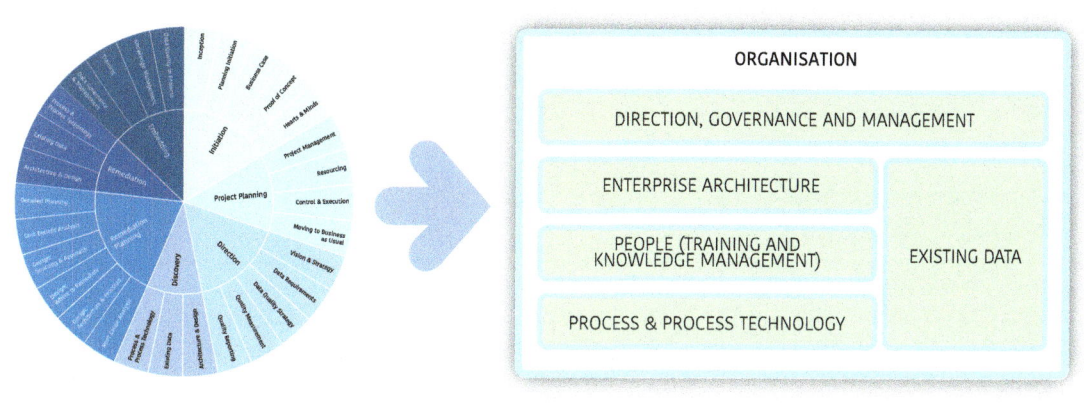

The stages and phases of The Data Quality Blueprint are shown below. This is also the structure of the methodology section of the book where each of these will be discussed in detail.

Initiate	Initiate	Planning	Business Case	Proof of concept	Hearts and minds
Project Planning	Modules	Deliverables	Dependences	Resources	Project plan
Direction	Vision	Strategy	Requirements	Metrics	
Discovery	Architecture and design	Existing data	Process and process technology		
Remediation Planning	Design of the solution	Root cause analysis	Cost benefit analysis	Updated project planning	
Remediation	Architecture and design	Existing data	Process and process technology		
Embedding	Governance & management	Training	Knowledge management	Data quality in projects	

The above is a basic structure that I believe encompasses everything that should make up a data quality project which will solve data quality for the long term. It can also be tailored depending on the organisation. If an organisation already has documented processes and procedures (many do), and a documented data quality strategy, data requirements, and so on, then "direction" is going to be short. This does not mean that it can be omitted, but that most of the work has already been done for you, and you can move straight on to discovery.

11.12 Summary

In this chapter I started by outlining the various components that a data quality project needs to cover. Namely:

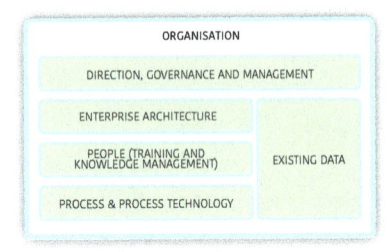

- Direction
- Governance & Management
- Architecture
- Existing Data
- Process
- People

I have introduced The Data Quality Blueprint, and shown how it covers the above in a logical manner that can be implemented via a single project. I have demonstrated how it covers the problem holistically, and how it covers all the elements of data quality within an organisation. The reader should be able to see that addressed in this way; a long lasting solution is possible.

This chapter concludes the high level overview of approach. From this point in the book I will be working towards a detailed description of the methodology and a detailed – and practical – description of how it can be put in place.

However, before this process can be start, a necessary evil is that all participants need to be on the same page in terms of the understanding of information within an organisation and how it flows within the business, and how, actually, is "quality" – or for that matter "data", going to be defined? This is the subject of the next section.

SECTION 4
BASIC UNDERSTANDING

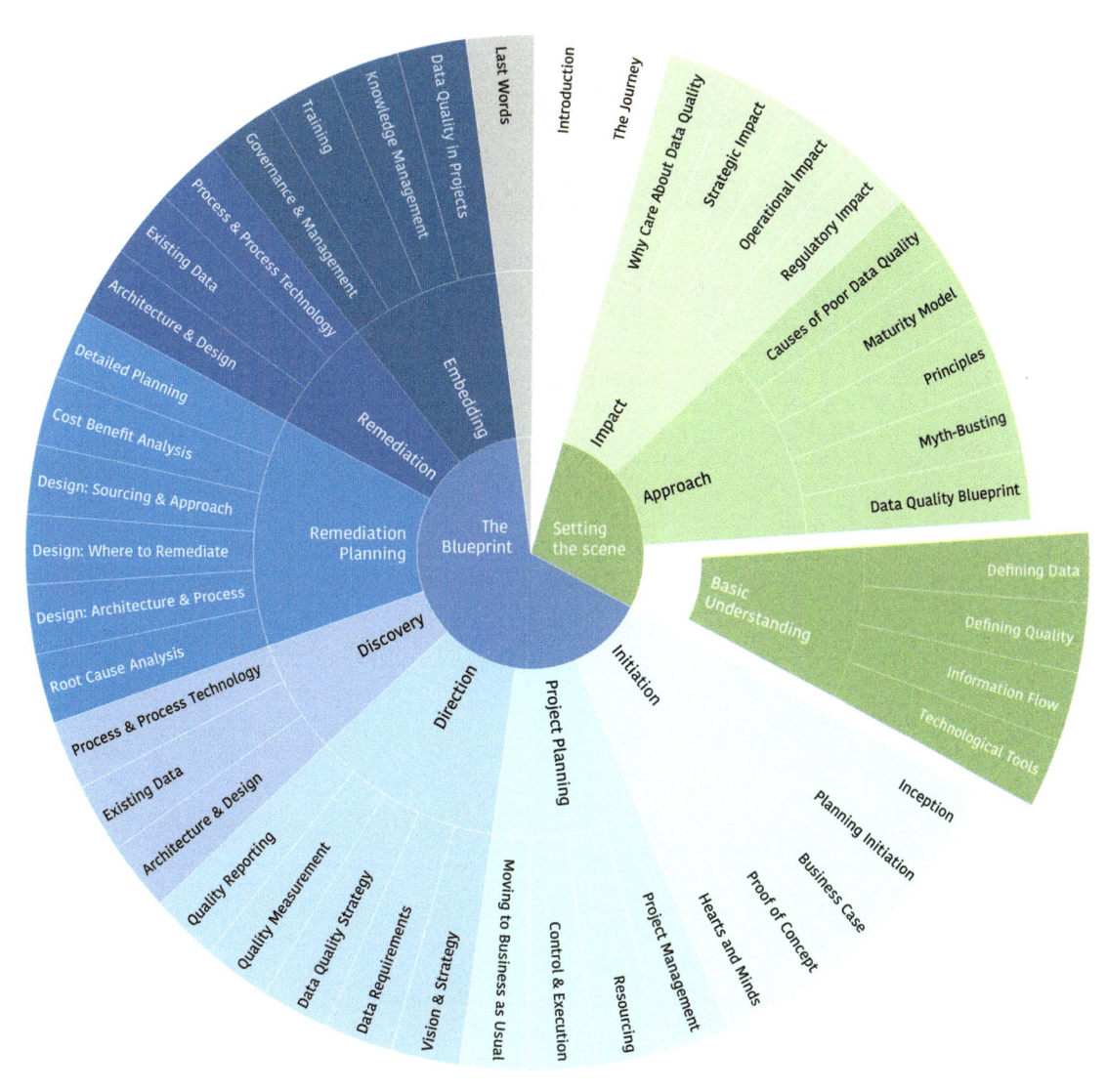

Let's get on the same page to start with

SECTION 4: INDEX

CHAPTER 12: Defining Data — 127

12.1	Structure	127
12.2	Introduction	127
12.3	Data can be defined by its audience	128
12.4	Data can be defined by its variability	129
12.5	Data can be defined by its use	130
12.6	Data can be defined by its purpose	131
12.7	Data can be defined by its structure	132
12.8	Data can be defined by the department that uses it	132
12.9	Data can be defined by its degree of normalisation	133
12.10	Summary	133

CHAPTER 13: Defining Quality — 135

13.1	Structure	135
13.2	Overview	135
13.3	Completeness	137
13.4	Existence	138
13.5	Accuracy	138
13.6	Consistency	139
13.7	Timely	139
13.8	Appropriate	139
13.9	Validity	139
13.10	Uniformity	140
13.11	Ease of use	141
13.12	Presentation	141
13.13	Trust	141
13.14	Uniqueness	141
13.15	Summary	142

CHAPTER 14: How does Information Flow? — 143

14.1	Structure	143
14.2	Overview	143
14.3	Channels	145
14.4	Channel Applications	145
14.5	Extract-Transform-Load (ETL)	145
14.6	Data Warehouse and Data Marts	146
14.7	Extracts and Reports	147
14.8	End User Computing	148
14.9	Putting it all Together	149
14.10	Data Lakes	149
14.11	Data Lineage	151

14.12	Data Models and Modelling	152
14.13	Summary	154

CHAPTER 15: Technological Tools for Data Quality — 155

15.1	Structure	155
15.2	Introduction	156
15.3	The Technological Marketplace	157
15.4	Profiling Tools	157
15.5	Profiling with Business Rules	158
15.6	Profiling and/or remediation with Reference Data	159
15.7	Remediation with Business Rules	161
15.8	Workflow Toolsets	162
15.9	Combo Tools	163
15.10	Data Governance and Management Tools	164
15.11	Integrated Stacks	165
15.12	Summary	165

SECTION 4: BASIC UNDERSTANDING

CHAPTER 12: DEFINING DATA

12.1 Structure

Within this section of the book I will be looking at the following topics:

1. Defining data
2. Defining quality
3. How does information flow?
4. Technological tools for data quality

This chapter covers the first of these topics.

12.2 Introduction

> "Data! Data! Data! I can't make bricks without clay!"
> **Sir Arthur Conan Doyle**

Data quality is difficult to define – everyone knows what it means, however there are thousands of definitions. Looking at "data" in isolation, I have known corporate consultants who find it useful to discuss four categories:

Data	This is the bald numbers-only – for example. "13", "26"
Information	This is data given meaning – "The number 13 bus", "26 minutes"
Knowledge	Is the next step, which makes the information more useful – "The No 13 bus takes 26 minutes to get into town"
Wisdom	This is the final step, which might be "The No 13 bus takes 26 minutes to get into town, except as they've closed the main road it's not running right now"

Even a brief search of the internet will return innumerable definitions of data, a number are shown below.

"facts and statistics collected together for reference or analysis." [28]

"Data is words, numbers, dates, images, sounds etc without context." [29]

"individual facts, statistics, or items of information:" [30]

"In computing, data is information that has been translated into a form that is more convenient to move or process. In other contexts, data has somewhat different meanings" [31]

"factual information (as measurements or statistics) used as a basis for reasoning, discussion, or calculation" [32]

Different actors will define data in relation to their own viewpoint. Each of these viewpoints has validity, and it is natural that a business leader is going to have a different definition of data than a database administrator, or for that matter a customer. For the sake of this book, which exists to aid understanding, I have considered various types of data definition, and examined the problem from a variety of angles, hopefully to illuminate the way each individual in an organisation sees data. If the business leader can understand how the IT analyst sees data, and vice versa, then comprehension and communication can start from a solid foundation – there is no point working through the process and then finding that what is actually being considered is fundamentally different. So how do various bits of the organisation define data?

12.3 Data can be defined by its audience

A business-focused way of defining data is by its intended audience. Whilst there are no rules as to the categorisation of data in this fashion, examples may be found below.

Classification	Explanation
Regulatory	Some data is primarily used by – and often defined by – the regulator. This may be summary data at a high level or detailed transaction-type data. Often (especially in UK financial services) the regulator defines both the data and the format which will be used to submit it. Regulatory data in many organisations is that data that has to be correct. It is the data where the effect of poor data quality may have the greatest impact. Regulatory data is also increasing fast both in terms of detail and complexity.
Board	A lot of data is primarily used by the board to underpin strategic decisions. Examples of such data could be:

---

28. http://www.oxforddictionaries.com/definition/english/data
29. http://www.bbc.co.uk/schools/gcsebitesize/ict/databases/0datainforev1.shtml
30. http://dictionary.reference.com/browse/data
31. http://searchdatamanagement.techtarget.com/definition/data
32. http://www.merriam-webster.com/dictionary/data

Classification	Explanation
Board	- Market Share
- Earnings per customer
- Profit per product
- Profit per division

This data is in the form of reports or embedded in reports or dashboards. In the same way as regulatory data, there is a significant problem if this kind of data is affected by poor quality, as significant, business-wide decisions will be incorrectly taken as a result. It should also be noted that the nature of this data is at a high level (i.e. summary or aggregate data rather than low level transaction data), and is calculated rather than directly input. This becomes important when board members ask data quality practitioners to concentrate on the numbers that are important to them – i.e. performance figures – not necessarily thinking that the performance figures are a summary of all the data that supports them, and you cannot "fix" performance figures without fixing the underlying data. |
Management	Data that is mainly used by management. This is, in a similar way to board data, data that is an aggregate of data at a lower level of the organisation but it is not at as high a level as would be utilised by the board. The challenge of this data is its variability and complexity. It may come in the form of reports or dashboards, but equally could be in the form of spreadsheets, data dumps, XML, web downloads, etc. The highest and widest variability of data is at this point of any organisation.
Line Management	Some data is primarily used by line management. For example, data that specifically concerns the performance of individual staff members will be used by line management only. Data KPI elements like contact centre throughput per agent, or documents handled per hour are likely to be aggregated at a higher level but exist in granular form only here.
User	Some data will only be used by the employee. This data will be purely operational data. Only an individual contact centre agent is ever likely to look at a customer date of birth field – everyone else at a higher level will be using aggregated data. Hence the granularity of the data used will increase as you move down the organisation.

12.4 Data can be defined by its variability

One of the most common ways of defining data from an IT perspective is by its variability. This loosely divides data according to its tendency to stand still and often as a result the ease with which it can be addressed from a data quality perspective.

Classification	Explanation
Static Data	Static data is data that never changes, or would not be expected to change. It is a reasonable assumption that once it is successfully captured it will not have to be captured again. Examples of such data are:

Classification	Explanation
Static Data	- National Insurance/Social Security Number - Date of Birth - Date of Death - Geographical hierarchies (i.e. London is in England, New York is in the U.S.)
Semi-Static Data	Semi-static data is data with the characteristics of static data, but that may change on a more regular basis. Examples of such data are: - Customer Name - Customer Title - Customer Address including postcode - Salary - Employer - Products held Most data quality (and data management) operations are largely concerned with static and semi-static data. Partly because it is much easier to keep an eye on something that does not move much, partly because it often has the greatest effect across the organisation.
Dynamic Data	Dynamic data is data that is changed and would be expected to change as further updates to the information become available; however, changes may or may not occur, and may occur either frequently or infrequently. Examples of such data are: - Bank balances - Loan balances - Interest rates
Streaming Data	Streaming data is data that is continuously changing and would be expected to continuously change. Examples of such data are: - Current time - Share price

12.5 Data can be defined by its use

Another way of defining data is its use within the business. This is a totally different definition to that of variability, and is a business-centric view.

Classification	Explanation
Visionary	The organisation needs to understand what information will be available in the future that will be necessary to effectively run their business. This information may not yet be in existence, it may exist but not be accessible, or it may simply not be used. An example may be location data. It is common for mobile phone applications to report the geographical location of the phone; however this information is rarely used. In the same way, bank account transaction data is rarely used to provide information to the organisation. This may not be the case in the future.

Classification	Explanation
Strategic	The organisation needs to understand and define what information is required to support its strategic aims. This will be defined in the data strategy. An example may be the number of customers. It is unlikely that the overall number of customers will be relevant to operational needs of the business, nor is it particularly relevant to the management of those customers, however it is likely to be a key metric to the strategic aims of the organisation, and the overall strategy may well be defined in those terms – e.g. "to double our customer base in 5 years".
Managerial	The organisation needs to understand and define the information that is required to manage itself. This will consist of mainly high level summary information covering all areas of the organisation. Examples of this kind of data may be sales per division, or total turnover.
Operational	Operational data will be significantly more granular than all other data and also contain much more information. For example, appointment times and the corresponding customer names for a particular day are operationally essential, but of limited value from a management perspective. However, the overall number of appointments and their times may be essential to plan staff cover, plan for busy periods, and potentially look at office planning. It is worth noting that in this case the appointment times for individual customers have no use whatsoever to any higher management of the organisation, but are critical to actually servicing customers. The level of the data in the organisation should not be confused with its importance.

12.6 Data can be defined by its purpose

Classification	Explanation
Metadata	Metadata is described as "data about data" and includes information such as report definitions, database schemas and field and table definitions. However it also includes data such as "how many rows are there in the customer database?" which will translate to "how many customers do we think we have?" which is noticeably more business focused. Or "how many blank addresses are there in our customer database?" which translates to "how many of our customers have we no way of sending mail to?" Hence whilst tempting, metadata should not be ignored by the business user or leader who is looking to understand and direct the improvement and management of data within their organisation.
Transactional Data	Transactional data is detailed data but it underpins most of the rest of the information in the organisation. The thing about transactional data is there tends to be a lot of it. A typical customer may make 100 transactions on their current account each month, but if an organisation has 1 million customers then that's 100 million transactions per month and 1.2 billion transactions per year. It is easy to see how using transactional data can result in a business facing the challenge of "Big Data" without going anywhere near social media or the internet.

Classification	Explanation
Hierarchical Data	Hierarchical data is data that describes the relationships between other bits of data. "John Smith is the line manager for Steve Jones, Steve Jones is the line manager for Tom Brown". "This company is the subsidiary of this company". Hierarchical data is often missed as it is considered inherent to the basic organisation of any data store, whereas in fact it has to be defined like anything else. However it is rarely written down anywhere.
Master Data	Master data is data that is relied on by many different parts of the organisation. Classic examples are customer details, name, address, data of birth, or similar. Master data can also include product data (type, price, name, stock number) and other data that will be widely used. It makes sense to have a centralised repository where all master data is stored and can be appropriately controlled.

12.7 Data can be defined by its structure

12.7.1 Structured data

Structured data is what we all recognise as data – specifically, tables with rows and columns. Structured data is easy for computers to work with and is efficiently stored in any of the typical database products that are on the market.

12.7.2 Unstructured data

Unstructured data is much more difficult to work with. Unstructured data may include emails or reports, but equally may include data such as audio (potentially in the form of call logs, which are stored in the individual contact centre applications but may not be in a searchable form) or it may also include pictures or video. The biggest problem is to translate unstructured data into structured data so that it can be used, but increasingly applications are being developed that will work directly with the unstructured data, especially text-based unstructured data such as emails. Free text searching is now almost common in enterprise database applications.

12.8 Data can be defined by the department that uses it

A common way of describing data in a business context is by the department that is using the data. This comes about because in a siloed organisation each department has a store of jealously-guarded information over which they exercise proprietary rights. Common descriptions include:

Classification	Explanation
Finance Data	Information that is used to create the company accounts, which is generated by transactional systems at an operational level. This includes interest payments, premiums paid, invoice amounts, etc. The nature of finance information is that the quantity is low but the quality is high, as there will be a high level of cross checking. A set of financial statements cross check themselves, as they have to be in balance. A non-balancing balance sheet is a sure way of telling that there is something badly wrong.
Customer Data	Information about the customer. Names, addresses, emails, title, gender, national insurance or social security numbers, mother's maiden name, next of kin, secondary contact details all the way to first school attended.
Product Data	Information about the product. Information such as release dates, when offers were in force, discontinuation dates, and also cost prices, selling prices, and amounts sold.
Marketing Data	Data that is used by marketing. In many organisations marketing are largely a law unto themselves when it comes to data. They draw data from everywhere, mash it together, and then use it to determine the propensity of customers to buy, and the ability of the organisation to cross-sell or up-sell products. As a result marketing data is often of significantly greater quantity but lower quality than the rest of the data in the organisation.

12.9 Data can be defined by its degree of normalisation

This is a technical way of describing data, but it is so commonly used, especially when talking about data in data stores that it is worth mentioning.

Data that is normalised is broken down into its component parts. An invoice may be broken down into multiple locations, one location holding customer name, the next holding customer address, the next product details. This means that it is easier to maintain structural integrity of the overall database, and it is easier to update. However, because the data is broken down into its component parts it is harder to read, because all the data needs to be joined up to re-create the record of, for example, an invoice. That's about all you need to know at this level. If you wish to know more, then do feel free to read E.F. Codd, **"Further Normalization of the Data Base Relational Model"**, 1971, or perform an internet search for an explanation of normalisation in data warehouses.

12.10 Summary

Within this chapter I have outlined the various ways of looking at data and how it can be classified. This has included defining data in a number of disparate ways, including:

- Its audience
- Its variability
- Its use
- Its purpose

- Its structure
- The department that uses it
- Its normalisation

I appreciate that this chapter is somewhat dry, and may come across as somewhat technical. It is probably the most technical of the chapters to date. However, my view is that without the business starting to understand some technical terminology, and the information technology function starting to understand some of the business-speak, then it is going to be very difficult to move forward. If both camps continue to stand apart and refuse to try and understand, little movement will ever be possible.

Whilst hopefully common sense, this establishes a baseline and I will use this information throughout the rest of the book when talking about how to plan and process remediation. In the next chapter I will continue this journey and take a look at quality, how it is defined, and what are the various facets that make up what can be called "quality" data.

SECTION 4: BASIC UNDERSTANDING

CHAPTER 13: DEFINING QUALITY

13.1 Structure

Within this section of the book I will be looking at the following topics:

1. Defining data
2. Defining quality
3. How does information flow?
4. Technological tools for data quality

This chapter covers the second of these topics.

13.2 Overview

> "Quality is never an accident. It is always the result of intelligent effort."
> **John Ruskin**

In order for an organisation to take steps to improve data quality, it first needs to define both data quality, and the parameters it will use to measure it. Without both there is no means of working out how bad your quality is, or proving the success, or otherwise, of a data quality project. Defining quality is more difficult than it might first appear. It is easy to say "accurate", but that's not helpful, and also leaves out a few elements of quality that are actually quite important. An example is "timeliness" – there's no use having "accurate" data six months after it would be useful. "Fit for purpose "or "suitable for the task required" are also descriptions that are commonly used, but that simply shifts the definition problem over to defining the words "fit" and "purpose".

The challenge is breaking down quality into its component parts which cover the whole spectrum of quality and are actually measurable. I think that given the point of this book is to improve an organisation's data quality, some time is justified in working out what data quality represents. Many books have attempted this. Most have a list that includes "completeness" but few, for example, include "ease of use". A few examples are shown below:

- **DAMA-BOK** – which has been often referenced in this book as it is an industry standard states: Accuracy, Completeness, Consistency, Currency, Precision, Privacy, Reasonableness, Referential Integrity, Timeliness, Uniqueness and Validity. [a total of 11]
- **ISACA's COBIT 5** – another industry standard of high repute, has a slightly different list: Accuracy, Objectivity, Believability, Reputation, Relevance, Completeness, Currency, Appropriateness, Concise, Consistent, Interpretability, Understandability, Ease of manipulation, Availability, Security. [a total of 15]
- David Loshin in "*The Practitioner's guide to Data Quality Improvement*" lists: Accuracy, Lineage, Structural Consistency, Semantic Consistency, Completeness, Consistency, Currency, Timeliness, Reasonableness, identifiability. [a total of 10]

The summary is that many people differ on the number of attributes that makes up data quality. This is no bad thing, but does mean it is sometimes difficult to pin down how data quality should be measured. What I have done in this chapter is to divide data quality up into the elements that I think it should have (thereby creating another list), explained the relevance of each element, and given an example of how it can be measured. My attributes of data quality are shown below.

Attribute	Description
Completeness	All data entries that should be populated are populated
Existence	No data entries are populated that should not be populated
Accuracy	The data reflects the real world
Consistency	The data is consistent within systems and between systems
Timely	The data relates to a timeframe that is consistent with its use
Appropriate	The entry is appropriate to its use
Valid	The entry meets business rules
Uniformity	The data should be uniform in terms of unit of measurement or expression
Ease of Use	The entry can be used for its intended purpose
Presentation	The data is presented in a manner that is understandable by the user
Trust	The entry is trusted by users
Uniqueness	The entry does not duplicate another entry unless it is appropriate to do so

I will now consider each in more detail.

13.3 Completeness

Completeness states that all entries that should be populated are populated. If there are 10,000 customers there should be 10,000 dates of birth. This is not quite as simple as might be thought. The statement above mentions every entry that should be populated. Here the important word is "should". Whilst every person will have a date of birth, they may not necessarily have, for example, an email address. Date of death is unlikely to be applicable to every customer unless you run a funeral parlour. National Insurance number may well apply to every UK adult, but what about children or foreign nationals? The measurement of completeness against any data set is trivial if your aim is to see the percentage of customers that have, for example, a populated date of birth. Unfortunately many organisations see data quality as equalling completeness but forget that merely having an entry in a field does not necessarily help. For example, in the cases below, every single record could be regarded as "complete" from a data perspective – in that the field is populated, but whether downstream systems (or downstream humans!) can accurately utilise the information is another thing.

Field Contents	Matters to consider
01/02/1980	Perfectly OK… but is it UK or US format?
1/2/1980	Not 8 digit format
01021980	Text string
1_2_1980	Text/special character string
19800201	Reversed text string
	String of spaces. No content. However not "Null" so could be considered "populated".
1 Feb 1980	Another text string, though could also be Microsoft Office date format.
1st February 1980	Text string, with special characters (superscript)
121980	This format can be 6, 7 or 8 digit format. 7 digits can be especially difficult to translate. For example, is "2111980" 2/11/1980 or 21/1/1980?
1.2.1980	Periods used instead of "/"
29252	Number of days since 1/1/1900 – a common date format

Hence "complete" needs to be taken with a pinch of salt. Even worse is the common use of a system default value (often 1/1/1900). This makes a mockery of any completeness measurement as every single date of birth on a system may be populated but the organisation cannot rely on a single one. Data is often considered "100% complete" when a significant percentage of the values are actually "unknown".

Anecdote

One insurance company had 10 million claims, but 2.2 million had loss codes of the system default value. Or, to put it another way, the company didn't know why it had paid 22% of its claims. The view of the company was that data in this particular system was "good". This is a common perception error – just because it is populated and hence "complete" doesn't mean that you actually have any useful data.

13.4   Existence

Existence is, in a way, the opposite of completeness. This means that no entries are populated that should not be populated. An example here could be date of death. It may appear to be stating the obvious, but if you have not died, a date of death should not be present. Few lists of data quality attributes will include "existence" of the data, most concentrating on completeness. Whilst it is tempting to roll the attribute of "existence" under "accuracy", accuracy should be seen as looking at a populated field and considering whether the value is correct, rather than looking at a populated value and determining whether it actually should be unpopulated. Data that breaks existence criteria is good at lulling you into a false sense of security. If you have an email address listed for the customer but actually the customer doesn't have an email address, how will you know? Who are you sending emails to? Existence is also hard to measure. The best way I have found is sample checking back to original application forms. It is also worth noting that in the same way to completeness, existence is totally skewed by default values, which populate everything with known inaccurate data.

13.5   Accuracy

Accuracy states that the entries on the system should reflect what they represent in the "real world". If the customer's name is "Smith" then "Smythe", "Smyth" or "Smithe" are incorrect. Equally, whilst an address of 34 Station Road may satisfy many data quality rules, it's not much good if the actual address is 43 Station Road. This attribute is again hard to measure as to the system – and to those querying the system – the data will look perfectly reasonable. Accuracy is a "hidden" data quality issue in that it is impossible from just looking at the data to tell whether it is right or wrong. Similar to existence, the way to check is to sample check back to original application forms, or to the call record.

Anecdote

On this subject, the accuracy of data in many organisations is pretty bad. I have been involved in checking accuracy many times and whilst the system record bears some resemblance to the original application form, it is not as much as you would expect. Common errors are mangled addresses where the expected word in put in place rather than the "real" one (one friend of mine lives at "Mountague" Road, and it is often re-spelt as the expected "Montague")

Misread or mis-scanned dates of birth abound, and a common problem is simply mixing up dates of birth and addresses amongst multiple joint applicants.

13.6 Consistency

Consistent data is data that is consistent both within the same system and also across systems. Within the same system the same types of data should be represented in the same way. The examples of dates of birth shown above in the "completeness" section are examples of inconsistent formats. Dates should be consistently in UK or US format, numbers should be of the same format, and addresses should have city names in the same field. Consistency across systems means the same data should be identical across different systems. Whilst it is sometimes necessary for performance reasons to have multiple copies of data (for example to have multiple copies of customer name/address details if the load on a single system for requests for this data from disparate applications would exceed capacity) the data should be consistent. Methods of ensuring consistency between systems include only one system being able to be updated by users, the others copying overnight on a batch basis and being otherwise read-only. Consistency is relatively easy to measure from a formatting perspective (i.e. one system using US dates and the other using UK dates), but much harder from a content point of view.

13.7 Timely

Another attribute of data quality is that data should be available at the correct time and be as up to date as it needs to be to fulfil business needs. Another way of putting this is that the data must be made available within a timescale that is commensurate with the use to which it is being put. For example, if sales figures for the previous month are only available a year in arrears, the value of that data is significantly (if not wholly) erased. Knowing where someone lived 10 years ago is only slightly useful. The data is complete, and may be accurate for the timescale, but whether it is still relevant may not be known. Timeliness of data can often be determined from the date of update of records, or file creation or modification dates.

13.8 Appropriate

Data should be appropriate for the use to which it is being put. Use of data that is not appropriate is common in many organisations where data is difficult to find or difficult to interpret. Because the real data is not available then a proxy is used which may, or may not, be an appropriate measure of the business metric required. An example might be measuring sales data by looking at production records. This may give an indication of sales (on the assumption that units manufactured are sold), but it is not as appropriate as looking directly at the sales figures themselves. One could argue that the production records plus the change in stock should equal items sold, but that still doesn't take account of units spoiled, broken, returned, etc, and it is still better to use the most appropriate measure rather than taking a proxy.

13.9 Validity

This attribute of data quality determines whether data conforms to business rules. These rules may be relatively simple (for example that dates of birth cannot be in the future) or may be more complex.

An example of the latter may be that the sum of the customer's current age and the length of the loan they are applying for cannot exceed customary retirement age. Equally data needs to be internally valid. For example, an address that states that the customer lives in "London, France" contains a valid entry in both country and city, but they are not valid with respect to each other. Determination of validity to business rules simply requires running queries, either manually or automatically against the database. A similar situation often exists with gender-specific pronouns. Mrs John Smith will most probably be incorrect.

13.10 Uniformity

Uniformity defines that data should be the same in all datasets and across datasets. By "same" here, we are not talking "same" in the same way as consistency, but in terms of, for example, weights and measures. For example, in a medical database, it is not acceptable if some weights are in kilogrammes and some in pounds. To give an example, consider the below data.

Name	Height
Mrs K Smith	172
Mr J Jones	70
Mrs L Andrews	5 10
Mr P Parker	1.8

Here the data is not uniform – different measures are used for different entries. In this particular case, one can see that the entries are probably centimetres, inches, feet & inches, and metres. However, this is because we have a good idea of the range in which human heights are distributed, and are given context by the heading. This may not be the case – for example sizes of components in a product database where a wide range (from millimetres to metres) is the norm. Uniformity would also be broken if prices are stated, without narrative, for 1 unit, 10 units or 100 units. There have been a number of high profile failures resulting from lack of data uniformity.

Anecdote

The Mars Climate Orbiter was a robotic space probe launched by NASA on December 11, 1998 to study the Martian climate.

However, on September 23, 1999, communication with the spacecraft was lost as it went into orbital insertion, due to ground-based computer software which produced output in non-SI units of pound-seconds (lb s) instead of the metric units of newton-seconds (N s) specified in the contract between NASA and Lockheed. The spacecraft encountered Mars on a trajectory that brought it too close to the planet, causing it to pass through the upper atmosphere and disintegrate.

13.11   Ease of use

Another often-overlooked component of data quality is the ease of use. The ease of use may be a combination of other attributes of data quality, such as format or presentation, however it is still a real world attribute that should be considered. How many times has data with a poor ease of use resulted in (expensive) hours transforming it into a useable state? Data that is unstructured is much harder to use than data that is structured. Equally, data that is buried in text is hard to extract. A printed report – or a PDF – is relatively hard to turn into structured data (though tools certainly exist for this purpose). Similarly, when USB sticks are banned, the data exceeds CD size, and emails are limited to 10mb, and the office has a wireless network, then shifting a high volume data file can be nearly impossible.

13.12   Presentation

Allied to ease of use is presentation. By "presentation" I am describing the way the data looks when you see it. Data formats are key to understanding of data, and can also easily mask its true meaning. As mentioned above, a common problem is formatting of dates, where strings of text on the lines of "20130102" are normal in computer systems. Before the data can be used the first question is whether it is in UK or US data format – the data itself does not tell you. Date formats are so commonly misinterpreted that when transferring data between systems it is often easier and quicker to export all date formats as text and then break them apart and recombine them at each interface rather than rely on the native date format of the exporting application being compatible with the native date format of the importing application.

13.13   Trust

This may be obvious but the data must be trusted by the users. Although a difficult criteria to measure, if data is not trusted it simply will not be used, and users will make up/create their own data from whatever sources that they can find, which may not be appropriate, or may simply be incorrect or out of date. It is therefore a fundamental criterion of good data quality that the data produced by the organisation's systems is trusted. In terms of measurement, trust is probably easiest measured by the use of questionnaires (i.e. "how much do you trust the data that you receive from the source systems, score 1-5").

13.14   Uniqueness

It is perfectly possible for every single one of the above criteria to be met, but for there to be another, identical data record. Duplication is endemic, especially with large or older organisations, and a customer may hold a number of products and be recorded separately for each. In older organisations, especially those where the customer experience spans many years (for example loans or mortgages), the data may have been transferred through many upgrades and migrations as information systems change over time, and duplication of records is a common side effect of multiple data transformations, as is loss and corruption of data. Marketing departments often have a separate database to the rest of an organisation, partly because they deal with a much wider range of individuals, and are likely to buy in data such as address lists from external organisations that may be of variable quality. They are also likely to retain historical records that are deleted from production systems.

A lack of uniqueness is a problem because it will increase costs, cause confusion, and may result in one record being updated for address changes and another left at the historical value.

Anecdote
A colleague of mine, on joining a new company, was in the process of being set up on the computer systems. They received a phone call from IT asking which of the 28 records on the system with an identical name applied to them. They happened to know there was only one other person in the company with the same name.
They had joined as the compliance director.

13.15   Summary

Within this chapter I have covered elements of data quality, including:

- Completeness
- Consistency
- Uniformity
- Trustworthiness
- Existence
- Timeliness
- Ease of Use
- Uniqueness
- Accuracy
- Appropriateness
- Presentation
- Validity

However, whilst the above represent my choice, there is no "correct" answer, and as long as the definition used covers the organisation's needs in terms of quality then there should be no argument. As can be seen, the word "quality" can be relatively complex to define.

When an organisation is talking about "data quality" it is important to understand and define what element of quality is being considered, and in what way. Be wary of those who use words like "right" or "correct" in relation to data quality as it may indicate that education is required.

This again may have come across as a reasonably technical chapter. Again, my view is that we need to ensure that everyone can talk to each other before starting a project where they will work together towards a common aim. It is also the case that many individuals have not necessarily thought about the components of quality before, and merely thought about data being "right". The breakdown of quality – or "rightness" – into its parts makes the problem easier to solve.

Now we have considered both data and quality, in the next chapter I will look at the way information flows through the organisation. This is important as without this understanding – on both sides of the fence – a large amount of effort can be wasted.

SECTION 4
BASIC UNDERSTANDING

CHAPTER 14
HOW DOES INFORMATION FLOW?

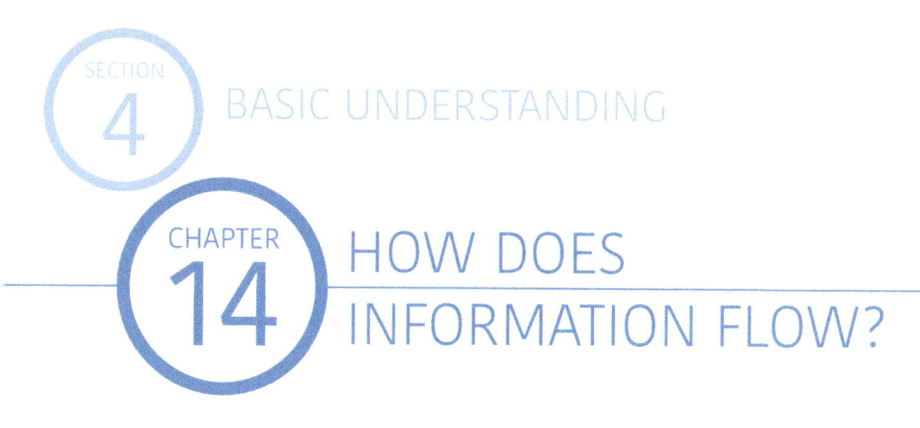

14.1 Structure

Within this section of the book I will be looking at the following topics:

1. Defining data
2. Defining quality
3. How does information flow?
4. Technological tools for data quality

This chapter covers the third of these topics.

14.2 Overview

> "An information ecosystem is a system with different components, each serving a community directly while working in concert with other components to provide a cohesive, balanced information environment."
> **Corporate Information Factory, W.H. Inmon et al, Wiley and Sons, 2001**

Information flows through an organisation from the initial contact of a customer to a contact centre or branch through applications and data warehouses to end user reports, board reports and potentially a regulator. Key to data quality is the understanding of this flow, understanding its component parts, and understanding how they interact. In this chapter I will walk through each component of information flow in a typical organisation, explaining its relevance to data quality, and how it interacts with the data landscape around it.

If this appears overly technical, and delving unnecessarily into the world of information technology, please bear with me. Back in the early 1980s W.H. Inmon coined the concept of the Corporate Information Factory. An organisation is exactly that, a factory. It is complex and interconnected. Ignoring that complexity and refusing to understand its components is a quick trip to never solving any data quality problem, or outsourcing the whole problem to the IT department, which is not the way to solve it.

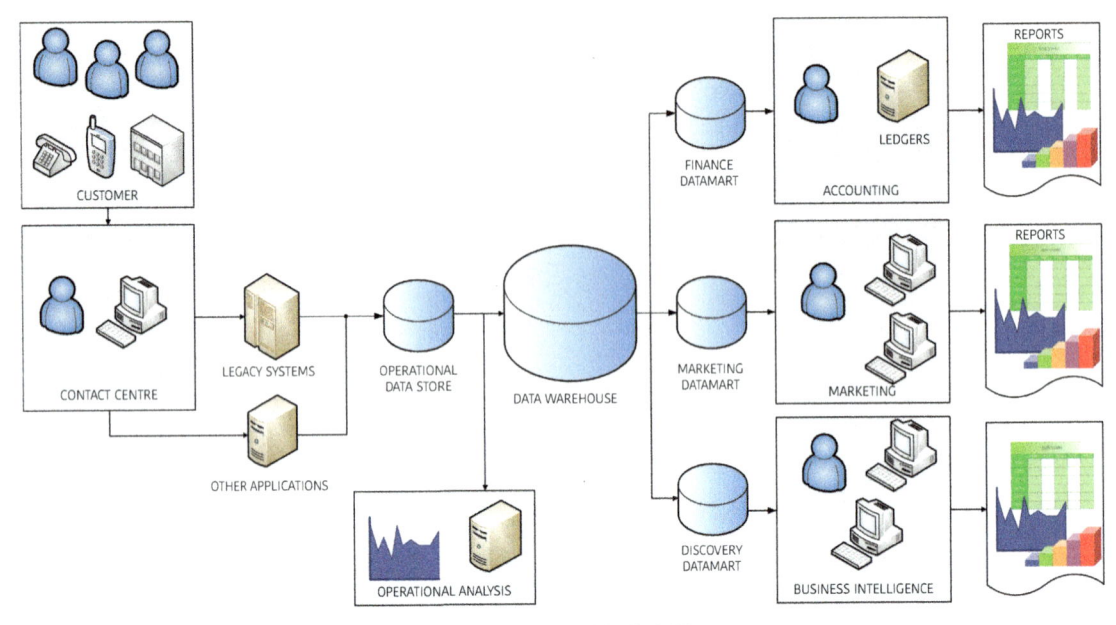

INFORMATION FLOW

Time and time again in this book I will come back to information flow. I will map remediation efforts to the information flow and show where is the best place for cleaning to occur. I will indicate the best place for a technological solution, and where manual efforts can be best directed. The understanding of information flow is critical for the data quality practitioner. A common perception is that IT owns the data and "provides" it to the rest of the organisation; however this is not really a good representation of reality. The business creates and owns the data, and IT owns the pipes that pipe it around the organisation. A typical (and much simplified) diagram showing the main data flows within a typical organisation is shown below.

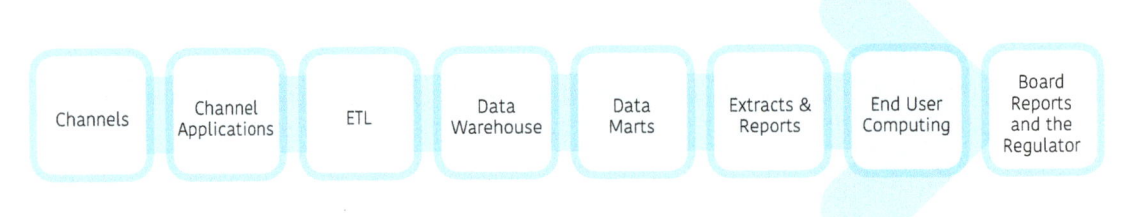

Channels → Channel Applications → ETL → Data Warehouse → Data Marts → Extracts & Reports → End User Computing → Board Reports and the Regulator

I will now consider each element of this chain in detail.

14.3 Channels

Channels are the customer touch-points. They are where the data first enters the organisation, be it via the customer typing their application into a website, the same data being typed by a contact centre agent, or at a branch. Other initial touch points may be a web search, a third party data feed, a text message, an email, or an entry in social media.

This sets in motion a range of activities. For the customer walking into the branch, the name is entered into a computer, this produces a list for the mortgage advisor of appointments the following day (operational data), it will go into a list that will inform the branch manager of how many appointments are being made for mortgage appointments (managerial data), it will inform the area manager of the demand for mortgage advisor resources and will, when aggregated over time, inform top executives of the waxing or waning demand for in-branch mortgage advice and whether other channels should require investment (strategic data).

The important fact is that at the channel boundary the data is being recorded for the first time. If we get it wrong here, it will run off and create a multitude of copies of itself in systems through the organisation, all of which will have to be amended at vast cost. Getting it right first time is much, much easier.

14.4 Channel Applications

Each channel is likely to have its own specialised computer application. Because the processes in-branch are so different from the website, each area will generally have different applications from different vendors, as not all vendors produce good software for every channel, and a quality conscious organisation will understandably choose best of breed for each application. The alternative is for the organisation to develop its own software; however it is generally much cheaper and quicker to use a vendor's solution than for every organisation to write its own applications. However, this approach has the side effect of fragmenting data. As proprietary application data stores have often a proprietary format, new customers from the branch will have a different data format from new customers via the website and this will be different from the data for new customers via the contact centre. It would make a lot more sense for all concerned if all the data was in one place and one format. The next stage in the information chain does exactly that, takes all the information out of each of the application stores and puts it in one place.

14.5 Extract-Transform-Load (ETL)

The next link along the chain is Extract Transform Load (universally acronymed to ETL). An ETL application will suck data out of the proprietary applications and transform it all into the same language [35] and load it into the data warehouse which will hold all the data for all parts of the organisation in one place. ETL may be "push" – where the source database runs a process which dumps a selection of records out to a file, or "pull" where the ETL application hooks into the source and extracts what is required. It is common for a separate application to manage the process, and

---

35. Can I ask all the IT guys reading this to stop twitching at this point as this is meant to be a simplified representation?

the transformation in the middle, rather than it being run by either end. There are many of these on the market, for example IBM's DataStage, Informatica's Powercentre, and many more. They will contain a set of instructions describing what is needed from the source and where it is located, what is needed in the target and where to put it, and what to do in the middle.

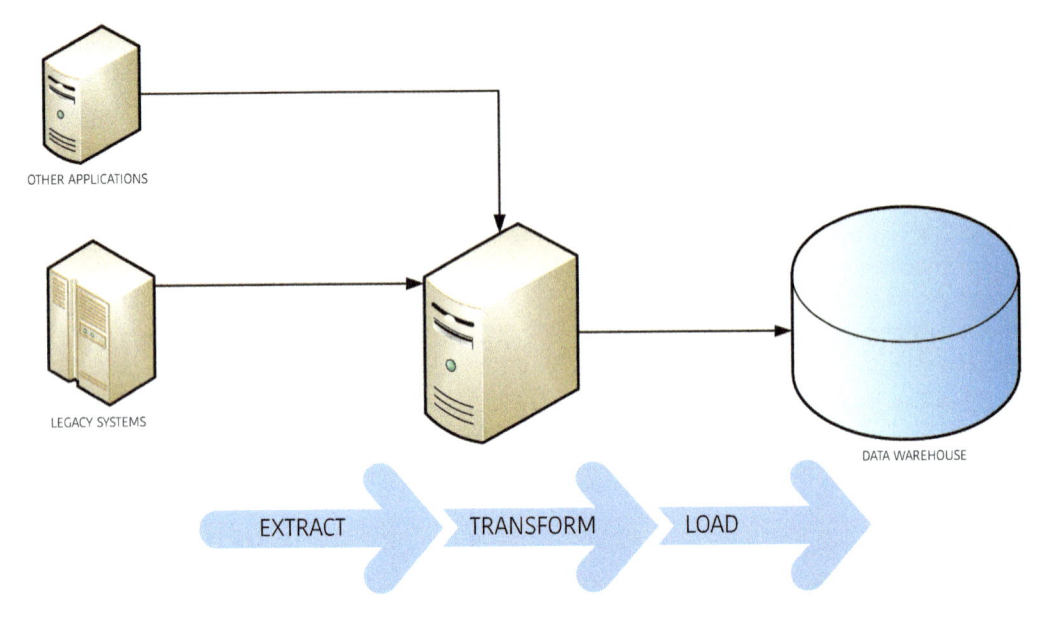

14.6 Data Warehouse and Data Marts

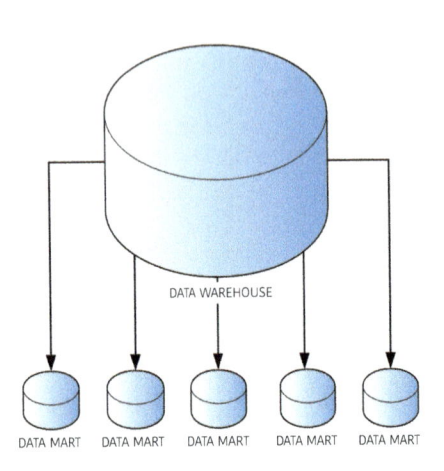

The next link in the chain is the data warehouse. The data warehouse is a huge database, holding all the data in one place. It is a big bucket of information that is specifically designed to have consistent format and gets around all of the problems inherent in application data stores. It will often be divided into separate areas, for example a landing area where data from source systems can be dropped in bulk before being carefully distributed across the warehouse.

The data warehouse is not perfect from a structure point of view for direct reporting. It is optimised for bulk in every way, not for picking selections of data of the kind common in reports. Therefore data is extracted out of the data warehouse (often using an ETL tool) into additional, department or use-specific databases which users can query using some form of reporting software. These are called data marts.

The data marts have a structure which will be optimised for reporting and will contain only a subset of the data (hence are faster to read) and will be structurally optimised for the job of reporting. It is not considered good practice for the data warehouse to be queried directly by users or for reporting to be done directly from the data warehouse. The effect of reporting directly from a data warehouse is a hybrid data warehouse design which does not adequately meet the needs of either reporting or bulk load.

14.7 Extracts and Reports

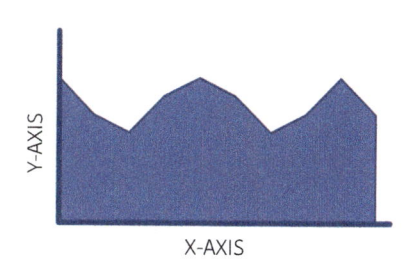

Extracts and reports are where the end users start to see the data. However there are a number of ways in which reports can be generated out of the data store. These are direct querying, the use of a business intelligence layer, pre-configured reports and visualisation tools. All are slightly different in terms of their characteristics, and hence I will briefly discuss each in turn.

14.7.1 Direct querying

Direct querying represents a scenario where an application allows a user to run queries directly against the data mart and return results. The advantage is that this is powerful, and allows the user total control over the information they require. The disadvantage is that you need a fairly tech-savvy user to understand the complexity within a raw database and know what they are doing. There are also considerable risks with this approach.

Anecdote
Every database user has written a query at some point in time and made an error in the syntax, and as a result created a monster. Pretty much as soon as you press "go" you realise…….the computer freezes, and looking back over the code (which is all you can see on the screen apart from the hourglass) you realise you've just tried to join a million customer records to a million customer accounts, messed up the syntax and the output is going to be a trillion records long, returning a result for each customer for each account. OK, most of the numbers will be zeros, but it's going to take forever.

Meanwhile, all your fellow colleagues are cursing you because you've just taken out the reporting data mart for the rest of the day. Time to find the Database Admin and beg them to pull the job from the inside (but who is probably having their lunch).

A similar situation occurred at one organisation where a marketing query took out the database for a day. Unfortunately poor design had resulted in some production routines being run out of this database. Result: the entire organisation stopped.

14.7.2 Pre-configured reports

Pre-configured reports are a way around this problem. The business gives the IT team requirements; the IT team builds the reports, tests them to make sure they don't crash the database, and then allows the business access. The reports may be available at a certain time every day, or may be run ad hoc when the target users wish to do so. The average business professional hates this way of creating reports as it gives them no flexibility. The average IT professional loves it, for pretty much the same reason.

14.7.3 A BI (Business Intelligence) Layer

A Business Intelligence layer is a half way house, where the users are given meaningful links into a reporting engine which allows arms-length access to the data. This enables the IT department to provision a data store with information that the business users require. The business users supply requirements to IT who will transfer the data elements (using ETL) on a regular basis – daily, hourly, whatever is required. The business users are then given free rein to create queries with this data. This is a reasonable compromise that enables the business users to play with the information but allows the IT staff a reasonable assurance that they will not be pulled off their lunch because someone has run a query that has taken the database down.

14.7.4 Visualisation tools

Visualisation tools are trendy at present. The way these work is to take a snapshot of the data and then let the user play around with it as they see fit, holding the data in local computer memory to allow fast reporting and manipulation. This is similar to a BI reporting layer except that the tools and queries are visually represented and constructed, and that the whole reporting layer is held in one application. It is also possible for such visualisation tools to be run on top of a reporting layer to allow rich visual reporting on pre-provided data.

14.8 End User Computing

End user computing is one of the larger uncontrolled and unmanaged areas within most organisations. The growth has been partially fuelled by the inability of end users to gain the information they need out of the main systems, either due to lack of access to the data, lack of flexibility, or poor data quality. The increasing power of desktop and laptop computers – and the emerging power of tablets – hand in hand with the ease of use, intuitive interfaces and accessibility of desktop productivity tools, has meant that each individual is often their own report writer, business intelligence guru and data architect.

This, of course, has advantages for the individual, but now many reporting structures in most organisations are based on data and application constructs which are undocumented, uncontrolled, have massive critical person vulnerabilities, and are equally extremely likely to have large errors. It is relatively common for reporting to be based on "George's Spreadsheet" or "Ann's Database" which – if the organisation is lucky – will be held on a shared (and hence backed up) drive but more likely will be residing on the local hard drive of a PC or laptop, ready to be forever destroyed by an errant cup of coffee.

This is typical in environments where data quality is poor, as business users, unable to obtain data of sufficient quality directly out of source systems, will extract the best fitting data they can, and then play with it until it meets requirements. This is one of the reasons why having poor data quality increases organisational risk.

Anecdote
One organisation performed an investigation into the extent of its end user computing problem and found that its critical month end reporting was based on 400,000 MSExcel spreadsheets.

14.9 Putting it all Together

If we put all the above together it results in a simplified architecture diagram as below. Here I have included end user computing in the "reporting layer".

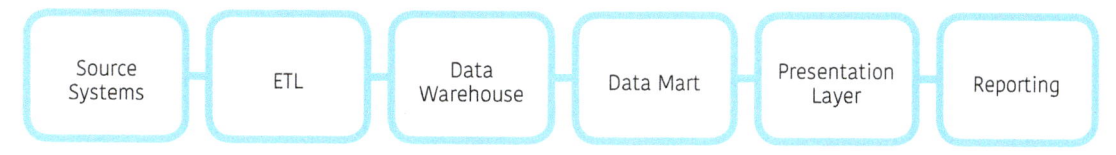

Source Systems → ETL → Data Warehouse → Data Mart → Presentation Layer → Reporting

This is wholly representative of the data flow within many current organisations, and I will use the simplified diagram repeatedly in the rest of the book.

14.10 Data Lakes

A relatively recent change to the architecture discussed so far, which has been standard for years, is the advent and use of the data lake. A data lake is a large storage facility – often based on open source architecture (Hadoop is the most popular product at time of writing) – where all the data in the organisation is dumped in the same format as in the source systems. In addition to internal data, the data lake may contain additional data from social media, reference organisations such as the government or proprietary websites, or the internet in general. A modification of the above diagram to account for the concept of a data lake is shown below.

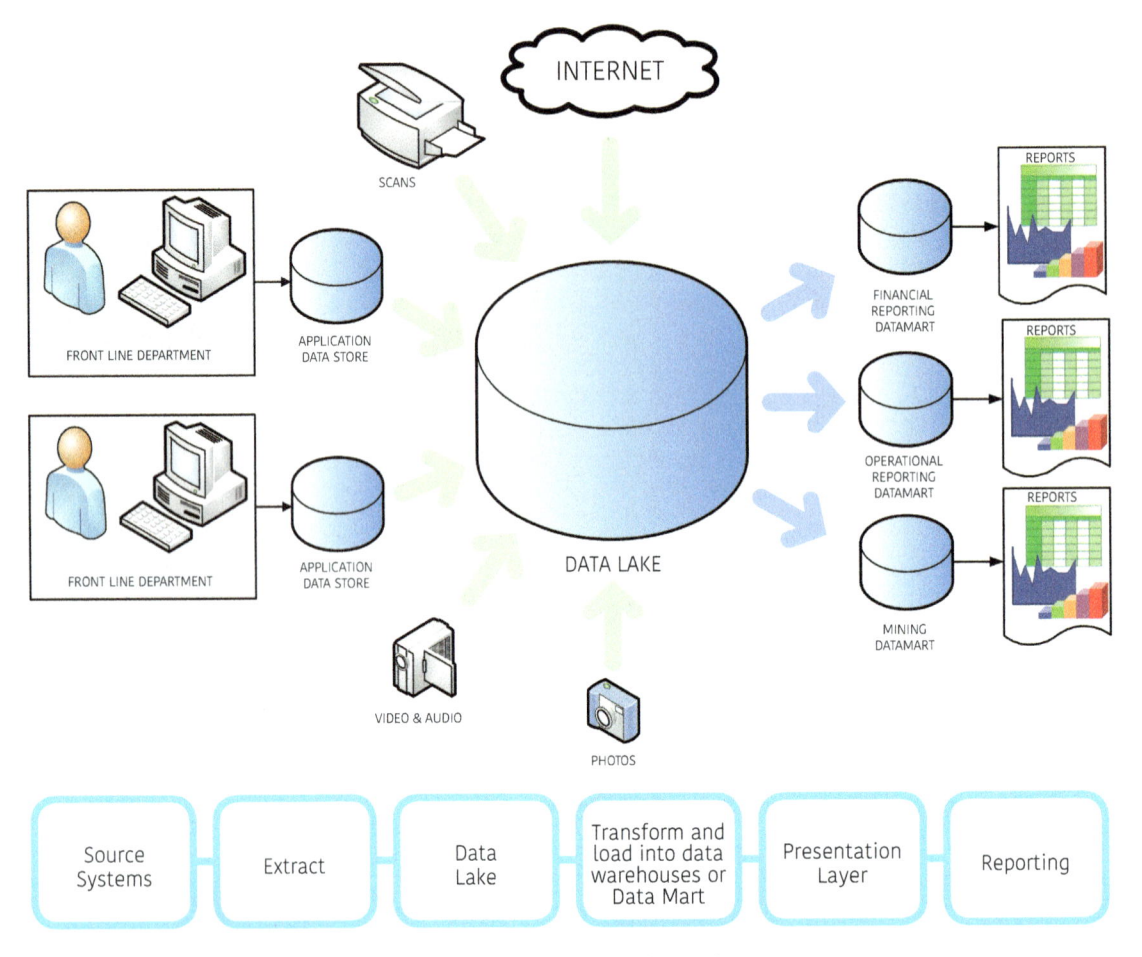

A data lake has a number of advantages over the traditional systems.

- Any data can be thrown in and nothing is going to break as a result as the lake is an uncontrolled dump.
- A data lake enables an organisation to add data to their overall store easily and quickly, with all the worrying about how it will be used to come at a later date.
- The data lake enables greater analytic flexibility as the analysts are not constrained to just the data in the data warehouse.
- A data lake decouples the generally unstructured and ad hoc process of discovery and mining from the formal and rigid processes of regulatory and financial reporting.

The data lake solution also inverts the normal Extract-Transform-Load paradigm. In a data lake solution data is sorted when it is pulled out of the lake, rather than when it is put in, which means that transformations and load can be limited to only the data needed, rather than covering everything. There are, however, disadvantages of a data lake architecture:

- Tracing lineage of data is often difficult or impossible.

- Governing data is often difficult or impossible.
- Working out the right data to use is often difficult or impossible.

Data quality is often abysmal. A Gartner article, recent at the time of writing this book, noted wryly that "there are no barriers to entry into many data lakes".[36] A subsequent blog post added:

"By its definition, a data lake accepts any data, without oversight or governance. Without descriptive metadata and a mechanism to maintain it, the data lake risks turning into a data swamp." [37]

14.11   Data Lineage

Data lineage is the traceability of data from initial contact with the organisation to its final destination. It is the understanding of where a data element came from and where it is going to. In most organisations data lineage is – at best – poorly understood, let alone documented. Data lineage is invaluable when looking at information flow within the organisation. However, the definition and documentation of data lineage is often avoided by organisations as it is seen as a monstrous task with little benefit. However, data lineage enables:

- An end-to-end view of business rules which allows the identification of gaps.
- An end-to-end view that improves the ability of the organisation to manage and govern data.
- An end-to-end view that allows efficient design of data architecture to eliminate redundancy.
- New systems to be implemented more effectively and efficiently.
- Data quality management to be easier as it is possible to see where poor data is coming from and what it is feeding.
- Root cause analysis to be easier for the same reason.
- Reuse rather than recreation of information.

In addition, data lineage can be established at different levels and at different times. It is perfectly possible to start with high level data lineage and build this out over time as resources are available. Hence whilst potentially an enormous task, it can be attacked in bits, each bit is useful of itself, detail can be evolved over time as required, and it is of great benefit to all areas of the organisation.

Anecdote
It is not unknown for data lineage to be totally a mystery. One organisation took two years to find out the source of some data, as the data was dumped on a server in an outlying office on a monthly basis and no-one knew who or what put it there. This was, naturally, critical reporting data.

---

36.   The Data Lake Fallacy: All Water and Little Substance, Gartner, July 2014
37.   http://www.gartner.com/newsroom/id/2809117

14.12 Data Models and Modelling

> "A frequently overlooked aspect of data quality management is that of data model quality. We often build data models quickly, in the midst of a development project, and with the singular goal of database design. Yet the implications of those models are far reaching and long-lasting. They affect the structure of implemented data, the ability to adapt to change, understanding of and communication about data, definition of data quality riles, and much more. In many ways, high quality data begins with high quality data models".
> Steve Hoberman, *Data Modeling Made Simple: A Practical Guide for Business and IT Professionals*, Technics Publications, 2005.

Related to data lineage is the concept of data models. A data model describes the way in which data entities are related, and hence gives a logical structure of data within an organisation. In relation to data quality a good data model can make life easier, however a poor, overly complex, unstructured or simply non-existent data model can make the pursuit of data quality hard. Whilst at a high level data models appear to be stating the obvious, as they become more detailed they provide a strategically valuable information structure.

At its highest level, a conceptual data model may costs of nothing more than what is called an entity relationship diagram.

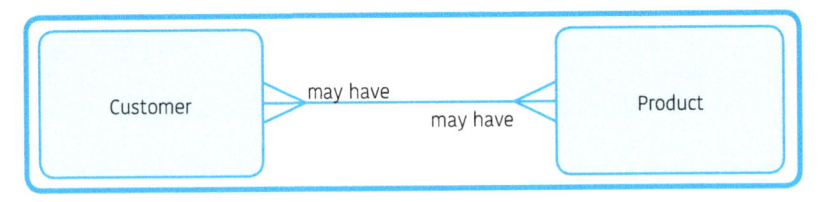

This example, with two entities (customer and product), reads from left to right and right to left respectively: *Each customer may have one or many products: Each product may have one or many customers*. This (which is a many to many relationship) is not very helpful from a database design point of view. As a result, a better representation may be:

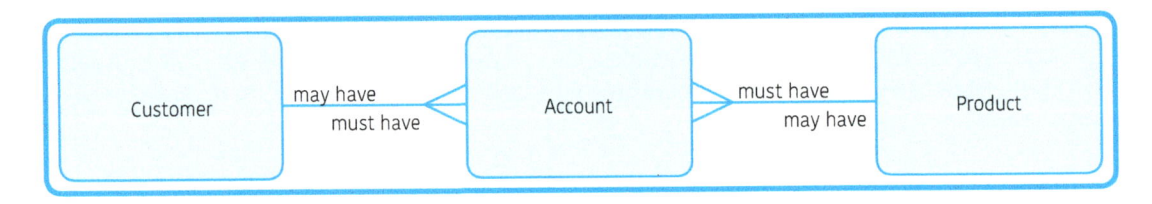

This reads (left hand side): *Each customer may have one or many accounts; each account must have one and only one customer*. The right hand side reads: *Each account must have one and only one product; each product may have one or many accounts*. We can then start building this out into more detail (and ignoring the account and product area from now on to keep matters simple).

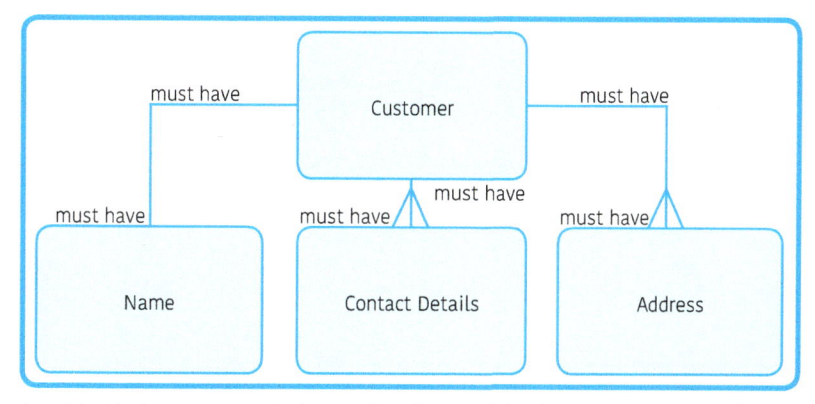

```
                    must have              must have
                 ┌──────────┐
                 │ Customer │
                 └──────────┘
                       must have
   must have      must have         must have
  ┌──────┐    ┌─────────────────┐  ┌─────────┐
  │ Name │    │ Contact Details │  │ Address │
  └──────┘    └─────────────────┘  └─────────┘
```

It is noticeable that we are entirely dealing here with abstract concepts of entities that are related. We start moving down into the next level (the logical data model) when talking about the attributes each entity may have. For example, name may have components such as:

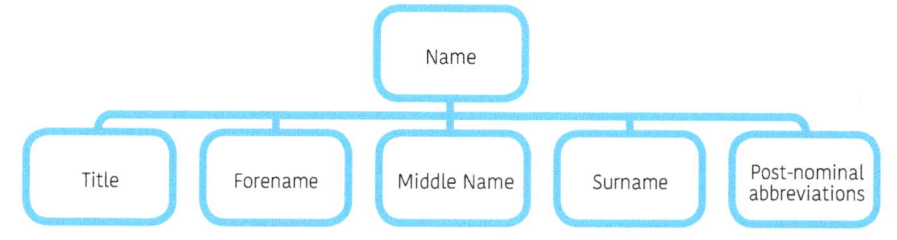

```
                        ┌──────┐
                        │ Name │
                        └──────┘
   ┌───────┬────────────┼────────────┬──────────────┐
┌─────┐ ┌──────────┐ ┌─────────────┐ ┌─────────┐ ┌───────────────┐
│Title│ │ Forename │ │ Middle Name │ │ Surname │ │ Post-nominal  │
└─────┘ └──────────┘ └─────────────┘ └─────────┘ │ abbreviations │
                                                 └───────────────┘
```

A data model tells an organisation how to structure its data and how data elements are related. A data model may also incorporate business rules, for example how a product is described. If a data model is used consistency across an organisation then problems relating to incompatibility of data from different systems will be significantly reduced. This will lead to:

- reduced operating costs
- reduced implementation costs
- greater clarity of information
- significantly reduced interface complexity

A data model is valuable and useful to the organisation. Some organisations (IBM, Teradata and others) can supply data models that will support industry sectors, thus giving an organisation a pre-built solution to which the organisation can align.

Note: Data Models at different levels.

Data models are often described as conceptual, logical and physical. Conceptual data models are high level models of the area of interest (the relevant domain). They are in business language. The first diagram above would loosely correspond to a conceptual data model. Logical data models are more technical, and describe the detailed solution one level down from the conceptual model. The last diagram above might loosely be described as a logical data model. Physical data models show the detailed field-by-field relationships and are specific to the implementation.

14.13 Summary

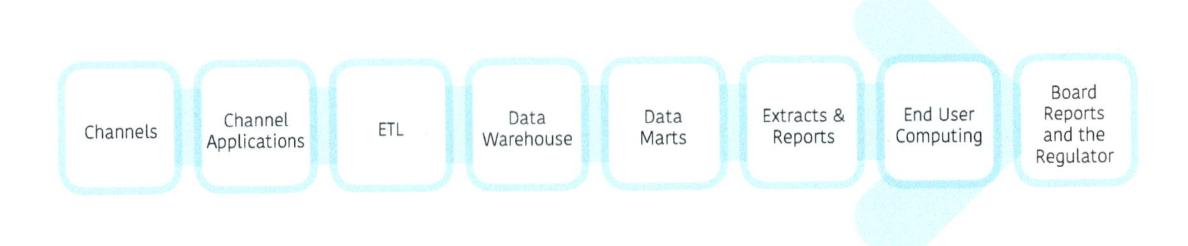

Channels → Channel Applications → ETL → Data Warehouse → Data Marts → Extracts & Reports → End User Computing → Board Reports and the Regulator

In this chapter I have outlined the typical information flow in an organisation, and the components that make up that flow. Whilst the above may appear a ramp-up in terms of technical terminology, here I introduce concepts that will be used throughout this book, and hence rather than continually simplifying every chapter a degree of terminology understanding can be used as a platform to both improve the ability of the reader to understand the book, and also as a lasting legacy to enable the reader to communicate with technical professionals on the ground.

A common aspiration within organisations is to find technology that can solve data quality problems and this is the subject of the next chapter, in which I will demonstrate that technology, whilst an excellent enabler of data quality remediation, is not an easy solution to all data quality problems, and needs to be used with care.

SECTION 4: BASIC UNDERSTANDING

CHAPTER 15: TECHNOLOGICAL TOOLS FOR DATA QUALITY

15.1 Structure

This section of the book covers the following topics:

1. Defining data
2. Defining quality
3. How does information flow?
4. Technological tools for data quality

This chapter covers the last of these topics.

15.2 Introduction

> "Data quality is not an IT problem. IT can help fix it, but the business must own the problem, However, technology will play a role in fixing many data quality issues, and organisations need to invest in a portfolio of data quality solutions such as profiling, cleansing, matching and enrichment."
> **Gartner Research vice president Andreas Bitterer**

I have mentioned a number of times that many organisations, publications, and worse, some consultants, approach data quality as a technological problem. This is not helped by some technology vendors occasionally selling their tools as the solution to all data quality ills. However it should constantly be in the mind of any organisation that technological tools are just that – tools to help perform a task. If the organisation has not yet determined what the task will be then this needs to be done before toolsets are bought. The solution should be orientated around the problem, and the tool bought, if necessary, to support the solution. This does not occur as often as it should. However, I do believe that there is a place for technology tools within The Data Quality Blueprint providing it is to support the people and processes that will do the driving. To give some examples:

- Technology can be a discovery tool, to define the data quality of the organisation and facilitate data profiling.
- Technology can be a discovery tool to find the data stores within an organisational network.
- Technology can compare information in several databases and match the information between them, so discovering where information is kept and in how many places.
- Technology can establish reference data for the organisation based on existing values or known data.
- Technology can be used to facilitate cleansing of data.
- Technology can be used to help keep the data good after remediation, via management of data dictionaries or data lineage.
- Technology can be used to constrain processes and procedures so it is more difficult for the data to end up in a poor state in the first place.
- Technology can be used to train staff on data quality, and can be used as a knowledge management tool.
- Finally technology can govern the remediation efforts and manage the data quality implementation by the use of a workflow.

In short, technology can be used in many ways to accelerate a data quality project. However rather than treating technology as an end in itself, in this book I have tried to treat technology as I believe it should be treated, as a tool that enables other tasks within the implementation. Within this chapter I will outline the various types of technological tools that are available at the present time to help a data quality project. I will discuss the merits of each, and also the challenges in using such tools.

15.3 The Technological Marketplace

The nature of a book is that it represents a publication date. Software, however, changes all the time. The risk in including references to software within a book of this type is that the software may move on, cutting edge software may become outdated, and new entrants to the market may produce a product that shines above all the rest. One way of approaching the problem, and the one I will take here, is to discuss each type of product and outline how it can help a data quality solution. To start the discussion, product types on the market at present include:

- Profiling tools
- Profiling with business rules
- Remediation with reference data
- Remediation with business rules
- Workflow toolsets
- Combination profiling toolsets
- Data governance and management tools
- Integrated stacks

I will now discuss each in more detail.

15.4 Profiling Tools

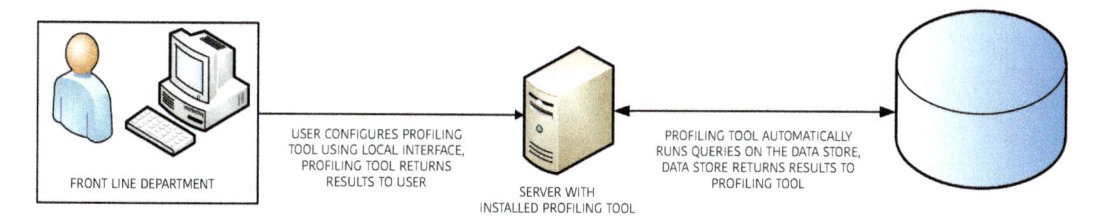

The most common type of tool sold as a "data quality" tool is a profiling tool. Profiling tools do what they say on the tin; specifically create a profile of the data. The output will typically include such characteristics as min and max values, patterns, and referential integrity. These tools do not try to remediate data, but to inform the user of its characteristics. A typical output (in this case from Oracle EDQ) is shown below.

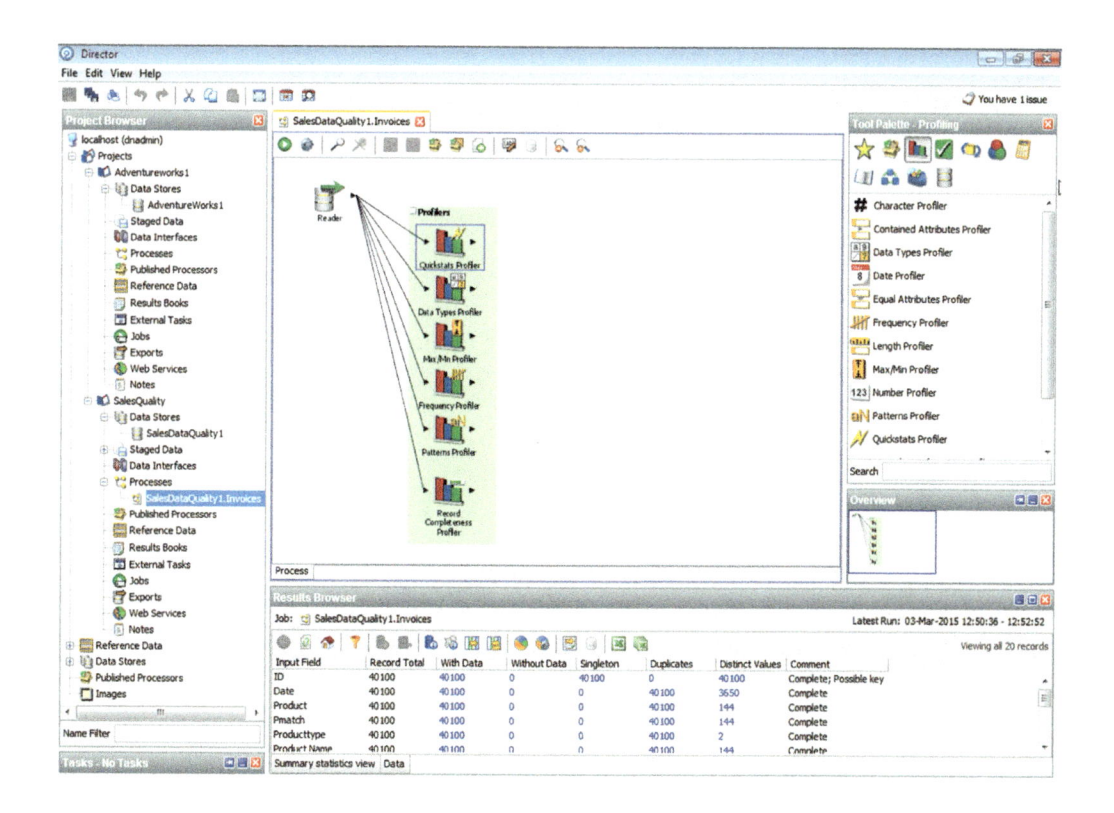

As an individual who has both used a number of these tools and has also performed many profiling exercises, at the time of writing these tools do not bring much functionality that is not already present with an experienced data analyst and a SQL querying tool. However, they are (much) faster. This kind of tool can automate many of the tasks that would take an experienced data analyst a significant time. For example, when running on modern hardware I have watched one tool profile every field in every table in a medium sized database in 10 minutes. This might compare with around a week or so for a data analyst to do the same. An intelligent third solution is for said data analyst to write a SQL script that is then run against every field in the database, which would probably take a day or so depending on size of said database.

Profiling typically will look to discover characteristics of the data as below.

- Primary key violations
- Foreign key violations
- Nulls
- Field types and length
- Business description
- Constraints
- Unique values (percentage of)
- Special characters
- Patterns and percentage of patterns
- Negative numbers (or positive depending on field)
- Max and min values
- Max and min length
- Top 10 values and percentages/numbers of these values
- Data breaking business rules
- Default values

Just to note – please see the "discovery" chapter for a more detailed discussion of the tasks included within profiling, including examples of each of the above.

15.5   Profiling with Business Rules

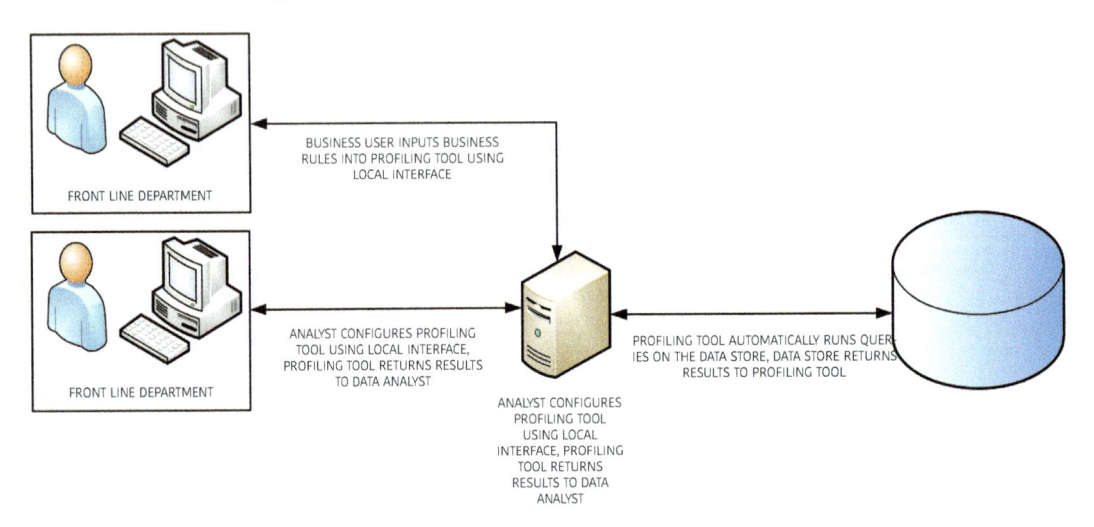

The next kind of tool to discuss is a tool which allows profiling with business rules. This is similar to "normal" data profiling as described above, but adds the ability for the user to set business rules and measure the data against them. The profiling will then not only identify characteristics as per the "standard" profiling set but also identify where the data breaks business rules. Examples may be subtracting a particular field representing customer date of birth from the current date to identify instances where customers are so old as for their age to be unbelievable (for example >120 years) or extremely young or even where the date of birth is in the future. It is possible to set up more complex rulesets, for example "that anyone borrowing money must be older than 18, so if a date of birth is found that is less than 18 with a credit balance then this is extracted out as an exception for further study".

It should be noted that no attempt is made to automatically remediate the data but this kind of toolset does allow exceptions to be identified. The kind of approach facilitated by this – and the first, simple profiling tool – will involve a number of actors, workflow and exception handling, which all will have to be co-ordinated manually.

It is also worth noting that in most, if not all cases, the business rules will need to be set up manually. Although some profiling toolsets come with some business rules built in, it is the nature of business rules that they are specific to the organisation and some time will need to be set aside to tune the toolset for the individual organisation. The configuration will also include the identification of the fields required for the rules – few, if any tools will automatically identify which field is the data of birth, or postcode. As a result setting such tools up will require discovery work with system and business subject matter experts to identify the correct fields and build the ruleset. This, however, will apply to almost every single toolset, not just those covering basic profiling or profiling with business rules.

15.6   Profiling and/or remediation with Reference Data

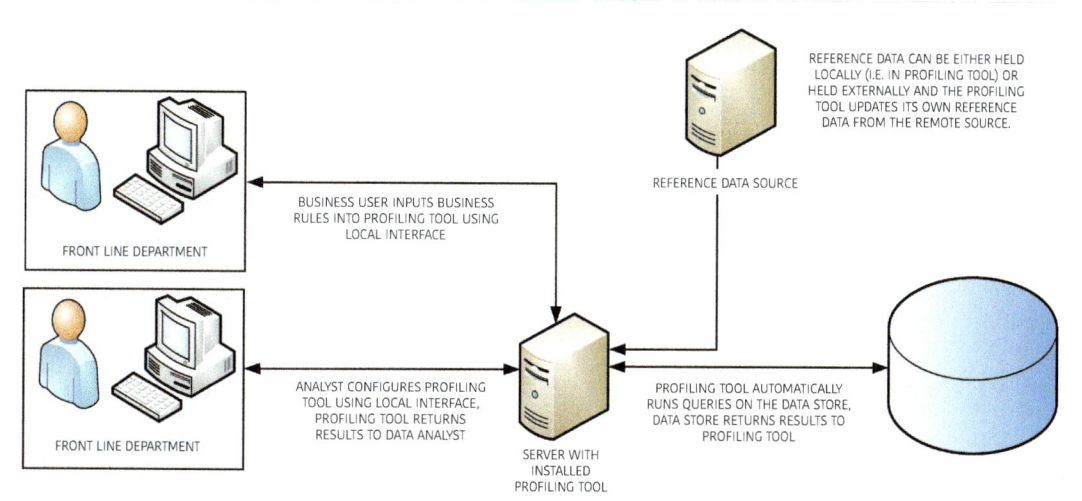

Several toolsets offer the ability to profile data against pre-prepared reference datasets. The reference sets can either be a known source of good data (for example valid zip code or postcode lists) or can be created by the user (for example product lists, departmental lists, staff lists). Here data will be highlighted where it does not meet a predefined set of valid values.

The Data Quality Blueprint

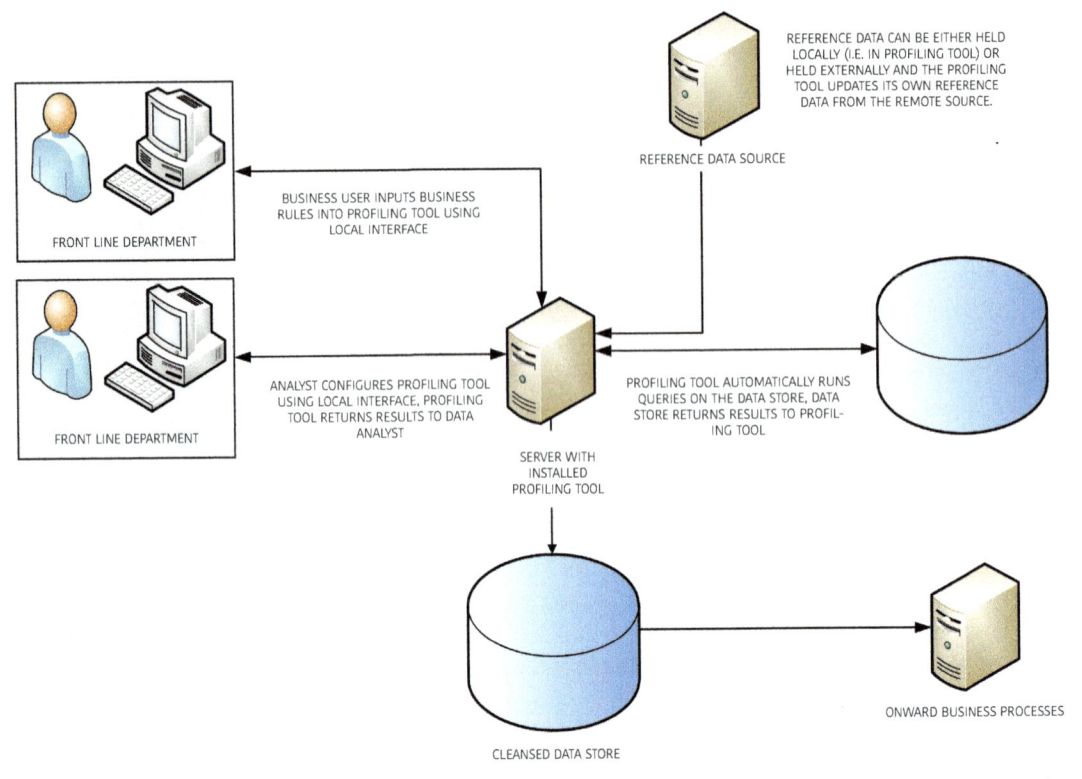

Some software may also automatically change data from "bad" to good based on predetermined mapping. For example a reference list could be mapped to remediate

- Stephne -> Stephen
- Tsephen -> Stephen
- Stephenn -> Stephen
- Stpheen -> Stephen

The danger with this approach, and why great care should be taken, is that often valid values are transformed, and the knock-on effect to the organisation is not considered. What happens to "Steven"? Or "Stefan", or "Stephanie", or "Stefanie", or "Stephe", or "Steff" or "Steve"? The law of unintended consequences can be quite significant here. As a result, whilst tempting, reference lists are not the automatic solution that many think they are and extreme care is required. The better examples of this kind of software will create a list of changes for review by a human being, however whilst this appears an ideal solution, in reality it is likely that no human will have the time to review changes which will be applied by the software without review as a result.

Example
In the US, the name "Stephe" is, although rare, perfectly reasonable as a forename, though uncommon in the rest of the world.

NAME
STEPHE
WORLDWIDE

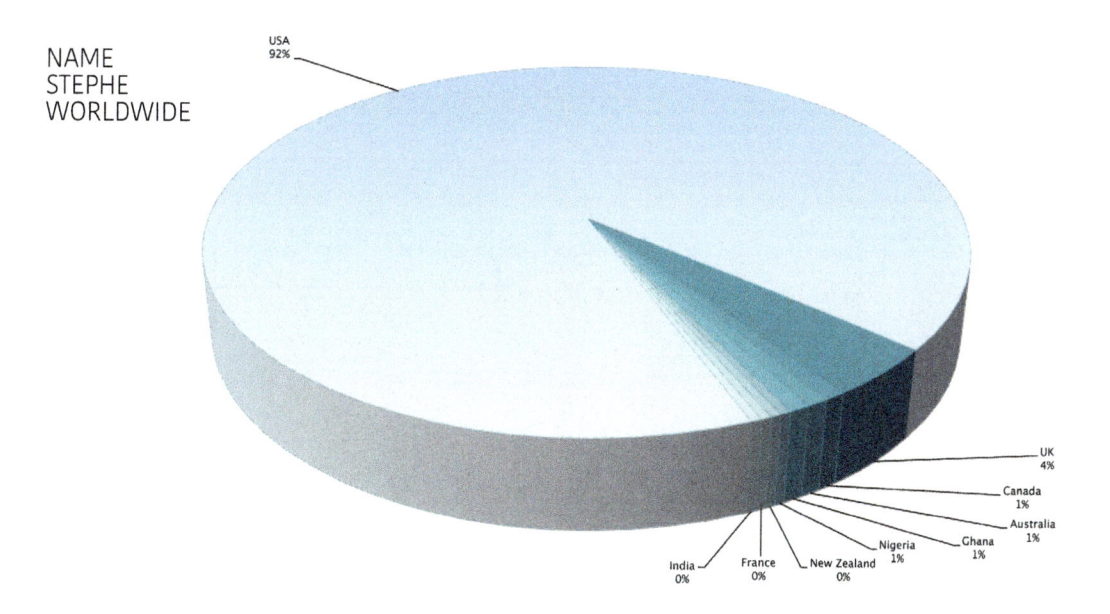

- USA 92%
- UK 4%
- Canada 1%
- Australia 1%
- Ghana 1%
- Nigeria 1%
- New Zealand 0%
- France 0%
- India 0%

If a reference list is used the following may occur.

Mrs Stephe Jones -> is electronically remediated to Mrs Stephen Jones

We now have taken correct data and turned it into incorrect data and caused a data quality problem. Also, the title doesn't match the forename. Hence a computer program may decide to change

Mrs Stephen Jones -> Mr Stephen Jones

Which is not going to help. Worse, if you also have a "real" Mr Stephen Jones, the next step may be the software looks at both records and merges them and you have lost a customer, their history, their products, and potentially are in breach of data privacy acts when you send the details of Mrs Steph Jones's account to Mr Stephen Jones. So you have created a data quality problem, lost a customer and have a legal problem, when you actually started with good data. Mrs Stephe Jones will not appreciate being electronically merged with Mr Stephen Jones. You then have a customer complaint problem as well.

15.7 Remediation with Business Rules

A related form of software is where data is automatically remediated based on business rules. These tools will examine the data, remediate what they can (potentially based on reference data sets as above), but can also remediate based on business rules. Similar to the above "profiling with business rules", the "remediation with business rules" will remediate what it can, then export exceptions that it cannot for further study.

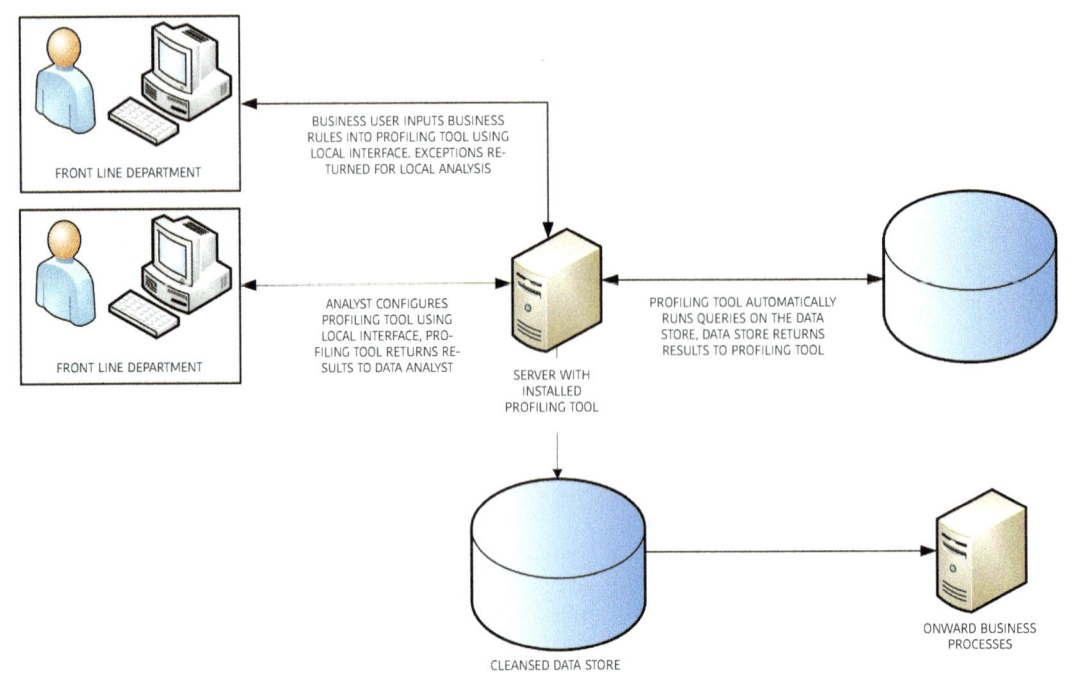

The advantages of this kind of tool is that often they will manage exceptions automatically, they can be implemented as part of ongoing data screening, and it absolutely accepts that the business has to be at the heart of the data quality remediation process. The disadvantage is that this approach can create a large number of exceptions for review – potentially into the thousands or tens of thousands, and therefore there is again the temptation for a hard-pressed reviewer to just let the software implement the changes – with all the risks that brings – without further review. In addition you still have to write the business rules; no (or very few) software tools will ever let you avoid that. However both of these disadvantages would also result from a manual remediation exercise.

15.8 Workflow Toolsets

The management of workflow is going to be essential in almost any medium to large scale remediation exercise. Workflow toolsets manage the remediation activity that will occur after profiling and remediation. Their functionality is to import exceptions from a profiling task – whether automatic or manual, and either basic, business rule or reference data based, and queue them into a workflow for examination, remediation and signoff. The users can then manage the remediation of the data in a real time basis and allocate the remediation tasks out. Management can see at a glance, at any point, the status of the remediation.

The advantage of workflow toolsets is that it is easy to manage the remediation activity from one place and new data remediation activities can be added all the time, making the tool a real hub of data quality remediation for the business. I would recommend workflow toolsets. Whilst it is possible to manage a remediation project entirely on spreadsheets it is easier to use a workflow, not least as there are a number available for no or little cost.

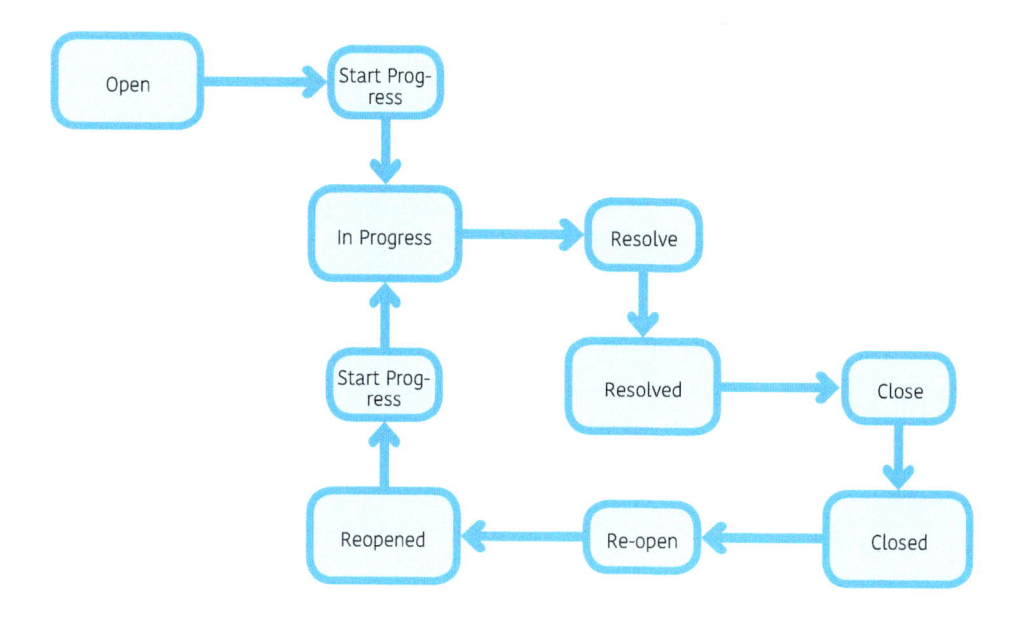

15.9 Combo Tools

Some of the best – and admittedly most expensive – tools combine many of the above elements into one tool.

- They will profile the historic data. They will also allow drill-down from summary results down to individual line item level.
- They will profile the data in relation to both built-in or user-created reference data and business rules.
- They will attempt to remediate the historic data in relation to reference data and/or business rules.
- They will then produce a list of exceptions for review.
- They will manage the workflow associated with these tasks.

These tools will significantly increase the throughput, reliability and management of data quality remediation.

The Data Quality Blueprint

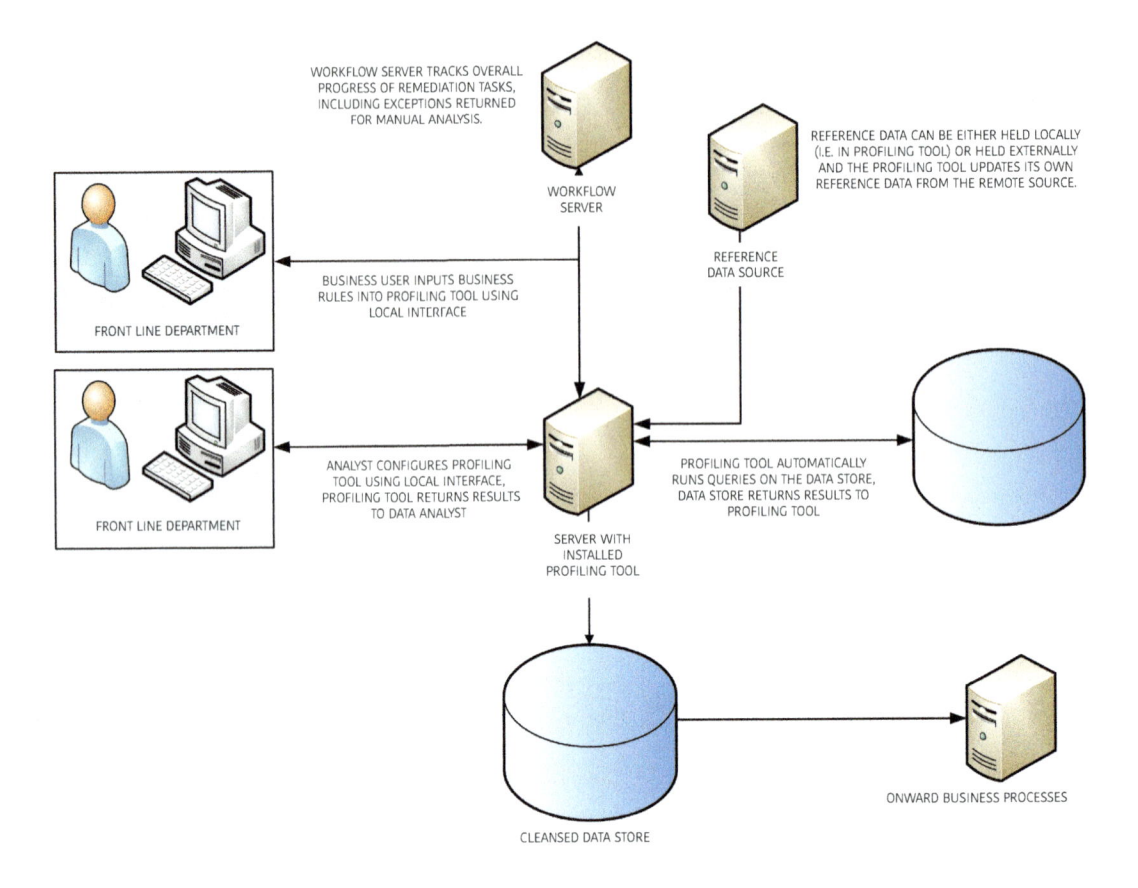

15.10 Data Governance and Management Tools

As well as data quality tools, there are also data governance tools. Whilst these do not cover the whole data governance landscape, if the organisation is looking to create or update a data dictionary and data requirements during the period of the project, then there are some excellent data governance toolsets coming onto the market. These enable an organisation to collaboratively define data definitions, as well as automate a signoff process. Many will also enable the documentation of data lineage, and some will automate this by importing data from ETL tools.

A good summary of the applications available in the marketplace covering data governance and data quality toolsets is **"Data Governance Tools"**, by Sunil Soares, MC Press, 2014.

Where I would recommend caution is that these tools are often sold as one-stop data governance solutions, which they are most certainly not. In my view the only way these should be implemented is in conjunction with a data governance strategy that includes people and process and is driven, much like I have advocated data quality, by the business. I will discuss more on data governance in the dedicated chapter on this subject later in the book in the "Embedding" section.

15.11 Integrated Stacks

Before leaving technology, it would be remiss not to mention the integrated stacks available from a number of the major software vendors, who have data quality modules that can be incorporated into their data landscape. These are the likes of SAP, Oracle, IBM and similar. Most of these organisations can offer some form of integrated data quality functionality, which will operate with other products from the same vendor. Hence the data quality tool will integrate seamlessly (at least in theory) with both the ETL toolset that transfers data from the source databases into the data warehouse and will also integrate with the data warehouse itself. Some of this additional software will also create a metadata library and a data dictionary and data lineage.

I will admit to having had mixed experience with these toolsets. I am aware of clients who have proclaimed that they work very well; equally I have known clients who have stated results that have been disappointing, and where the bolt-on data quality module has integrated poorly. It is the nature of any complex application landscape that some software plays nicely with others, and some other software does not, and to a certain extent it can be due to release versions of both the data quality software and the software it is trying to integrate to. In summary on this, I would suggest, like anything else, caveat emptor.

15.12 Summary

Within this chapter I have looked to outline how technology can help a data quality project. I would stress again that these technical tools are there to support, not replace, a business-orientated data quality methodology.

I have discussed the variety of types of tool on the market, and their capabilities and limitations. I have outlined the way that they work, and how, despite the stated view that technology is not the answer, that technology can significantly help a project of this nature. This chapter concludes the "technical" element of the book. At this point the reader, if not already au fait with the technical terminology, should know enough to have a sensible conversation with those that live in the technological world.

The next chapter will start the overall methodology proper and look in detail at the way in which data quality can be addressed in an organisation.

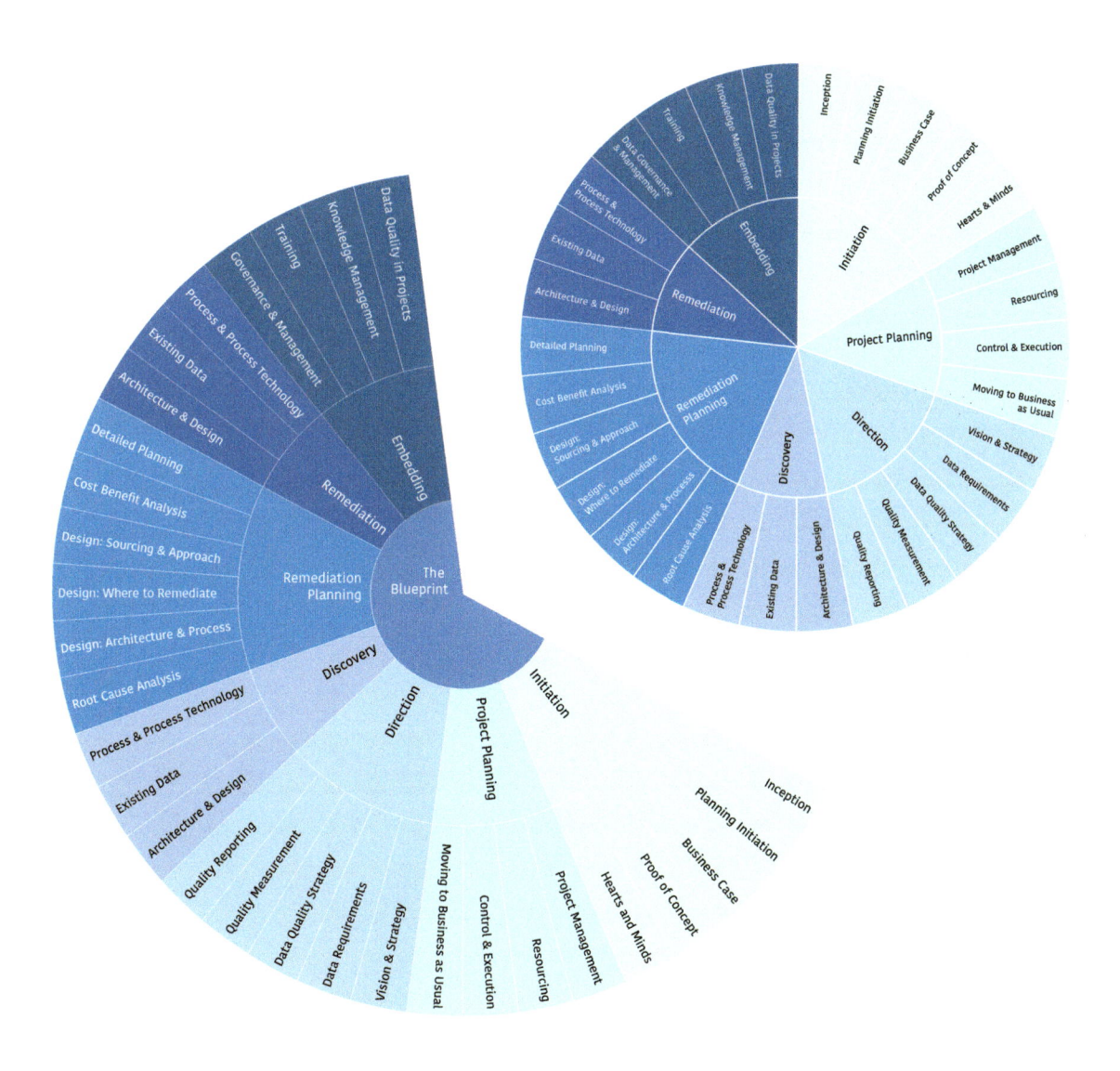

SECTION 5
THE DATA QUALITY BLUEPRINT

SECTION 5

THE DATA QUALITY BLUEPRINT

CHAPTER 16

METHODOLOGY OVERVIEW

To set the scene I will recap what I stated in the introduction. There are many data quality methodologies out there. This is not meant to be a replacement though it may be a complement. Actually, I think that over-engineering data quality approach is as much of a problem in itself. Hence regarding this as "A Methodology" is possibly giving it too grand a title. What I have tried to do here is to group together the tasks that would be involved in a typical data quality assignment, and put them in a logical order. Please don't think this the only path to nirvana. Many paths exist, and please feel free to take the elements you like out of this "methodology" and cut and paste with others that work for you or your organisation. Before I delve into the detail, a brief description of the steps is shown below.

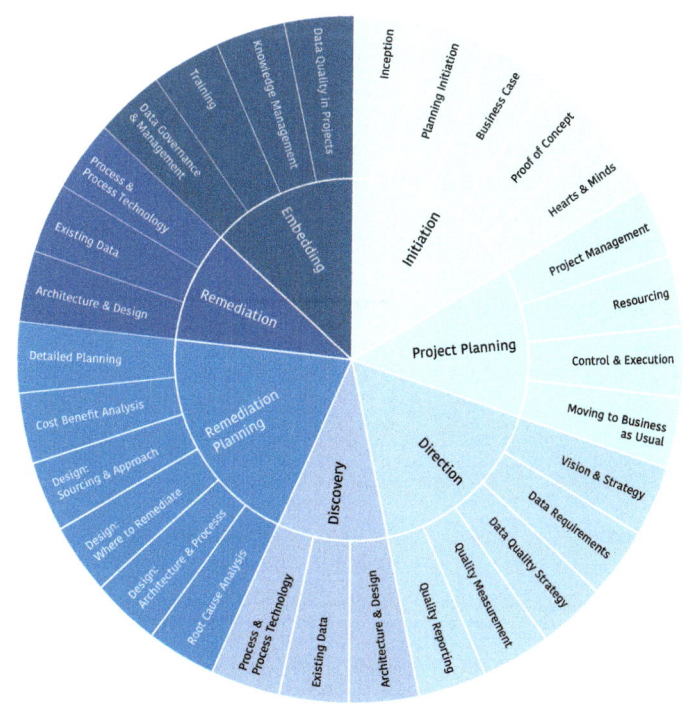

Initiation	The initiation stage sets the scene and lays the foundations for the rest of the project. It contains basics like development of scope, objectives and business case, as well as how to bring others on board and demonstrate to them the value of a data quality project.
Project Planning	The project planning stage takes the inputs from the initiation stage, and, assuming that a positive decision is made to continue with the project, will create a high level plan to the end of the project, including a detailed plan up to the remediation stage. The reason for this two stage planning process is that in reality you cannot create a detailed plan until you have completed the discovery stage, or to put it more succinctly, you cannot plan how to fix a problem until you know what that problem is.
Direction	Having completed the planning, the next stage is to define the direction. Hopefully, this is work the organisation has already completed, but if not then this will have to be performed. Without knowledge of what information the organisation needs, it will be impossible to make decisions on prioritisation and criticality for the rest of the project – the project will end up covering all data in every system. This is neither efficient nor effective.
Discovery	Next the project needs to find out the current situation. The purpose of this section is to define the nature and size of the problem. It does this by looking at existing architecture, data and process, and defining where they are deficient in meeting the information requirements of the organisation.
Remediation Planning	The remediation planning is a pivotal point of the project. Now that we know the problem we can take the high level plan created in the project planning stage and introduce more detail. This stage also takes the output from the discovery stage and looks for root causes, as several problems can potentially be addressed by changing one root cause. This makes the remediation more efficient. Finally this stage re-validates the business case, and the costs and benefits that will result from the project.
Remediation	Actual remediation of architecture, process and data. All of the preparatory work has been done, so this stage should be a workflow-driven factory of changes to the organisation, all performed in the most efficient and effective way with minimum disruption.
Embedding	Finally, it is important that all the good work undertaken by the data quality project is not lost. The data has to be kept good, and this will only occur if governance and management procedures are put in place, and staff receive training to enable them to contribute to an information quality environment. Lastly, knowledge management should ensure that the information created during the project will not be lost.

SECTION 5.1
INITIATION: OBTAINING BUY-IN

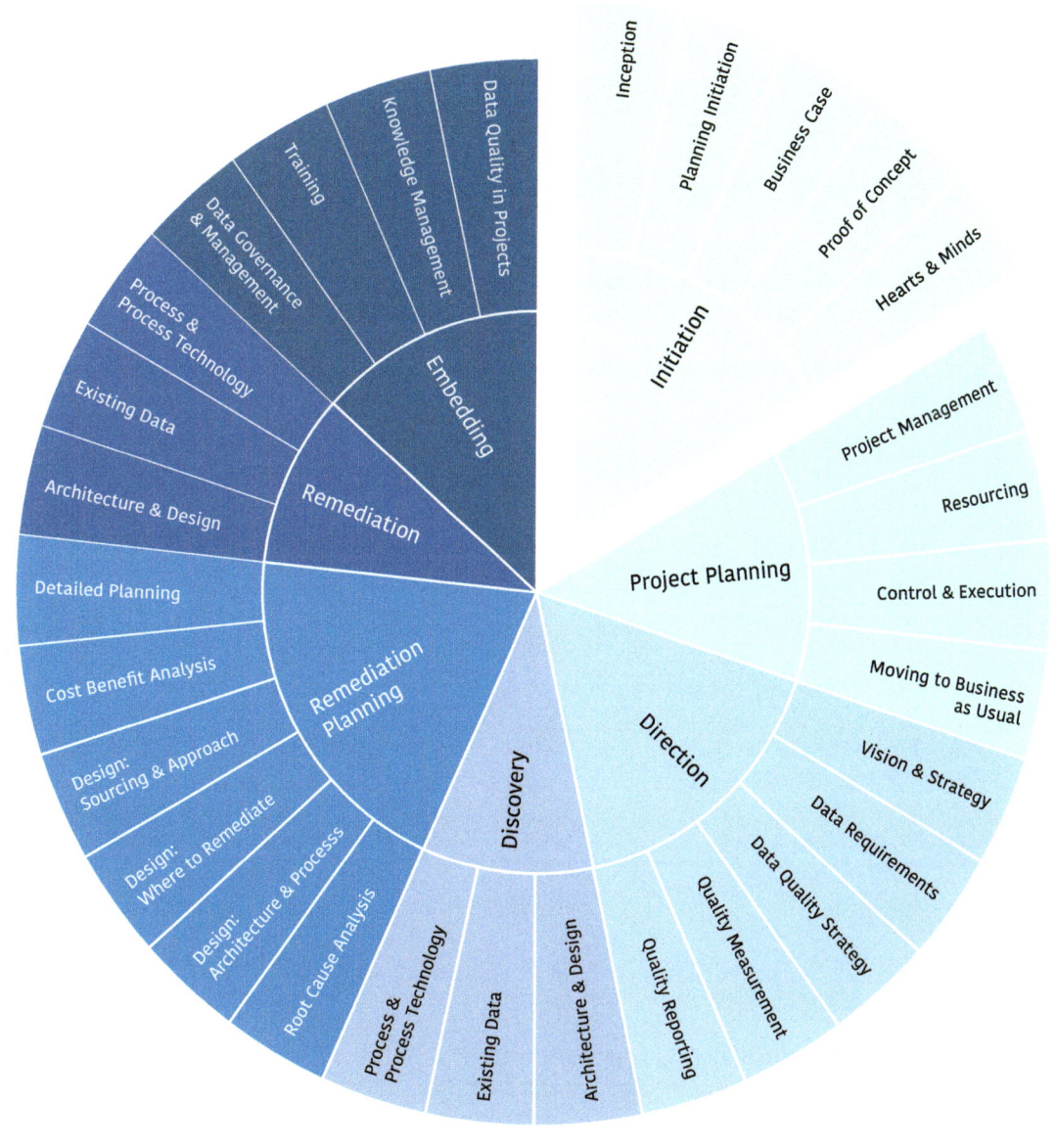

Initiation
- Inception
- Planning Initiation
- Business Case
- Proof of Concept
- Hearts & Minds

Project Planning
- Project Management
- Resourcing
- Control & Execution
- Moving to Business as Usual

Direction
- Vision & Strategy
- Data Requirements
- Data Quality Strategy
- Quality Measurement
- Quality Reporting

Discovery
- Process & Process Technology
- Existing Data
- Architecture & Design
- Root Cause Analysis

Remediation Planning
- Detailed Planning
- Cost Benefit Analysis
- Design: Sourcing & Approach
- Design: Where to Remediate
- Design: Architecture & Process

Remediation
- Process & Process Technology
- Existing Data
- Architecture & Design

Embedding
- Data Governance & Management
- Training
- Knowledge Management
- Data Quality in Projects

SECTION 5.1: INDEX

CHAPTER 17: Laying the foundations: Inception — 175
- 17.1 Structure — 175
- 17.2 The Basics — 176

CHAPTER 18: Planning the Initiation Stage — 181
- 18.1 Structure — 181
- 18.2 Overview — 182
- 18.3 What are the Inputs to this Stage? — 183
- 18.4 What Needs to be Achieved? — 183
- 18.5 How Long will the Initiation Stage Take? — 184
- 18.6 Resources for Initiation — 184
- 18.7 Initiation Plan — 185
- 18.8 Creating the Plan — 185
- 18.9 Other work in the planning stage — 186
- 18.10 Summary — 186

CHAPTER 19: Building the Business Case — 187
- 19.1 Structure — 187
- 19.2 Overview — 188
- 19.3 Background — 191
- 19.4 Reasons for Undertaking the Project — 191
- 19.5 Pain Points, Objectives and Scope — 192
- 19.6 Pain Points — 193
- 19.7 Objectives — 196
- 19.8 Scope — 197
- 19.9 Business Options — 199
- 19.10 Cost-Benefit Analysis — 200
- 19.11 Timescale — 201
- 19.12 Proof of Concept — 201
- 19.13 Risks, Assumptions, and Dependencies — 201
- 19.14 Summary — 202

CHAPTER 20: Creating a Proof of Concept — 203
- 20.1 Structure — 203
- 20.2 Overview — 204
- 20.3 Challenges of Proof of Concept — 205
- 20.4 Approach to a Proof of Concept — 206
- 20.5 Process-Based Approach — 206
- 20.6 Business Pound Value Based Approach — 206
- 20.7 Data Approach — 207

20.8	After the Proof of Concept	207
20.9	Summary	208

CHAPTER 21: Winning Hearts and Minds — 209

21.1	Structure	209
21.2	Overview	210
21.3	Timing of the message and repeating the message	213
21.4	Get the message at the right level	214
21.5	Liaison with existing functions	215
21.6	Communications Strategy	216
21.7	Principles	216
21.8	Propaganda: The Elevator Pitch and Day in the Life	216
21.9	User Stories	219
21.10	Stakeholder Analysis	220
21.11	Communication Planning	223
21.12	Targeting and Execution	227
21.13	Sustaining/Keep Happy	229
21.14	The Regulator	229
21.15	Further Reading	230
21.16	Summary	230

SECTION 5.1 — INITIATION: OBTAINING BUY-IN

CHAPTER 17 — LAYING THE FOUNDATIONS: INCEPTION

17.1 Structure

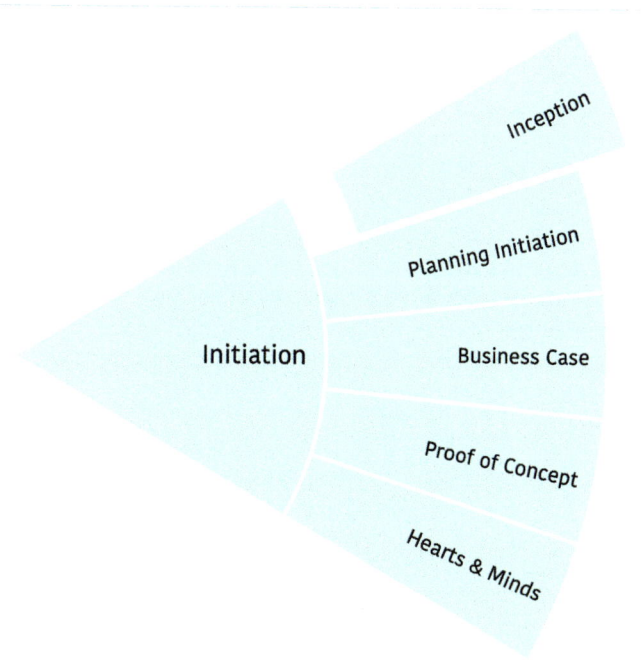

Initiation:
- Inception
- Planning Initiation
- Business Case
- Proof of Concept
- Hearts & Minds

This stage of The Data Quality Blueprint includes the following phases:

1. Laying the foundations
2. Planning the initiation stage
3. Building the business case
4. Creating a proof of concept
5. Winning hearts and minds

This chapter covers the first of these phases.

17.2 The Basics

Even before the start of the initiation stage, some basic tasks need to be undertaken. I am assuming that at this point either (a) a senior individual in the organisation has expressed a need for a data quality project and authorised internal spend on an inception phase or (b) an external consultant has replied to a Request for Proposal (RFP) and been invited in to perform the same. I am assuming that the reader is part of or is leading the response.

From the point of view of the book, I will talk of "the project" and "the project team" on one side and "the organisation", "IT", and "the business" on the other. It doesn't matter whether "the project team" are internal or external staff; they are a group of individuals who are dedicated to the task of running a data quality project. Their first task is the inception phase. This will normally take a few weeks, and will set up the rest of the project.

Here I am going to introduce a format I will use in most chapters from here on. Within chapters of the methodology I have included a table which is designed to help an individual involved with a data quality project. This table outlines the inputs, outputs, and dependencies, and the tasks that need completing for each section of the project. A reader following the book stage by stage can therefore see exactly what is required at each point. This allows each section to stand alone as a mini-project in itself, and will aid clarity in moving through the four hundred pages of text that detail the methodology. I am not going to go through every single task in detail – that would result in a book that was un-liftable – nor even necessarily mention them all, but each chapter will talk around the topics in each stage, outline the challenges, the approach and what needs to be considered. I would note that a full list of tasks is shown in the appendices.

The table below covers the key tasks, inputs, outputs and dependencies for the "Laying the Foundations: Inception" phase. After these tasks are complete the project, whether internal or external to the organisation, has authorisation for the initiation stage. It has also started work on critical deliverables and is in a good shape for moving on to the initiation stage itself. I will cover the planning of this stage in the following chapters.

INPUTS	TASKS

- Background information
- Project brief (if existing)
- Publically available information
- Request for proposal (RFP) – if existing
- Organisational diagrams
- Lists of systems and domains
- Organisational roles and responsibilities
- Key architectural documents
- Key data documents
- Key process documents
- Board reports (if available)
- Financial reports and management reports
- Financial accounts
- Application forms
	- Initial set-up
	  - Initial meeting with sponsor
	    - Arrange and attend meeting
	    - Identify key stakeholders
	    - Define initial problem statement
	    - Draft initial scope
	    - Draft initial objectives
	    - Document meeting
	    - Agree communications frequency
	    - Agree next steps
	    - Set up follow-up meeting
	    - Confirm actions to project sponsor
	  - Logistics
	    - Create daily log
	    - Create query log
	    - Create issue log
	    - Identify project team
	    - Determine availability

Chapter 17: Laying the foundations: Inception

OUTPUTS
- Initial problem statement
- Initial scope
- Initial objectives
- Daily log
- Query log
- Issue log
- Holiday tracker
- Draft onboarding document
- Initial task list
- List of key stakeholders
- Stakeholder map
- Interview schedule
- Interview material
- Meeting notes
- Update initial problem statement
- List of pain points
- Data domains in scope
- System domains in scope
- Process domains in scope
- Requirements for the project
- Expectations for the project
- High level project objective
- Low level (detail) objectives for the project
- Project definition
- Project approach document
- Work breakdown structure
- Technical and licensing requirements
- Project roles and responsibilities
- High level project plan
- Resourcing plan
- Draft communications plan
- Draft detail initiate plan
- Initial RAID Log
- Initial business case
- Project brief

DEPENDENCIES
- Access to stakeholders, including executive.
- Core team resources
- Agreement to spend resources on project

- Create holiday tracker
- Initial draft onboarding document
- Create project repository
- Create initial task list
- Assign task list to project team
- Organisational Understanding
  - Research background to organisation
  - Discover internal roles and responsibilities
  - Obtain details of organisational systems
  - Obtain details of organisational domains
  - Obtain details of organisational structure
  - Update list of key stakeholders
  - Upload documentation into project repository
- Initial Stakeholder Interviews (30 min - 1 hour max each)
- Identify stakeholders to interview
  - Draft stakeholder map
  - Request interviews
  - Prepare interview schedule
  - Prepare interview material
  - Perform Interviews
  - Document and confirm meeting notes with individual stakeholders
  - Upload interview notes into project repository
- Problem Statement
  - Update initial problem statement for interviews
  - Draft list of pain points
  - Agree with project sponsor and key stakeholders
  - Update as required
  - Upload into project repository
- Project Approach
- Scope
  - Define data domains in scope
  - Define system domains in scope
  - Define process domains in scope
  - Agree with project sponsor and key stakeholders
  - Obtain written signoff
  - Upload to project repository
- Objectives
  - Define requirements for the project
  - Define expectations for the project
  - Link requirements and expectations to problem statement
  - Draft high level project objective
  - Agree with project sponsor and key stakeholders
  - Obtain written signoff
  - Upload to project repository
  - Draft low level (detail) objectives for the project
  - Agree with project sponsor and key stakeholders
  - Obtain written signoff
  - Upload to project repository
- Project Definition
  - Create project definition
  - Agree with project sponsor and key stakeholders

- - Obtain written signoff
    - Upload to project repository
  - Approach
    - Define overall methodology to be used
    - Draft high level approach
    - Estimate timescales
    - Define project tasks at a high level
    - Create the project approach document
    - Upload to project repository
  - Work Breakdown Structure
    - Draft work breakdown structure
    - Agree with team
    - Upload to project repository
  - Technical and Licensing
    - Draft technical and licensing requirements
    - Agree with IT stakeholders
    - Upload to project repository
  - Resourcing
    - Define skill sets required
    - Define training needs
    - Confirm availability
    - Draft project roles and responsibilities
    - Upload to project repository

Initial planning
- Project Plan
  - Create high level project plan
  - Create resourcing plan
  - Draft communications plan
  - Create draft detail initiate plan
  - Agree with project sponsor and key stakeholders as required
  - Upload to project repository
- RAID Log
  - Brainstorm initial risks with team and/or key stakeholders
  - Brainstorm initial dependencies with team and/or key stakeholders
  - Brainstorm initial assumptions with team and/or key stakeholders
  - Brainstorm initial issues with team and/or key stakeholders
  - Document initial RAID Log
  - Agree with key stakeholders
  - Upload to project repository
- Draft Business Case
  - Create estimates of the cost of poor quality to the business
  - Create benefit estimates of the project
  - Socialise with key stakeholders if required
  - Draft initial business case
- Project Brief/SOW
  - Inputs

- Background
- Problem statement
- Scope
- Objectives
- Requirements
- Expectations
- Project definition
- Approach
- Work breakdown structure
- High level plan
- Resource plan
- Team structure
- Draft business case
- High level risks
- High level assumptions
- High level dependencies
- Creation and agreement
  - Create project brief
  - Presentation of project brief to sponsor
  - Obtain agreement and signoff for initiate stage
  - Present project brief to board
  - Obtain go decision and funding for initiate
  - Baseline and upload into project document repository

As the inception phase is the start of the project, there will be little information available. It is unlikely that there will be more than a high level Request for Proposal (RFP) – probably stating that there are "considerable problems with the data in the organisation". At this point as much background information as possible should be collected via public sources (for example the internet) and a meeting should be set up with key stakeholders such as the project sponsor and then key business and IT personnel, the former to gain a better idea of the problems facing the information and the latter to start a high level understanding of the data landscape.

Initial tasks will include the creation of a problem statement, an objective and a high level plan, initial risks and dependencies, proposed team structure and organisation, and a high level business case. At this stage all of these will be necessarily limited and high level, but will create a foundation upon which the rest of the project can build. The basic tasks also cover creation of a project brief and the statement of work (SOW). This will contractually govern the relationship between the organisation that is receiving services and the project that is giving them.

SECTION 5.1 INITIATION: OBTAINING BUY-IN

CHAPTER 18: PLANNING THE INITIATION STAGE

18.1 Structure

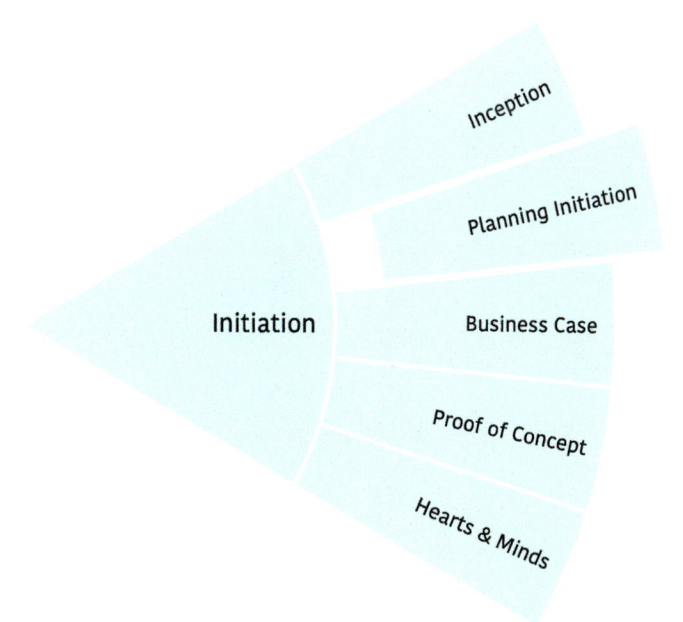

- Inception
- Planning Initiation
- Business Case
- Proof of Concept
- Hearts & Minds

(Initiation)

This stage of The Data Quality Blueprint includes the following phases:

1. Laying the foundations
2. Planning the initiation stage
3. Building the business case
4. Creating a proof of concept
5. Winning hearts and minds

This chapter covers the second of these phases.

18.2 Overview

INPUTS
- SOW and Project Brief
- All artefacts created or utilised in the previous stage

OUTPUTS
- Updated initiate plan
- Completed initiate project plan
- Draft full project plan
- Updated daily log
- Updated risk log
- Updated assumptions log
- Updated issues log
- Updated dependencies
- Updated query log
- Draft terms of reference
- Meeting schedule
- Draft terms of reference
- Agreed terms of reference for project and/or governance
- Agreed relationship with project management office
- Rules of engagement

DEPENDENCIES
- Access to stakeholders including executive stakeholders
- Core team resources
- Time commitment from stakeholders for forum participation

TASKS
- Plan
  - Update initiate plan
    - Confirm resourcing
    - Confirm skillets required from resources
    - Confirm availability of resources
    - Create internal RACI
    - Create external RACI
    - Define training needs for resources
    - Deliver training if required
    - Confirm draft timescales of project
    - Complete initiate project plan
    - Agree with project sponsor and key stakeholders
    - Baseline and upload into project document repository
  - Draft full project plan
    - Create draft full project plan
    - Socialise with team members
    - Update for feedback as required
    - Upload to project repository
- Initial Artefacts
  - Update daily log
  - Update risk log
  - Update assumptions log
  - Update issues log
  - Update dependencies
  - Update query log
  - Upload to project repository
- Forums
  - Steering Committee
    - Identify members
    - Draft terms of reference
    - Agree with key stakeholders
    - Brief members on purpose of meetings
    - Create meeting schedule
    - Upload to project repository
  - Data Design Authority
    - Identify members
    - Draft terms of reference
    - Agree with key stakeholders
    - Brief members on purpose of meetings
    - Create meeting schedule
    - Upload to project repository
  - Governance
    - Agree relationship with organisational governance
    - Agree terms of reference for project and/or governance
    - Agree relationship with project management office
    - Agree terms of reference
    - Agree appointment of project data steward
    - Brief members on purpose of meetings
    - Create rules of engagement

- Agree with key sponsors
- Upload to project repository
- Logistics
  - Agree hotel rates
  - Book hotels
  - Agree travel rates
  - Update on-boarding pack
  - Upload to project repository

Although the main planning of the project occurs in two stages (Project Planning and Remediation Planning), there is an element of planning to be undertaken in the initiation stage as well, to ensure that enough information is collated to allow the organisation to have a clear view of the benefits of the project and to hence obtain a green light for the forthcoming discovery stage. In this chapter I will cover the work that needs to be undertaken in the initiation stage.

18.3 What are the Inputs to this Stage?

The primary inputs to this stage will be the artefacts that have been created in Inception. These will be:

- Project Brief
- Detail plan of first few weeks
- Problem statement
- Skill sets required
- Project organisation
- Initial communications plan
- Statement of Work (SOW)
- Initial high level plan
- Work breakdown structure
- Training needs
- Project resource plan

As can be seen, the project is already off to a good start. Other inputs to this stage will be the knowledge of key individuals within the organisation which, together with some limited data, process and architecture discovery work, will enable these artefacts to be expanded.

18.4 What Needs to be Achieved?

Within the initiation stage of the project, work needs to cover some basics to ensure that the project can move on to the next stage. Work will include:

- Definition of scope and objectives.
- Critically, the creation of a business case for the project. This will include an initial architecture, data and process assessment, and an initial assessment of business options and a cost benefit analysis. The business case will underpin the whole project and demonstrate to the executive that the project is viable. At this stage the main objective is to prove the project is worth doing before significant costs have been consumed, and open the door to a more detailed discovery phase.
- A decision needs to be undertaken as to whether to include a proof of concept in the project.
- If it is decided that a proof of concept is necessary, implementation of the proof of concept.

- Work also needs to be undertaken to ensure that the project has buy-in from the business in general and key stakeholders in particular.
- Creation of a project initiation document – a more comprehensive project brief that will be a critical governing document for the project going forward.

As far as the planning stage is concerned, the requirement is to put together a plan to ensure that these outputs can be achieved.

18.5 How Long will the Initiation Stage Take?

The project initiation stage is not a long process. The inception phase would be expected to take 2-4 weeks, and the following initiation phase between 2 weeks to 2 months depending on the resources available, the scale of the organisation and the complexity of its data landscape. It will be longer if a Proof of Concept (PoC) is undertaken. It should be noted that this stage underpins the rest of the project and hence has to be done well. Skimping effort at this stage with the expectation that effort can be caught up later is a bad idea. Not only is it unlikely that resources will be available to play catch-up at a later date, but without this work buy-in will not be achieved and the benefits of good data quality will not be realised within the organisation.

18.6 Resources for Initiation

Like all projects there will be an initial team which will perform the start-up work. This team will be relatively senior.

- This will consist of the executive, and the senior business and IT sponsor for the project, together with the project manager. These individuals will build the overall team.
- The senior business and IT sponsors are essential at this point as the project will need these people to persuade individuals with critical knowledge within the various departments to spend less time on their day jobs and help the project.
- A project accountant will be required to build the costs and revenues to support the business case.
- A Project Architect/Architecture Lead will start to look at where the organisation is going and how the structure of the business supports its direction.
- There will likely be a small team (the "discovery team") who will be responsible for asking business subject matter experts (SMEs) about the current data quality pain points to support the business case. A similar team will look to discover how processes are failing from a data quality point of view – obviously these two teams can either be composed of the same individuals, or be in the same meeting to reduce the time taken from the business SMEs, but the focus is different, one set will work as data analysts and the other as process analysts.
- The data and process leads come on board to direct the discovery team and to start to assess the organisation.
- An addition at this stage is Quality Assurance, a separate section of the project reporting directly to the executive to provide an independent assurance on the progress of the project.

A diagram showing the project team and the interaction of responsibilities is shown below.

A wider discussion of the roles and responsibilities within the overall project is contained within the main project planning chapter which forms a central location within the book that contains all resource information.

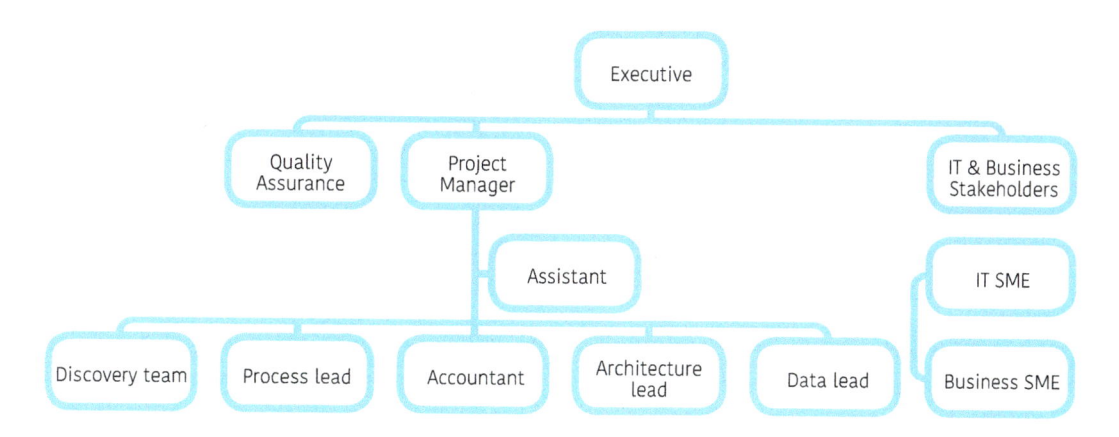

```
                            ┌───────────┐
                            │ Executive │
                            └─────┬─────┘
        ┌──────────┬──────────────┼─────────────────┬──────────────┐
   ┌─────────┐ ┌─────────┐                                   ┌──────────────┐
   │ Quality │ │ Project │                                   │ IT & Business│
   │Assurance│ │ Manager │                                   │ Stakeholders │
   └─────────┘ └────┬────┘                                   └──────┬───────┘
                ┌──────────┐                                  ┌─────────┐
                │ Assistant│                                  │ IT SME  │
                └────┬─────┘                                  └─────────┘
  ┌──────────┬──────┼────────┬──────────────┬──────────┐     ┌─────────────┐
┌─────────┐┌──────┐┌──────┐┌────────────┐┌────────┐          │ Business SME│
│Discovery││Process││Accoun││Architecture││ Data   │          └─────────────┘
│  team   ││ lead ││ tant ││    lead    ││  lead  │
└─────────┘└──────┘└──────┘└────────────┘└────────┘
```

18.7 Initiation Plan

The initiation stage needs to include the following, and this all should be included in the initiation plan.

- Business case
- Initial architecture assessment
- Initial process assessment
- Risk assessment & management strategy
- Option appraisal
- Proof of concept
- Implementing proof of concept
- Stakeholder assessment
- Ongoing communications
- Project Initiation Document (PID)
- Information gathering
- Initial data assessment
- Change capacity assessment & management strategy
- Analysis of poor quality cost
- Cost benefit analysis
- Planning proof of concept
- Communication strategy preparation & implementation
- Initial communications

One can see that this is a reasonable amount of work – the project plan at the back of the book lists over two hundred separate tasks in this area, and this is in no way an exhaustive list. The initiation plan needs to ensure that all project resources are in no doubt what they need to achieve and by when, and also what project products are pre-requisites for the creation of others.

18.8 Creating the Plan

It is often assumed that a project manager is responsible for the creation of the project plan. Whilst true, this does not mean that the project manager needs to be an expert on every task to be undertaken. The project manager is there to conduct the orchestra, not play every instrument, or to tell the violinist how to play. The project manager will need to draw on the expertise of the other members of the team to create the plan, and equally, the other members of the team need to be prepared to help create the plan that covers their area of work.

There is, unfortunately, a common misconception on both sides. Project managers are overstressed because they feel they do not have the expertise to guide the team, and some team members refuse to get involved in planning because "that's the project manager's job".

A common (and effective) approach is for the project manager to call a meeting of all team members to discuss the problem statement and the client requirements. From this session the task list can be generated, and the project manager can gain understanding from the team of the effort involved and the sequence required in each area. The project manager can then collate the information in a project tool and replay to the team in an iterative cycle.

Central to the planning process is the agreement of dependencies (what we need to do the job from the client/organisation/IT/business/third party suppliers), assumptions (the assumptions we have made when putting the plan together) and risks to delivery. Together with issues this is called the RAID log.

At the end of this process the plan for the initiation stage can be shown to the client, dependencies and deliverables agreed, and work started. I would also suggest that a very high level indicative plan of the overall project is created (assuming follow-on work from the initiation stage), which can then be built out in the following stages.

18.9 Other work in the planning stage

As part of the initiation planning work there are several other important tasks that need to be covered. The project needs to set up its own governance. This would typically consist of a steering committee, including the sponsor and key stakeholders, and the project manager. Rules of engagement need to be defined, as well as a reporting framework. The project needs to start interaction with the organisation's project governance process and understand what their requirements are.

I would strongly suggest that the project should set up a data decisions authority (of which more in the project planning section), and should create an initial RACI matrix (Responsible, Accountable, Consulted, Informed) to define who is involved in each part of the work, whether internal or external to the project, and the definition of their role.

18.10 Summary

In this short chapter I have outlined what needs to be achieved to plan the initiation stage. I have noted that for the whole project to be a success then this stage needs to be completed to a high standard to obtain the requisite buy-in from the organisation as a whole. I have outlined the resources that would be included within the initiation stage, why each resource would be required and what their responsibilities would be. Finally I have outlined the activities that the plan needs to include and how to create a plan. The objective is to introduce the reader, who, after all, may not necessarily be familiar with a project of this nature, to all the varying set-up tasks that would need to be undertaken if the project was performed for real.

In the next chapter I will look at one of the most critical area in the entire project, which is the creation of the business case which will underpin the rest of the project.

SECTION 5.1 INITIATION: OBTAINING BUY-IN

CHAPTER 19 BUILDING THE BUSINESS CASE

19.1 Structure

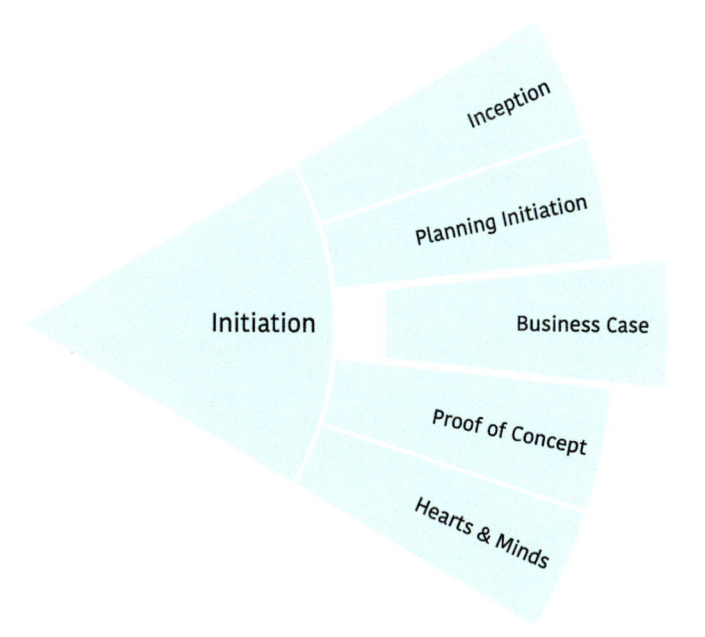

This stage of The Data Quality Blueprint includes the following phases:

1. Laying the foundations
2. Planning the initiation stage
3. Building the business case
4. Creating a proof of concept
5. Winning hearts and minds

This chapter covers the third of these phases.

19.2 Overview

INPUTS	TASKS

- All artefacts created or utilised in previous stages.
- Scope
- Objectives
	- Information Gathering
	  - From initial scope identify the architectural, data and process items in scope
	  - Document detailed scope
	  - Agree with sponsor and key stakeholders
	  - Identify key stakeholders across architecture, data, process
	  - Draft communications plan
	  - Agree with key sponsor and stakeholders
	  - Where stakeholders are to be interviewed, arrange interviews
	  - Where a questionnaire is to be used, prepare questionnaire
	  - Where a workshop is to be used, prepare workshop
	  - Send out questionnaire
	  - Distribute briefing information for workshops
	  - Distribute preparation material for interviews
	  - Perform interviews
	  - Run workshops
	  - Collate and document responses
	  - Collate and document pain points
	  - Upload to project repository

OUTPUTS	

- Detailed scope
- Draft communications plan
- Where a questionnaire is to be used, the questionnaire
- Where a workshop is to be used, the workshop preparation
- Questionnaire and workshop responses
- Pain points
- Initial list of architecture issues
- Initial list of architecture options for remediation
- Issues, impacts, and costs for remediation
- Domains in scope
- Systems in scope
- Data scope
- Initial list of data issues using documentation and output from interviews, workshops and questionnaires
- Initial list of data options for remediation
- Issues, impacts, and costs for remediation
- Process scope
- High level CRUD matrix
- Initial list of process issues using documentation and output from interviews, workshops and questionnaires
- Initial list of process options for remediation
- Issues, impacts, and costs for remediation
- Objectives in each area
- Scope in each area
- The overall cost of poor quality for the organisation
- Cost of remediation
- Cost benefit analysis of project
- Initial business case
	- Initial Architecture Assessment
	  - From project brief identify domains in scope
	  - From project brief identify systems in scope
	  - From project brief identify processes in scope
	  - Document architectural scope
	  - Identify key architectural documents
	  - Obtain key architectural documents
	  - Draft initial list of issues using documentation and output from interviews, workshops and questionnaires
	  - Estimate impact of issues
	  - Draft initial list of options for remediation
	  - Estimate cost of remediation
	  - Document issues, impacts, and costs for remediation
	  - Upload to project repository
	- Initial Data Assessment
	  - From project brief identify domains in scope
	  - From project brief identify systems in scope
	  - Document data scope
	  - Identify key data documents
	  - Obtain key data documents
	  - Draft initial list of issues using documentation and output from interviews, workshops and questionnaires
	  - Estimate impact of issues
	  - Draft initial list of options for remediation
	  - Estimate cost of remediation
	  - Document issues, impacts, and costs for remediation
	  - Upload to project repository

- Presentation pack for board

DEPENDENCIES

- Subject matter experts
- Executive time
- Access to key stakeholders
- Access to systems
- Access to processes and/or process documentation
- Architecture documentation
- System documentation

- Initial Process Assessment
  - From project brief identify domains in scope
  - From project brief identify processes in scope
  - Document scope
  - Identify key process documents
  - Obtain key process documents
  - Create high level CRUD matrix
  - Draft initial list of issues using documentation and output from interviews, workshops and questionnaires
  - Estimate impact of issues
  - Draft initial list of options for remediation
  - Estimate cost of remediation
  - Document issues, impacts, and costs for remediation
  - Upload to project repository
- Objectives
  - Collate issues from the initial assessment
  - Discuss with sponsor and key stakeholders
  - Update the objectives for the project
  - Document objectives in each area
  - Upload to project repository
- Scope
  - Update scope based on Objectives
    - Based on objectives and pain points define scope in terms of business areas
    - Define scope in terms of architecture
    - Define scope in terms of process and systems
  - Discuss and agree with sponsor and key stakeholders
  - Document scope in each area
  - Upload to project repository
- Risks, Assumptions and dependencies
  - Document high level risks, assumptions and dependencies using the RAID log as source
- Analysis of Poor Quality Cost
  - Collate details of pain points
  - Estimate financial impact of pain points
  - Draft the overall cost of poor quality for the organisation
  - Agree with key sponsor and stakeholders
  - Update as required
- Option Appraisal
  - Collate options for remediation
  - Estimate cost of options
  - Document cost of remediation
  - Agree with key sponsor and stakeholders
- Cost Benefit Analysis
  - Document cost benefit analysis of project
  - Agree with key sponsor and stakeholders
  - Upload to project repository
- Prepare Business Case
  - Draft template and agree with key sponsor
  - Add project definition
  - Add project approach
  - Add cost benefit analysis
  - Add risk assessment and management strategy

The Data Quality Blueprint

	- Add change assessment and management strategy
	- "Add data, process and architecture assessment"
	- Add pain points
	- Finalise initial business case
	- Agree with key sponsor
	- Socialise with key stakeholders
	- Prepare presentation pack for board
	- Present to board
	- Obtain signoff
	- Upload to project repository

"Without a business case, good data will lose to other priorities"
Tom Redman, 2012

A critical element of the initiation stage will be the creation of a business case to underpin the whole project. The business case starts life as the project brief and builds this out into more detail. It is important that nothing should be done that does not impact the bottom line in some (positive) way. Before any large project is undertaken, an investigation of business pain points and an impact analysis of these pain points should be made to prove the business case before further funds are approved. It is essential to make specific data quality issues directly relevant to the business rather than referring to vague and unformed statements of how poor data quality may affect some non-specific business issues. The objective here is to make the business case watertight and limit the ability for the business case to be criticised.

Barclays

FSA fines Barclays £2.45m for providing inaccurate trading data

City regulator penalises Barclays Capital for 'serious weaknesses' in its transaction reporting

Common statements I have heard include: "well, that won't be a problem here because...", "we're different, that won't work here", "we tried and it didn't work before", "Well, of course, whilst I agree what you are proposing would be the ideal situation, here in reality..." The business case is essential to prove that what you are proposing will work, will work here, and will work this time. It should also be noted that it is not necessary to justify the whole data quality remediation project in one go – and neither should it be attempted. The business case should be looking to do enough to justify an initial exploratory phase of work, but also to give an idea of the scale of the savings possible for the whole project. In this chapter I look to step through the contents of the business case, outlining what it should include and why, and how the project can determine the contents.

A typical business case should contain the following components:

- Background
- Reasons for undertaking the project
- Objectives
- Scope
- Options
- Cost-benefit analysis
- Timescale
- Proof of Concept
- Risks

I will now discuss each of these in detail.

19.3 Background

The background section of the business case should provide basic information to enable a reader to orientate themselves and understand the project. The business case should stand alone, and not need supporting information. Not only is this better as all the information is in one place, but the business case is likely to be viewed or reviewed by many individuals who need a basic grounding in the project (and the organisation) as a whole. This is especially the case if external organisations or individuals without an intimate knowledge of the organisation are utilised for funding or oversight. The background section of the business case should therefore include information such as, but not limited to:

- Basic information about the company
- The background to the company
- The reason for the focus on data quality
- The reasons why it is important

It may also be useful to include information on how any data quality problem developed in the first place, for example that a recent acquisition resulted in siloed data and duplicated customers.

19.4 Reasons for Undertaking the Project

The reasons for undertaking the project will often divide into three areas, specifically those examined in detail in the earlier chapter:

- Data quality improvements to meet regulatory requirements
- Data quality improvement to meet strategic improvements
- Data quality improvements to meet operational improvements

The reasons for undertaking the project as described in this section of the business case should be designed to start the buy-in process. This section should outline business drivers that will convince a reader that the project is worth doing. For example:

"XYZ Plc is under pressure from the regulator due to inconsistent returns over the last 6 months. The regulator requested that XYZ plc undertake an investigation into this issue

and rectify the problems within 12 months. This investigation has recently completed and concluded that the inconsistency was due to underlying data quality problems in the customer and product database. The project is therefore proposed that will address these issues within the timescale required by the regulator."

Or, for another example,

"XLZ Plc recently undertook the first of three major data migration projects to migrate data to the new savings, loans and insurance platforms. Savings data was chosen as the first migration due to the comparative simplicity of the data. The migration ran 50% over budget and 12 months over time due to significant data quality problems in the underlying source systems, and was not able to complete the migration of all data. XYZ Plc has decided that before the second and third migrations are attempted that the data should be cleaned, given that this will result in significant business benefit as well as a reduction in risk that the migration projects will not deliver."

By the end of the "reasons" section, the reader should have a pretty good idea of why the project is being undertaken, and the high level drivers behind the business case.

19.5   Pain Points, Objectives and Scope

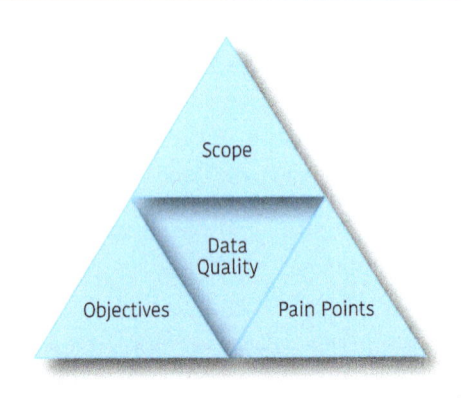

One of the first considerations for any data quality project must be the objectives and the scope. Specifically, what is the project trying to achieve and what parts of the overall organisation and its landscape are going to fall within its boundary. However, in some cases what the project is trying to achieve will be the resolution of some (or all) of the business pain points, which may not be known in detail or in full at the outset. As a result there is a three way relationship between scope, objectives and pain points.

The [objective] for the project is to solve the [pain points] within the [scope]. Scope, objectives and pain points will therefore inform each other. Typical options are:

A: SET PAIN POINTS FIRST. We discover the pain points (the places where an organisation is not working as well as it should and is causing issues for the customer, or for the staff) in the organisation. This determines scope, and the objective is to solve the problems.

B. SET SCOPE FIRST. We set the scope to "Division A", "the finance data", or "the data in the UK" and then restrict all work to the pain points in Division A, finance data or the UK. The objectives are then to solve those pain points.

C: SET OBJECTIVE FIRST. We set the objective as "improve our regulatory reporting" and the scope is then all data that contributes to regulatory reporting, and the objective is to solve the problems that are found in respect of the regulatory reporting.

Given this is a holistic approach the preferred option is the first, where the scope is set by the pain points. A fuller explanation is that we set a high level aspiration to improve data quality in the organisation ("Top Level Objective"). We then find out where the pain points are ("regulatory reports", "finance data") across the organisation. We then set an initial scope which covers those pain points, and undertake discovery work to identify the extent of the problems and the work needed to fix them. We then re-examine the scope based on which are cost-effective to fix. We therefore need to discover the business problems, determine what needs to be solved, and hence the objectives and scope of the project.

Pain Points
Data Quality problems facing the organisiation

Objectives
What we intend to do about them

Scope
Where are they located and what systems and processes will we need to touch to achieve this

In this chapter I will start with the consideration of pain points and objectives, and then go on to a consideration of scope. This phase is going to involve a lot of discovery work, principally interviews and workshops with key stakeholders.

19.6   Pain Points

The typical causes for poor data – at a high level – within any organisation have already been discussed at length in prior chapters. The "pain points" are the symptoms, which are likely to be the starting point for any project. Find out what is going or has gone wrong, work backwards to the cause, and then look at how to solve it. A detailed discovery phase should not be attempted at this stage; however the nascent project needs to establish a clear understanding of the problems facing the organisation so it can create more detailed objectives. "Improving the information available for strategic and tactical decision-making" is, after all, somewhat unspecific.

Those running the project need to start asking questions and listening carefully in a round of information-gathering interviews, workshops and questionnaires. This will enable them to start identifying pain points and hence building the detailed business case. This will involve talking to:

- Business leaders
- Departmental leaders
- The Business Intelligence (BI) team
- Business managers
- The IT team
- Database administrators
- Contact centre agents
- Process agents

The practitioner is looking for the pain points where poor data quality is hampering the ability of the people concerned to do their job, and (if possible) the root causes which are causing the data quality in the first place. These will form the basis of first the pain points, then the objectives and scope, and finally the operational business case. However what is the practitioner looking for? They are looking for comments on the lines of the examples below.

Business Leader

- "The sales figures from department A do not make sense. We've not been able to pin it down, but the figures appear to be internally inconsistent."
- "We cannot obtain sensible data from the system. "
- "We receive too much data and none of it makes sense."

BI Team

- "We spend most of our time cleansing the data on a monthly basis before being able to use it – the first two weeks of every month is spent amalgamating and cleansing data sets, the third performing analysis and the fourth preparing the presentation for the board."
- "We never get the information from Department G until the third week of the month – they say it is because of the difficulty of getting data out of the system."

Some of the best sources of information are long serving (long serving here is the target, not seniority) DBAs or contact centre staff. These people will be aware of data quality problems and will help you discover them. These people can and will give you an absolute wealth of information. Some real-life examples are listed below.

Contact Centre Senior Agent

- "Well, before the new system was in place we didn't have a field for email address, so we used to enter it in the comments field."
- "If we find duplicate customers we add "DO NOT USE" to the customer name and then put the right customer number to use in the notes field." [38]
- "We have a lot of problems with the automatic validation on the address field as the system doesn't contain a lot of the new addresses from the new estates built round here recently, so we just override it and type it in manually."
- "The details do not pre-populate from the initial contact application system through to the setting-up-a-account system, so we have to type them all in again." [39]
- "We can only update the "death registration flag" after receiving a form from Probate (department), and they have a two month backlog so until we get that we just append "DECEASED" to the customer name." [40, 41]

---

38. Next thing you check is if several thousand letters are going out every month to variants on "Mr John Smith DO NOT USE".
39. This is incredibly common. In several organisations they are printed out and then re-typed from the printout.
40. Yes, the organisation was mailing people with "Mr John Smith DECEASED" as the customer name. Even better, some of these people were not actually dead (data quality issues again) and were wandering into branches much agitated waving correspondence which stated they were dead. This resulted in what was internally known as "The Undead Project".
41. Another organisation I am aware of found 22 different spellings of the word "Deceased".

Long Serving DBA

- "Yes, we know the data structures are a mess, we had a new enthusiastic DBA who tried to sort it out by creating a new database and moving everything into it, but he only got half-way through the job before he was made redundant."
- "Marketing wanted a new database of their own, because the live database only contains active accounts, and they wanted to be able to mail people who used to be customers to see if they wanted to re-join the company, so we created a clone of the main customer database and mashed that together with the archive. It didn't really work but they wanted it with zero notice and got the CEO to lean on us to do it over a weekend in advance of a product launch on a Monday. We made best efforts and they appear to be happy."

Bear in mind that people are NOT stupid and genuinely will try and do their job as best they can. Unfortunately, unless they have been trained to do so (99% of the time) they may think of what is best for their own job, and may not think of the effect their actions will cause downstream.

> **FSA fines Commerzbank £595,000 over inaccurate trade reports**

Existing functions

A very good place to start looking for pain points are the areas of the organisation that have the responsibility for the future state of architecture, data and process and/or the responsibility for changing and designing them. This project will not have been the first, and previous projects will have had their own successes and failures. Learning of these is a very good way to identify pain points.

Equally, architecture, data and process change and governance functions are likely to have a very good idea of the problems facing the organisation, and whilst they may not be thinking in terms of data quality, they may well be aware of issues, and may even have attempted to solve them in the past. Talking to these functions both gains the project a wealth of information, but also can provide a way of not repeating past mistakes and not creating resentment in key individuals who see a project, with a mandate, doing what they have been recommending for years, but without the project involving them.

A note on regulation

Most organisations are regulated in some way. As stated in a prior chapter, the degree of regulation and the degree to which data quality issues are relevant to the regulator will depend on the organisation and sector. Health and defence industries, and the financial sector in particular, will have strong regulatory interest in data quality, and improving data quality is likely to be a regulatory-driven objective. In order to define the pain points in relation to regulatory reporting the project needs to understand:

- What are regulatory reporting requirements?
- What challenges are being experienced in meeting them?
- How is poor data quality affecting the ability to create the regulatory reports?

In order to achieve the above you need to speak to some fairly specific individuals within the organisation. These may be the Compliance Officer, the Chief Risk Officer, those responsible for creating regulatory reports or a designated liaison with the regulator. The above should furnish you with enough information to be able to determine the pain points for data quality in relation to regulatory reporting, and hence what the project needs to solve. These are the project objectives.

19.7 Objectives

The objective of the project is the desired final outcome. This will be a description of what needs to be achieved, and is the success criteria for the project. Assuming that you are following a pain point -> objective -> scope order of development, the objectives follow from the pain points. The objectives may simply be to eradicate the pain points. Therefore the high level objectives for a data quality project may be:

- Improving the information available for strategic and tactical decision-making.
- Saving money or increasing revenue through improvements in operational data quality.
- Enabling the organisation to meet and anticipate regulatory requirements.

However, these are also very unspecific. In order to obtain buy in and develop the business case the objectives for the project need to be clearly articulated. In this case the objectives need to be broken down. For example:

- Reduce customer duplication.
- Rationalise data structures.
- Reduce time cleansing data.
- Reduce the time creating the board report.

This moves the project on to a place where the project can start looking at the systems that support the creation of the board report and the state of the data in them, so defining scope. The project objectives need to be SMART. This is a common standard for objectives and stands for:

- Specific: General objectives like "Improve regulatory reporting" or "don't waste as much time and money on projects" is too general to be an effective objective. The more specific an objective the more likely it is to be successful.
- Measurable: The objective needs to specify how it will be measured.
- Achievable: It must actually be possible.
- Relevant: It needs to be relevant to the organisation and to the problem it is trying to solve.
- Timely: A timescale by which the objectives will be achieved needs to be set.

An example of SMART objectives in this context may be:

"The objective of the project is to remediate the asset data in a period of 12 months, and success will be measured by the achievement of signoff by the regulator that they are happy with the reports that are being provided."

Or, for another example:

"The objective of the project is to remediate the loan data that will be migrated to the new strategic platform. This needs to occur in the next 6 months, and effectiveness will be measured by the percentage of the data that is successfully transferred. The success target is set at 99% of customer records."

The point of the objective is to clearly state what the project is going to achieve, and to give the project as little wriggle room as possible in terms of what is considered a success. The project needs to know where it is going.

19.8 Scope

The scope of the project needs to be defined in the business case. This needs to cover the business areas, systems and processes in scope, and equally importantly, what is not included. At the end of the discovery of pain points you should have a pretty good idea of the problems facing the organisation from the perspective of data quality, and hence what the objectives of the project need to be. The limited discovery in relation to pain points also enables you ask some intelligent questions about scope and what is in and what is not in. For example, some systems may have a perceived horrendous data quality, and others may be considered quite good. In which case there may be a case for starting with the bad and leaving the good until later – unless "good" is business critical and "bad" is not. All of this will come out of the initial investigation.

What is scope must be answered somewhere at the beginning of the process as scope is critical to the development of the business case. It will come up again in both the discovery phase and remediation planning. This is because to a certain extent the scope of a data quality project should be variable – at least at the outset – and this is because the understanding of the data landscape will change over time and as the project progresses. In fact, the ideal scope should be up to and including the point where the last element of effort is exactly balanced by the gain to the organisation that results from that last element of effort, but that point is hard to define and difficult to measure, and most organisations will decide at the start of the overall process what elements of their data landscape will be affected by any subsequent work that is put in motion. This may be defined in a number of ways, which are described below.

19.8.1 Data by Subject

Defining data by subject is a common approach. Scope may include in an increasing order of difficulty:

- One element of customer or party data
- Customer (or party) data in its entirety
- Customer (or party) and product data
- Customer (or party), product and transaction data (for example, for an insurance business, party, product and claim)

Customer or party data is the most common scope of any data quality implementation, and in fact is often seen as the whole of the data quality problem. In many organisations customer data is shared across the organisation and so poor quality in this area will be especially visible. It probably has the greatest impact across the organisation of any data, and is also the easiest data to fix as it is the most stable of the information that any organisation holds. However, there is a perception that once fixed, this information will stay fixed. This is unfortunately incorrect, I refer to the soundbite that 6 million people change address in the UK every year.

Extension to product data is the next step, which is more variable than customer data (in most cases), and again is used across the organisation. The most common extension from this point is to incorporate transaction data. Analysis and understanding of the data quality of transaction data is rarely undertaken at most organisations as it is seen as inherently correct. This is not always the case.

19.8.2   Data by Location

A second way in which the scope of a data quality project can be defined is in terms of the location of the data. I have discussed in an earlier chapter the way in which information flows, and the nature of the various data stores that exist within a typical organisation. The questions regarding data remediation may circle around setting scope as being:

- Data in the source systems
- Data in the warehouse
- Data in the reporting environment

Remediating data within the source systems is by far the best idea, as you are attacking the problem at source, but has the disadvantage that the total number of data items that are in the source systems is much larger than the number used for running the business, and care has to be taken to ensure that a lot of redundant work is not undertaken.

It should be noted here that the data as it appears on application screens to a user is a tiny fraction of the data that actually resides within the systems. There is a common disconnect when business professionals describe "all the data in the system". What they actually mean is "all the data I can see" – which may be a relatively small number of fields (say, 200). IT professionals, who can see all the data, which will include metadata, print settings, logs, update times, "last modified by user" fields etc, then become frustrated when they think they have been asked to extract or remediate 2000 fields ("all the fields"), when actually the business professionals only really mean 200. I discuss ways of cutting down the total work in a later chapter.

19.8.3   Data by application

A final way in which data quality scope can be described is by the applications on which the data resides. As explained in the data flow chapter, within each application there may be a local data store. This may be close-coupled to the application and in a proprietary format, or may be remote and an open format. The applications are the "face" of the data to the business, and often business users will refer to data stores by the application which they associate with the input of the data, which may not necessarily represent the back end architecture.

For example, a branch system (call it "BranchApp") may hold no data itself, but write to a head office mainframe. The branch staff will refer to the data as being the data "in" BranchApp, whereas actually no data is held in that system. IT staff will refer to the data in the mainframe. Confusion will result when the data that is in scope is defined as the data "in" BranchApp. Understanding issues like this need to be addressed when deciding the scope of the overall project. That being said, delineating scope by application is a common way of approaching data quality projects. This may be because a particular historical application is known to comprise a certain proportion of the overall data landscape, or a certain system is perceived to have a data quality problem – often the case.

19.8.4 Scope decisions

The overall effort (and the overall cost and effectiveness) will be highly dependent on the answers to the questions discussed above. In addition, the scope has to be extensive enough to make a real difference to the operation of the organisation yet small enough to be manageable with the resources available. Typical questions to be asked to drive out scope might be:

- Where is the business cost in relation to poor data most obvious?
- What particular applications are most historical?
- What systems are most difficult to report from?
- Where does the majority of the data in the organisation reside?
- What challenges are there in accessing data in particular systems?

The project will need to consider such questions with the project sponsor in order to complete the business case.

19.9 Business Options

The business case needs to prove to the reader that the proposed option is the best option, and why. A business case will usually present a number of increasing cost options which will generally fall into the categories below. For each option the advantages and disadvantages should be detailed. One aim of the business options is to give assurance to the reader that a range of options have been considered.

Option	Comment
Do nothing	Cheapest, but clearly does nothing to help the current situation. However this option still needs to be considered. Unfortunately all too often projects are undertaken with no real consideration as to whether they are actually necessary or will actually solve the business problem.
Do minimum	The minimum is just that – the effort that just gets over the bar and just solves the immediate problem.
Do something	The problem with "do minimum" is that it is not cost-effective. The establishment of a project, the governance, upheaval, etc, will occur whether "do minimum" or "do a bit more" is chosen. Often a substantial increase in benefit can be gained by spending a bit more than the "do minimum" scenario and moving into the "do something" area.

Option	Comment
Do something more	A further increase to "do minimum". However there will be a point where the project starts to suffer from diminishing returns – i.e. where the effort imparted to the project is not outweighed by the benefits realised.
Do lots	Most expensive, but also most comprehensive. Similarly to the "do nothing" scenario, this is unlikely to be the option to be actually put in place, however it needs to be considered to examine the utility of the benefits that would come from this level of work – it is necessary to prove that it is not really required.

19.10 Cost-Benefit Analysis

The expected benefits of the project should be listed here with the – as far as possible – costs associated with them. The expected benefits will be derived from the information received from users outlined in the initial investigation. The earlier chapters in the "impact" section of the book went into some depth regarding the costs of data quality to an organisation. For the business case, the action is to collate this information and utilise it in a structured form to support the case for doing something about it.

Whilst sound-bites, as noted above, are great for getting buy-in, after people have laughed their fill about "The Undead Issue" the hard-as-nails question is "How much is this costing us?" Within the earlier chapters it was shown how a numerical value can be estimated against poor data quality costs, and this technique should be used here to give a rough idea of the potential benefits to the organisation – for example asking staff how long they spend cleansing data before they can use it. Equally, any project is going to have costs for implementation (sometimes called dis-benefits). In the case of a data quality project the dis-benefits in the short terms are going to be:

- Business costs (personnel time)
- IT Resource costs (personnel time)
- Technology costs (cost of laptops, licenses, and similar, if required)
- The disruption caused by a lot of business questions

When it comes to putting the business impact analysis together, a common format could be:

- Issue number
- Department
- Description
- Impact
- Proposed resolution
- Proposed impact of resolution (be realistic!)

It can be seen how the use of net present value calculations or payback periods could be used here.

You may find that many problems have the same cause, and it is possible to therefore propose one change that will have a measurable impact on the business through remediation of some element of either process or data. This is why a holistic approach is much more efficient than attacking each issue separately. However, we are only discussing the initial business case here. The business case need only be indicative at this stage. The business case will be expanded into much greater detail, with a much greater certainty, after the initiation and discovery stages. Therefore the business case needs only to prove enough that the initiation and discovery stage is given the green light. In addition, the initial estimation of costs and benefits can be used as a way of informing the data quality proof of concept.

19.11   Timescale

The business case needs to outline the timescale for the project. Here it is important to be realistic. A data quality project is not going to be completed overnight. Personal experience suggests that data quality remediation projects typically take from 9 months to 2 years. I would also suggest splitting the timescale into six parts along the lines of the project stages:

1. Initiation
2. Direction
3. Discovery
4. Remediation planning
5. Remediation
6. Embedding

This is in line with the methodology outlined in this book – and needs to make clear that go ahead/abort decision points exist all the way through the project, a subject that I will discuss in more detail in the Project Planning section. This is not – and should not be – a project where a decision on huge investment is required up front – it is a modular project where the business case is re-evaluated at each stage.

19.12   Proof of Concept

It should be possible – and is very effective – to prove the business case by building a proof of concept that will demonstrate in a small way the positive effects from improving the data quality in one element of the organisation. More on this topic in the next chapter, but any organisation should not be expected to make a decision to commit resources on faith, where it may be possible to demonstrate, by use of a proof of concept, the positive effects that a project of this nature will bring.

19.13   Risks, Assumptions, and Dependencies

There will be risks associated with undertaking a data quality project, and these risks need to be documented in the business case. Risks will include, but not be limited to, the risk that project will not be successful, key person dependencies, scope creep, infrastructure changes, regulation changes, and so on. In addition, there is the potential that if one project is given the green light, other projects may not be completed or may be delayed due to resources being tied up in the data quality project. At this point interaction may be required with an organisation-wide Programme Management Office (PMO) who can identify projects whose scope, objectives or resources will overlap. A full risk assessment should not necessarily be undertaken at this time, it fits better within project planning, but some of the more obvious high level risks should be included. Equally, high level dependencies and assumptions should be included in the business case.

Financial Services Authority (FSA)

Financial Services Authority fines Commerzbank £595,000

Financial Services Authority says Commerzbank failed to submit correct reports on 1.3m transactions

19.14 Summary

In this chapter I have tried to look at the reasons behind the business case and how the business case for data quality can be developed and outlined several methods of doing so.

I have discussed pain points, objectives and scope and explained the inter-relationship between them, and the approach to discovering pain points. I have outlined the contents for the business case and given examples of what should be included in order to best support the case for data quality within the organisation. As a result of this chapter, the reader should be able to understand the nature of a business case, and take steps to create one to support a data quality project.

In the next chapter I will move on to describing one of the most powerful arguments for a data quality project – the proof of concept.

SECTION 5.1 INITIATION: OBTAINING BUY-IN

CHAPTER 20 CREATING A PROOF OF CONCEPT

20.1 Structure

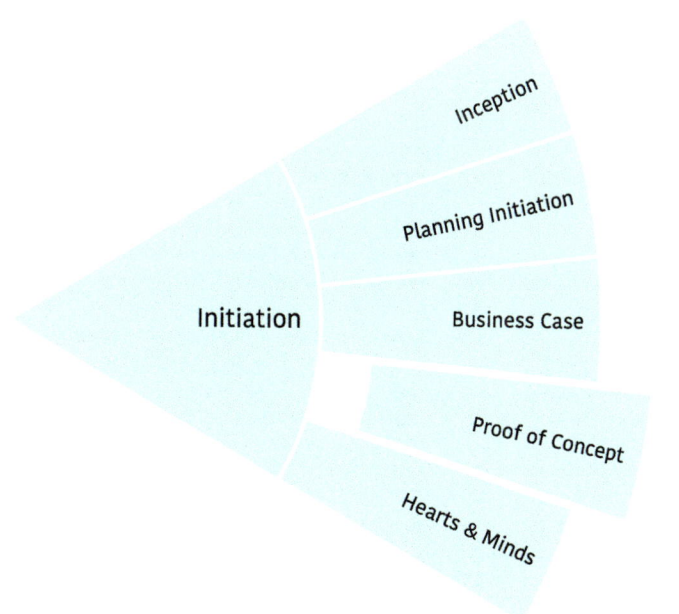

This stage of The Data Quality Blueprint includes the following phases:

1. Laying the foundations
2. Planning the initiation stage
3. Building the business case
4. Creating a proof of concept
5. Winning hearts and minds

This chapter covers the fourth of these phases.

20.2 Overview

INPUTS	TASKS
<ul><li>All artefacts created or utilised in previous stages</li><li>Business case</li><li>Pain points</li></ul>**OUTPUTS**<ul><li>Pain point to be addressed</li><li>Current cost of poor data quality in a specific area</li><li>How the effectiveness of the PoC will be measured</li><li>Expected positive effects of PoC</li><li>Expected negative effects of PoC</li><li>Implementation plan</li><li>Feedback from staff members</li><li>Other areas of the business that will experience costs/benefits</li><li>Costs and benefits</li><li>Final implementation documentation</li><li>Refined business case</li><li>Process improvements (in a defined area)</li><li>Data improvements (in a defined area)</li></ul>**DEPENDENCIES**<ul><li>Access to stakeholders</li><li>Ability to change process or data in a defined area</li><li>Access to subject matter experts</li></ul>	<ul><li>Planning Proof of Concept<ul><li>Determine if proof of concept required</li><li>Identify elements of the organisation where a PoC will show fast benefit</li><li>Identify pain point to be addressed</li><li>Determine current cost of poor data quality</li><li>Interview business and system owners of the area under consideration</li><li>Discuss implementation of a data quality proof of concept</li><li>Identify how the effectiveness of the PoC will be measured</li><li>Identify expected positive effects of PoC</li><li>Identify expected negative effects of PoC</li><li>Agree an implementation plan with the business and system owner</li><li>Document the implementation plan</li><li>Discuss and agree Implementation plan with sponsor</li><li>Upload to project repository</li></ul></li><li>Implementing Proof of Concept<ul><li>Remediate either data or process</li><li>Measure the positive and negative effects</li><li>Determine overall positive negative benefit</li><li>Obtain feedback from staff members involved (this is critical to identifying other benefits like improved customer engagement)</li><li>Obtain feedback from business owner</li><li>Identify other areas of the business that will experience costs/benefits</li><li>Interview (if required) downstream business owners to identify benefits</li><li>Quantify costs and benefits</li><li>Extrapolate the effect of rollout across the business</li><li>Write up implementation</li><li>Present results to sponsor</li><li>Finalise the implementation documentation</li><li>Upload to project repository</li></ul></li></ul>

If we assume that the driver for change is not regulation, governance or best practice but cost reduction, operational or revenue improvement or profitability, it is unlikely that any business leader is going to sign up for a full data quality project without some idea that the change is going to be a positive one – business case or no business case. The world is full of failed projects with good (paper) business cases. A pragmatic business leader will require some idea of how this is going to work. It is unreasonable for business leaders to be asked to spend funds on data quality initiatives without reasonable expectation of a positive result.

Whilst the data quality consultant, or those who suffer the effects of poor quality on a daily basis will know this without doubt, the same does not necessarily ring true of the executive. The executive sees growing profits and a healthy balance sheet despite background data quality problems. In this chapter I look to describe one of the most persuasive arguments for data quality within an organisation – the data quality Proof of Concept. This gives the executive decision makers a real feel for the benefits of a data quality project and how it will work in their organisation and the benefits that it can bring.

20.3   Challenges of Proof of Concept

> "Organisations Gartner has surveyed estimate that poor quality data is costing them on average $14M annually"
> **Gartner "Key Trends Driving the Change in Data Quality Technology"**

The Proof of Concept is a limited demonstration of the benefits of good data quality within the organisation, the point being to demonstrate real, living, business value coming out of data quality. Clearly defining the benefit of data quality improvements is a challenge as changes to data quality will ripple throughout the organisation. Although there may be a small positive change in a localised area resulting from a localised project, data quality improvements will change many areas of the business for the better, and will keep on giving positive change in the future, so measurement of an immediate change does not necessarily show the full picture. For example, an effort to reduce customer duplication will affect many areas of the business, and it is difficult to measure all of the changes. In addition many of the most significant changes are not easily measureable – how do you measure trust? How do you measure the pound value of reporting correct (rather than incorrect) figures to a regulator? Care must be taken with any Proof of Concept that all improvements are identified, otherwise the data quality effort is under-selling itself.

To use the example of 10% customer duplication:

- The customer numbers reported to the regulator are wrong.
- All customer mailings are costing 10% more than they need to.
- All queries that are run by every area of the business will take longer. Cumulatively this is likely to result in a significant time cost.
- Market share will be reported incorrectly.
- Cash flow and profitability predictions are likely to be wrong.
- Value/customer, earnings/customer and other similar metrics are incorrect.
- The customer themselves is likely to have a poor experience with the organisation as some contacts will be recorded under one customer number, some under another.
- Storage costs are 10% greater than they need to be.
- Maintenance costs will be higher.
- Remaining storage capacity is understated, hence large projects to upgrade IT infrastructure are likely to be undertaken earlier than necessary.
- The Disaster Recovery (DR) site is over-specified, and if it has to be used, it is likely to take longer to transfer operations.

20.4 Approach to a Proof of Concept

This being said, a proof of concept is perfectly possible and the raw data for the proof of concept may come straight out of a detailed impact analysis of the effect of poor quality on the business. There are three approaches, a processed-based approach, a business pound value approach and a data approach.

The method is to take a data quality cause-effect pair, improve the cause in a small way and then measure the effect.

20.5 Process-Based Approach

This approach takes one process within the organisation and measures the quality of the data generated. The effect of poor quality on the organisation in terms of cost or revenue is then determined. Steps can then be taken to improve the process and then re-measure the data quality and hence the change in cost or revenue. The benefits in terms of reduced cost or revenue against the cost of the process improvement can then be measured. For example, utilising the contact centre as an example and the cause-effect pair that is "x % of customer applications are rejected due to poor data quality":

1. Measure the general contact centre downstream data quality by measuring the data quality in customer applications from a subset of contact centre agents.
2. Take those agents and give them training on data quality, and tell them that the data quality of their work will be measured for the next two weeks.
3. Measure the improvement and the increase in time taken on calls. Call this (A).
4. Work out the percentage of applications that are rejected due to data quality issues.
5. Estimate the time costs of going back to the customer to ask for updated details or the £ cost of a rejected application. Call this (B).

If B>A then the proof of concept has demonstrated that improving data quality will return a positive investment.

20.6 Business Pound Value Based Approach

Here, the approach is to take one business area which has demonstrated that it appears to have data quality problems – for example marketing.

1. Determine the cause-effect pair. (In this case "we are mailing the wrong people or the right people multiple times.")
2. Determine how this can be addressed (design a solution in terms of data quality).
3. Address the quality issues for that element only. In the case of address data it may be that an extreme subset of the customer data file is used – perhaps individuals with a surname starting with an uncommon letter – "X", "Q" or "Z" – a small enough number that a proof of concept can be implemented for a small cost.
4. Measure and document the improvement, and the time required.
5. Demonstrate the positive return on investment.

The challenge is to accurately measure the improvement. For example, whereas there may be a direct cost in terms of mailings, there will be other cost reductions that will be difficult to determine, such as reduced costs as a result of less data to manage, reduced costs in terms of query time, and so on.

20.7 Data Approach

The approach here is to change the data and then measure the improvement in parts of the business that rely on that data. This is much more risky as there will be improvement in many different areas, so creating a valid and worthwhile proof of concept is more difficult. What is likely is that resources will be spent cleansing data, but the business effect will not be trackable, business leaders will be presented with a shiny clean data set and then say "that's nice but what benefit is that to me?". This is however the way in which many data quality projects are approached – the business case is largely built on hope and without firm metrics. The logic being:

1. We know we have a data quality problem
2. We know there is a lot of wasted time in the business resulting from our data quality problem
3. We will therefore clean up our data quality and that will solve the problem

Unfortunately, this does not give any real quantification of the problem or exactly how cleaning up the data is going to fix it. Where this approach does work is as an IT Proof of Concept. Using a real world example, if a business with 800,000 customers has 20,000 customer that are actually test cases in the live system ("Mr T Test" in this particular case) then deleting these should be possible without impacting the business in any way. The cause/effect pair in this case is "redundant data in our systems increases IT costs". It is then possible to make a number of measurements relating to data volumes – for example, run time of overnight batch jobs, running time of queries, and backup times. The change can then be implemented and positive improvement seen.

20.8 After the Proof of Concept

The next step after the Proof of Concept may be another proof of concept. It may be necessary to work round all areas of the organisation and demonstrate to all the benefits of data quality improvement. Approaching the problem in this way gives extremely powerful and tangible proof of the value of data quality to the organisation as a whole. It has the benefit of self-funding (in terms of the effort required to produce the proof of concept), and will win data quality advocates throughout the organisation. It is an important part of winning hearts and minds. You will need this to make a large-scale data quality initiative successful.

20.9 Summary

In this brief chapter I have outlined how a business-relevant Proof of Concept can be created and how that Proof of Concept will clearly demonstrate to business leaders how improvement in data quality can bring business benefit to the organisation.

I have outlined a number of approaches to the Proof of Concept and have given examples in each case of a Proof of Concept that will demonstrate the data quality business case. This should enable a reader to understand the importance of the proof of concept, and potentially will give ideas on how to create a proof of concept in their own project.

In the next chapter I will look in more detail at how the project can win the hearts and minds of the organisation.

SECTION 5.1 INITIATION: OBTAINING BUY-IN

CHAPTER 21 WINNING HEARTS AND MINDS

21.1 Structure

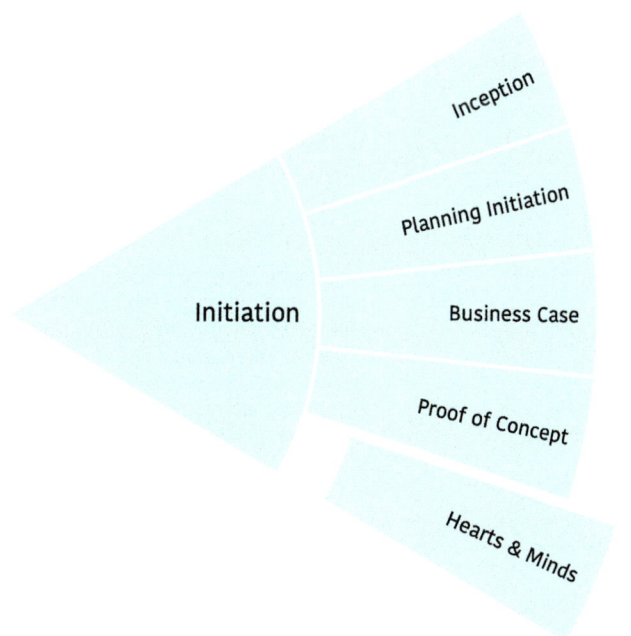

This stage of The Data Quality Blueprint includes the following phases:

1. Laying the foundations
2. Planning the initiation stage
3. Building the business case
4. Creating a proof of concept
5. Winning hearts and minds

This chapter covers the last of these phases.

21.2 Overview

INPUTS
- All artefacts created or utilised in previous stages
- Existing governance artefacts

OUTPUTS
- Updated key stakeholder list
- Stakeholder assessment template
- Interest/influence matrix
- External RACI
- Internal RACI
- Updated stakeholder assessment
- Strategy template
- Implementation plan
- Vision statement for the project
- Mission statement for the project
- Elevator pitch
- "Day in the life"
- Questionnaires
- Workshop material
- Presentation material
- Posters
- Communication plan
- Interview notes
- Interview plan
- Buy-in strategy

DEPENDENCIES
- Access to stakeholders
- Access to presentation facilities
- Access to workshop rooms
- Ability to mount posters

TASKS
- Information Gathering
  - Validate domains in scope
  - Validate business units in scope
  - Validate systems in scope
  - Update key stakeholder list
  - Input stakeholder information for all interviews, workshops and questionnaires created to date
  - Input organisation chart
  - Input business unit /organisation chart
  - Identify key system owners
  - Identify key process owners
  - Identify key data owners
  - Identify data stewards
  - Identify key influential personnel
  - Upload to project repository
- Stakeholder Assessment
  - Agree stakeholder assessment template
  - Create interest/influence matrix
  - Update external RACI
  - Identify information gaps
  - Schedule interviews to fill information gaps
  - Update stakeholder assessment
  - Agree with key sponsor
  - Upload to project repository
- Communications Strategy and Implementation plan
  - Agree strategy template
  - Define communications options
  - Define communication frequency
  - Draft implementation plan
  - Agree with sponsor and key stakeholders
  - Upload to project repository
- Initial Communications
  - Vision
    - Create vision statement for the project
    - Upload to project repository
  - Mission
    - Create mission statement for the project
    - Upload to project repository
  - Elevator Pitch
    - Create elevator pitch
    - Upload to project repository
  - Day in the life
    - Create "day in the life"
    - Upload to project repository
  - Interviews
    - Define approach from communications strategy
    - Define interviewees
    - Prepare briefing material and distribute
    - Arrange and conduct interviews

- Obtain feedback and apply to next interview
- Questionnaires
  - Define approach from communications strategy
  - Define recipients
  - Prepare questionnaire
  - Send out questionnaires
  - Obtain feedback and update approach as required
- Workshops
  - Define approach from communications strategy
  - Define delegates
  - Prepare briefing material and distribute
  - Deliver workshop
  - Obtain feedback and update approach as required
- Presentations
  - Define approach from communications strategy
  - Define delegates
  - Prepare briefing material and distribute
  - Deliver presentation
  - Obtain feedback and update approach as required
- Posters
  - Define approach from communications strategy
  - Define locations
  - Design posters
  - Mount posters
  - Obtain feedback and update approach as required

- Ongoing Communications
  - Frequency
    - Agree frequency and update as required
  - Interviews
    - Hold interviews
    - Obtain feedback and update approach as required
  - Questionnaires
    - Deliver questionnaires
    - Obtain feedback and update approach as required
  - Workshops
    - Deliver workshops
    - Obtain feedback and update approach as required
  - Presentations
    - Deliver presentations
    - Obtain feedback and update approach as required
  - Posters
    - Deliver poster campaign
    - Obtain feedback and update approach as required
  - Other methods (e.g. website, blog, etc)

"The void created by the failure to communicate is soon filled with poison, drivel and misrepresentation."
C. Northcote Parkinson

It is said in many speeches that people are what make any organisation special. Obviously special is a subjective term, and one person's special may be another person's awkward, irritating, obstructive or downright rude. Also, of course, one person will exhibit different behaviours depending on who they are talking to. For the practitioner trying to get data quality off the ground in any organisation, the people are the elements of the jigsaw that can ensure the project works or does not. It may sound like stating the obvious, but in order for any data quality initiative to succeed, it is absolutely essential that the people within an organisation:

- Understand why it is happening
- Understand the benefits it will bring
- Understand how it will be carried out
- Want it to succeed.
- Are willing to help
- Know how it will be measured.
- See the improvements in their daily work

Data quality improvement is not something that is imposed on staff – buy-in is critical. People are not all the same, so messaging has to be tailored to the recipient. It is truly amazing how many projects fail to do this. I have attended many presentations where either a 5 page deck has been presented to technical staff – who then wonder when the presentation will start, or (much more common) a 60-page deck is presented to executives (who have better things to do). It is not just length of communication, but content, approach, technique, level, and a myriad of other factors which can transform a project from a no-hoper to a certain-to-succeed. Most of these factors are people-related. When the project starts, or even before that – when it is but an apple in the eye of the sponsor or the consultant selling the work or the system integrator spying a problem, there will exist people within the organisation with:

- The will to make it work.
- A determination to ensure it doesn't.
- People who don't care.
- People who care, but in the wrong way.
- People who understand.
- People who have their own ideas on what constitutes data quality.
- People who think data quality is irrelevant.
- People who think data quality is a way of furthering their own agenda.
- People who hate projects.
- People who hate the sponsor, and will do anything to ensure the project fails, regardless of the business justification.

The more people you can move into the category of "willing to make it work", or at least "willing to play along" – the easier the whole process will be and the more likely the project is to succeed. It is worth spending the time and effort to get the buy-in, to start the positive thinking, and to ensure that as much as possible the hearts and minds of the organisation are with you. What I have tried to do in this chapter is to loosely tie together some of my experiences (the good and bad), together with some accepted approaches to people management in a way that will help the reader in the job of winning hearts and minds.

21.3 Timing of the message and repeating the message

The act of obtaining buy-in is not a one-off but an ongoing process. The project needs to both get people bought in but also keep them bought in. As a result the project will need to carefully nurture its stakeholders throughout the project lifecycle. There will be many meetings and many presentations and workshops over the course of the project. It is not the case that stakeholders will be approached just once. At the beginning of the project the information flow will be mainly from the stakeholders to the project, as the project seeks to understand the problems facing the organisation and how they can best be addressed. The information flow will then reverse, as the project socialises its intentions with the stakeholders, who will then feed back their comments and the information flow will reverse again. In some stages the project and the stakeholders will work together towards a solution.

In this chapter I will concentrate mainly on the first of the boxes below, that of obtaining buy-in, but as can be seen, the successful completion of the project depends on an ongoing successful relationship with stakeholders. In the project plan contained in the appendices you will see many separate stages where communication is occurring, and I have in no way covered all the conversations that will occur. For example, in a recent project I tried to have – as a minimum – a weekly conversation with the critical stakeholders, and a bi-weekly conversation with the rest. The first meeting is by far the most important though, as it forms the basis for the ongoing relationship, and, in any case, you don't get a second chance to make a good first impression.

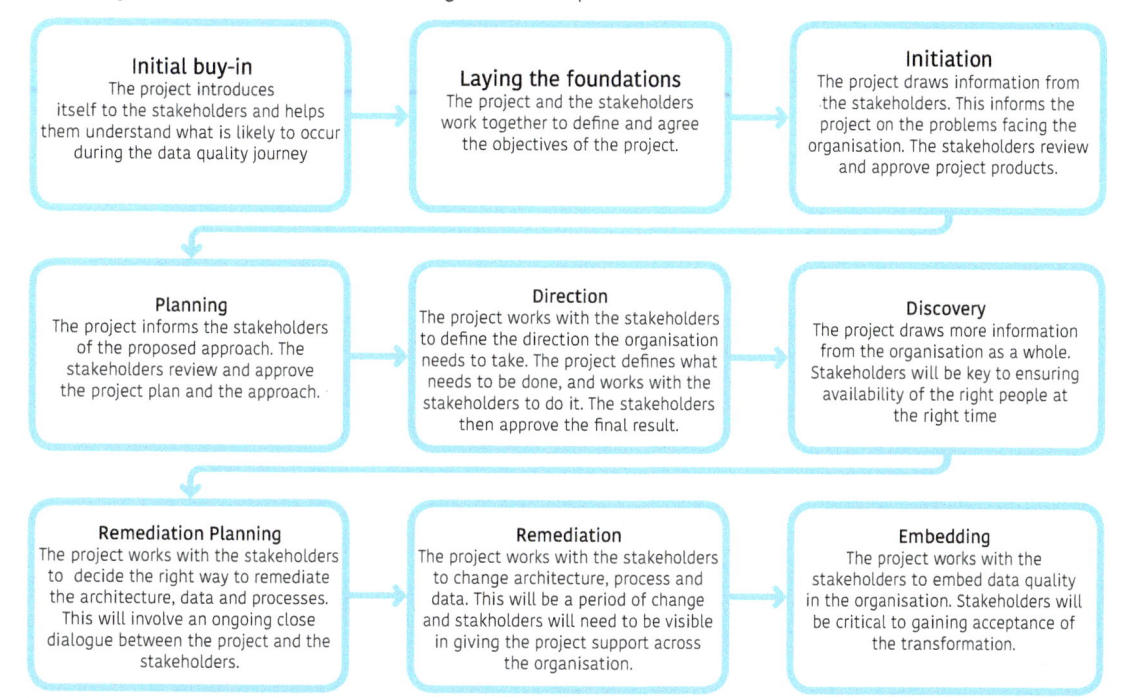

Initial buy-in
The project introduces itself to the stakeholders and helps them understand what is likely to occur during the data quality journey

Laying the foundations
The project and the stakeholders work together to define and agree the objectives of the project.

Initiation
The project draws information from the stakeholders. This informs the project on the problems facing the organisation. The stakeholders review and approve project products.

Planning
The project informs the stakeholders of the proposed approach. The stakeholders review and approve the project plan and the approach.

Direction
The project works with the stakeholders to define the direction the organisation needs to take. The project defines what needs to be done, and works with the stakeholders to do it. The stakeholders then approve the final result.

Discovery
The project draws more information from the organisation as a whole. Stakeholders will be key to ensuring availability of the right people at the right time

Remediation Planning
The project works with the stakeholders to decide the right way to remediate the architecture, data and processes. This will involve an ongoing close dialogue between the project and the stakeholders.

Remediation
The project works with the stakeholders to change architecture, process and data. This will be a period of change and stakeholders will need to be visible in giving the project support across the organisation.

Embedding
The project works with the stakeholders to embed data quality in the organisation. Stakeholders will be critical to gaining acceptance of the transformation.

21.4 Get the message at the right level

In order to effectively initiate, plan, implement and embed data quality communication is critical at every stage. Unfortunately, as previously stated it is often the case that data quality is communicated to all levels of the organisation in the same manner. The same language is used to the CEO as is used to the user, as is used to a Database Administrator (DBA). Depending on the specific CEO, or the specific DBA, this may not be appropriate.

It should be fairly obvious that the varying levels of the organisation are going to best respond to differing levels of communication. A CEO is going to have different priorities and different interests to the business user, and the same will apply to the DBA. A CEO is unlikely to be happy sitting through a presentation that discusses the details of field constraints when all they are bothered about is how this will affect the bottom line. Equally, a DBA is likely to feel that a presentation that is designed for a CEO does not contain enough detail to even begin to think about how it will affect them. This harks back to the discussions about different views of the organisation we had when talking about architecture earlier in the book. When thinking about communication we should consider the organisation in multiple levels, divided by level of technical interest (or the level of detail required) and also by the place at which the various individuals sit. An indicative matrix might be:

Level	Executive	Business	IT
High Detail	—	User	DBA
Medium Detail	CIO	Manager	Head
Low Detail	CEO	Head	—

It is easy – but wrong – to design a communications strategy based on a large presentation where bits are chopped out for the various user bases. The focus needs to totally change when presenting to each different audience. A CEO is going to spot a chopped-down IT-orientated presentation immediately and likewise the typical DBA.

Another unfortunately common trait is that the individuals at the bottom of the organisation are not deemed important enough to require (or deserve) a full explanation. "Oh, they are not interested" is a common refrain – "they just want their pay packet at the end of the week". I have heard this more than once. Whilst this may be true for some, the intelligence and engagement of coalface staff should absolutely not be underestimated. It is through their hands that data enters the organisation's systems. If they are not bought into the process then the project will in all likelihood fail.

There are other stakeholders outside the organisation who are often not considered within the communications strategy. Consider the regulator, who is going to be extremely interested in what a data quality project will do, how it is going to be achieved and what the results will be. Equally – and it depends on the relationship here – the auditors will certainly be interested in what is going on. Suppliers and customers are also going to be interested, but in a different way. What is communicated and what is the best strategy will depend on the stage of the project, what the project is trying to achieve, and who is the target of the communication.

Lastly, if there are multiple people who are going to be responsible for delivering the project message, make sure they are all delivering the same message.

21.5 Liaison with existing functions

A data quality project – especially one that is looking at the organisation holistically, will be interacting with all areas of the organisation, and may well propose change in order to improve the quality of information within the organisation. As such it has the potential to upset many people.

Many individuals throughout the organisation may have attempted to improve data quality over time, and the reason the data quality project exists is presumably because they have been un-successful. However just because the data quality project has a mandate and a problem to solve does not mean that pre-existing initiatives should be ignored, and certainly the people involved in pre-existing initiatives will be a mine of useful information as to what works and more importantly what does not work. These people need to be brought into the project and treated with respect, as otherwise, if the project continues with blinkers on, ignoring them, at the minimum great resentment will build up and the project will have created an enemy, at worst the project will waste time and resources making all the same mistakes as prior projects, and be ineffective at the same time. I repeat the mantra of doing as little work as possible. The project should never think it knows best, and approaching the organisation with knowledgeable humility is a much better approach than arriving with an attitude problem, however strong the mandate.

The same applies to existing change functions. Bring them in, and let them help. In fact ask for their help. The project (especially if being run by an external agency) is not an expert on the organisation and how it reacts to change. Performing a change management assessment is not as good as living with the organisation and trying to implement change on a daily basis for years.

Finally, the same applies to architectural, business process and data management functions. These functions, if they exist, will not appreciate a project coming in and running roughshod over their hallowed ground. Central to winning the hearts and minds of an organisation is not annoying people. Bring these people in and make them part of the project team and ask them the best ways of developing the solution. It is likely that all of the problems that a data quality project is looking to solve will have been faced before, solutions will have been proposed, and potentially implemented. That the solutions may not have been effective may not have been the fault of those designing or implementing them

In short, the project may consider itself as linking knowledgeable individuals and bringing them together under an umbrella that happens to have a strong mandate. This is a much better approach than creating resentment, anger, and repeating the mistakes of the past.

21.6 Communications Strategy

The exact how, where and why of how to communicate can be rolled together into a communications strategy. So, how do you build a communications strategy? There are some key stages, which I have outlined below.

- Set overall principles
- Propaganda:
  Elevator Pitches and Day in the life
- Stakeholder analysis
- Communication planning
- Targeting and Execution
- Sustain/Keep happy

I will now look through these phases in more detail.

21.7 Principles

The first thing to re-iterate is that winning hearts and minds is related to people. Many projects work on the basis of "we are implementing this technology solution, like it or leave". These may not be the words actually used, but that is certainly the mission statement. This is not a way to bring people along with you. It is a way to build resentment and guarantee your project to failure. If you can help people realise and understand how their life will change for the better after the end of the project, then you are much more likely to get participation and (most importantly) active participation. Equally, different styles are necessary for each individual within the organisation. This should be noted – each individual. Not each department, not each business area, each individual. When you encounter a blocker (and anyone can be a blocker) then you need to understand what makes them tick and how you can overcome their resistance, and this means understanding them as an individual. You need to understand;

- What their objections are.
- Why they have those objections.
- Is it because they don't really understand what has been proposed?
- Is it because they feel threatened?
- Is it because they have another agenda you don't know anything about?
- Is it because they have family problems that are causing stress which is spilling over into their working life?

You need to be the person they see as the gateway to less stress, less work and an easier life. This is convenient, as often that is exactly what a data quality project will bring them.

21.8 Propaganda: The Elevator Pitch and Day in the Life

21.8.1 The Elevator Pitch

The data quality practitioner will bump into many critical individuals in unforeseen places. One critical element in communication of any data quality project (and in winning the hearts and minds) is being able to get across in a short timescale what you are looking to achieve and why, and with luck, why it will benefit either the organisation or the recipient.

These are commonly called elevator pitches in that they pre-suppose a scenario where you get into a lift with your "target" and then – given this fortunate moment – have the time for the elevator to move between floors to transfer as much information as you can in as best a fashion as possible. You need to get really good at elevator pitches. Having one to hand, in the back pocket, so to speak, will make your life and the life of the project considerably easier if trotted out at regular intervals. A selection of pitches to give to different target levels of the organisation is even better.

21.8.2 Regulatory

In a highly regulated industry it may be much simpler to win hearts and minds as the organisation needs to address data quality issues in order to continue in operation without significant unwelcome attention. The current challenges some organisations are having with BCBS 239 & Solvency II in the financial industry being a case in point. When using the regulatory boot to sell a business case, the sales points are:

1. Data quality is an increasing focus of the regulator.
2. You need to be able to demonstrate that you are on top of the problem.
3. You need to be able to demonstrate that you don't have a problem.
4. Otherwise you will be in trouble.

To build this type of sales pitch, the practitioner will need a good knowledge of the regulation that faces the industry, how this knowledge is relevant to data quality and a good knowledge of the data landscape of the organisation. Real life elevator pitches have been:

Executive level

"Within our industry an increasing number of critical regulations are coming in place which mandate data quality. These are: (Insert Relevant Regulations Here)

Data quality is linked to these regulations because : (insert direct links to regulation). There are some situations where poor data quality resulted in large fines or unwelcome attention from the regulator.

Therefore we recommend addressing data quality issues – or at least undertaking work to identify if we have any data quality issues and how they affect us – before the regulator comes knocking."

Senior and Middle Management Level

"As a result of current regulatory attention we need to ensure that our data quality is up to scratch, especially in relation to the numbers that we supply to the regulator. As a result I am working with [INSET NAME OF SPONSOR HERE] to initiate a project that will look at data quality across the organisation. I would be really interested in talking to you to know your views about existing data issues that are affecting you and your team."

21.8.3 Non-regulatory Elevator pitches

Again, real life elevator pitches below.

"It's become increasingly obvious through feedback from users, managers and customers that we have a data quality problem in the organisation, and we want to do something about it. We reckon we can save money, but at the same time make lives easier if we clean up our act. I'm working with [INSERT NAME OF SPONSOR HERE] on a project that will look at data quality across the organisation. I would be really interested in talking to you to know your views about existing data issues that are affecting you and your team."

"If we want to really compete with the market leaders we need to clean up our data quality.

Our competitors are making decisions before we can even start to think. It is all about quality – we spend too much time cleansing data that should be right from the start. Let's clean it up, and it will mean we can make better decisions and be faster and more responsive. We'll save money and keep the regulator happy too."

I'm sure that by this point the idea is obvious. From my own point of view, I would say that a typical elevator pitch divides into three sections.

- What are we doing?
- Why are we doing it?
- Why is it important that YOU (the listener) are involved?

Look for a maximum of about 100 words and get delivery speed to about 30-40 seconds. Practice it until you are pitch and speed **perfect**. Then use it on everyone you talk to. You will notice in the above examples that the last point is about buy-in. If you can make people feel valued (and they will have value to contribute) then your chances of getting productive buy-in are vastly increased. People like to have their views considered, they like to have input and they (generally) want to help.

21.8.4   A day in the life

Another effective sales tool that can be used for data quality projects is the idea of "the day in the life". This is also known as future state vision, but at a more granular level. A day in the life is a detailed description of what the future will look like after the project is finished and how the day to day operation of the individual will have changed. It goes without saying that this must be both different and better than the current state. From the data quality perspective this may include:

- Not having to explain to management why the number of customers via your report is two customers different from the number of customers from their report.
- Not having to amalgamate lots of data from many sources to do your work.
- Extracting data from the system and it being complete, with no gaps, and containing the information you want.
- The data being right when you get it, and not having to put through many manual amendments.
- You won't have to spend time working out which data is the correct data.
- From the CEO perspective, all departments will sing the same tune.

The "day in the life" makes the concept live. It takes what could be a dry and boring subject and transforms it into a vision-with-reality, something that people throughout the organisation can relate to. It is also something that needs to be pitched at the appropriate level, and – in the same manner as elevator pitches – more than one may be required.

21.9 User Stories

An interesting approach to winning hearts and minds is to create user stories. User stories are most often utilised as a technique of requirement creation for agile software development. The problem with data quality is that, despite the impacts mentioned earlier in the book, it is often very difficult for the data quality practitioner to convince stakeholders that data quality will really make a difference to their everyday life. User stories complement the "day in the life" and highlight the problems caused by data quality throughout the organisation.

A user story is in the form of: "As a <role>, I want <goal/desire> so that <benefit>". For data quality, user stories may include:

- As an executive, I need to know that the information I base my decisions on is correct so I can have the confidence I am making the right decisions.
- As a departmental manager, I need to be confident that my staff are not wasting time re-creating data in order to ensure they are productive.
- As a company accountant, I need to know the figures are reliable so I can use them to calculate the most effective use for the organisation's money.
- As a data analyst, I need to know the data is correct to ensure I am providing genuine insight to the business.
- As a departmental manager, I need accurate information on the performance of my staff so that I can manage feedback and training.
- As a regulator, I need to have confidence in the information supplied to me by the organisation so I can manage the industry effectively.
- As a consumer I need to know that the information provided to me is accurate so my interactions with the organisation are as efficient as possible.
- As a shareholder I need to know that the annual accounts are accurate in order to enable me to make the best investment decisions.
- As a shareholder I need to know that the annual accounts are accurate in order to enable me to judge the effectiveness of the executive.
- As an investor I need to be able to rely on the information given to me by the organisation so I know that my investment is safe.
- As a call centre agent I need to be able to access accurate information in order to give the customer the best possible service.
- As a member of the branch staff all interactions with the customer depend on information. Without good quality information I cannot do my job.
- As a member of the risk and compliance function I need trustworthy and accurate information in order to accurately gauge the risk exposure of the organisation.
- As a marketing professional I need to be confident of the information in the organisation so I can suggest the right products to the right people.
- As a marketing professional I need to be confident of the information in the organisation so I can understand the current product use, what customers want, and hence design attractive products.
- As a treasury professional I need good information on the current financial risk, so that I can mitigate it.

- As a member of the customer complaints team I need good information on how a customer has been treated, in order to ensure I can take the best action.
- As an auditor, I need good information in order to gauge the organisations risk profile and give an accurate report on going concern.
- As an auditor, I need to be able to trust information systems, as I rely on information systems to provide the evidence to prove my findings.

My view is that user stories can throw into stark relief the consequences of poor quality information, and the way in which poor quality information affects all areas of the organisation. Especially for organisations familiar with the more traditional use of user stories, this approach may prove effective.

This approach also opens the overall project up to a regular review of the user stories. Is the departmental manager confident their staff are no longer wasting time re-creating data, and if that is the case, can the project be said to have achieved at least one of its goals?

21.10 Stakeholder Analysis

21.10.1 Seniority is no guide

The people most affected by data quality in the organisation on a day to day, operational basis, are unlikely to be the most senior people. The people who will be affected daily by poor data quality will be the upper and middle management. On the other hand, the people who you really need to buy in are the people who do the primary data capture and manipulation. A table covering the perceived level in an organisation against the nature of their view and their ability to directly affect data quality is shown below.

Area	Organisational Perceived Level	General feeling	Overall view	Ability to directly affect data quality
Board	High	Valued	Will have a holistic view	Low
Upper Management	High	Valued – they have departmental budgets, responsibilities, are consulted on changes. They have titles like "Head of Information Management"	Will have a holistic view	Low
Middle Management	Medium	Undervalued		High
Operational Management	Medium	Undervalued. Feel that middle and upper management don't really know what it is like to actually run the organisation, and don't have to deal with the day to day operations.	Unlikely to have a view of how their actions affect downstream	High

		Are likely to see data quality initiatives as simply another burden imposed from on high, and in terms of quality will likely to do their best but also likely to do what is most expedient.	departments	
Team leader	Low	Will feel entirely unvalued by the organisation. Will see themselves as un-cared for. Worse, will have probably raised data quality issues in the past and probably have been ignored.	Unlikely to care about downstream departments	High
Coalface worker	Low	Will feel entirely unvalued by the organisation. Will see themselves as un-cared for.	Unlikely to care about downstream departments	Extremely High

As the table above shows, there is an inverse relationship between the seniority of an individual within the organisation and their ability to directly affect data quality. Whilst winning hearts and minds, it is not enough to concentrate on a few senior stakeholders. You need to drill down to the base level, make people feel valued, and get their buy in – a failure to do this is why some data quality projects do not succeed.

21.10.2   Methodologies

There are many ways of ranking stakeholders and I will go through a number of the key ones that can help a project.

RACI

A RACI matrix is a popular way of categorising people and their attitude to a project. As a starter I think it is a reasonable approach. RACI stands for Responsible, Accountable, Consulted and Informed.

- "Responsible" is the person (or persons) who are responsible for a deliverable. They are the guys who will actually put pen to paper or fingers to keyboard and do the work.
- "Accountable" is the person where the buck stops. They are accountable for the work being done, though they may – or may not – do the work themselves. Only one person can ever be accountable for one item, and ideally it should be a named individual – committees are bad at being accountable as it is difficult to nail down who is actually going to be the accountable individual.
- "Consulted" is people whose views need to be taken into account.
- "Informed" describes those who need to be kept in the loop, but are not going to interact in any other way.

The usual approach here is to take all the deliverables and create a RACI matrix, an example below.

	Person A	Person B	Person C	Person D
Deliverable 1	A	R	C	C
Deliverable 2	R	I	C	A
Deliverable 3	AR	C	C	C

The problem with RACI, in my opinion at least, is that it does not go far enough. For example, "Informed" means what, exactly? Does it mean they get copied in to the emails, or invited to the meetings, and the weekly meetings, or just the monthly ones, or do they just receive a newsletter? How will people be consulted? Face to face, receive hundreds of emails asking if they have any views, invited to meetings, and so on. It is the lack of an individual approach and the treating of people as broad-brush groups that falls short here. What is the preference for the individual? Many senior people are in back to back meetings during the day and then catch up with their emails at evenings or weekends. For them a face to face meeting will cut into already busy time but a detailed email can be perused at leisure – or they may not want a detailed email but just highlights. The project needs to communicate in the manner that is most likely to please the individual you are trying to communicate with. People can get annoyed by too much communication of the wrong sort as much as by not enough, and you cannot afford to throw away the goodwill of any individual. At the least, a line at the bottom of an email stating that "we have contacted you according to your preferences, if these change, or you would like a different level of interaction with us and the project, then please let us know" can work wonders.

Power/Interest Grid

Another useful tool is the power/interest grid. By mapping key stakeholders onto the grid above it is possible to define the level and type of effort required to keep them happy.

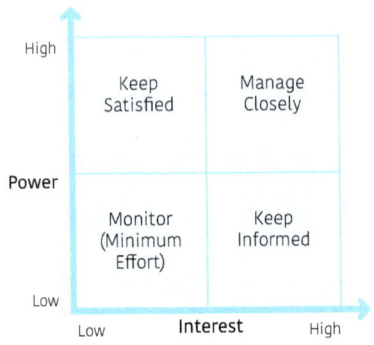

In the top right are the people who you must actively engage and satisfy. These are the high interest, high power individuals. People with high power but low interest need to be kept satisfied, and the work should be performed with this goal in mind. They do not need regular updates; they just need an occasional state-of-the-nation communication. Low power but interested people need to be kept informed. However, these people can be key to the successful performance of the project. Many individuals performing primary input will come into this category. Lastly are individuals with low power and little interest. These individuals need to be monitored but little else.

Combination grid

Personally whilst I think the above two methods are good, neither tells the whole story. Given each project is different, I think that a better approach is using a grid specific to the project that covers the elements that are going to be relevant for the project, and then using this in conjunction with the RACI. An example of this kind of approach is shown below.

	Position	Influence	Interest	Business Area	Preferred communication method	Key Concerns	Key Benefits	Capacity
Stakeholder 1								
Stakeholder 2								
Stakeholder 3								

Of course, there may be people who want to be contacted in a different way depending on their interest in the deliverable in question. This can be accounted for by amending the grid above. This covers the stakeholder analysis element of the communications strategy, at this point it is time to move on to the planning.

21.11   Communication Planning

Methods of engagement for stakeholders vary wildly, and are not just limited to interviews. Methods of engagement can include:

- Interviews
- Surveys
- Focus groups
- Workshops
- Weekly/monthly/daily updates
- Posters in the office

The more time invested in a stakeholder the more valued a stakeholder is going to feel. Interviews will best convey the message that the interviewee is valued by the project. It is perfectly possible to use this to help the buy-in of critical individuals – the more time you spend with them, the more important and bought-in they will feel.

21.11.1   Interviews

For interviews, preparation is absolutely essential. Before the interview you should know:

- Who the person is, and what their position is in the organisation
- How they will be directly affected by the data quality project
- Will this be a negative or positive effect?

- For any of the negatives, how you can mitigate them (they will ask, and having the answers – and believable answers – up your sleeve helps a lot)
- How will their staff be affected?
- Are they, personally, likely to be with the project or against it?
- Have they raised any data quality issues recently?
- Do you know of any data quality issues that personally have affected them?

A badly prepared interview is a good way of wasting your time, the interviewee's time, and turning them from potentially a willing helper to a blocker. You cannot afford this kind of failure. An interview is often seen as simply a way of extracting information from the stakeholders – it should not be – an interview is a key way in which you sell the project to the stakeholders and how you obtain their buy-in. Examples in the table below:

Information received	Likely current situation	Interview tip
Interview with the CEO has indicated that the monthly reports are always late and full of errors	The CEO gives grief to the person supplying the report. Probably on a monthly basis.	When talking to the person who supplies the information to the CEO, ask about supply times for the board pack. Stress that data quality improvement will mean that less work will be have to be done to create the board pack, and it can be done quicker.
CEO says that the number of customers is always different depending on who you talk to	CEO sends round many emails querying figures	Stress that in the new world not only will it be much more likely that the figures will agree in the first place, but that there will be an escalation point for all data quality concerns.
Coalface staff complain that much of their time is spent trying to work out which of the myriad customer numbers with similar names is the correct one	That they will get around the situation by duplicating customers, and the problem becomes self-sustaining	Point out that both data and process are being looked at during the project, and that there will be an escalation point for all data quality issues available to everyone. With coalface staff, they really need to be bought on board, and are often undervalued by the organisation. Special love and care needs to be taken here to combat probably many years of complaints not being taken seriously.

What you need to take away:

- What they want from the project
- What they want from you.
- How are they prepared to help?
- What can they bring to the project?

What you need to think about:

- If they are implacably opposed, how will you manage this?

- Is the project going to affect their job security? (If they currently spend most of their time data cleansing then what will they do in the new world?)
- If they are opposed, how can they be won around?
- Do they have an agenda they will try and use you or the project to promote?

21.11.2   Online Surveys

Surveys have the advantage of being really efficient ways of gathering information, but the disadvantage that they come across as impersonal. The other disadvantage is that the annoyed and irate will tend to out-shout (in terms of response rate) the happy and fulfilled. We have all answered surveys which are irrelevant, or ask stupid questions, so (and this may appear common sense) some thought has to go into online surveys. Surveys, although often seen as a way of getting information out of people, can also be a way of getting information into people. For example, consider the two survey questions below:

Example 1

"How much time do you spend performing rework on data that comes out of the source systems?"

Example 2

"By improving data quality across the board, we are trying to reduce the amount of work that people need to do on a day to day basis to improve the quality of the data that comes out of the source systems. In order to do this we need to work out how much time is spent doing this work. We think this work should be unnecessary if the data quality was good but we want to be sure that there is a clear benefit to our approach.

Hence can you let us know how much time you spend reworking data that comes out of the source systems?"

The difference in terms of the respondent is clear. The second question gives:

- Information on why the question is being asked
- Makes it more personal
- Makes it clear that the reason for asking is to help the respondent
- Makes it clear that the approach is business-focused
- Is, frankly, a lot nicer to answer

The first question turns people off; the second promotes buy-in.

21.11.3   Focus groups/Workshops

Focus groups or workshops get all the active participants into the same place at the same time. This can be extremely effective – with all individuals in the same place decisions can be taken quicker (there is no blocker where five other people need to be consulted every time a question is asked) and participants can feed off each other. Facilitation is, however, key. Large meetings will fail to deliver as focus can be lost; meetings start within meetings as individuals with their own agenda interfere with the overall progress, and particularly vocal individuals can dominate the meeting leaving others, less vocal but with no less valid a point of view, without a voice. It is necessary in any such situation to employ a facilitator who will bring authority to the meeting, manage the participation, and keep the meeting on track, as well as understanding that some people prefer to give immediate answers and others prefer to give their answers after a period of reflection.

21.11.4   Posters

Posters have the disadvantage that they are one-way and passive, but have the advantage that they are cheap and can hit a large audience. You have to be wary of using posters, and if you are going to put them up you need to be non-discriminatory. The best posters are those which are in all areas of an organisation, from the boardroom to the canteen, and give actual, relevant, useful information, such as:

- Purpose of project
- Timeline
- What's going on and when?
- How it will affect each area of the organisation

Pease note: staff will notice if the prevalence of posters drops off as the seniority of the location increases, and they will feel devalued.

21.11.5   Bulletins

By bulletins I mean electronic posters. These have been sent out via email in every organisation I have ever worked in or with, and are as a rule ignored by the recipient. Messaging and language is key, and often neither are performed well. Because bulletins have to be approved by the executive, they are often in executive speak, but then are sent out to the workforce, who don't speak that language.

Typical examples include bulletins which talk about how "Sarah" is going to take over some department or other, and drive forward growth, and how "Steve" is going to move into Sarah's old position which represents an exciting opportunity for him. Most recipients are asking "Who is "Sarah?" "Who is "Steve?" "Why should I care?"

Even if they are in the right language, people don't read them. Even when they are relevant, people don't read them. The number that are relevant are vastly outweighed by those that are not. If your organisation has a great track record here, super, but on my experience I would not bother. However, if the organisation already runs a regular bulletin then consider adding a project section.

21.11.6 Presentations

I've put these at the end as they are possibly the most ineffective way of communicating, but equally the most used. Someone senior stands up and talks in an excited manner about the changes to come, but the language they are talking and the language that the listeners need to receive are totally different. If done well (rare) then presentations can be effective, interesting, engaging and productive. This is not the norm, and "Death by PowerPoint" is a phrase that has now entered the language. If you have to use presentations, key areas to think about are below:

- What language does the presenter speak and what language do the attendees speak? If you get a CEO to present to the IT department you are wasting everyone's time.
- Think about duration. A slide deck longer than about five slides and the average CEO will find something better to do. Really, if you can't get a simple, high level message across in five slides then there's something wrong with the proposal. Equally, if it is to a technical crowd and its only five slides long then they will expect more detail.
- Think about level of technical information within the presentation. As a rule of thumb, if you are presenting to C-level execs and the presentation contains the word "database", you are off track. Again, a technical crew are likely to get confused if it is not in there.
- There is no point putting someone out front who cannot understand the questions from the target audience. Consider an expert panel to answer questions.

CEO's deal in finance, sales and profits, technical staff deal in systems and data, business owners deal in people and relationships and workflow. Do not mix messages.

21.12 Targeting and Execution

Targeting of messaging is critical. The typical way in which large projects – such as data quality – are communicated to the organisation is as follows.

Area	Organisational Perceived Level	General Messaging	Ability to directly affect data quality	Effect
Board	High	Individual 1-2-1 face to face meeting, generally with several senior DQ experts	Low	Buttresses Perception of Value
Upper Management	High	Individual 1-2-1 face to face meeting	Low	Buttresses Perception of Value
Middle Management	Medium	Workshops/Focus Groups	High	Often confusing as level of delivery is never right for everyone

Area	Organisational Perceived Level	General Messaging	Ability to directly affect data quality	Effect
Operational Management	Medium	Workshops/Focus Groups	High	Often confusing as level of delivery is never right for everyone
Team leader	Low	Posters and a presentation from one of the DQ experts	High	Negative "We don't really care about you or your opinion"
Coalface worker	Low	Posters in the canteen	Extremely High	Negative "We don't really care about you or your opinion"

The point is obvious. However, the common response when any alternative is suggested is that it would cost too much, or not enough quality information will come out of it.

Some of the most productive conversations I have ever had are when talking to junior staff – especially long-serving ones. You will often get all the data quality problems laid out for you, plus the reason why they have occurred, plus all the ways in which management have tried to address the problem and the reasons why each of these ways failed. I personally would suggest a different communications strategy, but obviously each organisation is different and tailoring is required.

Area	Organisational Perceived Level	General Messaging	Ability to directly affect data quality	Effect
Board	High	Individual 1-2-1 face to face meeting, generally with several senior DQ experts	Low	Meets expectations
Upper Management	High	Individual 1-2-1 face to face meeting	Low	Meets expectations
Middle Management	Medium	Individual 1-2-1 face to face meeting	High	We care about you and what you think
Operational Management	Medium	Individual 1-2-1 face to face meeting. Potentially not every single operational manager (ask them), but a significant selection	High	We care about you and what you think
Team leader	Low	Workshops for everyone, and 1-2-1 meetings with long-serving staff	High	We care about you and what you think
Coalface worker	Low	Workshops for everyone, and 1-2-1 meetings with long-serving staff	Extremely High	We care about you and what you think

21.13 Sustaining/Keep Happy

21.13.1 Repeat the message

It is unlikely that a message will be received and understood if it is only announced once, which is why a combination of communication methods, communicating the same message, should be used and used on a repeated basis. Whilst I have mentioned posters above, they are a good way of providing a constant update to the project messaging, as they can provide a constant reminder – in stairwells, lifts and canteens – of what the project is trying to achieve. It makes sense to repeatedly communicate to members of the organisation so that they are aware of overall progress and also to ensure a continued buy-in. Scheduling repeats will reinforce the message that the organisation cares about the views of its staff and the hard work that has gone in to getting the right message out to the right people in the first place. These scheduled repeats can be timed to project checkpoints. An interesting variation on this is to embed updates into the screensaver on staff computers.

21.13.2 Taking on board feedback

All feedback is valuable. If one person comes to you with a problem it is never just that person. Other individuals will have the same views, thoughts, or questions. Feedback is valuable even if it is wrong. If an individual comes in with an item of feedback that clearly indicates that they have not read the poster, or not attended the presentation, or cancelled the 1-2-1, then the question that needs to be asked is "why?". It is not their job to give their heart and mind to you, it is your job to win it – hence failings in perception are as much a fault of those that have allowed that perception to exist in the first place. For feedback, take it seriously. Log it, write it down, and think about it. This about why that person has given the feedback, why they have their views, how it will affect their buy-in to the project, and what you can do about it.

21.13.3 Bringing people in

One of the best ways of bringing people along with the project is to make them part of it. If people think that they have made a significant contribution they are much more likely to support the project and have a vested interest in its continuing success. The most effective way of utilising those who have bought totally into the project is to use them as ambassadors for the project themselves.

21.14 The Regulator

It is important to ensure that the regulator knows the journey on which you are about to embark. First of all, most regulators will react positively to news that data quality is going to be significantly improved within one of the organisations within their care, and informing the regulator is likely to gain a positive reaction. It should not be considered that the regulator should not be informed because they will then know that the data was not of a good enough quality in the beginning. The regulator is more than aware of the quality of data that exists within the market (refer here to the senior supervisor's report on counterparty data from the introduction), and is known to be acting to persuade companies to improve.

Ideally, the regulator should be involved at every part of the process, and having the regulator on board will actively smooth any issues that are likely to occur. Communication is a key factor in ensuring that the upheaval that is likely is actually seen in a positive, rather than negative light. Many of the processes that are required by a regulator are time-specific, and this timescale may be under threat if significant changes are being made to the data. Therefore, early, open and honest communication with the regulator will not only be helpful, but vital. For level of communication, the most suitable approach will be to share the overall concept and intention at a high level up front – for example the same level as would be appropriate for the executive – but make it clear that greater detail is available as and when required.

21.15 Further Reading

- *The Project Management Communications Toolkit (Effective Project Management)*, Carl Pritchard, Artech House Publishers, 2013
- *Project Management Communications Bible,* William Doe, John Wiley & Sons, 2008
- *Communication skills for project and programme managers*, Melanie Franklin, Stationary Office, 2008
- *Project Management Communication Tools*, William Doe, 2015
- *Managing Project Stakeholders: Building a Foundation to Achieve Project Goals*, Tres Roeder, John Wiley & Sons, 2013
- *Making Projects Work: Effective Stakeholder and Communication Management (Best Practices and Advances in Program Management Series)*, Lynda Bourne, Auerbach Publications, 2015

21.16 Summary

In this chapter I have tried to outline how to make the job of introducing, managing and running a data quality project easier. This is done by bringing the rest of the organisation with you and obtaining their buy in. Rather than trying to implement the whole project on your own against the wishes of the organisation you then have others who are working to help you. I cannot stress how important this is to the success of the project. I hope that this chapter has convinced the reader of this, and also shown them the ways in which the messaging of the project can be used to convince the people to support it.

In the next section I will look at the way in which a large data quality project can be managed, and the specific elements of project management that should be considered if an organisation is looking to implement data quality on a larger basis.

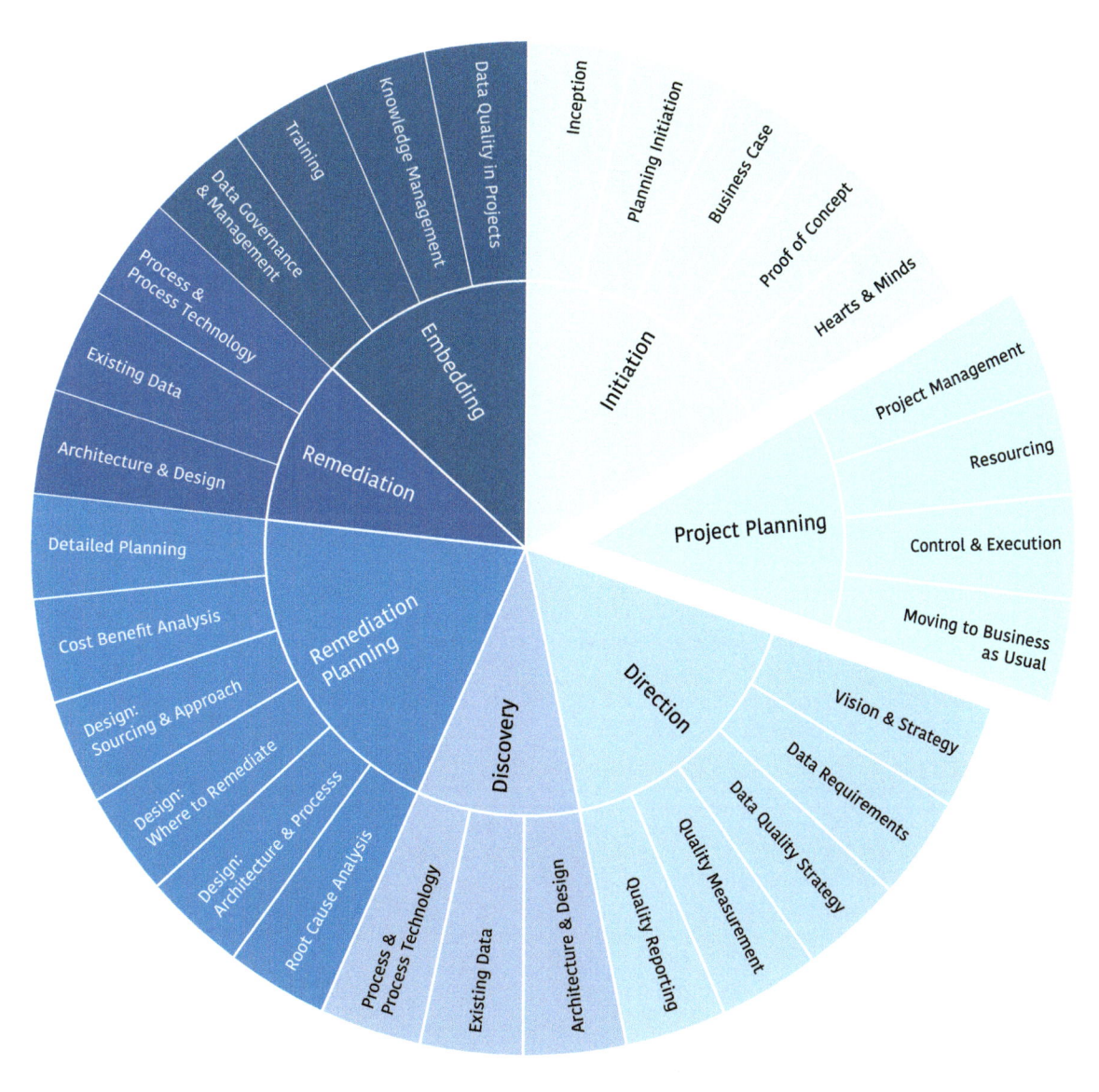

SECTION 5.2 PROJECT PLANNING

SECTION 5.2: INDEX

CHAPTER 22: Project Management — 233

22.1	Structure	233
22.2	Overview	234
22.3	Data Quality as a Modular Project	237
22.4	Planning the Rest of the Project	238
22.5	Objectives and Success	239
22.6	Business Case	240
22.7	Risk Assessment	240
22.8	Assumptions and Constraints	241
22.9	Issues	242
22.10	Dependencies	242
22.11	Deliverables	243
22.12	Change Capacity Assessment	244
22.13	Work Breakdown Structure	245
22.14	Project Plan	246
22.15	Project Initiation Document (PID)	248
22.16	Mapping Project Stages to IT Architecture	248
22.17	Summary	250

CHAPTER 23: Resourcing — 251

23.1	Structure	251
23.2	Overview	252
23.3	Key Roles	253
23.4	Organisation	255
23.5	Resource Profile of the Project	262
23.6	Summary	262

CHAPTER 24: Control & Execution — 263

24.1	Structure	263
24.2	Overview	264
24.3	Project Stages	264
24.4	Workflow	267
24.5	Further reading	268
24.6	Summary	269

CHAPTER 25: Moving on to Business As Usual — 271

25.1	Structure	271
25.2	Overview	272
25.3	Approach	273
25.4	Transitioning the Project Team	273
25.5	Problems to be Faced	274
25.6	End Project Assessment	275
25.7	Summary	276

SECTION 5.2 PROJECT PLANNING

CHAPTER 22 PROJECT MANAGEMENT

22.1 Structure

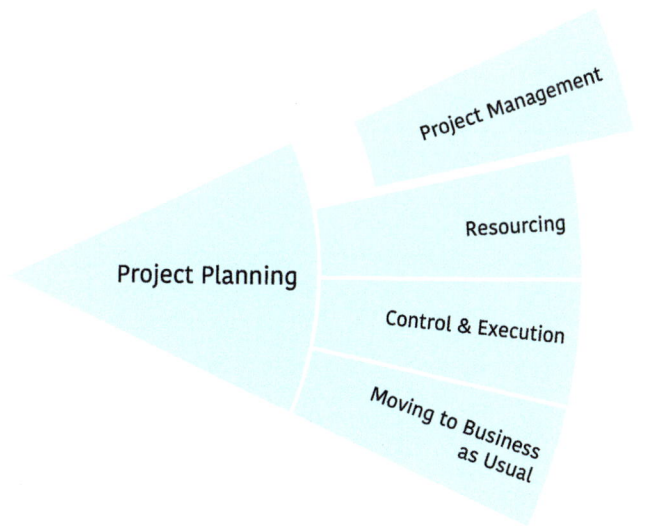

This stage of The Data Quality Blueprint includes the following phases:

1. Project Planning
2. Resourcing
3. Control & Execution
4. Moving on to Business as Usual

This chapter covers the first of these phases.

22.2 Overview

INPUTS
- All artefacts created in earlier stages

OUTPUTS
- Updated requirements
- Updated definition of systems in scope
- Updated definition of domains in scope
- Updated definition of processes in scope
- Draft deliverables list
- Detailed description of deliverables
- Mock-up of deliverables
- Change assessment template
- Change capacity assessment
- Change mitigation strategy
- Risk assessment template
- Definition of risk appetite
- Risk assessment
- Updated work breakdown structure
- Draft of task list
- Draft reporting template
- Reporting strategy
- Reporting template
- Change management strategy
- Change management template
- Updated risks
- Updated assumptions
- Updated dependencies
- Updated issues
- Software requirements
- Draft project plan
- Project initiation document

DEPENDENCIES
- Access to stakeholders
- Organisational PMO if available
- Software requirements (e.g. MSProject, workflow tools)
- Access to change and risk management function if available

TASKS
- Scope & Objectives
  - Requirements, Expectations, Scope
    - Update expectations as necessary based on initiation stage
    - Update requirements as necessary based on initiation stage
    - Update definition of systems in scope if necessary based on initiation stage
    - Update definition of domains in scope if necessary based on initiation stage
    - Update definition of processes in scope if necessary based on initiation stage
    - Agree with sponsor and key stakeholders if required
    - Document and upload to project repository
- Deliverables
  - Create draft deliverables list
  - Discuss and agree with sponsor and key stakeholders
  - Create detailed description of deliverables
  - Ideally create mock-up of deliverables
  - Discuss and agree with sponsor and key stakeholders
  - Upload to project repository
- Change Capacity Assessment and Management Strategy
  - Create and agree change assessment template
  - From interviews, workshops and questionnaires assess capacity for change
  - Identify change issues
  - Discuss with key sponsor and, if required, key stakeholders
  - Estimate impact of issues
  - Document change capacity assessment
  - Identify mitigating actions
  - Identify residual risk to change
  - Prepare change mitigation strategy
  - Agree with key sponsor
  - Upload to project repository
- Risk Assessment and Management Strategy
  - Create and agree risk assessment template
  - From interviews, workshops and questionnaires assess risks
  - Define the risk appetite of the organisation
  - Query whether data quality risk has been differentiated between departments
  - Identify risks of pursuing a data quality project
  - Identify impacts of individual risks
  - Identify the risks of NOT pursuing a data quality project
  - Identify impacts of individual risks
  - Create overall risk assessment
  - Identify treatment of risks (e.g. Mitigate/ignore/etc)
  - Create risk management strategy
- Detailed Approach

- Modules
  - Define project modules with go/no go decision points
  - Discuss and agree with sponsor and key stakeholders
  - Document modules
  - Upload to project repository
- Work Breakdown structure
  - Update work breakdown structure
  - Discuss with relevant project resources
  - Update as required
  - Upload to project repository
- Task list
  - Create first draft of task list
  - Discuss with relevant project resources
  - Update task list
  - Discuss and agree with sponsor and key stakeholders
  - Upload to project repository

- Control Strategy
  - Reporting
    - Discuss reporting strategy with sponsor and key stakeholders
    - Draft reporting template
    - Document reporting strategy
    - Agree with sponsor and key stakeholders
    - Upload to project repository
  - KPI
    - Discuss project KPI with sponsor and key stakeholders
    - Draft reporting template
    - Define source for KPI
    - Document approach for KPI reporting
    - Agree with sponsor and key stakeholders
    - Upload to project repository
  - Workflow
    - Agree use of workflow with the engagement team
    - Source workflow tools as required
    - Set up basic workflow
    - Agree roles and responsibilities (e.g. review/perform)
    - Document roles and responsibilities
    - Upload to project repository
  - Change management
    - Discuss change management strategy with sponsor and key stakeholders
    - Draft change management strategy
    - Discuss with engagement team and steering group
    - Draft change management template
    - Agree with sponsor and key stakeholders
    - Upload to project repository
  - Traceability matrix
    - Create template
    - Populate template with deliverables and requirements
    - Note updating the traceability matrix will be an ongoing task throughout the project
  - RAID
    - Update risks

- Update assumptions
- Update dependencies
- Update issues
- Project Plan
  - Create draft project plan
  - Socialise with engagement team
  - Update as required
  - Socialise with key sponsor
  - Update as required
  - Socialise with key stakeholders
  - Update as required
  - Socialise with steering group and/or board
  - Update as required
  - Obtain written signoff
  - Upload to project repository
- Project Initiation Document
  - Update project brief into a full initiation document
  - Update problem statement
  - Update project definition
  - Update scope and objectives
  - Update RAID
  - Update business case
  - Update team and roles
  - Update resource plan
  - Update risk management strategy
  - Add change management strategy
  - Add results from POC
  - Add communication management strategy
  - Update project plan
  - Finalise project initiation document
  - Agree with executive sponsor
  - Agree with board (if required)
  - Receive written signoff
  - Upload to project repository

I described in an earlier chapter how the overall methodology fits together. When embarking on a data quality project, some degree of management and planning is vital as the project will touch every area of the organisation. Even a small scale remediation exercise will require planning and project management. For large scale remediation the management and planning overhead is likely to be significant. Unfortunately, data quality projects are often undertaken because "our data quality is abysmal" or "something has to be done" or "we need better data quality" with no documented (or even thought out) strategy around what is the "something", or how it is going to be achieved. What is "abysmal" for example? Or, for that matter, "better"? When does the "something" need to happen? Far too often the business or IT (rarely both) or a tiny data quality team, are tasked with doing "something". Putting a decent level of management around the "something" is common sense. The assumption is that this section follows on from the initiation stage and therefore some investigation and limited discovery work, some stakeholder identification and management, scoping, business discovery (i.e. what are the existing pain points), and the preparation of the business case have been completed and the project has the green light for formal project initiation. This chapter will therefore cover the project management that will be required to deliver a full remediation project. This will include:

- Stages of the project
- Timing
- Objectives
- Risk assessment
- Assumptions and constraints
- Issues
- Dependencies
- Deliverables
- Change Capacity Assessment
- Detailed planning
- How the project will flow
- Business case

I have now worked on over twenty data quality projects. I have also managed both data quality and other large information management projects. Whilst I would never put myself forward as an authority on project management, I have tried to include in this section thoughts and ideas that I think will smooth the way of other people who are approaching a data quality project, potentially for the first time. I have also placed in the appendices a list of artefacts that could be used to facilitate a data quality project, as well as a full data quality project plan.

22.3 Data Quality as a Modular Project

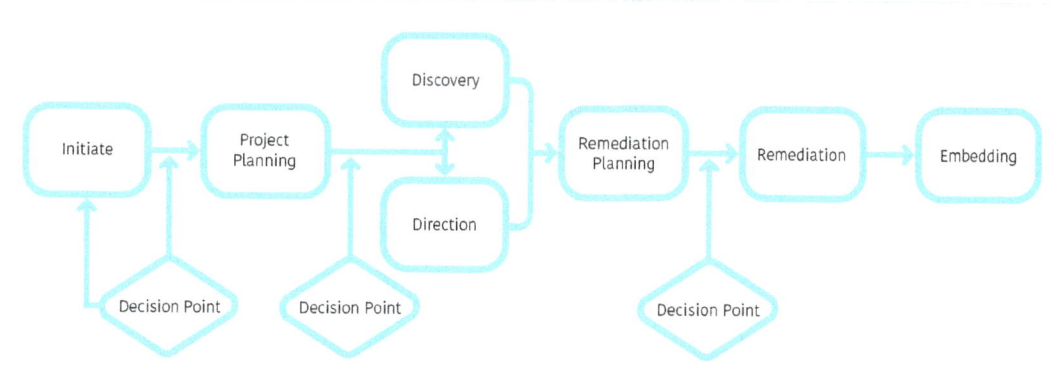

At the end of the Initiate stage there is a decision point to go into full planning. If the Initiate stage is not showing significant benefits then either the whole project needs to be abandoned or the Initiate stage needs to be re-examined to ensure that it is picking up all positive outcomes.

At the end of the Project Planning stage there is a decision point which will justify the project as a whole at a high level (as the detailed business case will have been completed) and the following two sections (Direction and Discovery) in particular.

There should not be a decision point before the detail remediation planning stage. This is because the previous two stages are information definition and discovery stages. Analysis needs to be completed before a decision point can occur.

At the end of the Remediation Planning project stage there is a decision point which will justify the remainder of the project (i.e. the remediation effort) with detailed figures for both anticipated cost and benefits.

There should not be a decision point between Remediation and embed as the Embedding phase should be a given, otherwise the whole project will simply need to be repeated within a few years.

Data quality projects should be modular projects with multiple decision points. Data quality projects should not be "all or nothing", either in terms of timescale or in terms of resources. I have always seen a data quality project as progressive, with each section both forming the platform off which the next section will spring, but also justifying the next stage in terms of effort and business case. The project as a whole – and certainly in this book – breaks up into discrete chunks, each of which can be seen as units on their own. Hence the "Laying the Foundations" stage forms the business case for the initiation stage, which forms the basis for the "Discovery" stage (strategy and requirements being a necessity regardless), and the "Remediation Planning" stage justifies the remediation. Technically, direction can be carried out in parallel with the discovery phase, but there needs to be a continuous feed between them to ensure that the discovery stage is aligned to the information needs of the organisation. This, and related decision points, are shown in the above diagram.

At each point it should be possible to say "yes, this project will result in defined benefits to the organisation". Hence if, after a promising foundation stage, the discovery stage results mean that the organisation has to think again about the whole project, then it is perfectly possible to stop at that point and rethink. In fact, that is precisely what the "Remediation Planning" stage requires – that when you have real information from across the organisation rather than the limited information from initiation and discovery, the remediation effort needs to be re-planned. The overall planning of the project, therefore, is split into three chunks – one small one before the initiation stage to plan that stage on its own, another after initiation and another after the discovery stage has been completed.

A note here of importance. Just because the project can be broken up into chunks does not mean that that certain stages – and most specifically and importantly the "embed" stage – can be left out. Leaving out the "embed" element will mean that the most likely outcome is that the project will be a failure, and will have to be repeated at a later date. This is analogous to a mechanic building a machine at vast cost and then the owner never oiling it. It may be the world's greatest machine, but without basic maintenance it is likely to break down. At this point, the owner may state that "clearly it was not a good machine", which shows a lack of understanding on their part. In the same way, the data quality machine needs oiling. It may be the world's most successful project, but without the last element – that of embedding it into the organisation – then data will drift into poor quality again. For those that like withdrawing the funding for projects when they are 90% complete – **You Have Been Warned**.

22.4 Planning the Rest of the Project

It is worth here recapping on the overall project stages that need to be undertaken after the planning stage has been completed.

Stage	Objective
Direction	The objective of this stage is to define the overall data strategy, data requirements, data quality requirements and data quality metrics, based on the corporate vision and strategy. This can be done in parallel with Discovery. It is likely that there will already be assets in place within any business that cover elements of this work, so this stage may well be more collation of existing resources and bringing them together, and then examining what they mean for data quality.
Discovery	The objective of this stage is the definition of the current state architecture, exiting data and process and where it is deficient compared with the required standard.

Remediation Planning	The objective of this stage is collation of discovery results and the planning of the remediation work so that the remediation work is undertaken in as efficient and effective a fashion as possible.
Remediation	The objective of this stage is to change current architecture, process and existing data to the planned to-be state in a controlled fashion.
Embedding	The objective of this stage is to ensure that data quality remains good after the project close, and to do this by implementing governance, training and knowledge management. Note that parts of this stage (notably governance and training) can be performed in parallel with other stages after direction.

Within each of these stages the project needs to understand:

- How it will measure success
- What dependencies it will have
- What deliverables it will have
- What resources it needs
- How it will control and execute the stage

Lastly, the project will need to understand how it will close down and move data quality into business as usual.

22.5 Objectives and Success

Every project should have a defined objective. We have already discussed objectives at a high level in the "Initiation" section, and I would expect a data quality project to have an objective on the lines of the example below:

The primary objective of the project is to improve data quality in our reports to the regulator.

A secondary objective is to improve data quality in data that is used by the board and management in order to improve decision making.

A third objective is to define data quality metrics and implement a data quality reporting process that will enable the success of the project to be measured and will form part of ongoing monitoring of data quality.

In scope are all data items that are required in regulatory reports, board reports or management reports.

Alternatively the objective could be, at a high level:

The objective of this project is to improve the quality of information in the organisation. This will be achieved by a review of the architecture, processes and existing data. The detailed scope of the remediation will be defined after a discovery phase that will identify areas where poor data quality is impeding the ability to deliver accurate reporting to regulator, board or management, or to serve the customer.

For each objective the project needs to define success. This may be in terms of a timescale for completion, or an achievement of business value, or acceptance that an audit point has been cleared. The nature of the objectives are likely to be different for each type of data and each type of business – there will not be a "one size fits all" objective for data quality. For example, in a risk-based financial services retail lender, customer income may be critical and require a high degree of data quality; however, customer email address may be significantly less critical. In another organisation where sensitive documents are distributed by email, the quality of the email address may well be critical to operations. In every part of the project, the relevance and reference back to the objective needs to be considered. There is no point remediating data which is of no use to the business, or wasting time and resources remediating data to a higher standard than is required.

22.6   Business Case

The business case for the project, which we discussed in detail in the initiation section, is not a one-time effort. The business case needs to be re-evaluated throughout the project as it is possible that initial assumptions that underpinned the initial business case may turn out to be incorrect, especially during discovery stage. At every single stage of the project, and especially when risks crystallise, the business case should be revisited to ensure it still supports the continuation of the work.

22.7   Risk Assessment

A risk assessment is an assessment of all the risks that may occur in a project and how they are going to be treated. The risk log is one element of the RAID log. A good practice at the start of a project (of any kind) is to brainstorm with the project team everything that could possibly go wrong, however absurd it may appear at the time. This produces an initial list (the risk log), which should note how likely it is to occur and what would be the impact if it did. This gives an overall ranking of the risks.

Risk	Probability	Impact	Composite
Critical staff member leaves	20%	60%	12%
New CEO Cancels project	2%	100%	2%
Cannot access data sources on a timely basis	50%	80%	40%

It is then possible to rank the risks and then decide how they can be addressed. In general, there are four potential actions to be considered for any risk.

Action	Explanation
Avoid	The most common approach to a risk is to take steps so that it cannot occur. This may involve changing the approach to the project or performing tasks in a different order. For example, if there is a risk that data may be changed in the data stores without proper authorisation then it is possible to design a process to ensure that this cannot happen.
Accept	Accept that if this happens then there will be an effect on the project, but no further action is taken. This approach is often adopted if there is little that can realistically be done to avoid, mitigate or transfer, or the risk is either improbable or has little impact.
Mitigate	Occasionally known as risk reduction, this is taking steps to reduce the likelihood of the risk crystallising into anything that may affect the project, or taking steps to mean that if it does crystallise then the effect on the project is smaller and hence the risk can be accepted.
Transfer	Transfer the risk to someone else. An obvious example of this is taking out insurance. In return for a payment, the risk is now someone else's problem.

After considering each risk, and deciding on an action to take, there will be a residual risk. The project then needs to consider whether this residual risk can be accepted. Risks also need to be tracked to monitor whether initial assumptions made (for example, probability) change over time. New risks that occur over the duration of the project need to be added to the risk log and the same process of assessment and mitigation undertaken. The management and tracking of risks comes under project management. It is also worth considering upside risks/opportunities. There is a possibility that the project may go particularly well if certain events occur, and it is worth thinking what actions will be taken in that event. For example, if the data sources are available in advance of the date initially promised then will there be personnel on hand to start profiling early?

Lastly, risks need to be communicated to the wider organisation, especially the project sponsor. Not least as they may be able to do something to mitigate, but more importantly because if any of the risks materialise then it will help if the project sponsor knew it was a risk in advance rather than it coming as an issue out of the blue.

22.8 Assumptions and Constraints

A list of assumptions is a basic requirement in any project. In the same way as risks, a brainstorming session with the project team at the beginning of the project can drive out the assumptions and constraints that underpin the project. Examples of basic assumptions may be:

- We will be able to have access direct to the source systems.
- The project will assume that the systems in scope are limited to system 1, system 2, system 3.
- The project will assume that the new subsidiary is not in scope.
- The platform upgrade will be complete by the end of the project's discovery stage.

Examples of constraints may be:

- We can only have access to stakeholders for X hours a week.
- We can only change data whilst production systems are not in operation.

Assumptions and constraints have to be documented, and ideally should be part of the project brief and all contract documents, so that if they are violated then the project can call out that a base assumption that will materially affect their ability to deliver is no longer valid. The assumptions and constraints log (generally just regarded as the assumptions log) is another element of the RAID log.

22.9   Issues

Any issues that occur during the project need to be documented. It should be noted here that a risk has not happened, an issue has. In order for an issue to be documented in the issue log then it has to be affecting the project. When documenting issues, a clear and concise format that can be easily understood by non-technical individuals is recommended. Senior individuals will want to read the detail and it will not help if they cannot understand it. A useful method is the Situation-Complexity-Options-Recommendation format, where, for each issue, the description is:

Situation: What's occurred?

Complexity: Why is it a problem?

Options: What can we do about it?

Recommendation: What we think is the best option and why.

Also included in the documentation should be an issue owner, and a timescale when the issue needs to be resolved (be realistic, "yesterday" is not a viable timeframe and just annoys people). The issue log is another element of the RAID log.

22.10   Dependencies

Critical to the success of the project will be the degree it is supported (or not) by the rest of the organisation. It is certainly invaluable to call out these dependencies at the start and make it clear that the project cannot meet its objectives in the timescales promised if the rest of the organisation (or potentially other organisations) does not support it. The dependencies should be agreed with both the supplying organisation/department and the project itself, both in terms of nature and in terms of due dates. It is also wise to describe the dependencies in enough detail that there is no cause for debate if there is argument at a later date. Examples of dependencies are shown in the table below.

No	Dependency	On Whom	Date Required	Why Required
1	A business Subject Matter Expert (SME) allocated full-time to the project between project start date (as defined in the project initiation documentation) and the defined signoff date of the remediation.	New Lending (Mortgages)	1/1/20XX	In order to document the new lending process
2	Data extract from the lending system. This needs to include all fields as listed in the data profiling approach document, and include all loans and mortgages, not just those that show an outstanding balance. [42]	IT	1/1/20XX	In order to start the profiling work for that system
3	Data masking [43] of the production data. This masking should be limited to personally identifiable fields only, specifically forename and surname, account number, and the first six address fields.	IT	1/1/20XX	So that offshore agents can access and profile the data
4	Supply of profiling tool. This profiling tool should meet the specifications as detailed in the profiling approach document.	IT	1/1/20XX	So that profiling can proceed as efficiently as possible

In a large programme a whole matrix of dependencies will exist between projects, and with other parts of the organisation outside the project environment, and third parties. Management of these dependencies can become an industry in itself, so it is advisable to make sure that they are defined clearly, concisely, and agreed with all parties, and also that they are real – nothing annoys someone more than breaking their back to meet a dependency to find that actually it's not going to be needed for weeks and the person asking for the dependency was simply building in some contingency. The dependency log is another element of the RAID log.

22.11   Deliverables

Any data quality project will have deliverables. Some of these deliverables will be external to the project – in that they will be delivered to stakeholders for review and signoff, or to external organi-

---

42. A lot of data quality issues result in mortgages having a positive balance (i.e. the bank owes the customer). There are a few totally legitimate reasons for this to be the case but in general if a mortgage account is showing that the bank owes the customer money, something is wrong.

    It should also be noted that the project will often need to supply requirements of its own in order that other parts of the organisation can meet the dependencies. For example, in the case of (2) above, IT are likely to come back with the questions: "What fields do you want?" & "What time range of data?"

43. Data Masking is the process of disguising personally identifiable fields either for the purposes of data security, or to allow access to the data from a country with different data laws. Data masking can be done quite scientifically, so that it is still possible to profile the data. For example, "John" may be replaced with "Jaly", where the initial letter and capitalisation remain as-is, and the rest of the letters are scrambled, however vowels are kept as vowels and consonants as consonants.

sations. Some others will be purely internal to be used at a later date by the project itself.

Deliverables should be listed at the beginning of the project with agreed dates when they will be provided – potentially in the project contract documentation. This is both to provide a means of the organisation keeping tabs on the project and making sure that it is delivering to schedule, and to ensure that deadlines exist and work does not slip because there is no deadline for fulfilment. A sample list is shown below.

No	Deliverable	By	Date Required	Signoff
1	Data profiling for lending system	Project Profiling Lead	1/6/20XX	Lending Manager
2	Agreed project plan (high level)	Project Manager	1/1/20XX	Executive Sponsor
3	End project report	Project Manager	To Be Agreed	Executive Sponsor
4	High level data lineage diagram	Project Data Architect	1/2/20XX	Enterprise Architect

In respect of deliverables, it is essential (especially if their signoff is a contractual event or a pre-requisite for funding or for moving on to the next stage of the project) that the format of the deliverable is agreed with the reviewers beforehand. There is nothing so depressing as submitting deliverables for review to find that one reviewer states that the document is not what they expected, they are not signing it off, and a large amount of work may need to be re-performed.

Another thorny question relates to document and physical deliverables. Document deliverables are literally that – they are documents that are delivered. Physical deliverables are actual changes made to the architecture, data, systems, applications or processes that are not a document as such, but equally need to be delivered. However the same applies to both document and physical deliverables in that the nature of the deliverable should be agreed beforehand. If the physical deliverable is going to be an updated database, the project needs to answer questions such as: Which database? Which fields? How will they be updated? What are the success criteria? And if the deliverable is not accepted, how is the database put back to where it started?

A typical list of artefacts for a data quality project, some of which may or may not be "formal" deliverables, is shown in the appendices.

22.12   Change Capacity Assessment

A change capacity assessment is a product that examines at the way in which a project wishes to change an organisation, and then looks at the capacity of the organisation to implement or adapt to that change. Note this is also called a change readiness assessment or similar. In the case of a data quality project, and especially one where they are starting from a low state of maturity, then the degree of change may be considerable, and some consideration needs to be made of the ability of the organisation to process this change. Drivers to any organisation's capacity for change will include, but not be limited to:

- Leadership style
- Amount of existing change in flight
- Management style
- Employee flexibility
- Culture and values
- Organisational complexity

If there is already a large amount of change occurring, then the organisation may not be able to accommodate more. In this case it may be better to leave further change until things have settled down. Equally, a young, flexible workforce is likely to accept change more easily than an older, less dynamic workforce.

The initial investigation work should give a good idea of the capacity to change, and it is possible to add into that assessment questions on the attitude to change and the performance of past transformational projects. I am not going to delve into the mechanisms of change assessment here but it is necessary to state that a change capacity assessment will be required and the project needs to ensure that it is done.

22.13   Work Breakdown Structure

A work breakdown structure is a breakdown of the project into logical blocks. It is a precursor to a full plan, and shows the components of each logical stage of the project. An example, for a subset of the discovery stage of a data quality project, is shown below.

Within a work breakdown structure there should be no overlap between work items. Each work item should contain at a sublevel all of the deliverables that are needed for it to progress and all of the deliverables, both end and interim stages should be captured.

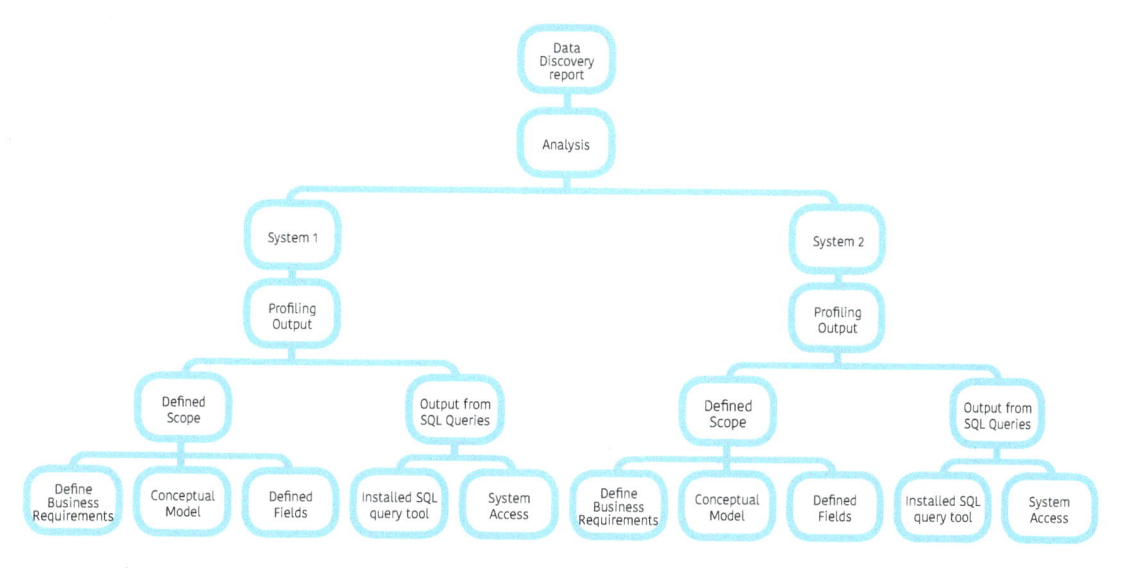

It should be noted that the work breakdown structure includes outputs, not actions (which are contained in the task list or the project plan). A work breakdown structure can be continued to a very high level of detail, but where the detail stops is up to the practitioner. There will be a point where subdividing work items any further makes little sense, and will create an overly confusing diagram or introduce levels of detail that are not relevant to the reader. The work breakdown structure however is a key enabler for the project manager to create the overall plan.

22.14 Project Plan

The project needs to create an overall project plan that shows what tasks are will be undertaken, when, and how those tasks relate to each other. The project plan will be the governing document for the project manager. They do not necessarily need to create every element themselves – they can ask the experts for each area to provide sub-plans – but they will need to collate responses, identify interdependencies and create the overall plan.

A key inclusion in this book is a full detailed (1500+ tasks, level 3+) project plan for a data quality project, which is included in the appendices. This is an amalgam of a number of real plans created for real organisations, and includes the tasks within each stage of the project. This project plan should be sufficient to enable a first draft of a data quality project plan to be created, and will also aid in the overall understanding of the effort by the project manager, which should also accelerate the planning stage.

Project plans are usually divided into levels, at increasing levels of detail. Every organisation will have its own standard as to the degree of detail at each level. Level zero is always the highest level, and will commonly consist of one line "do data quality project", with a specified duration of the whole project timescale. Level 1 breaks this out further, and so on. By the time the plan reaches level 3 then I would submit that there is little point extending to further detail without making the plan unwieldy and turning its maintenance into a full time job. The plan in the appendices would be in my view potentially too detailed to actually use to manage a project, and could easily be collapsed slightly in real life for ease of use, but the detail is useful for a newcomer to data quality as it shows, blow by blow and step by step, exactly what needs doing.

What I will do here is take a quick look at the data quality project plan at level 1 and 2 to demonstrate some key points.

22.14.1 Level 1 plan

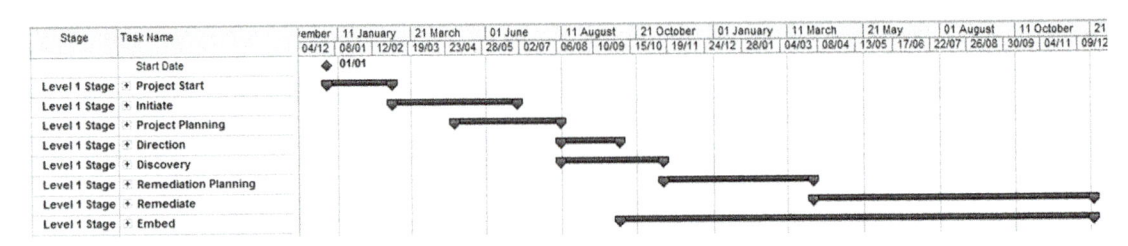

Stage	Task Name	Start Date
Level 1 Stage	+ Project Start	01/01
Level 1 Stage	+ Initiate	
Level 1 Stage	+ Project Planning	
Level 1 Stage	+ Direction	
Level 1 Stage	+ Discovery	
Level 1 Stage	+ Remediation Planning	
Level 1 Stage	+ Remediate	
Level 1 Stage	+ Embed	

Looking at the sample plan what will be instantly noticeable is the overall level 1 plan is not sequential. Certain elements start at the same time, others overlap. Whilst it would be logical to approach the project as a pure waterfall the real world does not operate like this and there will be an organisational expectation that the project progresses as fast as possible, given resource constraints.

As a result there are some time savings that can be made. Planning can in theory start after the business case is signed off, and does not have to wait until after the Proof of Concept or the communications have been completed. With care, Direction, Discovery and Embedding can start simultaneously, though it is better if (as shown above) Embedding waits until the direction is in place. Remediation planning, however, cannot start until direction and discovery are completed. These changes significantly shorten the overall project from a "waterfall" based approach, and experience indicates that this would be a preferred solution for most organisations.

22.14.2 Level 2 plan

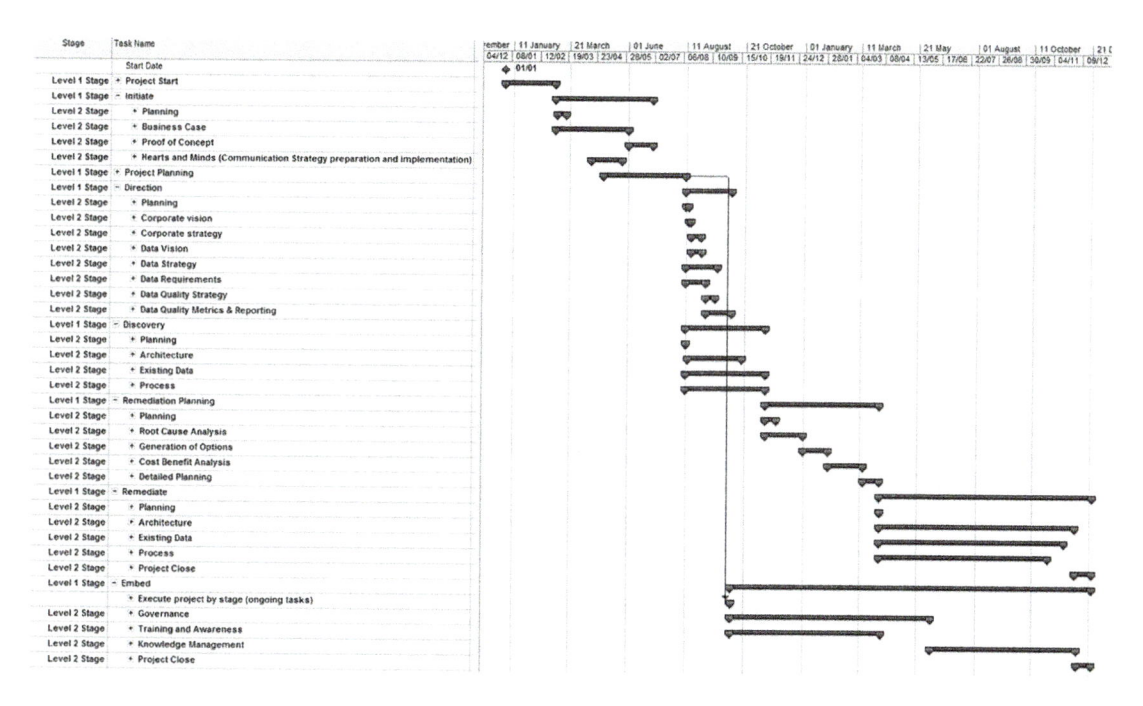

Stage	Task Name	Start Date
Level 1 Stage	Project Start	01/01
Level 1 Stage	Initiate	
Level 2 Stage	Planning	
Level 2 Stage	Business Case	
Level 2 Stage	Proof of Concept	
Level 2 Stage	Hearts and Minds (Communication Strategy preparation and implementation)	
Level 1 Stage	Project Planning	
Level 1 Stage	Direction	
Level 2 Stage	Planning	
Level 2 Stage	Corporate vision	
Level 2 Stage	Corporate strategy	
Level 2 Stage	Data Vision	
Level 2 Stage	Data Strategy	
Level 2 Stage	Data Requirements	
Level 2 Stage	Data Quality Strategy	
Level 2 Stage	Data Quality Metrics & Reporting	
Level 1 Stage	Discovery	
Level 2 Stage	Planning	
Level 2 Stage	Architecture	
Level 2 Stage	Existing Data	
Level 2 Stage	Process	
Level 1 Stage	Remediation Planning	
Level 2 Stage	Planning	
Level 2 Stage	Root Cause Analysis	
Level 2 Stage	Generation of Options	
Level 2 Stage	Cost Benefit Analysis	
Level 2 Stage	Detailed Planning	
Level 1 Stage	Remediate	
Level 2 Stage	Planning	
Level 2 Stage	Architecture	
Level 2 Stage	Existing Data	
Level 2 Stage	Process	
Level 2 Stage	Project Close	
Level 1 Stage	Embed	
	Execute project by stage (ongoing tasks)	
Level 2 Stage	Governance	
Level 2 Stage	Training and Awareness	
Level 2 Stage	Knowledge Management	
Level 2 Stage	Project Close	

The level 2 plan breaks into the next level of detail. Where parallel development is possible then the plan has assumed this will be the case, with the constraint that work is approached in packages and integrity of the overall solution is not lost. Here the reader can see that the discovery work for architecture, data and process proceeds simultaneously and the same applies to the remediation. Also, training and governance run simultaneously. These decisions are based on real-life requirements to shorten the project timescale and perform the work as efficiently as possible.

22.14.3 Level 3 and below plan

This is only in the appendices and as stated runs to over 1,500 individual tasks. These are the detailed tasks required to complete the overall plan. An example may be "arrange initial meeting with key sponsor". It is the intention that the example project plan will be an aid to any practitioner looking to launch a data quality initiative.

The Data Quality Blueprint

22.15 Project Initiation Document (PID)

At the end of the planning stage the Project Initiation Document (PID) needs to be created. This is one of the most important documents in the project. Its starting point is the project brief, which is built out into the business case. This is then further expanded into the project initiation document, which contains a detailed description of how the project will get from its start point to its objective. The PID will draw on the project plan, the resourcing, the dependencies, deliverables, risks, issues – in fact almost everything involved in the management of the project. It will also be an evolving document that will continue to be updated at every stage all the way through to the close of the project.

22.16 Mapping Project Stages to IT Architecture

An interesting question to consider is how the various tasks to be undertaken during the lifecycle of the project will fit within the overall technology architecture of the organisation. This will inform the skill sets of the resources required.

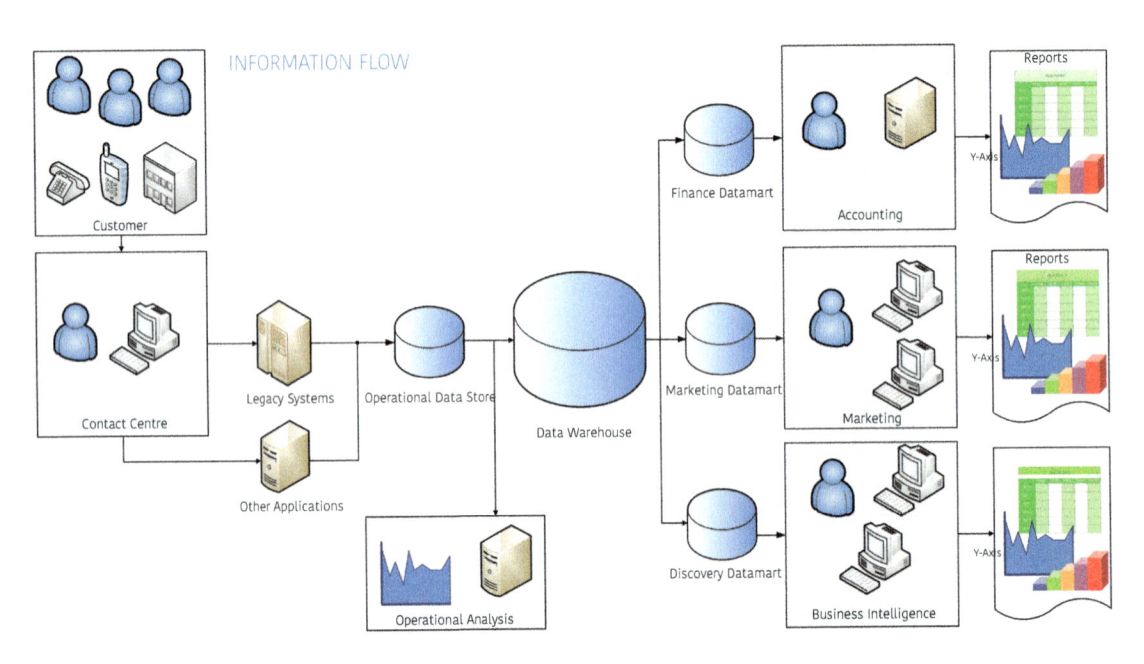

Here I will use the description of the organisational technology landscape developed in an earlier chapter, specifically the diagram above. This I have considerably simplified to another diagram introduced earlier.

22.16.1 What do you do where?

A high level diagram showing the elements of the overall architecture that are relevant in each stage is shown below.

Data Quality Project	Source	ETL	Datawarehouse	Datamarts	Presentation	Reporting
Initiation	Understanding of nature and location of source data, basic profiling and data lineage.	Understanding of how ETL is used and how transformations are documented, and understanding of data lineage.	Basic understanding of datawarehouse data scope and the data models used.	Basic understanding of datamart data scope and data models used.	Understanding of the information requirements of the organisation for reporting and analytics and the pain points in data usage.	Understanding of the information requirements of the organisation for reporting and analytics and the pain points in data usage.
Project Planning	Project Planning will involve all parts of the architecture.					
Direction	Understanding of operational data requirements and data quality requirements.				Understanding of end user information requirements and optionally implementation of data quality metrics.	Understanding of end user information requirements.
Discovery	Detailed data profiling against data requirements and business rules.	Discovery of transformational changes enacted during ETL, to discover data lineage, and to discover hidden Data Quality transformations.	Discovery of what is actually used in the data model, so as to reduce effort in profiling and remediation.	Discovery of the data model, so as to reduce effort in profiling and remediation.	Discovery of the data model, so as to reduce effort in profiling and remediation.	Using end user computing to discover the ways in which end users remediate data to expose deficiencies.
Remediation Planning	Remediation Planning will involve all parts of the architecture.					
Remediation	Remediation of source data by enhancement or replacement with remediated data.	Changing ETL tools to increase robustness, improve visibility of "hidden" data quality transformations.	Adding constraints, and triggers, potentially updating the data model.	Adding constraints, and triggers, potentially updating the data model.	Simplification of processes around data retrieval.	Simplification and reduction of requirement for end user computing.
Embedding	Training users and operationalising data management.	Training users and operationalising data management.	Training users and operationalising data management.	Training users and operationalising data management.	Training end users on information governance.	Training end users on information governance.

- Initiation will touch every element of the data architecture, but it will be a light touch only. It should include basic gathering of information on the number of sources, the location of pain points, and how data quality is perceived in the organisation, and why it has reached the current state.
- Project planning does not heavily interact with the architecture as it takes the outputs from the initiate phase and uses them to plan the remainder of the project.
- The direction stage works with the organisation to understand exactly what information is required. If there is any interaction with the architecture it would be associated with the creation of reporting metrics for measuring the quality of the data. Whilst measuring data quality on an ongoing basis should be as far towards the end of the information flow as

possible as data quality should always be measured at the point where it is used, discovery will primarily interact with the source systems and the data use layer. It will include both the detailed profiling of the source systems and the understanding of the processes that result in their population, together with measuring quality at the point of use to discover degradation that may occur within the information flow.
- Remediation planning does not directly touch the architecture, as it takes outputs from the previous stage and utilises these to create a detailed project plan and workflow that can be used to guide the remainder of the project.
- Remediation will also interact with almost every area of the architecture as it looks to change the overall architecture, process and data of the organisation to improve both current and future data quality. However, remediation of the actual data should always take place as near to the source of the data as possible. This is discussed in more depth in the remediation planning chapter.
- Embedding is mostly concentrated on people and process, and not architecture-related.

22.17 Summary

Within this chapter I have given an overview of the way in which a data quality project should be a modular project, and how its objectives should be set and success measured. I have introduced the reader to the various elements to the project, outlined the concepts of dependencies and deliverables, and how they are fundamental to the overall project management. I have discussed the project plan and explained how it relates to the various stages of the project, and mapped the project to the architecture of the information systems.

This section has not tried to define in detail all project artefacts, or how to run a project, as there are many publications that exist that effectively cover this ground. However, it has looked to give an introduction to those who may not have extensive familiarity with the subject. In the next section I will look at the resourcing of the project in detail, the skills and roles that are required and how they should be organised at each stage of the project.

SECTION 5.2 PROJECT PLANNING

CHAPTER 23 RESOURCING

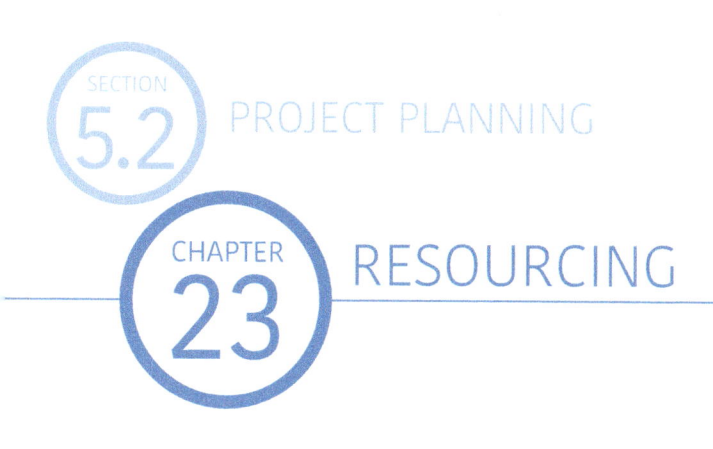

23.1 Structure

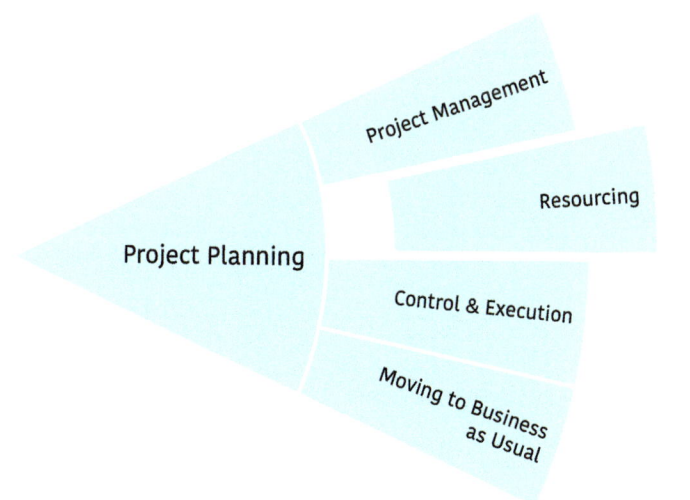

- Project Planning
  - Project Management
  - Resourcing
  - Control & Execution
  - Moving to Business as Usual

This stage of The Data Quality Blueprint includes the following phases:

1. Project Planning
2. Resourcing
3. Control & Execution
4. Moving on to Business as Usual

This chapter covers the second of these phases.

23.2 Overview

INPUTS
- Artefacts created in earlier stages of the project
- Project plan
- Resource availability
- Resource skills

OUTPUTS
- Resource plan
- Resource estimation
- Required skill sets per project stage
- resource profile over the project lifecycle
- Resource-leveled project plan
- Internal RACI
- Initial list of organisational personnel required
- Availability schedule

DEPENDENCIES
- Access to team members
- Access to business subject matter experts
- Access to IT subject matter experts
- Access to key stakeholders

TASKS
- Resource Plan
  - Required skills
    - Determine required skill sets per project stage
    - Determine resource profile over the project lifecycle
    - Identify available skills and hence skill gaps
    - Requisition relevant resources
    - Interview and onboard new team members
    - Verify final list of team members
    - Verify training needs of team members
  - Availability
    - Discuss project with proposed team members
    - Verify availability
    - Verify holiday plans
    - Agree with team members start and end dates
  - Plan
    - Take project plan and add resourcing
    - Allocate tasks to individuals
    - Create internal RACI
    - Perform resource leveling
    - Socialise resource plan with team members
    - Obtain feedback
    - Update plan as required
  - Organisational resourcing requirements
    - Create initial list of organisational (as opposed to project) personnel required
    - Distribute to departments concerned
    - Agree and document availability
    - Verify this fits in with plan dates
    - Update plan as required
  - Software and licensing
    - Define and agree software required during project lifecycle
    - Agree licensing and delivery schedule
    - Agree environment access
    - Agree purchase responsibility
    - Agree installation responsibility
    - Agree installation timescale
    - Document, obtain signoff, and upload to repository

> "Get the right people. Then no matter what all else you might do wrong after that, the people will save you. That's what management is all about."
> **Tom DeMarco**

One of the critical inputs when starting a project of this nature will be the number and nature of people required to make the project a success and whether these people will be available. Whilst it might be assumed that these personnel will be dedicated to the project, this is incorrect. These requirements will apply not only to the project personnel, but also to the organisation itself as subject matter experts will be required to pass their knowledge to the project so it can achieve its aims. These subject matter experts may come from IT, and be experts on the source systems, data warehouses or business intelligence systems, or may come from the business and be experts on processes or business outcomes. They are unlikely to be full time.

Within this chapter I will start by outlining key roles that will be necessary for the project to engage. I will cover what they will be required to do and when they will be needed. I have gone slightly further and, for each stage of the project in turn, outlined a representative organisational structure for that element of the project, and how the roles fit into that structure. I have also shown how the project organisational structure will change over the period of the project, and where resource requirements are at their greatest.

This chapter should give any potential project manager a good idea of the resources required in order to begin to socialise the overall effort involved to the executive, and to enable sourcing of individuals with the requisite skills.

23.3　Key Roles

23.3.1　Executive

Executive buy-in to the project is essential. Executive buy-in does not consist of appointing a project manager and signing off a budget. Whilst these are worthy tasks, the executive needs to be involved and engaged with the project, and be there to wield the executive boot if required. The executive needs to continuously emphasise the importance of the project to both staff and fellow board members, and to perform this task well they need to know enough about the project to justify it in a business context.

Whilst the executive do not need to be experts, they need to know the basics, and in the case of the business case, some of the details as well. The executive also needs to understand that the data quality project will require additional effort above the normal day to day job for much of the organisation. They need to understand that business leaders should be allowed time to work on the project, and if this is the case, that other tasks are likely to suffer. The executive needs to be able to accept – and in some cases mandate – the use of business time to improve data quality.

23.3.2　Project Management

The project management skills that are needed for data quality projects are not significantly different from other large projects that may have a number of separate work streams. Any project management methodology can be utilised, and as in other areas of this book where there is a large body of knowledge in existence, I will make no attempt to re-write exceptionally good publications in a necessarily limited space.

23.3.3 Project Management Office

Project Management Office (PMO) performs housekeeping for the project. This will include defining standards, collating information and chasing timelines. The project should not underestimate the amount of administration it takes to keep a project of any size operating as a cohesive unit. A project management office within the project provides a central point for this administration.

Within larger organisations, there may be a permanent organisational PMO consisting of specialised staff that operate across all projects and perform the project administration. This has the beneficial side effect for the organisation that there is a central view of all projects and what they are trying to achieve. In addition, projects which are impacting the same systems or parts of the organisation can be identified early and appropriate management put in place. A PMO of this nature is an excellent place for overall project governance. There are many advantages to simply hooking into an existing organisation-wide PMO. Those who work in the office will be experienced, competent practitioners, and many templates will already be defined. There may be standard ways of working that the data quality project can utilise, and also standard ways of resolving problems. In addition, the PMO may – having performed the task on many occasions – be able to simplify potentially arduous tasks like obtaining access to systems and environments.

23.3.4 Business Leaders

What was said about the executive applies to business leaders as well, but to a greater degree. The operational business is the creator and user of the information, and its leaders need to be intimately involved in its remediation. The operational business also owns process and procedures, and any proposed changes need to be discussed and agreed with the business leaders. Therefore business leaders need to be involved in and more importantly engaged with the project. They need to know the business case, but they also need to know how the project will progress. They will need to allocate staff to help with the data quality effort, and these will need to be the experienced, competent staff – precisely the staff that business leaders will be most unhappy to lose. It is essential that they know why the project is required and what benefits it will bring to them. Their buy-in will be critical to success.

23.3.5 Information Technology

IT will be heavily involved in any data remediation. The data is held on IT systems, and matching records, running database queries and suchlike is more likely to be in the skillset of the typical IT professional than that of the typical business professional. It is essential that the IT department is engaged with the project rapidly, and then kept on board. The effective integration of IT into a data quality project can easily make the difference between success and failure. In terms of IT involvement, essential individuals to be involved in a project should be:

- A senior IT sponsor. This is hopefully the Head of IT, CIO or similar, who have the authority to allocate resources and, importantly, make sure they stay allocated.
- IT project manager. Someone who can bring the disparate IT elements of the project together and who understands the IT landscape.

- A senior DBA who understands the business, and has the knowledge of the various transforms of the data over the years and why they have occurred. Note that this person is going to be difficult to get hold of and keep allocated to the project.
- Application owners, who understand the way in which data is held in their applications and how their applications interact with the data warehouse (if applicable), and how processes and procedures in the applications affect the data. It should be noted that this may result in proprietary representation.

In addition, it is likely that a significant number of developers will be required.

23.3.6   Remediators

A data quality project will require resources to perform manual remediation where necessary, to examine exceptions that are created by any automatic remediation tools, as well as management of workflow and process change. As mentioned elsewhere in the book, of the many remediation projects I have been involved with, the number of individuals working on data remediation has been up to 200-500 Full Time Equivalents (FTE) for between 12 and 18 months.

These numbers were reached over time. Remediation work has initially been undertaken by one of the teams in the contact centre. Over time, this team has grown, then split into more teams as the volume of work started to back up. Finally it moved to another building/floor where there was space, and continued to both grow and specialise. All to shrink back into nothing at the end of the project.

23.3.7   Data quality centre of excellence

The organisation may already have a data quality centre of excellence, which exists to promote data quality and address data quality issues. This may be left over from a previous project, or be created as part of a current one. In either case, it makes perfect sense to bring them under the wing of the data quality project, if they are not there already. The centre of excellence may form the core of the data quality project, but may also comprise a collection of SMEs who are able to be parachuted in to a hot spot of poor data quality within the organisation to look at the situation and recommend solutions.

23.4   Organisation

In this part of the chapter I will walk through each stage of the project and suggest the resource requirements and organisation.

23.4.1 Stage 0 – Laying the foundations

At the very start, the project needs key personnel only. The basic start-up tasks (in "laying the foundations") can be completed by the project manager with an assistant if required. This stage covers basic tasks such as definition of the problem statement and the creation of the project brief. Engagement would also be expected from the executive and key IT and Business sponsors, so they are aware of the project and its intentions. Other individuals who may be involved at this stage are the leads for Architecture, Process and Data, but it is unlikely at this point that this would be a full time involvement.

Note: For clarity, the diagram above shows "business" as opposed to "project" resources with shading.

23.4.2 Stage 1 – Project Initiation

When the project moves into the Initiation stage there is a slight ramp in resources. Here the lead members of the three major teams (Architecture, Data and Process) will come on board full time, and IT and Business SME resources will work with them. The team will include:

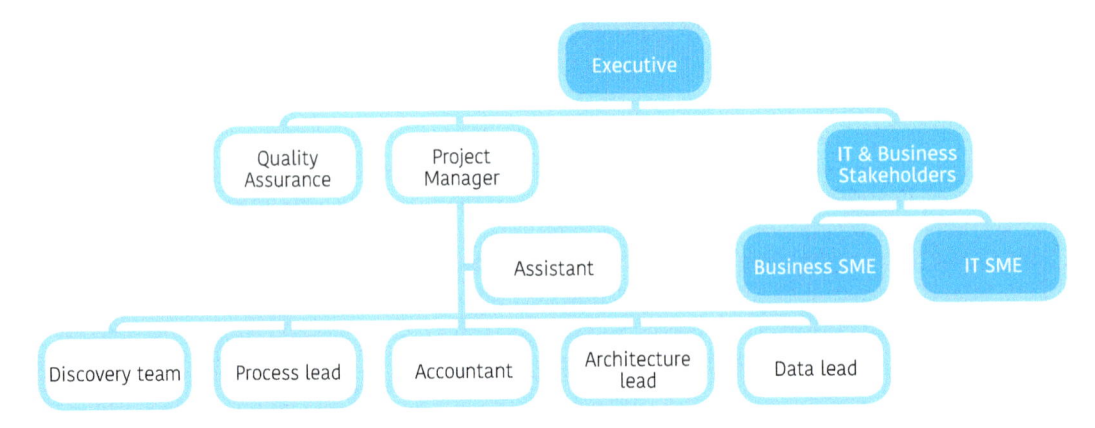

- The executive.
- The senior business and IT stakeholders, who are essential as the project will need them to persuade individuals with critical knowledge within the various departments to fit in project work in addition to their day job (the IT and Business SME).
- A project accountant will be required to build the costs and revenues in to support the business case.
- A project architect/architecture lead will start to look at where the organisation is going and how the structure of the business supports its direction.
- There will likely be a small team (the "discovery team") who will be responsible for asking business SMEs about the current data quality pain points to support the business case. A

similar team will look to discover how processes are failing from a data quality point of view – obviously these two teams can either be composed of the same individuals, or be in the same meeting to reduce the time taken from the business SMEs, but the focus is different, one set will work as data analysts and the other as process analysts.
- The data and process leads come on board to direct the discovery team and to start to assess the organisation.
- An addition at this stage is quality assurance, a separate section of the project reporting directly to the executive to provide an independent assurance on the progress of the project.

23.4.3 Stage 2: Direction.

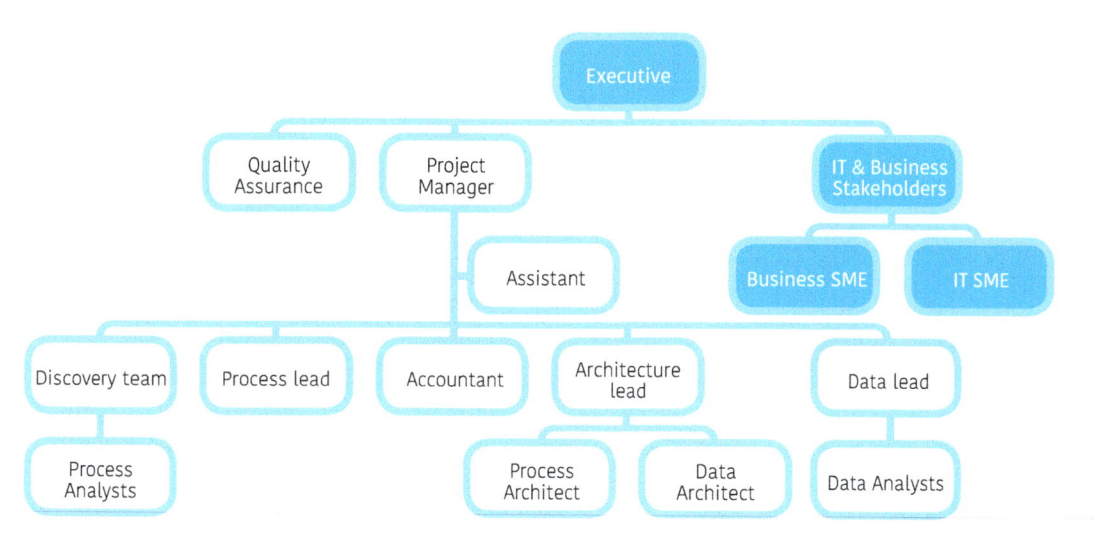

```
                            Executive
         ┌──────────┬──────────┴──────────────────┐
    Quality      Project                    IT & Business
   Assurance    Manager                     Stakeholders
                    │                        ┌────┴────┐
                Assistant                Business SME  IT SME
   ┌──────┬──────┬──┴────┬──────────┬──────────┐
Discovery Process  Accountant  Architecture   Data lead
  team    lead                     lead
    │                           ┌────┴────┐        │
 Process                     Process    Data    Data
 Analysts                   Architect  Architect Analysts
```

The next stage is direction, defining where the organisation is going. This requires several additional roles to the initiation stage.

- A strategy lead. This is someone who is experienced at taking the business requirements and translating them into data and process requirements at a strategic level. This could be a senior business analyst, or a more specialised role, or even a Chief Data Officer (CDO) or part of their team. The important element of this role is that it needs to be able to see the world from both a business context and an IT context.
- The discovery team is now split into process and data analysts, reporting to their respective leads.

It is worth noting here that the process analysts and data analysts are not technically required during this stage. There will be some need for data work if the organisation has not yet established any information requirements, however, this could be covered by the data lead and business SME. One of the reasons I would advocate starting the discovery stage early is to allow a clean pick-up of these resources that could move straight on to data profiling and process analysis.

What will be required is additional time from the executive, or any part of the organisation that is responsible for setting its strategy. These people need to inform the project where the organisation intends to go, in order that the business requirements for information can be defined.

Finally, also worth noting is that the accountant would probably not be allocated full time to the project at this point either.

23.4.4   Stage 3 – Discovery

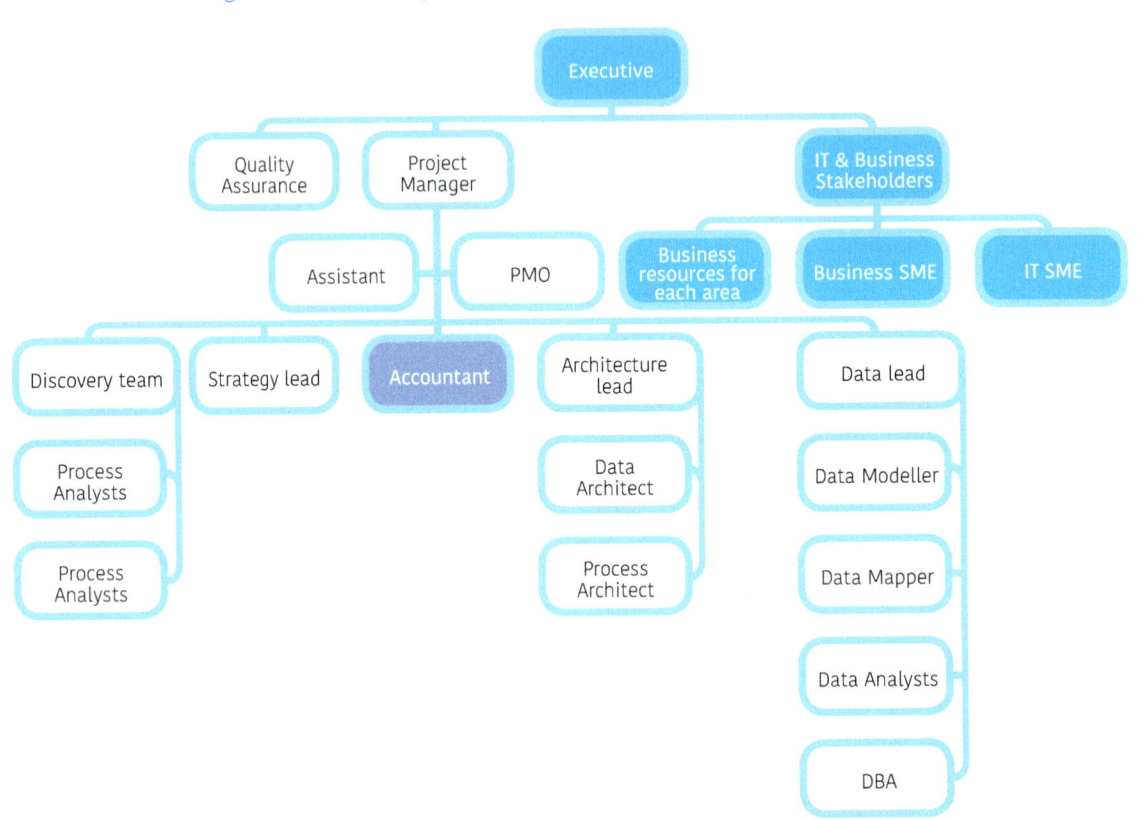

```
                                    Executive
                                       │
        ┌──────────────┬───────────────┼────────────────────────────┐
        │              │                                            │
     Quality        Project                                    IT & Business
    Assurance      Manager                                     Stakeholders
                      │                                             │
              ┌───────┴──────┐                     ┌────────────────┼──────────┐
          Assistant         PMO               Business         Business SME   IT SME
                                            resources for
                                              each area
        ┌─────────┬──────────┬─────────┐
    Discovery  Strategy  Accountant  Architecture          Data lead
      team       lead                    lead
        │                                 │                    │
     Process                            Data               Data Modeller
     Analysts                         Architect
        │                                 │                    │
     Process                           Process              Data Mapper
     Analysts                         Architect
                                                                │
                                                            Data Analysts
                                                                │
                                                              DBA
```

The next stage is discovery, and at the start of this phase a number of additional resources will need to come on board. This stage starts the documentation and analysis of architecture and processes, the mapping of data flows and profiling of data sources, and specialised professionals will be required. At this stage the project will need frequent access to business and IT subject matter experts, in order to understand data and process, and ideally such resources should be dedicated to the project.

- The architecture team is likely to remain small and senior.
- The database administrator (DBA) can look at the database in situ and extract data for use

by the data analyst. The DBA can also look at constraints on the database and understand how the data has been created. Good data analysts will be able to do the same. A DBA will also be able to track information to and from the major data stores, examine Extract-Transform-Load processes and understand data lineage.
- Process mappers will be required to document processes, and process analysts to analyse them.
- The data analyst role will be required to understand and profile the data. The data mappers will be required to understand and document data flows and data lineage. Data profiling can be done manually (via SQL queries or scripts) or via a profiling tool, and the approach adopted will determine the number of resources required.
- A data modeler will be useful to understand and/or develop the conceptual model of the source systems and thereby direct the profiling in the most efficient manner possible.

23.4.5   Stage 4 – Remediation Planning

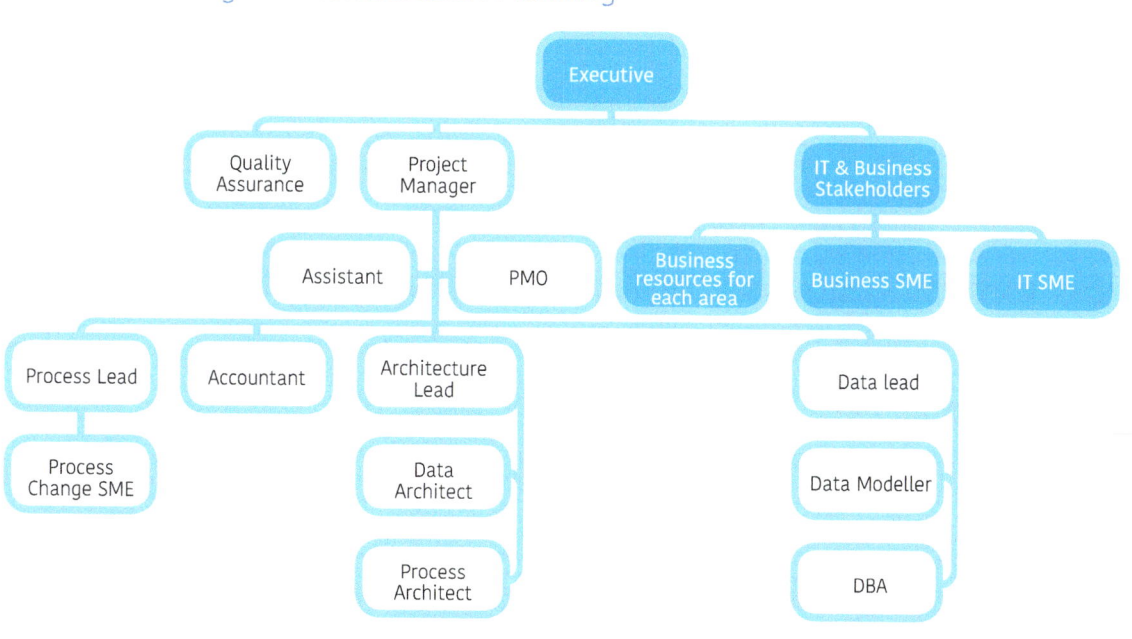

The next stage is remediation planning. This stage will shrink the overall project team as all the work from the discovery stage is consolidated. The objective of work in this stage is to decide exactly what will be remediated and how. The overall structure will resemble the original project initiation stage with a couple of additions:

- A Database Administrator (if one is not already in place) is at this point a welcome addition to the team to understand the data issues and how they can be addressed. This will not only cover the IT remediation work to bulk update records with good data, but also the constraints that can be placed on the databases as a preventative control.

- A process change expert is another addition to the team at this point, in order to take the inputs from the process analysis and process mapping and to translate this into a plan for process change.
- The accountant – mostly part time during the project – will become more involved due to the requirement for financial analysis.

23.4.6 Stage 5 – Remediation

The next stage – remediation – will see a significant expansion of the overall project team. At this point the project would be expected to bring in remediation teams, each headed by a team leader, to complete remediation tasks, whether it be architecture, process or data. The number and nature of these teams will depend on the scale of the remediation work to be undertaken and the skills required as a result. The project will also require a ramp up in terms of the resources it requires from the organisation, especially if there is widespread use of manual remediation utilising business-as-usual processes to remediate customer or product information.

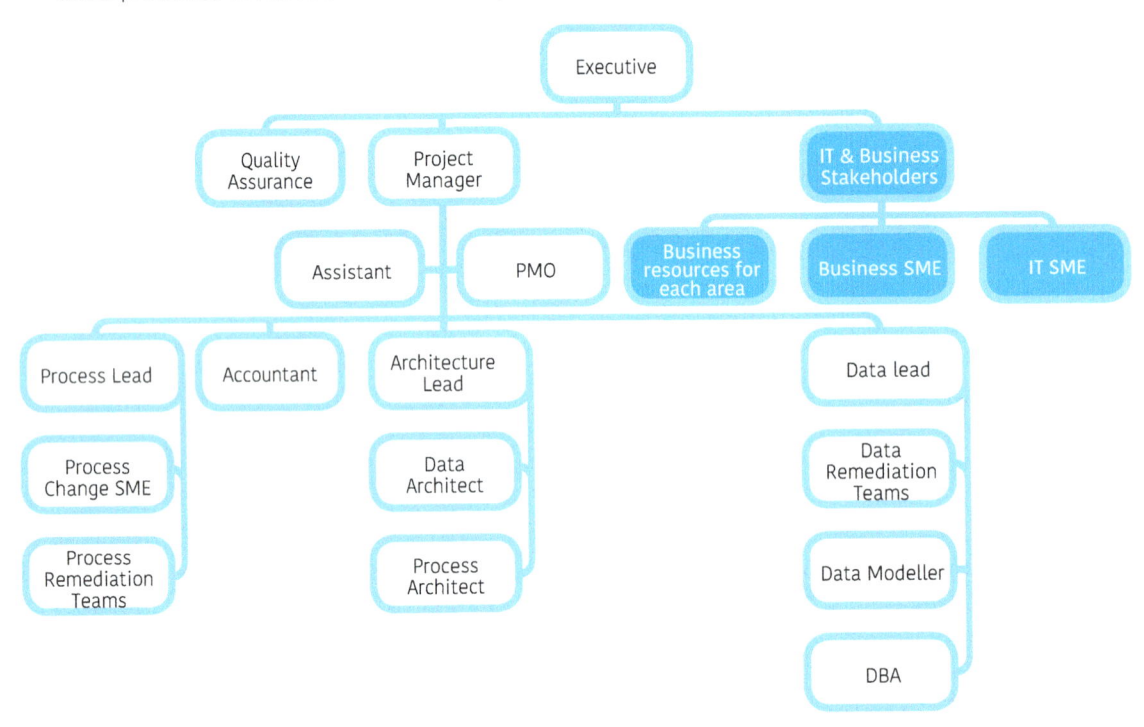

I will give an example from my own experience. In one project there was:

- A team purely working on the data quality of death registrations
- A team working entirely on product data
- A team working on customer details, with sub-teams looking at title, name and address

Additional tasks may well be required. For example, a specific (and critical) task will be workflow management; however, I have not added a specific role as have assumed this could be covered by the Project Manager, or preferably their assistant.

Other roles

Another new role at this stage would be one monitoring customer interactions – specifically customer complaints. There will be significant changes to customer data in this stage, and if these changes go wrong, the customer is likely to complain. Whilst obviously no organisation wishes matters to get to that stage, customer complaints are a useful long-stop to pick up the hopefully small number of issues that are missed by testing and quality assurance (there will be some). It also should be noted that the project should continue to involve senior business representatives from each area to understand what is occurring with their data, and to ensure it is in line with business expectations.

23.4.7   Stage 5 – Embedding

Embedding is the last stage of the project described in the book. At the point of entering the embedding stage the project team will shrink again, but will now require different specialists. It is perfectly possible, for example, for the governance and training to run at the same time at other stages as there is no personnel overlap. New entrants into the project for this stage will be:

- Knowledge management. The project will require a specialised practitioner to design and implement the process by which knowledge is shared and retained within the organisation.
- Training. The project will require a trainer to design and give the training to the organisation.
- Data Governance. If data governance is not already present in the organisation, and it

is the intention to stand up data governance as part of the embedding stage, then it is necessary to bring in a data governance practitioner.

23.5 Resource Profile of the Project

The above covers the roles required at each stage of the project, however, how does it all come together?

Over the entire data quality project there are two resource peaks, the first the discovery stage and the second the remediation stage. Both stages require significant number of resources to investigate and then remediate systems and process. In between is the planning phase, which typically requires less resources, and the final embedding stage is also not resource-heavy. Clearly the most appropriate solution here is to keep a core team for the majority of the product duration and supplement them with specialists as and when required.

However this does not consider the resources required from the "host" organisation to help remediate the data quality. A data quality project is going to utilise a significant amount of business and IT resources to:

- Help document processes.
- Describe data pain points.
- Test the results.
- Answer data and process-related queries.

My view would be that the majority of the business SMEs will be required in the discovery and planning phase, with a tail-off during the remediation and embedding phase. The actual remediators – probably the bulk of the project staff – will be required during the remediation phase, depending – as previously discussed – on the method of remediation.

23.6 Summary

Within this chapter I have taken a detailed look at the resourcing implications of a data quality project. This includes the nature of the resources, the number of these resources and when they will be required over the period of the project. This information should enable an organisation – or a project manager or data quality practitioner – to start to plan at a high level what will be required in terms of skills within a data quality project and to pull together a high level resource plan.

In the next chapter I will discuss the control and execution of a data quality project in order to ensure that it best meets its objectives.

SECTION 5.2 PROJECT PLANNING

CHAPTER 24 CONTROL AND EXECUTION

24.1 Structure

This stage of The Data Quality Blueprint includes the following phases:

1. Project Planning
2. Resourcing
3. Control & Execution
4. Moving on to Business as Usual

This chapter covers the third of these phases.

24.2 Overview

INPUTS	TASKS
■ All artefacts created or used to this point	■ Execute project by stage ■ Plan and update workflow as work items are completed ■ Allocate and manage resources, both in-project resources and also subject matter experts. ■ Update plan for new information and as work items are completed ■ Update product and task lists as required. ■ Create and deliver weekly reporting ■ Create and deliver monthly reporting ■ Create and deliver stage reporting ■ Manage deliverables ■ Update risk assessment for new risks and changes to risks and risk profile ■ Update assumptions ■ Update dependency log and manage dependencies ■ Update issue log and report and manage issues ■ Update daily log as required
OUTPUTS ■ Updated plan ■ Updated risk assessment ■ Updated dependency log ■ Updated assumptions log ■ Updated issue log ■ Updated resource estimation	
DEPENDENCIES ■ Access to stakeholders ■ Project resources ■ Business resources ■ IT resources ■ Technical resources	

A data quality project is similar to any other large, multi-stage project and execution will rely on traditional project management tools and skills. There is nothing particularly special about a data quality project and most experienced project managers will be perfectly capable of delivery.

The only element of project management that may be different in a data quality project is that there will be a large number of moving parts. The project, depending on scheduling, may be simultaneously performing discovery work on architecture, process and data, or remediating architecture, process and data as well as starting the governance and training elements of the project. Whilst I have no intention of turning the book into a description of best practice project management – there are many, many publications in existence, plus several well-known methodologies – this chapter will first cover a few topics for those whose knowledge of project management is less extensive.

24.3 Project Stages

A typical project will pass through four stages:

Initiation → Planning → Execution → Close

We have covered initiation and planning already, and close is covered in the next chapter, so what tasks fall into execution? Work done in execution will cover:

- Progress management
- Risk management
- Monitoring of performance
- Monitoring of quality
- Issue management
- Change management
- Monitoring of cost
- Resource management

I have already covered risk assessment in an earlier chapter. Risk management is the continuation of this process throughout the life of the project, where new risks are identified, assessed, and action taken to mitigate, avoid, accept or transfer that risk from the project. Issue management is also covered elsewhere. This is the process of tracking issues from when they were initially raised through to their resolution. Monitoring of cost will mainly cover the monitoring of time, and will be closely linked to timesheets and analysis of time spent against tasks achieved.

Monitoring of quality is the monitoring of deliverables. Each deliverable should be listed in a deliverables log, held centrally and written into the contract, and the progress against each deliverable reported. Part of the reason for this is ensuring that the deliverables meet the expectations of the organisation. Here I would suggest agreeing and documenting the format and contents of every deliverable with those who will be signing it off as complete. I would also advocate the utilisation of a quality assurance function on the project to independently monitor the quality of the deliverables. Monitoring of progress, which I will cover briefly here, will come down to the plan, products and the deliverables.

Monitoring by plan

The easiest way to manage a data quality project is by reference to a plan. This breaks down the overall project into time-boxed tasks which can then be marked as complete. Most modern project planning aids will make this process easy indeed and after the initial effort to create the plan, following it should be straightforward. It is worth creating high level summaries of work as it is unlikely that senior individuals will drill down into the detailed tasks, but will merely want to know "how remediation is going". Preparing a plan that can be rolled up to a level consistent with answering such questions will make the project manager's life easier later on.

The risk with control by plan is that any project changes over time and the plan will also change. For a data quality project, the effort required will be unknown until the discovery phase has been completed. I therefore suggest the creation of three planning phases. The first mini-planning phase at initiation covers just that stage. The first major phase (and the second overall) plans at a high level for the overall project, but at a detail level only for the direction and discovery elements of the project. The third validates the original plan and updates it for the "real" information now to hand. There is a danger that the organisation may see the initial plan and assume everything will be over quickly, but then the discovery phase uncovers a heap of horrors and this timescale needs to be extended. The messaging should clearly be: "We'll take a guess at long it will take to remediate, but we don't know, and will have to revise the estimate later when we have done more work."

Monitoring Products

A useful way of looking at projects is utilising a product flow diagram. This treats each part of the project as a deliverable in its own right, and adds dependencies to products upstream and from products downstream. This is product based planning. An example may be:

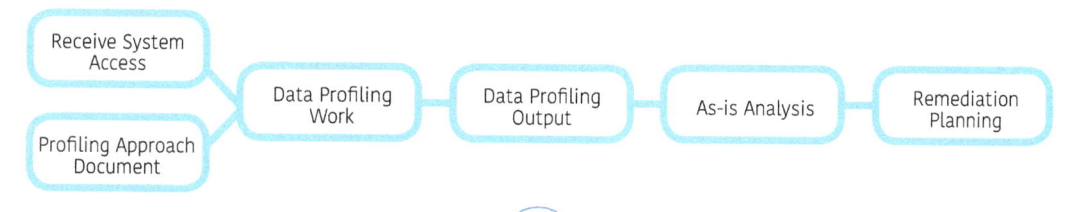

In this example, the deliverable "access to systems" and the deliverable "profiling approach document" are pre-requisites for the data profiling work, and so on. This gives a means of control for the overall project which can map how each element of the project relates to every other element of the project. This is often represented by a dependency matrix or dependency diagram. It is possible to control the project and determine the overall level of completion, as well as the risks to the overall project and the way in which each element relates, in this manner.

Change Management

Management of change will be an inevitable task on any project. There are many change management methodologies but one I have come across more than once and works effectively is outlined below.

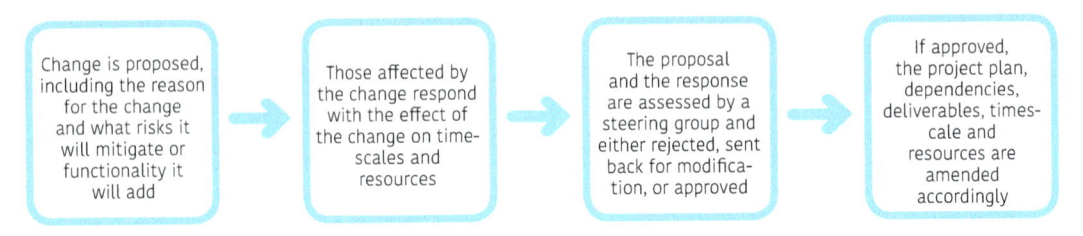

Change is proposed, including the reason for the change and what risks it will mitigate or functionality it will add → Those affected by the change respond with the effect of the change on timescales and resources → The proposal and the response are assessed by a steering group and either rejected, sent back for modification, or approved → If approved, the project plan, dependencies, deliverables, timescale and resources are amended accordingly

Change is always contentious, and if the project is looking to change anything I would strongly recommend having a thorough read through the "hearts and minds" chapter to ensure that when change is proposed, all those affected by it are consulted in advance. I have more than once carefully primed key stakeholders before a difficult meeting and then the one I could not get hold of caused all the problems. Deal with problems before the meeting.

Reporting

Whatever the nature of the project, it is likely that the project manager will be required to report on a regular (probably weekly) basis detailing:

- Progress against plan
- Risks arising
- Deliverables
- Issues arising
- Near future dependencies

Control by reporting is the traditional way of managing projects, where each team submits a report weekly to the project manager detailing the progress on their work, and the project manager then rolls these reports up into a weekly report to the executive.

A lot of senior executives quite like the cadence of this approach, and I will admit I have a fair amount of time for it myself. It means that the information arrives and can be browsed at leisure, usually over the weekend when there's hopefully not a lot else going on and time can be dedicated to think about the project, where it is going, what needs to be achieved, and how all of this is affected by the report that has just been given to you on a Friday afternoon – and then prepare a list of queries for the project team to give to them on Monday. However, several major project methodologies (notably PRINCE 2) criticise the approach of regular reports as creating a lot of unnecessary paperwork.

The "manage by exception" approach recommends setting a target and a variance, and the report only gets created if the variance is exceeded – or is likely to be exceeded. It will depend on the executive whether they are happy with this approach, and each person is different in the degree of reassurance that is required from the project management.

24.4 Workflow

As mentioned one of the characteristics of a data quality project is a large number of moving parts, and tracking them all can be a large amount of effort in itself. A workflow tracks the progress of each task from the point where the work is started through to completion. This allows a high level holistic view of the overall progress of the work to be easily created. Workflow stages are shown in the diagram below.

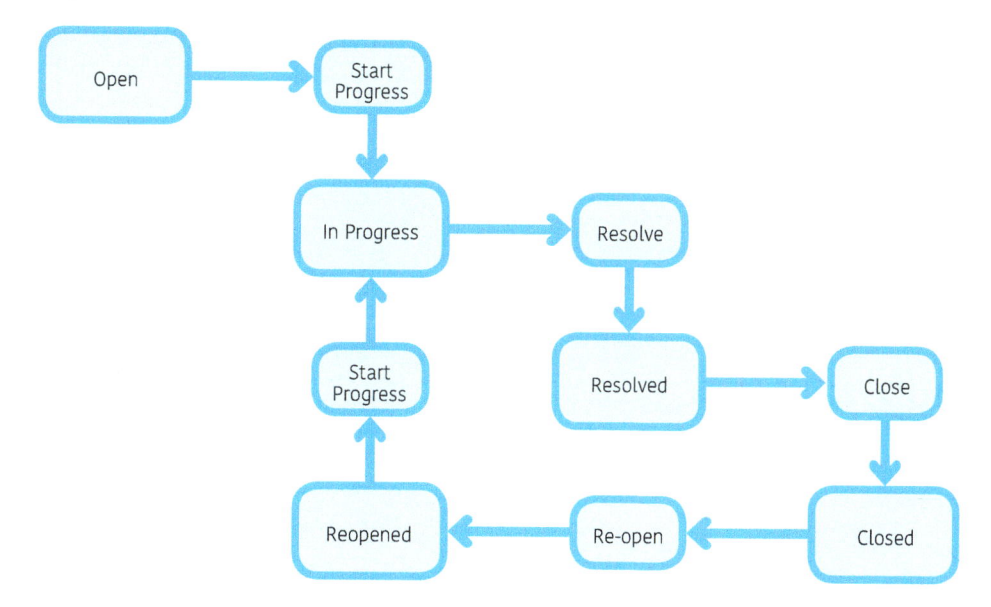

```
Open → Start Progress
         ↓
       In Progress → Resolve
         ↑              ↓
       Start         Resolved → Close
       Progress                    ↓
         ↑                      Closed
       Reopened ← Re-open ←────────┘
```

I have already mentioned that in a data quality project some stages can be independent from each other and can take place concurrently, but this does make management more complex. Remediation in particular may consist of hundreds of separate mini-projects to remediate elements of data or process. Tasks may be:

- Contact customers and determine 300 dates of birth.
- Contact customer and determine 10,000 NI numbers.
- Match 100,000 addresses against the Royal Mail postcode index and remediate the addresses if they do not match the Royal Mail format.

When tracking the individual data-related work streams there is a useful measure – the number of records. It becomes more difficult when tracking remediation of processes. It helps to use a similar format for the purpose of recording both process and data stages. An example is shown in the table below.

Element (Data Quality)	Element (Process)
- Business data quality measure affected - Number of records - Remediation type - Owner - Stage - Current KPI - Estimated completion time - Time taken to date	- Business data quality measure affected - Complexity of process - Remediation type - Owner - Stage - Current KPI - Estimated completion time - Time taken to date.

For day to day management of the remediation it is preferable to use a workflow tracker. A simple spreadsheet may serve the requisite purpose, but if not there are many workflow monitoring tools in the marketplace, some of which are freely available. Examples of a workflow record in a simple spreadsheet format are shown below.

Element	No	Remediation Type	Owner	Stage	Current KPI
Blank titles	45,216	Automatic – assignation by perceived gender	IT	In Progress	74% Complete
Blank titles where automatic assignation not possible	3,000	Manual	Contact Centre	In Progress	5% Complete
Title does not match forename	2651	Manual	Contact Centre	In Progress	Complete

24.5 Further reading

- *Managing Transitions: Making the Most of Change*, 3rd Edition, William Bridges, Nicholas Brealey Publishing, 2009
- *Managing Successful Projects with PRINCE 2*, TSO 2009
- *Teach Yourself Successful Change Management in a Week,* Mike Bourne, Teach Yourself, 2012
- *Project Management For Dummies,* Nick Graham, John Wiley & Sons, 2015
- *Visual Project Management: Simplifying Project Execution to Deliver On Time and On Budget*, Mark Woeppel, Pinnacle Americas, Inc, 2015
- *Project Management Step by Step: How to Plan and Manage a Highly Successful Project*, Richard Newton, Pearson Business, 2007
- *A Guide to the Project Management Body of Knowledge (Pmbok Guide)*, Project Management Institute, 2013
- *The Change Manager's Handbook*, Harley Lovegrove, Linchpin Publishing, 2015

24.6 Summary

Within this chapter I have looked at the project management of the execution stage, including risk, issue, cost and quality management, change management progress monitoring and reporting. I have also explained the concept of workflow and how it can be used to manage large numbers of concurrent tasks.

This chapter has continued on the theme of explaining in detail how a project of this nature will work at a high level and what elements of project management will be especially relevant for a data quality project. Again, it is understood that the reader may not necessarily have exposure to this kind of project environment, and I would wish to make sure, before discussing the operation of the project in detail, that this ground is covered.

In the next section I will cover the last stage of the project, which is project close and moving on to business as usual.

SECTION 5.2 PROJECT PLANNING

CHAPTER 25: MOVING ON TO BUSINESS AS USUAL

25.1 Structure

This stage of The Data Quality Blueprint includes the following phases:

1. Project Planning
2. Resourcing
3. Control & Execution
4. Moving on to Business as Usual

This chapter covers the last of these phases.

25.2 Overview

INPUTS	TASKS
■ All artefacts created or utilised to date	■ Finalise risk assessment taking account of all project risks. Include risks to BAU that have been identified
OUTPUTS	■ Finalise dependency log, indicate any remaining dependencies and their stage
■ Final risk assessment	■ Finalise assumptions log
■ Final assumptions log	■ Finalise issues log including any unresolved issues
■ Final dependency log	■ Document lessons learned and feed into knowledge management framework
■ Final issues log	■ Document any unfinished work
■ End project report	■ Perform team appraisals and give feedback
■ Team appraisals	■ Finalise workflow and note where items are not closed
■ Lessons learned	■ Document tasks remaining or required to complete work
■ Any detail of unfinished work	■ Complete final project costs, and compare with budget
■ Change assessment	■ Create end project report. This covers the performance of the project against objectives, key data quality KPIs before and after remediation, project costs and time measured against budget
DEPENDENCIES	■ End Project Report
■ Access to stakeholders	- Data quality assessment
■ Access to BAU teams	- Budget assessment
	- Timescale assessment
	- Benefits review plan
	- Lessons learned
	- Outstanding issues
	- Create end project report
	- Agree with sponsor and key stakeholders
	- Obtain written signoff
	- Baseline and upload into project document repository
	■ Agree ongoing communications with project team and key stakeholders
	■ Agree ongoing knowledge management with team and key stakeholders

I have stated elsewhere in the book that the objective of a data quality project is largely to make itself redundant. At the end of the project, there will be a number of outcomes.

- Remediated data
- Remediated processes (to ensure that data does not have to be remediated again)
- (Potentially) Remediated architecture
- A sound understanding of how the organisation will deal with its data landscape in the future in respect of data quality.
- Data governance and data management framework
- Training delivered
- Knowledge management delivered

The end stage of the project is to finally hand over remediated data and processes into business as usual, to wind up the project, and to measure the realised benefits before everyone packs up on a job well done. Within this chapter I will briefly discuss the considerations concerning moving the project to business as usual. This will include winding down the project team or bringing them into the data governance effort. I will also look at specific problems to be faced and the ways of facing them.

25.3   Approach

A data quality project combines business process re-engineering, data remediation and architecture remediation. Each part – indeed each data element or process – can transition to business as usual when required. There is not necessary for a "big bang" approach where the whole project moves to business as usual at the same time.

Business process re-engineering will involve identifying and measuring problems with data quality, and identifying the process that caused them. The practitioner will need to design a new process, test this process, and implement this process. Finally the process will need to be re-examined to ensure that the predicted benefits have been realised. At the end of this process the process is embedded into business as usual.

The steps for taking the remediated data and process and embedding them into the new world are covered in remediation of data and process. Unlike many projects (especially software projects) a data quality project does not "go live", but is a continuous incremental improvement from day to day. The only exception to this would be if the information was being collated into a new "golden source" – potentially as part of an MDM project – which is then "switched on" at a point in time representing a typical "go live" date. However the scope of this book is not MDM, but a practical look at how to remediate data which is solution-agnostic.

However, there will be a process to take the project as a whole to a conclusion. This will involve:

- Handling artefacts over to the relevant departments (knowledge transfer and knowledge management – discussed later).
- Documenting the various improvements that have been made to architecture, data and process.
- Determining whether the project has realised the overall benefits in the business case.
- Preparing a statement to the board in relation to the final costs and success of the project.
- Releasing personnel back to their departments or (if temporary staff) releasing them from the organisation.

In addition there will be the final wrap-up and management of the workflow. The project needs to be happy that all elements of workflow have completed satisfactorily.

25.4   Transitioning the Project Team

An important consideration in the winding up of the project is what to do with the core project team. These individuals have lived and breathed data quality for some time and are likely to be an effective functional unit with a considerable knowledge of data quality. My personal view is that if we consider that embedding forms one of the last phases of the project, and this includes data governance, these individuals would be an excellent place to start to allocate data steward responsibilities, or to form a governance board. They will most certainly have views on data governance, and will be quite keen to ensure that their good work within the data quality project is not wasted. Alternatively, it is possible to embed these individuals in departments (potentially the departments from which they were originally sourced) as data quality champions.

25.5 Problems to be Faced

There are specific issues that will only occur at the end of the project. I mention these here, but have not gone into solutions, as this would require another book on subjects varying from change and configuration management to code merge. All of these topics are well covered by others elsewhere. What I will cover here is a few pointers on areas that may cause a concern.

Where is the remediated data and how are you going to move it so that all parts of the business use it?

One of the challenges with data quality remediation is that whilst it is relatively simple to take a static data set and remediate it in isolation, updating live data – especially data that is in constant use, is considerably trickier. It is better to update the data that applications are already using, because this doesn't involve remapping all the applications to different data stores, but then the data is in hundreds of disparate places, will shortly start to diverge, and the problem will recur. The potential of a Master Data Management (MDM) solution has already been mentioned, where a separate project can bring all the data into one place and then ensure that all parts of the business use that one data store. The approach of a well-managed shift of data from development through testing to production also addresses the problem (and is described later in the data remediation chapter) but could be onerous for a small organisation.

How are the new processes going to be integrated?

There will be a point where old processes stop and new begin. How is this going to be managed? This is addressed within the chapter on process remediation. Luckily, as opposed to data, once a process has been remediated then it should remain working until otherwise changed. It is, however, important to make sure that the processes work together. Care has to be taken to not introduce gaps in the control framework, and overall process architecture design has to be considered as part of the project to ensure that such situations do not occur. Part of the end state and the transition to business as usual is looking at that organisation-wide operation in a holistic manner; coming out of the detail and understanding how all the moving parts are working together.

What happens if it starts getting worse again?

A (hopefully) rare problem, at least if The Data Quality Blueprint is followed, is what happens if the data quality in the organisation starts to degrade again? Now the project is complete, the team disbanded, and there may not be the resources available to go and re-solve the problem.

The key here is to catch any degradation early. If a certain department starts creating poor data then this needs to be picked up fast, before it reaches the stage where the problem has got too big to solve. Reporting metrics need to be sufficiently detailed to identify the cause of poor data quality and to allow drill-down to enable a hit squad to identify, and remediate quickly. The retention of this "virtual" hit squad – especially in large organisations – may be a legacy of the project. This is a group of individuals with data quality experience (another possibility for the data quality team post-project), who can descend on a part of the organisation where it is all going wrong and help them to address their problems.

Rewriting the past?

A critical consideration in relation to data quality is that the data quality project will be changing information on the organisation's systems. This is generally seen as a good thing, as it improves the quality of the information that can be used for reporting, mining, and decision-making. However in many cases it is rewriting the past. For example, imagine an organisation where sales location has been incorrectly set to a default value of the head office. Reports to executive on the relative profitability of regions, regional sales figures, etc, will be grossly distorted. Updating the data quality then results in a large shift of the data from the pre-remediated state.

This may (at best) raise eyebrows, and executives and managers need to be aware that their world-view may have to change as a result of the better information within the information systems. At worst, such data has been published – in accounts, to investors, shareholders and the regulator. Careful management is key. The executive has to understand that this above scenario is possible, and they need to plan in advance how it will be managed. Going to the regulator and explaining that regulatory submissions have been wrong for 10 years is unlikely to win friends. On the other hand it is certainly better than not telling them and them finding out in another way.

25.6   End Project Assessment

It is mentioned above that it is wise to look at the overall organisation's landscape after the project has completed and to assess how the landscape has changed as a result of the project. This is the end project assessment. This should include:

- Review of the business case
- Review of the objectives of the project
- What has been done, what has been changed?
- Review of responsibilities for business as usual
- Summary of follow-on actions
- Lessons report – what went well, what didn't
- Summary of costs and benefits
- Recommendations for the future

The end project assessment draws a line under the project and is a formal closure. This document should be presented to and signed off by the executive sponsor.

25.7   Summary

In this chapter I have covered the work that needs to be planned in respect of moving data quality from the project into business as usual. I have outlined for the reader the overall approach and also suggested various ways of utilising the project team. It should be mentioned here that this chapter represents a high level overview only, as the embedding of the remediated data and processes are also included in the chapters on remediation.

In addition, a more detailed consideration of how data quality can be embedded in any organisation is included later in this book. In the last few chapters I have taken the reader through considerations in respect of the project planning, and what would be required in each stage in terms of resourcing, and also given an indication of the overall timescale of the project.

The project has now created a large number of artefacts, understands at a high level the landscape of the organisation, and knows where it is going and what needs to be achieved. Hopefully the roadblocks in terms of understanding, scope and buy-in have been removed and the project can point itself at the future and keep going. In the next section I will be looking in detail at the "Direction" stage of the data quality project, to understand the organisation's direction and mapping this to what the project needs to achieve.

SECTION 5.3 DIRECTION

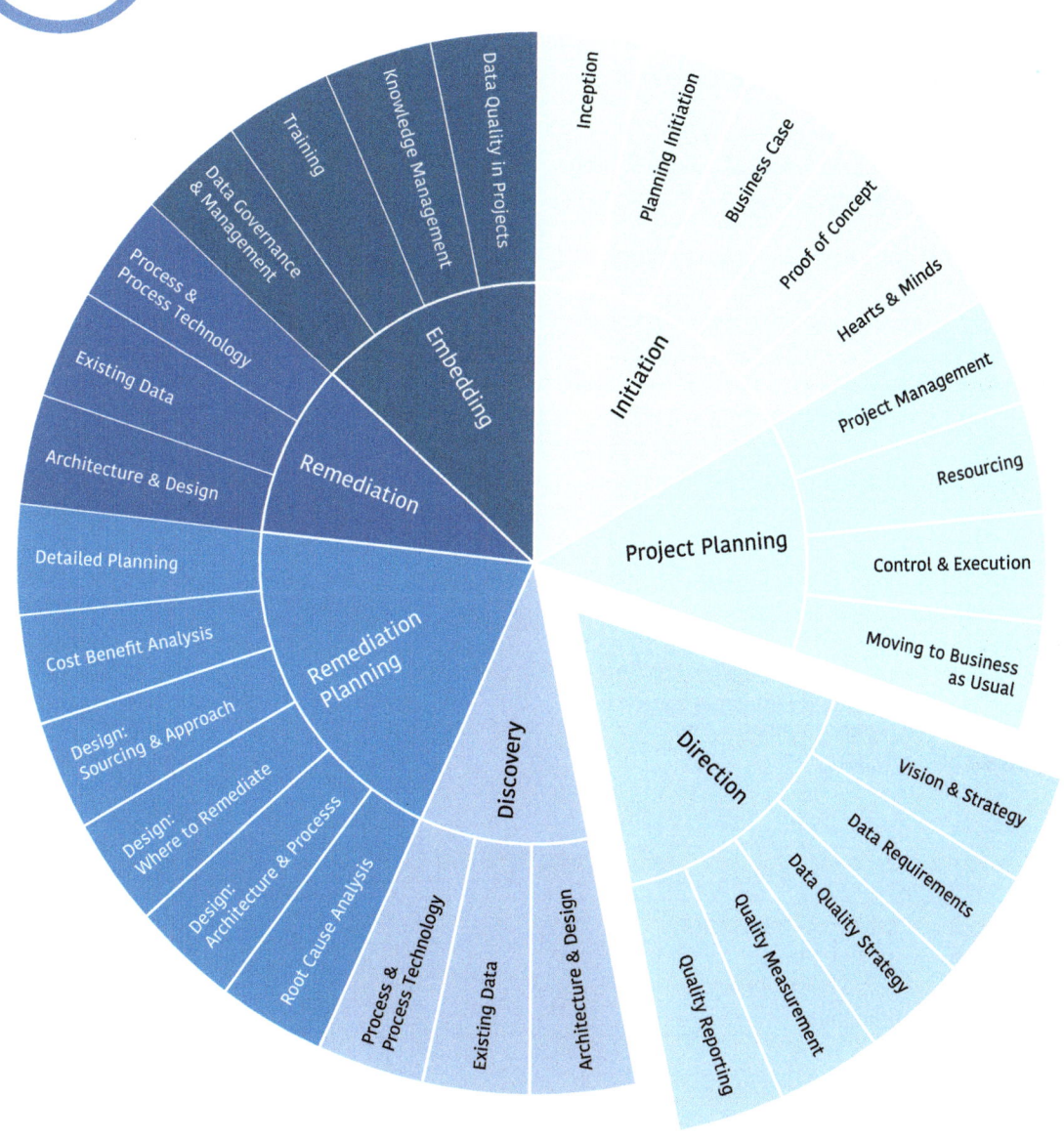

Where are we going and what do we want to achieve?

SECTION 5.3: INDEX

CHAPTER 26: Vision and Strategy — 281
- 26.1 Structure — 281
- 26.2 Overview — 282
- 26.3 Corporate Vision & Strategy — 283
- 26.4 Data Vision — 284
- 26.5 Data Strategy Overview — 284
- 26.6 Key Components of a Data Strategy — 285
- 26.7 Summary — 291

CHAPTER 27: Data Requirements — 293
- 27.1 Structure — 293
- 27.2 Overview — 294
- 27.3 What are Data Requirements? — 295
- 27.4 Where do Data Requirements come from? — 295
- 27.5 What should Data Requirements include? — 297
- 27.6 How to Approach Detailed Data Requirements — 300
- 27.7 Data Quality Requirements — 301
- 27.8 Summary — 302

CHAPTER 28: Data Quality Strategy — 303
- 28.1 Structure — 303
- 28.2 Overview — 304
- 28.3 Data Quality Strategy Overview — 304
- 28.4 Data Quality Implementation Plan — 310
- 28.5 Data Quality Policy — 310
- 28.6 Summary — 311

CHAPTER 29: Quality Measurement — 313
- 29.1 Structure — 313
- 29.2 Overview — 314
- 29.3 Introduction of Metrics — 314
- 29.4 Types of Metrics — 316
- 29.5 How to get the Metrics — 318
- 29.6 Summary — 322

CHAPTER 30: Quality Reporting — 323
- 30.1 Structure — 323
- 30.2 Overview — 324
- 30.3 What Should Reporting Include? — 324
- 30.4 Technical Data Quality Reports — 325
- 30.5 Reporting on Specific Business-Relevant Data — 325

30.6	Reporting the Data Quality in Existing Reports (data reliability reports)	326
30.7	Reporting the Effect of Poor Data	326
30.8	Timing of Reports	326
30.9	Types of Dashboards	327
30.10	Proof of Concept	327
30.11	Reporting Tools	327
30.12	When Should Dashboards be Created?	328
30.13	Summary	329

SECTION 5.3 DIRECTION

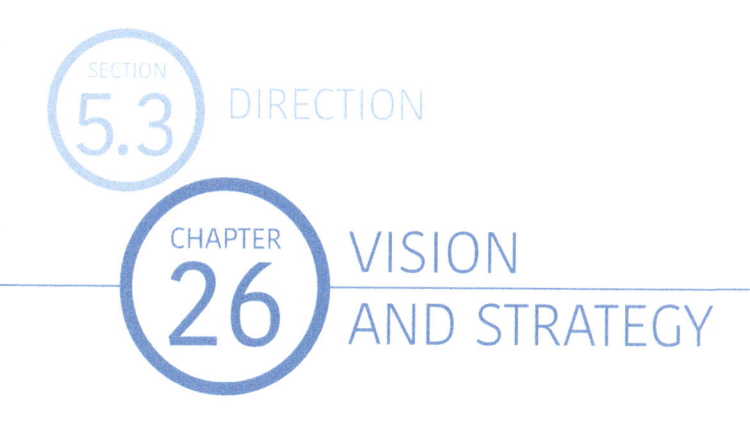

CHAPTER 26 VISION AND STRATEGY

26.1 Structure

This stage of The Data Quality Blueprint includes the following phases:

1. Vision & Strategy
2. Data Requirements
3. Data Quality Strategy
4. Quality Measurement
5. Quality Reporting

This chapter covers the first of these phases.

26.2 Overview

INPUTS
- All project artefacts created or used so far
- Corporate vision
- Corporate strategy
- Data architecture
- Data strategy (if available)
- Business architecture
- Application architecture
- Infrastructure architecture

OUTPUTS
- Data impacts of corporate strategy
- Data requirements for corporate vision
- Map of corporate vision to data vision
- Template for data strategy
- Data vision
- Data strategy

DEPENDENCIES
- Access to stakeholders
- Access to executives
- Access to corporate strategy

TASKS
- Corporate Vision
  - Discuss corporate vision with sponsor and key stakeholders
  - Obtain or document the corporate vision
  - Upload to project repository
- Corporate Strategy
  - Discuss corporate strategy with sponsor and key stakeholders
  - Obtain the corporate strategy
  - Assess corporate strategy for data elements
  - Document data impacts of corporate strategy
  - Present to key sponsor
  - Upload to project repository
- Data Vision
  - Obtain data vision if it already exists
  - Determine vision for each functional area
  - Determine the data requirements needed to support the vision
  - Map corporate vision to data vision
  - Assess for data impact on current landscape
  - Present to key sponsor
  - Upload to project repository
- Data Strategy
  - Obtain data strategy if it already exists
  - Agree template for data strategy with sponsor
  - Input data and corporate vision
  - Create data strategy
    - Scope
    - Purpose
    - Define information requirements of the organisation
    - Key principles
    - Information acquisition
    - Information governance
    - Management framework, roles and responsibilities
    - Information policy and practice
    - Information management lifecycle
    - Data classification
    - Information protection
    - Knowledge sharing and collaboration
    - Delivery and communications
    - Technical implications
    - Analyse strengths and weaknesses of organisation
    - Analyse strengths and weaknesses of competitors
    - Analyse strengths and weaknesses of the market
  - Draft data strategy
  - Present to sponsor and other critical individuals and gain feedback
  - Finalise data strategy
  - Receive written signoff
  - Baseline and upload into project document repository

> "Information should ultimately support the goal of any enterprise—to deliver value for its stakeholders—which translates to enterprise goals that should be achieved"
> **COBIT 5, *Enabling Information*, ISACA**

Before anything else, before the first process is examined or the first database is interrogated, any data quality practitioner should ask – "where does this organisation wish to take its information?" A common failing of many data quality projects is the inclination to start work before they know where they are going, resulting in at best a waste of resources or, at worst, effort that actually makes achieving the organisation's final goals less achievable. The starting point of any strategy – data or otherwise – must always be the corporate vision, as this defines the destination. This vision will be set by the board of the company, the executives whose job it is to control its future direction. The vision may reach out a decade; the strategy is usually 3-5 years.

In this chapter I will discuss the overall "statement of direction". I will start with the corporate vision and corporate strategy, which detail how the vision will be achieved. The corporate vision then defines the data vision – and the data vision and the corporate strategy define the data strategy. I will then give a breakdown of the components of the data strategy – what it needs to include and in what detail. This should clearly define the direction that data will take within the organisation. This information is needed before continuing to the next chapter which will discuss data requirements.

26.3 Corporate Vision & Strategy

Defining where you are going is the first step in trying to get there. Before anything else the corporate strategy needs to define how the corporate vision will be achieved. Worryingly some (incorrectly, in my view) consider that the data strategy can evolve independently of the company strategy, or even be defined by the IT department. The data strategy and data quality strategy must be specifically defined to support the company strategy.

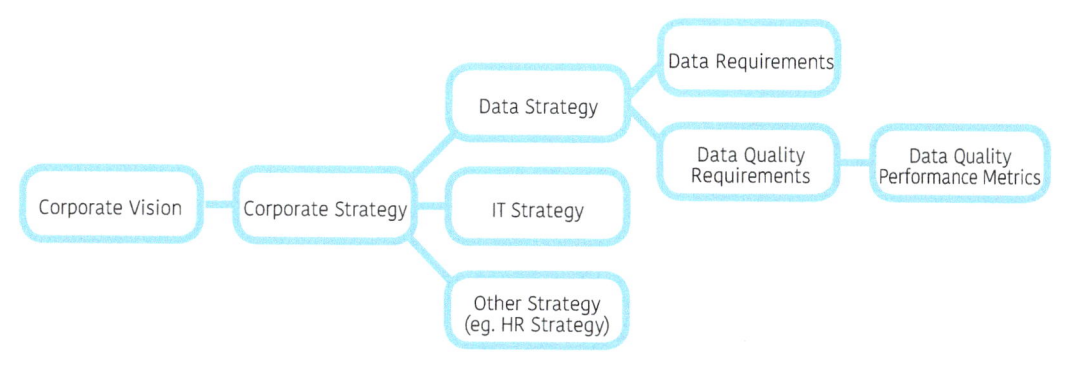

If the data strategy is developed independently of the organisation's vision and strategy, it will naturally diverge from it, and may – as a result – actually hinder its achievement.

For example, if the corporate strategy, carefully considered and fully achievable from a market perspective, is to grow the number of customers by 50%, however the systems only have a small capacity for future growth, then the systems will constrain the strategy and the tail is wagging the dog. The corporate vision defines the organisation's strategy, which defines the data strategy and IT strategy (and recruitment strategy, HR strategy, etc) and these define the data requirements (where you want to get to). The data requirements define the data performance metrics (how you will measure your data quality and hence the project success) and the policy and procedures (how you'll achieve this quality). This order of precedence is shown in the diagram above.

26.4   Data Vision

It is, of course, possible to go from the corporate vision straight to the corporate strategy and then to the data strategy. However, there is a value in the concept of a "data vision". The data vision is how the organisation would like to use information in the future.

For example, I was recently told of a insurance company's future state vision which was on the following lines: the organisation tracks a policyholder's car in real time. When this tracking indicates the car has had an accident it automatically contacts the policyholder via smartphone. If the customer indicates that an accident has occurred the organisation automatically despatches a recovery vehicle, medical care, accident assessors, and a drone to take photographs of the accident scene and then uploads all the data in real time to the customer's phone where they can accept or reject the claim details. The organisation then sends a self-driving courtesy car to take the customer onwards to their destination.

The above scenario will require an information vision. This will cover:

- Knowledge of the car whereabouts
- Knowledge of the smartphone whereabouts (no point if it's not in the car)
- Knowledge of the nearest drone location
- Ability to upload from a drone to central databases
- Ability to process a claim in seconds
- Knowledge of the whereabouts of the nearest courtesy car

The technology exists now, the availability doesn't. But it is a vision. A data vision, therefore, can and should be quite future-focused. However, if a company has a vision, it is important to ensure that current strategy supports that vision. Too many companies spend a fortune on expensive technology which does not actually improve their organisation – or is at best a tactical solution that will need to be unpicked later. Defining a data strategy is outside the scope of this book and in any case every organisation is different depending on its information maturity, its industry, its desired direction, and the journey it wishes to take. What I have done within this chapter is to document the contents of a data strategy.

26.5   Data Strategy Overview

From the starting point of the company strategy, the next stage is to define the data strategy. The DAMA-DM_BOK Guide states that:

> "Typically, a data strategy is a data management programme strategy – a plan for maintaining and improving data quality, integrity, security, and access. However a data strategy may also include business plans to use information to competitive advantage and support enterprise goals. Data strategy must come from an understanding of the data needs inherent in the business strategies. These data needs drive the data strategy." [44]

My personal view is that the above quote does not go quite far enough, and a data strategy should be more than simply a data management strategy. A data strategy should incorporate all the parts of the organisation's information landscape and clearly state what the future holds for each – albeit at a high level. I have seen data strategies that go down to a much greater level of detail and include the data policy. I would personally recommend against this as the two documents have different audiences. Those who wish to read the high level strategy are unlikely to be the same people who want to read the detail individual policies and procedures. I have included within the appendices a sample data strategy (loosely based on those I have written for real organisations) which gives a more "living" example.

I would urge the reader, if looking to create a data strategy, to use the internet to acquire examples. There are many available, primarily from public sector organisations, though it is becoming more common for private sector organisations to publish their information strategy as well.

26.6 Key Components of a Data Strategy

A data strategy should cover the following sections, which I will list, and then cover in detail.

- Scope
- Purpose
- Key strategic drivers for change
- Value of information resources
- Risk of undertaking the strategy
- Information needs of the organisation
- Key principles
- Data acquisition
- Information governance
- Information management
- Information policy and practice
- Information lifecycle
- Information security
- Information sharing
- Technical implications

26.6.1 Scope

The data strategy must clearly define its own scope and the parts of the organisation it covers. Especially in early stages of implementation the scope may be restricted – to, for example, finance – and then be rolled out at a later date. In many organisations there is often a fundamental misunderstanding of data, or how important data is, so it is necessary to be crystal clear where the scope ends and begins. For example, MRI (Magnetic Resonance Imaging) scans may not appear to be data in terms of the classical spreadsheet or database. They are clearly vitally important to an organisation (and the patient!), and are held in databases. They are information, and will be used for a number

---

44. *Data Management Body of Knowledge, DAMA-BOK*, Technics Publications, 2010.

of processes and procedures, surgery and the like. I would submit that they absolutely are data, and should be treated as such. They therefore should have an owner and have defined quality requirements. A clear and unambiguous definition of scope is essential when implementing a strategy and the scope should equally define what is not covered by the data strategy. The scope should list the business areas of the organisation and which are in or out.

26.6.2 Objectives of the strategy

The objective of the data strategy needs to be defined. This definition need only be at a high level. For example, a typical set of objectives for a data strategy is shown below:

- To align the information of the organisation with the corporate direction and principles.
- To set out roles and responsibilities for the governance, management and control of information.
- To define the high level information principles of the organisation.
- To define the approach to determine the information requirements of the organisation.

The strategy also needs to include the following information, and can either include this within a "background" section or in separate sections of their own.

Key strategic drivers for change	Why the strategy is being written and implemented
Value of information resources	How the organisation values data. What it considers important
Risks of undertaking this strategy	The organisation needs to demonstrably understand risks of undertaking the data strategy. In every case the operation of improving data will require resources, and likely scarce resources.

26.6.3 Information needs of the organisation

The data strategy needs to define the information needs of the organisation. This does not need to be done at great detail. Whilst this may appear obvious, the overall data strategy for, say, a postal delivery firm may involve a wish for customer location – so post can be delivered to people, not addresses. If so, this has implications for the data model, data architecture, timeliness of information within the systems, and would have some major implications for the overall data strategy. Categorisation of the information requirements may facilitate definition. The example used below is one of the taxonomies covered in the earlier chapter which covers the definitions of data.

Visionary	The organisation needs to understand and define the information that will be available in the future that they will need to effectively run their business. This information may not yet be in existence, it may exist but not be accessible, or it may simply not be used. An example may be location data. It is common for mobile phone applications to report the geographical location of the phone; however this information is rarely used. In the same way, bank account transaction data is rarely used to provide information to the business.
Strategic	The organisation needs to understand and define what information is required to support the strategic aims of the business. This may be market data, it may be information on competitors, it may be information on customers or suppliers.
Regulatory	The organisation needs to understand the information needs of its regulator. Depending on the regulator this may be high level information only, or, in some cases, may run to hundreds of pages of requirements. There also may be more than one regulator – in the U.K. financial services regulatory reporting is to both the PRA and the Bank of England, and they have separate requirements.
Management	The organisation needs to understand and define the information that is required to manage itself. Often this is aggregated operational data, but the point is that it is different from operational data.
Operational	Operational data requirements must be defined. It is likely that operational data is significantly more granular than all other data requirements and also contains many more fields. For example, appointment times and the corresponding customer names for a particular day are essential operationally, but of limited value from a management perspective (though the overall number of appointments and their times may be essential to plan staff cover, plan for busy periods, and potentially look at office planning).

26.6.4   Key Principles

The data strategy should document the key principles behind the collection and use of data within the organisation. Principles are high level and should be clear and easy to understand. They should also be wide-ranging enough to be applicable to many situations. An example set might be:

- Information is an asset and should be treated as such.
- The use and collection of data will support the needs of the organisation.
- Data will be captured once and captured correctly, hence reducing rework.
- Information will be effectively governed and managed.
- There will be a single version of the truth. (Although for performance reasons it may be necessary to hold multiple copies of the truth, a single source will populate these copies in a manner that ensures coherence between them.)
- Data will be classified (confidential/restricted/private, or clinical data and patient data.)
- Data will be shared with those who have a right to access it.
- Information will be fit for purpose.

Matters to note here are that the number of base principles should be limited indeed. More than 5-10 is certainly overkill. To give examples, below are two real-life (and publically available) examples of data principles that are enshrined in data strategies.

> **Financial Conduct Authority: Data Principles**
> - Effectively governed and controlled
> - Clearly specified
> - Fit for purpose
> - Strong and rich at a baseline level
> - Collected appropriately
> - Managed and stored in an appropriate technology solution
>
> SOURCE FCA data strategy September 2013

> **Department for Work and Pensions: Data Principles**
> - Information is a valued asset
> - Information is managed
> - Information is fit for purpose
> - Information is standardised and linkable
> - Information is re-used
> - Public information is published
> - Citizens and businesses can access information about themselves
>
> SOURCE DWP Information Strategy April 2012

26.6.5 Data Acquisition

It has been repeatedly mentioned within this book that correct information capture is the most effective way of ensuring data quality. The well-known principle "garbage in, garbage out" applies to information. If information capture is poor, no amount of cleansing or remediation is ever likely to be effective. It is therefore justifiable, in my view, to include a separate section on information capture within the data strategy. The data strategy can define the touch points where information enters the organisation, and state that data quality will be an intrinsic objective within the process of capture. Touch points may include:

- Contact centre
- Post
- Website
- Branch
- Internet downloads (e.g. Halifax House price index)
- Trading software (e.g. Bloomberg Terminal)

A point of note is that one of the example data strategies used above (that from the UK Financial Conduct Authority) specifically states as one of its principles that data should be "collected appropriately". They have given more detail, and go on to state:

"All data will be collected through controlled channels to ensure that it can be consolidated, catalogued, directed and accessed across the FCA. We will ensure that we speak to suppliers of data before we make a formal request. Collection mechanisms will be easier to use and flexible to evolve, without significant lead time and costs for the industry." [45]

This gives a very good example of the level of detail to be included within a data strategy. I would note that considerably more detail on the various entry points of data into an organisation is covered in both the chapter on information flow and also in the remediation section ("where to remediate").

26.6.6 Information Governance

The data strategy should include reference to and a high level description of the information governance framework of the organisation. The purpose of this framework is to align data management with the principles and aims of the organisation. The description of information governance in the data strategy may be high level, or may go into more detail and include terms of reference and ways of working. However, I would advise against the latter for the same reason as not including detailed data policies, in that the readership of the data strategy would not normally be focused on that level of detail. In the same way the data strategy can set out the roles and responsibilities necessary, within the governance framework, for implementation. Whilst individual names would not be expected the strategy could include roles and responsibilities, for example "Head of Data Governance", and the roles of "Data Owners" and "Data Stewards". In addition, the terms of reference for governance forums, and how these interact with the existing organisational governance structure may be defined. However a more appropriate solution is to consider a separate information management strategy, which can then cover both data governance and data management. A considerably more detailed description of data governance is included within the embedding section, and examples of detailed roles and responsibilities are included in the appendices.

26.6.7 Management framework, roles and responsibilities

As with information governance, the data strategy should include some description of data management. At a high level, it may only be necessary to identify the components of data management. The example components below are from the DAMA Body of Knowledge: [46]

- Data architecture management
- Data operations management
- Data quality management
- Data security management
- Data warehouse and BI management
- Data development
- Metadata management
- Document and content management
- Reference data management

It is of course possible to cover data management, and components thereof, in greater detail within the data strategy, but this would normally be the responsibility of the information manage-

---

45. FCA data strategy September 2013
46. Data Management Body of Knowledge, DAMA-BOK, Technics Publications, 2010

ment strategy rather than a (deliberately high level) data strategy. In a similar way, a data strategy is the wrong level to include specific references to individual data controls, however should include a high level description of the purpose of those controls and/or references to a document that do contain the detail. This would normally be the information policy, or the documentation that is associated with individual processes.

26.6.8 Information Policy and Practice

The information policy will give the detailed processes and procedures that will translate the data strategy into an applicable instrument. However, the information policy itself should be distributed as a separate document. It is akin to the information security policy, and in a similar way should be distributed to all new joiners (and periodically to existing staff) who must then sign/date to confirm acceptance and compliance. The data strategy merely needs to mention the existence of the information policy and note that all members of the organisation are required to adhere.

26.6.9 Information Management Lifecycle

The data strategy should mention the data management lifecycle. There are many definitions of the information lifecycle, some proprietary which may happen to coincide with the elements of applications packages, some are more general. The typical components of an information management lifecycle would be expected to include:

- Planning (or data requirements)
- Data capture and/or receipt
- Organise/Classify
- Use
- Maintain/Manage
- Archive
- Destroy

A data strategy should outline how the organisation will approach each part of the lifecycle. This may not necessarily be in detail, and may potentially be at the level of principles. An example may be that an organisation will destroy records only after a minimum legal retention period.

26.6.10 Data Classification

Data is typically classified for security and management. A typical classification would be "restricted", "confidential" and "public". The data strategy can state, as a minimum, that all data items in scope will be classified. How they will be classified and how this will affect their treatment may also be included, but this is probably too much detail for a document at this level. Typically this is included within data security documentation.

26.6.11 Information Protection

Information protection – i.e. data security – could easily be a book in itself, and no attempt will be made here to delve into a subject already covered effectively and comprehensively elsewhere. However, in terms of high level principles, the theory is that information should be made available to those who are entitled to use and see it, and denied to those who are not. A data strategy should set out how this will be achieved – at a high level. A typical approach is to directly refer to a number of documents that will cover information security, as well as supporting documentation on an intranet site.

26.6.12 Knowledge sharing and collaboration

Sharing of information is critical to its effective use, and if an end user needs information for their role, however cannot access it, it is likely that they will simply re-create it. In the same way that the data strategy should outline how data will be protected, it also needs to outline how it can be shared effectively throughout the organisation. This may mean that "private" stores of data are not allowed and all data must be held in a central repository, which may not necessarily be willingly accepted by all employees.

26.6.13 Other implications

The data strategy should include its relevance to the other elements of data management. These may include:

- Corporate and data architecture
- Creation and maintenance of a data dictionary
- Creation and maintenance of data lineage
- Archiving and storage
- Maintain/Manage
- Archive
- Destroy

It should be noted that the above act to support the strategy, not the other way around. The data strategy is the master document and draws authority from the corporate strategy. Too many data strategies take as a base the existing IT landscape and then write a pseudo-business justification for the pre-existing situation, possibly with a few tweaks on data management and/or quality. This is not a data strategy, this is a verbose justification of the IT department's view of the world, and the data strategy needs to be business-driven. Data strategies of this type are depressingly easy to spot.

26.7 Summary

Within this chapter I have discussed my view of how the information strategy needs to support the corporate vision, and outlined what such a strategy needs to include. I have described how the data strategy supplies the overall framework to inform and govern the decisions made in relation to information, and it is imperative that it is defined first. Hopefully the reader at this point will understand that it is otherwise inevitable that decisions will be made which, at best, do not further the progress of the organisation to its eventual destination, and, at worst, prevent the organisation from fulfilling its potential and actively impede its progress.

In the next chapter I will discuss data requirements, which are the detailed description of what data will be required to support the data vision and data strategy, and also the quality requirements for that data.

SECTION 5.3 DIRECTION

CHAPTER 27 DATA REQUIREMENTS

27.1 Structure

This stage of The Data Quality Blueprint includes the following phases:

1. Vision & Strategy
2. Data Requirements
3. Data Quality Strategy
4. Quality Measurement
5. Quality Reporting

This chapter covers the second of these phases.

27.2 Overview

INPUTS	TASKS

■ All project artefacts created or utilised so far
■ Corporate vision
■ Corporate strategy
■ Data architecture
■ Data strategy (if available)
■ Business architecture
■ Application architecture
■ Infrastructure architecture
	■ Template and timescale
	  – Define template for requirements
	  – Define timescale for the definition of requirements
	■ Regulatory
	  – Discuss regulatory reporting requirements with regulatory reporting manager
	  – Identify regulatory reports required
	  – For each report define fields needed and meaning (often available via regulator's website)
	  – Collate into regulatory data requirements
	  – Note and add any quality requirements

OUTPUTS
■ Data requirements
■ Data quality requirements
	■ Board
	  – Obtain existing board reports
	  – Obtain existing financial accounts
	  – Discuss with key sponsor or board and identify missing information
	  – Define data required to support the vision and strategy
	  – For each report define fields needed and meaning of these fields
	  – Collate into data requirements
	  – Note and add any quality requirements

DEPENDENCIES
■ Access to stakeholders
■ Access to executives
■ Access to corporate strategy
	■ Managerial
	  – Obtain existing management reporting
	  – Discuss with users what information is missing or required
	  – Potentially use workshops to define requirements
	  – For each report define fields needed and meaning of these fields
	  – Collate into data requirements
	  – Note and add any quality requirements
	■ Operational
	  – Obtain application forms and customer reports
	  – Discuss with users their information needs
	  – For each report define fields needed and meaning
	  – Collate into data requirements
	  – Note and add any quality requirements
	■ All areas
	  – Collate and rationalise requirements
	  – Document requirements and circulate for review
	  – Update as required
	  – Discuss and agree with sponsor and key stakeholders
	  – Upload to project repository

After defining the data strategy, the next stage is to define the data requirements. The data requirements describe the information necessary for the organisation to undertake its activities. As the objective of the data quality project is to take the data from its current state to a state where it meets these requirements, understanding of the data requirements – and their definition if they are not available – is essential. In this chapter I will explain the nature of data requirements, and why they are needed. I will give examples of these requirements and show how they can be built out into data quality requirements. These are a prerequisite to take the process further, as before any project to remediate data quality begins, it is necessary to define a baseline, and how that baseline must be improved. Following chapters will define how a data quality strategy can be put in place to achieve these now-defined data quality requirements.

27.3 What are Data Requirements?

Unfortunately, "Data Requirements", "Data Standards" and "Data Dictionary" are words that have many meanings. This is not helped by other terms such as "Data Specifications", "Data Lexicons", and so on also being freely used. For the purposes of this book, I am going to adopt the following set of definitions.

A data dictionary is a centralised repository showing data meaning. It may also include information on lineage, format and owners. A data catalogue, data definitions or data lexicon cover the same ground. Data standards are the defined manner in which various data operations should occur. These include standards for data modelling, standards for data definitions, and so on. Data requirements are created by businesses for giving to those who provide them with the data within the context of a system implementation project or similar. Data requirements are the precise criteria, specifications, and rules for the definition, creation, storage and usage of data within an enterprise, and data quality requirements are fairly obviously those requirements which specifically relate to data quality. Data quality requirements are what the data quality project is trying to meet.

The data requirements are clearly an invaluable tool in the management of data throughout an organisation. In fact, without the data requirements little management is possible as it is not possible to determine to what standard the data is being managed, and it is impossible to measure the quality of the data or the effectiveness of any operation involving data. Surprisingly, despite this, many organisation launch on data quality projects with no real idea of requirements.

Anecdote

Once when an organisation was creating the specification for a new system, the existing data fields were documented in great detail. One particular calculated field caused a great deal of problem and investigations were undertaken to work out exactly how the legacy systems calculated the result.

A lot of investigation later concluded that the way the field was currently being calculated was actually wrong, and did not meet business expectations. The thing was, it had been wrong for twenty years – and no-one had noticed.

27.4 Where do Data Requirements come from?

We have already mentioned that the data strategy should specify the information requirements of the organisation, and we also noted that these requirements would be at a high level. Therefore the data strategy is the starting point for more a detailed creation of data requirements which will take this information to the next level.

We also mentioned earlier how data can be described by its use. Whilst there are many approaches to defining data requirements, I will use here as an example the taxonomy of:

- Regulatory Data
- Board Data
- Management Data
- Operational Data

The first step is therefore regulatory data.

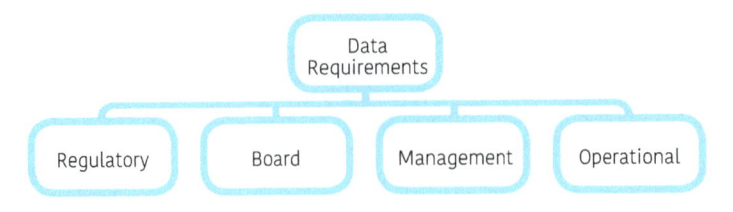

```
                    Data
                Requirements
        ┌───────────┼───────────┬──────────┐
   Regulatory     Board     Management  Operational
```

27.4.1 Regulatory data requirements.

The first point of call for regulatory data requirements is the regulator. Fortunately, most regulators will define, usually in great detail, precisely the information they require from the organisations under their care. If we take the example of financial services, regulatory data is largely covered by:

- Bank of England reporting
- Council of Mortgage Lenders reporting
- EBA COREP and FINREP reporting
- FCA conduct reporting
- PRA regulatory reporting
- PRA treasury reporting

Each of these reporting sets and the data items they contain are specified in great detail by the regulators themselves. For example, at the time of writing, all the Bank of England forms, definitions and requirements for reporting are clearly specified on their website.[47]

Using this information from all regulatory bodies it is possible to draw together a schedule for all regulatory requirements for the organisation relatively easily.

27.4.2 Board Reporting

It is likely that a large proportion of the board reporting requirements will already have been included within the regulatory reporting requirements. However there may be many data requirements that are at a lower aggregate level than required or simply unneeded by the regulator, or may be outside the regulators remit.

The starting point for a project that is looking to define data requirements is the board reporting packs. The board reporting packs will be provided to the board for every meeting. They will normally contain a large amount of data, and this can be used to build up the board data requirements.

---

47. http://www.bankofengland.co.uk/statistics/Pages/reporters/defs/default.aspx

A second place to look for board data requirements is to look for the history of ad hoc reporting requested by the board over the previous year. This can normally be found by asking the business intelligence function or the divisional or business unit leaders what has been requested.

A third place to look for board requirements – especially in less mature organisations that may not really know what they want, is publications which list data items that the board may wish to consider. Specifically I can recommend the publications "*The Multidimensional Manager*"[48] and "*The Performance Manager*"[49] which both give a reasonably comprehensive list of data items that the average board (and management) may require.

27.4.3 Operational Data

The next category I would like to consider is operational data – I will come back to management data shortly. Operational data is the most granular in the organisation, and may, as previously noted, include appointment times, customer data (names, addresses), product data, as well as data used by departments such as marketing who will draw in data from everywhere.

By far the best way (in fact almost the only way) of identifying this data is going to talk to the departments themselves and if necessary walking through the processes with an operator and noting the data they use.

27.4.4 Management Data

The reason I have left management data until last is that by the time the practitioner has worked their way through regulatory data, board data and operational data it is very likely that most of the management data will have already been covered. Where management data differs is in its variability of format – it comes in all kinds. However this is likely to be a result of aggregation and presentation, rather than the actual data items themselves. The other advantage of leaving management data until last is that wading through thousands of documents, databases, spreadsheets and so on will be very time consuming indeed. I would suggest leaving it until last and then picking up anything not covered in the other categories by exception.

27.4.5 Pulling it all together

At this point, the practitioner should have a large spreadsheet with a long list of data items and who needs them. The next stage is to build out the requirements and to create more detail for each data item.

27.5 What should Data Requirements include?

Data requirements should include, for each item that is relevant:

---

48. *The Multidimensional Manager,* Connelly, McNeil & Mosimann, Cognos, 1999
49. *The Performance Manager,* Connelly, McNeil & Mosimann, Cognos, 2007

- A name and domain to which it relates
- An explanation or description
- A pattern, if required
- Valid values, if applicable

An example is shown in the table below. I would also suggest that data requirements should also include the meaning and criticality of the data item, and also whether it has regulatory relevance. For calculated data (e.g. loss ratio or similar) the method of calculation should be included.

Name	Domain	Explanation/Description	Pattern	Valid Values
C_DOB	Customer	Date of Birth	DD/MM/YYYY	NN/NN/NNNN
C_Title	Customer	Customer Title	TT TTT TTT TT TT	Mr Mrs Miss Ms Dr
C_DOD	Customer	Date of Death	DD/MM/YYYY	NN/NN/NNNN

Data Requirements may not just include static data, but can also include calculations, and in fact would be expected to do so. Not all data items are simply input, many are derived. For example:

- A "net sale" amount may be calculated as "total amount – tax".
- Gross mortgage debt may be calculated as "debt at beginning of period + accrued interest to end of day less the payments made in period".

The key is to be precise. In the case of the first example, what tax, or, for that matter, what total? In the case of the second example, how do we define period? Is it calendar month, accounting period, and is it from the first day of the period or the last day of the previous period? How is interest accrued, is it including the day of calculation or not? For "payments", is this all payments, or capital payments only, and if a repayment mortgage, where each payment consists of a capital element and an interest element, which bit are we counting? Data requirements need to be detailed enough that they could be given to an IT developer who could build the payment in the system and would never need to come back to ask questions. The data requirements should also include the desired format of the data. To take the example of address data which is typically more of a mess than most other customer data, a typical subset of the customer database may look like the table below.

One can see that there is no consistent address format, with the address fragmented in several different ways across the available fields. Amongst other problems, this makes de-duplication nearly impossible.

Address 1	Address 2	Address 3	Address 4	Address 5	Address 6	Address 7
1 Station Road	Sutton Coldfield	Birmingham				
Dunroamin	1 Station Road	Wylde Green	Sutton Coldfield	Birmingham	West Midlands	

Dunroamin	1	Station Road	Wylde Green	Sutton Coldfield	Birmingham	West Midlands
1	Station Road	Wylde Green	Sutton Coldfield	Birmingham	West Midlands	
Dunroamin	1 Station Road	Birmingham	West Midlands			

Here, requirements could state:

- Address 1 = Name (if applicable)
- Address 2 = Number
- Address 3 = Street
- Address 4 = District
- Address 5 = Minor Town (if applicable)
- Address 6 = Postcode Town
- Address 7 = County

This gets around the data quality (consistency) problem. After remediation the above should look like the below, which is comparatively easy to de-duplicate.

Address 1	Address 2	Address 3	Address 4	Address 5	Address 6	Address 7
	1	Station Road		Sutton Coldfield	Birmingham	
Dunroamin	1	Station Road	Wylde Green	Sutton Coldfield	Birmingham	West Midlands
Dunroamin		Station Road			Birmingham	
	1	Station Road	Wylde Green	Sutton Coldfield	Birmingham	West Midlands
Dunroamin	1	Station Road			Birmingham	West Midlands

As an aside, the reason that address data is generally so poor is that in a contact centre the agent will fill in fields in the order the customer gives them. The customer may not necessarily give all the fields in the same order at the same time. Also, there is a difference between the answer to:

"What is your address" and

"What is your house number" followed by "what is your street name".

The above example in the table may also not necessarily get picked up under data validation, as every single one of the lines in the first example is a valid address, and if mail was sent to that address it would reach the relevant customer. It is only when an attempt is made to de-duplicate customers that issues will then arise.

Anecdote:
One organisation performed a brief data quality investigation into the address data on a primary

system. The investigation showed that there were 19,000 addresses in the data store. Of these, 12,000 had no postcode at all (i.e. blank) and a further 1,700 had incomplete postcodes.

27.6 How to Approach Detailed Data Requirements

Needless to say, the creation of requirements at this level of detail is not an overnight job. However some acceleration is possible. Personally, I would suggest documenting all the fields relevant to the project with best-guess definitions and then sending out the file to business subject matter experts to validate and fill in the rest. This approach may appear a waste of time – subject matter experts are, unarguably, the best people to create the definitions. However, I would submit that it is quicker to perform a "first pass" at the definitions and then let them tweak/re-write what you have already written than to ask them to create from scratch. If something is wrong they will certainly be keen to change it – lest it become law – and by giving many examples of detailed (and good) definitions it is less (psychologically) easy for them to write poor ones.

If a data field is going to have a list of valid values, the valid values have to be defined. Some thought will need to be put into this, especially if the valid values list will be used to constrain the data entry. For example, in respect of the "customer title" field, the following entries will occur to most people:

- Mr
- Mrs
- Miss
- Ms
- Master
- Dr
- Rev

However, other perfectly valid values may include:

- Constable
- Sister
- Sergeant
- Lord
- Colonel
- Monsieur

A good way of determining valid values is to start with an existing data set and work from there. An existing data set will include all of the valid values – and probably a fair few invalid values too, but after chopping out the clearly invalid, the remaining set has the advantage of being easy to create and also tailored to your organisation. Prioritisation is the key here. Do not try and define every field in the database – you'll be there until the end of time – typical data warehouses will have 20,000-30,000 fields. Prioritise those data elements that are relevant for the business reporting or operations – you should find that these are a small percentage (potentially less than 10%) of the total. Typically reporting requirements for an institution will be comprehensively covered by significantly less than 1,000 data fields. Here I will mention two organisations in the UK financial sector. For one of these 550 fields covered reporting requirements, another managed to get away with just 350. A later part of the book looks at a way of working with a data modeller and the overall data model to determine the fields that require work, and a similar approach can work well here.

In the case of the country codes mentioned earlier you can pick these up freely from the internet. In other cases (e.g. postcodes) a valid list may have to be purchased and then kept up to date. The challenge with this approach is if your customers are special cases that don't fit the pre-defined list. Defining a field as a certain format for U.K. National Insurance numbers is not going to work if you have U.S. customers who will have social security numbers instead. Look at your data first.

The problem with "reference data sets" is that they have to be tailored after receipt, and it is much harder to think of outlier values and add them in rather than be presented with a comprehensive list and cut values out that are not required. Certain lists are thankfully easy – country codes for example. In the case of country codes there are a defined number, and an international standard. Others – like title – are trickier.

Anecdote
One organisation had many thousands of unique entries in its title field. Whilst reasonable examples represented most of the total they also found: [50]

MRS	MRS.	MR MRS	MR AND MRS	MR & MRS
MR,MRS	_MRS	MR&MRS	MR.MRS	MRMRS
MR& MRS	MRSS	MR MRS	MR. & MRS.	MR.AND.MRS
MR + MRS	MR.MRS.	MR/MRS	MR &MRS	MRSD
MRSE	MR. MRS.	MRS MR	MR MRS	MR&MRS.
MR+MRS	_MRS.	GMRS	MMRS	,MRS
MRAND MRS	MR NAD MRS	MR, MRS	MR-MRS	DMRS
_MR MRS	_MRS	DR AND MRS	DR & MRS	MR AMD MRS
.MRS	MRS,MR	___MRS	MR. & MRS	MR 6 MRS
MR. MRS	MRSA	MRANDMRS	MR SAND MRS	

This gives you an idea of the sheer number of potential entries (and inventiveness of operators) you can get if you allow a free text field, even in a relatively easy-to-enter and standard field. I will admit to finding this kind of data fascinating. This information tells you:

- There is clearly no validation whatsoever on the title field.
- People are pushed for time.
- There are lots of typing errors.
- Operators are not incentivised on quality.
- No-one whatsoever is checking the quality of the data input.

27.7   Data Quality Requirements

Data quality requirements can also be written into the data requirements. Data quality requirements define the acceptable quality for each element of data from the business perspective. Examples may be:

- Over 95% of addresses must have a valid postcode.
- 99% of customers must have a valid title.
- 99% of customers must have a valid date of birth.
- Default values for claim type cannot exceed 10% of claims.
- 90% of retail customers must have either a valid postcode or a valid address.
- 70% of customers must have a populated email address. For online customers this should be 95%.
- 80% of customers should have an alternate contact number.
- Customer age cannot exceed 120 years old.

---

50. Actual data changed but examples representative.

- Customer date of birth cannot be in the future.
- 80% of customer phone numbers have to have been validated in the last year.
- All sales data must include data from the first day of the month, to last day of month, inclusive. The only exceptions are backdated transactions.
- All invoices must have a date.
- All invoice numbers should be unique.
- A maximum customer duplication of 1% is allowable.
- For regulatory reporting purposes, customer balances are reported at midnight on the last day of the month.
- The minimum score on the annual data trust survey should be 80%.
- Any customer record needs to score 80% across all of the standard five business rules.

For each element, the organisation needs to define the minimum acceptable quality requirements. These may relate to business rules that cover validity, specific dimensions of data quality (e.g. completeness), or may be spread across a number of dimensions. The data quality requirements inform both the data quality strategy and the data quality metrics.

Anecdote
One organisation was suffering a problem due to poor data quality in relation to customer employment. They found that the most common employment for their customers was apparently "Astronaut". This was, of course, the first selection available in the drop-down list in the new customer screens, and agents, pressured by throughput, were choosing the first available valid selection regardless of what the customer actually told them as it took too long to find the right entry.

Another individual noted to me in conversation that in their previous organisation a disproportionate number of customers were entered as "Abattoir Worker" for the same reason. Another organisation had a high proportion of Palestinian mortgages. This was because the top entry in the drop down list was supposed to say "Please Select", but because of space limitations had been abbreviated to PS, which unfortunately matched the country code for the state of Palestine.

Of course, this is a process issue (of which more later), but it does rather indicate how things can get in a mess.

27.8 Summary

In this chapter I have discussed data requirements and data quality requirements, why they are important, the various types of requirements and the way in which an organisation can approach the creation of requirements.

I have also looked specifically at data quality requirements, and discussed how they can be used as a measured baseline for a data quality project. Data quality can then be improved and the change in quality (and thence the success of the project) determined by reference to the data quality requirements.

In the next chapter I will discuss the data quality strategy. This is the detailed approach which describes how the desired data quality can be achieved.

SECTION 5.3 DIRECTION

CHAPTER 28 DATA QUALITY STRATEGY

28.1 Structure

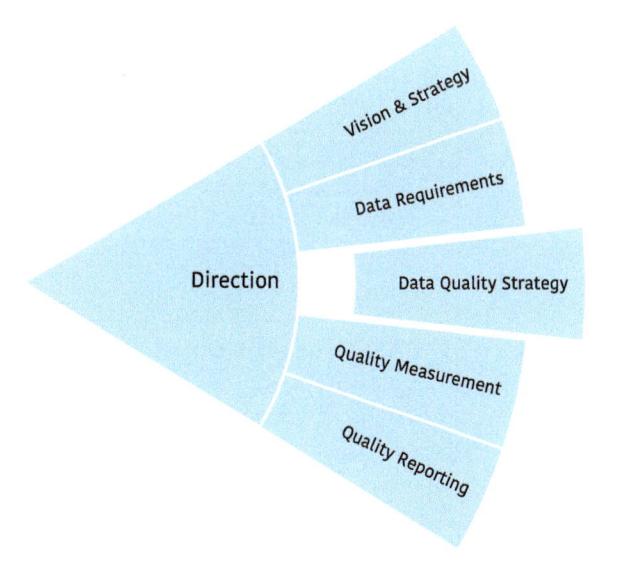

This stage of The Data Quality Blueprint includes the following phases:

1. Vision & Strategy
2. Data Requirements
3. Data Quality Strategy
4. Quality Measurement
5. Quality Reporting

This chapter covers the third of these phases.

28.2 Overview

INPUTS
- All project artefacts created or used to date
- Corporate vision
- Corporate strategy
- Data architecture
- Data strategy (if available)
- Business architecture
- Application architecture
- Infrastructure architecture

OUTPUTS
- Data quality strategy
- Data quality process framework
- Data quality governance

DEPENDENCIES
- Access to stakeholders
- Access to executives
- Access to corporate strategy

TASKS
- Relate data quality strategy to data strategy
- Determine how data quality relates to and supports the corporate vision
- Determine how data quality relates to and supports the corporate strategy
- Agree template for the data quality strategy with sponsor
- Create data quality strategy
  - Scope
  - Exemptions
  - Purpose
  - Objectives
  - Benefits
  - Data quality governance
  - Data quality process framework
  - Risk appetite
  - How to deal with breaches and urgent issues
  - Data archiving
  - Data remediation
  - Data reconciliation and control
- Draft data quality strategy
- Present to sponsor and other critical individuals and gain feedback
- Finalise data quality strategy
- Receive written signoff
- Baseline and upload into project document repository

After the business has defined its data strategy, and then defined the data requirements and data quality requirements, it can then – and only then – start to look at how to define how it is going to achieve those requirements. This is the data quality strategy. Defining a data quality strategy without defining the data requirements acceptable for your business will lead to effort wasted in performing irrelevant tasks with no defined direction and little business benefit. Within this chapter I will walk through the contents of the data quality strategy and what detail it should contain. The purpose is to inform the reader so that if there is a necessity to create a data quality strategy within their organisation then this should give them the understanding to do so. Data quality policy is touched on but not expanded in detail, partly due to limitations of space, but mainly because the exact contents of a data quality policy are much more bespoke to the organisation in question.

In the same way as data strategy, there are a number of publically available data quality strategies on the internet, and I would encourage the reader, if faced with the task of creating one, to use this valuable resource.

28.3 Data Quality Strategy Overview

The data quality strategy describes the organisation's strategy to meet its data quality requirements. It should not be confused with the data strategy, however often is. This is because many organisations fail to think about the holistic nature of data and how it should be aligned to the organisational strategy. Data is seen as an IT problem, so therefore the only elements of data that require a strategy are those relevant to quality, everything else being covered in the IT strategy. Typical contents of the data quality strategy are described below and a full example is included in the appendices.

28.3.1   Scope

The data quality strategy should clearly define its own scope and the parts of the organisation covered. Whilst it may be natural to assume "all" as a default, the data quality strategy may initially only cover a subset of the organisation. It is essential that departments and staff are clearly aware of what is "in" and "out". There is, unfortunately, often a presumption, that when faced with governance requirements, every effort is made to ensure that "this doesn't mean me". Equally, there is often a fundamental misunderstanding of what data is, or how important data quality is. A clear and unambiguous definition of scope is essential. A sample scope statement might be:

> *"This document applies to all financial information wherever it may be created or used in the organisation. Whilst this includes regulatory reporting and accounts information, this will also include all information at a greater level of detail, such as information on interest payments, balances, accruals and prepayments, but also incidental charges, cash payments and individual invoices.*
>
> *For the avoidance of doubt, it should be considered that if the data concerned is expressed in currency of any nature, then it will be covered by this document."*

This may be wide ranging, but at least unambiguous. It is often advisable to define exemptions as well. For example, an initial data quality strategy may concentrate on customer and product data only. Equally, non-financial data may not be in scope, or the strategy may exclude data from a certain division.

28.3.2   Purpose and benefits of the strategy

It is important to define the purpose of the strategy. This enables a reader to understand what the strategy is trying to achieve. An example set of objectives may include:

- Raise awareness of data quality throughout the organisation.
- To define the framework for the management of data quality in the organisation.
- To define escalation processes for data quality issues.
- To defines roles and responsibilities for data quality.
- To outline the roadmap for the improvement of data quality.
- To describe the principles behind data quality in the organisation.

The strategy should detail the anticipated benefits of implementing the strategy. These should, in the same way as the overall data strategy (with which they should agree and support), define exactly what will be the benefit, in business terms. Any project to improve data quality will have to prove business benefit in order to get the funding it requires to start, and the starting question should always be:

- How does it support the business aims?
- What will be the benefits to the business?
- What numerical cost/benefit will be delivered by data quality?

Example benefits of a data quality strategy are shown in the example in the appendices, but may include:

- Improved customer satisfaction.
- Improved information capture at source to support efficient and effective analysis.
- Enhanced management information for internal use to drive service delivery and analysis of customer care.
- Demonstration of board ownership for good data quality.
- Increase ownership of data quality with management and operational staff.
- Clarity within the organisation in respect of data quality.

28.3.3   Why Data Quality matters

Whilst it may appear odd to include this here, several organisations I am aware of have included a section not un-akin to the first few chapters of this book (on the impact of poor data quality) within their data quality strategy and I think it helps in the overall understanding. It is important that no reader is under any misapprehension that data quality is fundamental to achieving business aspirations. Unfortunately in many cases some education is required, and including this section in the strategy can help buy-in and support.

28.3.4   Principles

Although a data quality strategy may simply cascade principles down from the data strategy, a data quality strategy may also have principles of its own. For example, the below principles are taken from the Leicestershire Country Council Data Quality Strategy.

Leicestershire Country Council Performance Data Quality Principles [51]

- **Awareness** – relevant staff recognise the need for good data quality and how they can contribute;
- **Definitions** – relevant staff know which indicators are produced from the information they input and how they are defined;
- **Systems** – are fit for purpose and staff have the expertise to get the best out of them.
- **Validation** – there are validation procedures in place as close to the point of input as possible;

---

51.   Source: Leicestershire County Council Performance Data Quality Strategy 2010-2011.

- **Data supplied by third parties** – aiming to ensure information produced amongst our partners is as reliable as our own and that risks where reliability is in doubt are effectively managed
- **Output** – performance indicator data is extracted regularly and efficiently and communicated quickly;
- **Presentation** – performance indicators are presented so as to give an easily understood, accurate and transparent picture of the Council's performance to the public, external inspectorates, partners, Council Members and staff.
- **Risk, continuity and knowledge management** – strategic and operational risks in relation to performance data are managed. Arrangements for business continuity should be implemented to ensure that specialist knowledge in relation to performance indicators and data quality is not lost.
- **Monitoring and Review** – it is important to continuously review the arrangements for securing data quality.

It can be seen how these principles are geared towards data quality as opposed to data as a whole. It should be noted at this point that Leicestershire County Council were commended for the clarity of their data strategy by The National Archives and that the data quality performance strategy is written in the same clear and concise manner. I would personally note that their strategies, which are available via their website, are excellent examples to which the reader can refer.

28.3.5 Strategic aims for Data Quality

The data quality strategy should define how data quality improvement intersects with the strategic aims of the organisation. As has already been mentioned in the case of the overall data strategy, it is essential that data quality is driven by the business and its strategic aims, and unless data quality supports those aims it is arguable whether it should be undertaken. Examples of strategic aims for data quality may include:

- To improve customer retention and attract new customers by improvements in customer service.
- To enable organisational growth by more effective marketing.
- To enable improved governance and management of the organisation.
- To enable effective decision making on strategic issues.

A note here is that the aims are strategic, long term and affect the whole of the organisation, and are business, rather than data or technical aims.

28.3.6 Operational aims for data quality

The quality of the information held within any organisation's systems must support its day to day operations. All processes that exist within the organisation which use data should be able to rely on its quality. The data quality strategy, as well as stating the above, should note that the quality of data (and the nature of the data) required within the organisation will depend on its use. If we consider, for example, compliance and regulatory reporting, performance measurement, marketing, customer service, data cleansing and finally risk management, each of these will require different levels of data quality, but all are operational elements of the business.

To perform the operational activity of mailing a customer it is desirable, but not strictly necessary, to have a full address AND a full postcode. In the UK, at least, a house number and postcode is normally enough. However, for the data management activity of cleansing and de-duplication, it is clearly ideal to have as much information as possible, and a full address AND postcode are useful in that they provide mutual confirmation of the other's accuracy. Equally, emailing the wrong customer with a marketing campaign is irrelevant (assuming personal information is not used). Emailing the wrong customer with, for example, a loan decision or a statement is another matter and very serious.

The risk appetite of the organisation is critical to data strategy and data quality. It should not be expected that the risk appetite will be the same across all departments, data types and classifications, and hence a tailored risk appetite would be expected. The data quality strategy needs to state how it supports the varying risk appetite of the organisation.

28.3.7   Data Quality Management

In the same way that the data strategy will define the management over data in a general way, the data quality strategy will take this concept down to the next level of detail, and define the management framework around data quality. The management section should include:

- Data quality management framework
- Roles and responsibilities specific to data quality
- How data quality will be monitored and reviewed
- Systems, process and procedures relating to data quality
- Data quality risks and risk management
- How to ensure quality over data supplied by third parties

I have referred to the DAMA framework a number of times in this book, and the specific activities that they list as being critical elements of data quality management are; develop and promote data quality awareness; define data quality requirements; profile, analyse and assess data quality; define data quality metrics; define data quality business rules; test and validate data quality requirements; set and evaluate data quality service levels; continuously monitor and measure data quality; manage data quality issues; clean and correct data quality defects; design and implement operational data quality measurement procedures; monitor operational data quality measurement procedures; audit data quality management.

This is a reasonably comprehensive list and would be an excellent starting point for any organisation to look at the structure and tasks required for data quality management.

28.3.8   Data Quality Stakeholders

The data quality strategy should define its key stakeholders of which there will be many who are directly affected by both the data strategy and data quality strategy. Whilst some will be within the organisation – such as data users, the executive board, and so on – it should also include those outside the organisation. For example, a major data quality initiative will significantly improve the customer experience, and the customers should be considered stakeholders. Equally, the regulator should be considered a stakeholder, as well as suppliers and all other third parties who interact with the data of the organisation. Stakeholders can and will include, but are not limited to:

- Customers
- Suppliers
- Staff
- Regulators
- Government
- Shareholders
- Directors and management
- Process owners
- Internal business stakeholders

The effect of the data quality strategy on each should be considered. At the level of the data quality strategy however they only need to be mentioned as stakeholders in the strategy.

28.3.9 Data Quality Process Framework

The data quality strategy should define the data quality process framework, covering processes in the event of the identification of data quality issues. An example is outlined below.

Contact → Initiate → Assess → Implement → Escalate

Contact	How a data quality incident is created should be considered. Any individual within the company or customer, supplier or regulator may cause a data quality incident, or may identify a need to raise one.
Initiate/Engage	The process by which the data quality professionals engage with the initial report of the incident and then log the incident and bring it forward into the assess stage.
Assess	The process framework should define how the particular data quality incident should be assessed and against what criteria. Some data may be more critical than others and the criticality of the data may change. For example, shareholder address information may be particularly critical ahead of a rights issue and less critical at other times.
Implement	Implementation of the solution. This may be against the single record identified by a customer, or a whole class of records of which the customer's record is one.
Escalate	Finally, the process should define and describe how the matter should be escalated if any one of the parties involved is unhappy with the way in which it has been dealt with.

It is worth including the process to be followed in relation to urgent issues as well. At some stage a data quality issue will be discovered that is urgent enough to not use the normal channels. This should also be covered in the process section, or can be a separate section of its own.

28.3.10   Data Reconciliation and Control

The data quality strategy may define how data should be reconciled when moving from one part of the organisation to another or from one system to another. This may be formalised in greater detail in an ETL strategy or ETL standards; however, the data quality strategy should specify that both the movement of data between systems is important, and that standards should exist for its control. This reflects two points made a number of times within the book that interfaces are often critical points in an organisation where data goes wrong, and also that the organisation, when considering data quality, needs to consider the organisation as a whole rather than business or system silos.

28.3.11   Data Remediation

The data quality strategy may include information covering the remediation of data quality separate from the process framework. The strategy may define specifics regarding remediation – for example it may be possible to run remediation activities at a certain time – many organisations have a specific time of the year in which data remediation and/or duplication efforts are undertaken (often over Christmas in the UK).

28.3.12   Education and Training

The data quality strategy needs to outline how the organisation will educate and train staff on the importance and relevance of data quality. I will discuss training in much more detail in the training chapter, but the data quality strategy needs to state that training on the importance of data quality, and of the processes to ensure data quality, is critical to success.

28.4   Data Quality Implementation Plan

The data quality strategy can contain the process for its own implementation. This may, however, be covered in a separate document. In either case, the implementation plan needs to include typical sections such as the objective of the data quality project, what will it achieve and measures of success, a project plan, a project timeline, and implementation steps. In the event of a separate implementation document not being produced then this information will need to be included within the data quality strategy.

28.5   Data Quality Policy

After the data quality strategy is defined it is possible to define the data quality policy. This is at a lower and more detailed level and covers the precise way in which the data quality strategy will be achieved. Examples of elements that may be specifically within the data quality policy and in no higher level document could be:

- Data entry principles (e.g. "if you don't know, don't guess").
- Action on discovering a data quality issue.
- Who are the local representatives for data quality?

Anecdote
A colleague once told me that in an early part of their career they were a data entry clerk in an insurance company, transcribing claims onto the data systems. Their targets were 120 motor claims or 80 property claims a day. No-one mentioned quality.

28.6 Summary

In this chapter, I have discussed the components of a data quality strategy. I have covered each of the components in turn and given a little more detail of what should be included. This should enable a data quality practitioner to work with the organisation to write an effective data quality strategy. To this end, I have included in the appendices a full data quality strategy which a reader is welcome to use or adapt within their own organisation.

In the next chapter I will take a detailed look at data quality measurement, the metrics used, and where they are appropriate.

SECTION 5.3 DIRECTION

CHAPTER 29 QUALITY MEASUREMENT

29.1 Structure

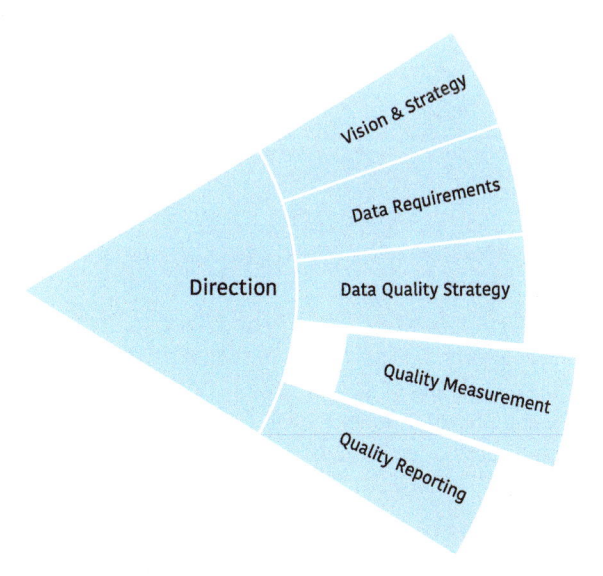

This stage of The Data Quality Blueprint includes the following phases:

1. Vision & Strategy
2. Data Requirements
3. Data Quality Strategy
4. Quality Measurement
5. Quality Reporting

This chapter covers the fourth of these phases.

29.2 Overview

INPUTS	TASKS
■ All project artefacts created or used to date ■ Corporate vision ■ Corporate strategy ■ Data architecture ■ Data strategy (if available) ■ Business architecture ■ Application architecture ■ Infrastructure architecture	■ Collate data requirements and quality requirements ■ For each requirement identify critical data items ■ For each critical data item define metrics ■ Map requirements and metrics to each business process ■ Create "basket" of metrics ■ Discuss and agree with sponsor and key stakeholders ■ Draft reporting suite ■ Update as required ■ Draft approach for capture of metrics ■ Create proof of concept mock-up of reporting ■ Discuss and agree with sponsor and key stakeholders ■ Update as required

OUTPUTS

- Data requirements and data quality requirements
- Critical data items
- Metrics for each requirement
- Basket of metrics
- Draft reporting suite
- Proof of concept or mock-up

DEPENDENCIES

- Access to stakeholders
- Access to executives
- Access to Corporate Strategy

In order to measure both the initial state of data quality and importantly the success (or otherwise) of any data quality remediation efforts, it is necessary to define performance metrics for data quality. In this chapter I will give an overview of data quality performance metrics, and briefly discuss the appropriateness of each type of measurement. I will consider the performance metrics that are appropriate for different types of data and conclude with a discussion on how these metrics can be obtained within the organisation. The following chapter will discuss how such metrics can be rolled into a reporting framework.

29.3 Introduction of Metrics

Data quality performance metrics are those metrics that enable measurement of the achievement of data quality requirements. In addition, business information owners need to be given tools to identify, categorise, and quantify data quality issues while setting targets. These tools and processes promote business ownership of data quality. The organisation should develop and document metrics that business information owners can utilise to continuously measure, monitor, track, and improve data quality at multiple points across the organisation. The two main tasks are:

- Identify pre-defined business quality requirements for the selected data.
- Define quality metrics for each identified critical data element.

The metrics should not look to define the business rules for each data item. It is outside the scope of data quality metrics to define the rules for each data item, a process that lies within the exercise of determination of data requirements. Data quality metrics simply look to measure the adherence (or otherwise) of the existing data to the defined data requirements.

29.3.1　Appropriateness

The type of performance measurement appropriate for any individual data item is dependent on the systems on which it is stored, the measurement capabilities, and the type of data. The performance metrics used should be commensurate with the data that is being measured.

For example, once an item of static data – for example date of birth – has been correctly recorded, it should never need to be checked again. New items of data that are coming into the organisational information stores should be checked for quality, however the frequency of the check needs to match the risk. It would be inappropriate to instigate a process to check the customer date of birth on a monthly basis, and equally would be inappropriate to check the property loan-to-value once every twenty years. The nature of the data, and the risk associated with error, drive the kind and frequency of the metrics that need to be produced to measure its quality.

29.3.2　Definition of Measurement

The organisation needs to define how data quality is measured. This is not the same as the definition of the data, but is the definition of the measurement of the data. For each measurement a detailed definition should exist. For example:

- Postcodes are considered "missing" if the entry is either NULL or is all blanks.
- Postcodes are considered "partial" if they consist of four or fewer characters which do match the first four characters of a valid entry in the Royal Mail index
- Postcodes are considered "invalid" if the value in the data field matches the correct pattern but does not match any entry on the Royal Mail index
- Postcodes are considered "incorrect" if the field value matches the Royal Mail index but does not match the correct customer address.

Crafting these definitions is an art in itself as there can be no loophole left. In the example of the above, the logic should be applied in the order given.

29.3.3　Cause or Effect

It is also possible to look at performance metrics in relation to whether you are measuring the cause or effect of poor information. For example, in the case of customer addresses, it is possible to check the process for entering the data, the data entered, the immediate effect of entering poor data (for example, mail being returned), or the business consequence (i.e. having to go and find the correct address). In general it is better to pick up errors as early as possible, so in this chapter I will concentrate on measuring data quality as high in the information flow as possible, by looking at cause.

However analysis of subsequent issues does form an important part of data quality performance measurements and I will touch on this at the end of the chapter. An example here would be the monetary effect of each percentage error in postcode to the business.

29.4   Types of Metrics

29.4.1   Capture of customer and product data

The initial capture of customer information is a key process within the organisation. The source of this data will be the customer, either directly or via the product application form, website, or similar. The objective of the metric is to determine the efficacy of the data information capture. For example, metrics could include:

- % of customer names captured correctly
- % of customer addresses captured accurately
- Use of correct field names

Separate to data specific to the customer, there is data captured specific to the product held by the customer. This will include:

- Correct product used
- Correct product details entered

The source of this data will again be the customer, either directly or via the product application form. To check this data it is necessary to physically match the product application form (or the customer call) to the application and thence to the resulting data on the system. Whilst some of this can be done automatically (for example if the customer is entering details in a website), some has to rely on sample checking. The amount of data needed to be checked will depend on the total volumes, however, a suggestion is at least 1% and preferably 5%, the latter giving a very good confidence level.

As well as sample checking there are also inter-relationships between the fields on a form or screen that can be checked automatically. These can be part of the application validation. For example, it is possible to create performance metrics to match the type of product held on the system (adult, child) to the date of birth of the applicant. An adult should not be applying for a "young saver" (or similar) account. Equally there is a strong correlation between home phone number and address (in terms of country or region code), and postcode can be mapped to region or county. It is possible to create a suite of metrics around capture of customer and product data to measure the efficiently of the process.

29.4.2   Existing customer and product data

It is not cost effective to check the full historical product base against application form or call data, and metrics will be limited to that achieved using high level profiling tools only. This profiling will be undertaken as part of the discovery phase of the project. Therefore, whilst most of the metrics outlined above will stand, it is the expectation that remediation activities will result in a cleansing of the historical data, and the performance metrics will measure the effectiveness and progress of this cleansing activity. Examples may be:

- Nulls in critical fields
- Blanks in critical fields
- Invalid data in critical fields
- Out of range data
- Data invalid by business rules
- Invalid keys
- Invalid inter-relationships between fields

Unfortunately the above does not provide a solution to assure accuracy. This can only be done by either checking with the customer or cross-referencing with a known good data source. It is possible to sample check back to historical records, but this is laborious and slow.

29.4.3   De-duplication

De-duplication runs should occur on a regular basis as historical data is cleansed. I would suggest that de-duplication should occur quarterly at a minimum. The results from de-duplication should perform part of the data quality performance metrics, both in terms of the number of matches, and in terms of the type, age and product to which they apply. The simplest method of de-duplicating data is to concatenate a number of critical fields and then perform a count on how many exist. For example:

- Forename (John)
- Surname (Smith)
- DOB (01011980)
- Postcode (B755JY)

Create one field as a combination of them all.

[JohnSmith01011980B755JY]

Then count how many of the above are held on the systems. Clearly some degree of intelligence needs to be applied in relation to duplication and the data that is required to support it. A large number of blanks or default values in any field will negatively affect de-duplication efforts. The example below is going to end up with a lot of potential (and inaccurate) de-duplication:

[Forename ("John"), Surname ("Smith"), Date of Birth [Missing], Postcode [Missing]]

Equally if the organisation has historically not captured full forenames then it is possible to end up with thousands of false positives. An important note about de-duplication efforts is that every single one that is not a perfect match should be carefully considered before individuals are merged. With a large data set, people often do have the same name and date of birth (especially for common names) and having a human in the loop to ensure no individuals are inappropriately merged is critical.

29.4.4 Performance metrics on dynamic data

Dynamic data is data that not only changes, but is expected to change. Examples could include:

- Bank account balances
- Customer balances
- Current outstanding invoices
- Current debt
- Arrears performance

For performance metrics the challenge is to determine the quality of information. In most cases the information is aggregate information based on static or semi-static data. Examples in this category include invoices, claims, agreements or payments. It could be argued that once the underlying data is assured in terms of its quality, then the aggregate data it supports should be considered cleansed. Sadly this is not necessarily the case. In many cases, the calculations are complex and it is easy for mistakes to occur. The typical ways of checking dynamic data will be:

- Recalculation
- Parallel running
- Out of range exceptions
- Data not matching business rules

For example, high interest payments but a low interest rate, or high or low values. These metrics can be obtained either via a snapshot extract from the running system, or via continuous auditing (of which more later).

29.4.5 Performance measures on streaming data.

Streaming data is data that not only changes, but does not stand still. Examples of this kind of data include time and share prices. The challenge with measuring the data quality on this data is that by the time you have checked, the data has changed again. As a result checking the quality of this kind of data will consist of:

- Checking against a reference source.
- Checking integrity (time should only ever move in one direction).
- Checking against expectations (e.g. very large movements in share prices should be investigated).

29.5 How to get the Metrics

29.5.1 Manual Interrogation Tools

Interrogation tools are by far the most common of measurement methods. Interrogation tools can be run against the data, results collated and reports created. This method is unfortunately time and labour intensive. The advantage is that the tools themselves are relatively easy to obtain and often free, and the approach is flexible – adding additional metrics is quick.

29.5.2   Automatic Interrogation Tools

Similar to manual tools, these are run on a regular basis against datasets. The advantage is that they are much quicker than performing the job manually. The disadvantage is that setting up the data sets for analysis is sometimes a time consuming process. Tools are often sensitive to the quality and format of the incoming data, and data integration and transformation becomes an important element of creation and distribution of data quality metrics.

29.5.3   Traditional Reports

Another common approach is to utilise the enterprise reporting solution to create quality reports on the data. This has the advantage that the reports will be created on a monthly/weekly basis without any human intervention, and hence will always be available – after the initial expenditure of time to set them up. The disadvantage is that reports created in this manner are not flexible (given they are often set up either by an IT department or a third party), and adding additional measures to the reporting solution may take time and cost.

29.5.4   Continuous Auditing

Continuous auditing is a technology-enabled automatic method of examining data on a real time basis and then automatically highlighting exceptions for manual examination and rectification. This is performed by installing auditing software either at the end of a process or between two processes, and checking all data that comes through the process against a set of rules placed in advance. The advantage of this type of checking is the sample set is 100%. The disadvantages are potentially many thousands of false positives and that the rule set has to be carefully tailored. However, over time, and with a carefully tuned rule set, these tools can be effective. Continuous auditing tools can be used for exceptions, patterns, transgression of business rules, trend analysis, and so on. Continuous auditing tools often face resistance from IT security. Due to their nature they often require a high degree of access to applications and data, and this will normally break IT security policies. Getting buy-in from IT to install such tools is critical.

29.5.5   Sample Checking

For some elements of data quality, it is only possible to obtain metrics by sample checking from the source of the data, in most cases the customer application form or telephone call. This is because high level data interrogation can only check whether the data on the system is valid against the business rules set for that particular data item – for example that a postcode is valid against the Royal Mail postcode database, or that a customer National Insurance number conforms to the rules set for the format for a National Insurance number.

It is not possible, using high level interrogation, to check that the NI number held is accurate for that particular customer, except in a relatively limited way, for example checking whether the NI number recorded matches another individual already held. As a result, to determine metrics it is necessary to determine the accuracy by which the data is transcribed from the initial customer call or application form onto the information systems.

It is clearly not possible to check this process for each transaction; however, it can be effective to check a sample of the transactions to determine the efficacy of the data capture methodology. This process may be manual, and in many organisations such checking is already performed by the QA teams responsible for the individual areas or by Internal Audit as part of a regular cycle of auditing processes within the organisation. Whilst it is possible for technology to enable the scanning of application documents or phone conversations to allow this checking to be performed automatically, the process – based on my own experience – is fraught with error at the current level of technology. However the metrics obtained though these parts of the organisation can and should be included within the overall data quality metrics.

29.5.6   Patterns

Pattern checking uses the technique that humans use to determine the quality of data all the time. It is the "does it look right?" test. For example, retail sales in the UK would normally be expected to be higher in December than in November due to Christmas. Most organisations have a good idea of how metrics will change on a month by month and week by week basis. Business rules can therefore be put in place to highlight potential data quality issues as they occur. The danger is that data may be within expectations but actually be wrong or, worse, that the data may be manipulated to "look right" and mask a serious problem.

29.5.7   Recalculation

An effective way of measuring the accuracy of data is to re-perform the changes that transition data from one stage to another. This can be done on an ad hoc basis, all the time (parallel running of the entire calculation), or on a sample basis. A popular way of performing this check is what is called a "proof in total". For example, if for each account:

[interest paid on the balance] = [balance] x [the interest rate] x [time since the interest was last paid]

Then the same logic should apply for the total of all accounts – total balance multiplied by average interest rate multiplied by the number of days since the end of the last month should equal the same amount as the sum of all of the individual accounts. These high level checks are effective in identifying major errors and were commonly used when I was working in an audit capacity.

29.5.8   Cross Checking

Cross checking is a powerful and effective check on data quality. Examples are:

- **Contact Address = Property Address (for a mortgage customer)**
  An important performance metric in terms of data quality involves determination that the customer address is the same as the property address. Whilst there are good reasons for the address to be different (buy-to-let, power of attorney, etc) in most cases the address should be the same.

- **IT Access List = HR Employee List = Payroll**
  This is a particularly effective cross check for data quality within an organisation, as in theory all three lists should be the same. If HR are paying someone who does not have access to the building according to the security department then that is worth highlighting. If the organisation is not paying someone who does have such access that would be peculiar indeed.

29.5.9 Customer Complaints

It is effective to use customer complaints as a metric for data quality, providing that there is the ability for the customer complaints team to be able to flag complaints as relating to data quality issues. Even if not, an analysis of customer complaints can reveal a wealth of information in relation to the issues facing data quality in the organisation. Customer complaints are especially effective at identifying situations where both the original data capture and the rectification process have failed, and all controls have failed along the line. Each customer complaint should be a gold mine of critical information as to where the organisation can be improved. All too often customer complaints are dealt with in the most expedient way possible, possibly using form letters, which may or may not relate to the original complaint, and hence introduce yet another layer of failure on top of the many that have already occurred. Customer complaints are some of the most useful information available to the organisation. Typical issues identified by customer complaints are:

- Failures in death registrations. Customers get upset when they are opening letters addressed to deceased relatives when the customer has already advised the organisation of the situation.
- Failures in transcription of addresses and especially names. No-one likes their name being spelt incorrectly.
- Failures in product setup – "I didn't get what you told me I was getting".

Again, these metrics should be included within the overall data quality metrics.

29.5.10 Returned Mail

If you send out mail and the postal service are unable to deliver it then it is most often returned to sender. In most organisations, the terminology used to describe invalid addresses held is "gone-aways" and I will use that here. I have been directly involved in a number of organisations that use a gone-away process, which often follows a three step procedure.

Number of returned mail items	System Flag	Effect
1 item of returned mail	Gone-away Flag 1	No effect
2 items of returned mail	Gone-away Flag 2	Mail restricted to essential or legal communications only (for example notification of Annual General Meeting)
3 Items of returned mail	Gone-away Flag 3	No mail sent to this address

Every time a mailing occurs, the returned mail should be the sum of new gone-aways and those gone-aways marked as 1 or 2 depending on the mailing. The gone-away process as described above places a system around the mechanism for recording invalid customer addresses, and also flags addresses where there is evidence to assume that the customer address is actually incorrect. The gone-away process can therefore act as a start point for investigation and rectification of customer address errors.

29.6 Summary

I have in this chapter covered a number of ways of generating metrics and also matched this to the type of data that is being measured. The matching of type of data to the type of metric is summarised in the table below.

Data Type	Primary Method	Secondary	Tertiary
Static and semi-static data (e.g. customer date of birth, customer address)	Sample checking (calls, application forms)	Continuous auditing, reporting	Customer complaints, gone away
Dynamic data (e.g. customer account balance)	Sample checking (calculations)	Continuous auditing reporting	Parallel running
Streaming data (Share price, Time)	Parallel running Source comparison	Continuous auditing	

I have discussed the various performance metrics that can be used to measure data quality. In the next chapter I will cover when reporting metrics should be put in place, the timing of reporting, and the types of dashboards that can be employed. I will finish by covering in brief the tools that can be employed for data quality and how they can be deployed in the organisation.

SECTION 5.3 DIRECTION

CHAPTER 30 QUALITY REPORTING

30.1 Structure

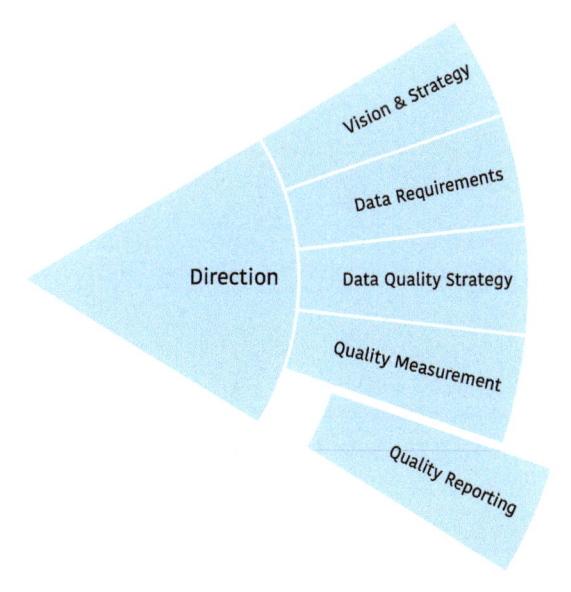

This stage of The Data Quality Blueprint includes the following phases:

1. Vision & Strategy
2. Data Requirements
3. Data Quality Strategy
4. Quality Measurement
5. Quality Reporting

This chapter covers the last of these elements.

30.2 Overview

INPUTS	TASKS
■ All project artefacts created to date ■ Corporate vision ■ Corporate strategy ■ Data architecture ■ Data strategy (if available) ■ Business architecture ■ Application architecture ■ Infrastructure architecture	■ Define measurement criteria ■ Define source data for reporting ■ Define timing and frequency of reporting ■ Design dashboards ■ Agree approach with users and sponsor ■ Create POC (mockup, not functional) ■ Obtain feedback and update ■ Determine mechanism for obtaining source data ■ Define data integration approach ■ Define data quality data model ■ Define data quality metadata ■ Design target database (if applicable) ■ Implement extraction and transformation of data ■ Implement dashboarding tool ■ Implement dashboards

OUTPUTS

- Data quality measurement integration approach
- Proof of Concept dashboard
- Reporting approach
- Data quality metadata repository
- Data quality dashboard

DEPENDENCIES

- Access to stakeholders
- Access to executives
- Access to corporate strategy

In the previous chapter I have discussed the data quality metrics, and the contents of the reports. In this chapter I will look at the contents of the reporting – what it should include – and how the reporting should be presented. I will also look at the way that data quality metrics can be included in exiting reports and finally will briefly touch on the timing of reports.

30.3 What Should Reporting Include?

Data quality reporting should include:

- **Technical reports** – covering the technical status of data quality in terms of poor data – this is very matter-of-fact, and raw – reports will state that "we have xx% of email addresses". Try and limit this kind of reporting to a minimum.
- **Reporting on specific business-relevant data** – slightly better in that the raw data is made business-relevant. These reports cover monitoring of business areas of interest and monitoring the reliability of the business data. These reports cover specific areas – for example that "the part of the organisation responsible for production of customer statements does not have customer addresses" or "the contact centre don't have customer phone numbers".

- **Reporting the state of data quality in current reports** – this is adding next to a figure such as "gross total customer mortgage balance" that "xxx account had a negative balance and xxx were null". This is quite an effective report from the business perspective – albeit one that has a large possibility of making the business not trust a thing that they are told.
- **Reporting the effect of poor data** – This is the by far the most hard hitting and best in terms of presentation to the business user and the execs. This is the report saying "because of the poor quality of our data, our capital requirement may be incorrect by £3,000,000". This is the kind of reporting that will get action, will smooth the way for the rest of the project, will result in barriers magically disappearing before the project's eyes, and will suddenly mean that resources become available. If you can possibly get an example of this last form of report in the pack, in any way, it will be worth it.

30.4   Technical Data Quality Reports

These reports monitor the status of the databases or data loads and focus mainly on the "objective" dimensions of data quality, such as:

- Accuracy
- Consistency
- Validity
- Completeness
- Currency
- Uniqueness (non-duplication)

These reports are prepared for single data elements and may be grouped into logical units, such as by system, product or brand. They are used to monitor the status of data quality, identify potential issues or areas for follow up, and can be used to display the results for data quality improvement achieved through use of data quality tools. They are the easiest to set up, but really should be limited to internal reporting within the data quality teams as they have limited business relevance. For technical folk this kind of report has the most meaning – it is, after all, talking in terms of raw data and facts. Unfortunately, in terms of the executive it has the least meaning, if any. Avoid this kind of reporting. At worst, it can reinforce the view that data does not matter and has little relevance. If possible, move the reporting into the business facing reports that will mean more to the business user – and the execs.

30.5   Reporting on Specific Business-Relevant Data

These business reports focus on specific data quality issues and are intended for business motivation. For example, "the marketing department needs to have customer email addresses for at least 95% of customers, while only 35% is currently populated." This may lead to a subsequent requirement for the percentage of actual, correct and completed email addresses. These reports:

- Change the culture and approach of data entry employees to the actual data entry process and perception of data quality as an important attribute of data entered
- Allow management to focus on data quality activities on areas important for the business
- Provide measures that may be used to motivate the data entry team.

The drawback of these reports is that they are not directly relevant in terms of pound value. They indicate a data deficit, and a potential effect (e.g. that marketing cannot email customers), but they do not draw a line between the two, and most certainly don't draw a line between this and "as a result, we estimate that we have lost xxx cross sell opportunities with a total revenue of £xxx,xxx".

30.6 Reporting the Data Quality in Existing Reports (data reliability reports)

These are usually not standalone reports, but summarised indicators in the regular business reports. The aim of data reliability monitoring is to indicate whether the business report may be trusted. These reports:

- Create internal "buy-in" for data quality management and capture the attention of decision makers
- Change the culture of business.

The main disadvantage of these reports is the same as the advantage; they make the business question everything they are told, and this may not be politically advisable in some climates.

30.7 Reporting the Effect of Poor Data

This is the most difficult area for reporting. This is answering the question "how much money is our data quality costing us?" Some degree of thought has to go into this kind of reporting, but it is also the most effective and business relevant. Examples are shown in the table below.

Cause	Metric
Number of customer applications dropped as a result of poor data quality	Estimated lost revenue and profit
Potential errors in risk metrics	Estimated excess capital
Total invalid addresses	Estimated mailing overspend
Number of customer complaints that are directly related to data quality	Aggregated cost of complaint in terms of time cost processing complaint and subsequent rectification

30.8 Timing of Reports

The timing of data quality reports will depend on the cadence of the business process that is being measured, together with the effort required to create the metric and the sensitivity or criticality of the poor data quality to the business, and also the anticipated speed of response. For example, there is little point reporting on static data on a daily basis, equally there is no point reporting daily on data if it takes a year to rectify. A suggested frequency is shown in the table below, however in reality this will vary depending on the organisation and will be different for each organisation.

Time Period	Type of data	Reason
Hourly	Not really relevant for data quality	
Daily	Primary data capture	If someone is doing this wrong they need to be stopped fast
Weekly	Operational data quality metrics	
Monthly	For most metrics monthly is a reasonable compromise	
Quarterly	Duplication	De-duplication normally takes time, though I am aware of some organisations that de-duplicate daily

30.9   Types of Dashboards

The useful subject of how dashboards should be put together and how they should present information is covered in great detail by other books. What I will do here is talk at a high level. The reason for dashboarding is that presenting reams of output to the executive level is undesirable. They don't have time and are generally not interested. The quicker, easier and more efficiently that you can get information across the better. At the time of writing visualisation tools are particularly in vogue for dashboarding and can be utilised to convey information extremely effectively.

30.10   Proof of Concept

A powerful tool when it comes to demonstrating quickly what data quality reporting can achieve is a proof of concept dashboard. If based on dummy data they can be created in a short time indeed (an hour or less) and presented to the management of the organisation so that the project can work with them to refine the reporting framework. This kind of mock-up is useful in managing expectations, though most managers in my experience are impressed when even basic data quality reporting is presented to them. A more detailed mock-up based on actual data is another (and desirable) possibility. This is certainly an area of the overall project where prototyping can be effective.

Prototyping, if you are not familiar with the term, is developing on the fly, where a developer and the eventual recipients of the dashboard sit together and rapidly develop the final design between them. This avoids the time delay of requirements definition and validation and then subsequent development. In fact, in relation to a data quality dashboard, I would strongly suggest this method as the users of the dashboard are unlikely to realise what is possible. This may well be the first time they have ever seen a data quality dashboard, given the maturity in the industry.

30.11   Reporting Tools

If you listen to many vendors then you can be easily convinced that it is impossible to perform any reporting on data quality without a suite of tools, a horde of consultants, some shiny new kit, a lot of training and quite a lot of money. This is (fortunately) not true. It is true that bespoke tools make things easier, but the same effect can be created with the use of basic office productivity tools and a degree of knowledge.

I know it is somewhat heretical to say this – but if you are the point where you have defined data strategy and requirements but are not into the discovery and remediation as yet then knocking up a few dashboards with basic office productivity tools will be faster and more productive than using bespoke toolsets.

Source Application → Source Data Store → ETL → Landing Area → R Analytics → Access → Excel

One of the better data quality implementations I have come across was actually created using SAS for bulk extraction and manipulation, Microsoft Access for collation and comparison, and Microsoft Excel and PowerPoint for presentation. You could equally well use open-source R for extraction and manipulation, and Open Office for manipulation, or use office database and spreadsheet tools (which most organisations already have), and end up paying no more in licence fees than you do already. Is it easier to use a data quality tool? Absolutely yes. Is it absolutely necessary? Absolutely not.

Where data quality tools shine (again, in my opinion) is:

- Automating profiling in bulk (no-one wants to be spending hours running queries against a database every month – but a few queries on critical fields is fine).
- Workflow (managing exceptions and their remediation).
- Business definition management (and, specifically, nagging people to approve definitions).
- Management of data quality "on the fly".

None of these elements – whilst important at a later point of the process – are necessary at the start of the process. Hence, my suggestion is not to buy them until you are absolutely sure that you are going to get good use out of them. Like many tools, the point is to do a job you already do better. Not to buy a tool and then wonder what you will use it for.

30.12 When Should Dashboards be Created?

An interesting question to address is when should the reporting on data quality be put in place? Should it be at the beginning of a data quality project or at the end? My personal view is that there is considerable value in putting in place the reporting metrics for data quality as early in the process as possible. This is assuming that a number of the larger questions have been addressed, such as what data, why, and whether the data is relevant to the overall organisation. Hence reporting can be put in place immediately after the direction stage. Of course, a straw man of the metrics can actively help their determination. Other considerations include:

- The reporting will be needed to govern the performance of the remediation effort, measuring both the before and after state.
- Some reporting will be almost certainly an output from the profiling.

- Putting the data quality reporting in place quickly gives a visible output from the project at an early stage.
- Seeing data quality statistics at an early stage incentivises the rest of the project – there is nothing like a report that states that the organisation only has 10% of customer email addresses to put some meaning and business relevance into the project.
- Seeing reporting figures moving in a reassuringly positive direction makes it feel like the project is achieving something – both to participants who can feel their hard work is paying off, but also to executives who can see some return for the invoices they are signing off each month.

30.13   Summary

In this chapter I have outlined the way in which data quality can be measured on a practical basis. The intention is to enable the business to emplace KPIs that can form the basis of dashboarding in terms of the overall data quality of the organisation, but also, and more importantly in the context of this book, to enable management visibility of the effectiveness of any data quality remediation project. I have also talked about when an organisation should put in place data quality reporting.

This chapter should enable a data quality practitioner to effectively discuss the nature of data quality reporting within their organisation and to promote the most effective kinds of reporting in order to manage data quality, and alert the management and board to data quality issues.

I have finished by talking briefly about how tools can be included within the architecture of the organisation, and briefly mentioned the advantages and disadvantages of specific data quality tools (or profiling tools) over general office productivity tools.

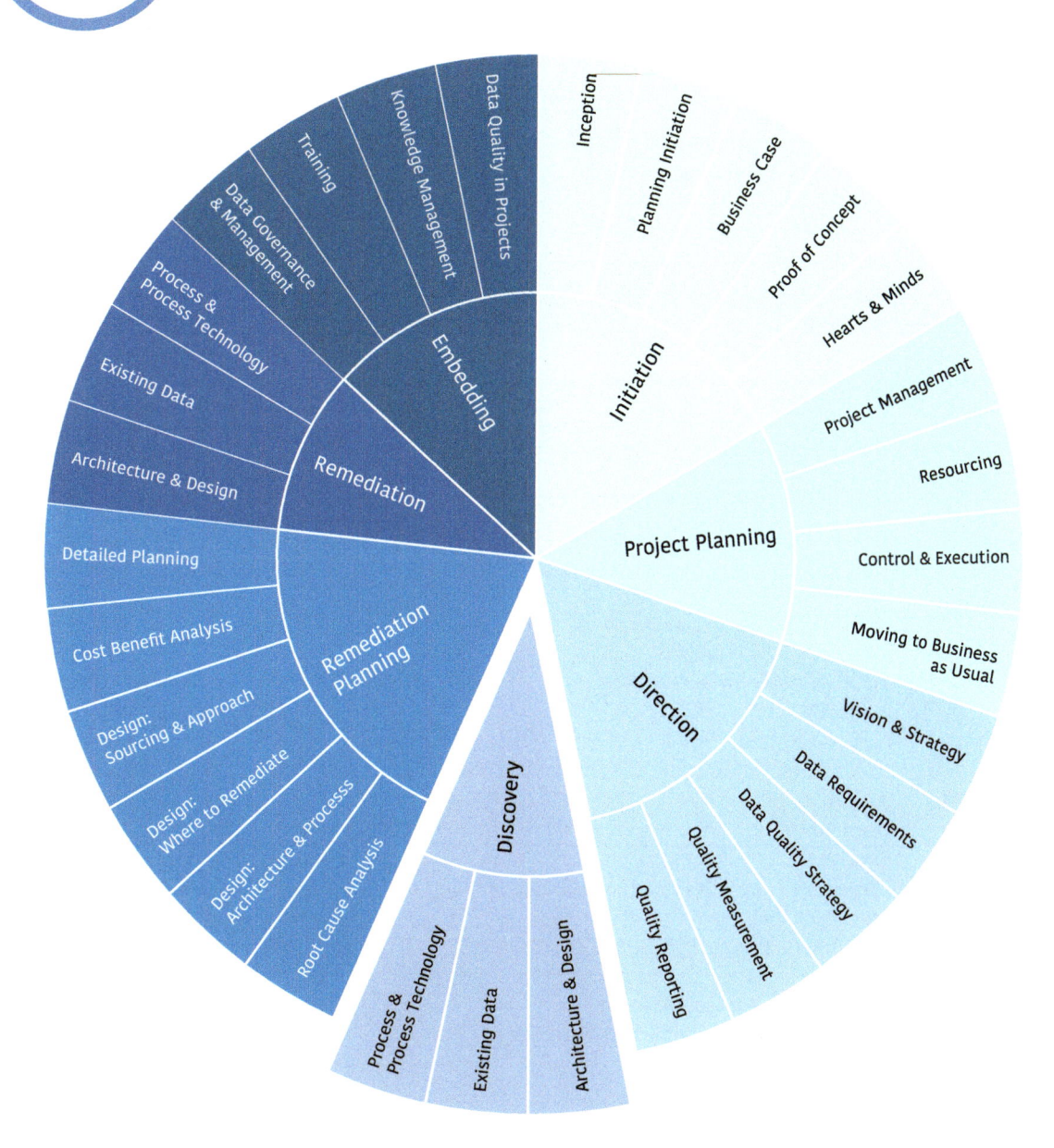

SECTION 5.4 DISCOVERY

Initiation
- Inception
- Planning Initiation
- Business Case
- Proof of Concept
- Hearts & Minds

Project Planning
- Project Management
- Resourcing
- Control & Execution
- Moving to Business as Usual

Direction
- Vision & Strategy
- Data Requirements
- Data Quality Strategy
- Quality Measurement
- Quality Reporting

Discovery
- Process & Process Technology
- Existing Data
- Architecture & Design

Remediation Planning
- Root Cause Analysis
- Design: Architecture & Process
- Design: Where to Remediate
- Design: Sourcing & Approach
- Cost Benefit Analysis
- Detailed Planning

Remediation
- Architecture & Design
- Existing Data
- Process & Process Technology

Embedding
- Data Governance & Management
- Training
- Knowledge Management
- Data Quality in Projects

Where are we going and what do we want to achieve?

SECTION 5.4: INDEX

CHAPTER 31: Section Overview — 333

CHAPTER 32: Discovery: Architecture & Design — 335
- 32.1 Structure — 335
- 32.2 Overview — 336
- 32.3 Engage the Existing Architecture Function — 337
- 32.4 Step 1: High Level Definition and Scope — 338
- 32.5 Step 2: Plan — 338
- 32.6 Step 3: Detail Investigation and Description — 339
- 32.7 Step 4: Assess Architecture — 339
- 32.8 Step 5: Architecture Assessment Deliverable — 346
- 32.9 Summary — 346

CHAPTER 33: Discovery: Existing Data — 347
- 33.1 Structure — 347
- 33.2 Overview — 348
- 33.3 Engage the Existing Data Function — 349
- 33.4 Step 1: High Level Definition and Scope — 350
- 33.5 Step 2: Plan — 352
- 33.6 Step 3: Profiling — 354
- 33.7 Dynamic Data — 355
- 33.8 Streaming Data — 357
- 33.9 Step 4: Data Assessment — 357
- 33.10 Step 5: Data Assessment Deliverable — 357
- 33.11 Summary — 358

CHAPTER 34: Discovery: Process & Process Technology — 359
- 34.1 Structure — 359
- 34.2 Overview — 360
- 34.3 Engage Existing Process Functions — 362
- 34.4 Step 1: High Level Definition and Scope — 362
- 34.5 Step 2: Plan — 364
- 34.6 Step 3: Detail Investigation and Description — 365
- 34.7 Step 4a: Process Focused Assessment — 366
- 34.8 Step 4b: Data Focused Assessment — 367
- 34.9 Step 5: Process Assessment Deliverable — 369
- 34.10 Common Problems — 369
- 34.11 Summary — 370

SECTION 5.4 DISCOVERY

CHAPTER 31 SECTION OVERVIEW

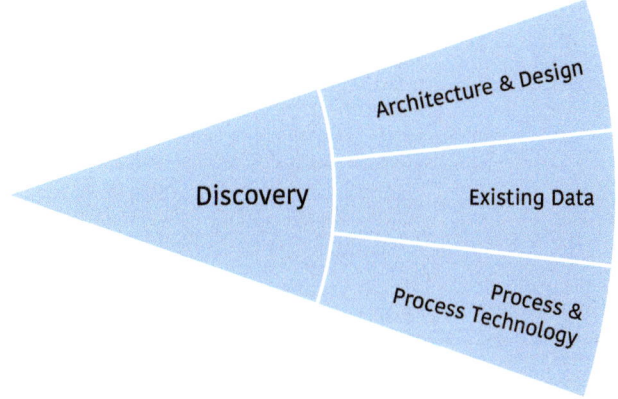

Discovery: Architecture & Design, Existing Data, Process & Process Technology

The next stage in our data quality journey is to determine the current situation. This discovery stage covers the analysis and assessment of the overall architectural organisational design, the familiar task of profiling the existing data, and also the less familiar task of business process assessment, where the project looks at the way business processes contribute to poor quality data. The reason this stage is placed here is that assessment should be made in full knowledge of the information requirements of the organisation, otherwise it is likely, if not inevitable, that much time will be wasted. The approach for each of the three assessments, architecture, data and process, follows a similar pattern. In short, the process is definition of scope, definition and/or documentation of the element to be assessed, a planning stage, an assessment stage and a final delivery stage.

Definition → Documentation → Assessment → Product Delivery

For architecture, the documentation of architectural elements needs to occur before they can be assessed, and the same applies to process. For existing data this "documentation" stage is the profiling itself. The delivery of results should be in the same format over all three disciplines. It is only the assessment phase that differs. For architecture and process the assessment is for risks to good quality, for data it is the actual analysis of the data itself, directly measuring the data quality. A high level view of the three phases is shown in the diagram below, which explicitly demonstrates the commonality in the approach.

Discovery: Architecture & Design	Discovery: Existing Data	Discovery: Process & Process Technology
Step 1: High level definition and scope	**Step 1**: High level definition and scope	**Step 1**: High level definition and scope
Step 2: Plan	**Step 2**: Plan	**Step 2**: Plan
Step 3: Detail Investigation and Description	**Step 3**: Profile Data	**Step 3**: Detail Investigation and Description
Step 4: Assess Architecture	**Step 4**: Assess Profiling Results	**Step 4A**: Process Focused Assessment
Step 5: Deliver Assessment Results	**Step 5**: Deliver Assessment Results	**Step 4B**: Data Focused Assessment
		Step 5: Deliver Assessment Results

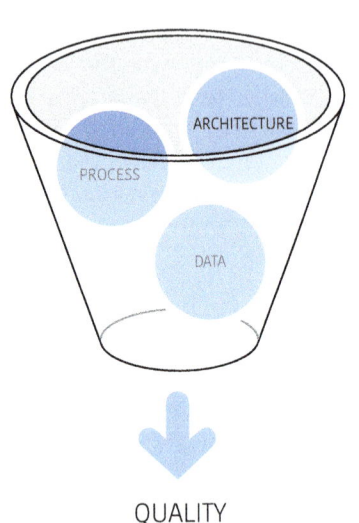

In theory the discovery stage for architecture, data and process can proceed simultaneously. The skill sets are different for each "leg" and hence different resources would be used as a matter of course. This lends itself to a very efficient project execution and is far better than analysing each section sequentially. However, all three discovery phases should work hand in hand. A process may look risky, but only the analysis of the data coming out of the process can prove that the risk has materialised. Equally, the assessment of architecture and process will identify good places for the data team to look more carefully. The data results can also inform where process and design has failed. Whilst there is therefore significant benefit in running all three simultaneously for efficiency of timescale, it is essential that the elements interact and work together.

QUALITY

SECTION 5.4 DISCOVERY

CHAPTER 32 DISCOVERY: ARCHITECTURE AND DESIGN

32.1 Structure

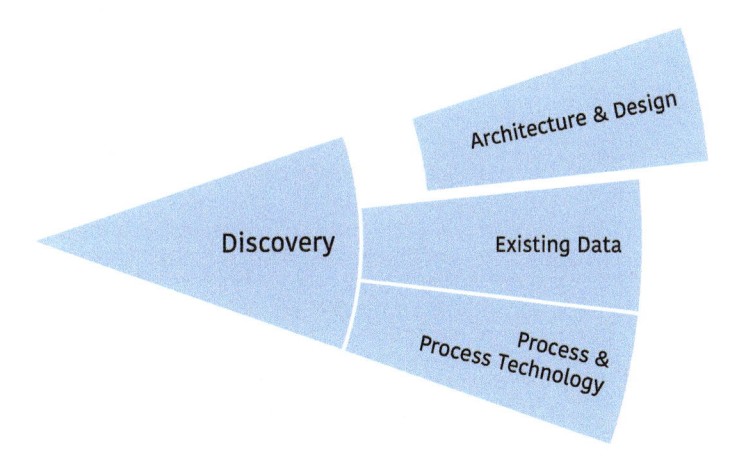

This stage of The Data Quality Blueprint includes the following phases:

1. Architecture & Design
2. Existing Data
3. Process & Process Technology

This chapter covers the first of these phases.

32.2 Overview

INPUTS
- All artefacts created or utilised in the data quality project to date
- Architectural artefacts
- Conceptual architectures
- Data architectures
- Business architectures
- Technical architectures
- Infrastructure architecture
- Data lineage
- Data models

OUTPUTS
- Data architecture assessment approach
- List of key personnel
- Exception process
- Necessary architecture documentation
- Architecture issues/pain points
- Data architecture assessment

DEPENDENCIES
- Access to stakeholders
- Access to architects

TASKS
- Scope
  - Confirm domains in scope
  - Confirm systems in scope
  - Confirm business units in scope
  - Validate scope against pain points, objectives and requirements
- Plan approach
  - Draft reporting template
  - Divide architecture into functional areas
  - Divide architecture into information flows
  - Divide architecture into business processes
  - Allocate specialists to separate areas
  - Define and document timescales
  - Identify key personnel to interview
  - Understand data requirements of the organisation
  - Define architectural notation
  - Create approach document
  - Upload to project repository
- Exception Process
  - Document exception process
  - Determine escalation points/people
  - Determine required timescales for exception turnaround
  - Discuss exception process with process and business owner
  - Obtain buy-in to exception process
  - Agree SLA for exception process
  - Deliver exception process document
  - Upload to project repository
- Documentation Review
  - Collate existing architecture documentation
  - Where documentation does not exist create documentation
  - Identify areas where architecture looks to be inadequate
  - Identify areas where (from previous interviews) there are data quality issues
  - Document issues
  - Upload to project repository
- Architecture review
  - Arrange and perform interviews
  - Identify pain points
  - Document pain points
  - Confirm architectural issues with key personnel
  - Document issues
  - Upload to project repository
- Architecture Assessment
  - Collate pain points
  - Collate issues raised from documentation assessment
  - Assess the architecture in relation to its effect on data quality
  - Assess the impact resulting from each of the issues

	- Document the impact - Estimate the cost of the impact - Agree with key stakeholders - Create architecture assessment - Upload to project repository

A fundamental component of the ability of an organisation to achieve its information quality aspirations is the structure of the organisation. This structure is its business processes, data stores, applications and infrastructure. Many organisations have grown organically over time, or have implemented multiple tactical solutions with no consideration of the end state thereby created. Organisations are therefore often a spaghetti of applications, data stores and infrastructure, all looking to support an organisation where business processes are continuously trying to adapt to a changing world. To say the least, the result is often sub-optimal.

When looking to assess data quality, consideration of the individual processes or data fields is essential, but equally essential is stepping back and looking at the organisation as a whole. Within this section we are covering not only the business and technological design, but the high level design of, and interfaces between, the technology and the organisation.

Poor choice of technology can make data quality harder to achieve. It is worth taking some time to understand the technological makeup of your data solution and where technology is blocking your achievement of optimal data quality. Within this book the architecture and design covers the high level technological solution to information quality, and the process assessment considers the way in which technology supports the individual process. This continues the approach taken of considering technology as integral to the organisation and processes rather than a separate component in itself.

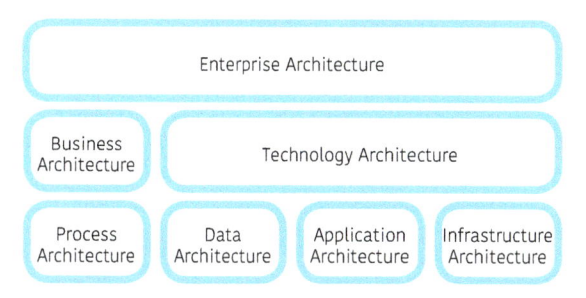

In this chapter I will detail how the organisational architecture can impact data quality, how it should be assessed, what that assessment should cover, and also give examples of how poor architecture can cause data quality problems. I will also discuss how architectural problems should be documented in order to have consistency across the whole discovery stage of the project.

32.3 Engage the Existing Architecture Function

I have mentioned before the importance of utilising existing knowledge, to smooth the progress of the project and to prevent the project repeating the previous mistakes. At the start of the discovery phase, if the project has not already done so, then the project needs to engage the existing architecture function and make sure that they are aware of the project, and are ideally helping with the project if not embedded within it.

Even if a formal architecture function does not exist, individuals will exist which who have been thinking about the long term architectural strategy for the organisation. The project needs to make sure they are involved.

32.4   Step 1: High Level Definition and Scope

The starting point for the architectural discovery process is to determine scope in terms of domains, systems and business divisions. The discovery process needs to create high level overviews of the architecture, before it can drill down into more detail. Architectural definition documents should ideally be available to the data quality practitioner in any organisation that has an enterprise or data architecture function, but often this function is either under-developed, new, or doesn't exist at all, and hence the data quality practitioner, looking to source architectural artefacts, may have to create the documents themselves. Views that need to be initially created will include:

- Organisational diagrams (which will almost certainly exist)
- High level application structure
- High level data stores
- High level business architecture

This may involve asking individuals within the organisation to draw the business as they see it from their perspective. Architecture is much based on viewpoints and views (where you stand and what you can see from that point) and the result of asking many different individuals to draw the same diagram is likely to result in an exceptionally informative and diverse view of the business. Architectural diagrams are quite powerful documents, and often visually simplify complex concepts. Once an overall structure is created it is then possible to plan the approach to understand how the architecture will affect the quality of the data.

32.5   Step 2: Plan

The next stage is to take a step back and make a high level assessment at an organisation and business-level of how the existing architecture will affect the overall data quality of the organisation. The objective is to identify where further detail investigation is needed and also, to a lesser extent, what skills may be required from the team. The data quality practitioner is primarily looking for examples of poor or awkward integration, or complex or poor design. Examples may include:

- The poorly integrated new acquisition
- The department without a home
- Complicated reporting lines
- Randomly "busy" areas of a diagram indicating lots of small elements with no container framework
- Parts that are added on by the creator as afterthoughts ("oh, and of course I forgot, there's the department in Solihull")
- Anything that appears to indicate an interface between old, legacy world and new, shiny, modern world

Mostly, when it comes to overall design, simple is better than complex, as complex introduces many more opportunities for error. It will be impossible for any assessment to look at every area of architecture in great detail. In most organisations the task is too big by far. Some degree of prioritisation needs to occur, and this needs to be aligned towards the most risky areas. The assessment of which areas are the most risky is based on the high level assessment, as well as the assessment previously undertaken in the initiation stage.

Anecdote:
Nothing to do with data quality, but a long time ago I was a baby auditor, doing a stocktake at a foundry. The foundry had an old and a new part, and 20 ton crucibles of molten steel ran on over-head rails. The rails in the new part of the factory were slightly different sizes to the rails in the old part of the factory.

Watching the juggling that occurred as the operator tried to nurse the crucible (which was swaying to and fro containing the aforesaid 20 tons of molten steel) between the two sets of rails (legacy and new world) was watching an accident waiting to happen.

..and so it is with data.

32.6 Step 3: Detail Investigation and Description

After the planning has identified areas where there may be problems, it is time to delve into the architecture in detail. The high level documentation may already exist, but for a proper assessment it will be necessary to expand this. Here the practitioner will flesh out the understanding created in the definition phase. This may also involve delving into the technology to see where data feeds come and go, what actually connects to what, and how. The architecture practitioner will draw on all the initial investigation undertaken in the initiation stage, and this may well involve going back to the people contacted in the initiation phase and asking them who can give more information on a problem that they identified.

32.7 Step 4: Assess Architecture

The next stage is assessment. For each part of the architecture, the data quality practitioner needs to ask the question: "How does the architecture affect the quest to improve data quality?" Here the data quality practitioner needs to identify any situation where the architecture places a hurdle over getting things right first time. The example given earlier of siloed data sets is an obvious one, but other examples are shown below. This is in no way a comprehensive list of potential high level architectural issues – any organisation is likely to generate several hundreds of varying levels of severity. This work should be performed carefully and at an increasing level of detail to fully understand the problems facing the organisation. Rarely are poor solutions deliberately created. Poor solutions evolve from not enough budget or time, and projects that don't complete or have last minute budget cuts. The objective is to understand why the organisational design is in its current incarnation, what effect it can have, and eventually what can be done, if anything, to fix it.

Whilst I have given a number of examples, in this particular area there is little substitute for experience, which is why I would consider experienced architecture practitioners as essential parts of the project team. The examples should give the reader a feel for what is being covered in the architecture analysis, and how.

Anecdote:

A long time ago I was working at a major retail bank. As is often the case with temporary occupants, we were given a few isolated desks in an outlying and forgotten part of the head office, and after dusting off the desks and shooing a few old copies of newspapers into a bin; we got on with our work.

Next to where we were working was a bank of six desks, with six ancient (green screen) computers on them. These machines were turned on, showing a password and username prompt which had burned into the screen over clearly, many, many years. No-one ever came near them; no-one ever touched them. They were covered in dust. After a while I asked what they were used for. The answer was: "Oh, no-one uses them, but if we disconnect them the mortgage system falls over".

Clearly the mortgage system was, somewhere in its labyrinthine complexity, calling out to see whether these machines existed or not. You can easily see how clearly many generations of managers had looked at this problem, realised that solving the application architecture was going to be a massive job (looking through potentially millions of lines of code) and decided to ignore it as the simplest solution – and make sure the machines were never switched off.

32.7.1 Example 1: Historical systems/applications

Question	Reason for question
Are there any historical systems/applications?	Historical systems do not tend to store modern data well. For example there may not be fields for email address or mobile phone number

Why is this important?	What can we do?
It may not be possible to remediate data as the system may not support data of the required quality. Staff, looking to do their jobs to the best of their ability, may use alternative fields to store essential information. The "comments" field may be commonly used to store email addresses, as it is unlikely to have any validation checks on it. Email addresses are commonly just a jumble of words, special characters ("@") and numbers which will not pass validation checks on other fields. Not all staff members may consistently do this – others may use a different field.	■ Can we replace the historical systems? ■ Can we introduce agreed workarounds so that at least everyone is doing the same thing?

32.7.2 Example 2: Siloed Data

Question	Reason
Are there many copies of customer data?	The more copies, the more confusion around which is correct, the more they are likely to diverge

Why is this important?	What can we do?
Multiple silos mean that every job has to be performed multiple times, ballooning cost of remediation.	- Collapse the silos. Much easier said than done - Ask business owners whether the data is being used - Temporarily delete the data, and wait for someone to scream. If no-one screams within three months, it is probably safe.

32.7.3 Example 3: Multitudinous Feeds

Question	Reason
Are there are many feeds?	- Complex feeds with complex transformations are risky from a data quality point of view. They are generally "black boxes" which are scheduled to run overnight, most of the time no-one knows what they do, they are generally poorly documented, and often have no owner. Modern organisations are lousy with complex feeds. - In once organisation I worked in there were 7,000 (yes, seven thousand) data feeds into ONE department.

Why is this important?	What can we do?
Complex feeds will often transform data. The transformation may be incorrect. The transformation may have worked well at the time it was written. Now? Who knows? The transformation may auto-populate with default values, The transformation may contain hard coded numbers, the feed may drop data it doesn't like, The feed may rely on lookups to tables of, for example, current products, which may or may not be being updated or even exist. In all cases, the problem is that the data is being modified, added to or deleted and no-one really knows how or why – it is a hidden activity.	The "proper" way of doing it would be to analyse each one and work out whether they are necessary. With large volumes it may actually be easier to either: - Create another feed that does the job of 10 others and then switch the others off. - Switch the others off anyway, and see who screams.

32.7.4 Example 4: Too many applications

Question	Reason
Application Spaghettification	Multiple data sources, multiple feeds, multiple data standards, often proprietary, multiple data models

Why is this important?	What can we do?
My personal view is that this is a (bad) symptom of the general IT department's natural inclination to buy kit as the solution to any problem. Part of the problem that this book was written to try and solve.

This is one of the key selling points of the large single vendor stacks which incorporate multiple functions into one single monolithic system – Oracle, SAP, etc.

However my view is that if organisations could stop the IT department buying kit, and actually think about what is the best solution to the problem as opposed to what is currently the shiniest thing on the market a lot of these problems could be avoided. | The traditional way is to buy a new application, and migrate all the data from the legacy systems into the new application (an exercise in itself). Of course, what actually happens is that the legacy systems are never actually switched off, resulting in simply another application being added to the mix. Right idea, wrong result.

The best way to approach this is to start by obliterating the systems, but that comes with its own risk. Finding out who is using them and for what helps, and migrating the data to something sensible. At this point beware of end user computing, as the users then re-create the old system on someone's desktop machine. |

32.7.5 Example 5: Siloed business processes

Question	Reason
Are there are any siloed business processes?	Each part of the organisation does the same thing, just very slightly different

Why is this important?	What can we do?
The problem for remediation in siloed business processes is that process discovery and remediation will have to be performed multiple times. Common reasons for this are the unintegrated new acquisition, or multiple divisions.	There is an opportunity to amalgamate processes to a service orientated architecture, where one part of the organisation is a specialist in customer on-boarding, another in further advance lending, etc

32.7.6 Example 6: The secret data factory

Question	Reason
Are there are any secret data factories?	One part of the organisation invests a lot of time and money into solving their data quality problem. They may involve a third party consultant to help them, or even a third party remediation agent. They build a bespoke data warehouse, populate it, and as far as they are concerned have solved their data quality problem. The trouble is that no-one else knows about it.

Why is this important?	What can we do?
From a data quality view, the data quality practitioner will get half way through the project to find that all the answers are squirreled away in a forgotten corner of an abandoned office. It's quite annoying.	Understand what the secret data factory has achieved and how it has done it. Analyse whether its approach would work in the wider organisation. Get the owners and creators on board so they can work with the project.

32.7.7 Example 7: Choke points

Question	Reason
Are there are any choke points?	Choke points are where demand for a business process has far exceeded the capacity of the business area to keep up.

Why is this important?	What can we do?
This is likely to cause a number of data quality problems. First, within the part of the organisation under pressure quality is likely to come a poor second to throughput, and second other parts of the organisation are likely to attempt to find/create/invent a variety of totally ungoverned process short-cuts to work around the problem. None of these will be overly concerned about data quality.	Understand the impact of the choke point on data quality. If the risk is unacceptable then raise as an issue to the organisation.

32.7.8 Example 8: The new acquisition

Question	Reason
Has the organisation ever expanded through acquisition?	New acquisitions take time to integrate into the wider organisation. They will come with their own applications and data stores for everything from HR management to customer on-boarding. None of these will match those of the new parent. This pseudo-separation can last decades.

Why is this important?	What can we do?
It has been said that interfaces are where data quality most commonly goes wrong. A separate company will create many of these interfaces. It is arguable that the most risky situation is the half-integrated old acquisition, where a series of tactical and half-baked solutions have tried to integrate the data, and never quite succeeded.	Understand what is and is not integrated, and what can be integrated. Understand the quality differences between the new and old data, and how they are being amalgamated.

32.7.9 Example 9: The rapidly growing or "cool" division

Question	Reason
Is one area of the organisation growing fast, or being seen as the future for the organisation?	A rapidly growing part of the business, or one that is seen as a shining star for any reason, may well consider that it has carte blanche to ignore the processes, procedures or control that will control data quality, or will be growing so fast that there is no time to do things "properly". Beware of anything with "Digital" in the title!
Why is this important?	**What can we do?**
It is much better to stop poor data quality entering the organisation in the first place than to let it enter and then cleanse it later. The most likely scenario is that the promise to cleanse the data later will never occur and the organisation will be saddled with poor quality data for the foreseeable future.	The project needs to understand what is being done and why, and what has been created. Some long and hard conversations may have to be made with the new division and they may need to devote additional resources to coming into line.

32.7.10 Example 10: The half-finished project

Question	Reason
Have there been any projects that have closed whilst only half-completed?	A half-finished project will be likely to have left a lot of loose ends which are then tied up in a haphazard and uncontrolled fashion.
Why is this important?	**What can we do?**
Project products are often created with core functionality first, and controls and testing completed towards the end. Projects that are not completed often leave untested and poor quality products in use in the organisation's information systems environment. These may be feeding poor quality data into the organisations systems, or corrupting good data already in place.	- Make a list of the loose ends and the solutions that have been used to complete them and how they will create risks against data quality. - It may be the case that the data quality project has to address some of these.

32.7.11 Example 11: The shiny kit

Question	Reason
Has the organisation recently bought or installed any new elements into its information landscape?	An organisation may spend a large amount of funds on an application, and then will try and make the most of the expenditure by using the new purchase for purposes for which it is not explicitly designed. This may especially be the case if the vendor has over-promised that the shiny new kit can solve many problems in order to persuade the organisation to buy.
Why is this important?	**What can we do?**
The use of an application or database for a purpose for which it is not necessarily designed risks the information that is being processed.	Understand the capabilities and limitations of the shiny new kit. If its use poses unacceptable risk to information quality, stop using it.

32.7.12 Example 12: The tactical solution

Question	Reason
Has the organisation implemented any short term tactical solutions in order to meet short term needs that are intended to be updated later?	Most organisations are full of short term solutions. An issue is identified and a tactical solution is put in place as a sticking plaster to hold the information flow together until a better solution is found. In the normal course of events they will never be replaced.
Why is this important?	**What can we do?**
Solutions that are implemented quickly, with limited – if any – testing, outside the normal governance process are often causes of major information quality issues.	Understand the capabilities and limitations of the tactical solution. Understand its original purpose and what can be done to reduce risks. If risks are unacceptable then the organisation should look to modify or replace the solution.

32.7.13 Example 13: No reference architecture

Question	Reason
Has the organisation a reference architecture so that different divisions or jurisdictions are constrained to do things in the same way?	Complexity breeds poor quality. With different countries all using different applications or data connected in different ways there is no consistency or, for that matter, economies of scale.

Why is this important?	What can we do?
With no reference architecture it is very difficult to create good quality aggregate information. Meaning is likely to be different in each jurisdiction. The total number may add up, but it will be composed of apples and pears.	Understand the effect of differing architectures on the data quality. Focus on the elements that cause the data quality pain and try and make all jurisdictions perform at least that element in the same way.

32.8 Step 5: Architecture Assessment Deliverable

After the detailed discovery work the next step is to collate the issues under the four architecture headings, specifically business, data, application and infrastructure. At this point themes should start to emerge in the way the organisation approaches information architecture and information change. The nature of the deliverable will be similar to the example below.

Area	Domain	Issue	Impact
Business architecture	Multiple customer on-boarding areas	Multiple similar processes	Higher risk of poor quality
Data Architecture	Customer Data	Multiple copies of data	High customer duplication. Multiple "golden sources"
Data Architecture	Credit Risk Data	2,000 incoming data feeds	High complexity, high risk, poor management
Application Architecture	Website Applications	Complex application landscape	No clear data standards as each application uses proprietary data model

32.9 Summary

In this chapter I have outlined how architecture should be considered within a data quality discovery process. Largely I consider most of this common sense; in the same way that individuals can see what looks wrong within an actual building I believe that most individuals can see what is wrong within architecture, providing that it is presented in an appropriate way. I have lost count of the number of times I have been talking to a manager at the organisation who has presented a beautiful diagram but with a messy element stuffed into one corner.

On asking about this the response has started "ah, yes, the old building/server/database/division [delete as appropriate]". It is likely that most of the data quality problems will either be there, or at the interfaces between that area and the rest of the organisation. This chapter will give the data quality practitioner the ability and understanding to look for the bits that don't fit.

SECTION 5.4 DISCOVERY

CHAPTER 33 DISCOVERY: EXISTING DATA

33.1 Structure

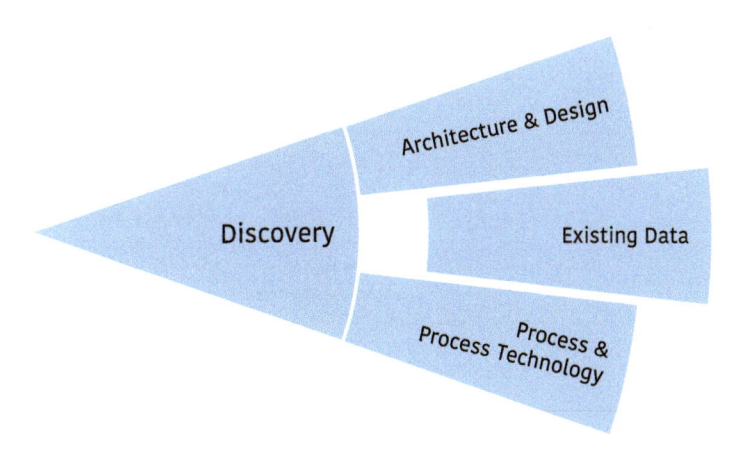

This stage of The Data Quality Blueprint includes the following phases:

1. Architecture & Design
2. Existing Data
3. Process & Process Technology

This chapter covers the second of these phases.

33.2 Overview

INPUTS
- All artefacts created or used by the project to date

OUTPUTS
- Data assessment approach
- List of pain points
- Exception process
- Profiling task list
- Profiling planning document
- Data profiling results
- Existing data assessment

DEPENDENCIES
- Access to stakeholders
- Access to data stores
- Access to data models
- Access to source systems or extract from source systems
- Profiling tool if deemed necessary

TASKS
- Scope
  - Identify domains in scope
  - Identify systems in scope
  - Validate scope against pain points, objectives and requirement
- Approach
  - Plan Approach
    - Obtain existing system documentation
    - Obtain conceptual model of system(s)
    - Discuss conceptual model with system and business subject matter experts
    - Input pain points from initial interviews/workshops/questionnaires
    - Create profiling task list (fields to be profiled)
    - Agree fields to be profiled (and not profiled) with business
    - Agree profiling approach including reporting template and milestones
    - Deliver profiling planning document
    - Agree with business stakeholders
    - Upload to project repository
    - Update dependencies, assumptions and risks
    - Determine and document extract and/or data source requirements
    - Team identification and allocation to system or domain
    - Team training
  - Exception process
    - Design and document exception process
    - Determine escalation points/people
    - Determine required timescales for exception turnaround
    - Discuss exception process with system and business owner
    - Obtain buy-in to exception process
    - Agree SLA for exception process
    - Deliver exception process document
    - Source system access
    - Request access to source systems
    - Enquire about level and nature of masking and determine if it will cause an issue with profiling
    - Agree schedule for availability of data (if extract) or access to systems and data (if direct access)
    - Document schedule and include within plan
    - Obtain extract or access
    - Profiling tool
    - Determine if profiling tool required
    - Identify and source profiling tool if required
    - Determine appropriateness for organisation (i.e. whether it meets requirements)

- Install profiling tool and ensure it can access data.(this may take a long time - I've seen two months)
- Perform training on profiling tool if required
- Profile
  - Agree template with key stakeholders
  - perform profiling work - System 1
  - Perform profiling work - System 2
  - Perform profiling work - System 3
  - Perform profiling work - System 4
  - Perform profiling work - System 5
  - Create profiling results
  - Upload to project repository
- Existing Data Assessment
  - Perform initial investigation of cause
  - Identify "headline issues"
  - Collate into stakeholder groupings (e.g. all the issues that need to be presented to each stakeholder)
  - Present back to business and IT (and exec) stakeholders
  - Document business feedback and revisit causes
  - Create profiling deliverable
  - Create existing data assessment
  - Socialise deliverable with stakeholders
  - Upload to project repository

For most organisations with a large amount of historical data the challenge is both to remediate the existing data and then prevent the problem recurring. The Data Quality Blueprint separates the "recurring" problem out and addresses it through process and architecture improvement, leaving the existing data problem to be tackled in isolation. This task should only ever have to be performed once, as the transformation of business processes should ensure that incoming data quality will remain high and the organisation will not simply add poor quality new data on top of good quality historical data. It is now time to start on the discovery of existing data quality.

Most organisations will face several problems at this point:

- Not knowing where the data in the organisation is located.
- Not knowing its quality.
- Not knowing what it is used for.

Within this chapter, I have covered the methods available to discover the data sources in the organisation, to assess and profile them and to collate and present the results of this work. This will then provide a base for the work to be undertaken in the remediation planning chapter.

33.3 Engage the Existing Data Function

I have already mentioned engaging the existing architecture function within the organisation and the same applies to data. The project needs to be talking to any existing data governance or data management function, as well as critical database administrators and data users. As already stated, they will have a wealth of information, and the project does not want to waste time and resources repeating past mistakes.

33.4 Step 1: High Level Definition and Scope

Defining the scope of the problem is necessary before an organisation is able to define an approach to solve it. This first step is to find out the location of the data and how it is used in the organisation. In large organisations this may be a substantial task as data is scattered across many servers and databases in many geographical locations. In multi-site or multi-country organisations, finding out where the data is located may appear extremely challenging and a logical approach is required. There are, overall, three approaches to data discovery. Which one is used will depend on the exact data landscape of the organisation. In some cases the sources will be well known, in others there will be a voyage of discovery. In each case, the intention is to build up a picture of the data landscape and where the major data stores exist.

33.4.1 Bottom-up

Bottom-up process starts with the identification of data sources. Whilst there are a number of applications that are designed to help with data quality tasks, there are none that I am aware of that will automatically scan an internal network and report every data source. As a result system discovery will best occur through discussions with long-standing members of staff, or, if all else fails, tracking data from one application to another. This will give you a starting point in terms of how much work is going to be necessary. In reality the major data sources for the organisation may be few in number – even a large insurance company is unlikely to have more than a dozen claim handling systems, and similarly, core banking systems are likely to be limited in number – though each country may have a subtly different implementation. What will swell the numbers is the hundreds, possibly thousands of specialist and ancillary applications that interface with the core systems. If identifying core systems then you should be looking to create a catalogue of data sources of the nature below.

No	Data Source	Business Unit	Domain	No of fields	No of records
1	COCLM	Commercial	Claim	7000	10,000,000
2	PLINS	Personal	Claim	6000	50,000,000
3	PARINS	All	Party	1000	1,000,000
4	SPCL	Personal	Claim	1000	100,000
5	PolicySys	Personal	Policy	1000	20,000,000
6	PolicySysC	Commercial	Policy	1000	2,000,000
7	MISYS	ALL	Claim, Policy	1500	10,000,000

There is a risk that in larger organisations which may have hundreds of servers with thousands of databases and tens of thousands of tables, a high level approach like this will still not identify the critical table which is pulled down off the internet every night by a member of staff in an outlying office. Another approach is needed.

33.4.2 Top-Down

This will be the better approach in larger organisations where no-one really can identify where the data comes from and how it is used. The approach here is to analyse the information used by the organisation and then analyse from where it is sourced. Stages are shown in the graphic below.

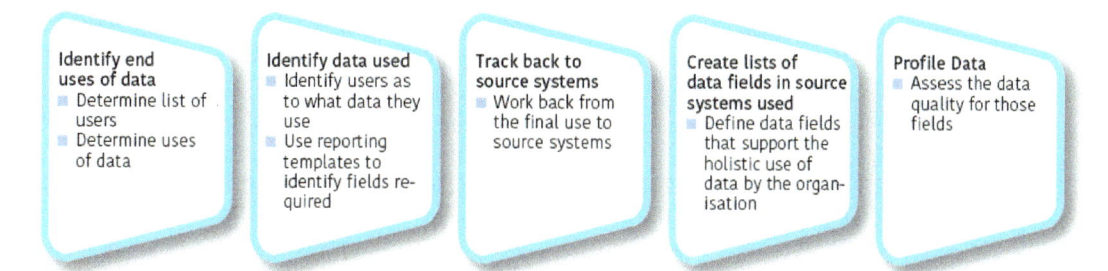

Identify end uses of data
- Determine list of users
- Determine uses of data

Identify data used
- Identify users as to what data they use
- Use reporting templates to identify fields required

Track back to source systems
- Work back from the final use to source systems

Create lists of data fields in source systems used
- Define data fields that support the holistic use of data by the organisation

Profile Data
- Assess the data quality for those fields

Start with the end users. The executive, management, team leaders and operational personnel, and ask for examples of the information they use on a daily basis and the regulatory reporting requirements. This may already have been covered within the definition of data requirements. What may be surprising at this point is how few data items (in total) are used. As stated earlier in this book, a total number of less than 1,000 would be expected in most (even large) organisations.

Expect a large degree of overlap between the various departments. The more senior users will be interested in the overall picture (aggregated figures) rather than the detail. For example, the balance on one mortgage account is useful to the contact centre when the customer rings to ask what is outstanding, but not interesting to the executive. The executive is going to be interested in the aggregated mortgage balance.

The next step is to track back to the relevant data stores. Whilst this may take time it allows a more targeted profiling approach and will save time in the long run in a large organisation. In a small organisation it may actually be simpler to profile everything on the basis that tracking through the spaghetti of databases and extracts and feeds will take longer (and cost more) than sourcing a team of relatively junior staff and starting them performing profiling tasks, or acquiring a profiling tool and letting it run overnight.

33.4.3 Middle-out

If you have a large, known store of data (many businesses have) – a data warehouse or similar – it may make sense to start there. The data warehouse will have feeds in from source systems and feeds out into management reporting, and it is therefore possible to determine the data lineage. An important point is that it helps considerably if the data warehouse is stable. Many data warehouses are in a continual state of improvement/redesign/rebuild and it will be more difficult to try and track data through a data warehouse that is simultaneously being rebuilt. Also, tracking the extracts from the data warehouse only works if you know about them. If users have free rein to extract data from the data warehouse then it may be difficult to discover all the data feeds, and implementation of logging/tracking will be required to identify who is extracting data and what data they are extracting. The disadvantage is this still will not pick up the aforesaid critical table which is pulled down off the internet every night by a member of staff in an outlying office.

33.4.4 Hybrid

In most cases the most sensible approach is "attack from all sides". A sample set of actions may be:

- Look at the main data store and identify critical tables containing the primary business data. Start a team of profilers going on these tables.
- Simultaneously look at the data that is contained in the high level board reporting and extrapolate downwards into its component parts (for example, "earnings per customer" has to contain the data element "earnings" and "customer". "Earnings" can be broken down into its component parts relatively easily, at which point you have an idea of the data that will be needed to be profiled).
- Have a chat with the operational users and get them to walk you through the process, noting the data they use. As process walkthroughs will be occurring as part of the process discovery work, there is an opportunity for synergies by chatting to the process team and letting them know what you need.
- Have a chat with the users who gave the stories which were used in the initiation stage, and ask them to supply more detail.

The intention here is to build up the picture of the organisational data stores. After the data stores have been identified it is then possible to start to undertake the exercise to profile the data to find out its existing quality.

33.5 Step 2: Plan

After identification of the source systems, the next stage is to have a good look inside them and see the state of the data and how it measures up against the defined data requirements. In this way the creation of data requirements at an early stage of The Data Quality Blueprint enables a reduction in workload here. Planning the profiling will take in inputs from the data source discovery and the data modelling work to determine an approach of which systems to profile first, and how, and what is being looked for.

Whilst it is possible to set a team of enthusiastic profilers out to profile everything in existence, it is highly unlikely that this will be necessary, because only a small subset of the data within the source systems will be needed by the organisation. A rough rule of thumb I have carried with me for years is that the ratio of total fields within a database to the proportion actually used for reporting is 10 to 1, though I have seen up to 100 to 1 (one system, 30,000 data fields, but only 300 used for reporting). The number of fields used for operational activities is going to be much higher than that used for reporting, but it will still be a small subset of the total. This offers an opportunity to reduce the overall amount of work within the exercise by restricting profiling to critical fields only. How is this done? The place to start is the data model.

33.5.1 Data Modelling – cutting things down to size.

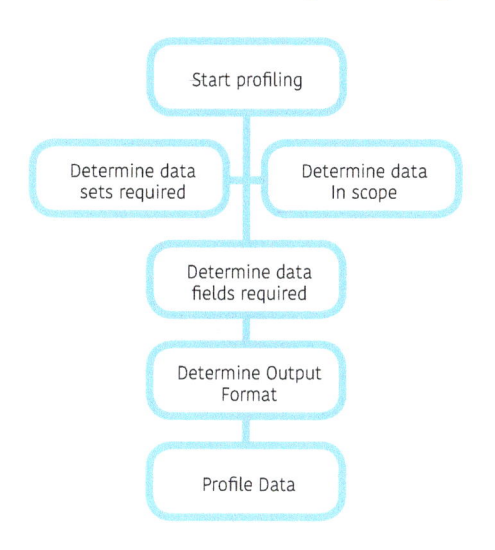

```
Start profiling
    |
    +---------------------+
    |                     |
Determine data      Determine data
sets required        In scope
    |                     |
    +---------------------+
              |
      Determine data
      fields required
              |
      Determine Output
           Format
              |
        Profile Data
```

You will recall in the section on information flow I explained the nature of data models. To recap, the data model is a logical representation of the structure of the data system. It will define the data within the system used for customer fields, and the nature of these fields, and the data within the system used for product, and so on. Data models come in a number of levels of detail – the top being the conceptual data model, followed by the logical data model, and finally the physical data model.

The data model – and the data modeller who understands it, together with some subject matter experts who understand what is required for the business, can provide a fast and effective way of prioritising the profiling. This can be done on a common sense basis.

For example, print settings – of which there may be thousands – are unlikely to be business critical. Equally metadata may be useful information, but is unlikely to require profiling. Even a worst case scenario is unlikely to require more than 30-40% of the total fields in a database being profiled. Then the organisation has successfully cut its workload by over half. Whilst it may appear laborious to work through every field in a database and decide whether it needs profiling, it can be done quickly and effectively. A group of people in a room, a list of fields on a screen, and a determined attitude can make to-profile-or-not-to-profile decisions on thousands of fields in a day. It's not an interesting day, but it is effective.

It may also be helpful to divide the data into a number of logical blocks – for example "before the new system was implemented" and "after the new system was implemented" or "data that relates to a new subsidiary" or "data produced by the contact centre" as opposed to "data produced by the website". There are likely to be wildly differing data quality metrics between the various logical blocks of data. This also enables the organisation to plan its approach.

33.5.2 How to profile

I would submit there are three ways of performing profiling. Manually, semi-automatically, and automatically. I have experience of all three. Manual profiling simply described running queries against a database using SQL and a database management system or query tool. These are queries of the nature of:

"Count * from Customer.Title where Customer.Title is NULL".

This is boring and labour intensive. However, if you have many cheap staff it means that you can start the work immediately. Semi-automatic is pretty much the same, except that the queries are included in a script which is run against each field or each table and outputs to a file. Automatic profiling uses one of the many automatic profiling tools available on the market. It is much faster, but the tools are not cheap. Typical timescales for full profiling of a 1000 field database might be two weeks for 5 staff for full manual, a few days for the same staff for semi-automatic, and a day for 1 member of staff and an automatic tool, most of this day being setting the tool up for the specific database. Unfortunately, given typical procurement timescales and approval requirements, it is (depressingly) often faster to go manual or semi-automatic than waiting for the all-singing, all-dancing tool to arrive.

33.5.3 Output

Another task is agreeing the output format for the profiling with the organisation as a whole. The output from the profiling work is the first time the organisation will see "inside the box" on data quality, possibly ever, and a surprising number of people will be interested in the results. Expect requests from the BI team, the management information team, the source system SMEs, the business managers, and potentially the executive. Make the output look polished and not just a pile of numbers in a spreadsheet.

33.6 Step 3: Profiling

The nature of the detail tasks within profiling will depend on what the organisation considers to be its main concern – remember that there is no point solving a problem that does not exist. However if we consider the previously defined attributes of "good" data, then the attributes of "bad" data are the opposite. Typical data profiling will include:

Profiling Content	Explanation
Primary key violations	For example, if there are two customers with the same customer number.
Foreign key violations	E.g. if a customer is stated as having an account XXXX, but there is no account XXXX.
Nulls	Null does not represent 0, or blank, it simply represents "unknown". As such it is quite an important variable for data quality, as sometimes knowing what you do not know is as important – or more useful – than knowing what you do know.
Field types and length	For example, CHAR(40) – character field with a maximum length of 40 characters
Business description	e.g. "Customer first name". This is not necessarily a result of the profiling, but business meaning will need to be included for the step of matching issues to process, or grouping issues together
Constraints	E.g. Key constraints or table or field constraints (if known)
Unique values (percentage of)	Values that only occur once. For a key, this should be 100%

Special character	Characters such as £, ^, *, #, @, (, %, !, etc.
Patterns and percentage of patterns	Patterns are normally expressed in a code – for example "John" may be ULLL (Uppercase, Lowercase x3) or John9999 may be ULLLNNNN (N= Number)
Negative numbers (or positive depending on field)	Self-explanatory. A positive loan balance or a negative savings balance would both be worth highlighting.
Max and min values	Self-explanatory. Common poor quality indicators are values of 99999999 or similar.
Max and min length	Self-explanatory.
Top 10 values and percentages/ numbers of these values	This is a useful way of identifying default values, "blanks" – i.e. not null but no content, or similar.
Data breaking business rules	For example that balance cannot be negative (overdraft) if age of customer is less than 18.
Default values	Some values can be set up to self-populate as a new record is created

The business intelligence team can significantly help the data quality practitioner in the initial discovery phase, as they are likely to have significant knowledge of the data, its shortcomings, and also may have the profiling and discovery tools readily available to undertake a deep dive into the data sources. Hopefully, the business intelligence team have been involved already in helping to define the strategy and, as end users, helping to define the requirements that will be used to measure the data. As users of significantly more data than almost any other area of the organisation business intelligence will identify data quality issues rapidly and effectively, and utilising the experience in data mining already existing within the business intelligence function is likely to be an efficient way of discovering data quality.

33.7 Dynamic Data

Most of the conversation so far has been restricted to static and semi-static data. However this will be merely a subset of the overall data held within an organisation. To give an example, 1 million customers, each with one bank account, with 20 transactions per month, each containing 5 data points (date/time, amount, target sort code, target account number, narrative), and with 50 elements of static data per customer, will create, in one year 50 million static/semi static data points and 1.2 billion dynamic ones. Over any significant period the amount of dynamic data will vastly exceed the amount of static and semi static data. The quality of dynamic data is a harder proposition to measure, however the root cause may be easier to find as it is almost certainly going to be computer-based or calculation-based.

Anecdote

A banking organisation had an issue that one of their customers performed some mathematical analysis on their interest payments (there's always one) and realised that the bank were calculating the interest incorrectly. The subsequent investigation quickly uncovered that ALL interest payments for a certain type of account were incorrect, and it was a relatively easy matter to fix.

What was not an easy matter was restitution of all the thousands of borrowers with the payments that they should have received, especially when the difference in the correct and incorrect amounts was normally very, very small (as in pennies).

When it comes to dynamic data, there are a number of sources of information:

Source	Description
Testing	Sources of information: - Initial testing of systems - Current testing of systems Thankfully, most IT systems are relatively competent at adding up; the problem comes with definitions (which again refers to the important of establishing definitions for data and data types at the start of the process). When the systems were set up there is likely to have been testing to ensure that calculations are being performed in the appropriate manner. These can be revisited to see if anything has been missed. It is also possible to perform testing on the current systems state.
Users	Reports that come out of IT systems are, by nature, dynamic. They are also used to manage the business on a day to day basis, as well as being integral to operations. The primary source of information in relation to the accuracy (or otherwise) of dynamic data will be the users – primarily managers and analysts – in the business. It is unlikely that they will have day to day exposure with individual customer data fields, but they will have day to day exposure with aggregate reports, and will almost certainly have a long history of trying to get the information that they need out of the system. As such they are likely to know where reports do not tally, which reports commonly give an erroneous result, and which data does not match between departments and products. Of course, a report being incorrect may simply be the result of a badly written report, but again, users are likely to have a good idea where this is the case and where the underlying data is incorrect. Users of systems will be fine tuned to the quality of dynamic data, and hence will be a first port of call in terms of discovery of data quality issues. Almost all users will be able to point to reports which are "wrong" or are inconsistent with other reports, or on occasion simply farcical.
Customers	Customers and customer complaints provide another source of knowledge. Unfortunately most customers will automatically assume that calculations coming from an organisation's systems are correct, and not query them. This is not always the case – as mentioned in one of the anecdotes. However, if a customer queries the system calculations close attention should be paid.

33.8 Streaming Data

Most difficult of all is data that is continuously changing – how can you measure the quality of data that never stays still? In the same way that the quantity of dynamic data exceeds the quantity of static and semi-static data by orders of magnitude, the quantity of streaming data will be likely to exceed the quantity of dynamic data by orders of magnitude. Think, for example, of the amount of data flowing through a stock exchange. At this point I am going to make a decision and state that looking at the quality of streaming data is largely outside the scope of this book. I thought long about this, and came to the conclusion that there are relatively few organisations where data at this velocity is a critical issue (stock exchanges as mentioned above are one, organisations that make use of real-time telemetry are another) and these organisations are relatively specialised. Space is already at a premium in this book, which is – in most areas – looking at its subject from a high level and not delving into the detail. Spending time discussing the solutions to a problem that most organisations will never face appears slightly absurd when I don't have space to discuss (in the detail I would like) problems that will affect every organisation.

Thankfully in relation to entirely dynamic data there is not much of this data in most organisations. One that is worth mentioning is time. Time is a data field woven into probably every system that exists on the planet, and the determination of time and the quality of the data field that appears on every transaction, every "update" field, every receipt and every reservation is immediately relevant. It is worth an organisation looking at the time field and checking whether it is actually correct. Luckily, there are many resources to do exactly that, and by far the easiest method is comparison to a known "golden" source, of which there are many, and not only that, most are set up to be used as references. However, do not neglect time. As was found in relation to the Year 2000 problem, wayward time fields can have unexpected and unanticipated effects, and if, in your profiling, you come across a field with a timestamp in it, give thought to how you will determine how this field can be validated.

33.9 Step 4: Data Assessment

The next step is to analyse the results. Here themes will start to appear in the existing data, and these may point to either design or process issues and hence feed into both the process and architecture assessment. The assessment work will collate the issues into groups, covering headline issues, quick wins, and potentially those issues requiring further analysis. This can then be presented back to the stakeholder groups. At this point the root causes of a number of the issues may be discovered, as key stakeholders recognise what has caused the problem. This feedback is vital in truly understanding the root causes and planning remediation.

33.10 Step 5: Data Assessment Deliverable

The deliverable from the data discovery element of the work also fits into a standard format as shown in the example below.

Area	Field	Issue	Impact
Customer data	Postcode	10% null postcodes	Mailings, duplication
Product data	All	Many legacy products records	Old data un-needed, should be archived from the production database
Customer data	NI number	3,000 Invalid records	De-duplication, taxation implications

33.11 Summary

Within this chapter I have covered the ways in which the apparently overall overwhelming problem of poor data quality can be split into chunks and brought to a manageable size. This chapter gives the practitioner an approach to discovering the sources of data, and then detailing the individual problems with each data set.

I have covered discovery from top down, bottom up and middle-out, and have covered the work required relating to data discovery both in relation to traditional static and semi static data and also touched on dynamic and streaming data.

After this process the practitioner – as the organisation as a whole – should have a comprehensive understanding of what is wrong with data in the organisation. The next stage is to look at the processes and start to work out how the data ended up in this state.

SECTION 5.4 DISCOVERY

CHAPTER 34: DISCOVERY: PROCESS AND PROCESS TECHNOLOGY

34.1 Structure

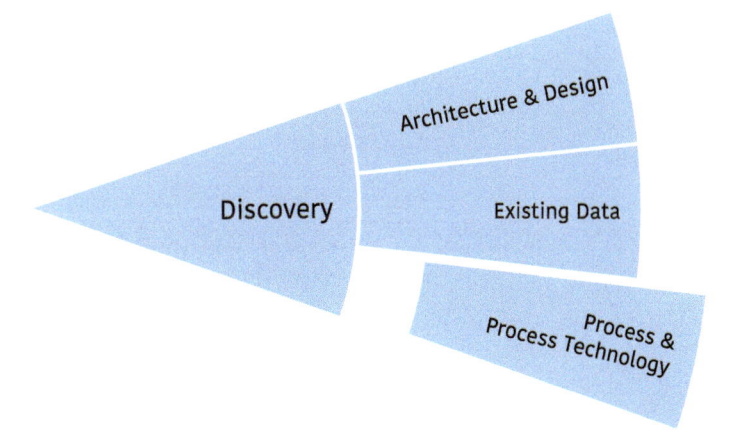

This stage of The Data Quality Blueprint includes the following phases:

1. Architecture & Design
2. Existing Data
3. Process & Process Technology

This chapter covers the last of these phases.

34.2 Overview

INPUTS
- All artefacts created or used by the project to date

OUTPUTS
- List of processes in scope
- CRUD Matrix
- Holistic process map
- Process assessment task list
- Sampling criteria
- Process assessment approach
- Assessment planning document
- Dependencies
- Exception process document
- Process documentation
- KPIs
- Process issues
- Potential process improvements
- Process assessment

DEPENDENCIES
- Access to stakeholders
- Access to process users
- Access to systems if necessary
- Process documentation tool if required (or use MSVisio or similar)

TASKS
- Scope
  - Identify domains in scope
  - Identify processes in scope
  - Validate scope against pain points, objectives and requirements
- Approach
  - Plan Approach
    - For each domain identify a domain owner
    - Discuss with the domain owner the processes that lead to data creation or change
    - Discuss with users and process owners the processes that lead to data creation or change
    - Create and document known list of processes
    - Document interactions between processes
    - Create CRUD Matrix
    - Create holistic process map
    - Replay to domain owners
    - Obtain process documentation
    - Create process assessment task list
    - Note processes not to be assessed and why
    - Define type of assessment per process
    - Define sampling criteria (if sampling used) and expected output
    - Define assessment approach including reporting template and milestones
    - Create assessment planning document
    - Upload to project repository
    - Define dependencies
    - Baseline and upload into project document repository
    - Determine if tool required
    - Source and install toolset
    - Team identification and allocation to system or domain
    - Team training
  - Design exception process
    - Design and document exception process
    - Determine escalation points/people
    - Determine required timescales for exception turn-around
    - Discuss exception process with process and business owner
    - Obtain buy-in to exception process
    - Agree SLA for exception process
    - Deliver exception process document
    - Upload to project repository
- Fact-finding
  - Interview process users and walk through process - Domain 1
  - Interview process users and walk through process - Domain 2

- Interview process users and walk through process - Domain 3
- Interview process users and walk through process - Domain 4
- Interview process users and walk through process - Domain 5
- Document process interactions
- Identify and document elements that affect data and data quality
- Model current processes (if necessary)
- Identify and document KPIs
- Benchmark current process
- Agree documented process and issues with user and domain owner
- Document issues with current process
- Upload to project repository

■ Process Assessment
- Perform initial assessment of issues with current processes in respect of data quality
- Identify headline issues
- Identify potential process improvements
- Collate into stakeholder groups (i.e. all issues relating to each stakeholder)
- Present back to business stakeholders
- Document feedback and revisit as required
- Create process assessment deliverable
- Socialise deliverable with stakeholders
- Upload to project repository

As discussed earlier in the book, the exercise of cleansing existing data is only part of the story. In order to make sure the data stays good the organisation has to examine the processes that feed data into their data stores. This step starts with identification of existing processes and discovery of how and why processes are failing to supply the organisation with good quality data.

Analysis of process is undertaken in two ways. First, the processes themselves can be examined through a data quality lens and issues identified where the process is failing to deliver good quality data. This may be through lack of control, overly complex process, or poor technology. Secondly, the data coming out of the processes can be examined to see where process failures have occurred. The first is a process driven approach, the second a data driven approach. Both are valuable.

In this chapter I will first look at the procedure for identifying the processes in scope and cover the first step which is basic process documentation. I will then discuss the way in which existing processes can be examined in the light of data quality using both of the above approaches, and how individual issues can be identified. Finally, and in preparation for entry into remediation planning, I will discuss how existing process problems should be documented in order to have consistency across the whole discovery stage of the project.

34.3   Engage Existing Process Functions

I have already mentioned that the project needs to engage existing architecture and data functions, and the same applies to process. This is absolutely essential, not only due to the knowledge these individuals will have, but also immeasurably helps the project in discovery, design, and implementation, as well as ensuring that these critical people do not resent or end up opposing the project.

34.4   Step 1: High Level Definition and Scope

Processes within an organisation that are relevant for data quality are those that create/capture, transport, transform (update/delete) or read/use data. Especially relevant to data quality are the data creation processes, as an error at this stage will cascade through the organisation resulting in errors at all points downstream.

34.4.1   Data Creation

Data creation processes will include, but will not be limited to:

- Downloads of information from websites. This may be data from a recognised authority (for example the Halifax House Price Index or Land Registry data, or information released by the Office of National Statistics) to ad hoc data that is being used off the web. This can vary considerably in authority and accuracy, and may come with copyright issues (potentially company documents or images) or be simply incorrect. Web-based information may also include information such as the current time or weather information which may be used by anyone within the organisation.
- Data captured from third parties via direct transmission. This includes invoices, EDI links to suppliers or customers and information from banks or regulators.
- Data captured via phone lines in voice form. This includes a contact centre or simple phone call with clients, suppliers or customers. In the case of the former it is common practice to record all contact centre calls, and there is potentially a large database of customer-sensitive data in voice form, probably on an application database. In the case of the latter it is unlikely it will be recorded in voice form but records may include contemporaneous notes or emails confirming points discussed.
- Data captured by company employees and entered into company systems. The example here is the company contact centre, where many agents may be typing data into application systems.
- Data automatically created by systems. These include date or time stamps on record updates, system logs, and so on.
- Data created via the company website. In the case of companies that allow customers to apply online for products or quotes, or order products for delivery via the web, the management of this information will be critical.
- Data captured from mobile devices. This includes both the company's own mobile devices and data captured from third party and customer devices.

- Data captured via conversations with other human beings. These include notes of meetings, recordings of meetings, or simply information transmitted via speech.
- Finally, of course, there is information acquired via email, which may comprise a large proportion of the total. We include within email those messages that come from and are transmitted to individuals outside the organisation. These are likely to contain sensitive company data.

34.4.2   Data Transport

Data transport processes will include, but will not be limited to:

- Extract-Transform-Load operations, where data is moved out of line-of-business applications and thence into a data warehouse. These transport operations may be automated, include manual elements, or may be wholly manual. ETL operations are likely to include transformations.
- Physical transport in terms of CD/DVD/Blu-Ray and USB devices. These can hold a phenomenal amount of data. This type of transport is well known to carry a high risk of data loss and hence reputational damage, and is hence banned by many organisations, with USB and optical disk drives being disabled on company laptops to limit the use of such devices. However banning their use does not absolve the organisation from considering their management.
- Transmission via company intranet.
- Transmission via the internet (either securely via shared encrypted storage – data rooms, SharePoint and the like) or via ftp.
- Transmission via email.

34.4.3   Data transform (update/delete)

Data transformation processes will include, but will not be limited to:

- Extract-Transform-Load operations as above.
- End user computing using such applications as Microsoft Excel.
- Slightly higher end applications like IDEA and Microsoft Access.
- Scripts.

To say that there is massive scope for data quality issues within data transformation is to understate the case. In fact, many of the major issues within data that I have experienced over the last 20 years have been due to data transformation which was not transforming as intended. Where issues most often occur is in the transformations that occur within "transform" of the Extract-Transform-Load (ETL) process, especially as the ETL is often a black box where the inner working is only known to the original developer, who has since left the organisation. Since then a script, ETL, or similar has probably been running every night but no-one has any idea what it is doing.

34.4.4   Data read/use

Finally, data use processes will include, but will not be limited to:

- End user computing such as Microsoft Excel and Access, which are both widely used as data manipulation tools.
- Presentation and report writing. Data that is inserted into reports should have the source and nature of the data that is used clearly defined. It is common practice to hear the refrain "where did you get those figures from?" Traceability of information through the organisation is key to trust of data (one of the key data qualities) and key to understanding differences between different data interpretations.
- Financial Models. Big users of data are financial models, including cash flow models, asset and liability models in a bank, profitability models, and so on. The data that flows into models should be clearly defined as to its nature and source.
- Marketing will be heavy users of data, as they will wish to run analytics to determine the propensity of existing customers to buy, and also to use large scale customer data such as addresses (email and postal) for mailshots.

Data use processes are the touch points where the data reaches its final destination, either the management to make a decision or the customer. Even if the rest of the process stream is correct this will be the area, if you get wrong, that most noise will be made. This does not mean that this part is where the most action should be concentrated – the data creation process is still the most important – but it is often the case that data quality efforts are focused – incorrectly – on data usage precisely because of the noise that bad data at this point creates.

34.5   Step 2: Plan

The next step after the discovery of the overall process landscape is to define those in scope for the project. Clearly the project cannot cover every process in the organisation, so how is the scope curtailed? For data creation, although the above list of processes appears daunting, the majority can be addressed by concentrating on where the largest proportion of customer data enters the organisation. These will be contact centres, web and branch, and in most organisations the first two are likely to form the vast majority of the data capture effort.

A useful technique for understanding the processes in scope is the CRUD Matrix. CRUD stands for Create-Read-Update-Delete. Every process can be listed and those that affect data can be clearly identified.

Account Close Process	Create	Read	Update	Delete
New customer setup		✔		
Regulatory Reporting		✔	✔	
Change of address		✔	✔	✔
De-Duplication	✔	✔		
Strategic planning		✔		✔

Additionally, the specific data processes under consideration can be looked at from the perspective of data quality only, and then cut down further into those processes that can cause data quality issues. This will leave a small subset of the total processes within the organisation as worthy of effort in respect of data quality, specifically:

- New customer setup (contact centre and web).
- Change /update customer record (contact centre and web).
- New product for existing customer (contact centre and web).
- New product setup.

This is now a relatively small and manageable package of processes which will often cover 80-90% of all data creation in the organisation.

For data transport processes, in a similar way it is possible to determine the processes that most directly affect the business operations and where impact of poor quality is greatest. In general the largest impact on data quality is likely to be the transport of information from the data capture applications to the destination, be it operational data stores or a data warehouse. We are ignoring the possibility of an employee losing a data disc containing millions of customer records – in which case the process definitively needs improvement, and data quality is likely to be the least of the organisation's worries for the immediate future at least.

In exactly the same way the most critical data transformation processes will be the transformation from source systems into data warehouses and data marts. This is especially the case when moving data from the application databases, as the data structures are likely to be only understood completely by the application vendors (who are likely to charge for support, and are likely to have a limited number of technical individuals who understand the data model). Hooking into the application databases to extract data is fraught with error. In addition, the nature of such transformations themselves is likely to be poorly understood. To establish the scope that is necessary for data usage, the scope is again best factored towards elements which cause the greatest impact – specifically regulatory reporting and board level decisions.

34.6   Step 3: Detail Investigation and Description

The next step is process mapping. By far the best approach to process mapping is to walk through the process with the individual who performs the process in real life. This is important as the way in which a process is actually performed is likely to significantly differ from the way in which it is supposed to be performed (or the way it is documented). For example, the official process document may specify that a search is undertaken for existing customers matching a current customer's name and date of birth, and new accounts/ product/ enquiries linked to the existing customer. However, this check may not be performed in practice resulting in many duplicate records.

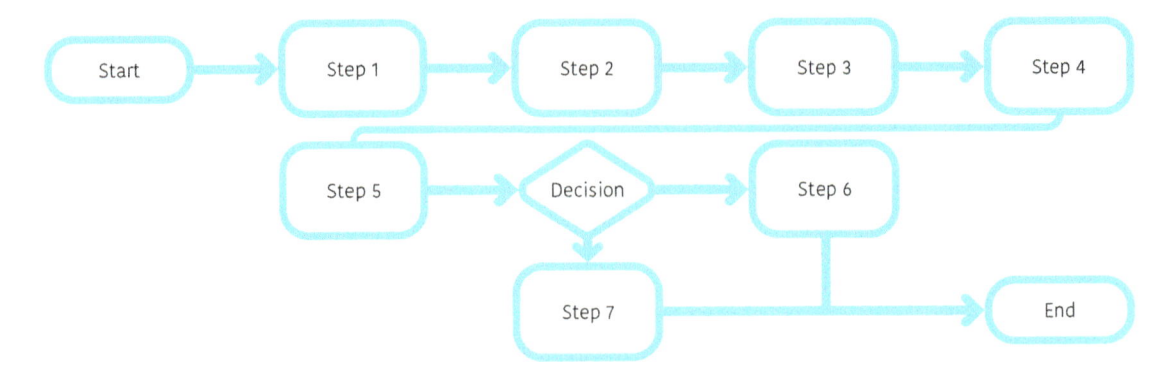

A process map can be created in any of the recognised formats, but an example is above. The objective of the process mapping is to gain understanding of the process and to help identify data quality issues. It also translates the processes into a portable format which can then be utilised, together with the results from the architecture and data discovery work, to plan the remediation.

34.7   Step 4a: Process Focused Assessment

As previously mentioned, the overall approach for discovery is to use a processes focused and data focused approach in tandem. I will discuss each in turn. A process focused approach looks at the process as it occurs in the organisation from the perspective of data quality. It looks to where the process does not facilitate the creation of good quality data first time, or does not have controls in place to pick up errors or omissions that degrade data quality. A data quality process assessment should look for:

- Lack of quality checks
- Lack of duplication checks
- System constraints (e.g. if there is no mobile phone field, where does the operator put the data?)
- System failures (e.g. what occurs when the system fails to recognise a postcode)
- Click-through (e.g. an operator pressing "next" four times)
- Poor or no validation

In cases like these, chatting through the process with the operator will produce much useful information. Useful questions to ask may be:

- What happens if you put in a future date of birth?
- What happens if you put in a date of birth that indicates an age of less than 18?
- What happens if you put a numeral in a name?
- What happens if you put in the same date of birth and name as another customer?
- What happens if the postcode is not recognized?
- What happens if the system thinks that the postcode and address are not compatible?
- How do you deal with really difficult-to-spell names?
- Is there any linkage between title and name?

- How do you account for house names?
- How do you account for Scottish flats?
- How do you input mobile numbers?
- Is there any commonly used data for which there is no field?
- What do you use the notes field for?
- What fields can you leave empty?
- If you don't have a value, do you input default values?
- Are there any bugs in the system you have to work around?
- What happens if a customer gives you two phone numbers?
- What happens if a customer gives you two addresses?
- How do you ensure that the customer name is spelt correctly?
- How do you validate address?
- Is there a defined process about which address field goes in which box?

The aim here is to discover how processes affect data quality, the identification of any constraints and the identification of how the quality of input is managed.

Matters to note: It is especially important to ensure that customer names are captured correctly as there is often no real validation possible on a customer name field other than it is (normally) restricted to alphanumeric characters. Addresses are the same but worse – there is typically little validation on an address field as almost anything goes in terms of valid addresses.

34.8   Step 4b: Data Focused Assessment

The next step is a data focused approach. This is often fascinating from a data professional's perspective as looking at a data set that has been in existence for a long time is almost like a geologist looking at a particularly interesting strata of rock, or, possibly more appropriately, a forensic scientist looking at a crime scene. The data will hold evidence of process failures and system changes over time. A small subset of examples from my own experience:

- Finding 20,000 "Mr. Test Test" in the live database. Investigation revealed that someone managed to implement a poorly tested script on the live database which was creating several hundred test records every second before it was eventually stopped. Of course each of these was linked to a dummy address and a dummy product too.....
- Noticing many apparent customers where staff had entered "Don't use this customer number, use [another customer number] instead" in a prominent note field. This revealed process quality issues with customer setup.
- Noticing that many customers had the word "DEAD" after their name identified an historical process issue where it was not possible to mark a customer as inactive so agents had marked the fact in the name field. Note here that the customer was not actually deceased, just the account was "dead".
- As mentioned elsewhere in the book a high number of missing dates of birth were eventually tracked to a process issues with a new employee with a predilection to enter dates in US format. When the Extract-Transform-Load (ETL) program then picked these up from the

application system it considered many of the dates not convertible to the format the data warehouse required, so inserted null values instead. Hence 01/01/1990 transferred OK (same in either format), 04/11/1990 transferred OK (but was wrong – it transferred as 4th November 1990 and should have been 11th April 1990) but 04/15/1990 created a null.

The existing data is an often fascinating map telling you where data quality issues exist in the upstream processes. The approach is simple and based on common sense. Within the analysis of existing data there will be fields that are of good quality, fields that are of bad quality and some in the middle. These can be further subdivided into data that is simply missing and data that exists but is of poor quality. For the data that is simply missing the questions to ask are was it ever captured, or was it captured but has since been lost? For data that exists but is of poor quality, it is necessary to discover why it is of poor quality, and that will depend on the nature of the deficiency.

For example, a fairly clearly misspelt address (e.g." 1 Stationn Road") is almost certainly a mistake by the initial individual capturing the data and points towards training, typing or poor checking. Whilst, again, it is tempting to simply see this as "operator error" – which it may be – it may be worth investigating some way of stopping a recurrence. A simple method would be to change the address entering process so all addresses are based on a postcode lookup system. This also has the advantage of creating a consistent address format. There needs to be a system for capturing new addresses (not yet on the postcode system) or for where customers insist on giving their house a name ("Dunroamin" or similar). The advantage of looking at the entire data set as opposed to walking through with one agent is that the agent assigned to the walkthrough is likely to be one of the most experienced. Whilst this may appear an advantage, a senior operator will not demonstrate to an "auditor" (for that is how you will be seen) the shortcuts that are commonly undertaken in real life.

Whilst a process based approach is vital for completeness, the existing data should always be checked as it can be relatively quickly interrogated and often offers "quick win" solutions that will markedly improve the data quality with little effort. In the case of the examples above, the 20,000 test cases were deleted (resulting in an instant reduction in overnight processing times).

For new data that is coming into the business the analysis inherent in the data discovery phase is an excellent starting point to determine the reason why the data has got in such a poor state in the first place. Tracking back to the guilty processes from the data is not a difficult job, and will involve utilising the data itself and conversations with users to determine what went wrong and how. For example, taking the example of a telephone field where someone, at some point, has written:

"01234 976543 between the hours of 9-5 but then ring 07700 123456 in evening because he lives with his mum".

There are clearly a number of issues here. First, however strange it might appear (and however tempting to smile and blame the agent), the agent has clearly wanted to be as helpful as possible to the business in recording the best way to contact the customer. So the source of the problem is in helpfulness, not poor performance. In fact, the above entry might be critical in the case of contacting a customer in an emergency. The reasons for such an entry may be:

- No mobile phone field in the entry application form at the point when the entry was made
- No "notes" field
- Poor training
- No space for all the information given by the customer to be recorded.
- Poor application database validation.

None of which really have anything to do with the agent themselves. In fact, the above entry is almost certainly likely to be a failing in the application systems, and the root cause is poor application design and/or implementation. As to which one would require further analysis.

34.9 Step 5: Process Assessment Deliverable

In a similar way to the output from the data-focused assessment, the process-focused assessment will provide insight into the processes within the organisation. An example output is below.

Process	Fields	Issue	Impact
New customer entry	Name, DOB	No check for existing customer	Duplication of customer records
New customer entry	Postcode	No validation	Incorrect postcodes captured
New customer entry	Postcode	System allows nulls	Impact on de-duplication efforts, customer contact
New customer entry	Date of birth	No application validation	Future and extreme past dates of birth are allowed

34.10 Common Problems

I will finish off this chapter by listing some of the common causes of poor data quality within processes. Based on my own experience, top reasons include:

- Free form fields in any application
- No database validation
- Poor training
- Applications poorly implemented
- Staff do not consider (or are not measured) on good data quality
- No clear data requirements or data quality requirements
- No entry checking
- No quality assurance function
- Poor engagement with users of the data
- Pressure on throughput
- Applications not suitable for the task in hand
- "Tactical" deliveries.

34.11 Summary

In this chapter I have looked at the ways in which existing processes can be examined through the lens of data quality. I have started with the identification of the processes within the organisation and how they can be documented. I have continued to explain how the overall scope of the project can be determined and then the approach to process assessment. I have explained both the process focused approach and also the data focused approach. I have also outlined how process issues can be documented.

After this chapter, I have described all elements of the discovery work. The data quality practitioner, and the organisation, can now see why it is necessary to look at every part of the organisation in a holistic approach, because every part of the organisation affects data quality if poorly executed.

In the next section we will look at bringing all the discovery work together, the determination of root cause, and the subsequent planning of the remediation project.

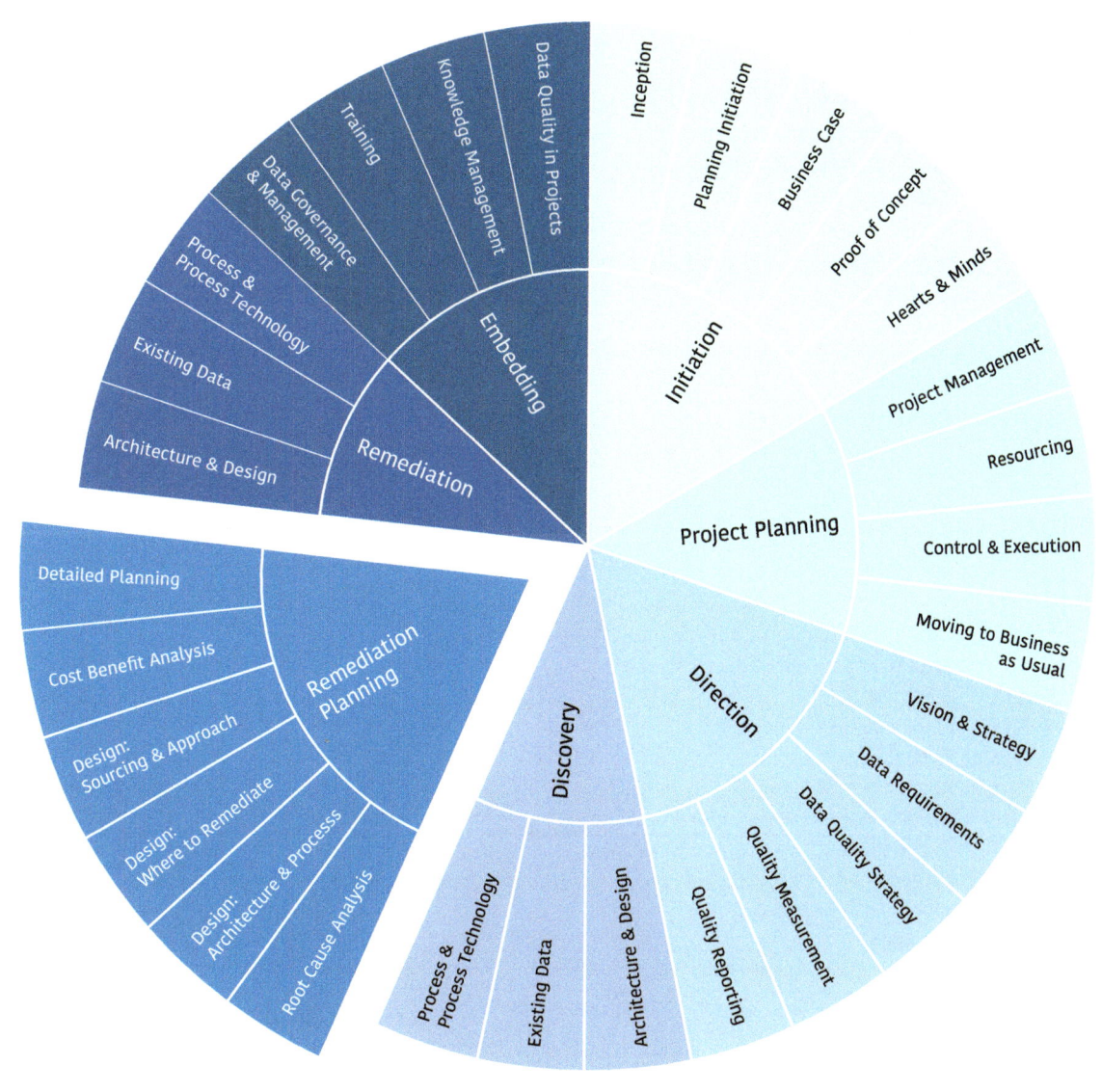

SECTION 5.5 REMEDIATION PLANNING

SECTION 5.5: INDEX

CHAPTER 35: Section Overview — 375

CHAPTER 36: Root Cause Analysis — 379
- 36.1 Structure — 379
- 36.2 Overview — 380
- 36.3 Step 1: Consideration of Architectural Issues — 382
- 36.4 Step 2: Identification of Root Causes — 383
- 36.5 Step 3: Collation of Results — 385
- 36.6 Step 4: Link Root Causes — 386
- 36.7 Step 5: Assign Degree of Responsibility — 387
- 36.8 Step 6: Assigning Cost — 388
- 36.9 Summary — 389

CHAPTER 37: Remediation design for Architecture and Process — 391
- 37.1 Structure — 391
- 37.2 Overview — 392
- 37.3 Generation of options — 393
- 37.4 Architectural Design — 393
- 37.5 Process Design — 406
- 37.6 Process Controls — 408
- 37.7 Summary — 411

CHAPTER 38: Remediation design for data: where to remediate — 413
- 38.1 Structure — 413
- 38.2 Overview — 414
- 38.3 At Source — 415
- 38.4 Within ETL — 415
- 38.5 In the Lake (if applicable) — 417
- 38.6 In Data Warehouse & Data marts — 417
- 38.7 In the presentation & reporting layer — 418
- 38.8 After the presentation layer — 418
- 38.9 Where is best and why — 419
- 38.10 Summary — 420

CHAPTER 39: Remediation design for data: sourcing and approach — 421
- 39.1 Structure — 421
- 39.2 Overview — 422
- 39.3 Scope and Approach — 422
- 39.4 Replace or Remediate? Replace — 423
- 39.5 Replace or Remediate? Remediate — 424
- 39.6 Sources of Good Data — 425

39.7	Best Source Analysis	432
39.8	Summary	434

CHAPTER 40: Cost Benefit Analysis — 435

40.1	Structure	435
40.2	Overview	436
40.3	Recap from the Root Cause Analysis	437
40.4	Step 1: Option Costing	437
40.5	Step 2: Benefit Valuation	438
40.6	Step 3: Option Appraisal & Assessment	438
40.7	Step 4: Baskets of Options	440
40.8	Step 5: Reviewing the Business Case	441
40.9	Step 6: Building the task list and deciding on the final plan	442
40.9	Summary	442

CHAPTER 41: Detailed Planning — 443

41.1	Structure	443
41.2	Overview	444
41.3	Questions that the plan needs to answer	445
41.4	Step 1: Roadmap	445
41.5	Step 2: Task List	446
41.6	Step 3: Detailed Planning	447
41.7	Step 4: Responsibility and Resourcing	448
41.8	Step 5: Dependencies & Deliverables	448
41.9	Summary	448

SECTION 5.5 REMEDIATION PLANNING

CHAPTER 35 — SECTION OVERVIEW

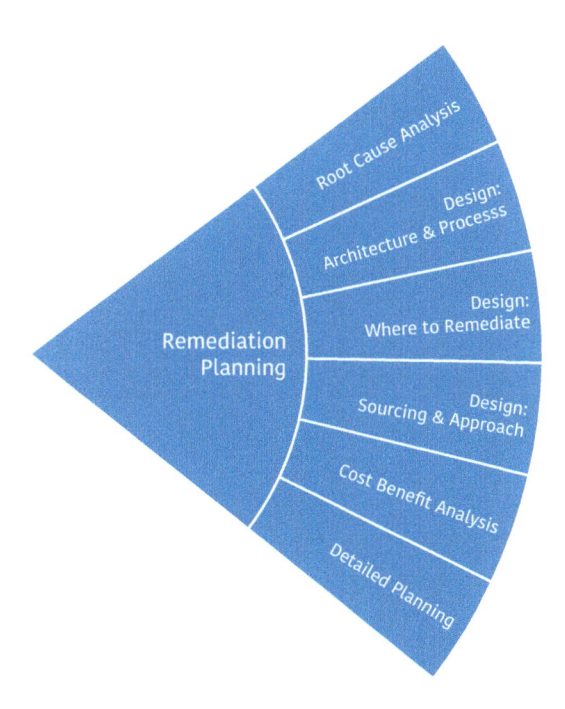

- Root Cause Analysis
- Design: Architecture & Processs
- Design: Where to Remediate
- Design: Sourcing & Approach
- Cost Benefit Analysis
- Detailed Planning

(Remediation Planning)

The discovery phase discussed over the last few chapters informs the rest of the project. The objective of the remediation planning phase is to take the information that has been accumulated in the discovery phase and use it to plan the remediation activity.

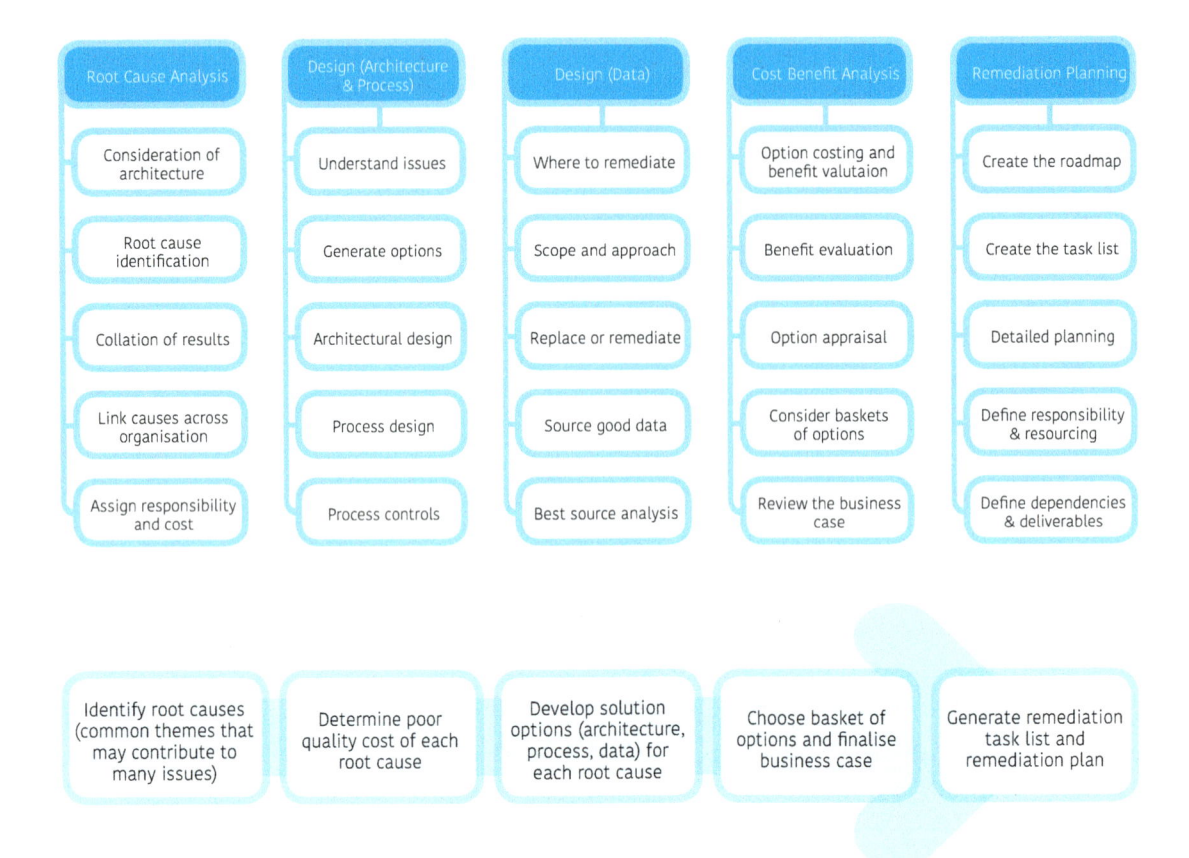

The Data Quality Blueprint

Root Cause Analysis	Design (Architecture & Process)	Design (Data)	Cost Benefit Analysis	Remediation Planning
Consideration of architecture	Understand issues	Where to remediate	Option costing and benefit valutaion	Create the roadmap
Root cause identification	Generate options	Scope and approach	Benefit evaluation	Create the task list
Collation of results	Architectural design	Replace or remediate	Option appraisal	Detailed planning
Link causes across organisation	Process design	Source good data	Consider baskets of options	Define responsibility & resourcing
Assign responsibility and cost	Process controls	Best source analysis	Review the business case	Define dependencies & deliverables

| Identify root causes (common themes that may contribute to many issues) | Determine poor quality cost of each root cause | Develop solution options (architecture, process, data) for each root cause | Choose basket of options and finalise business case | Generate remediation task list and remediation plan |

A most important principle of the methodology is that the organisation should not rush off and remediate the first bit of incorrect data it finds. The Data Quality Blueprint recommends that the organisation should understand what is required and the best solution before taking action. There is no point remediating a data set if the processes that feed that data set are broken. Like many other areas of human experience, a little planning reaps rewards; allowing the actual work to be done faster, more effectively, and cheaper than would otherwise be the case.

In this section I will cover:

Root cause analysis	Root cause analysis takes all the issues that have been surfaced by the discovery stage and looks for common themes. This process enables dependencies between issues to be identified and hence exposes synergies within the remediation effort.
Remediation design (architecture and process)	Remediation design takes the output from the root cause analysis and creates options for remediation. I have split this into two sections. Architecture and process covers the changes to the organisational design and the processes that support the supply of data to operational data stores and the use of data from them.

Remediation design (existing data)	The next section (two chapters) covers the remediation design for existing data. This includes the decision whether to remediate or replace, how to identify the best source of data for your organisation, and where in the overall information landscape it is best to perform the remediation.
Cost benefit analysis	Cost benefit analysis takes the baskets of options identified by the previous two stages, costs them and compares them with the benefits they create. It revalidates the business plan and makes the final decision as to what will be included in the remediation.
Remediation planning	The remediation planning is the detailed planning of the individual tasks necessary to remediate. It uses all the work so far to build the task list and plan for the forthcoming remediation stage.

SECTION 5.5 REMEDIATION PLANNING

CHAPTER 36 ROOT CAUSE ANALYSIS

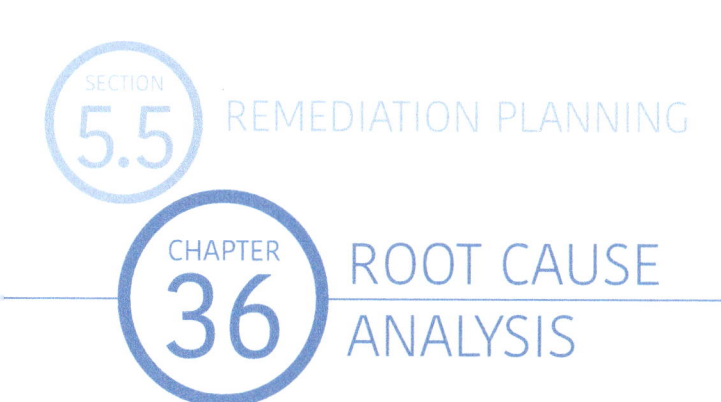

36.1 Structure

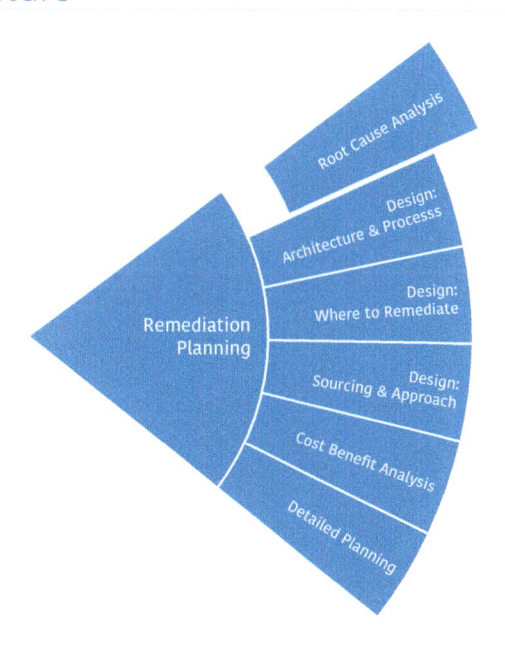

This stage of The Data Quality Blueprint includes the following phases:

1. Root Cause Analysis
2. Design for Architecture and Process
3. Data: Where to Remediate
4. Data: Sourcing Data
5. Cost Benefit Analysis
6. Detailed Planning

This chapter covers the first of these phases.

36.2 Overview

INPUTS
- All artefacts created or utilised by the project to this point.
- Results from architecture discovery
- Results from data discovery
- Results from process discovery

OUTPUTS
- Impact of architectural issues
- List of root causes
- Cost of each root cause
- Root cause analysis

DEPENDENCIES
- Access to key stakeholders

TASKS
- Consider Architectural Issues
  - Assess architectural issues for major items
  - Determine impact of these issues on the rest of the project
  - Decide if they are important enough to be addressed first or will have significant impact on the project
  - Document key concerns
  - Discuss with sponsor and key stakeholders
  - Prepare impact analysis of either doing or not doing them first
  - Based on impact analysis present recommendation to sponsor and key stakeholder, together with impact on the project
  - Feed decision into remediation planning
- Root Cause Analysis
  - Identification of Root Cause
    - Input issues from architecture assessment
    - Input issues from data assessment
    - Input issues from process assessment
    - Define approach and method to be used for root cause analysis
    - For each issue track back to root cause
    - Document root cause analysis
    - Socialise with key stakeholders
    - Update for feedback
    - Upload to project repository
  - Collate results
    - Collate root causes
    - Assign to architecture/process/data/direction/etc
    - Group root causes
    - Identify common root causes
    - Discuss with stakeholders
    - Update for feedback
    - Upload to project repository
  - Link root causes across organisation
    - Create organisation-wide root cause list
    - Identify key root causes
    - Analyse interaction of root causes
    - Create final root cause list
    - Upload to project repository
  - Assign degree of responsibility
    - For each issue allocate responsibility to a root cause
    - Collate results
    - Discuss with stakeholders
    - Update for feedback
    - Upload to project repository
  - Assign cost
    - Input business case
    - For each root cause assign the poor quality cost for

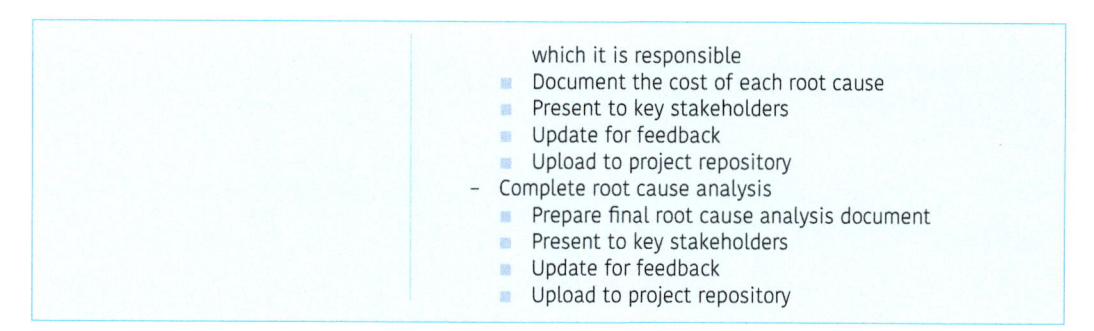

		which it is responsible
		■ Document the cost of each root cause
		■ Present to key stakeholders
		■ Update for feedback
		■ Upload to project repository
		− Complete root cause analysis
		■ Prepare final root cause analysis document
		■ Present to key stakeholders
		■ Update for feedback
		■ Upload to project repository

Remediation planning is a pivotal point of the project. All work from the discovery and direction stages is collated, and root causes for data quality issues determined. A plan is created to remediate issues – architecture, data or process – in the most efficient way – and to create the future state.

Initiation + Planning + Direction + Discovery = Remediation Planning

Remediation planning represents a point in the project where lessons learned from previous stages can be incorporated into the overall plan. A brief rest can be taken from the "doing" and a taking stock and re-assessment can be made of the business case, the reasons behind the project, and whether the overall project still financially stacks up. The remediation planning stage is a critical part of The Data Quality Blueprint. The approach understands that in order to solve issues most efficiently you need to understand the issue and the reasons – whether design or process – that have caused them. This means that rather than attacking many symptoms the organisation attacks one root cause. In this chapter I will look at root cause analysis in more detail.

Identify root causes (common themes that may contribute to many issues) → Determine poor quality cost of each root cause → Develop solution options (architecture, process, data) for each root cause → Choose basket of options and finalise business case → Generate remediation task list and remediation plan

The diagram above shows where this fits into the overall remediation design process. This chapter will cover:

■ Consideration of architecture issues
■ Asking why

- Fishbone or Ishikawa analysis
- Discussing the methods to group and link root causes
- Assigning poor quality cost to root causes
- Taking this through to cost benefit analysis.

This first stage enables the organisation to identify the most efficient and effective way of remediating the data quality in their organisation.

36.3 Step 1: Consideration of Architectural Issues

As explained elsewhere, architectural issues may result in unnecessary or repeated remediation, and the remediation of architectural issues should be included as part of the overall data quality project. The first task is to look at each of the large scale architectural issues identified during the discovery phase and analyse their effect. An abbreviated example of this analysis is shown in the table below.

Issue	Effect on data quality and remediation	Criticality	Effort required to remediate
Siloed data between departments	Remediation will have to be performed multiple times	High	High – data restructuring of the organisational data stores would be required
Large numbers of unused databases	Reduction in the number of databases would reduce the complexity and risk that the wrong data is used in the future	Medium	Low – it may be possible to simply turn them off
Overly complex data structure	Will increase effort	May be low – in that the unused or unneeded data can simply be ignored	May be low
Data is transferred into reporting systems once a month	Data is not timely due to the lag between refreshes	High – board are unhappy with the data being out of data	May be very low – it may simply require running a data transfer once a week rather than once a month

For major architectural issues the organisation will need to discuss the best way to proceed. For example, in relation to siloed data, options include collapsing to one data store, creating a "golden source" to replace most departmental data, or creation of multiple golden sources (e.g. remediate multiple times). This is a business decision based on the effort required. If the overall effort is high, then it may be necessary to perform further analysis and design and potentially form a separate project. However, that does not mean that the effect on data quality can be ignored, or that easy-to-fix architectural issues should not be addressed.

36.4 Step 2: Identification of Root Causes

36.4.1 Introduction

Identification of root causes involves looking at issues raised and how they interact. A classic example would be the consideration of the cause of poor customer address data quality. Causes could include the process in the contact centre, a bug in the website, poor data input, a bad scanning system, or could equally be due to the systems that transfer data from one part of the organisation to another (The Extract-Transform-Load process). The organisation must find out what and why before deciding the path forward. The objective of this work is to enable the organisation to avoid abortive work, and to get the best bang for the buck in terms of remediation effort.

36.4.2 Method 1: Asking Why

A simple way of looking at root cause analysis is often termed the "five whys". The objective is to ask why until you cannot do so any more. Despite the name, the particular number of whys is not fixed at five, but you continue until the answers start to feel like root causes. For a particular example, this may be:

Step 1	Agents in the contact centre are choosing the first item on a drop down list for employment status, and as a result 20% of our customers are now listed as "abattoir workers". Why?
Step 2	Because it is difficult to find the right employment type for the customer. Why?
Step 3	Because the list is very long and out of date, and does not represent many newer jobs, especially those within the IT sphere. Why?
Step 4	Because the list was put in place quickly when the system was built, and there was little thought to its suitability for the business. Why?
Step 5	Because the requirements were poorly specified. Why?
Step 6	Because insufficient time was given to requirements analysis and an off the shelf package was assumed to be able to do the job.

Here the root cause is historical and cannot be retrospectively amended. In this particular case the solution may be re-writing the list, or just accepting that a drop-down list is not the way to solve this particular problem. In the future, the organisation can understand that spending a bit more time on requirements capture and solution analysis may pay off.

The only problem with "asking why" as an approach to root cause analysis is the potential to head down a particular tunnel of thought and not consider other reasons that may equally contribute to the same problem.

For example, whilst poor requirements analysis might be a root cause in relation to system problems, an equally important issue may be that staff are incentivised on throughput and don't care about finding the right employment type, or even that the application is old and buggy and scrolling fast down a list causes it to crash, and so on. A useful way of getting around this problem is to use fishbone, or Ishikawa analysis.

36.4.3 Method 2: Fishbone analysis

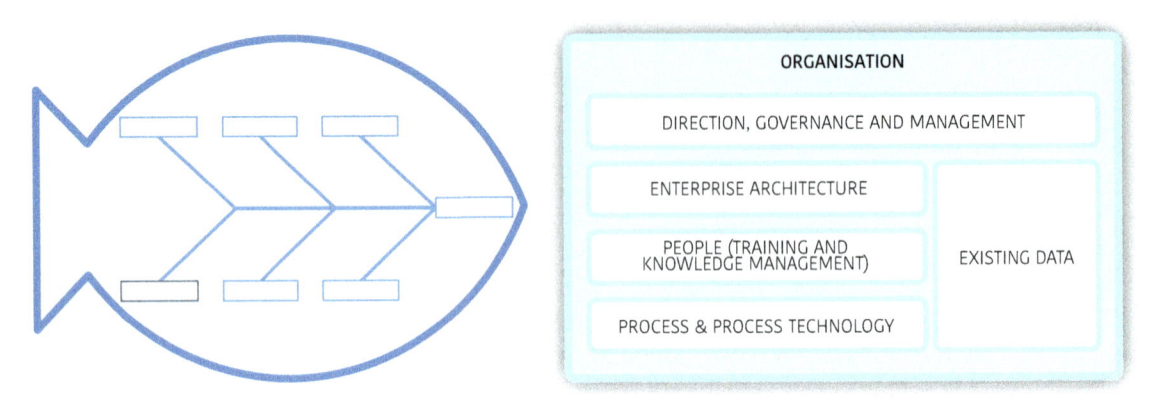

Fishbone analysis (also called Ishikawa analysis after Kaoru Ishikawa) is a technique of root cause analysis dating from the 1960's. The objective is to show that a single event may have many causes. This addresses the problem identified in the previous section. The "bones" of the fish represent categories of causes that contribute to the overall issue. Categories represented by the "bones" will differ from one organisation to another, and may also differ based on the nature of the issues. In this case, if we look back to the original causes of poor data quality in an organisation as introduced earlier in the book, we can see how the "bones" of the fishbone analysis can be tailored to align with this taxonomy.

In this case, Direction, Governance, Architecture, Process, People and Existing Data could all be utilised as "bones".

For example, poor initial input is likely to cause issues in data quality in customer address, date of birth, NI number, etc. However "poor initial input" is not in itself a cause, but is likely to be a symptom of incentivisation on throughput (People); badly performing input systems (Process Technology); the problem that data quality is not measured (Process, Governance and Management); or poorly designed processes (process, or if it is the interaction between processes, architecture). On the other hand there may be a different reason for poor quality in the postcode – for example that the reference data is out of date (existing data). The strength in fishbone analysis is that it allows categorisation and analysis of various causes that all lead to the same problem.

I personally believe that a combination of asking why and fishbone analysis can result in the best of both worlds. Fishbone analysis brings the breadth, and "asking why" the depth.

36.5 Step 3: Collation of Results

The first step in root cause analysis is to map each data quality issue back to the root cause(s), utilising either or both of the analysis methods described above as the means of discovery. This process will create a large number of root causes lists and/or diagrams. A single generic example is shown in the diagram below.

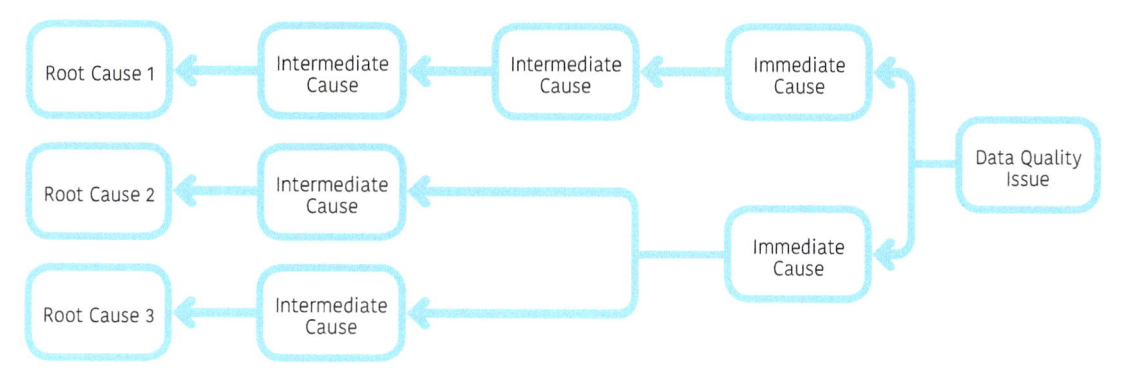

The next step is to collate the results across the organisation and to identify common root causes. We can also map these root causes against the categories mentioned above (Governance, People, Process, Architecture, and so on). I have expanded the above diagram to show this stage.

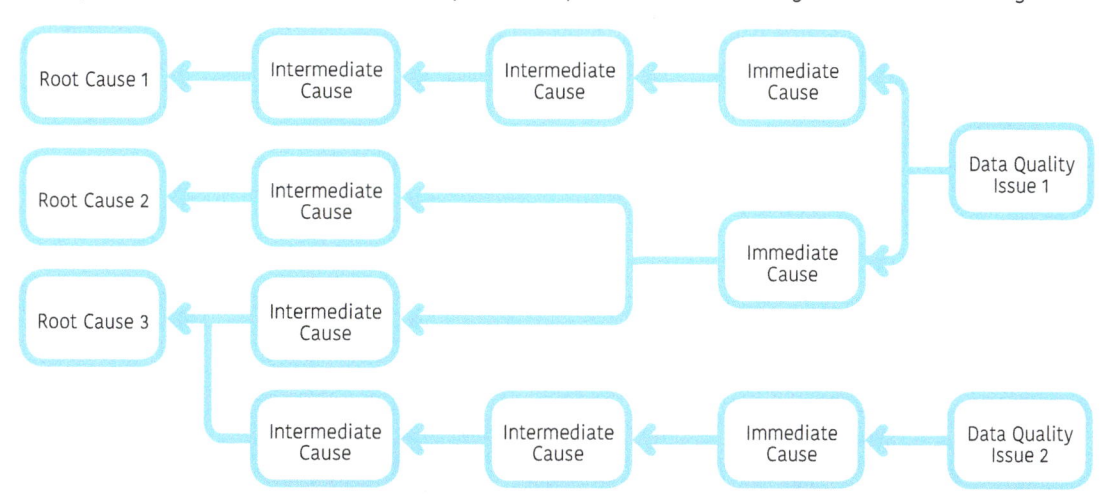

After the above work has been completed many diagrams of this nature will be produced, one for each data quality problem. It is then possible for the project to approach the diagram from the left, and look at where the same root causes are causing data quality problems elsewhere in the organisation. For example, in the diagram above we can see that "Root Cause 3" is the sole cause of "Data Quality Issue 2" and a contributor to "Data Quality Issue 1". This discovery of root cause enables the remediation effort, in a later stage, to work in the opposite direction along the cause-effect chain, utilising what used to be a negative connection as a means of propagating a positive one.

The Data Quality Blueprint

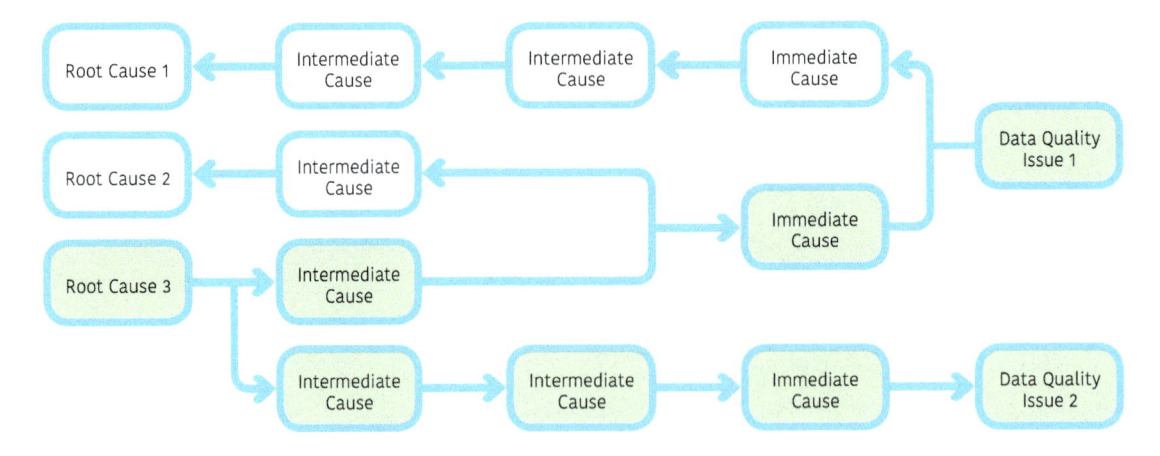

36.6 Step 4: Link Root Causes

The next step is to link root causes across the organisation. This process allows the identification of themes.

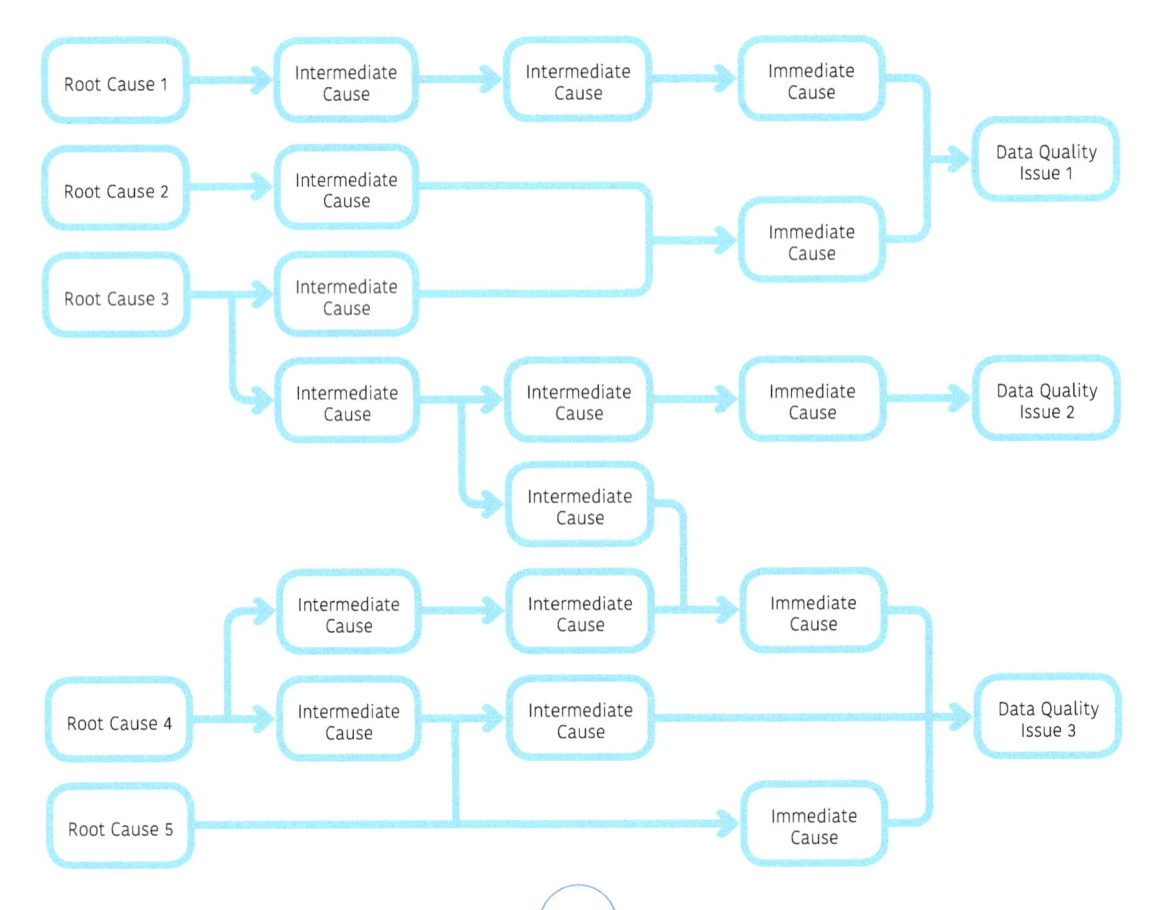

The start point is the overall diagram of root causes and data quality effects. In the example above, we can see three data quality issues, and five root causes. Unfortunately the interactions of root causes can get very complex, and I would suggest in a real scenario to utilise a table/spreadsheet to show the relationships rather than a flow diagram. This makes life much easier, but for demonstration purposes in this book the flow diagram shows the inter-relationships more effectively.

In the example, Root Cause 3 is common across all the data quality issues. It looks from an initial analysis that it would be particularly effective to start remediation here, however what is not known yet is the degree to which each root cause contributes to each data quality issue.

36.7   Step 5: Assign Degree of Responsibility

Therefore the next step is to work out how much each cause contributes to each issue. There is no point starting to work on detailed design for a root cause that does not contribute to the overall problem in a meaningful way. This is very difficult to do objectively, but some subjective analysis is possible. I have continued using the same examples below.

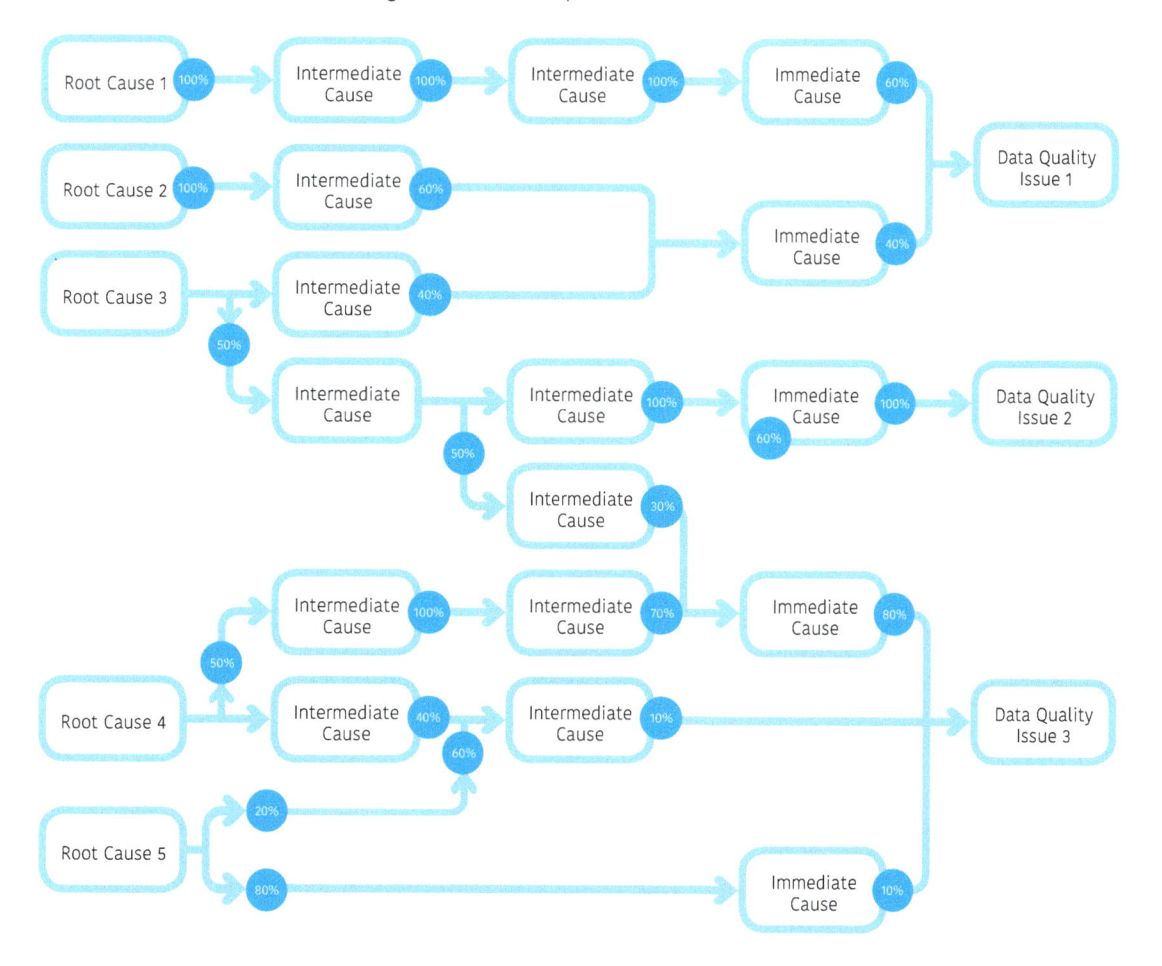

Here we can see that

- Root cause 1 causes 60% of Issue 1.
- Root Cause 2 Causes 24% of Issue 1 (60% x 40%)
- Root Cause 3 Causes 16% of Issue 1 (40% x 40%), but also 100% of Issue 2, and 24% of Issue 3 (80% x 30%)
- Root Cause 4 causes 4% (10% x 40%) of issue 3 through one branch, and 56% (80% x 70%) through another, making a total of 60%.
- Root cause 5 causes 6% of issue 3 through one branch and 10% through another, making a total of 16%.

We can now use this analysis to map costs to causes. Again, I would strongly recommend performing this task in a spreadsheet. Whilst the diagrammatic approach works for small numbers of issues, the diagram would become overly complex for analysis in even a very small organisation. An example is shown below.

	Issue 1	Issue 2	Issue 3
Root Cause 1	60%		
Root Cause 2	24%		
Root Cause 3	16%	100%	24%
Root Cause 4			60%
Root Cause 5			16%

36.8 Step 6: Assigning Cost

We can now look to assign cost to each of the data quality issues, and thence to each of the root causes. This work draws on the information from the business case. With the root cause analysis complete, the cost for each issue can now be divided amongst the causes. This may be relatively unscientific, but it is possible to apportion a percentage of the estimated benefit across the relevant causes.

If, therefore, the cost of Data Quality Issue 1 is £1,000,000, that of Issue 2 is £3,000,000 and that of Issue 3 is £4,000,000, then the apportionment to root causes is as follows:

	Issue 1	Issue 2	Issue 3	Total
Root Cause 1	£600,000			£600,000
Root Cause 2	£240,000			£240,000
Root Cause 3	£160,000	£3,000,000	1,080,000	£4,240,000
Root Cause 4				£2,400,000
Root Cause 5				£640,000

This analysis enables the organisation to spend time developing remediation options for the root causes that are costing the organisation the most money and not to waste time on problems that in reality are minor. This process is a way in which The Data Quality Blueprint reduces the overall effort and allows the organisation to use scarce resources in the most efficient manner.

It can be seen from the above that Root Cause 2 actually contributes very little to the overall poor quality cost and may be able to be ignored. It can also be seen how we are starting to build up a business case for each issue. When looking at options for remediation a multi-million pound solution is clearly not going to be palatable for Root Cause 1, but may be appropriate for Root Cause 3.

In terms of effect on the data quality of the organisation, Root Cause 3 ranks highest, followed by 4, 5, 1 and 2 in that order.

36.9   Summary

In this chapter I have looked at the way in which root causes can be identified, using both "asking why" and fishbone analysis. I have covered the method of identification for the prioritisation of remedial actions, and looked at assigning cost to each of the root causes to inform the option development. This chapter has introduced the data quality practitioner to the concepts of root cause analysis. By the end of the chapter they should be able to effectively apply root cause analysis to their own organisation if required, and to continue this analysis to group root causes across the organisation and assign data quality costs to each.

SECTION 5.5 REMEDIATION PLANNING

CHAPTER 37 REMEDIATION DESIGN FOR ARCHITECTURE AND PROCESS

37.1 Structure

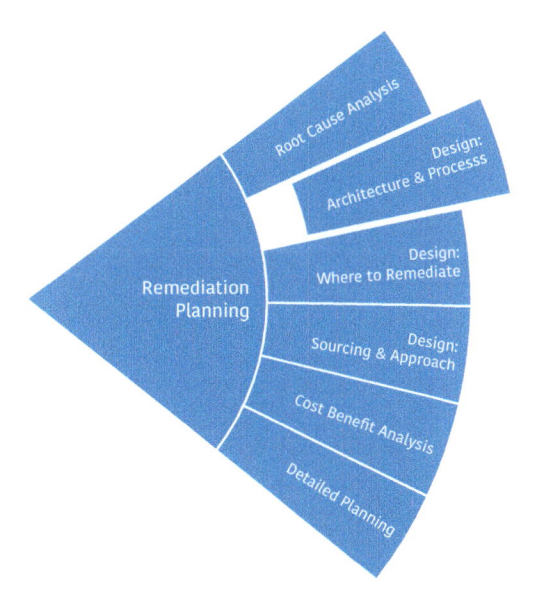

This stage of The Data Quality Blueprint includes the following phases:

1. Root Cause Analysis
2. Design for Architecture and Process
3. Data: Where to Remediate
4. Data: Sourcing Data
5. Cost Benefit Analysis
6. Detailed Planning

This chapter covers the second of these phases.

37.2 Overview

INPUTS	TASKS

■ All artefacts created or used by the project to date.
■ Results from architecture discovery
■ Results from data discovery
■ Results from process discovery
■ Results from root cause analysis
	■ Architectural Design
	  - Understand architectural scope
	  - Engage organisations architectural function
	  - For each architectural root cause understand issue
	  - For each architectural root cause consider options
	  - Discuss with architecture function
	  - Determine and document most appropriate options
	  - Ensure alignment with long term architectural roadmap
	  - Document architectural roadmap
	  - Define transition states (if required)
	  - Present to key stakeholders
	  - Update for feedback
	  - Upload to project repository
	■ Process Design
	  - Understand process scope
	  - Engage process owners
	  - For each process root cause understand issue
	  - Ensure process correctly documented
	  - For each process root cause consider options
	  - Discuss with process owners
	  - Generate process design
	  - Determine and document most appropriate options
	  - Ensure alignment with future process roadmap
	  - Document process roadmap
	  - Define transition states (if required)
	  - Present to key stakeholders
	  - Update for feedback
	  - Upload to project repository

OUTPUTS	
■ Architecture design options ■ Architecture roadmap ■ Process design options ■ Process roadmap	
DEPENDENCIES	
■ Access to stakeholders	

After the root cause analysis has identified the reasons for poor data quality within the organisation, the next stage is to look at what can be done about them. Here I will refer back to the diagram introduced in the "causes of poor data quality" chapter.

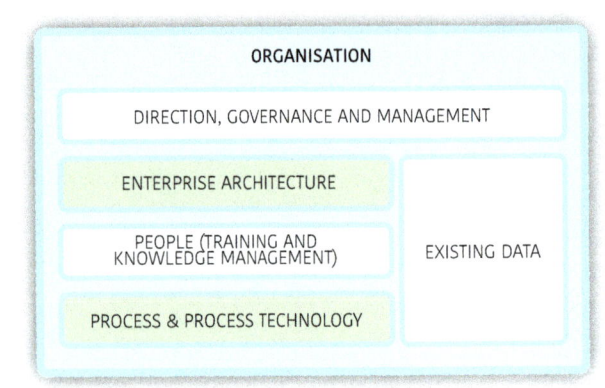

```
ORGANISATION
┌─────────────────────────────────────────┐
│ DIRECTION, GOVERNANCE AND MANAGEMENT    │
├──────────────────────────────┬──────────┤
│ ENTERPRISE ARCHITECTURE      │          │
├──────────────────────────────┤ EXISTING │
│ PEOPLE (TRAINING AND         │  DATA    │
│ KNOWLEDGE MANAGEMENT)        │          │
├──────────────────────────────┤          │
│ PROCESS & PROCESS TECHNOLOGY │          │
└──────────────────────────────┴──────────┘
```

So far, in this book, I have covered direction – the project knows where it will be going. The later "Embedding" chapter will cover governance and management, as well as training and knowledge management. In this section we address architecture, data and process. Each root cause will feed a number of quality issues, and for each poor quality issue there may be potentially a number of root causes. This chapter will cover architecture and process.

Identify root causes (common themes that may contribute to many issues) → Determine poor quality cost of each root cause → Develop solution options (architecture, process, data) for each root cause → Choose basket of options and finalise business case → Generate remediation task list and remediation plan

37.3 Generation of options

"It is very common to find that the data to support many of the business information needs is simply not available at the levels required, or that it is of such bad quality that it is impossible to use. Resolution of these types of issues often requires fundamental changes to business processes."
Tim Berners Lee

Given we know the root and intermediate causes, the next step is the generation of options for remediation, for both architecture and process.

Often, in remediation design, there will be short term, long term and medium term solutions. In general, the further up the cause chain the harder the cause will be to fix and the longer it will take before the fix brings results.

"Management unaware of the importance of data quality" may be a common root cause, but making sure that management are well aware of data quality issues does not change the here-and-now poor quality data going into the systems from existing processes. It will take time for management, newly enthused about data quality, to put into place training budgets and a reward system for good data quality, as well as the infrastructure that can enable data quality reporting, even if the money was immediately available to do so.

Whilst a solution of the root cause will eventually solve the issues, in the short term there is a need for an effective band-aid to make things better. This may be a quality assurance review covering data entry, or having a think about the employment field drop down list and amending it so that it is both shorter and more relevant to customers. As a result there may be a short term fix which will show instant results and a long term fix that will prevent the problem ever re-occurring.

Care should be taken not to fall into the trap of concentrating on easy long term options that will not actually solve the problem on a timely basis, but will give the impression of a solution. In most cases the long term options are a given necessity, and the tricky decision is between several short term options each of which will have some immediate effect on the data.

37.4 Architectural Design

37.4.1 Overview

We have considered in an earlier chapter within the discovery stage the way in which architectural issues may cause poor data quality. To recap, the particular examples I mentioned at this point were:

- Historical systems/applications
- Multitudinous feeds
- Siloed business processes
- Choke points
- The rapidly growing or "cool" division
- The shiny kit
- No reference architecture
- Siloed data
- Too many applications
- The secret data factory
- The new acquisition
- The half-finished project
- The tactical solution

The project has by now combined these issues with the issues from data and process discovery, and identified root causes. It now needs to examine the root causes that apply to architecture and to look at options for remediation, and design solutions that will remediate them.

As this can appear slightly abstract, I will give a number of real-world examples of architectural change. All of these are examples that I have come across in my career, and may give the reader a greater understanding of the impact – and complexity – of architectural change. I will also look to relate each to data quality.

37.4.2 Centralisation

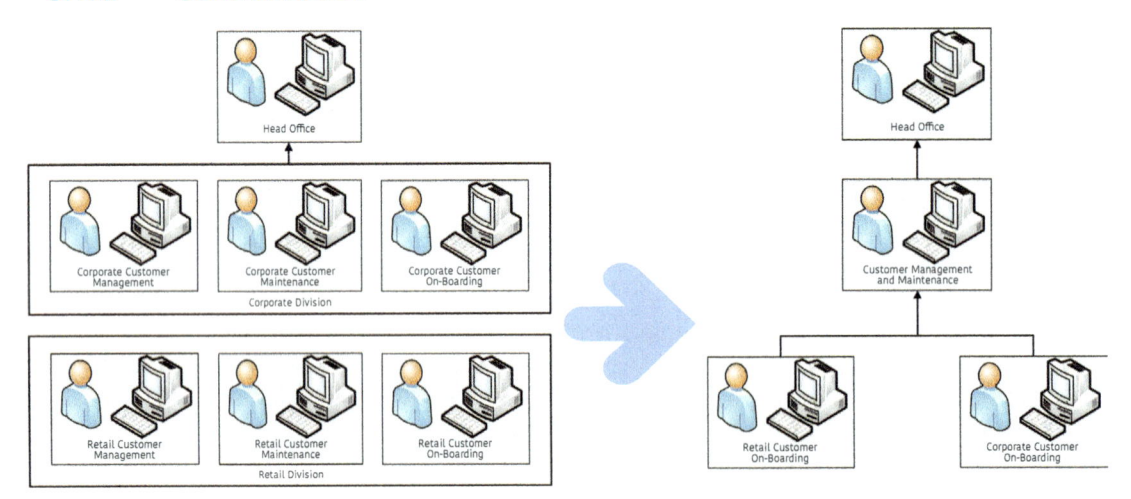

Most readers will have seen the scenario where departments basically doing the same thing in a variety of disparate locations are collapsed into a single central unit, generally for the purpose of cost saving. From a data quality point of view, the advantage of centralisation is that one set of processes, centrally controlled, are less risky than disparate processes geographically dispersed. It is the "it's easier to look after if it is all in one place" view.

37.4.3 Federalisation

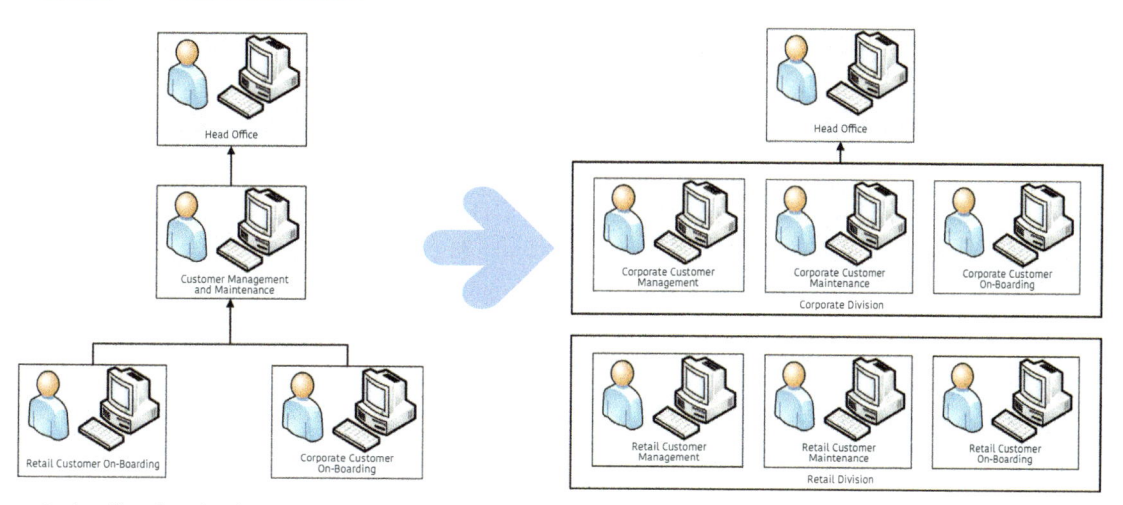

Federalisation is the opposite, and may occur when centralisation has failed, or where it is recognised, for whatever reason, that individual departments, countries, or business lines have more that differs than is common. It may then be more efficient to promote separate solutions than to combine all solutions into one unit. From a data quality point of view, federalisation is most beneficial where differences are so pronounced that fitting all departments into one data model or process involves so many workarounds that the processes (or data) may as well be separate in the first place.

37.4.4 Supplementation

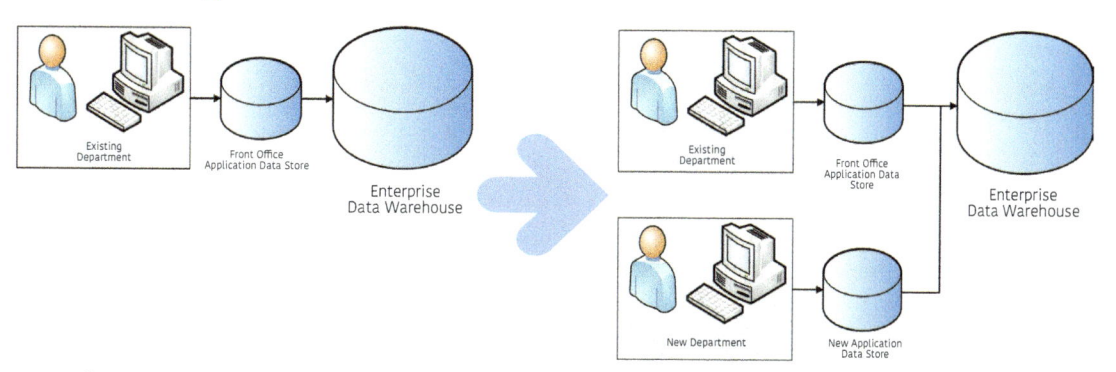

Another extremely common change is where existing data is left as is and a new process is piped into it. This may be the new department, the new acquisition, or the new product. It can be easily seen that this is the first step into a siloed organisation, and as further elements are "supplemented" the problem will inevitably get out of hand. However supplementation is easy and quick, and easy and quick often wins over "right". From a data quality point of view, the big risk is the place where the two data flows meet. Does the "new" process have the same view of "customer" as the old? Does it have the same view of "customer balance"? Extreme care needs to be taken whilst amalgamating data from two different sources.

37.4.5 Reversing the pipes

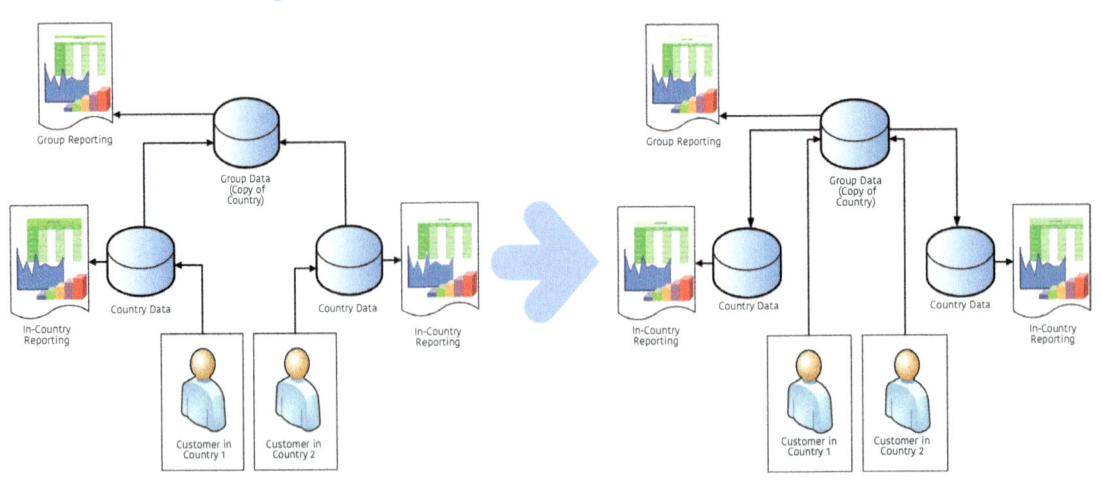

This scenario occurs when centralisation continues to feed the individual data systems, but from the opposite direction to the original situation. An example would be where rather than customers ringing up country call centres who create the initial data, which then feeds up to group reporting, the customer calls a global central call centre and then copies of the data are syndicated to the countries for in-country reporting. It is an interesting architectural solution which in theory brings a number of the benefits similar to centralisation, but without the disbenefits, as the countries still have their own "copy". However a problem that still remains is whether all of the country's data fits into the global model. If not, then awkward workarounds will occur which will cause more problems than they solve.

37.4.6 Data Lake

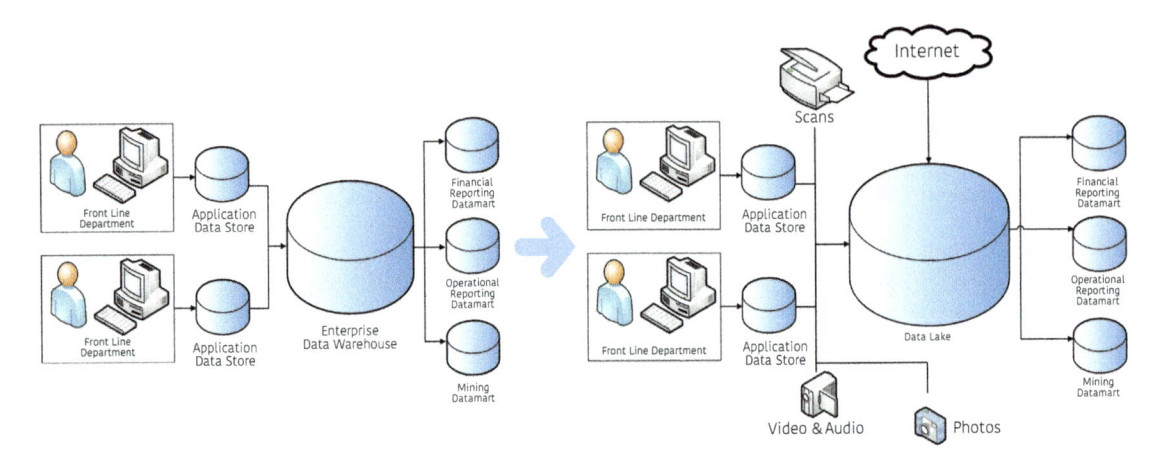

A data lake is a relatively recent solution that was a result of the rise in big data storage solutions. A data lake is a data storage solution which provides a pool of data, or all types, for use by the organisation. This data may include data from traditional front-office sources, but equally may include information from social media or the internet, or from reference data providers. Whilst the diagrams above may look superficially similar the advantage of data lakes over traditional data warehouses is that you can throw anything at them. The arrangement of the data is not specified by the lake, so many different types of data can co-exist in one place in many formats and languages. Traditional structured data – no problem, emails – no problem, audio – no problem, video – no problem. They are massively scalable and represent a way of creating a vast and varied storage solution relatively quickly. This is in comparison to getting data into a data warehouse which may take time and effort as data is carefully tailored to the language used by the warehouse.

At present the jury is still out on data lakes. Many organisations have spent heavily in this area without the promised nirvana occurring. There is an argument that a data lake merely moves the effort from upstream of the enterprise data store to downstream, but few could argue the potential flexibility and scalability offered by a data lake can be a considerable advantage to the organisation.

From a data quality point of view the problem with a data lake is that there are generally no barriers to entry. Any old rubbish can be chucked in and thereby enter the information flows of the organisation. Whilst there are data management tools available for big data platforms they are not as mature as for more traditional data platforms and in many cases require bespoke coding.

37.4.7 MDM (1)

Master Data Management (MDM) is an architectural change where, rather than each front end system, or department, maintaining their own copy of customer data, this data is held centrally and maintained centrally. From a data quality point of view, this means that each update to customer data (for example address changes) only has to be performed once, as the data is shared across the organisation. It also has the advantage of central management, so quality can be enhanced in one place and the benefits shared by all. The creation of a MDM solution, performed well, offers the possibility for a step change in the ability of the organisation to process and use high quality data.

37.4.8 MDM (2)

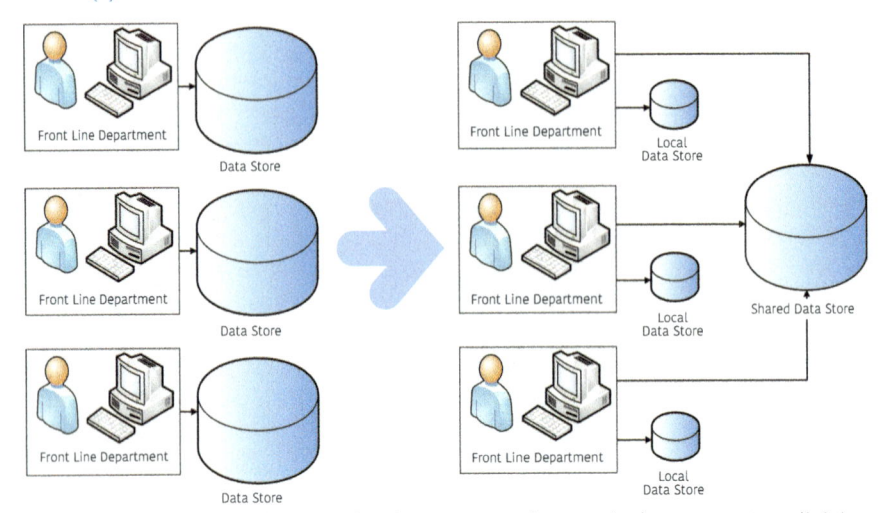

A second variety of MDM is where the organisation accepts that each department or division will have data that is specific to them, and is not shared with any other part of the organisation. However it also accepts that much data – often customer and product data – is common. This variety of MDM allows the individual division to keep their own data store for information that is specific to that division, but then mandates the use of an enterprise-wide data store for the shared data.

From a data quality point of view, this form of MDM has some similarity with federalisation, in that it allows a scenario where the data that is difficult to fit into a 'one-size-fits-all' global MDM solution can be federated, but also allows the organisation to reap the benefits of centralised master data.

37.4.9 Simplification

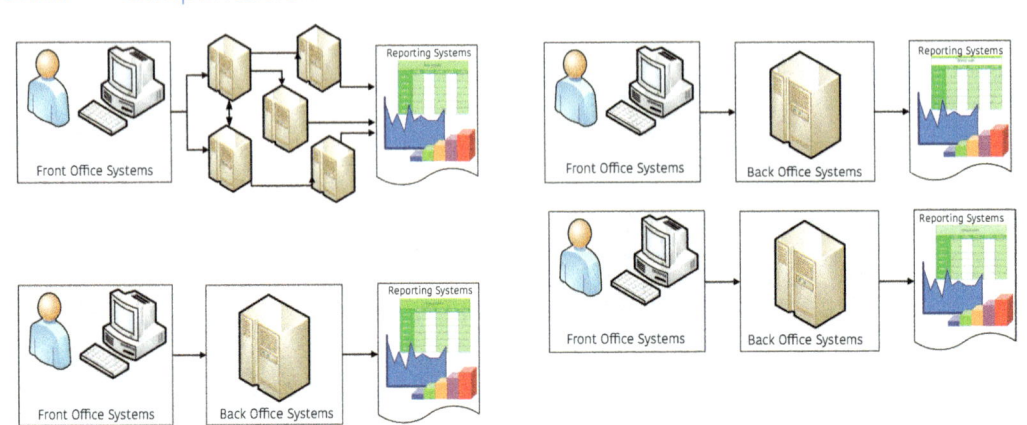

A very common type of architectural change is simplification. The scenario shown at a high level in the diagram above is in no way uncommon, and as organisations have grown organically over time in some cases the data architecture resembles ungoverned spaghetti, with links all over the organisation. As interfaces are where data quality typically goes wrong, simplification reduces complexity, cost and the risk to data quality.

37.4.10 Data Quality Layer

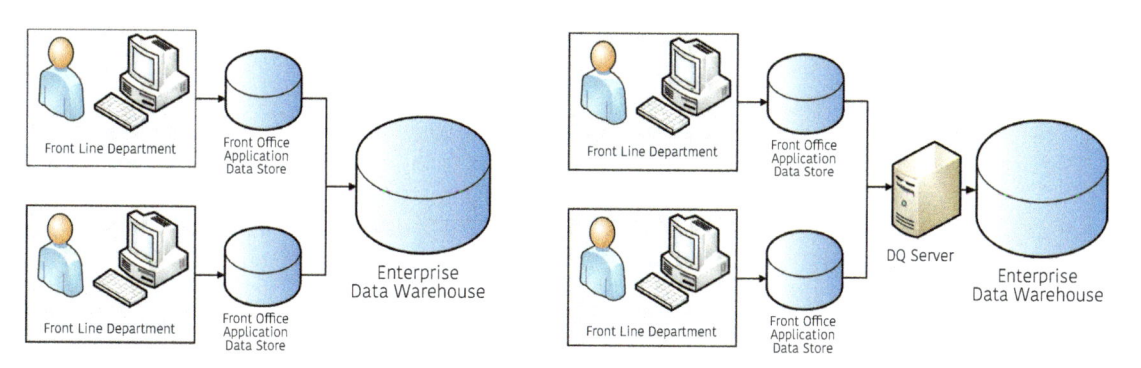

I have mentioned elsewhere in the book the various architectural options for data quality remediation, and have made the point that ideally any data quality remediation should occur as near to the source systems as possible. I also mentioned this rarely occurs.

The best situation that commonly occurs is where the data quality layer is placed immediately downstream of the source systems, and it is this architectural change that is shown in the diagram above. The data quality layer sits between the source systems and the enterprise data warehouse. Poor quality data is imported from the source systems into the data quality solution (which may be embedded in ETL) and then output, cleansed, into the data warehouse. The disadvantage of this solution – as noted elsewhere in the book – is the break in data lineage between the source systems and the data warehouse. As a result reports run directly off the source systems directly (for example operational reports showing daily totals) will no longer match the reports run off the data warehouse (for example monthly performance figures).

37.4.11 Encapsulation

Encapsulation – there are various terminologies for this – gets around the problem of how to make all systems appear to speak the same language when in reality they do not. In addition it does this without going to the trouble of actually doing the job properly and replacing the systems concerned. I would submit that encapsulation should only really ever be a short term solution, as it can be considered inefficient and messy. However some encapsulation solutions can exist for decades as the promised "final" upgrade never occurs.

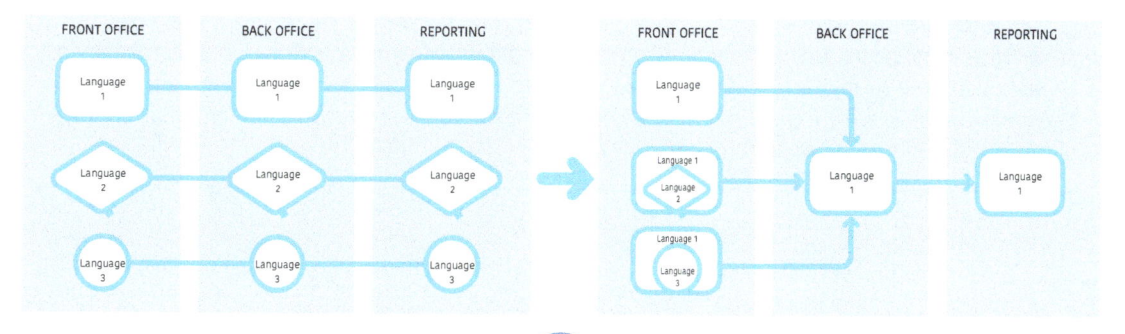

An example here would be if a legacy front end application writes to a legacy database. It is possible to buy a brand new database and then create a structure inside it that acts exactly the same as the old, legacy database.

In this case all the front end applications can operate exactly as they did before, but have the advantage of the shiny new kit which is now in – rather than out – of support.

From the above description, you will be aware that I personally believe that this is a somewhat bad idea. However in cases where there are only enough funds to implement one element of a solution properly, this can be an effective stop-gap until a final solution is deployed. From a data quality point of view, this solution introduces additional and theoretically unnecessary complexity and interfaces, and is likely to have a negative, rather than positive, effect on quality.

37.4.12 Data Model Changes

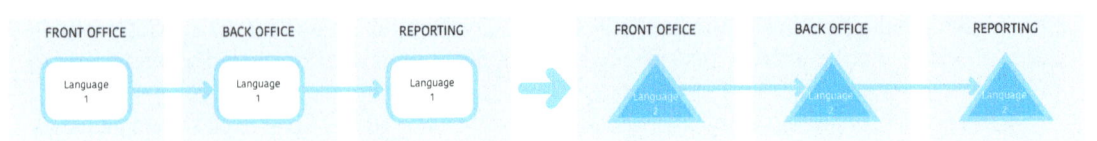

A fundamental base level architectural change is to change the data model. As described earlier in the book, the data model is the underlying structure of data within the organisation and represents the organisations view of the necessary structure of information to support its functionality. Unfortunately functionality changes over time, and when an original assumption might be that the organisation would not offer insurance products, later decisions may result in this view changing and hence data relating to insurance products may have to be woven into the existing data model.

Another example is the concept of connected parties. If an organisation is looking to identify financial crime, then the concept of individuals who are not actually customers, but control customer accounts (examples like power of attorney) needs to be included within the overall data model.

The importance of data model changes cannot really be overestimated. The meaning of every element within the organisation may change, resulting in a change to every process, data transport, data warehouse and database. A change to the data model changes the language that is built-in to every report, extract, and application in the organisation.

There can be several reasons for a data model change. A typical reason is the purchase of a new core system, which works in a different way to the old. Changing the new system to match the old data model (and hence effectively interface with all the other organisational systems) may not be possible or desirable, and hence it may be necessary to change the data model downstream to facilitate transfer of information.

From a data quality point of view, changes to the data model are very risky. Extreme care needs to be undertaken to map one data model to the next. For some areas, months of careful analysis may be required to ensure the effective transfer of information and to ensure the information flows within the organisation are not broken.

37.4.13 Removing blockers

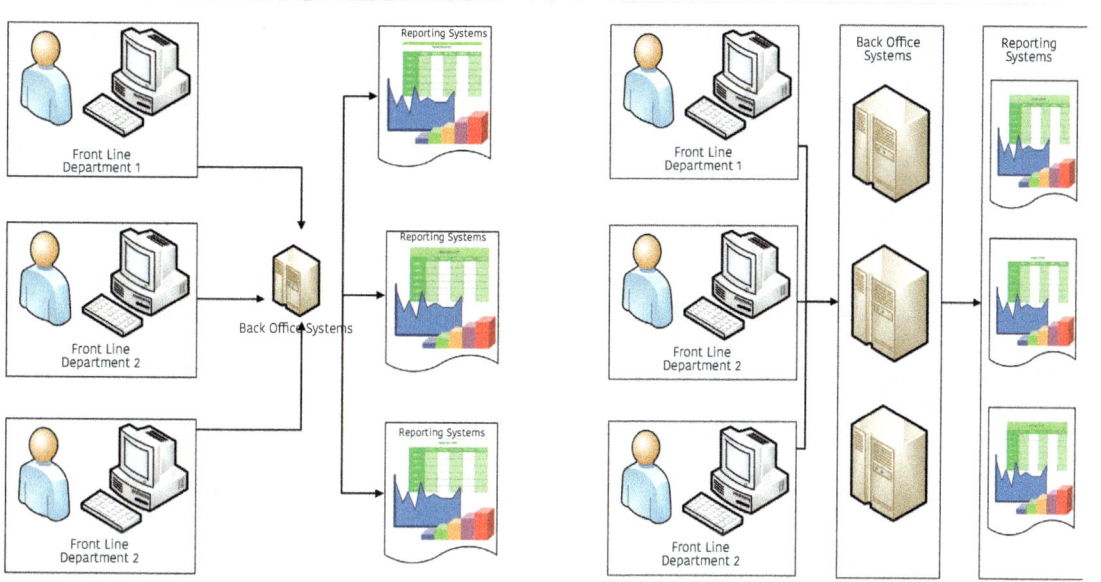

A very common type of architectural change is the removal of blockers. This is especially relevant to data quality, because if one part of the organisation is a blocker to others – either by lack of throughput or excessive bureaucracy, or for any other reason, then the rest of the organisation will look to work around the blocker. This increases data quality risks as workarounds are often either informal and/or poorly governed.

From a data quality point of view, an architectural change to remove a blocker decreases risk, increases throughput, and overall increases the opportunity for the organisation to get data quality right.

37.4.14 Globalisation

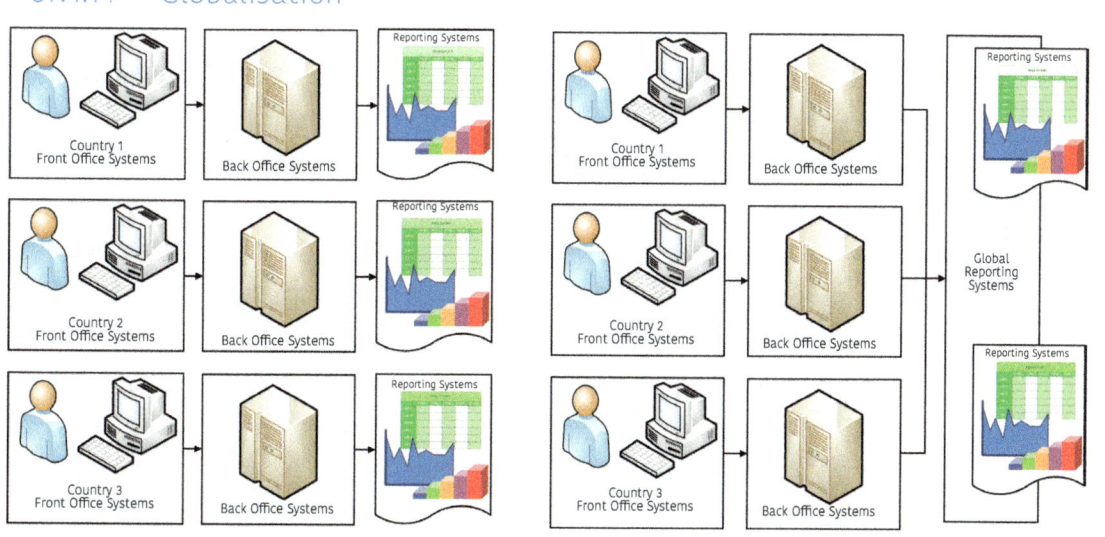

Globalisation is a very common scenario. At the start of the process the organisation may have several different divisions existing in each country. Each division does their own thing, with their own applications, data stores, data models, and report to the individual country regulator.

When moving to a global model all of these differences need to be ironed out, so that at a group level all the countries operate in the same way, allowing results to be amalgamated for group reporting.

A further variation of this is the introduction of a mandatory global reference data architecture. Here organisations mandate the type and nature of data architecture for any division joining the group. This may result in major upheaval for the individual division as it has to remake all its systems to fall in line with the global model.

From a data quality point of view, globalisation often creates initial chaos, as it is found that all of the various reporting systems in each country speak different languages. However, after this has been addressed, the overall effect to the organisation is positive.

37.4.15 Virtualisation

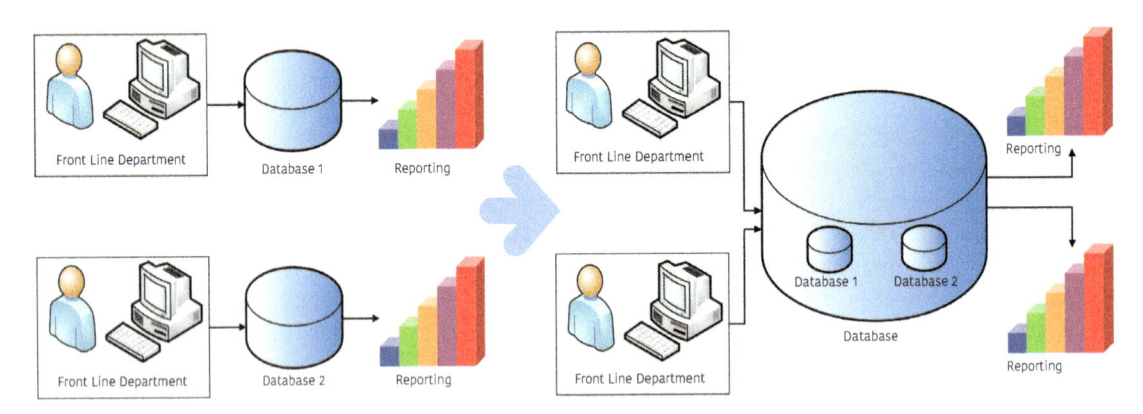

Virtualisation is not necessarily a change in architecture, but it is an enabler to the flexibility and management of architecture. A virtualised environment has many "virtual" machines running on one physical machine. This enables rapid changes to architecture, as in reality all the various servers and databases are figments of the imagination of a larger machine, and can be replicated, moved around, and changed at will.

From a data quality point of view, the effect of virtualisation is minimal as the change is to the underlying infrastructure architecture.

37.4.16 Capability and redundancy

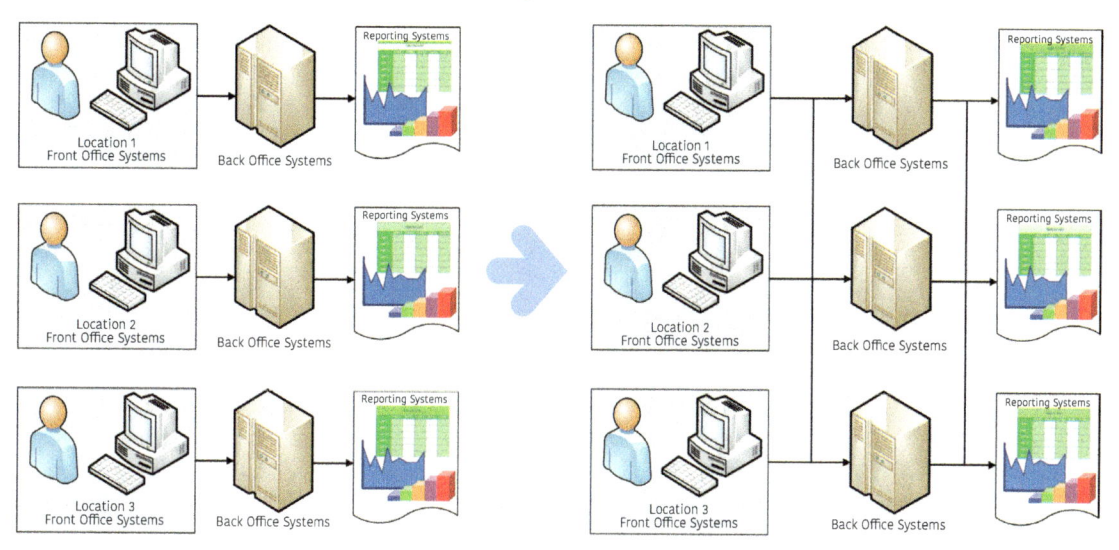

There are various ways that the resilience of the organisation to issues can be improved, and one of these is to increase the linkage between systems, so that one system can do the job of another.

From a data quality point of view, this change does not normally cause issues as the change is to the infrastructure architecture rather than the data architecture. However care should be taken when systems are replicated that the data flows in the same way from each of the redundant systems.

37.4.17 Timing

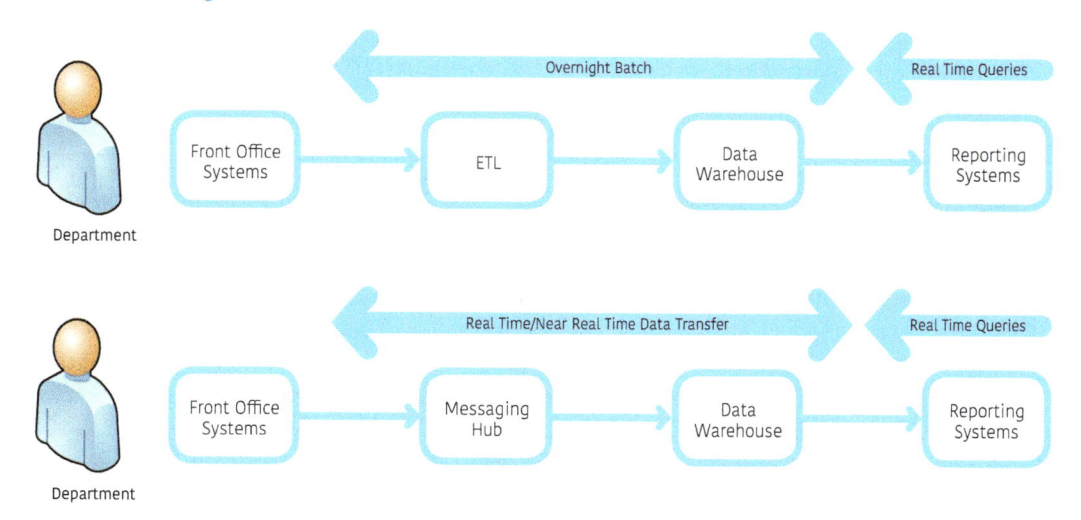

Historically, computer systems have worked on a batch basis, where a set of processes occur and then the data created by those processes is transferred overnight into a downstream system. With increasing globalisation, and the increasing move to 24 hour operations, that "batch window" is shrinking.

Now organisations look to process information in real time or near-real time (minutes). This requires a change in the architecture to an architecture based on a messaging approach, where information is passed between systems as soon as (or very shortly after) it is recorded.

As everything is now on the move, care must be taken in respect of data quality. This is an architectural change that takes static data moved on a batch basis, to a second-by-second transmission. Extreme care needs to be taken that data arrives in the same state as transmitted, and that messages are controlled in respect of data quality.

37.4.18 Unification

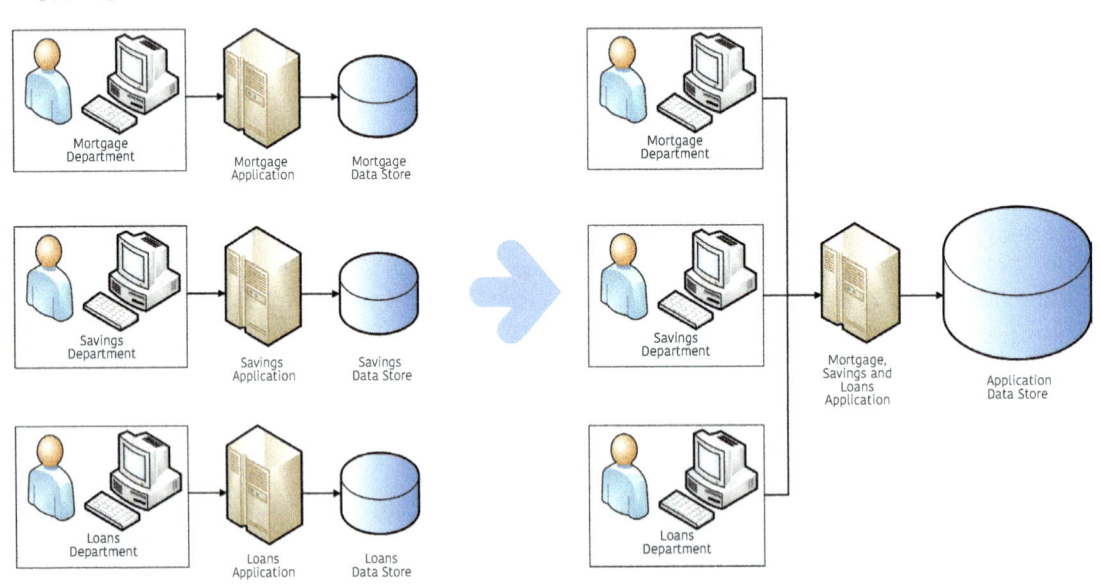

Unification occurs when there are a number of processes all using different approaches and/or different applications. The movement onto one application unifies the data, reduces complexity, and creates a common platform for reporting.

This change also increases staff mobility, as the applications used across the organisation are now the same, so it is possible for staff to move to branch from the contact centre, or to the savings department from the mortgage department. Everything looks the same. This change also reduces overall training costs as there is only one system to be trained on.

From a data quality point of view this architectural change is generally positive, as it unifies the data in one place, and in one model, and in a model which is interoperable between departments. As such it enables a holistic view of the organisation across all data sets.

37.4.19 Collapse of the clones

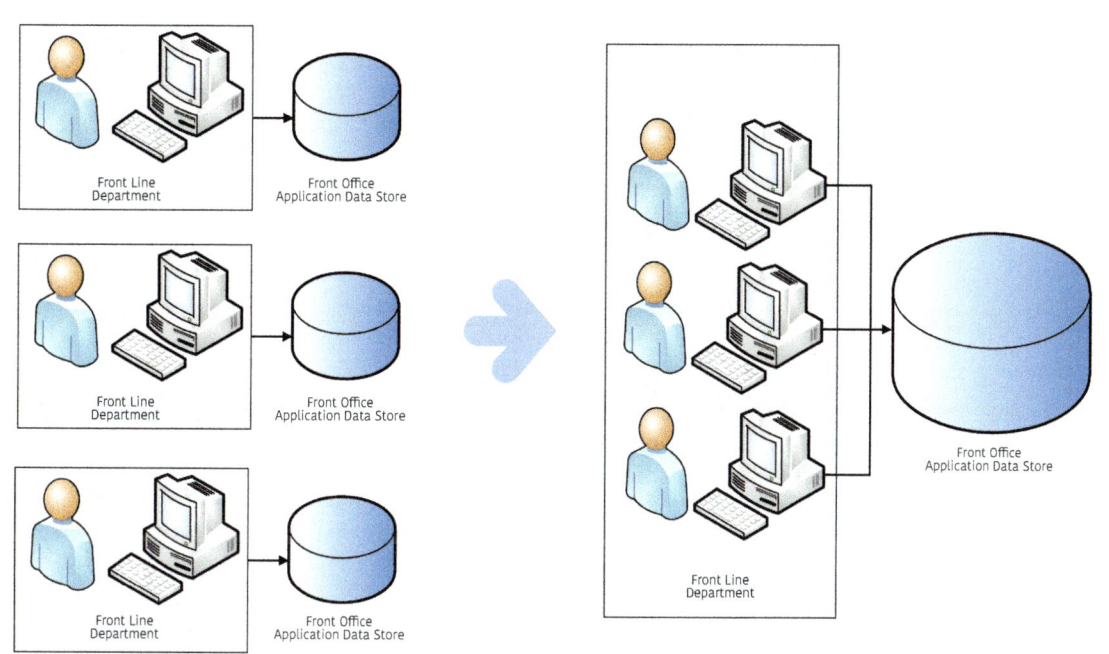

The final example of architectural changes is where there are many departments, all doing more or less the same thing in the same way. Each is a clone of the others. This may occur when an organisation buys a competitor, and apart from some rebranding, leaves the competitors systems and processes in place. Collapsing the clones places all the information together and also reduces the number of applications. From a data quality point of view, this kind of change is generally positive, as it means that all data is now in the same language and the same place, allowing for much more effective management.

37.4.20 Alignment with enterprise architecture

As has been mentioned before, a very important point is that it is essential to engage with the organisational architecture function, if it exists, and with those responsible for long term architectural change if it doesn't. In many organisations there will already be a roadmap for the future state architecture, and in reality many of the problems that are identified by the project are likely to have already been identified and the most appropriate solution already determined, and potentially documented and agreed. A data quality project running around and performing abortive work re-discovering the wheel will not help anyone.

The data quality project needs to ensure that any architectural solution supports, and is aligned with, the overall future architectural direction. Changes need to be agreed with the architecture function, and if there are deviations from the long term architectural direction, and especially if there are changes that make the achievement of the long term architectural vision more difficult, this needs to be thoroughly discussed. Whilst it may be necessary, if such decisions are made the reasons for them need to be understood.

37.4.21 Summary on architectural design

The above examples are in no way a comprehensive list of the way in which architecture can change. Every organisation is different and will face different problems. However it should give a feel for the potential changes that may be necessary and the reasons that they may occur. It will be the role of the enterprise architect, and the business process, data and application architects, to design in detail a solution that addresses the root causes for each individual organisation.

The above looks at the design of architectural change, the next stage is to discuss how the process changes are designed, managed and implemented.

37.5 Process Design

Following on from the architectural design, the next step, in terms of granularity, is to look at the individual processes. A large part of the poor data within any organisation is likely due to faulty processes in the past (and present) and it is equally likely that a significant proportion of the root causes will relate to process failure.

The data quality project needs, therefore, to consider how to change processes so that they create better quality information. To change a process to improve the data quality, a holistic approach should be taken. Change will cover not only the processes themselves, but the controls around those processes – the controls that act to ensure that the process does what it should.

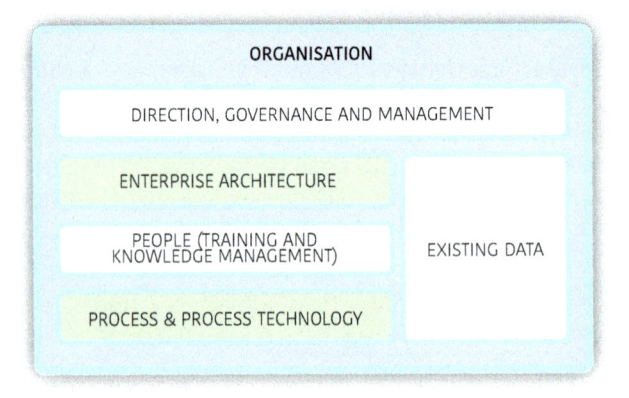

```
ORGANISATION
  DIRECTION, GOVERNANCE AND MANAGEMENT
  ENTERPRISE ARCHITECTURE
  PEOPLE (TRAINING AND KNOWLEDGE MANAGEMENT)      EXISTING DATA
  PROCESS & PROCESS TECHNOLOGY
```

We have mentioned above that Direction, Governance and Management, Training, Existing Data are covered elsewhere in the book, and architecture is covered in the above pages. Here we look at process and process design.

It may be that the root cause analysis will identify a process as requiring remediation. This section examines the way in which that design can evolve. Redesign of process within the approach recommended in The Data Quality Blueprint is intended to embed data controls and to minimise the likelihood of poor data quality propagating throughout the organisation. The remediation will need to consider many factors, including the impact on both the individual area of the organisation, and on data quality. The old process will need to be benchmarked, and the new process tested, and the positive impact measured. First, however, the design needs to be considered, which I will discuss next.

In the discussion of process discovery processes have been divided into those that create or update data, those that transport data, those that transform data, and those that read/used data. The same pattern will be used here.

37.5.1 Data Create/Update

For data creation or update, it is especially important to ensure that quality criteria should be included within every process requirement, specification and design, together with how the data quality relevant to the process will be measured. The reason is that – as mentioned before in the book – once poor quality data is entered into information systems it is very hard to reverse out the poor quality. SiriusDecisions, a sales and marketing research firm, quantifies data quality using the 1-10-100 rule, which says "*It takes $1 to verify a record as it's entered, $10 to cleanse and de-dupe it and $100 if nothing is done, as the ramifications of the mistakes are felt over and over again.*"

The specifics of the requirements will depend on the process, the nature of the data and the risk appetite of the organisation for errors in that individual type of data. The objective is for the organisation to carefully think through the process and understand where barriers exist to getting the process right first time, and act to remove them, or supplement the process so that the risk of poor data quality is reduced.

To give an example of a practical change in process that will increase data quality, it is often the case that a customer is asked to type their email address twice in a web form. This is an example of a simple and easily implemented change that vastly improves the quality of the captured data.

Whilst this is a relatively obvious example, it is necessary to understand – for each process – both the quality specification, which the organisation can obtain from the data quality requirements discussed in an earlier chapter, and also how changes in the process will help meet that quality specification.

37.5.2 Data Transport

In the case of most data transport processes, checksums and check digits can be baked into the data transport process, as well as simpler checks such as total number of rows and totals of numerical fields.

When little can be done to influence the data model for proprietary applications, then there will naturally be a transformation between the application and downstream systems. In these cases the Extract, Transform, Load (ETL) operations should be simple, clear, and above all well documented, so when someone decides to duplicate the extraction or add another transformation to the data then they know what they are doing. When it comes to extracts from a traditional data warehouse, data should be exported in a manner that provides the most information and the best description of the data that is exported.

The objective is to ensure that at each stage in a data transport process checks exist to ensure that data has arrived in the same state that it was transmitted.

37.5.3 Data Transformation

For data transformation processes, effort should be put into ensuring that data is not adversely affected by the transformational process and that unintentional transforms are not made. Especial care should be taken that data is not deleted in the process.

For example, when transforming formats, it is common for some programs to take fields that the program cannot convert into the desired target format and set them as null. This is reducing the quality of data.

If it is necessary to make changes to the data during transformation, the rule should be that any change to the data has to be in the direction of improving quality or it should not be implemented at all. Inserting default values is not improving quality issues, it is masking quality issues.

37.5.4 Data Read/Use

For data use, the most effective way for data quality to be included in reports is to reconcile the information in the reports back to source data. This enables the regulator or the board to have confidence that the information in the reports is a representation of the source. Large gaps between source systems and reports in terms of data are likely to cause recipients – understandably – to doubt the entire information flow in the organisation.

An alternative is to have a hierarchical report format, starting with aggregate results which are progressively broken down as the report progresses. This builds confidence in the data as the lineage is transparent.

For board reports it is possible for the quality metrics relating to the data items being reported to be included as KPIs. This is a somewhat courageous strategy and the practitioner risks being told to go away and come back when they are certain what their numbers are!

37.6 Process Controls

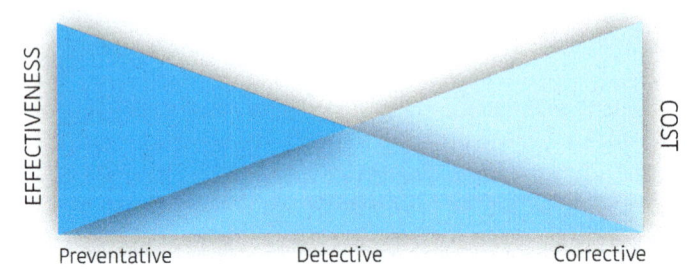

In the book "Poor Quality Cost" – quoted at the very beginning of this book, Harrington creates the concept of poor quality cost as the cost incurred by the organisation as a result of not doing things right the first time. It is the cost of all the controls, checking, double-checking, reporting, all there because the organisation cannot trust processes to get it right first time.

Data quality in processes often comes down to control: The aim is to make it as difficult as possible for a mistake to occur, if it does occur for it to be automatically corrected, and finally if not corrected the mistake needs to be identified as soon as possible as an exception for investigation. This is traditionally summarised as preventative controls, corrective controls and detective controls. It is far more cost-effective to prevent something going wrong than to find and correct it after the fact. This is why this book focuses on getting data quality right – cheaply – first time rather than picking up and correcting errors at great expense later. Remember the mantra is to do as little work as possible.

If we use the analogy of a physical (paper) file, the data that refers to the location of a physical file is easy to get wrong. To correct it – to find the physical file – in even a small organisation – can take many, many hours of searching by many people. If this is a critical item such as a medical record then ignoring the problem and hoping it will turn up sometime will not work – it has to be found.

37.6.1   Process Control: Preventative

Preventative controls are designed to stop an event happening in the first place. They may be as simple as asking a customer to type their email address in a website form twice, or may be deeply hidden within the database to stop an application updating a telephone number outside a prescribed format.

37.6.1.1   Non-technical preventative controls

- **Process design.** Already mentioned is the way in which process design should consider quality and make it as easy as possible for the process to succeed. Any part of the process that makes it easy to get data quality wrong needs to be removed.
- **Training.** Staff education on the effect of data quality is a key preventative measure. Often, the staff themselves will understand the requirement, but may not have considered that it matters, or will not necessarily join up the causes of the poor quality with their own behaviours. For example, the oft-quoted creation of many abattoir workers due to the length of a drop-down list may be seen as irrelevant to the account creation process if occupation is not used, but may be very relevant to the effectiveness of the marketing department.
- **Incentivisation.** It is unfortunately the case that call handlers are not incentivised in any way on data quality. Their incentivisation is either on throughput, or sales, or both. This means that when they come across a difficult entry – for example foreign names and places – then their incentive to ensure that the data that is entered is correct is unfortunately often nil. Their incentive is to enter the data as fast as possible and sell the customer a product. It is however perfectly possible to incentivise staff in relation to data quality. Checking of data quality by a supervisor and reward of the call handlers on that basis is a trivial step to take, but it is almost never taken. However it will make a massive difference to the quality of the data input. I have seen evidence of such a change at a number of organisations I have worked with.
- **Appropriate access to data.** Another unfortunate common scenario is that an unenlightened IT department will decide which data the business needs and then severely restrict the business access. Unfortunately the unenlightened IT department is unable to correctly judge what the business do and do not need. The result is business users simply find another way of getting the information, possibly from a spreadsheet held by their friend in accounts, or

a data dump that looks like what they need, or try to source it externally. This wastes their time, and pollutes the data within the organisation with data that is now both uncontrolled and unreliable. It is far better for IT to work with the business to ensure that the data that they need is available.

37.6.1.2 Technical Preventative Controls

Technical preventative controls may include:

- **Good and appropriate design.** The design of information systems should make it easy for data quality to be kept high. If the majority of customers come from the United Kingdom or USA do not place "United Kingdom" or "USA" under "U" at the bottom of a 200-country alphabetical drop-down list.
- **Constraint.** It is perfectly possible – indeed recommended – to set up databases so that it is impossible to enter data that does not conform to basic rules. A telephone number should contain no text, a gender two possibilities [52], a date of birth should not normally occur in the future [53].
- **Triggers.** Triggers can be set up in databases highlighting more complex issues, for example more complex business rules. Does the input indicate that the individual is BOTH under 18 AND earning more than ten times the average salary AND applying for a low-value loan AND living at an address that is known as a high-value area? If so, an exception may need to be created.
- **Data Models.** The data model of the organisation should be clear, consistently applied, and strictly controlled. Whilst relatively easy at the conceptual level, this becomes harder at the logical and especially physical (i.e. the actual database) level. For example, names should be descriptive, so that the content of the field is not ambiguous. Field names in tables such as "Col1, Col2, Col3, Col4, Col5" make unraveling the spaghetti later in the day (when individuals are trying to work out where data comes from) a much harder task.

37.6.2 Process Control: Detective

Detective process controls are there to highlight, after the event, that a process has produced a defective result, and to mark it for remediation. Some of these controls can be at a high level, some a low level, some may exist in data stores – for example reports that will highlight if incorrect data has been loaded into a database – and some will be embedded into an application to highlight as soon as possible when an issue has occurred. Detective controls will include, but are not limited to:

- **Triggers.** As above these are an automatic action that takes place after a pre-determined

---

[52] More accurately "commonly" two possibilities. I am well aware of systems where many more genders are used, being Male, Female, Male transitioning to female, pre-op, male transitioning to female, post-op, female transitioning to male, pre-op, female transitioning to male, post-op, "prefer not to say", etc. I know of one organisation which used nine genders. This is important in health sector where – due to the drugs transitioning people may be prescribed – it materially affects other drugs that can be prescribed.

[53] Except in maternity wards, health insurance, doctors surgeries, forms for paternity or maternity leave, etc.

effect. For example, when an invalid date is loaded into the warehouse, a trigger can take an action to alert the organisation that something has gone wrong.
- **Reconciliation reports** – especially across systems – are an effective high level control. As previously mentioned, these may take the form of comparing the number of people who the HR department think they are paying with the number of people building security think should be able to access the building via their access cards. A further check may be to those people that IT Security can log in to the organisation's systems.
- **Batch totals are an effective detective control**. When data is transmitted across systems a total is included of the sum of all the parts of the transmission. A quick and simple check is then possible to see if all the items that were transmitted actually arrived.
- **In-line auditing**. It is possible to place auditing systems in line with the information flows of the organisation to highlight when it detects data that is outside pre-determined ranges.
- **Data quality reports are detective controls**. Many organisations create reports on data quality. Whilst not ideal on their own, they should be part of the on-going assessment of data quality in the organisation and are a detective control.

37.6.3 Process Control: Corrective

- In process corrective controls work much like auto-correct within many popular word processing applications. Common errors are automatically corrected by the process without further user intervention. Dates of birth are a typical use of this kind of control. If a date of birth is entered where the last two digits are, say, smaller than 99 but later than the current year then the preceding two digits must be 19. 1816-1899 is not a normally valid date of birth for living customers and neither is 2016-2099.
- Other corrective controls. Here we are talking of data remediation, which is extensively covered elsewhere in the book.

37.7 Summary

In this chapter I have stepped through in some detail the process of designing a remediation strategy for architecture and process. I have given a number of examples of architectural design, and have related each of these to their effect on data quality. I would note that the exact nature of architectural change will depend on the individual organisation, as all organisations are different.

I have also looked at process design, and how data quality can be baked into the individual processes that create, read, update and delete data. I have discussed process controls and how they can be used to limit poor data quality.

The practitioner should now be able to look at architectural and process design and work with the relevant architects to create a design for their own organisation that will maximise its data quality.

In the next chapter I will consider the remediation design for data, and where in the organisation it is best to perform this vital work.

SECTION 5.5 REMEDIATION PLANNING

CHAPTER 38: REMEDIATION DESIGN FOR DATA: WHERE TO REMEDIATE

38.1 Structure

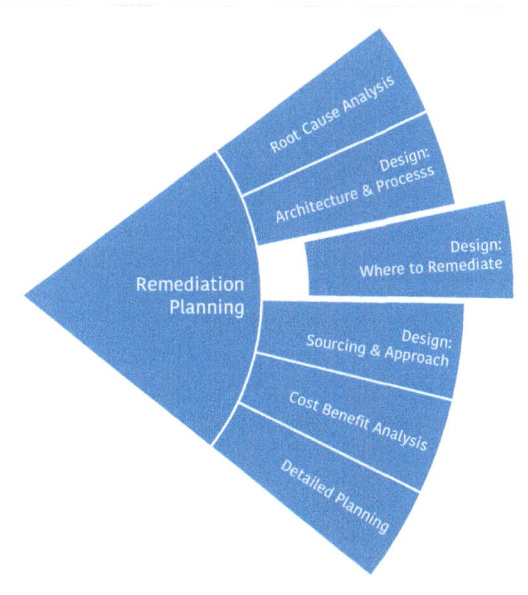

This stage of The Data Quality Blueprint includes the following phases:

1. Root Cause Analysis
2. Design for Architecture and Process
3. Data: Where to Remediate
4. Data: Sourcing Data
5. Cost Benefit Analysis
6. Detailed Planning

This chapter covers the third of these phases.

38.2 Overview

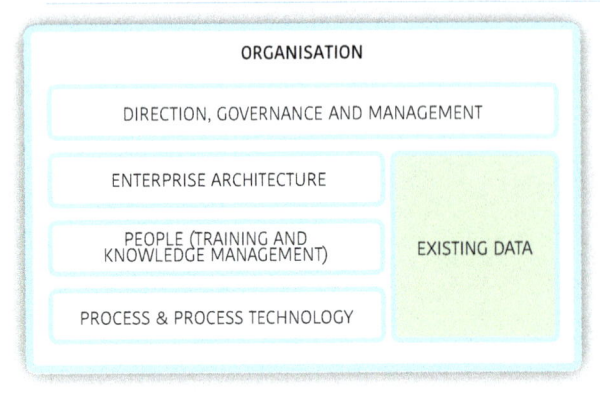

The previous chapter has covered the design of remediation for architecture and process. Other sections have covered direction, and governance. Knowledge management and training are covered in the "embedding" section later in the book. The remaining section is the remediation design for existing data.

ORGANISATION
- DIRECTION, GOVERNANCE AND MANAGEMENT
- ENTERPRISE ARCHITECTURE
- PEOPLE (TRAINING AND KNOWLEDGE MANAGEMENT)
- PROCESS & PROCESS TECHNOLOGY
- EXISTING DATA

The diagram below shows where this fits in the overall remediation design stage.

Identify root causes (common themes that may contribute to many issues) → Determine poor quality cost of each root cause → Develop solution options (architecture, process, data) for each root cause → Choose basket of options and finalise business case → Generate remediation task list and remediation plan

Remediation design for existing data covers two topics:

- What data are you going to remediate? Will you remediate the source data, will you look to replace or rectify the data in the data warehouse, or in the reporting layer.
- How are you going to remediate the data? Will you replace or rectify? How will you source better data to enhance your own? How will you integrate the new data with the existing data, and how will you move the new data to a point where it can be used?

Unfortunately, it is very common indeed for remediation of data to be performed in the wrong place, and to the wrong data. What I would like to do in this chapter is to cover where remediation should fit into the enterprise. This then opens the floor for discussion of how to remediate the data in more detail.

If we go back to the description of data flow then we can examine where remediation should fit.

Source System → Extract - Transform - Load → Data Warehouse → Data Mart → Presentation Layer → Reporting

In a typical organisation the data flows from source applications through to decision points at the end of the process. Clearly, there are any number of other architectures that exist within organisations (in fact the above architecture would not necessarily be recommended as a current greenfield solution), but the above is still common. An alternate "data lake" architecture that is becoming increasingly common is shown below.

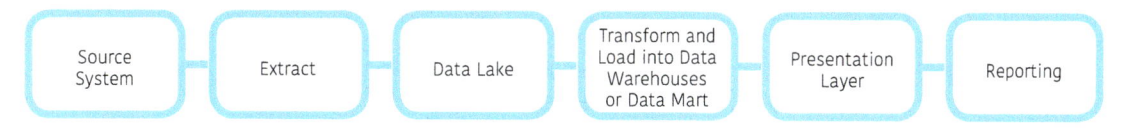

Source System → Extract → Data Lake → Transform and Load into Data Warehouses or Data Mart → Presentation Layer → Reporting

In this chapter I will explain where data quality fits in to the above and what works best. The approach I will use is to step through the different options available; at source, within ETL, in the warehouse, or within or after the presentation layer.

38.3 At Source

Embedding data quality at source is both the best way of solving data quality problems and by far the cheapest in the long run. Making sure the data quality is good up front means that all the problems with poor data quality downstream – in ETL, the data warehouse, the data marts or the presentation layer – simply don't occur anymore.

Rather than data quality remediation having to be performed many times with multiple departments performing the same cleaning routines, often utilising high value staff, the problem is sorted one and for all. This is unfortunately also the least common way in which data quality is addressed.

The reason is that it requires effort up front. Many organisations appear quite happy to let half the financial management team spend most of their time correcting data quality issues, as this is hidden cost. Solving application data problems at the source often requires a high-visibility project (with associated high visibility costs) and perceived-difficult-to-implement process improvements. The only danger of attacking data quality at source is that there is more potential for abortive work if all the data is cleansed, rather than just the data that is actually needed downstream. However, careful management and attention to data lineage can avoid this risk.

38.4 Within ETL

38.4.1 Extract

It is extremely rare that any data quality effort is performed on the extract stage of Extract-Transform-Load. This is because the extract stage is there to do exactly what it says on the tin – to move information out of the source systems to a landing area. A landing area is either a table in a database or a flat file. What does occur in extract is limitation of the extract to the records that meet certain criteria, such as "occurring in the last month" or "having a balance greater than zero". This is precisely the reason why data quality issues should be addressed at source, upstream of any such criteria being applied. For example, if a data quality error in processes results in balances being incorrectly zero, and the first extract only extracts accounts with a positive balance then the data quality error will cascade through the whole organisation.

A note on flat files

Flat files are the lingua franca of the data world – every application understands them, and every application can export to them. When moving files around a data landscape with many proprietary formats, a flat file is often the easiest and least risky way of doing it. A typical example is where the values are separated by commas. Hence

Forename	Surname	Account Number	Country
John	Parkinson	0123456	U.K.

Becomes on export

Forename,Surname,Account Number,Country

John,Parkinson,0123456,U.K.

The separator doesn't have to be a comma – it can be Tab, Pipe (|), or any character that a computer can produce. Care is required to ensure that whatever character is used to separate fields will not exist in the data, otherwise additional fields will be created – a notes field can make a total mess of comma separation as people often will include commas in the notes (hence a note saying that "Claimant's car damaged the wall of two properties, numbers 32 and 34" will be split into 2 fields on export due to the comma in the middle). One instance I am aware of ended up using the symbol for Japanese Yen (¥) as the only character that didn't already exist in the data itself.

38.4.2 Transform

A common location for the positioning of data quality is within the transform of Extract-Transform-Load. The data is often being transformed from the language of the source application into the language that is being loaded into the downstream systems, so this is a logical place for data quality.

A typical transform might be that the source system uses 8 digit account numbers, but the target requires 12. The transform script may therefore "pad out" the source data with "0000" at the beginning.

Unfortunately the transform element of Extract-Transform-Load is often a black box of a multitude of apparently minor data transforms. Care must be undertaken to ensure that any changes are carefully documented, preferably within the code itself in the form of comments, and in a format that another individual coming to the code to work out why everything has gone wrong months or years later can understand. For example:

- 'Source system xyz produces 8 digit account numbers, target system abc accepts 12 digit account numbers, hence pad out with 0000 to ensure compatibility with target system abc" is good.
- "Acc Num xyz +4x0 -> abc" is less than helpful.

There are several proprietary applications on the market that manage Extract-Transform-Load a lot better than traditional scripts. These applications will provide better visibility of the transforms that are taking place as data is moved around the organisation. Several of these proprietary systems (well-known products at time of writing such as IBM Data Stage and Quality Stage and Informatica Powercentre and Data Quality) also can contain add-ons that will cleanse data in transit.

The problem in making data quality changes on transform is that the downstream information no longer matches the source data – data lineage has been broken. A report from the source system to identify customers in a particular location will not match the same report from downstream systems. There are now two versions of the truth, and managers will therefore distrust both. Whilst it is admittedly a common place for data quality to be implemented in organisations, it is not as good as source. An additional reason for source being best is as mentioned above, the transform script can only work with the data it is given. If it looks to extract "sales in the last month" and source invoice date data is wrong, no amount of transformation within ETL will rectify the issue that incorrect data has been chosen in the first place.

38.4.3 Load

There should not really be any changes to data in the "load" stage. The "transform" element should get the data into a state that is compatible with the target systems, and then load it into those systems. Care is required within "load" for the auto-rejection of entries that do not meet target specifications (i.e. the "transform" job has not been done well enough). An exception is if the organisation is running a data lake environment then an approach known as "schema on read" can be used. This bundles the transform and load together downstream of the data lake. In this case the comments regards transform are as in the section above.

38.5 In the Lake (if applicable)

This is definitely not the place to address data quality as a data lake is designed to be a "warts and all" data store, where information exists in its rawest form. The data lake will also contain a large amount of data that is rarely – if ever – used by the organisation and any attempt to remediate data quality in the lake will result in redundant work. Saying that, at least one vendor advocates embedding data quality in the lake but only on data specifically identified as business critical.

38.6 In Data Warehouse & Data marts

The data warehouse and data marts are also not the place to try and address data quality problems. The data warehouse should hold data in a stable, non-volatile state and whilst it can enforce data quality, it does this by refusing to accept, for example, social security numbers that do not meet the correct format. Remediating the data should not be the job of the data warehouse or the teams that manage it. Exactly the same applies to the data marts. There are many issues related to trying to change the quality of the data whilst it resides in a data warehouse or data mart:

- As in the case of any other solution that is not changing data in source, it cannot recover data quality that has already been lost upstream.
- It breaks data lineage and creates multiple versions of the truth.
- Worse, the data warehouse is supposed to be the single source of the truth – creating multiple versions within the data warehouse is likely to cause distrust, additional complexity and error. For example which table should be referenced, the old, uncleaned, or the new, cleaned? Obviously the latter is the correct answer, but it causes confusion and some will get it wrong.
- The data warehouse is not optimised for the kind of operations that data quality changes will involve; therefore it is a resource-hungry way of solving the problem.
- A data warehouse should be non-volatile storage. The data should remain the same over time. Changing the data within the data warehouse breaks that principle.
- The volume of data in a general data warehouse is so large that remediation is likely to be ruinously inefficient.
- The data warehouse is likely to be a "black box" to everyone but a small group of IT users, who will be the only people who are allowed to directly change data within it.

Overall, changing the data in the data warehouse or the data marts is not ideal.

38.7　In the presentation & reporting layer

The presentation and reporting layer should be relatively thin and contain a limited amount of complexity. It should simply be formatting and aggregating information that already exists in the data mart. Unfortunately, the ideal world is not present, and the presentation layer will be likely to end up compensating for all the data issues accumulated in all previous stages. Most organisations as a result have significant buried data quality remediation complexity within presentation and reporting. However, for exactly the same reason as embedding data quality within Extract-Transform-Load is a bad idea, the problem with embedding data quality within the presentation layer is that it cannot recover data quality lost upstream and it breaks data lineage.

The data that is used for reporting now does not match ad-hoc reports that are pulled off the data warehouse or data marts, and they are also different to the reports that are pulled off the source systems. There is now a multiplication of sources of the truth. The situation is worse when the presentation and reporting layer is self-service.

This is because many organisations, given the proliferation of easy to use self-service data analysis tools (Excel, Qlikview, Tableau, etc) prefer that the analysts and reporting managers are simply given access to the data and will do the reporting themselves. If data quality is implemented in the presentation layer very expensive individuals are then building data quality solutions in an ad-hoc manner. This uses time and resources that could much better be used in many other ways.

38.8　After the presentation layer

Depressingly, this is by far the most common way that data quality is addressed in many organisations. Poor data exists all the way through the overall data flow, causing confusion at every point.

As a consequence vast effort is then expended by expensive staff at the far end to sort the problems created because the data does not make sense. Reports and extracts that are created by the systems are not suitable for users, so end user computing occurs in common office productivity toolsets to make the data fit for purpose. This common problem has already been mentioned right at the start of the book in the section covering the operational impacts of poor data quality.

38.9   Where is best and why

By far the most efficient and effective place to remediate data quality is in the source systems. As soon as the best data is not held in source then there are instantly two versions of the truth. Practically, the further "upstream" – i.e. towards source – any data quality remediation occurs the better, so within Extract-Transform-Load is better than in the presentation layer, and anything is better than the common solution of individual users using common productivity tools to cleanse data.

However it is worth discussing an interesting variation. This is utilising a Master Data Management (MDM) solution, where the source systems either do not hold the source data, or only have a reference to a cleansed, "gold" source.

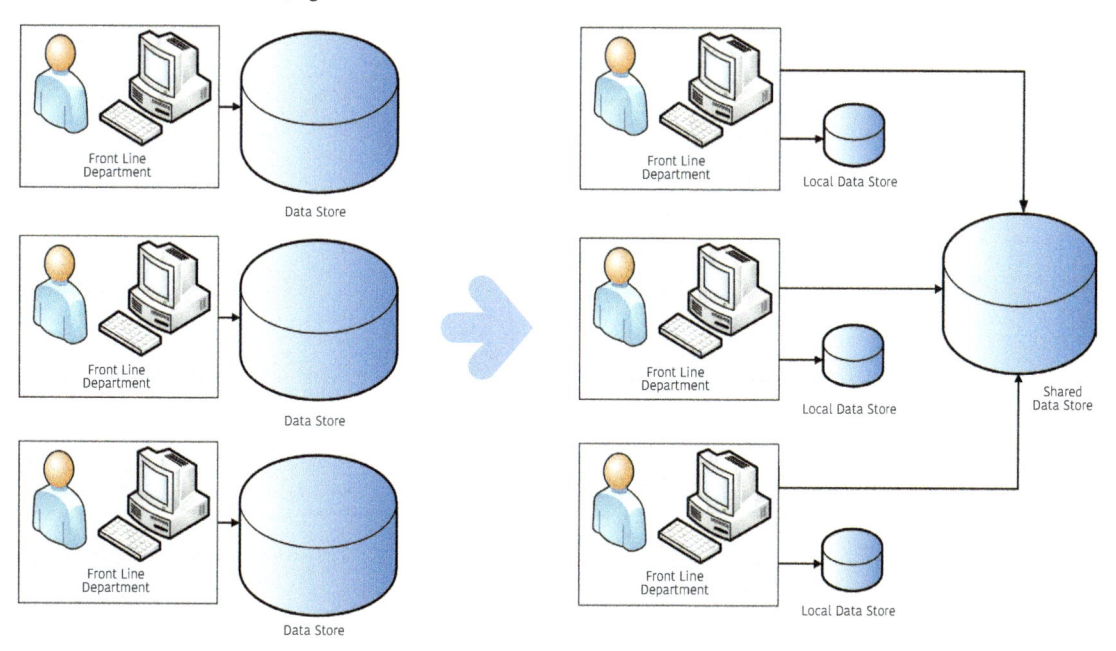

The source systems hold a key or identifier to a record (e.g. a customer). The MDM solution – a separate database – holds the detail, but holds that detail for all sources. A record created in a source application is held in an enterprise-wide data store that is common to all systems, and when the source application wants the data it uses its "key" to go and find it. This is shown in the diagram above. The local application holds only a small amount of application-specific data within its own environment and for anything that is used enterprise-wide refers to the separate MDM solution. The advantage of this approach is that the information is only held once, and shared across the enterprise.

It should be noted that there are many variants of MDM. In some all the data is held in the MDM database, in others it all still resides in the application data stores but keys are shared so that data can be matched between them. The above shows the most common implementation I have come across to date.

38.10   Summary

Within this chapter I have shown where data quality fits in to the overall data flow within a typical organisation. I have explained why implementing data quality changes downstream of the source is a bad idea because data quality cannot be recovered downstream and it creates multiple versions of the truth. I have also briefly introduced the concept of MDM architecture and shown how this can also provide a good data quality solution.

I hope that this chapter will give the reader the understanding to resist – strongly – when someone attempts to force a sub-optimal solution on the data quality practitioner or the project. In the next chapter I will look at where to source good data before the work of cost benefit analysis, building a final plan and starting the remediation work in earnest.

SECTION 5.5 REMEDIATION PLANNING

CHAPTER 39: REMEDIATION DESIGN FOR DATA: SOURCING AND APPROACH

39.1 Structure

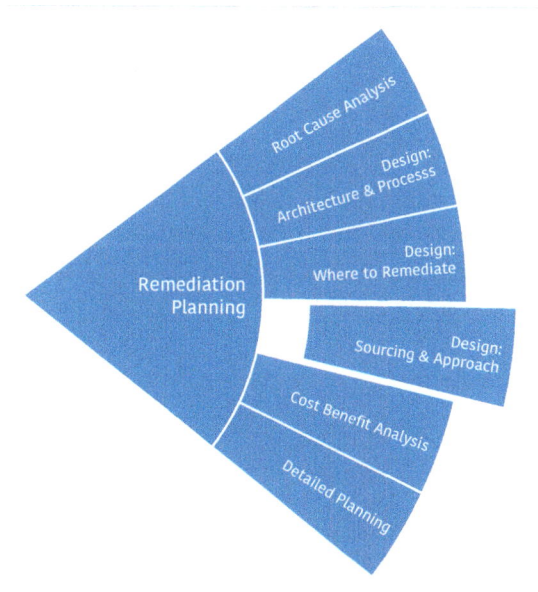

This stage of The Data Quality Blueprint includes the following phases:

1. Root Cause Analysis
2. Design for Architecture and Process
3. Data: Where to Remediate
4. Data: Sourcing Data
5. Cost Benefit Analysis
6. Detailed Planning

This chapter covers the fourth of these phases.

39.2 Overview

INPUTS	TASKS
■ All artefacts created or utilised by the project to date. ■ Results from architecture discovery ■ Results from data discovery ■ Results from process discovery ■ Results from root cause analysis	■ Understand data scope ■ Engage data owners, data governance and data management ■ For each data root cause understand issue ■ For each data cause consider options ■ Discuss with data owners, data governance and data management ■ Generate options ■ Determine approach for remediation ■ Define the replacement data required ■ Source replacement data ■ Perform best source analysis on replacement data ■ Document data roadmap ■ Determine and document most appropriate options ■ Present to key stakeholders ■ Update for feedback ■ Upload to project repository
OUTPUTS	
■ Data options ■ Remediation approach ■ List of the replacement data required ■ Best source analysis ■ Data roadmap	
DEPENDENCIES	
■ Access to stakeholders	

The discussion of where to remediate data leads into the next phase in The Data Quality Blueprint, which covers how existing data will be remediated. The diagram below shows where this fits into the overall remediation design stage.

Identify root causes (common themes that may contribute to many issues) → Determine poor quality cost of each root cause → Develop solution options (architecture, process, data) for each root cause → Choose basket of options and finalise business case → Generate remediation task list and remediation plan

This phase includes examination of options for replacement or remediation of existing data, and if the former where the replacement data is going to be sourced. It is necessary to consider these options now as the remediation approach will affect the cost, and therefore the cost-benefit analysis. The detailed mechanics of remediation as a step by step process will be covered in the data remediation chapter later.

39.3 Scope and Approach

The first decision to make is what data you will remediate. We have mentioned a few times that there is no point wasting time remediating data that is of no use to the business. This is why The

Data Quality Blueprint recommends first working out the data required by the business and to what standard (data requirements and data quality requirements). Assuming that this is completed, then there will be a large pile of poor quality data that needs work. The best approach to tackling the detail of the remediation is to take the problem apart and attack each element as a separate mini-project. Therefore data can be split into domain and system, and may be further split into business divisions or operational areas.

Data issues should also be grouped by issue. It may be that several areas of the organisation are having a problem with customer addresses. This would not be surprising if they are reliant on the same data store. Remediating one data store will then have a wide impact. What will be interesting is if one area of the organisation is having problems with addresses and another is not, as it could possibly indicate that the first data store could be realigned with the second.

Fortunately many data elements are related but not interdependent – as such remediation of one data item may considerably decrease the difficultly in improving others, but is not dependent on it. For example, remediating forename and remediating title are technically independent, however if forename remediation is performed first, then titles – at least in terms of gender-specific "Mrs", "Mr", can be inferred.

Another example of this approach is address data. Addresses are often in a wide variety of formats – sometimes so wide that one wonders whether they are dependent on the mood the agent was in when they were typing the address. Within the typical customer database can be found examples akin to the below.

CustID	Address 1	Address 2	Address 3	Address 4	Address 5	Postcode
234	1 Station Road	Sutton Coldfield			Birmingham	B56 1PG
346	"Dunroamin"	1 Station Road	Wylde Green	Sutton Coldfield	Birmingham	B56 1PG
646	1	Station Rd	Wylde Green	Sutton Coldfield	Birmingham	B56
897	1 Station Rd	Wylde Green			Birmingham	

Merging these customer numbers is going to be difficult in their current state. However, if you can determine which of the two postcodes is correct, then the addresses can be repopulated using correct data, and then merged. Solving one data quality issue – the postcode – solves a number of others. Therefore choose your direction carefully and in a manner to make the greatest effect with the least effort. This is a central principle of The Data Quality Blueprint, to do as little work as possible.

39.4 Replace or Remediate? Replace

The next decision to make is to choose between replacing the existing data with new, or to remediate what you've got. Replacing the existing data may be a required option when the current data is so bad that no amount of cleaning will help, but it is more likely when the current data is simply non-existent or corrupt (for example, if no email addresses have ever been collected).

This approach creates a new, "golden source" from scratch without using current data or only using a limited subset. The new source then replaces the current data, and existing applications and reporting will be then pointed to the new source. Even in this situation the old records will still probably be used as keys, and the new data mapped onto them.

The Data Quality Blueprint

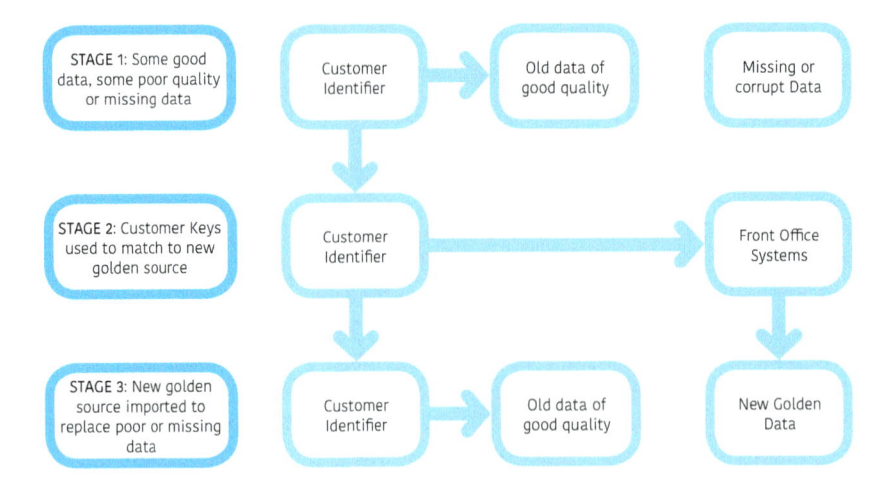

STAGE 1: Some good data, some poor quality or missing data
- Customer Identifier → Old data of good quality
- Missing or corrupt Data

STAGE 2: Customer Keys used to match to new golden source
- Customer Identifier → Front Office Systems

STAGE 3: New golden source imported to replace poor or missing data
- Customer Identifier → Old data of good quality
- New Golden Data

To create the new golden source, there are a variety of possibilities; it is possible to contact the customer directly via mail, email or phone, or to use a reference data set. This kind of recreation of customer data from scratch has its own challenges. For example, how do you contact the customer when you cannot rely on the contact or security details?

Alternatively a small amount of data can be given to a third party who will auto-populate a new golden source based on the data that is supplied to them (e.g. customer name, date of birth and postcode). This is heavily dependent on the quality of the data that they are given. Sources of good data will be discussed later in this chapter.

39.5 Replace or Remediate? Remediate

39.5.1 Automatic Remediation

The capabilities of technical data quality tools were covered in an earlier chapter, and will be mentioned again here. A common approach to remediating data is to use data quality tools and/or reference data to enhance the current data. Whilst care has to be taken to ensure that good data is not overwritten, this can be effective, especially in the case of small lists with formalised names and abbreviations, such as countries, states, counties and postcodes. It is also possible to automatically remediate addresses based on the postal/zip code and a large reference set. Automatic remediation of names is more difficult due to the large number of (valid) alternate spellings and the high degree of customer dissatisfaction if names are not spelled correctly. For example, Caren, Karyn, Karin, Caron, Karon, are all used as alternatives to the more common Karen. Filtering out the misspellings from the individualistic alternatives requires care. It is also possible to utilise reference data sets held by external agencies, of which more later in this chapter.

39.5.2 Manual Remediation

Analysis-driven manual remediation is another common method of remediating data. The stages are:

Profiling

- A detailed analysis of the data (profiling) which will detail completeness, uniformity, consistency, uniqueness and validity

Source Analysis

- An analysis of accuracy and existence by tracking a sample back to original source documents

Quality Analysis

- Further analysis covering ease of use, presentation, appropriateness, timeliness and trustworthiness

The analysis enables the creation of a holistic picture of the data quality within an organisation. From this point it is possible to enter the remediation planning stage as usual. The output from the analysis feeds directly into tasks that can be remediated manually. The contact centre (or similar) is given the task of remediating each deficient item, potentially contacting the customer to confirm details in the process. This is a labour-intensive way of approaching remediation, but it will get there eventually. No extra technology needs to be purchased, and the changes are being made in the right place – on the source systems.

39.5.3   Hybrid Approaches

As might be suspected, the most effective approach is a hybrid one – use external agencies where they hold data of sufficient quality and granularity to provide an effective solution, to use automatic remediation where possible, and to otherwise either remediate or replace the data via a contact centre and customer interaction. All of remediation comes down to replacing bad data (or non-existent data) with good data, and there are a whole range of ways of doing this. I will discuss sources of good data next.

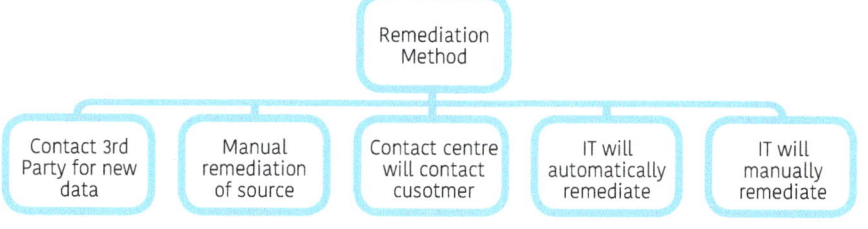

```
                      Remediation
                        Method
   ┌───────────┬───────────┬───────────┬───────────┐
Contact 3rd   Manual    Contact centre   IT will      IT will
Party for new remediation will contact   automatically manually
   data      of source   cusotmer       remediate    remediate
```

39.6   Sources of Good Data

In order to remediate data it is necessary to replace the current data with data of better quality. The remainder of this chapter covers where to get this data and how to determine the best source.

39.6.1 The good data is obvious

Often, when data is of poor quality, it is easy to determine what good quality should look like. Elsewhere in the book, I gave examples of typographical mistakes in the title field. I will use the same examples to demonstrate a remediation approach.

MRS	MRS.	MR MRS	MR AND MRS	MR & MRS
MR,MRS	_MRS	MR&MRS	MR.MRS	MRMRS
MR& MRS	MRSS	MR MRS	MR. & MRS.	MR.AND.MRS
MR + MRS	MR.MRS.	MR/MRS	MR &MRS	MRSD
MRSE	MR. MRS.	MRS MR	MR MRS	MR&MRS.
MR+MRS	_MRS.	GMRS	MMRS	,MRS
MRAND MRS	MR NAD MRS	MR, MRS	MR-MRS	DMRS
_MR MRS	__MRS	DR AND MRS	DR & MRS	MR AMD MRS
.MRS	MRS,MR	___MRS	MR. & MRS	MR 6 MRS
MR. MRS	MRSA	MRANDMRS	MR SAND MRS	

I would submit that it is perfectly possible for a reasonable person to determine the correct values. You don't need to buy expensive replacement data, as you can have reasonable confidence that "Mr amd Mrs" is incorrect. I would submit that a large percentage of incorrect data within information systems is possible to remediate in a similar way. Performing the remediation is straightforward, as the same reasonable person can run down a list of titles and match the actual entries to a specific set of known valid variables, even if the list is several thousand values long and the reasonable person takes a couple of days. This list can then be run against the database and the values changed automatically. For example:

Old Value	New Value	Old Value	New Value	Old Value	New Value
MRS	Mrs	MR NAD MRS	Mr and Mrs	MR &MRS	Mr and Mrs
MR,MRS	Mr and Mrs	__MRS	Mrs	MR MRS	Mr and Mrs
MR& MRS	Mr and Mrs	MRS,MR	Mr and Mrs	MMRS	Mrs?
MR + MRS	Mr and Mrs	MRSA	Mrs	MR-MRS	Mr and Mrs
MRSE	Mrs	MR MRS	Mr and Mrs	DR & MRS	Dr and Mrs
MR+MRS	Mr and Mrs	MR&MRS	Mr and Mrs	MR. & MRS	Mr and Mrs
MRAND MRS	Mr and Mrs	MR MRS	Mr and Mrs	MR & MRS	Mr and Mrs
_MR MRS	Mr and Mrs	MR/MRS	Mr and Mrs	MRMRS	Mr and Mrs
.MRS	Mrs	MRS MR	Mr and Mrs	MR.AND.MRS	Mr and Mrs
MR. MRS	Mr and Mrs	GMRS	Mrs	MRSD	Mrs? (look where "D" is on the keyboard)
MRS.	Mrs	MR, MRS	Mr and Mrs	MR&MRS.	Mr and Mrs
_MRS	Mrs	DR AND MRS	Dr and Mrs	,MRS	Mrs
MRSS	Mrs	___MRS	Mrs	DMRS	Dr and Mrs?
MR.MRS.	Mr and Mrs	MRANDMRS	Mr and Mrs	MR AMD MRS	Mr and Mrs
MR. MRS.	Mr and Mrs	MR AND MRS	Mr and Mrs	MR 6 MRS	Mr and Mrs
MRS.	Mrs	MR.MRS	Mr and Mrs		
MR SAND MRS	Mr and Mrs	MR. & MRS.	Mr and Mrs		

The above reduces 49 different invalid entries to 4 valid entries (and took 5 minutes), three entries (with question marks) where more investigation may be required. A simple query run against a database overnight would immediately result in a significant improvement of data quality, and a significant improvement in customer satisfaction. I would doubt many customers are enthused regarding the competence of an organisation that sends letters addressed to "Mr nad Mrs".

39.6.2   Your own systems

The next easiest source of good data is the organisation's own systems. In a multi-product, many-customer environment, it may well be possible to source data from other information systems. In this case duplicated information can be your friend. Possible sources may include, but are obviously not limited to:

Source	Description
Similar data	Similar (or the same) addresses can have the same postcode. Certainly the first part of the postcode is likely to be the same. It can be possible to populate totally unknown data with partially known data if a similar address is used as a reference point.
Duplication	Duplication can, on occasion, be your friend. Two sets of data for the same person, or address, may yield a composite data set that is better quality than either.
Different product data	Different product data can be a source of information. Some product data sets (for example mortgage data sets) hold considerably more information about the customer and their address than product data sets such as savings accounts (where address data is likely to be badly out of date). Mortgage data sets (because of the nature of the product) are likely to include correct, current details of the house the customer is living in. Given that customers often have more than one product with the same company, it is possible to populate bad, historic or simply missing data in savings accounts from good data in mortgage accounts.
Recent product data	More recent product data can help too. If two products are held by the same customer, with two different addresses (or one partial address) then it is possible to use the more recent source as the "golden source" and to re-populate the historic data with the more recent data.
Historic data	Occasionally, this works the other way too. Especially if there has been a systems migration which has caused data problems, going back to historical archives to find customer data is occasionally necessary.
Paperwork	If all else fails, original application form and files may be a source of data. It is manual, but possible. Issues may occur if there is a significant discrepancy between the paper applications and the details on the system. This is especially prevalent in historical trustee files, where it was often the intention that the child would be the account holder and the parents trustees, however many data creators, seeing Mr and Mrs, would put these first, and then subsequently add the child. If you have problems such as these, and there is no other way of solving it, the paper records may be necessary.

39.6.3   Your staff

You should never discount your own staff as sources of information, as they may have relevant information that you can use to help cleanse your data. Staff will certainly have information on postcode data for the local area (especially if the organisation is locally-orientated or has a strong regional bias). Staff may well also be customers (likely if there is a staff discount) and will be able to help remediate their own accounts. A surprising percentage of the total can occasionally be remediated in this way, depending on the organisation, its sector and its location, and the relevant legislation [54]. In some sectors, any business that does not have 99.9% (at least) correct data on their staff accounts should be working harder.

39.6.4   The Customer

For customer information the customer is clearly the best source of information. However, customers have their own ideas about spelling and formatting, especially in relation to addresses, may have illegible handwriting, and will make mistakes. In addition, however you package the communication, asking a customer for details which the customer perfectly reasonably believes that you should already possess can cause reputational issues. It is of course possible to mail customers and ask them to confirm data, assuming that you can manage the message correctly. Sometimes a regulatory boot can be used – "we are required by the regulator to" – assuming that the excuse is correct, of course. Equally, it is possible – especially in smaller companies – to simply say that "we are moving to new data systems and would like to use this opportunity to ensure that the data that is held is free from any defect, and would welcome your help in this important matter". This approach is common enough that I have such a letter from a local car dealership on my desk as I am writing this paragraph.

Anecdote
Customers can sometimes be too helpful. For one data quality mailing the organisation was attempting to determine who would receive a share payout. One individual was mailed twice, as the organisation incorrectly had her on the database once with her maiden name, and once under her married name.

This individual dutifully replied that both were correct, and would have received a double payout, once under each name, if she had not returned both forms in the same envelope.

39.6.4.1   Mail

A common approach is to mail all customers with a reconfirmation document – similar to the car dealership above. This approach has been adopted by several large organisations. In one case I am aware of 3.2 million customers were mailed with a request to reconfirm their data. For historical data in particular the use of customer data confirmation is a powerful tool in both analysing and remediating data quality. It may appear to be a sledgehammer to crack a nut, but the advantage is that it does, actually, crack the nut. Many alternative approaches deliver glancing blows at best.

---

52.   It may be impossible, illegal or against policy for a staff member to access their own account

One challenge with this approach is the problem that without an address it is not possible to send a form to a customer for them to confirm their address. However, where the organisation does hold a valid address this is an excellent way of both confirming data held by the organisation and capturing historical data not currently held. The results from such operations also provide an excellent way of determining the overall data quality within the organisation. Clearly this approach is self-limiting to those customers who reply to the customer data confirmation mailing. However with a customer data confirmation included as part of an existing large mailing operation (e.g. the Annual General Meeting mailing) sufficient responses can be gained to enable an extrapolated analysis of the data quality of the organisation as a whole. The organisation needs to accept that this will be a "best case" answer given that those customers with poor data quality records will either not receive the mailing (poor address) or be so historical as to have limited incentive to participate.

In the case of the mailing of 3.2m customers mentioned above, a total of 2.6m (80%) responded, and of those 1.9m (59%) advised of changes to details. To put it another way, before the remediation process, the organisation had incorrect data on nearly 60% of its customers, and didn't know whether it did or didn't have correct data on another 20%. Of the total of 1.9m customers that advised of changes, 900,000 of those changes had to be performed manually.

Issues with this approach can be an often poor response rate (direct mailings will typically get a 8-10% response rate – the above 80% mentioned in the anecdote above was an anomaly due to there being a share handout to customers), input or scanning errors (again using the example above, there were 40,000 respondents whose forms had to be manually input because the scanners couldn't read the customer's writing), or poor address data simply means you may mail the wrong person.

39.6.4.2 Online

If there is an online portal that customers can access, there is an opportunity to persuade customers to check their own data. The data already exists in their online account, and persuading them to check it is correct may be merely a matter of asking the customer to tick a series of boxes before being allowed to continue. The advantage of asking the customer to remediate their own data is that they do know the accurate value. Customers will know how to spell their own name and will get their date of birth correct. Getting a customer to type their own name – especially if it is an easy name to misspell – is much better than any other way of collecting the data. Dates of birth are considerably trickier, especially if it is a pick from a drop down list – it is very easy to pick the wrong day when presented with a grid of 30 numbers.

Issues with this approach are data entry errors and data transcription errors, however mitigation strategies can include:

- Online customers can be asked to type data twice
- The use of address lookups on postcode
- The use of constrained entry criteria – i.e. a drop-down list for country of residence

Whether this approach can be utilised for an individual organisation will depend on the level of interaction expected from the customer. However, it is relatively easy to measure how many phone calls are taken on a daily/monthly basis, or how many website visits are received, and how many of these are unique customers. It is possible to calculate the degree of penetration that a phone or online based approach will achieve in the required timescale. For example, if 10% of customers contact the organisation each month then, even with repeats, a 9 month period will provide a high proportion of customers an opportunity to reconfirm their details. A decision can then be made to mail the remainder or contact them in some other way. This strategy particularly works when the interaction with the customer is performed on a yearly cycle – for example insurance companies where policies typically last 1 year.

39.6.4.3   Email

Email has the advantage that it potentially has one of the highest response rates (up to 25% for online surveys), and is also possibly the easiest and least invasive way to contact the customer. The disadvantage with email is that customers are understandably wary of any email that asks them to "confirm their details" as this kind of email is routinely used by scammers to harvest personal details for nefarious reasons.

39.6.4.4   Phone

A contact centre is an excellent source of remediated data. Depending on the industry customers may contact the organisation on a regular basis. An organisation with a yearly reset would normally expect around 5-10% of customers to ring the contact centre each month. In this case a pop-up confirmation can be designed so that the contact centre agent is prompted to confirm data every time a customer rings. This form of data confirmation can be totally hidden from the customer. The customer will think it is a security check, or part of confirming sensitive records or it can even be sold as "we will soon be using more of your customer data to confirm your security in order to make the access to your account more secure. As a result we will be confirming email addresses and phone numbers which may be used in forthcoming security questions." The customer doesn't need to know it is because you're trying to cleanse your data. Similar to the online approach, it may only take half a year to gain quality data on the majority of your customers. The data can be used to remediate existing data or to create a new "golden source" of data in a new database.

39.6.4.5   In Person

If you have customers who actually visit your offices or branches, a similar scenario can be used with the difference that the customer is standing in front of the agent and is clearly identifiable.

39.6.5   The government

The government (in the case of this book the UK Government) holds considerable information on those living in the country. This information is not generally accessible by organisations or the public, however – and especially in recent years in response to the increasing interest in genealogy – much data has been released that can be used to cleanse personal information held in information stores. One information source that has been available for a long time is, however, the electoral roll. There are two releases of the electoral roll, the full roll and the edited roll. Both are updated yearly. The full roll contains details of everyone eligible and registered to vote, the edited roll contains the same, less those who have chosen not to be on the edited version of the roll. The edited roll is available in full to anyone for a charge, and at present contains the details of 18 million UK adults. Historical rolls are also available going back until 2001. It is entirely possible to use the electoral roll to mass cleanse your data and to match names and addresses against known "good" data.

39.6.6 Third Parties

There are a number of external agencies who hold data and represent a viable alternative source for the organisation undertaking a data quality project. It should be noted that this area is changing very rapidly and at the time of writing is very much at the cutting edge of data management. At present there are four main paradigms.

- Clean, good data can be bought/sourced from a third party and then the organisation itself can cleanse its own information using this clean data.
- The external third party can be supplied with a copy of key fields (for example, customer name, social security or National Insurance number) can then populate other data such as address, email, etc, and then supply good data back to the organisation.
- The external third party can take a full copy of the customer data and then, using their own sources, plus data analysis, cleanse the data. This is effectively remediation-as-a-service (RaaS). The data can then be imported back into the organisation. Alternatively the organisation may establish an externally hosted data store that is managed by the third party to quality requirements and service level agreements (data management as a service – DMaaS).
- The organisation can utilise external data stores for key fields. This is a new service that has come on the market in recent years. Several providers host external clean stores of critical data – common examples are legal entity information and corporate hierarchical data. When looking to identify customer data the organisation looks to the external third party and pipes in clean data in a standard format. The external third party sells the information to multiple organisations, and also receives feedback from those vendors on errors, where corrections will then benefit everyone. Organisations that provide reference data solutions include Euroclear and Smartstream, Swiftref, and the Clarient entity hub.

In terms of third parties that are currently offering one or other of these services in the United Kingdom, the names and services are changing all the time. The Royal Mail offers services such as returns management service (the gone away index) – which can be used to update address when mail is returned. Other services offered by the same organisation include NCOA (National Change of Address); Update NCOA Alert, which can help with fraud (e.g. people applying for finance in the name of the person who used to live there); supply of the postcode address file (29m postal addresses, 1.8m postcodes); a bureau service to clean data, which can also update data with dates of birth, telephone numbers, or lifestyle details and NCOA suppress, which tells you when customers leave their addresses.

Other organisations can offer remediation as a service – i.e. the organisation will offer to cleanse your data for you, and most will also sell databases of valid data. They will also offer to perform a data audit to determine your current data quality. A short and non-exhaustive list is shown below.

Organisation	Website
CCR	http://www.ccr.co.uk/
Data360	http://www.data360.co.uk/
W8 Data	http://www.w8data.com/
UK changes	http://www.ukchanges.com/
Experian	http://www.edq.com
CNM	http://www.cnm.co.uk/
Data-8	http://www.data-8.co.uk/
Postcode Anywhere	http://www.postcodeanywhere.co.uk/

Of course, it is necessary for any prudent organisation to assess the capability of any third party and also the quality of the data that they hold, to consider the benefits that bringing in a third party will generate against the cost of doing so, and compare this approach with the other approaches described earlier in the chapter.

This process – best source analysis – is described in the next section.

39.7   Best Source Analysis

The next step after considering sources of data to remediate or replace poor quality data is to determine the best source of data. Note that this will not necessarily simply be the best in terms of "best quality", but will be a balance between a number of factors. Best source analysis is the process by which you analyse and ultimately choose the data that will be used to update your data. Factors to be considered will be the metrics of data quality, which I listed in a previous chapter. Specifically;

- Completeness
- Existence
- Accuracy
- Consistency
- Timely
- Appropriate
- Validity
- Uniformity
- Ease of use
- Presentation
- Uniqueness

In order to determine which source is best to update your existing (poor) data, it is necessary to gauge and weight the various options available so as to get the best fit for your organisation. A short list below holds indicators of quality which are worth considering if a full analysis of the potential replacement data is not possible:

- Who typed the data – customer, contact centre, customer complaints? Typed by customer (e.g. into a webform) is better than typed by staff (e.g. from a contact centre). Typed by staff from a paper document is likely to be better than typed by staff from a contact centre due to the time constraints. However equally staff in a contact centre can ask for clarification and customer handwriting is often illegible. Typed twice by customer (e.g. email in a web form) is better than typed once.
- How was it communicated – typed, over a telephone call, handwritten?
- Who formatted the data – what system does it reside in, who was the person who loaded it?

- What constraints existed at the time of input? Many old systems were limited to six digit dates (03/05/94) or a limited number of characters for each part of the address field.

Other factors that relate to the data will be:

- Cost – both in terms of cash cost for the data and resource costs to implement.
- Suitability – If the main problem with the data is lack of postcodes, data that is lacking in postcodes is (obviously!) not going to be the best source, even if the same data source is fully complete and accurate in respect of the other elements of the address.

39.7.1 Scoring Matrix

Each data source should be ranked based on the perceived quality of the data, the use to which it will be put (i.e. the gaps in the existing data), and other factors such as cost. Ranking each source using a matrix is a useful technique. To take an example mentioned above.

Characteristic	Score
Typed twice by customer	10
Typed once by customer	8
Typed by contact centre based on a typed form	6
Typed by contact centre based on a phone call	4
Typed by contact centre based on a typed form	2

This can then be incorporated into an overall matrix with weighting to establish a final score. The weighting will be different depending on the gaps in the current data and what the organisation is trying to accomplish. An example of a matrix of this nature is shown below

Data Source	Quality/ Implementation	Attribute	Weighting	Score
Source 1	Quality	Completeness	10	9
		Existence	10	9
		Accuracy	10	10
		Consistency	9	8
		Timely	2	6
		Appropriate	1	5
		Validity	1	7
		Uniformity	1	3
		Ease of Use	1	4
		Presentation	1	5
		Uniqueness	1	2
	Implementation	Ease of Use	10	5
		Timeliness	10	6
		Cost	10	8

This will naturally lead the organisation into a decision matrix on the lines of:

Data Element	Source	Weighted Score
Postcode	Source 1	89
	Source 2	74

It is then easy not only choose a source, and also to demonstrate the thinking and justification behind the choice of source. This approach also enables judgement to be made between competing sources.

Data Element	Source	Weighted Score
Postcode	Source 1	89
	Source 2	74
Name	Source 1	67
	Source 2	90
Title	Source 1	34
	Source 2	62

It is possible to gain an overall score for each source for every element of data, and the most cost-effective source of data utilised. The organisation is then aware of both the source data and its quality issues from the discovery work, and the source of the data that will replace it. In most cases these decisions will also naturally determine how the remediation will be completed. Creation of one million new records will almost certainly be performed by the IT department as a manual solution would be too time-consuming. Remediation of a small number of records can be done manually. If the data is being bought from third parties then there is clearly the possibility – subject to relevant regulations – to pay the third party to integrate the data as well.

39.8 Summary

In this chapter I have discussed the remediation of existing data. I have covered the options of replacement or remediation and the sources of data that can be used for cleansing. I have finally discussed best source analysis and how the decision on the replacement data can be made. This enables the reader and the organisation to make an informed decision on the means of data quality remediation.

This logically follows on to the cost benefit analysis, where the options created within remediation design for architecture, process and data are considered from a financial point of view.

SECTION 5.5 REMEDIATION PLANNING

CHAPTER 40 COST BENEFIT ANALYSIS

40.1 Structure

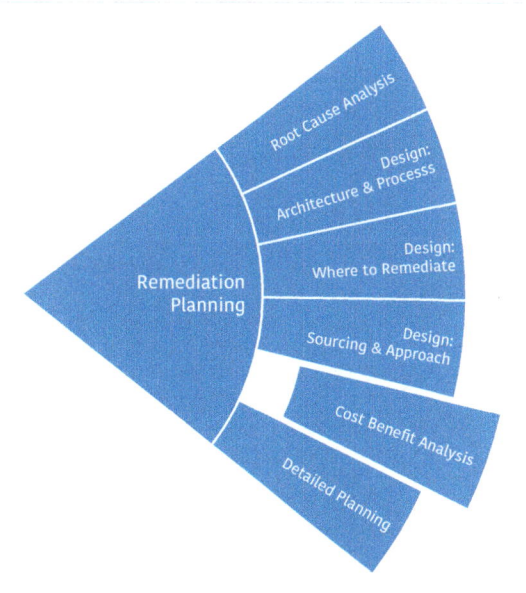

This stage of The Data Quality Blueprint includes the following phases:

1. Root Cause Analysis
2. Design for Architecture and Process
3. Data: Where to Remediate
4. Data: Sourcing Data
5. Cost Benefit Analysis
6. Detailed Planning

This chapter covers the fifth of these phases.

40.2 Overview

INPUTS
- All artefacts created or used by the project to date.
- Results from architecture discovery
- Results from data discovery
- Results from process discovery
- Results from root cause analysis

OUTPUTS
- Option costs
- Estimated benefits
- Option appraisal
- Option baskets
- Cost benefit analysis
- Updated business case

DEPENDENCIES
- Access to stakeholders

TASKS
- Option Costing
  - Input options from design process for architecture, data and process
  - For each option cost solution
  - Agree cost with key stakeholders
  - Document options costing
  - Upload to project repository
- Benefit valuation
  - For each option determine whether it will solve problem and to what degree
  - Assign benefits to each option (% of problem solved)
  - Agree benefit valuation with key stakeholders
  - Document benefits
  - Upload to project repository
- Option appraisal
  - For each option group the issues
  - Identify options to treat each root cause
  - Identify synergies where applicable
  - Identify dependencies where applicable
  - Analyse whether the identified options will create an effective solution
  - Identify transition states (if any)
  - Prepare estimation of cost for each option
  - Document costs and benefits (i.e. perform an option appraisal)
  - Agree option appraisal with key stakeholders
  - Upload to project repository
- Option baskets
  - Collate options into baskets
  - Calculate resulting financial impact
  - Draft Impact/effort grid
  - Identify quick wins
  - Create priorities for baskets
  - Create final draft list of work for remediation
  - Discuss with sponsor and key stakeholders
  - Update for feedback
  - Upload to project repository
- Review Business Case
  - Review business case in light of current information
  - Discuss any changes to the business case with key stakeholders
  - Obtain additional approvals if necessary
  - Document changes to business case
  - Obtain signoff
  - Upload to project repository
- Create task list
  - Create final task list for remediation

It has been repeatedly noted in this book that the remediation effort needs to pay for itself in terms of business value, and this point of the methodology is where it comes together. Cost benefit analysis is a critical part of the overall remediation planning. At this point all the discovery work is done, the difficulty of the overall effort is known, and underlying root causes have been identified. The potential options for remediation of architecture, process and data have been considered and a series of options created. The diagram below shows where this fits into the overall remediation planning stage.

Identify root causes (common themes that may contribute to many issues) → Determine poor quality cost of each root cause → Develop solution options (architecture, process, data) for each root cause → Choose basket of options and finalise business case → Generate remediation task list and remediation plan

In this chapter it is all about numbers. The cost benefit analysis puts numbers to the effort and effectiveness of data quality remediation so that the organisation can decide what is in its best interests to remediate. This then follows through to the next chapter which covers the detailed planning of that remediation.

40.3 Recap from the Root Cause Analysis.

The starting point for the cost benefit analysis is the work performed in the root cause analysis. Here I will continue using the example developed in the preceding chapter, looking at five root causes and three data quality issues. These are shown in the table below.

	Issue 1	Issue 2	Issue 3	Total
Root Cause 1	£600,000			£600,000
Root Cause 2	£240,000			£240,000
Root Cause 3	£160,000	£3,000,000	1,080,000	£4,240,000
Root Cause 4				£2,400,000
Root Cause 5				£640,000

40.4 Step 1: Option Costing

The first stage in the cost benefit analysis is option costing. For each of the proposed solutions for the issues identified in the discovery phase, and the options identified in the remediation design phase, it is necessary to define the cost of the work. This can be equally well defined when creating the remediation design, however it makes sense to perform this task here as the remediation design will from necessity be fragmented across architecture, process and data, whereas the cost benefit analysis collates these all together and addresses them as a unit.

Costing can include licence costs for any required software, costs for the data itself if being provided by a third party, potential costs to the third party for the effort of cleansing, personnel costs, lost production costs, potential consultancy costs, and so on. In short, everything needed to build up a holistic view of the cost of the remediation. For the example we are using, such an analysis may look like the below.

Root Cause	Solution	Cost
Root Cause 1	Solution 1	100,000
	Solution 2	200,000
	Solution 3	150,000
	Solution 4	400,000
Root Cause 2	Solution 1	130,000
	Solution 2	300,000

40.5 Step 2: Benefit Valuation

The organisation would not necessarily be expected to try and address every root cause in full, as there will be a form of diminishing returns as each successive work package offers less and less in terms of return. It is therefore necessary for the project to decide to what extent each solution is a viable way of addressing each problem.

Root Cause	Cost	Solution	Cost	% of Cause remediated	Benefit
Root Cause 1	£600,000	Solution 1	100,000	100%	£600,000
		Solution 2	200,000	90%	£540,000
		Solution 3	150,000	50%	£300,000
		Solution 4	400,000	100%	£600,000
Root Cause 2	£240,000	Solution 1	130,000	50%	£120,000
		Solution 2	300,000	100%	£240,000

40.6 Step 3: Option Appraisal & Assessment

40.6.1 Bringing it together

The analysis can now be concluded with a valuation of each cause and remediation pair, and a calculation of the net effect of each. An example is shown below.

Root Cause	Cost	Solution	Cost	Benefit	Net
Root Cause 1	£600,000	Solution 1	100,000	£600,000	£500,000
		Solution 2	200,000	£540,000	£340,000
		Solution 3	150,000	£300,000	£150,000
		Solution 4	400,000	£600,000	£200,000
Root Cause 2	£240,000	Solution 1	130,000	£120,000	-£10,000
		Solution 2	300,000	£240,000	-£60,000

With the creation of the above table we can now see how the work to date is starting to identify the most cost-effective solutions to data quality problems. The particular example above would indicate that the idea of remediating Root Cause 2 at all is distinctly dubious, and possibly the organisation either needs to look again at solutions (to find a super-low-cost one) or just accept that Root Cause 2 will not be remediated.

An additional objective of this exercise is to identify linked solutions, where either solving one issue will solve another (synergies between solutions) or solving one cause will make another issue worse. The practitioner can now collate issues, causes and results. This approach enables the individual cause-effect pairs to be determined and individually assessed for effectiveness if remediation of the actual root cause is deemed too expensive or time-consuming. This analysis will also identify where the same cause is common to a number of problems. Can the organisation solve many issues with one bit of effort, or, whilst solving one issue, would a small extra bit of effort mean three more can also be addressed?

40.6.2   Step 4: Effort/Effect map

At initial planning a lot of unknowns were present in the data quality project. As a result of these unknowns there would have been much in the way of assumptions and guesswork in the business case and the time and resource estimates. Now the practitioner can revisit those estimates and validate those assumptions, to ensure that the project is still viable and will still give a positive business value. In all likelihood, because of the additional information that has surfaced over the period of the discovery phase, the effects of data quality improvement will be higher than originally estimated. With the new information, the practitioner can start to rank the individual data quality remediation tasks in terms of their profitability. For each cause effect pair the organisation needs to determine:

- Effort required – this will be in terms of man days and cost
- Business effect – in currency.

This enables an effort/effect map to be created, an example being shown below.

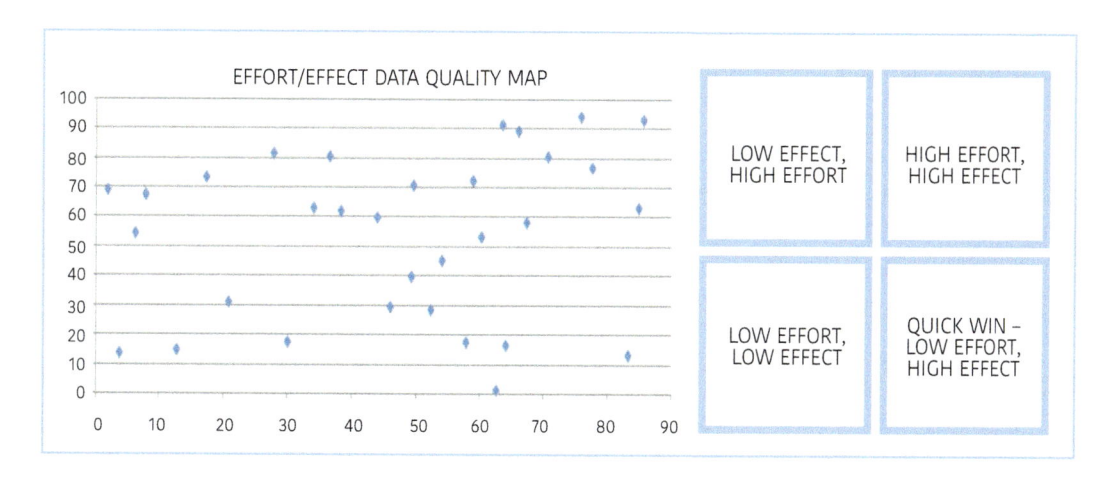

Now it is possible to divide problems into "quick wins" where a minor and simple change will make a noticeable difference, through to difficult issues where many or difficult changes will need to be made to provide a solution. This enables the formulation of an overall plan.

High effect, low effort	Quick wins. Implemented quickly to give a rapid measurable effect on the data. These are definitely ones to put in the plan first.
High effort, high effect	The two central categories should be the next set of tasks after the quick wins. At any point where the effect equals or exceeds the effort then the task is being rewarded. However high effort options may require additional analysis and approval.
Low effort, low effect	
High effort, low effect	This are definitely things to park until you've either run out of things to do or a better way of approaching them presents itself

To be brutal about it, anything that falls above a 45 degree line in the graph above should absolutely not be attempted unless it brings some other form of benefit, for example strategic enablement or the ability to subsequently perform higher value work.

40.7 Step 4: Baskets of Options

Much as it would be tempting to simply continue the project until the last element of effort returns exactly the same amount of reward, unfortunately organisations do not work like that and there will be dependencies amongst the individual cause, effect and remediation groups. The practitioner needs to divide the remediation problems and solutions into logical groups.

These may be groups that all together support a single goal. It may also be true that one high value remediation work package cannot proceed until several lower value (or negative) work packages have been completed. It is likely that some work will need to be performed not because the data is causing issues in a current process, but because it will hinder, or even prevent, a future planned process.

These considerations may be grouped by area of the organisation (e.g. source data), by department (e.g. finance), or by ease of remediation, and may contain a mixture of short and long term solutions.

An example would be when the organisation wishes to use analytics in the future and feels that cleaning its data is a pre-requisite to the future initiative. Another good reason is that if a lot of work is to be performed then it makes sense to do it all "whilst the hood is up", even if the business case is marginal. The organisation can then design a range of option baskets, potentially broken down by department or system to decide what the final remediation work will include.

The organisation can now complete the cost benefit analysis. This exercise considers the data requirements of the business, determines which data quality initiatives are necessary to implement, and in what order, to most effectively and efficiently improve the data quality of the enterprise.

	Existing Data	Process	Architecture	Net Value
Option 1	Do Nothing	Do Nothing	Do Nothing	0m
Option 2	Cleanse all critical customer data in system 1	Remediate data capture Processes	Collapse silos	2.4m
Option 3	Cleanse all critical customer data in system 1&2	Remediate data capture and transport processes	Migrate data from legacy system hence removing feeds	3.0m
Option 4	Cleanse all critical customer data in system 1-3	Remediate data capture, transport and reporting	Establish reference data architecture	3.3m
Option 5	Cleanse all critical customer data in system 1-4	Remediate all processes		3.5m
Option 6	Cleanse all critical customer data in system 1-5	Remediate all processes		4.0m

This gives the executive a clear view of the business case for the remediation, the options available, and importantly the numbers are backed by analysis which can be used to demonstrate the rigour of the process undertaken.

40.8   Step 5: Reviewing the Business Case

Armed with the above, the executive and the practitioner can go back to the business case and have a long hard look at the assumptions. The question to be asked is whether the project is still viable. At this point the most likely outcome is that the project will divide into:

- Quick wins – do these anyway.
- Larger, major effort elements (like architecture remediation that will have effects across the business in multiple ways) – will probably need separate business cases and possibly separate projects.
- Medium effort, medium-to-high effect elements that could go either way.
- Medium-to-high effort, but low effect items that will be placed out of scope.

It is inevitable that the business cases will have to be rewritten with the new information. This however should not be a major task as all the information is in place as a result of prior work. It is also critical to obtain a final signoff from the executive on the plan and the amended business case before the remediation work starts in earnest.

40.9 Step 6: Building the task list and deciding on the final plan

The organisation can now create the task list for the remediation stage of the project. This can contain an individual costing for each of the remediation tasks and the associated benefit. This enables a clear prioritisation of the tasks to be performed. The organisation can now move onto the final detailed plan.

The next stage is to take this list and group it into logical blocks to further improve the overall efficiency. For example, it there may be interdependencies so one task must be completed before another. It may make sense to remediate one issue first if it has a particularly time-critical business benefit (for example, regulatory compliance).

40.10 Summary

Within this chapter I have discussed the critical element of cost-benefit analysis. I have discussed how the organisation can cost the remediation effort, and taken the reader through the step by step process to do this. This enables the reader to understand the cost-benefit analysis process, and to actively contribute to it in their own organisation.

I have also shown how value can be assigned to individual tasks, and how those tasks can be brought together into baskets of options to present to the executive for signoff.

The next chapter will cover the preparation of the detailed remediation plan before moving on to the remediation work itself.

SECTION 5.5 REMEDIATION PLANNING

CHAPTER 41 DETAILED PLANNING

41.1 Structure

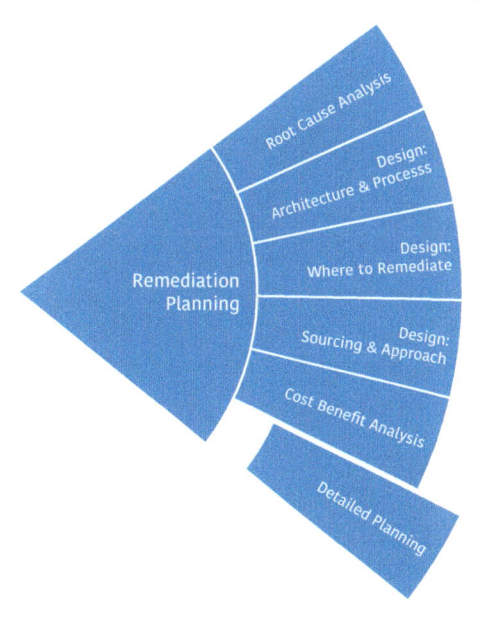

This stage of The Data Quality Blueprint includes the following phases:

1. Root Cause Analysis
2. Design for Architecture and Process
3. Data: Where to Remediate
4. Data: Sourcing Data
5. Cost Benefit Analysis
6. Detailed Planning

This chapter covers the last of these phases.

41.2 Overview

INPUTS	TASKS

• All artefacts created or utilised by the project to date.
• Results from architecture discovery
• Results from data discovery
• Results from process discovery
• Results from root cause analysis
• Results from cost benefit analysis
• Initial project plan
	• Roadmap
	  – Create high level roadmap for remediation stage
	  – Validate with team members and subject matter experts
	  – Validate with business and IT owners
	  – Upload to project repository
	• Detailed planning
	  – From initial planning and remediation roadmap create draft detailed plan
	  – Identify dependencies (external and internal)
	  – List document and physical deliverables and agree with stakeholders
	  – Update RAID log
	  – Socialise proposed remediation plan with business users
	  – Agree resources with business users (e.g. subject matter experts)
	  – Agree resources with IT (e.g. environments, databases)
	  – Agree dependencies with providers
	  – Resource level plan
	  – Finalise detailed plan for remediation
	  – Discuss with sponsor and key stakeholders
	  – Update for feedback
	  – Upload to project repository

OUTPUTS	
• Updated remediation task list • Dependencies • Updated RAID log • Remediation plan • Remediation priorities • Detailed plan to the end of the project	
DEPENDENCIES	
• Access to stakeholders	

As previously discussed, The Data Quality Blueprint recommends three planning phases. One at initiation, another before the start of the main project, and a third after the discovery work has been completed, immediately before the remediation. This chapter covers the last of these.

Initiation Planning
Detail for initiation, high level for the rest of the project

Project Planning
Detail up until the end of Remediation Planning, high level for Remediation

Remediation Planning
Detail for the whole remaining project (i.e. remediation) - finalisation of project plan

At the beginning of the project, assumptions are made in respect of timescales and resources, on necessarily limited information. This planning phase creates the initial project plan. The project plan cannot be fully completed until after the discovery phase, the assessment of root causes, and the final decision as to what will be remediated. Now we take this to greater detail and plan the individual tasks to remediate the organisation.

Identify root causes (common themes that may contribute to many issues) → Determine poor quality cost of each root cause → Develop solution options (architecture, process, data) for each root cause → Choose basket of options and finalise business case → Generate remediation task list and remediation plan

The diagram above shows how this fits into the overall remediation planning stage. Discussions here will focus on the questions the plan needs to answer, the creation of a roadmap, the allocation of responsibility and finally the detail of the planning.

41.3   Questions that the plan needs to answer

The project plan can now give a task by task description for the rest of the project. This includes how remediation will occur, and the timeline for doing so. This plan must answer a number of questions:

- What data is required to be remediated and why?
- What data items are a prerequisite for remediating other data items? For example remediating the postcode allows the remediation of the whole address to be performed much faster.
- The method of remediation. Data replacement, remediation of current data, or leave as-is?
- Who will perform the remediation? Will it be in-house, or an external agency? Or will it be in-house using data from an external agency?
- How will architectural issues affect the overall remediation? If there has been a decision to – for example – merge siloed data how will this be done, and in what sequence?
- What is the timescale and what are the resources needed?

The plan must be at a level of detail that enables each part of the project, and each resource on the project, to be in no doubt what their responsibilities are, what will be occurring and when.

41.4   Step 1: Roadmap

The detailed remediation plan should follow the same process as the original project plan. Namely roadmap, work breakdown structure, task list, and then detailed plan. The inputs for this process are the existing plan and related artefacts, the output from the discovery and remediation planning stages so far, and in fact almost everything created by the project to date.

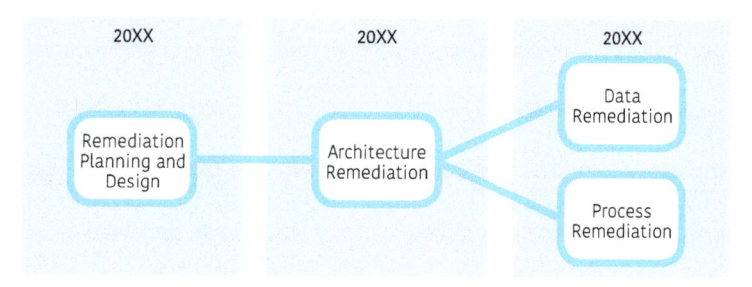

20XX: Remediation Planning and Design → 20XX: Architecture Remediation → 20XX: Data Remediation / Process Remediation

Step 1 to create the final plan is the roadmap. A roadmap will detail what is going to occur, when, and in what order. It is a precursor to the final remediation project plan. At a high level, this may well look as simple as the above – which could be created based on the original project plan.

This roadmap can be used at a high level to guide the overall project timescale and serve as a basis for the detail. The next stage is the building out of the plan into successive levels of detail where first the high level tasks are created and then greater detail to the level of individual tasks. For example, "remediate customer occupation" will require new data to be sourced, existing data to be replaced, and the data quality to be measured before and after the process, and so on.

41.5 Step 2: Task List

The detailed task list includes all the tasks required in the project, together with who is doing them and – at a high level – how it will be done. This list is supplied by the decisions taken at the end of the cost benefit analysis. An example of a task list can be seen below.

No	Root Cause No	Affecting Data Issues No	Nature of remediation	Source of new data	Automatic or manual	Responsibility
			Remediate	Royal Mail	A	IT
			Replace		A	Business
			Delete	n/a	M	

The task list is a clear record of everything that needs to be achieved in the project. It can be used as a progress marker, and provides a statement of remaining scope. All of these items will be invaluable as an input into the final stage, which is the creation of the detailed project plan itself. If an agile approach is being used this task list can be compared to the product backlog.

Example
Another (insurance) company had a large number of claims where, in 70,000 cases, the cause of the claim had not been filled in by the claims handler (or, more accurately had been filled in with default values). In most cases it was actually possible to fill in this field (which was critical for pricing purposes) from other details available within the claim documentation – often the comments field on the same database (if the comment field stated; "house fire after lightning strike" hence cause could be filled in as "lightning").

However, there was no way of doing this automatically. This would be manual search and remediate, as a human being would have to read the comments fields and judge whether they gave enough information to populate the cause of claim.

41.6 Step 3: Detailed Planning

After the task list has been created it is possible to update the overall project plan with details of exactly what is going to be achieved and when. Specifically, the start and end date of each task, what needs to be completed before this task can start (its predecessors), and what other tasks rely on it (its successors). It should also include resourcing – who will perform each task. Whether any particular project planning tool is used is not relevant. The requirement is for a plan of the tasks within the project and how they interact, how long they will take, and what needs to occur before they can start. The latter feeds the dependencies for the final plan. In addition to the planning elements above, it is necessary to add some other items. This will include:

- Review and signoff personnel – who is going to certify that the remediation has been done correctly? What are the success criteria?
- How will the project ensure that the remediated data is actually used by the business?
- How will the project prove that the business case has been met?
- How will the project incorporate checkpoints to govern progress?

An example of a detail portion of a project plan is shown below. You will note that this is down to the detail of tasks only lasting a few hours. This, if anything, is too much detail, as creation of a plan at this level of detail will be a massive endeavour. However, in this context it serves to identify the complexity of effort that will be necessary to remediate one element of data.

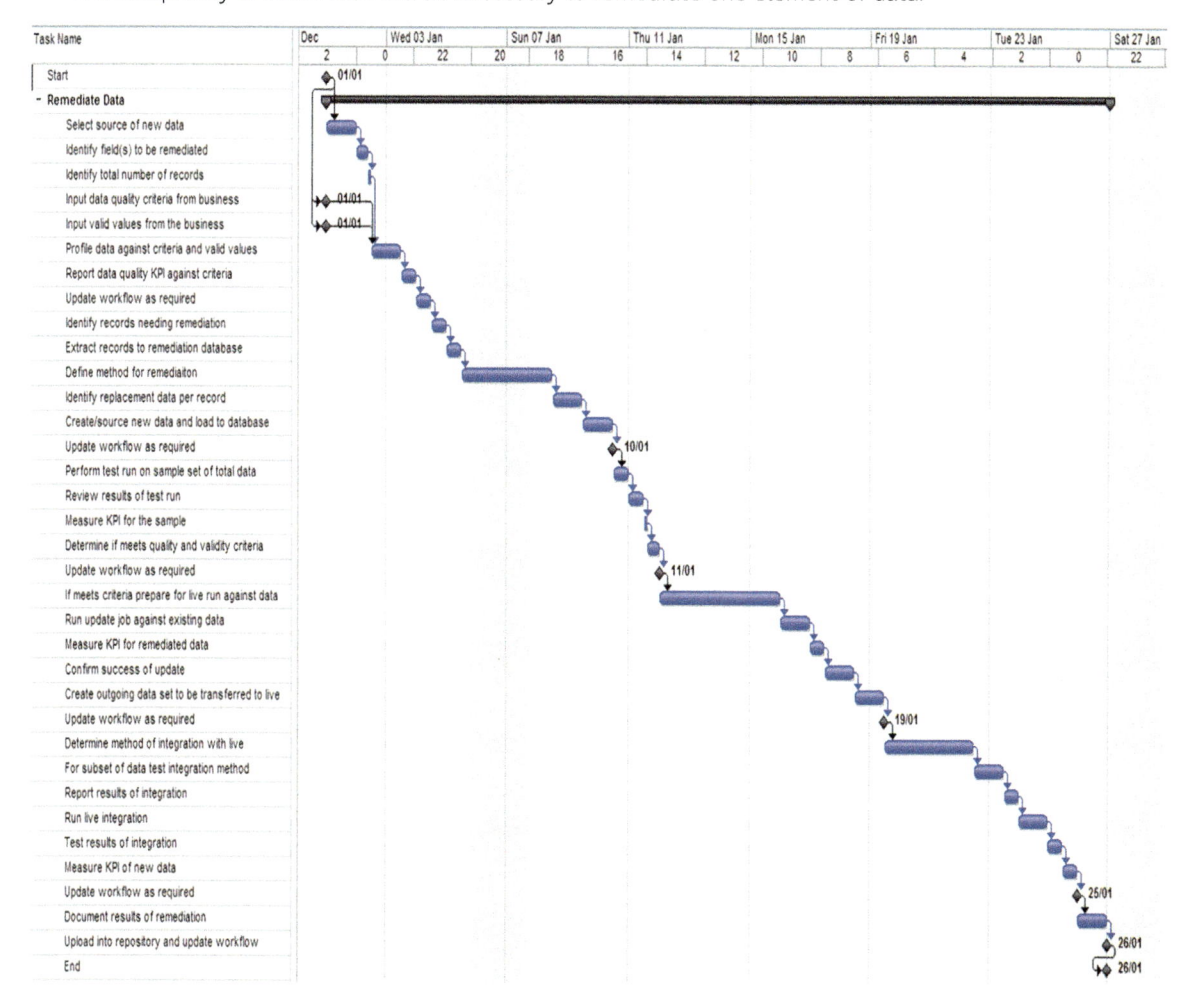

41.7   Step 4: Responsibility and Resourcing

It is often assumed that the actual doing of the remediation will fall into the remit of the IT department. This may be the case for some elements of the remediation, but not always. Whilst some updates – the bulk update of fields in a database for example – will have to be performed by IT, other tasks are best performed elsewhere. For example, customer information updates could be performed by a dedicated team in the contact centre. This can be usefully done where information from a customer is required to update details. For example, for remediation of customers where the organisation holds the telephone number but not address, calling the customer is probably the easiest and most direct method of proving good data. Equally some critical or sensitive updates should be performed by the business unit (see example).

Anecdote

One organisation had a backlog of around 40,000 death registrations – i.e. deaths notified but not verified, and hence not yet flagged as deceased. Hence many of their supposedly active customers were actually deceased. This was causing headaches all over the organisation, in customer service and customer complaints as angry relatives phoned in, there were issues with accounts being locked as no-one had used them for a long time, etc, etc.

However, given the sensitivity of the issue, it was not possible to bulk update with death flags. There really was no alternative than working through the backlog. This resulted in the death registrations department growing by a factor of ten, and dedicated training being performed to induct new staff to the point where they could deal with the complex probate and death registration process.

41.8   Step 5: Dependencies & Deliverables

In the same way as the cost benefit analysis will need to revalidate the initial business case, the detailed remediation planning will need to revalidate the initial project plan, including the dependencies and deliverables. This will include both those external to the project (for example, access to data) and also those internal, as some remediation will depend on other remediation being in place first. Architectural issues may have to be resolved first, to avoid duplicated work. There may also be some clear priorities to either data or process remediation. For example, if remediating address information and using external agency information to do so, it would make sense to make the postcode field as perfect as possible before applying the external data.

41.9   Summary

In this chapter I have looked at the detail of the remediation planning. This takes the original project plan, and revalidates it given the additional information now available. This now enables the project manager or data quality practitioner to create a project plan that will take the project through the next stage and to the end of embedding. The project now knows what it is going to do, and how. It might appear odd that this only occurs at this stage, and many hundreds of pages into the overall methodology. However in The Data Quality Blueprint the methodology looks at the problem as a whole, performs research on the interlinking of business problems and how they affect quality, and hence enables a solution that is efficient, effective, and, most importantly, doesn't have to be done again.

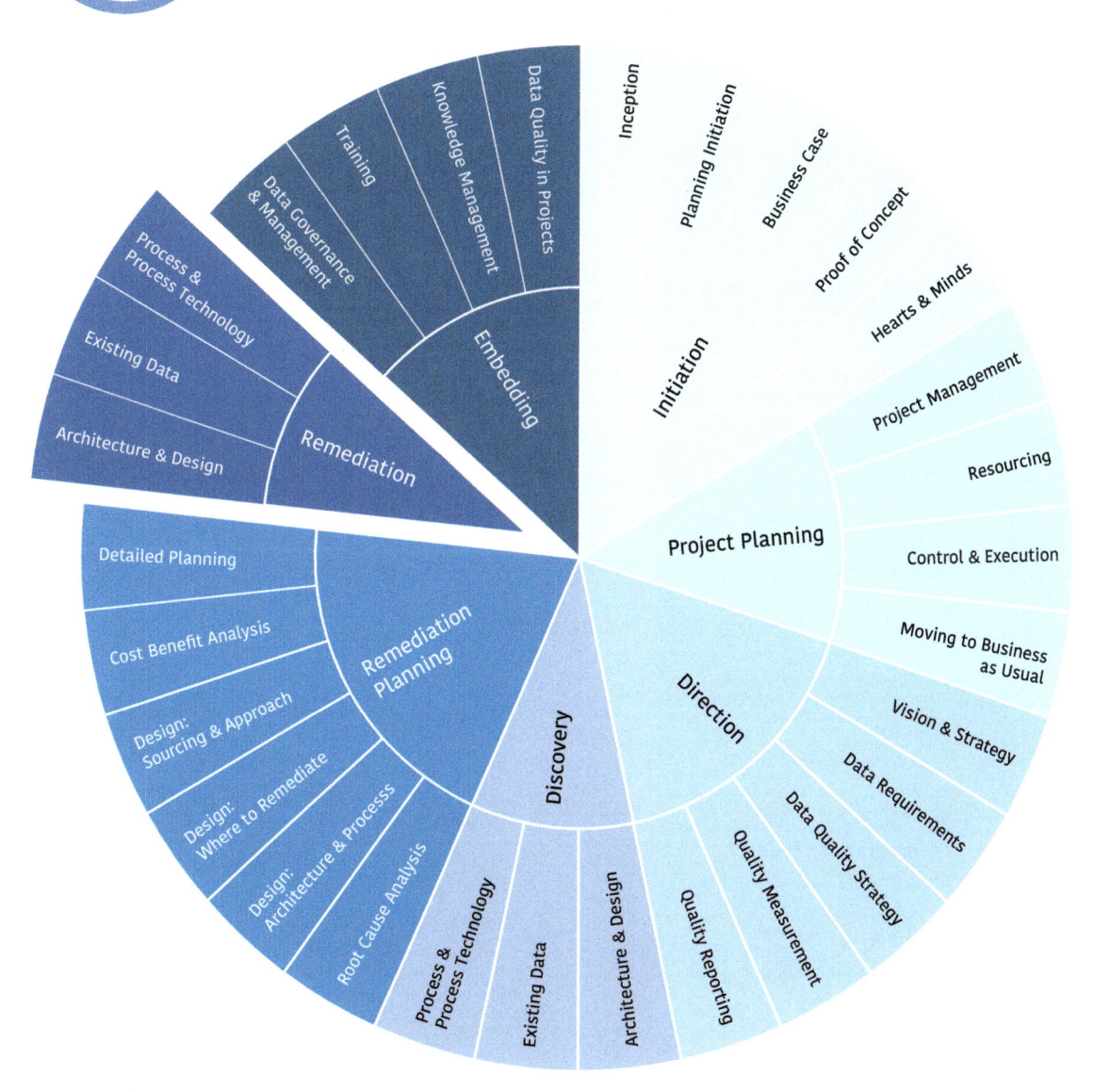

SECTION 5.6 REMEDIATION

Section 5.6: Index

CHAPTER 42: Section Overview — 451

CHAPTER 43: Remediation: Architecture & Design — 453
- 43.1 Structure — 453
- 43.2 Overview — 454
- 43.3 Where to start — 455
- 43.4 How to approach Architectural Change — 456
- 43.5 Architectural Change Frameworks — 460
- 43.6 Example of Architectural Change — 463
- 43.7 Summary — 464

CHAPTER 44: Remediation: Existing Data — 465
- 44.1 Structure — 465
- 44.2 Overview — 466
- 44.3 Types of Remediation — 468
- 44.4 Manual Remediation (BAU) — 468
- 44.5 Manual Remediation (dedicated back office) — 469
- 44.6 Remediation by or with IT (Bulk update) — 470
- 44.7 Remediation by use of Specialist Remediation Toolsets — 475
- 44.8 Other Approaches — 475
- 44.9 Workflow — 476
- 44.10 Where do we stop? — 477
- 44.11 Summary — 477

CHAPTER 45: Remediation: Process and Process Technology — 479
- 45.1 Structure — 479
- 45.2 Overview — 480
- 45.3 Scope — 481
- 45.4 Approach — 482
- 45.5 Considerations for Process Change — 483
- 45.6 Implementation — 487
- 45.7 Testing — 488
- 45.8 Workflow — 489
- 45.9 Where do we stop? — 489
- 45.10 Further reading — 490
- 45.11 Summary — 490

SECTION 5.6 REMEDIATION

CHAPTER 42 SECTION OVERVIEW

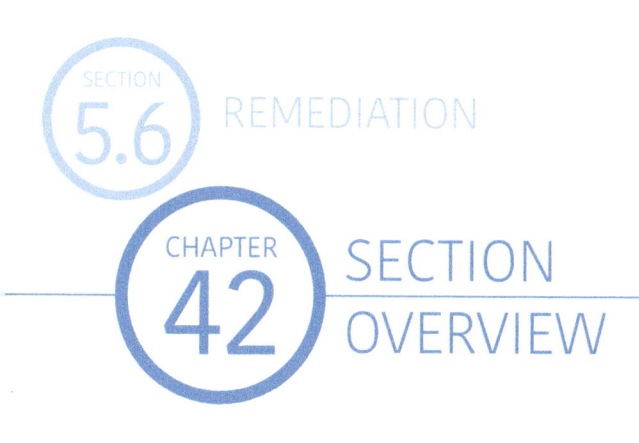

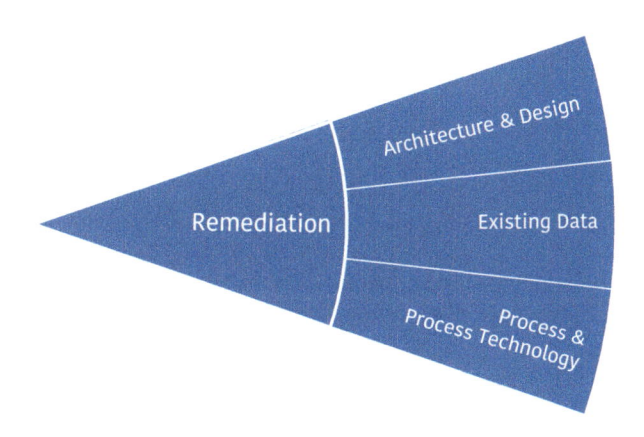

In contrast to many books on the subject, the actual remediation of data quality issues forms a relatively small part of this book. The reason is that much of the difficult work has already been completed, and with all preparation done the actual work is much easier. To use an analogy, replacing an individual component within a car engine may not take much time in comparison to the overall process, which will involve fault-finding, discovery of the actual issue, isolating and removing the faulty component, sourcing a new component, and then – after replacement – trying to make sure that the issue does not reoccur (which may of course involve driver education).

So it is with data quality. It is possible to write an entire book on this part of the data quality journey, but that is not the intention here. Here we cover a wider approach at a higher level. The contents of this section are therefore a relatively broad brush description of the remediation process, looking at approaches to remediation and the process flows of changing architecture, data and process from bad to good. I have not, in this section, looked to step through each of the project tasks (shown in the graphic and at the beginning of each section) in detail, as we have to an extent already discussed these earlier in the book. Here I will cover questions and decisions that the project needs to consider on the remediation journey.

The Data Quality Blueprint

Architecture and Design	Process	Data
Define Methodology	Finalise Future Process	Use task list to finalise appeoach
Finalise solutions	Evaluate Options & Test	Identify good data
Migration Planning	Plan Implementation	Plan Implementation
Implementation Governance	Implement POC	Implement remediation
Architecture Change Management	Roll out, review and report	Re-integrate data

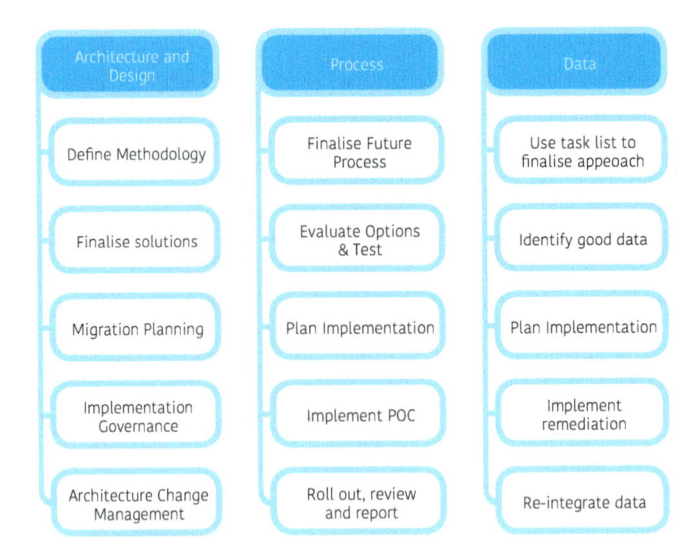

The approaches for architecture & design, process and data are slightly different.

- For data the work is to amend existing data, either utilising common sense or, where this is not possible, new, good data to replace or remediate the current data set. This new data has to be sourced from another location. As a result the effectiveness of the solution is dependent, partly, on the new data and the effectiveness of its integration.
- For process, the work is largely internal. It is amending the existing process to improve the quality of the data output.
- For architecture, the work can be complex, as it involves changing the way in which the organisation is structured, to remove those elements which impede the correct flow of information.

As a result, the approaches as described within the following chapters differ. However all are looking to move the organisation from an inadequate current state to a desired end state which will support the organisation's requirements for high quality information.

SECTION 5.6 REMEDIATION

CHAPTER 43: REMEDIATION: ARCHITECTURE & DESIGN

43.1 Structure

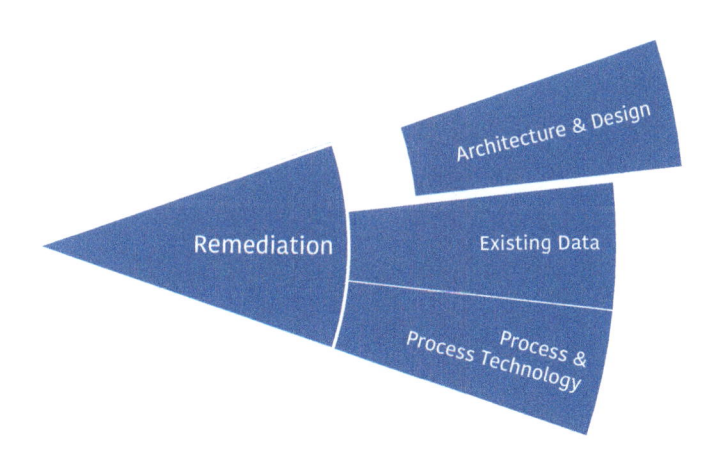

This stage of The Data Quality Blueprint includes the following phases:

1. Architecture & Design
2. Data
3. Process and Process Technology

This section of the book will step through each of these areas in detail looking at how remediation can be approached. This chapter covers the first of these phases.

43.2 Overview

INPUTS
■ All artefacts created or utilised by the project to date. ■ Current as-is architecture diagrams and artefacts ■ Results from architecture discovery

OUTPUTS
■ Remediated architecture ■ Workflow status reports

DEPENDENCIES
■ Workflow management tool ■ Architecture change skills and methodology ■ Executive buy-in ■ Access to stakeholders

TASKS

■ Architecture-specific final planning
  – Discuss and define methodology in consultation with key sponsor
  – Document process issues changed or altered by the changes to architecture
  – Document data issues changed or altered by the changes to architecture
  – Define architectural issues to be addressed
  – Define architecture changes using the remediation plan for architecture
  – Define transition states from remediation plan
  – Refine and complete implementation plan
  – Agree with sponsor and key stakeholders
  – Upload to project repository
■ Start transition #1
  – Start governance
  – Measure KPI
  – Update architecture (note in reality all tasks below will interact and whilst can be considered separately the implementation will need to be carefully planned and orchestrated between them)
    ■ Update business architecture
    ■ Update process architecture
    ■ Update data architecture
    ■ Update application architecture
    ■ Update infrastructure architecture
  – Ratify that changes meet plan including KPI
  – Document lessons learned
  – Update implementation plan for next transition based on lessons learned
  – Agree with key sponsors and obtain decision to proceed to next transition
■ Start Transition #2
  – Start governance
  – Measure KPI
  – Update architecture (note in reality all tasks below will interact and whilst can be considered separately the implementation will need to be carefully planned and orchestrated between them)
    ■ Update business architecture
    ■ Update process architecture
    ■ Update data architecture
    ■ Update application architecture
    ■ Update infrastructure architecture
  – Ratify that changes meet plan including KPI
  – Document lessons learned
  – Update implementation plan for next transition based on lessons learned
  – Agree with key sponsors and obtain decision to proceed to

>   next transition
>   - Start final transition
>   - Start governance
>   - Measure KPI
>   - Update architecture (note in reality all tasks below will interact and whilst can be considered separately the implementation will need to be carefully planned and orchestrated between them)
>   - Update business architecture
>   - Update process architecture
>   - Update data architecture
>   - Update application architecture
>   - Update infrastructure architecture
>   - Ratify that changes meet plan including KPI
>   - Document lessons learned and changes to architecture
>   - Agree with key sponsors and obtain signoff
>   - Complete architecture remediation

Entire methodologies have been written about how to change architecture within an organisation, and the common theme is that it requires care. Architecture is baked in to the structure of the organisation on all levels. To use an analogy of a house, it is relatively easy to move the furniture around, but really quite hard to move rooms around.

To continue the analogy, the project may find that fundamental to solving data quality problems within the organisation is that rooms are in the wrong place. Hence it may on occasion be better to solve this root cause rather than trying to patch up a fundamentally broken structure. In this chapter I will look at where to start in the process of addressing architecture remediation. I will introduce some of the more well-known architecture change frameworks and describe one in detail. I will then take an example and demonstrate how the change methodology (in this case TOGAF) can be applied to a large architectural change.

As in other parts of the book, wholesale architectural change is a subject in itself and I would suggest that this is not attempted by inexperienced individuals. This is particularly the case with architecture, and this chapter is very high level and broad brush. The inherent complexity in architectural change is one of the reasons why I advocate the presence of data, process and enterprise architects within the project team.

43.3   Where to start

An organisation should ideally consider the effect that architecture is going to have on the quality of its data, and act to mitigate this problem if one exists. Fundamentally architectural remediation requires a rethink of the way the organisation fits together, as remediation of one element of the architecture (for example, data architecture) is likely to have a knock-on effect on the business, technology and application architectures. However, it is still better to rectify "The Wrong Architecture" than to try and solve an unsolvable problem.

A classic example is multiple sources of data in the organisation. There is no point remediating dozens of sets of customer data individually. Not only will this take excessive time, but by comparing data sets a full, good data set may emerge. Alternatively, it may be necessary to think about implementing a "golden source" solution, where the disparate data stores are replaced by one source to which all the others refer. In a case like this, it would make sense to deal with the architectural issues before starting any more direct remediation activities.

However, due to the complexity in architectural change, the organisation may decide that solving the architecture problem is not for the current project and that instead it should concentrate on the easy wins, or rectifying the existing data, rather than trying to "boil the ocean". This decision will be covered in the detailed cost-benefit analysis. In the case of this book, the critical consideration is how the architecture is affecting the quality of the information, not how perfect (or otherwise) the architecture may be.

43.4 How to approach Architectural Change

43.4.1 Validation of solution

The original solution first needs to be validated. Before any architectural change occurs, an even more detailed assessment needs to be made of the as-is state, and how the movement to the target state will positively impact the organisation. This validation will cover all the elements of architecture affected, business and business process, data, applications and infrastructure.

This detailed assessment is vital. It is perfectly possible for a solution to look very plausible from a high level, but only when being planned in detail does information appear that will change the effort involved. The project needs to ensure that the high level view is supported by the low level facts.

43.4.2 Define objectives

The implementation needs to clearly define its objectives. What is it trying to achieve? How will it be achieved? Importantly, how will it be measured? SMART (Specific, Measurable, Achievable, Relevant, Timely) objectives have been introduced earlier in the book, and the same applies as the smaller scale of an individual implementation. An example of an objective may be:

To replace the current 100 feeds into the finance department with 5 feeds, within six months from project start. This is in order to simplify the current complex manual integration required within the finance department and reduce the number of days required for the process from the current 10 to 2, and with significantly better quality output.

This objective clearly states what will occur, why it is occurring, and how it will be measured (number of feeds, and the reduction in number of days of effort from the finance department).

43.4.3 Transition states

The initiation stage or the discovery stage has defined the current state architecture. The remediation planning stage, described earlier, will have identified which of these issues need to be addressed, and defined the final architectural design. It also may or may not have identified transition states that the architecture will pass through on the way to the final design. If not then this will need to be performed here.

Transition states are intermediate states that facilitate the transposition of the organisation from one architectural state to another. Performing architectural change in this manner is less risky

Chapter 43: Remediation: Architecture & Design

than making a "big bang" change from one state to the next. The analogy of architectural change being akin to moving the rooms of a house around has been previously used, and in some cases the foundations of the new extension have to be put in place before work can continue to build new rooms. There will be a number of sequences that could occur, and the selection of the optimal sequence is the not-inconsiderable task of the enterprise architect.

An example of MDM transition states might be as below. The initial state is separate data stores. The next stage is one department migrates its customer data onto the MDM solution, and retains its own data store for specialist data. Then the next department does the same, and finally the third.

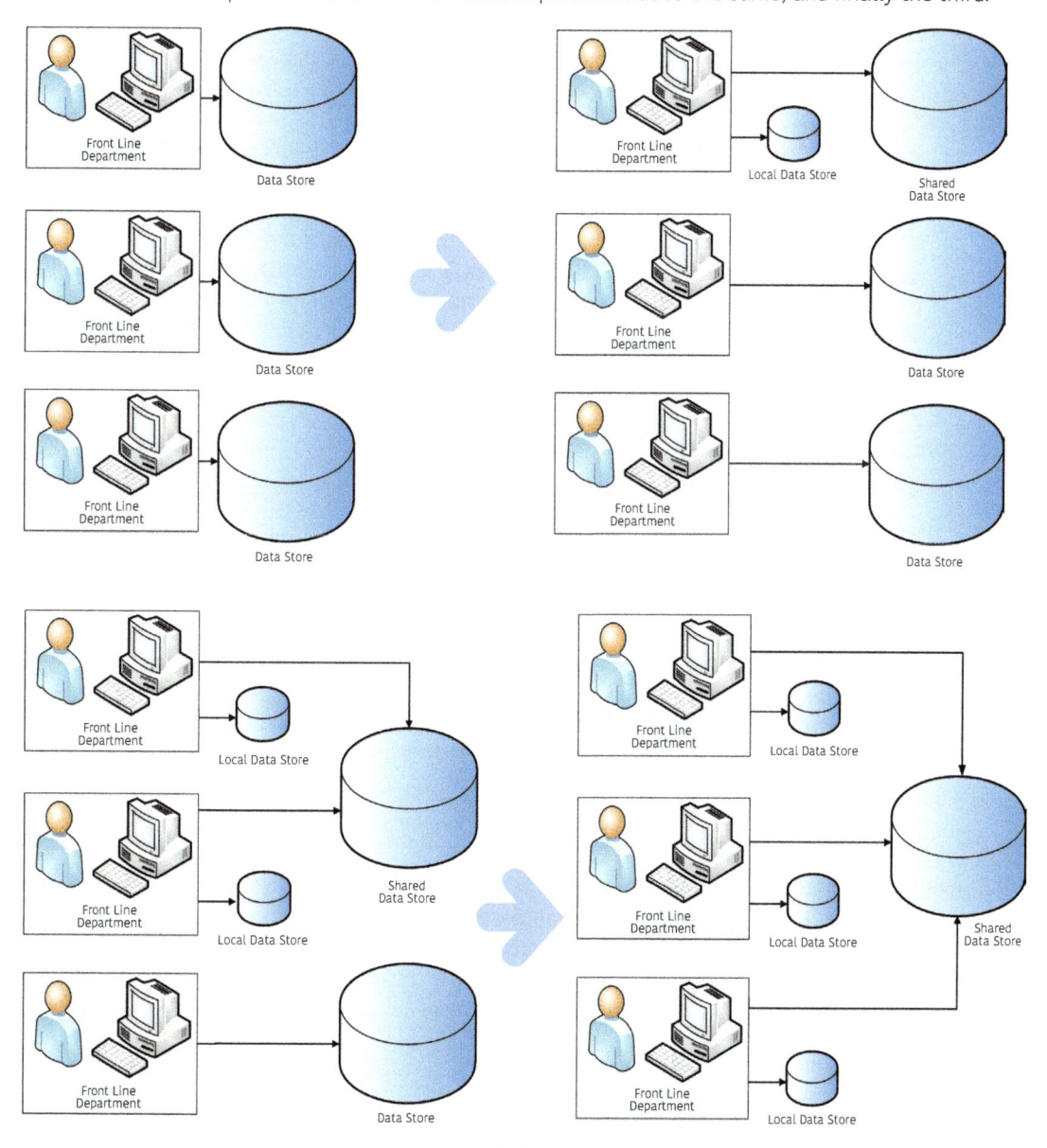

Another example is the replacement of individual accounts departments in many sites with one central account department. First one site is migrated in, then the next, until all have been consolidated. The architectural implementation not only has to consider the start and end states, but also all the intermediate states. What will occur, for example, when half the sites have migrated? What will the organisation look like? How will processes work?

43.4.4 Governance of architectural change

For each element of architectural change there needs to be governance. The change methodology needs to control the overall change in order to ensure that it is delivered as anticipated, and materialises the expected benefits, and is in line with the organisation's risk appetite. The governance will include, but not be limited to:

- Auditing the overall design, and transition states against the overall organisational principles. These may include data principles, security principles, and risk and compliance principles.
- Ensuring the proposed changes support the organisational attitude to risk, and/or that transition states are managed to minimise risk to the organisation.
- Ensure that business continuity is considered in each area of change. What will occur if there is a disaster during the change process, how will the business recover? Typically business continuity is established after a steady state is achieved. Not only does the organisation need to ensure that at each transition point a business continuity plan exists, but that it is continuously updated as the change progresses.
- Ensuring an appropriate review or quality assurance mechanism is in place for the project.
- Ensuring a transparent link between the requirements of the overall project and what is being delivered. It is surprisingly easy for the original requirements to get lost as solutions are developed, and continuously refined, until a point is reached where the solution is technically mature, but shifts in functionality over time have meant that the original aim is no longer achieved.
- Ensuring that roll-back procedures are in place in case the change does not deliver the promised benefits, or (worse) actually creates problems more severe than those originally identified.
- An important stage is monitoring. The execution of the architectural change starts with as-is, and moves to each of the transition states in turn. The change is validated at each step, and the progress towards the overall goal monitored.

43.4.1 What are the impacted areas?

An important consideration is the identification of the impacted areas within the organisation. Architectural change is often upheaval. It is absolutely necessary to ensure that the parts of the organisation impacted are fully on board with proposed changes, and are prepared to support the project. The change needs to be explained to those areas. Equally which individuals are impacted needs to be determined. The architectural change will need to answer questions such as:

- How will job roles change?
- How will processes change?
- What effort is required from the business/IT areas?

- What information is needed from the business/IT areas?
- Who are the key stakeholders?
- Will applications change – if so, what departments use those applications?
- What infrastructure will change?

43.4.2 How will the change impact business operations?

The change needs to be feasible from a business operation point of view, and this includes all the transition states. There is little point designing a transition state that will result in the organisation having to cease operations for any period of time. Realistically, a weekend is likely to be the maximum time it will be feasible for information systems to be "down". In reality, this window is getting squeezed as organisations move towards 24/7 operations.

It may be necessary, for example, to design the architectural change so there is a degree of parallel running, with business operations operating in both old and new architectural states for a period, and sharing the load between them until the new operation is proven.

43.4.3 Define success factors, especially business success factors

It is necessary for the project to define the success factors for the architectural change. Unlike process or data changes, architectural change is more commonly a facilitator for data quality improvement, rather than an operation that results in improvement in itself. As a result, the measurement of success may be in the ability of the organisation to proceed with a subsequent process – for example remediation of data after many data sets have been merged into one.

Equally, simplification of architecture may result in simplification of process (for example, as one process is now required where there used to be three). It is important to understand that architecture as a facilitator is as much a contributor to data quality as changing the data itself.

It is important that success factors are clearly measurable, in line with SMART objectives.

43.4.4 Interaction with other areas of the project

The reason that the organisation is undertaking architectural change is to improve data quality. Depending on the nature of the architectural change it may well affect other areas of the project. If the architectural change affects business processes, then the process analysts and process designers will of necessity been involved from the inception. Process architects and data architects need to ensure that they understand the nature of the changes and are involved at every step. Equally, other areas of the project need to understand what is changing, why, and what effect it will have on them.

An example might be that if business processes are going to be merged, then this will affect the process section of the project. The process analysts and architects need to be involved to ensure that changes are made in a wholly positive direction. This may appear an obvious statement, because any changes should be driven by the need to improve data quality, and the previous work on direction and remediation planning should have ensured a holistic approach. The important consideration is for the project not to become siloed at the remediation stage.

For example, if merging of data silos is performed to improve the ability of the organisation to remediate data, the effect on upstream processes needs to be taken into account. If there is now only one downstream database, how will the multitude of upstream processes feed into it, and how will the data quality of those processes be maintained?

43.4.5 Are there any dependencies, and is there a natural sequence?

Allied to the concept of transition states, there may be dependencies between different elements of the solution, and as a result there may be a natural pattern to the overall change. For example, it will not be possible to run management information from the new database until it holds data. Therefore there is a natural dependency from management information to database population.

43.4.6 Plan solution

The next stage is planning and executing the change. It is likely that architectural change may be of a scale that functional change management needs to be set up. Equally, however, if the change is merely the deletion of feeds then this is less necessary.

43.4.7 Proving benefit and success

One of the most important areas to consider when implementing architectural change across the organisation is how to prove the overall benefit of the change to the organisation, and how to prove that the change has been a success. We have mentioned above the establishment of success factors. The success of the change and the benefit it delivers need to be measurable.

43.5 Architectural Change Frameworks

Fig.: TOGAF Architecture Development Method (ADM)

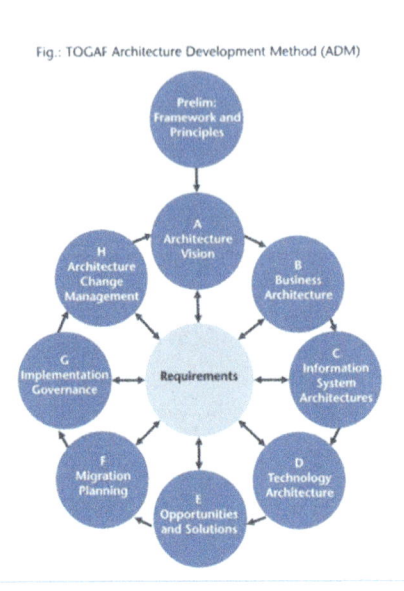

To change from one architecture to another you need a framework. Several frameworks exist for architectural change. In this book I will refer to the TOGAF framework, which at the time of writing had reached version 9.1. The TOGAF framework grew out of the US military architectural framework, but since 1995 has been adopted, modified, enhanced and published by The Open Group. The Open Group is a consortium of organisations with an interest in architectural change and an interest in pushing forward the disciplines of architecture, enterprise architecture and managed architectural change. The (9.1) version of the TOGAF Architecture Development Method is shown in the diagram. [55]

at the process is similar to that described in this

---

55. Reproduced with permission from The Open Group

book. The TOGAF framework sets an architectural vision for the organisation, performs discovery and analysis work, plans how to get to the vision from current state and then implements the solution. This process is very much followed by The Data Quality Blueprint. This is entirely deliberate. I have, in fact, tried to follow an approximate analogy to the TOGAF framework within this book, first because the TOGAF framework is a simple and effective way of managing change, but second because data quality fits across many areas of the organisation in the same way as architectural change. A side effect is that The Data Quality Blueprint is entirely compatible with the TOGAF Framework. [56]

I have no intention of repeating the 600+ pages of the TOAGF manual. However, I will step through the TOGAF framework in my own words to give an idea of how architectural change can be approached. The stages of the TOGAF framework are described below.

Stage	Description
Requirements	Requirements management is just that, and is the section of the TOGAF framework that will manage the architecture requirements of the organisation. It should be noted here that this phase looks to perform a number of tasks. The organisation will identify requirements and the requirements management phase will look to ensure that these requirements are available for every element of the architecture development method throughout the project.
Preliminary Phase: Framework and Principles	The preliminary phase covers the elements that relate to the set-up of the overall method. This includes the way in which the organisation sets architectural standards and principles, and also the framework to be used. The preliminary phase will also start defining the requirements for the overall architecture and the business drivers as to why architectural change is necessary. This preliminary phase is about defining "where, what, why, who, and how we do architecture" in the enterprise concerned.
A: Architecture Vision	The architectural vision phase is similar to that of the corporate vision, described much earlier in this book. It is the development of the high level "where are we going" statement, and defines what will be delivered as part of the overall architectural development methodology. It also will look to develop a statement of architecture work that will be used to govern the project to implement the new architecture in the organisation.
B: Business Architecture	The business architecture element takes the architecture vision, and looks to develop a business architecture that will support the vision and will hence deliver on the business goals. Note that the business architecture is the way the business fits together, and is the first part of the four elements that take the organisation's vision and translate it into a target state. In architecture, as in data quality, business leads the way. This phase will assess the current business architecture, note issues and gaps, and design a future target state that will address them.
C: Information Systems Architecture	Information systems architecture is split into two elements, data and application. It can easily be seen how this is directly relevant to data quality, as this phase of the overall architecture development methodology will directly address architectural

56. ArchiMate®, DirecNet®, Making Standards Work®, OpenPegasus®, The Open Group®, TOGAF®, UNIX®, and X® logo are registered trademarks and Boundaryless Information Flow™, Build with Integrity, Buy with Confidence™, Dependability Through Assuredness™, FACE™, IT4IT™, Open Platform 3.0™, Open Trusted Technology Provider™, the Open 'O' logo and The Open Group Certification logo are trademarks of The Open Group.

	issues in the data architecture. This phase takes the overall architecture vision, and the business architecture developed in the previous phase, and uses this to determine a data and application architecture that will support both. In the same way as the previous phase, this phase will assess the current data and application architecture, note issues and gaps, and design a future target state that will address them.
D: Technology Architecture	In the same way, the next stage of the architectural development methodology looks at the technology architecture. This is the nuts and bolts – or in this case servers and networks – that will support the overall architecture. It takes its lead from the business, data and application architecture and looks to create a technology architecture that will support them. In the same way as the previous phase, this phase will assess the current technology architecture, note issues and gaps, and design a future target state that will address them.
E: Opportunities and Solutions	This phase is an aggregation phase. All the various roadmaps and design architectures are taken together and a complete framework for the target architecture is developed, incorporating all elements. This phase will also look at approaches to the overall implementation of the target architecture, as to whether it is necessary to create intermediate steps between the current architecture and the defined future architecture that will support the business vision.
F: Migration Planning	After determining the future vision, the next step is to define how the organisation will get there. The migration planning phase will finalise both the target end state architecture and also the way in which it will be achieved. This will include intermediate architectural steps (if necessary) and how transitions will work from one step to another.

This phase will also look to identify how the architectural change will fit in with the rest of the organisation. This will include how it will interact with the business and IT elements being changed, how it will interact with business as usual, and also how it will interact with the organisation's change function. |
| G: Implementation Governance | The objective of the next phase is to ensure that the implementation of the target architecture is performed correctly. This phase will be looking to ensure that the delivered architecture meets business needs, is what was required, and delivers what was promised. |
| H: Architecture Change Management | The final phase of the architectural development methodology is analogous to the "embedding" stage in The Data Quality Blueprint. It is the phase that keeps the architectural development on line in the future, and that the overall governance framework is put into place. |

Other architectural change frameworks apart from TOGAF exist. In fact, TOGAF was not even the first, though it is arguably the most popular. Given that Wikipedia (queried in 2015), listed 38 different frameworks, and also noted that this was not in any way a comprehensive list, I am certainly not going to go into them all. Another that is worth mentioning is the Zachman framework, which marked the emergence of architectural frameworks into the mainstream consciousness.

43.6 Example of Architectural Change

The above section is a little dry, so I will try and make the architectural change a little more real by walking through an example. I will again use the example of siloed data. Let us assume that we have five silos of customer data.

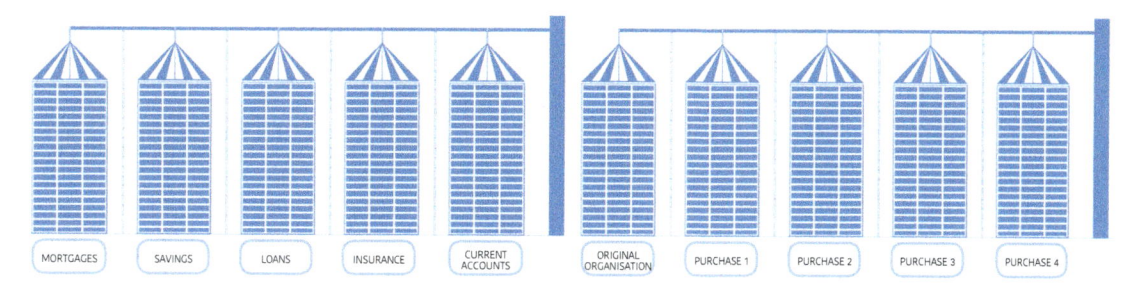

This may be because the organisation has five product categories (say, mortgages, savings, loans, insurance, current accounts), or may have bought/absorbed four other organisations and hence ended up with five sets of customer data, some of which may or may not overlap. The actual effort of merging these five silos is complex in the extreme, but I will look at this from a high level, and from the point of architecture only. Architectural change as a discipline comes in when planning how to get from the current state to the target state.

- A preliminary stage would be necessary that sets out the framework to be employed – for example a decision to employ the TOGAF ADM.
- Phase A is Vision. From a methodology perspective, the most important task at this point is to decide what the organisation wants. Is one set of customer data appropriate? There might be a wish to retain separate data systems if there was a strategic intention to sell off one of the silos. In this case, I have assumed that the intention is to amalgamate them all, in which case the target state is one (admittedly large) silo.

- The Requirements phase would pick up and manage the requirements for the overall project – this may be business, data, application or technology requirements.
- Phase B will examine how business processes can be amalgamated, how the organisation will work with only one silo, what will have to change and how the business moves from one state to another.
- Phase C will take the work already accomplished and move onto the amalgamation of data stores. This will be a daunting task, and transition states will be critical. Will the business merge all data at once – 5 to 1 in a "big bang" approach, or will it amalgamate two silos first as a pilot (possibly the largest and smallest, or the two smallest, whichever works better) and then add in a silo at a time? Data that flows into and out from the existing silos will have to be re-routed.
- Should the data be moved, then de-duplicated (as in the diagram above), or is it better to de-duplicate, then move? The same will apply to applications. There may be a set of applications per silo, and they may – or may not – be compatible. There will have to be a decision to turn one off, migrate data, and do this in a controlled manner.
- Phase D will look from the technology perspective. Currently there may be five servers, five back-up sites, five sets of network infrastructure. These will have to be amalgamated and this stage will determine how this will occur.
- Phase E then brings this all together. This phase will set out a roadmap for the overall architectural change, and also the combined end state vision.
- Phase F takes the output and will plan how to deliver the change. In this particular case it will involve the whole business as the information flows throughout the business will be fundamentally reorganised. It may be possible, with careful design, for one silo (the biggest) to remain unchanged, if everything else is merged into it, and for the impact on the overall organisation to be minimised.
- Phase G is actually about governing the change. The project may be in full flow, with many moving parts. Phase G will look to ensure that the implementation is put in place according to the roadmap and plan.
- Phase H will finally ensure that an architecture governance framework is in place, to try and ensure that the situation never occurs again.

43.7 Summary

Within this chapter I have examined architectural change in detail. I have discussed the difference between architectural change and process and data change, and noted that it may be necessary to minimise architectural change, or to create a separate project, rather than trying to boil the ocean and correct large scale architectural issues. For those issues that are considered in scope I have discussed the approach to remediation, and given examples of specific areas that will need to be considered.

I have also introduced the reader to the TOGAF architectural development methodology, stepped through this at a high level and then given a practical example of how this can be applied to a real-life problem of siloed data.

In the next chapter I will move on to discussing the approaches to remediating existing data.

SECTION 5.6 REMEDIATION

CHAPTER 44 REMEDIATION: EXISTING DATA

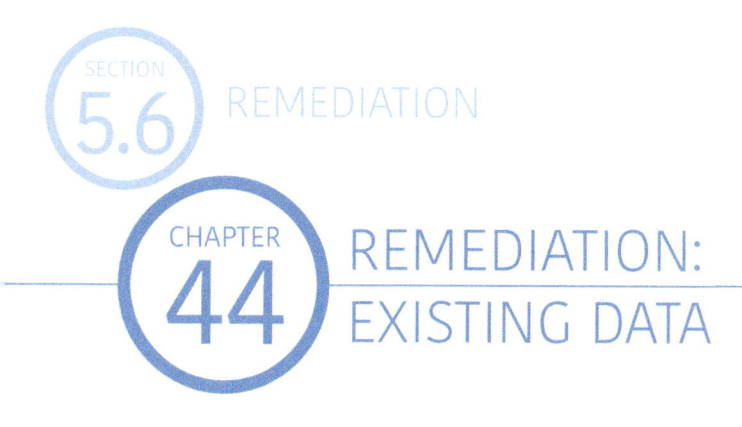

44.1 Structure

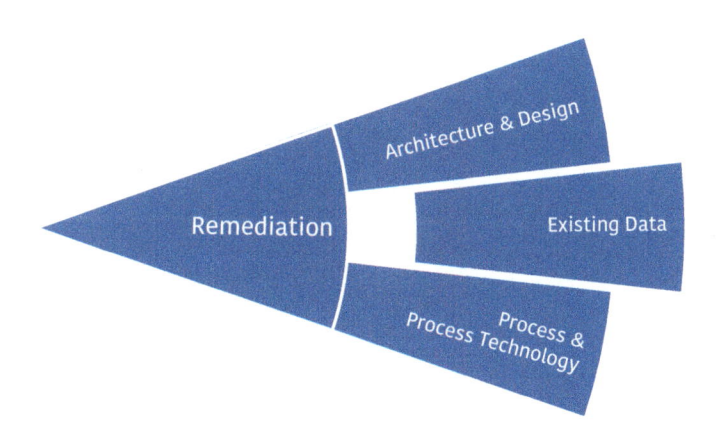

This stage of The Data Quality Blueprint includes the following phases:

1. Architecture & Design
2. Existing Data
3. Process and Process Technology

This chapter covers the second of these phases.

44.2 Overview

INPUTS	TASKS

■ All artefacts created or utilised by the project to date.
■ Remediation plan
■ Output from data discovery
 	
OUTPUTS
■ Task plans
■ Integration plans
■ Populated databases
■ Proof of concept
■ Remediated data
■ Workflow status reports
■ Initial and remediated KPI
 	
DEPENDENCIES
■ Target database
■ Scripting skills
■ Environments
■ Workflow management tool
■ Process change skillets
■ Applications
■ Manual remediation teams
■ Physical locations for teams
■ IT infrastructure
■ Access to key stakeholders
■ Access to IT
■ Access to business
	■ Validate plan still on track
	  - Validate resource availability for stage
	  - Validate scope against pain points, objectives and requirements
	■ Data Specific final planning
	  - Discuss approach with key sponsors utilising data remediation plan
	  - Define approach for each data set (manual/automatic)
	■ Manual
	  - Planning
	    ■ Identify teams to perform remediation (set up teams if necessary)
	    ■ Determine team locations (if a dedicated team look to co-locate)
	    ■ Identify toolsets required for team
	    ■ Identify access required for team
	    ■ Discuss toolsets and access with IT
	    ■ Agree timescales for implementation of infrastructure
	    ■ Identify training needs and deliver training
	    ■ Identify any need for process documentation
	    ■ Create process documentation
	    ■ Implement and initiate workflow
	    ■ Create final task plan
	    ■ Agree and signoff with stakeholders
	  - Data Issues Block M1
	    ■ Identify data (likely on production systems)
	    ■ Calculate initial data quality KPI
	    ■ Define success criteria
	    ■ Identify new source of data
	    ■ Allocate data remediation tasks to teams
	    ■ Perform remediation
	    ■ Prove updated data quality KPI
	    ■ Determine whether success criteria is met
	    ■ Update workflow
	    ■ Confirm data quality KPI
	    ■ Document results
	    ■ Obtain signoff of remediated data
	  - Data issues block M2
	  - Data issues block M3
	  - Data issues block M4
	  - Data issues block M5
	■ Automatic
	  - Planning
	    ■ Define and agree approach for environments (i.e. where is data remediated)
	    ■ Implement and initiate workflow
	    ■ Test environment access
	    ■ Create working database in relevant environment
	    ■ Test access to target data

- Test access to source data
- Upload source data sets if required
- Test any toolsets
- Create integration plan
- Agree and signoff with stakeholders and IT
- Data Issues Block A1
  - Preparation for remediation
    - Identify data
    - Extract cut of target data into working database
    - Validate data cut
    - Calculate initial data quality KPI
    - Define success criteria
    - Define new source data
    - Take new source data into database
    - Define means of remediation
    - Document final plan
    - Update workflow
  - Proof of Concept
    - Use subset of data to prove remediation works
    - Prove updated data quality KPI
    - Determine whether success criteria is met
    - Update workflow
    - Document results and update plan for POC learning
    - Obtain written signoff and agreement for scale update
  - Implementation
    - Perform remediation
    - Prove updated data quality KPI
    - Determine whether success criteria is met
    - Upload cleansed data into cleansed repository
    - Document results
    - Receive written signoff and agreement for integration
  - Integration
    - Prepare for integration/replacement of original data
    - Integrate new data into original source (if required)
    - Validate integration
    - Confirm data quality KPI
    - Obtain signoff of remediated data
  - Documentation
    - Baseline and upload into project document repository
- Complete data issues block A1
  - Data issues block A2
  - Data issues block A3
  - Data issues block A4
  - Data issues block A5

Existing data is the millstone around the neck of many organisations stopping them from ever being as good as they should be. It impedes flexibility and decision making, and costs money every day. It's time to clean it up.

The detailed planning of the data remediation was discussed within the remediation planning section. This included the data to be remediated, the source that will be used to remediate or replace the data, how it will be done (automatically, manually, and so on), and by whom. However, it is not all plain sailing. Actually performing the remediation contains some tricky bits, and it is these that I will discuss in this chapter. This will cover:

- Some reconsideration of types of remediation and how they work
- Environments and environment access
- Establishment of a working database
- Isolation of target data
- Definition and measurement of success criteria
- Creation of a proof of concept
- Data integration

It is assumed in both the example project plan, and in real life, that the tasks of remediation of process, data and architecture will proceed simultaneously. There may be interdependencies – I have already mentioned that collapsing to a minimal number of copies of customer data (an architectural change) and then remediating this data is better than trying to cleanse them all. However, with the exception of interdependencies like this, the work on all three streams can proceed at the same time.

44.3 Types of Remediation

- Manual remediation (through business as usual)
- Manual remediation (dedicated back office)
- Remediation by IT
- Automatic remediation (using toolsets)

I will now discuss each of these in more detail.

44.4 Manual Remediation (BAU)

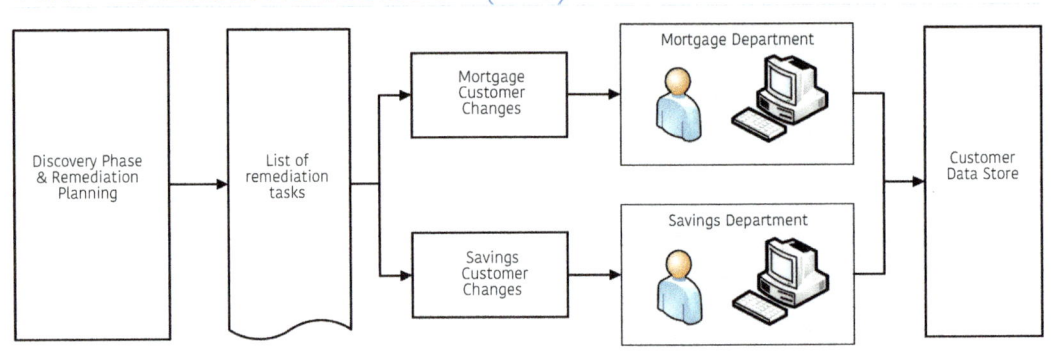

If the volumes are very small, then it is possible to allow the remediation of data to be performed by the business-as-usual teams as part of their normal everyday work. These teams are interacting with the systems on a day to day basis and updating customer data (for example) as part of their interaction with customers who ring up to change address/name/etc.

This only covers customer data but can cover product data as well, providing the agents have access to the right systems to do so (of which more later). The tasks that need to be achieved can be allocated to call centre teams who can work through them and be tracked doing so.

The big advantage of this approach is that it is very easy. No new systems need to be implemented, no new access rights granted. The big disadvantage is that it is slow, in fact the slowest of the approaches described here.

It is worth noting – especially if nonstandard or unusual changes are being implemented – that testing the changes to ensure that they propagate through the system as expected is advisable. The organisation should perform a limited test in a safe environment to make sure that changes will propagate through the system correctly. It is equally imperative that changes made are comprehensively quality assured.

However, overall, the risk of this approach is fairly low. Only one record is being changed at any one time by any one person, and it is possible to comprehensively quality assure the changes.

A disadvantage with this method is that agents typically have very restricted access to systems. Agents in the mortgage department may not be able to change details on the savings account information, even if these changes are trivial (e.g. change to title). As a result the second method is the remediation option that I have seen most often in practice.

44.5 Manual Remediation (dedicated back office)

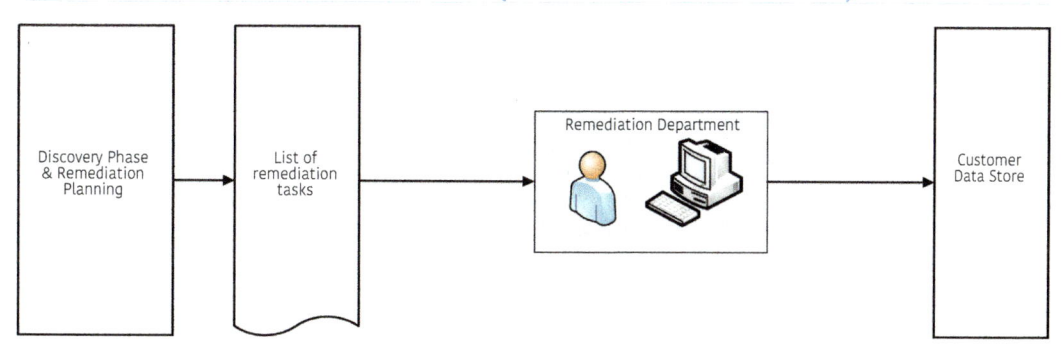

The second approach is that a remediation centre is set up with access to all the data-holding systems. The user interface is the same as the normal business-as-usual process (hence no additional software is required) but staff can – if faced with a remediation of title – open up and remediate the data in every system in turn. A large number of staff (I've seen 500) are employed to work their way through the backlog of quality issues.

This has the advantage of not impacting business as usual functions, not using any additional or non-standard software – staff are simply set up with comprehensive access rights – and can be located anywhere. A very common approach is to "seed" the remediation centre with extremely experienced staff who have worked within every department of the organisation over many years. They act as trainers for the other staff, who are often either junior or recruited in for the purpose. This leaves the business as usual teams more or less intact and does not impact customer service.

Again, the risk of this approach is fairly low. Only one record is being changed at any one time by any one person, and it is possible to comprehensively quality assure the changes.

44.6 Remediation by or with IT (Bulk update)

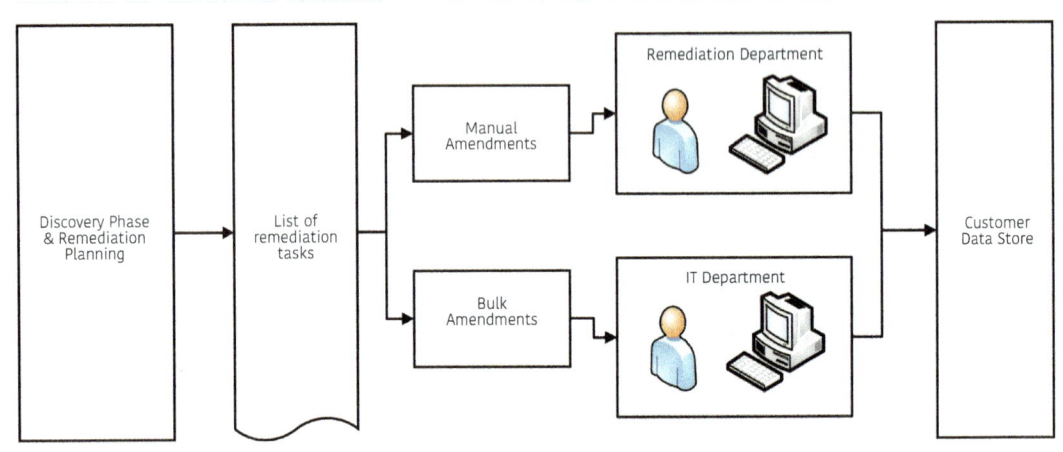

Remediation via direct access to systems by the IT department, in conjunction with the business, is another common approach, and is commonly implemented in conjunction with the back office remediation above. The problem with this method is that it is extremely high risk; a minor typing error can make the difference between remediating data and deleting the lot. A strong control framework needs to be implemented around these kinds of changes. Here I will discuss and explain the most common methods of risk mitigation in respect of bulk changes to data.

44.6.1 Environments and access

The starting point for bulk data remediation utilising IT systems is discussion with the client on environments and access. To put it bluntly, no normal organisation is going to allow you to hook directly into their production system and perform bulk updates of data without fairly extensive testing. The risk is simply too great. I have seen the results when an organisation tests solutions on their production system, and it takes a considerable time to clean up the mess later. The organisation is operationally supported by the production system and without it the organisation cannot function. It cannot pay customers, calculate interest payments, create new customers, or change addresses. Nothing should therefore touch production without thorough testing that proves nothing untoward will occur. So where is the testing done, and what are "environments" anyway?

Most organisations run between three and five separate environments. Software changes (and a script that is about to amend a million customer records is pretty high risk software) will typically move through each of the environments in turn. A traditional four environment system is shown below.

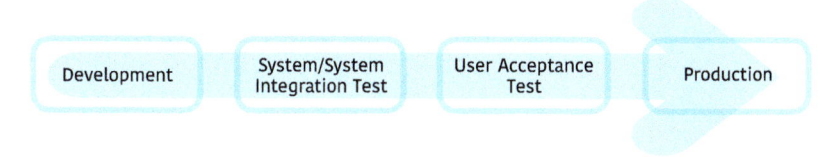

Development → System/System Integration Test → User Acceptance Test → Production

All environments are copies as far as possible from a software and hardware point of view. Development (Dev) is where software is built. System Integration Test (SIT) is where the organisation checks that the software plays nicely with other bits of software, User Acceptance Test (UAT) is where the organisation finds out whether the software will do what it is supposed to do.

The latest software and fastest hardware will be in the production environment, because that supports the business. In terms of data, there may be some dummy customer records in Development, System Integration Test will contain a bit more data, User Acceptance Test will probably contain the entire data set, and production ("Prod") will obviously contain live data.

There is a very clear set of checks and balances so that new functionality is checked and signed off before it moves into the next environment – a process known as "promotion". It is likely that in a large organisation a data quality project will need to follow this process. A script intended to modify a million customer titles will be run in Dev against a small subset. Moved to SIT and run again. If nothing untoward occurs it will move to UAT, where it will be run against the whole dataset, and then finally, when everyone is happy, it will move to Prod. In each case a set of test cases will be used to see whether the script has performed as planned.

For the project, as soon as any kind of funding is approved for data remediation, the project should be talking to IT about environments and access to these environments. Access to the environments in particular may well take time, as multiple authorisations may be required. You won't get access to Prod, and access to UAT will be limited. It will take time to set them up, and there may be licensing costs.

For profiling, assuming that the organisation does not just ask the IT department to extract a copy of the customer table and save it somewhere, the data profilers may be given access to UAT, with its copy of almost-live customer data. Typically the data from the "live" database may be copied over to UAT once a month to keep the data "fresh". The organisation will not allow the profilers to run queries against the Prod database (or at least, won't if they have any sense).

44.6.2   Getting the database

The next stage, after the environments are created or access is granted, is to set up what might be called a working database. It is possible to use the database already in the development environment (which should be identical to Prod in terms of structure and version, but won't contain much/any data), or it may be possible to set up a copy where data can be worked on. I prefer the latter as a separate database is a separate entity where the new source data can be stored and fine-tuned and the scripts can be developed. This database will exist in Dev.

New source data can be loaded from an external source into the working database. The data will be tuned to fit into the data model existing in the organisational database. A script will then be created to replace the dummy "old, poor" data with new data. If this works the source data and the script can move on to SIT.

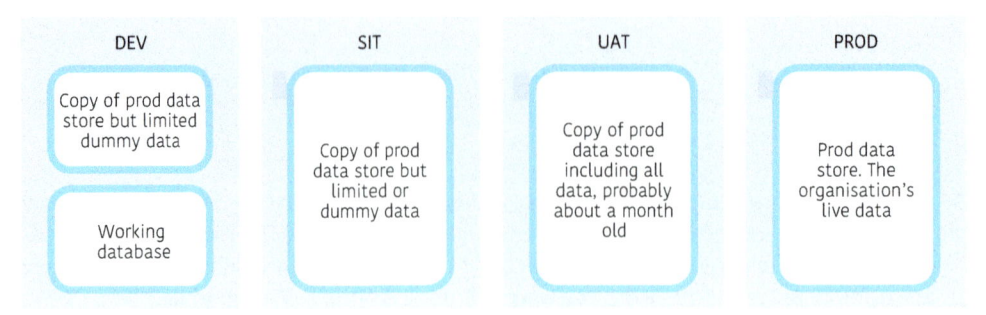

DEV	SIT	UAT	PROD
Copy of prod data store but limited dummy data	Copy of prod data store but limited or dummy data	Copy of prod data store including all data, probably about a month old	Prod data store. The organisation's live data
Working database			

44.6.3 Getting the data

The next item to think about is getting the data. Especially in the case of large financial institutions the amount of total records is significant, and requires a large storage volume. Dev and SIT are unlikely to be of a size to hold the entire customer database. However, in order to test the scripts that will replace the old data with new shiny data, test cases need to be crafted, and thus a representative set of dummy data needs to be created. For this exercise the place to start is the profiling results. The profiling results should inform the reader of all of the various possibilities in each of the data fields, and it will be possible to create test data that will include a representation of ever possibility within the live data. Within Dev and SIT, therefore, there should be a test data set, crafted by the profiling results.

The new source data should be loaded into Dev too. There may potentially be a problem if the replacement data is large. If, for example, there is a one to one relationship between new data and live data the Dev environment may be too small (i.e. not have enough storage) to hold it. Here you have three options:

- Talk very nicely to IT about the size of the environment and ask if they can increase it for free. In a virtualized organisation this may well be possible
- Pay for the hardware to increase the size of the environment
- Perform the remediation in chunks

In most cases the new data will be a set of amended data and many mapping rules (as in the case of the "Mr Sand Mrs" discussed earlier) and capacity should not be an issue.

44.6.4 Creating the remediation plan

The next stage is to create a remediation plan. The environments and data are in place, next is to agree what is going to be done and when. This will have been covered in some detail at the original planning, and again at the detail remediation planning, but now it's time to get down to real nuts and bolts – such as confirming the date and time a script will be run. Depending on the level of access to databases and environments it may be necessary to get into job scheduling [57], but this is far too detailed a discussion for this book, so just be aware it exists and that someone may mention it to you.

44.6.5 Isolation and extraction

Depending on the exact situation it may be possible to extract live data into the UAT system (or even, if you are lucky, development) where testing can take place. Here you need to isolate the data that is required and extract it into a "safe working environment". It will be necessary to lean heavily on the system subject matter experts who will make you aware of the tables and fields that require changing.

44.6.6 Testing

Another art form briefly mentioned previously is the creation of test scripts. Test scripts will need to be created for every single type of change that is going to be made. If this appears onerous then I would submit that it is much better than getting to UAT and then having to rewrite everything. The test scripts will cover every possibility of change, and will not only test that changes are made in line with expectations, but also that correct data is left alone and not changed.

44.6.7 User Acceptance Testing

Do not skip UAT. UAT should be an environment where the database exists with a copy of the user environment. Once the script and good data has been uploaded into UAT, testing need to make sure that everything is as required. This means that data is being displayed on screens correctly (amazing things can go wrong here), that new drop-down lists are functional and selectable, and populate the database correctly. It is – and should be – an onerous and thorough test, where everything that can go wrong should be tested. The next step after this is Prod, and if all the customer names turn up as "****************" on the screens of the contact centre agents when talking to real customers then the success and benefits of the project will be seriously questioned.

44.6.8 Implementation

This, finally, brings the project to the point where it can actually start to remediate data. By this point the organisation has determined:

- The data that it needs to run its business by the creation of a data strategy, data quality strategy and data quality requirements.
- It has assessed its current data against those standards and performed a gap analysis.
- It has planned how it is going to close that gap (remediate or replace the data) and what data it will use to perform this work.
- It has undertaken a detailed planning exercise and knows the order in which it will perform the remediation.

---

[57] Job scheduling covers the area by which rather than scripts or processes being run manually, they are scheduled by a scheduling engine, which will open and run applications and/or scripts in a specified order. It will plan, track and execute jobs on multiple platforms, environments and applications. A well known product at time of writing is IBM's Tivoli.

It is now time to perform the work. At this point, because of the work that has been done beforehand, this task should go relatively smoothly. However there is still a structure to follow if an organisation wishes to perform the work well. For each individual element of the remediation, the work involves:

- Isolating the data that is to be remediated from the "dirty" whole. This is so that work can be completed on this element in isolation. Different elements of data may require remediation in different ways. For some fields the method of remediation may be manual, for others a bulk update. It will help a lot if the dirty data is physically separated.
- Creating KPIs at various points throughout the remediation cycle. It is important to track the progress of the remediation, and to be able to say at the end of the process that the data quality has been improved and by a specific percentage.
- Creating rollback procedures. Throughout the remediation process, it is necessary to ensure that careful logging of the work is undertaken, so that if required the original data can be reinstated if there are any problems. Again, the KPIs taken can be used to check the reinstatement of the data has been completed correctly.
- Keeping workflow updated on a regular basis so that the project as a whole has clear visibility of the progress of the remediation.
- Careful reintegration of the new data with the old. This may mean creating a new, "golden source", separate from the old data, or updating the old source data with the new. If the latter is the case great care must be taken to not create more problems than were started with.

This process is explained diagrammatically below.

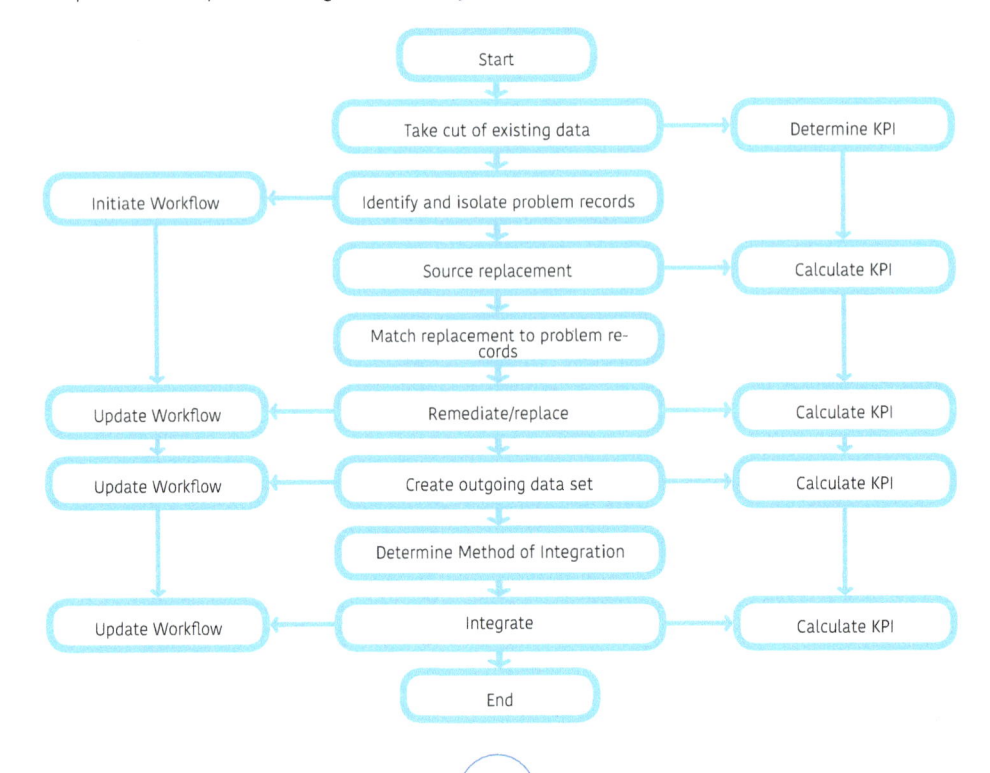

44.7   Remediation by use of Specialist Remediation Toolsets

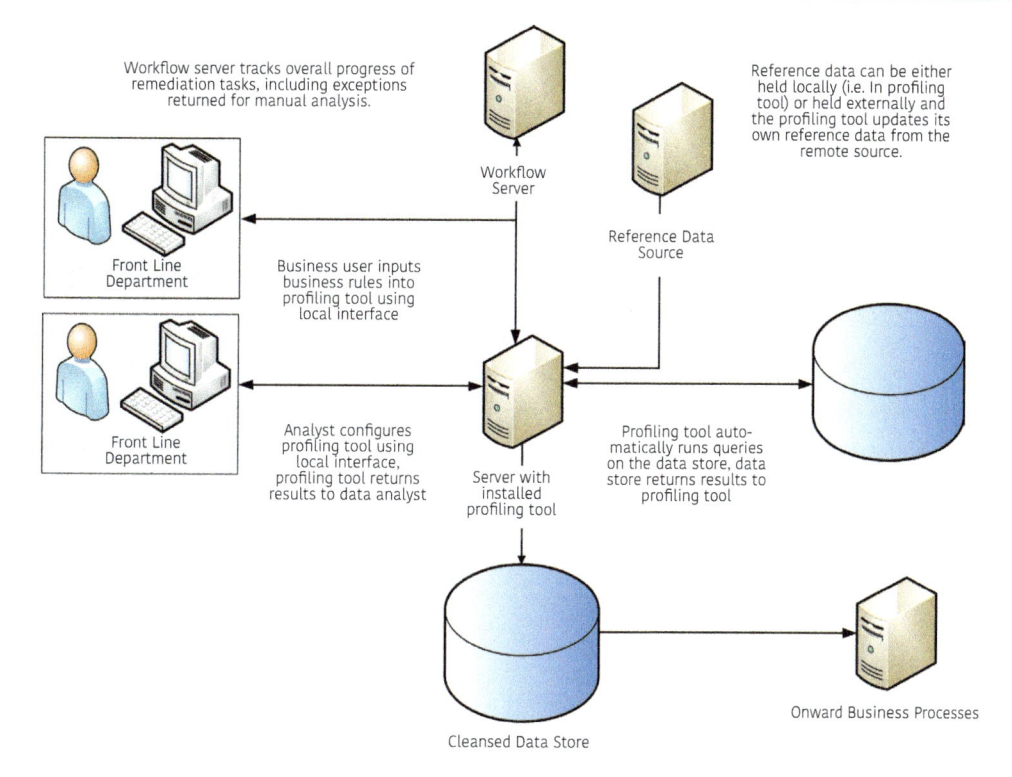

Diagram: Workflow server tracks overall progress of remediation tasks, including exceptions returned for manual analysis. Front Line Department users interact with a Workflow Server and a server with installed profiling tool. Business user inputs business rules into profiling tool using local interface. Analyst configures profiling tool using local interface, profiling tool returns results to data analyst. Reference data can be either held locally (i.e. in profiling tool) or held externally and the profiling tool updates its own reference data from the remote source. Profiling tool automatically runs queries on the data store, data store returns results to profiling tool. Outputs flow to Cleansed Data Store and Onward Business Processes.

The types of applications available in the marketplace to automatically update data have been discussed previously, and do not need repeating. I have also discussed the way care needs to be taken when using the tools so as to avoid the scenario of them becoming "black boxes" where data goes in, different data comes out, but there is little understanding or control over the process that occurs in between. As a result, whilst the data may have improved, it is occasionally difficult to determine whether the organisation has simply exchanged one set of data problems for another. Very careful operation and thorough quality control over changes is the key here.

That said, these tools do bring with them the opportunity for a significant reduction in the time taken for remediation, with only the exceptions being identified for manual handling.

44.8   Other Approaches

44.8.1   Less thorough processes

It is possible, especially in small organisations, that the above reasonably rigorous approach might not be followed. Certainly I have worked with many organisations that have implemented changes directly into Prod, though they generally regret it later. If organisational controls are lacking I would strongly suggest the project implements a rigour of its own. I would suggest the project creates its own working database on a disposable server and thoroughly tests the implementation of data changes before any change is made to the live data, whatever the organisation itself says. For example, creating a dummy "UAT" server with a full copy of production data and running bulk data changes against this database will at least give you the comfort that nothing horrible should go wrong.

44.8.2 Proof of Concept

Another technique that can be employed to calm nerves is to perform a proof of concept. This is, as discussed previously in the book, a small-scale implementation of the data changes against a limited range of data. The project can then see if the script works, whether it didn't and if so what needs to be changed.

44.9 Workflow

The objective of a workflow (if you have not come across the term before or read the section on project management) is to monitor the progress of multiple tasks against a predefined list of states. It is a management tool to control and monitor progress.

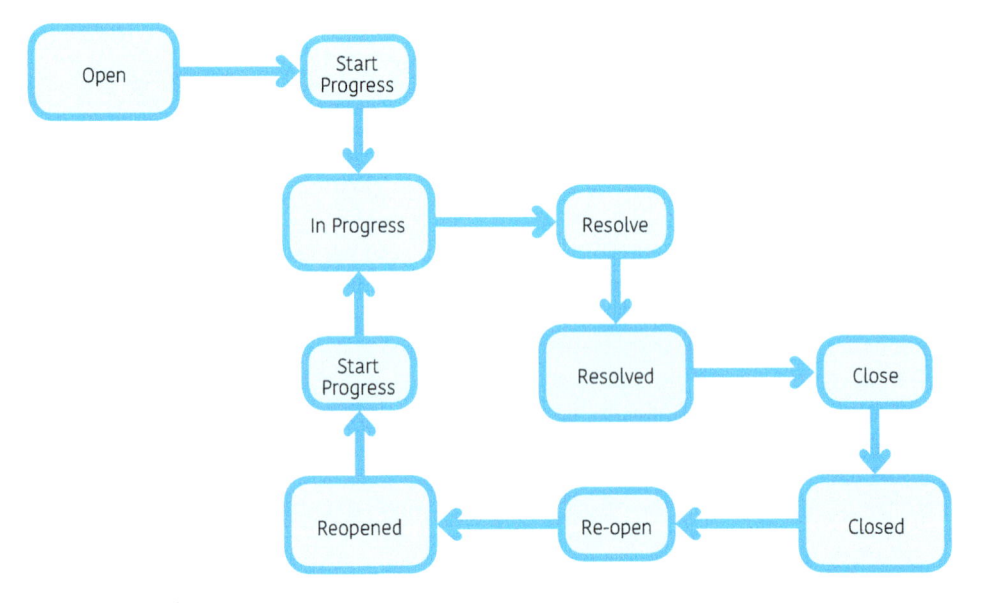

From Wikipedia:
A workflow consists of an orchestrated and repeatable pattern of business activity enabled by the systematic organization of resources into processes that transform materials, provide services, or process information. It can be depicted as a sequence of operations, declared as work of a person or group, an organization of staff, or one or more simple or complex mechanisms. [58]

---

55. https://en.wikipedia.org/wiki/Workflow

In order to effectively manage the remediation it is necessary to have a plan, and also to monitor the process of the remediation against that plan. It is also advisable to have a workflow tracker of some kind. In most cases a simple spreadsheet may serve the requisite purpose, but if not, there are many workflow monitoring tools in the marketplace. A typical example of a workflow management spreadsheet could be represented below.

Element	No	Remediation Type	Owner	Stage	Current KPI
Blank titles	45,216	Automatic – assignation by perceived gender	IT	In progress	74% complete
Blank titles where automatic assignation not possible	3,000	Manual	Contact centre	In progress	5% complete
Title does not match forename	2651	Manual	Contact centre	In progress	Complete

For a data remediation, there are likely to be a large number of separate workflows. There will be one to manage the overall remediation effort, but there will be workflows in each area of the organisation that is remediating data. They are an effective way of both orchestrating effort and also tracking progress. More detail on workflow is, as said, contained in the project management section.

44.10 Where do we stop?

It has been stated several times that an organisation needs to take care to constantly be aware of the business benefit of data quality remediation. The marginal cost of data quality remediation increases the closer an organisation nears to 100% data quality and every organisation needs to draw a line where increasing expenditure on remediation does not gain a commensurate return on investment. In reality, "perfect" data, like 100% data security, is an almost impossible dream that no organisation of any size will achieve due to the excessive time and cost – and impact on the business operations – to achieve that nirvana.

Data quality can easily become an end in itself with constant striving for a "perfection" that does not exist. One of the advantages of The Data Quality Blueprint is that this problem should never occur. If the steps have been followed appropriately, the criteria for meeting the organisation's requirements in terms of data quality have been defined at the start of the "Direction" stage. In addition, the measurement of data quality has been defined in the data quality performance metrics, so when performance metrics indicate that the organisation has reached the desired data quality, then halt proceedings.

44.11 Summary

In this chapter I have discussed the remediation of existing data, the correction, replacement and enhancement of the historical legacy of data within the organisation. This chapter has covered first how to approach the problem, and the differences between manual remediation by BAU, manual remediation in a remediation centre, and bulk change by IT. I have discussed each of these in turn and how risks can be mitigated.

For IT bulk change I have discussed the overall control to large scale implementation of change within the live data environment and how this would be managed. This gives those who may not be familiar with "environments" a basic understanding of how a large scale change would proceed.

I have described the step by step approach to performing remediation, and have covered how to manage the remediation process through workflow, and how to document the remediation so that it is consistent with architecture and process remediation.

In the next chapter I will discuss the remediation of process, that element of the organisation where failings have often resulted in poor quality data entering the information systems of the organisation.

SECTION 5.6 REMEDIATION

CHAPTER 45 — REMEDIATION: PROCESS AND PROCESS TECHNOLOGY

45.1 Structure

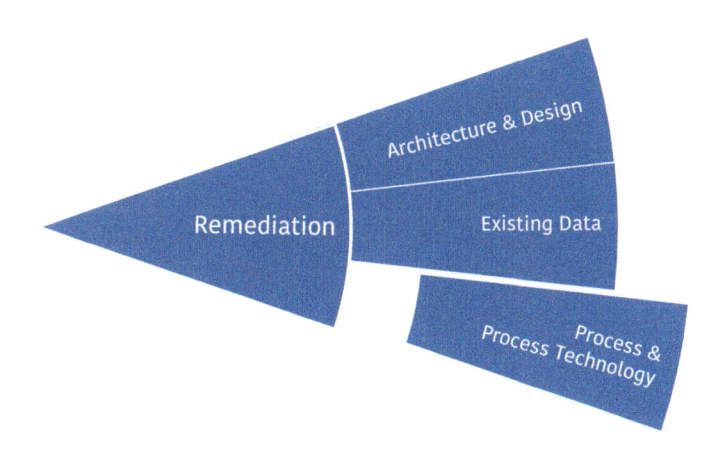

This stage of The Data Quality Blueprint includes the following phases:

1. Architecture & Design
2. Existing Data
3. Process and Process Technology

This chapter covers the last of these phases.

45.2 Overview

INPUTS
- All artefacts created or utilised by the project to date.
- Remediation plan
- Process maps
- Process architecture
- Remediation priorities
- Output from process discovery
- Output from data discovery

OUTPUTS
- Processes in scope
- Success criteria
- Future process options
- Results from pilot
- Remediated process
- Workflow status reports
- Initial and remediated KPI

DEPENDENCIES
- Workflow management tool
- Process change skillets
- Access to key stakeholders

TASKS
- Planning
  - Validate plan still on track
  - Validate resource availability for stage
  - Validate scope against pain points, objectives and requirements
- Process-specific final planning
  - Discuss issues with key sponsors utilising process remediation plan
  - Source documentation for processes in scope
  - Define and agree approach for remediation
  - Implement and initiate workflow
  - Test any technology required
- Process Issues Block 1
  - Preparation for Remediation
    - Define processes in scope
    - Collate process maps for processes in scope
    - Collate issues/pain points for processes in scope
    - Define KPI if not already done
    - Calculate data quality KPI on existing process
    - Define success criteria from remediation plan
    - Determine future process options
    - Evaluate and benchmark options
    - Determine final preferred option and agree with process owner
    - Update workflow
    - Plan implementation of pilot
    - Obtain signoff and agreement for pilot
  - Proof of Concept/Simulation/Pilot
    - Implement pilot
    - Create updated data quality KPI
    - Determine if success criteria met
    - Update workflow
    - Document results
    - Update implementation plan for lessons learned from pilot
    - Obtain signoff and agreement for full implementation
  - Implementation
    - Plan roll-out
    - Implement roll-out
    - Update workflow
    - Document results
    - Receive written signoff
    - Baseline and upload into project document repository
  - Complete process issues block 1
- Process issues block 2
- Process issues block 3
- Process issues block 4
- Process issues block 5

As mentioned in the process discovery section, remediation of process is informed by both the discovery work within process and the discovery work within data. This is why The Data Quality Blueprint recommends doing the discovery and then the remediation sequentially. In addition, the remediation planning process will collate root causes and hence make the remediation more efficient. Process remediation to improve the quality of data is in the territory of the established disciplines of business process engineering/re-engineering and business process management (BPM) and there are a number of good publications on the market which give comprehensive information on how to manage and change processes within an organisation. However, within this chapter I will give a view of process change as applicable to data quality, and an overview of the steps necessary.

Design of process should follow these guidelines:

- Simple is better than complex.
- Short is better than long.
- Doing something right once is better than doing it wrong and having to go back and fix it.

Note: you will have noted that the chapter is entitled "Process and Process Technology". This is because I view a process as both the steps undertaken to complete the task and the technology that supports it.

45.3 Scope

It will be outside the ability of any project at anything other than the smallest organisation to comprehensively redesign and implement change to every process in the organisation. There will be a trade-off between the work that can be accomplished and the time and money available to complete it. The scope needs to be vectored towards the most important element of the business and where any change to data quality will have the greatest impact.

An earlier part of the book introduced the CRUD (create, read, update, delete) matrix. Of these, processes that fall into "C" are the most important, as due to the well-known principle "garbage in, garbage out" it is not possible to obtain better quality data than that which you started with. Good data capture processes give data quality the best chance. Unfortunately, it is often the case that the processes around data capture are also those most routinely ignored by the people actually doing the job. This is because it is rare that value is placed on either the processes or – to their detriment – the people doing them. As a result, not only is primary data capture the area which has the greatest effect on data quality throughout the organisation, but it is also usually considerably neglected and where the greatest improvement can take place. It is almost always a "quick win".

Overall, the number of processes that have an impact on quality is likely to be small indeed, and any process change is likely to be a tweak to the existing process rather than a wholesale redesign. On the other hand, within the landscape of a larger project – such as a data quality remediation project – there will be many process changes being undertaken at the same time. In this case control and management of process change becomes a significant concern in itself.

45.4 Approach

It is a basic tenet of The Data Quality Blueprint that every process that creates, uses, transports or transforms data should have data quality baked into its design for success. Controls should also exist that act to ensure – as far as is practicable – that no process or procedure introduces errors into the data and there are no more issues with the data at the end of the process than at the beginning.

From the perspective of data process remediation there are a number of excellent publications on this topic, some of which are mentioned at the end of this chapter. Whilst each methodology has its own specific approach to process change, the basic steps are as listed in the table below.

Stage	Where in The Data Quality Blueprint	Description
Current process documentation	Discovery – Process	Document processes that critically affect data quality
Define process Problems	Discovery – Process & Business case	Identify areas where processes are causing data quality issues
Evaluate process	Remediation Planning	Evaluate the process and identify where it needs to change
Scope of change	Remediation Planning	Decide on the work that needs to be completed and what processes need to change
Benchmark process	Process Remediation or Discovery	As a first part of process remediation take KPIs of the process to measure the current data quality produced by the process
Set process goals	Remediation Planning or Direction	Sets the quality goals the process needs to achieve
Design future process	Process Remediation	Within each of the identified business processes where a data quality impact has been identified design changes to the process
Evaluate process options	Process Remediation	For each of the process change options evaluate in terms of ease of implementation, data quality improvement, cost-effectiveness, training required, etc.
Test	Process Remediation	Test the new process and how it will change the result
Plan implementation	Process Remediation	For each element of process change, plan how it is going to be implemented – for example, will one team in the contact centre change to the new process first, or all teams will change together? Will there be a parallel-run, where the results from the new process and the results from the old process are compared, etc?

Implement remediation	Process Remediation	Changing the process across the test area of the organisation
Re-benchmark process	Process Remediation	Measure impact of the new process in terms of data quality
Roll out process	Process Remediation	Changing the process across the whole organisation
Review and report	Process Remediation	Measure impact of the new process in terms of data quality

Within The Data Quality Blueprint, the discovery phase and the remediation design cover the first stages of business process change – specifically:

- Current process documentation
- Define process problems
- Evaluate process
- Scope of change
- Benchmark process
- Set process goals
- Evaluate process options
- Plan implementation

The elements to be considered here will be the test and implementation of process change. I will also look at the various ways to manage the overall process remediation effort at the end of this chapter.

45.5 Considerations for Process Change

45.5.1 Revalidate final decision

In a similar way to both architectural and data remediation, it is necessary to undertake a final analysis of the overall decision-making process to ensure that the work to be undertaken will meet the business objectives for data quality. This may appear an unnecessary duplication of effort, but it is still much better to check twice than do it incorrectly once.

45.5.2 Clearly document what is going to be done

Clarity is essential. The old process was documented in either the initiation stage or the discovery stage. The new processes need to be documented in a manner that is unambiguous. An effective means of determining the quality of the documentation is asking a sample of individuals to read the new process document and to explain the new process back to you. Good documented process descriptions will result in the same explanation from the majority of individuals. If there is significant variation between descriptions, then the documentation needs to be improved.

45.5.3 Parallel run or big bang?

Should the new process run in parallel with the old process or should the old process stop and the new begin with no overlap (a "big bang" approach). The big advantage with the parallel approach is that is allows the efficiency of the new process and the old process to be compared side by side "in real life". It also allows a phased transition where there can be a gradual shift from old to new. Another advantage is that it allows an easy reversion to the previous process if the new process is not working as efficiently as planned. The parallel run approach works particularly well in environments where there are a number of teams doing more or less the same thing, and the process can be transitioned team by team.

The disadvantage of parallel run is that it is more difficult when the process is supported by an application or other technological solution. It is unlikely that the IT department are going to be keen for the large scale production running and of supporting two entirely different solutions to the same problem.

It also doesn't work very well when there are a limited number of people performing a process. It is ridiculous, for example, for one person to use one process in the mornings and another in the afternoons, and similarly within a small team it is impractical for process differences to exist.

The other disadvantage of parallel running is that it means that the full advantage of the new process is only realised after a period of time (i.e. after the transition is complete) rather than immediately, however this is normally outweighed by the reduction in risk that parallel run allows.

45.5.4 Proof of concept/simulation

An alternative to parallel run is proof of concept or simulation. Whilst I have combined these two topics in one sub-heading, in reality they are very different beasts.

Proof of concept – which we have already covered in this book in an earlier chapter – is the use of a small, normally non-production version of the proposed system to be run in real life to demonstrate the benefits of the new process.

Simulation – as the name implies – is the modelling of a new process within a non-real-life environment – typically a computer – and the parameters of the simulation, and the nature of the simulation, are designed to accurately model real life as far as is possible. Simulation is an approach where the simple trial of a new process would be prohibitively expensive or risky, and it is essential to ensure – as far as possible – before any "real life" testing is done – that the organisation is confident of success.

The advantage of a proof of concept is that it is, actually, real life. Improvements will in theory accurately reflect reality. However the organisation needs to be careful here, as a proof of concept will naturally represent an environment where operators are learning and understanding a new process, and planned efficiencies may not be realised simply because of this fact. This is not a disadvantage of a simulation, which allows the modelling of the predicted steady state process after all learning has been completed.

45.5.5 Transition states

In a similar way to the change of architecture, it may be necessary, especially if the change to process is a large one, to design transition states intermediate between the original process and the final one. In reality, this is rare. The other problem with process transition states is that running a process as half one (old) process and half (new) process is unlikely to achieve much except confusion, and a substantial decrease in performance in terms of both throughput and quality.

45.5.6   Obtain feedback from stakeholders

The process architect needs to understand that however talented they may be, they are not the people who have been performing the old process every day for years and will be performing the new process day to day. The process architect should not consider that they know everything and should absolutely allow for modifications to the proposed process as a result of feedback from the operators.

Whilst tempting to dismiss any criticism of a new process as simple resistance to change and/or an unwillingness to learn anything new, such views should be held with caution. If a process operator states that "this new process will not work because...." then listen to them very carefully. It is much better to spend 30 minutes understanding their point of view than many embarrassing hours starting from scratch after a simulation or proof of concept which demonstrates that the new process is either worse than the old, or is simply unable to deliver the end product.

When getting feedback, be careful to include those upstream and downstream of the process in the feedback loop. A process may work effectively within the silo of the process operators themselves but may deliver rubbish downstream. Equally the new process may work well with current input, but may demand subtly different inputs which the upstream processes may not be able to deliver.

45.5.7   Governance

We have mentioned governance in terms of architecture and will certainly do so in terms of data, and it is equally important in terms of process.

Governance includes the integration of the processes of the organisation into the organisation as a whole, and the understanding of how processes support the organisation's aims. Equally process governance includes setting standards and quality measures for processes, and a mechanism for determining the manner in which processes measure up to these standards.

Governance will also include standards for process definition and process mapping, and also the description of the overall taxonomy within which processes reside. This will include the overall functional definition of the organisation and its departments.

45.5.8   Remove barriers if possible

A process does not exist in a vacuum, and is subject to many environmental factors which may or may not create barriers to the new process. Examples of barriers may be:

- Does the new process require more desk space than the old?
- Does the new process run significantly slower on the current computer equipment?
- Does the new process require updated ancillary equipment (lighting, monitors)

Failure to account for these may totally derail the attempt to improve process. Try and anticipate and remove them before they become an issue. To take one of the examples above, if a new screen requires scrolling down an inch every single time a customer record is opened this will be incredibly frustrating for the operators. If there is a critical field in that last inch of screen then the most likely occurrence will be it will simply not be filled in. Buy new monitors for the team.

45.5.9 Decide on timing

A quite important consideration that is often ignored up until the point where it becomes a problem is when, exactly, will the processes be remediated? Care needs to be taken not to choose the busiest time of the year for changing critical operational processes. Do not, for example, try and change retail sales processes on the run-up to Christmas. Equally, financial processes should not be changed near month-end, let alone year end.

Many organisations have a cadence that will allow for quiet periods and it is these periods that the project should consider as prime candidates for the timing of implementation. However do be careful. If a quiet period is followed immediately by a critically busy time of the year, then consider the impact of the process change not being embedded in time and running into the critical period, or the risk inherent in running the busy period on brand new processes.

45.5.10 Define success criteria

It is necessary for the organisation to determine whether the process change has been a success, and in order for this to occur then success needs to be defined. What is success? What quality improvement is required and, importantly, how will it be measured. This goes back to the concept of SMART objectives introduced earlier in the book.

45.5.11 Validate final processes

Before we move on and leave the new process in place, we need to ensure that it is actually being performed. There is no point designing and implementing what appears to be a successful process improvement if it turns out later that the process is not actually being followed and we are storing up a whole set of quality or business problems for later in the day.

For example, a process may deliver excellent quality results, but miss a critical check that in itself increases the risk to the organisation. Quality, throughput and staff satisfaction may all be green, but until the customer litigation arrives, or the regulator or auditor identifies an issue, the increase in risk may be hidden.

It is therefore worth performing a walkthrough of the final process to ensure that what should be being done is actually what is being done. Potentially this should be done more than once, for instance immediately after the process is in place and again after a week or a month has passed and the process is embedded.

Note: I mention above that during the process change, it is good practice to incorporate feedback and modify the process accordingly. Not every replacement process is right first time, and many need to be amended. As a final part of the process remediation it is therefore also necessary to revisit the documentation and ensure that it reflects the process as actually implemented.

45.5.12 Train

It may appear obvious, but in order to get the best out of the new process it is actually necessary to train people on it. Giving them a process description and a walk-through of screens is cheap, but ineffective.

Many data quality problems are caused by poor training and hence poor understanding of the downstream impact of getting processes right, and not simply short-cutting them to make them quicker or easier. Simply perpetuating the problem with a different process is neither effective nor clever.

The organisation needs to take the time to undertake proper training sessions, followed up by close mentoring, and on the job training. Yes, this is more expensive than simply dropping a process document on a desk and letting people read it, but it is much, much more effective. Remember one of the principles of the approach recommended in The Data Quality Blueprint is "do as little work as possible". That absolutely includes not doing work twice because you couldn't be bothered to do it properly the first time.

A much more detailed look at training is contained within the dedicated training chapter later in the book.

45.6 Implementation

For each individual process to be remediated, the process is similar to that for remediation of data. A step through of the process for remediation is below.

- It is necessary to create KPIs at various points throughout the remediation cycle. If this has not been already performed, the original process needs to be benchmarked so that it is possible to say at the end of the process that the data quality has been improved, and by a specific percentage.
- Process options need to be considered. There is likely to be a quality continuum from those changes that will result in a process that will definitely solve data quality problems, but will have adverse business affects, to those that will be easy for the operator, but not change the quality. For example, a process that calls for the customer name to be checked by 10 different people may well be robust, but equally is far too onerous. Also, there may be different options between business process and IT process.
- A final option is decided and tested. This can then be implemented as a pilot in a small area of the business to assess changes.
- Finally, the process change is rolled out to the entire organisation (or at least the areas of the organisation that use it).
- As in the case of remediation of existing data, it is essential to have a rollback plan in the event of the process not being as effective as hoped, or having a dependency on another element of the organisation which does not complete as planned (e.g. a dependency on a new software installation which is found to be faulty). It will be necessary to create and update a change log on a regular basis to track the changes that are being made.
- Keep workflow updated on a regular basis so that the project as a whole has clear visibility of the progress of the remediation.

The overall approach is shown in the diagram below.

The Data Quality Blueprint

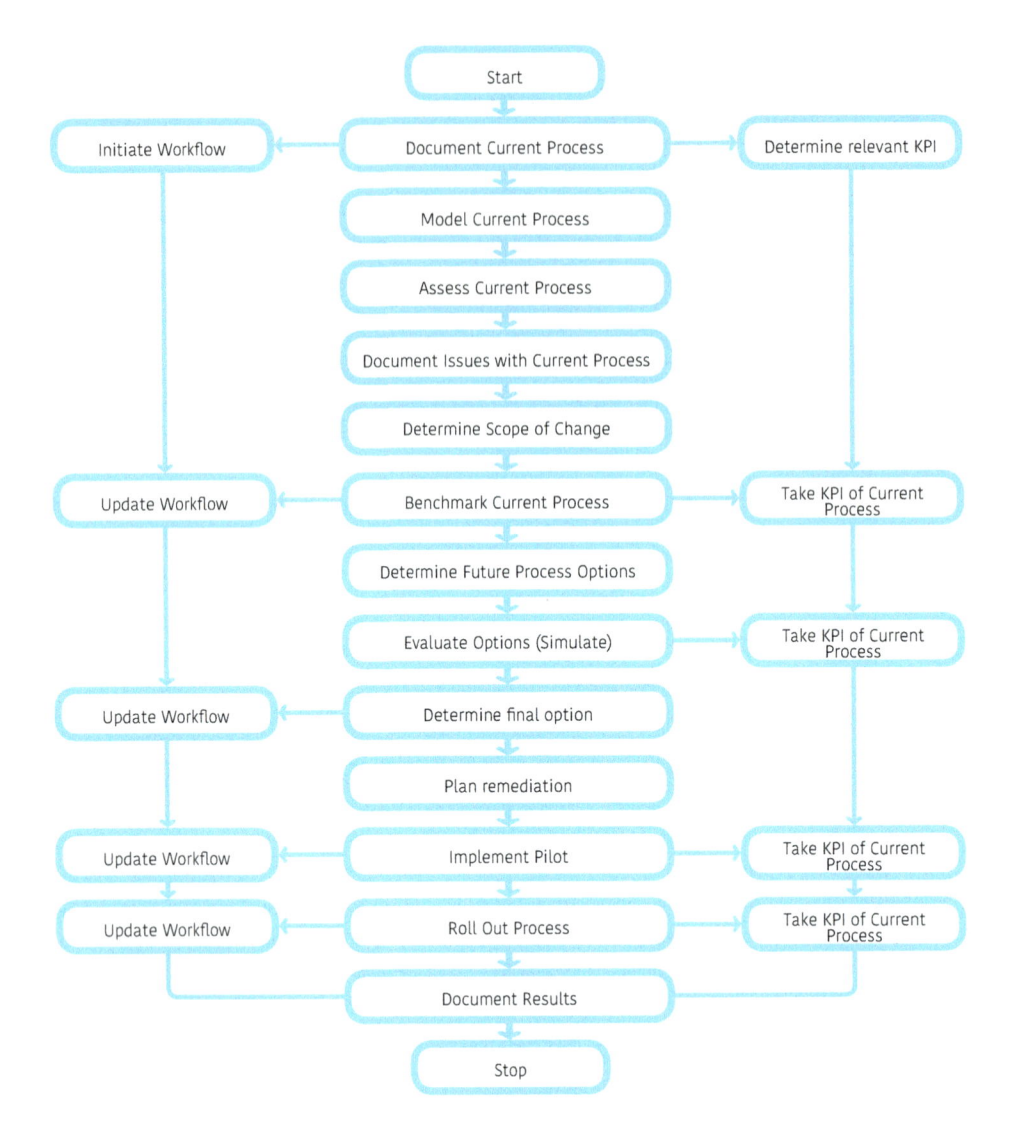

```
                              Start
                                ↓
Initiate Workflow ← Document Current Process → Determine relevant KPI
                                ↓
                      Model Current Process
                                ↓
                      Assess Current Process
                                ↓
                Document Issues with Current Process
                                ↓
                    Determine Scope of Change
                                ↓
Update Workflow ← Benchmark Current Process → Take KPI of Current Process
                                ↓
                  Determine Future Process Options
                                ↓
                  Evaluate Options (Simulate) → Take KPI of Current Process
                                ↓
Update Workflow ← Determine final option
                                ↓
                        Plan remediation
                                ↓
Update Workflow ← Implement Pilot → Take KPI of Current Process
                                ↓
Update Workflow ← Roll Out Process → Take KPI of Current Process
                                ↓
                        Document Results
                                ↓
                              Stop
```

45.7 Testing

I will mention briefly the approach to testing. In the same way as remediation of data there needs to be a rigorous approach to the change of business process. For business process this will not only include the propensity of the process to create quality information, but also to meet business requirements for the process, within a timescale that is commensurate with efficient resource use and supporting the ability of the organisation to improve the bottom line. As a result, testing cannot simply be focused on data quality, but also on these other factors, so as to ensure that data quality is not improved at expense elsewhere.

45.8 Workflow

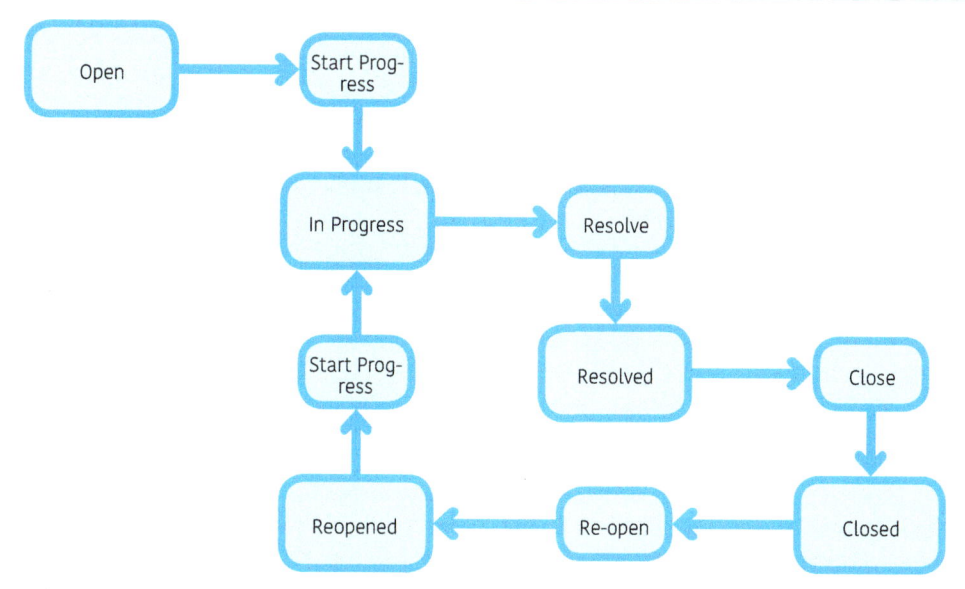

As in the case of remediation to data, it is necessary to operate and manage a workflow which will control the change process. As I have already covered the subject of workflow in both the project planning chapter and the remediation chapter I will not revisit the subject here, other than to show a possible template for recording the progress of the process remediation below.

Element	Description	Remediation Type	Owner	Stage	Current KPI
New customer set up	Add check for existing customer	Process redesign	Contact centre	In progress	Pilot in progress
New customer set up	Add check for existing customer	Process redesign	Branch	Not started	Not started
Report creation	Add data integrity check	Process redesign	Finance	In progress	

45.9 Where do we stop?

Similarly to data remediation, it is not possible to make any process 100% watertight, and the closer a process gets to 100% watertight then the more it costs for each additional element of quality improvement. In most processes there will be obvious elements which are significant in terms of data quality, and these should be the primary area of concern.

If The Data Quality Blueprint is being followed, the business should have defined its quality criteria at an earlier stage in the project, and the KPIs that are recorded as part of the process remediation will inform whether the process is now meeting criteria. If it is, then the work is done.

45.10   Further reading

- *Business Process Change*, Paul Harmon, Morgan Kaufman, 2007
- *Business Process Analysis*, Geoffrey Darnton, Requirements Analytics, 2012
- *The Basics of Process Mapping*, Robert Damelio, CRC Press, 2011
- *Business Process Management: Concepts, Languages, Architectures*, Mathias Weske, Springer, 2012
- *Fundamentals of Business Process Management*, Dumas et al, Springer, 2013
- *The Ultimate Guide to Business Process Management: Everything you need to know and how to apply it to your organization*, Theodore Panagacos, CreateSpace Independent Publishing Platform, 2012
- *Business Process Management*, John Jeston, Routledge, 2014

45.11   Summary

In this chapter I have discussed the remediation of processes. This has covered the scope and approach for process change. It has covered the step by step process for change and also noted where these steps fit within The Data Quality Blueprint. I have discussed critical considerations that will need to be addressed in any process change project, and also the management of that change and where the organisation should stop. I have also covered how to manage the remediation process through workflow, and how to document this so that it is consistent with architecture and process remediation

This now concludes the remediation section. If we are following the book in a logical manner, we have now remediated architecture, data and processes, and the data and organisation is in a good shape.

However, to really ensure that the information in the organisation remains excellent, we need to make sure all our hard work does not go to waste, and embed good practices and good behaviour within the organisation. This topic is the subject of the next section.

SECTION 5.7
EMBEDDING: KEEPING THE DATA GOOD

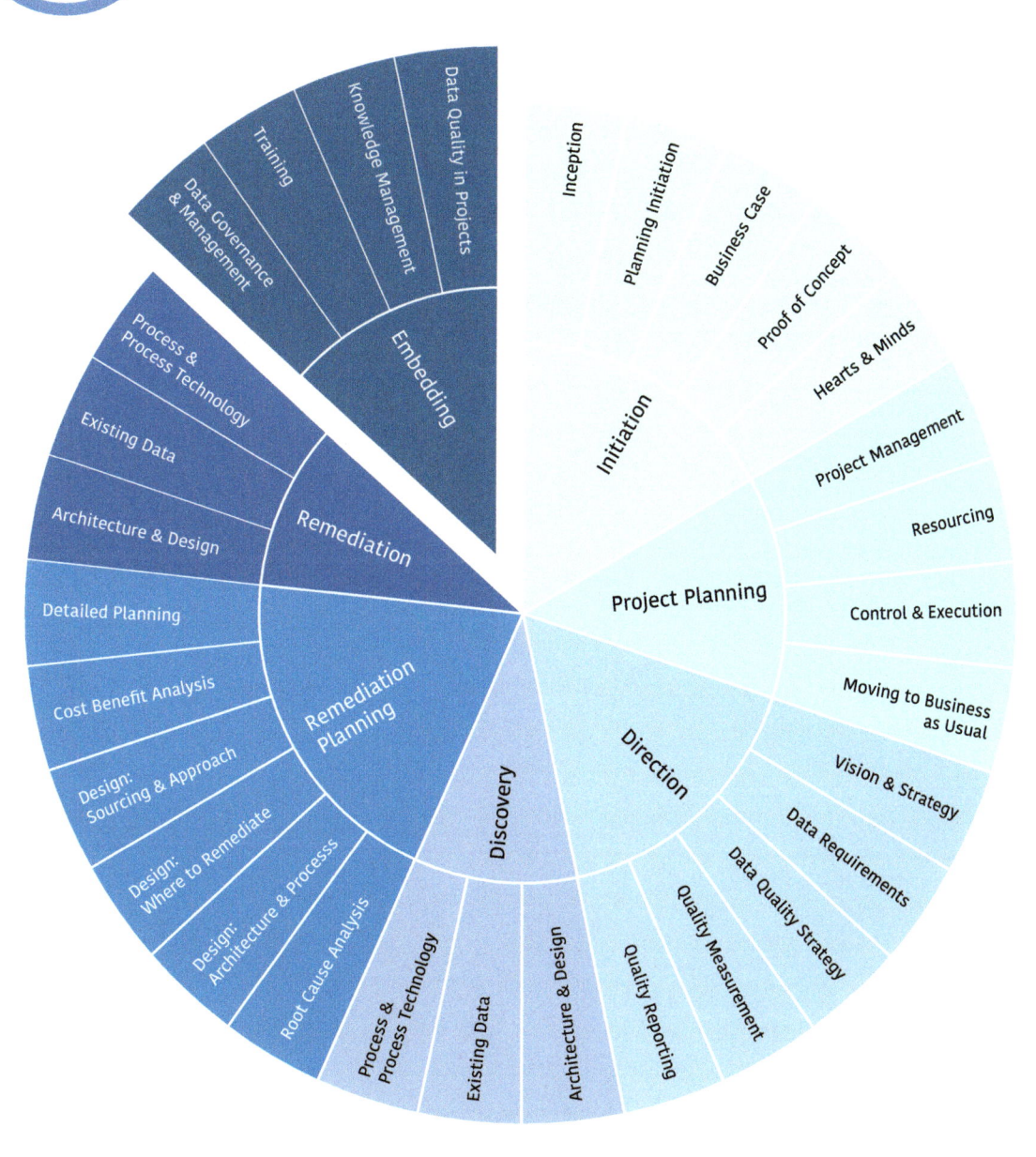

Embedding
- Data Governance & Management
- Training
- Knowledge Management
- Data Quality in Projects

Initiation
- Inception
- Planning Initiation
- Business Case
- Proof of Concept
- Hearts & Minds

Project Planning
- Project Management
- Resourcing
- Control & Execution
- Moving to Business as Usual

Direction
- Vision & Strategy
- Data Requirements
- Data Quality Strategy
- Quality Measurement
- Quality Reporting

Discovery
- Architecture & Design
- Existing Data
- Process & Process Technology
- Root Cause Analysis

Remediation Planning
- Design: Architecture & Process
- Design: Where to Remediate
- Design: Sourcing & Approach
- Cost Benefit Analysis
- Detailed Planning

Remediation
- Architecture & Design
- Existing Data
- Process & Process Technology

491

SECTION 5.7: Index

CHAPTER 46: Section Overview — 495

CHAPTER 47: Data Governance & Management — 497

47.1	Structure	497
47.2	Overview	498
47.3	Activities of Data Governance	501
47.4	Governance framework	502
47.5	Governance Actors	505
47.6	Governance: the role of Information Technology	507
47.7	Implementation of Data Governance	508
47.8	Measurement of Data Governance	509
47.9	Data Governance: Technology to the rescue	510
47.10	Data Management	510
47.11	Third Party Data	512
47.12	Further reading	512
47.13	Summary	513

CHAPTER 48: Training — 515

48.1	Structure	515
48.2	Overview	516
48.3	Who to train	517
48.4	How to train?	519
48.5	Specific Techniques	521
48.6	When to train?	523
48.7	Define training success factors	525
48.8	Further Reading	525
48.9	Summary	526

CHAPTER 49: Knowledge Management — 527

49.1	Structure	527
49.2	Overview	528
49.3	What is the Information?	530
49.4	Where is the Information	530
49.5	Who needs the Information	531
49.6	How do People try and find Knowledge?	532
49.7	So what is the Strategy?	533
49.8	Focus Groups	533
49.9	Project Blogs	534
49.10	After Project Review	534
49.11	Create a Data Governance function	534

49.12	Embed the Information within the Business Areas		535
49.13	Knowledge Bases (SharePoint or Intranet Sites)		535
49.14	Knowledge Map or Community Yellow Pages		535
49.15	Knowledge Cluster/Centre for Excellence/Community of Practice		536
49.16	Knowledge Fair		537
49.17	Bringing it all together		538
49.18	Further reading		538
49.19	Summary		539

CHAPTER 50: Data Quality in Projects — 541

50.1	Structure	541
50.2	Overview	542
50.3	Why is this Important?	542
50.4	Use of Embedded Data Governance and Project Governance	543
50.5	Project Data Forums	543
50.6	Data Quality Processes	545
50.7	Understand your Sources	545
50.8	Understand your Data	546
50.9	Communications	546
50.10	Summary	548

SECTION 5.7 EMBEDDING: KEEPING THE DATA GOOD

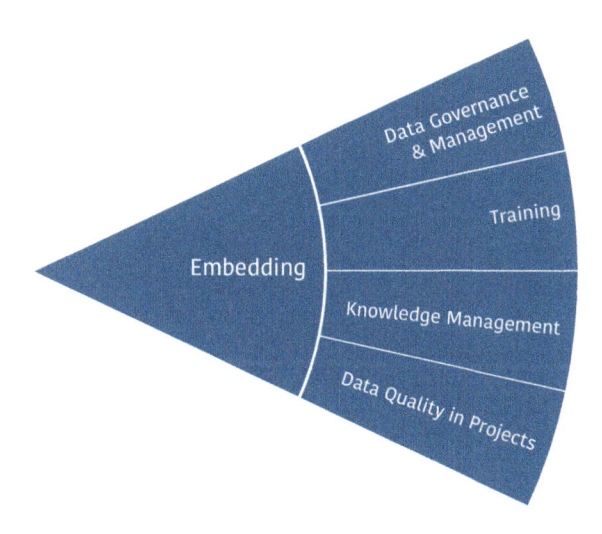

CHAPTER 46 SECTION OVERVIEW

Now that the business has achieved good data quality, the challenge is to keep it good. In order to do this, the new processes must be embedded into BAU, a governance framework must be established, knowledge needs to be maintained, and training imparted – otherwise there is a certainty that the organisation will be facing the same problems (and the same effort required to remediate) in a relatively short period of time.

Some of the embedding has already been discussed – for example, remediating processes so that they are less likely to cause poor data to be created or retained. However, it is necessary to look at the other components of embedding data quality within an organisation to ensure that the changes last longer than the next customer request to change their address.

If we look at the graphic below, which we created when discussing causes for poor data quality, we have now covered direction, and also the remediation of architecture, process & process technology, and existing data. The next stage is to ensure that the issues do not reoccur, and this is the role of governance, training and knowledge management. I have also covered in this section the scenario of looking at project data quality, in isolation from an organisation-wide initiative.

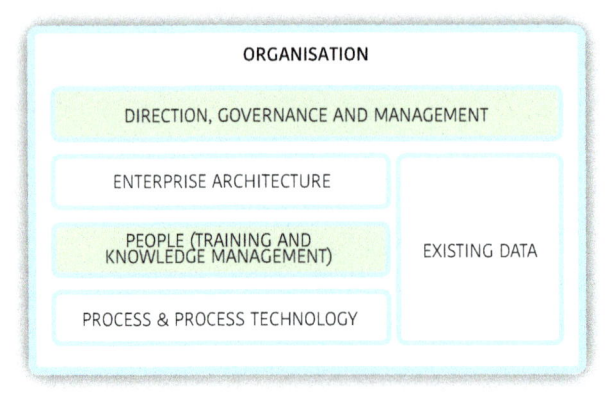

The Data Quality Blueprint

```
ORGANISATION

DIRECTION, GOVERNANCE AND MANAGEMENT

ENTERPRISE ARCHITECTURE

PEOPLE (TRAINING AND                    EXISTING DATA
KNOWLEDGE MANAGEMENT)

PROCESS & PROCESS TECHNOLOGY
```

It should be noted that the embedding does not in all cases have to wait until the data quality project has completed; data governance is a good thing to do whether a data quality project is being undertaken or not. Training is likewise. Knowledge management covers the retention of knowledge after the project has completed, so necessarily has to wait until that knowledge is available. The consideration of data quality in projects may be applicable either with or without a large data quality project within the organisation.

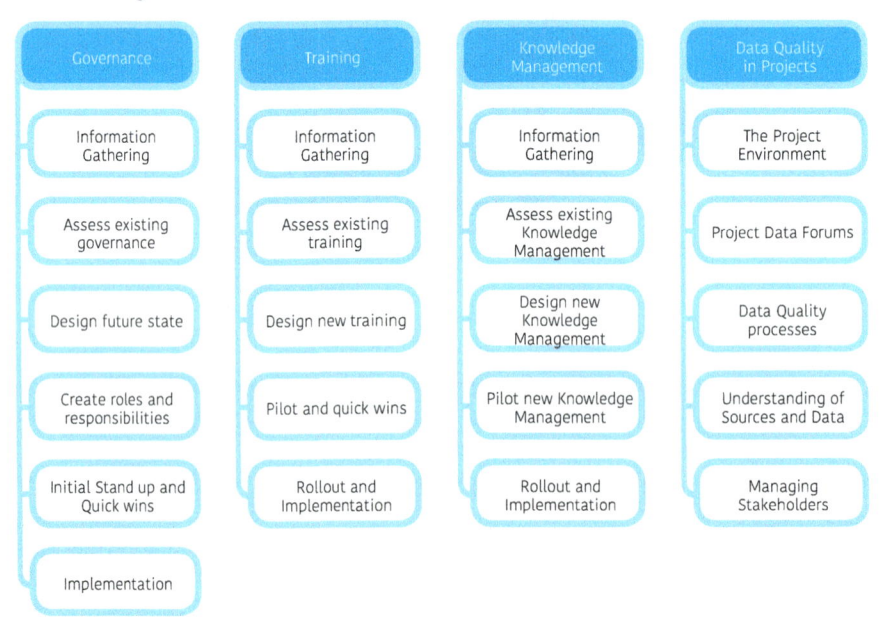

Governance	Training	Knowledge Management	Data Quality in Projects
Information Gathering	Information Gathering	Information Gathering	The Project Environment
Assess existing governance	Assess existing training	Assess existing Knowledge Management	Project Data Forums
Design future state	Design new training	Design new Knowledge Management	Data Quality processes
Create roles and responsibilities	Pilot and quick wins	Pilot new Knowledge Management	Understanding of Sources and Data
Initial Stand up and Quick wins	Rollout and Implementation	Rollout and Implementation	Managing Stakeholders
Implementation			

In a similar way to the previous section, I have not looked to step through the project tasks in detail. The process of assessment of existing governance, training and knowledge management against a desired future state, the creation of a roadmap and thence a plan is relatively standard fare and much less complex than the same process for architecture, process and data which I have already covered in detail. The challenge here is in the determination of the future state, and in the case of governance, training and knowledge management there is widespread misunderstanding of what is actually best practice. In this section, therefore, I have looked more to discuss what good looks like in these areas, and why.

SECTION 5.7 — EMBEDDING: KEEPING THE DATA GOOD

CHAPTER 47 — DATA GOVERNANCE AND MANAGEMENT

47.1 Structure

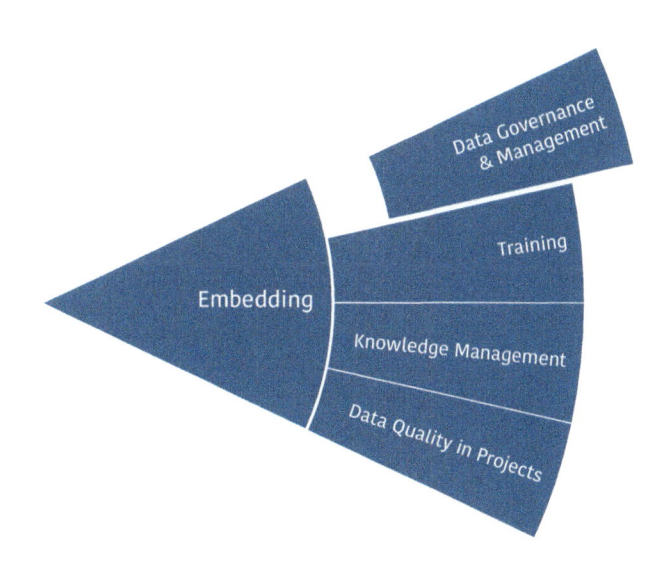

This stage of The Data Quality Blueprint includes the following topics:

1. Data Governance & Management
2. Training
3. Knowledge management
4. Data quality in projects

This chapter covers the first of these topics.

47.2 Overview

INPUTS
- All artefacts created or utilised by the project to date
- Corporate governance framework
- Existing information on data owners
- Existing information on data stewards

OUTPUTS
- Data governance framework
- Data governance roles and responsibilities
- Implementation plan
- Business pain points
- Sustainability plan
- Forum terms of reference
- RACI
- Stakeholder assessment
- Stakeholder map
- Communications plan
- Quick wins
- Project assessment framework
- Processes and procedures
- Sustainability plan
- Change capacity assessment
- Updated RAID
- Data governance deliverables
- Governance impact analysis
- Data governance scorecard

DEPENDENCIES
- Executive support
- Access to key stakeholders

TASKS
- Scope and objectives
  - Identify scope of data governance for this project
  - Define drivers for data governance
  - Define data governance goals
  - Agree with sponsor
  - Document and upload to project repository
- Initial Plan
  - Draft high level data governance implementation plan
  - Identify team members and training needs (if any)
  - Create resource plan and team organisation
  - Draft risks/assumptions & dependencies
  - Create initial cost estimates
  - Agree with sponsor
  - Document and upload to project repository
- Information Gathering
  - Identify key stakeholders (if not already done)
  - Obtain existing governance documentation (if any)
  - Obtain terms of reference for existing forums
  - Obtain lists of existing data owners/stewards
  - Attend forum meeting
  - Interview key stakeholders
  - Create and circulate governance questionnaire
  - Identify information needs of the organisation (if not already done)
  - Obtain existing lists of issues/resolutions
  - Hold information-gathering workshops
  - Create stakeholder assessment (if not already done)
  - Perform change capacity assessment if not already done
  - Perform risk assessment and update RAID
- Assess existing governance (if any)
  - Assess existing governance against best practice
  - Identify pain points from interviews/questionnaires
  - Identify cost impact of pain points
  - Identify areas or poor management or quality
  - Identify gaps in governance or management
  - Draft governance assessment
  - Draft initial business case
  - Agree with sponsor and key stakeholders
  - Finalise and upload to project repository
- Design future governance structure
  - Draft vision and mission statement for data governance
  - Create governance principles from the data principles in the data strategy
  - Socialise with sponsor and key stakeholder for agreement
  - Create elevator pitch
  - Draft framework design
  - Draft forum design
  - Draft RACI
  - Draft process design

- Draft terms of reference
- Draft data management and governance taxonomy
- Map the effects of governance to data quality pain points
- Identify any need for data governance toolsets
- Draft process for identification of owners and stewards
- Socialise all of the above with key stakeholders and update for feedback
- Upload to project repository
- Rollout and Sustainability plan
  - Update initial implementation plan
  - Create sustainability plan
  - Create communications strategy for governance
  - Create change management plan
  - Update costs and benefits
  - Create rollout and sustainability plan
  - Agree with sponsor and key stakeholders
  - Upload to project repository
- Roles and responsibilities
  - Identify data owners and discuss roles with them
  - Write data owner training
  - Identify data stewards and discuss roles with them
  - Write data steward training
  - Finalise data steward network
- Initial stand up and quick wins
  - Define scope for initial stand-up
  - Identify owners and stewards
  - Train owners and stewards
  - Convene initial forum meetings
  - Present to key stakeholders
  - Create project assessment
  - Identify and implement quick wins
  - Identify governance metrics
  - Document data governance deliverables
  - Create governance impact analysis
  - Draft process for identification of owners and stewards
  - Present to sponsor and key stakeholders
  - Design issue reporting forms
  - Start documentation of data lineage
  - Start documentation of data dictionary
  - Start creation of data standards
- Implementation
  - Identify immediate priority tasks and complete
  - Create data governance scorecard
  - Start project assessment
  - Create data governance processes and procedures
  - Agree with key stakeholders
  - Start information management assessment
  - Continue project assessment
  - Include data governance in intranet information
  - Implement data governance scorecard
  - Implement data governance toolsets

The implementation of data governance is absolutely a project in itself. This chapter gives an introduction to the much-misunderstood concept of data governance and a high level overview of the tasks that would be required for implementation, specifically in relation to data quality. As such after reading this chapter the practitioner will have the knowledge to understand the implementation tasks for a governance project that may be implemented alongside the data quality project, and also an understanding of the interactions between them.

To cover the misunderstandings first, data governance is the discipline of acting to align data management with the governance and risk appetite of the organisation. Data governance is not data classification management (sensitive, highly confidential, etc); running data quality reports (this is data quality management); data quality remediation; anything to do with access rights (data security management); or the process of building data models. There is also a common misconception that Data Governance is the same as Data Management. Again, this is not true. ISACA's COBIT 5 states:

The COBIT 5 framework makes a clear distinction between governance and management, i.e., they encompass different types of activities, require different organisational structures and serve different purposes. [59]

The DAMA-BOK [60] defines the two as follows:

Data Governance
"The exercise of authority, and control (planning, monitoring and enforcement) over the management of data assets" [61]

Data Management
"The planning, execution and oversight of policies, practices and projects that acquire, control, protect, deliver and enhance the value of data and information assets." [62]

The two are separate but complementary. Data governance has a wide remit, and will include in its tasks governance of all areas of data management. This will include (from the DAMA-BOK):

- Data architecture management
- Data development
- Data operations management
- Data warehousing and business intelligence management
- Reference and master data management
- Data security management
- Document and content management
- Metadata management
- Date warehouse and BI management

A Governance framework does not create good behaviour, but acts to create a framework where good behaviour is encouraged, where bad behaviour identified and sanctioned, where applicable

---

59. COBIT 5, Enabling Information, ISACA, 2013
60. Data Management Body of Knowledge, "DAMA-BOK", Technics Publications, 2010
61. Data Management Body of Knowledge, "DAMA-BOK", Technics Publications, 2010, p37
62. Data Management Body of Knowledge, "DAMA-BOK", Technics Publications, 2010, p18

laws are identified and applied to the organisation, where the processes and procedures of an organisation are developed against the background of good behaviour, and where the behaviour of the organisation is aligned with its overall direction. In addition, a good data governance organisation will act as a centre of excellence where those who wish to be compliant but are not sure how to achieve this can come and ask for advice.

Data Governance is also a subset of corporate governance, which represents the wider organisation – specifically being the way companies are directed and controlled. Within this wider umbrella of corporate governance exist other governance areas, such as Financial, IT, HR and Risk Governance. However data governance should not be tacked on to an existing governance structure as it has its own objectives which should not be diluted by having to share with other governance structures.

Data Governance is inherently linked with the data strategy, IT strategy, data quality policy and the corporate policies and corporate vision.

Within this chapter, I will outline the main elements of a data governance framework. I will concentrate on the elements that are most directly relevant to data quality. I will not spend excessive time covering, for example, data security, notwithstanding the importance of that element of data governance within the overall holistic governance framework of the organisation. At this point I strongly recommend both the COBIT 5 framework and the DAMA Body of Knowledge (DMBOK) as outlining in detail the approaches, industry standards and frameworks in existence for Data Governance.

I have quoted from both texts in this book and will continue to do so in this particularly relevant chapter.

47.3   Activities of Data Governance

We have discussed at some length what data governance is, but have not really delved into what data governance does, specifically the activities performed. Utilising the DAMA framework again, this splits the activities of data governance into data management planning and data management control, listing the activities undertaken by the data governance function as per the below:

Data Management Planning:
- Understand strategic enterprise data needs.
- Develop and maintain the data strategy.
- Establish data professional roles and organisations.
- Identify and appoint data stewards.
- Establish data governance and stewardship organisations.
- Develop and approve data polices, standards and procedures.
- Review and approve data architecture.
- Plan and sponsor data management projects and services.
- Estimate data asset value and associated costs.

Data Management Control:
- Supervise data professional organisations and staff.
- Co-ordinate data management activities.
- Manage and resolve data related issues.
- Monitor and ensure regulatory compliance.

- Monitor and ensure conformance with data standards, policies and architecture.
- Oversee data management projects and services.
- Communicate and promote the value of data assets.

I will not go into all of the above in detail, as most are self-explanatory. The above, together with the introductory text, should make it clear to the reader the scope and nature of data governance. One element worth mentioning is the creation of the data governance framework. The framework is the organisation which enables the performance of data governance. This covers the roles and responsibilities, the organisation itself, and enables all parts of data governance. Hence I will discuss the governance framework in more detail.

47.4 Governance framework

47.4.1 Introduction

A typical framework for data governance is shown in the diagram below. Before going through the structure in any detail, it is worth pointing out that a multitude of variations exist and that there is no one "right answer" to data governance structure. I am describing in this chapter a data governance function that operates across the whole organisation; however a federalised structure – where each area of the organisation has its own governance structure which reports to an executive steering committee – may work better depending on the organisation. Alternatively a virtualised structure that is scattered across the organisation may work for some. The consideration of the varying types of governance structure and their advantages and disadvantages is however beyond the scope of this book.

- Executive Board
- Information Governance Committee [1]
- Data Governance Board [2]
- Local Data Owners and Stewards

47.4.2 Executive Board

The board exists to govern and decide on issues that affect the organisation as a whole, and data governance is part of this. To be effective, data governance must have appropriate board-level representation. There may not necessarily be a "Data Quality Director" or "Data Director" in the same way as there will be an "IT Director" but there should be board representation.

---

[1] May also be called Data Strategy Committee, Data Governance Committee, Information Strategy Committee, Data Governance Leadership Team, etc. The name is not important, the responsibility for the direction of the governance of information throughout the organisation is.

[2] May also be called the Data Governance Working Group, The Data Governance Committee, Data Governance Forum, etc.

One of the biggest challenges facing executives today is that they need to get involved in managing information. Otherwise the information that they use to manage their organisations will be defined by IT. From a data quality perspective the board need to understand that information quality is almost a state of mind.

Note:
"IT" as "Information Technology" is largely misnamed. It is primarily focused on technology and makes technological decisions based on the technical merits or demerits of the case. It may be concerned with the movement of information between servers, databases and desktops, but is rarely – if ever – concerned whether the information meets the business needs. Some organisations are acknowledging this by splitting the role into CTO – Chief Technology Officer and CDO – Chief Data Officer, who may both report to the CIO or exist independently. This is a tacit understanding that CIOs have not covered the element of their role which covers information within the IT domain.

47.4.3   Information Governance Committee

The information governance committee (or the data governance committee) is the top level of the governance structure. It should be headed by a representative of the board who is tasked with data strategy, quality or governance. It needs to include the individual who is responsible for day to day data governance and key representatives from both the business (who use the data) and IT (who are responsible for the infrastructure that moves data around) and data owners (who are responsible for the creation of the data). There may also be representation from legal and regulatory departments, compliance and internal audit. The job of the information governance committee is to ensure that the data strategy supports the vision and strategy of the organisation, the risk appetite of the organisation, and to act as a top-level management to decide the process that must be followed to deal with major data issues, be they inside or outside the organisation. From a data governance perspective, this body is responsible for setting the data governance strategy (and hence the direction of governance in the organisation), approving the decisions of the data governance board and dealing with escalated issues. From a data quality perspective, the information governance committee needs to understand the way in which data quality will support the organisation's information needs, and also the management tasks that will be required in order for that to occur.

47.4.4   Data Governance Board

The data governance board is the functional heart of data governance within the organisation. This body will write data standards, assess and co-ordinate data management, and advise projects. It will consist of senior data stewards, and in a similar way to the information governance committee may also include representatives (albeit less senior) from IT and internal audit. Ideal members are those with a responsibility and interest for data in the organisation, as well as the seniority to act as arbiters in the case of dispute, whilst having the authority to align all areas of the organisation to the overall data governance strategy. From a data quality perspective – and assuming the absence of a specialist data quality board – the data governance board needs to understand the management tasks required to effectively manage data quality. It needs to ensure that data quality is both embedded in all the processes of the organisation and considered within the project environments.

47.4.5 Data Quality Board

The data quality board is an optional forum that may be separate to the Data Governance Board. It is specifically concerned with the data quality elements of the framework. It only forms one part of the various reporting entities that will report to the information governance committee. The role of the data quality board is to create, maintain, implement, and monitor policies, processes, and standards to ensure data quality. It is possible to think of the data quality board as an arbitrator of all data quality decisions. In the event of disagreement within the operational units, the data quality board decision overrides them. The data quality board should be chaired by the Head of Data Governance (or equivalent), and should contain representatives from both the operational units and the information technology areas, and both those in charge of infrastructure and those concerned with data, as well as specific individuals who are owners of operating systems that create or update data.

47.4.6 Summary visual representation of structure

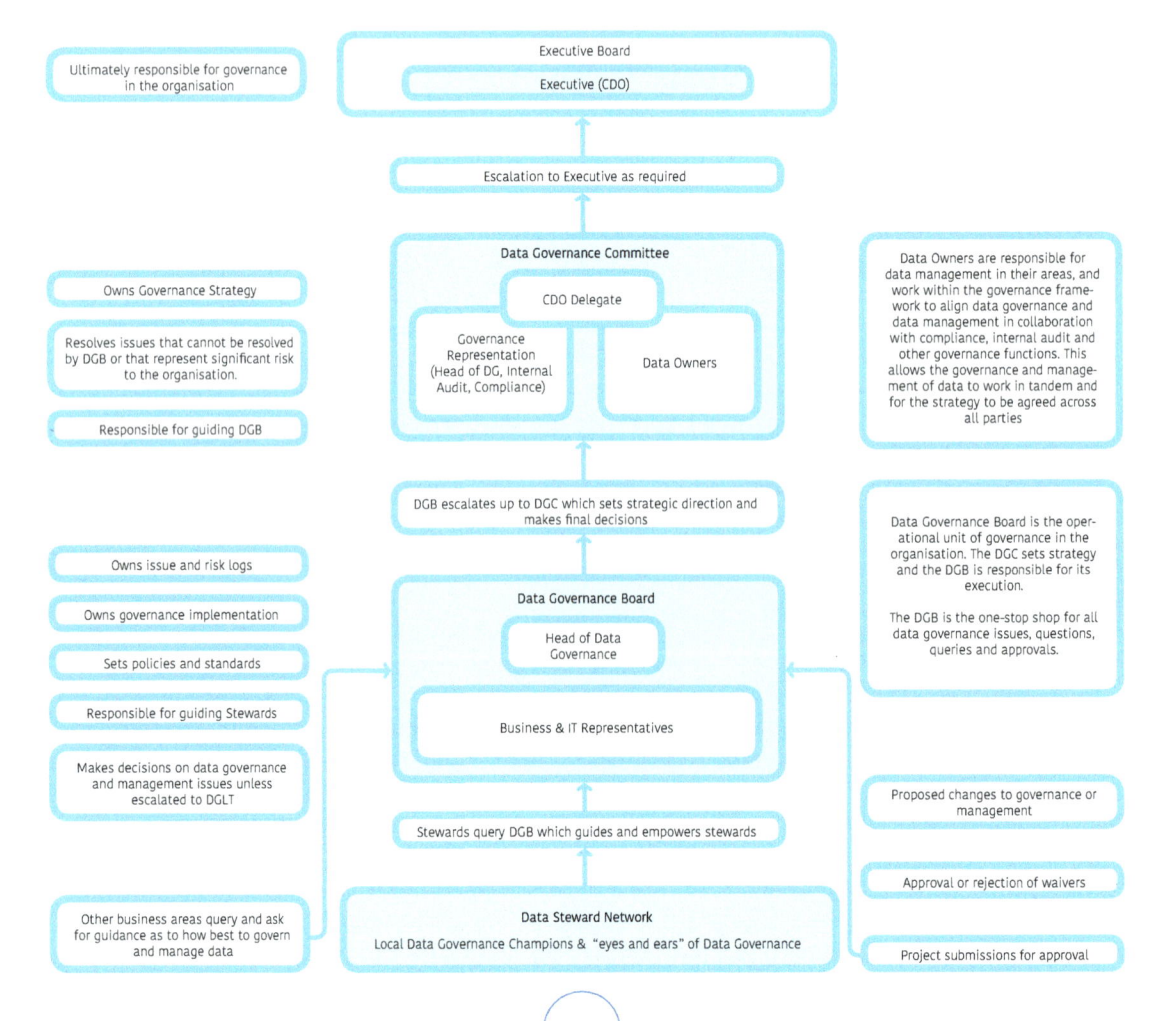

The previous diagram shows a potential framework including the various groups described above and the interaction between them (not including a data quality board).

47.5 Governance Actors

An example of the typical actors within the organisation is shown below.

A sample set of objectives and responsibilities is shown in the appendices.

47.5.1 CDO

The Chief Data Officer (CDO) is the individual responsible at board level for the quality of data within the organisation. They are ultimately responsible for the accuracy of the data which is used to manage the business. This is not a role that is undertaken in an individual's spare time. The CDO should work together with the Head of Data Governance and provide executive sponsorship for data quality and data strategy. The CDO's primary responsibility is for the strategy, planning and management of information in the organisation. The CDO must advocate a holistic approach to data quality, and should be business-focused. "Do we need a CDO?" is a question that is currently asked by a large number of organisations, and the more forward-thinking are coming to the conclusion that the answer is yes. I would go so far as to say that any organisation that states that it does not need a CDO is, by that statement, admitting a level of information maturity that shows they desperately need one.

47.5.2 Data Czar/Head of Data Governance

The Head of Data Governance is the individual within the organisation who has day to day responsibility for data quality and the implementation of the data strategy and the data quality strategy. This role should be full time, report to the CDO, and sit on the information governance committee. They should have a comprehensive knowledge of the factors that affect information quality in an organisation.

47.5.3 Data Owners

A number of definitions for "data owner" exist. The most common is the data owner as the person (or person in charge of the department) who has the responsibility for creating the data.
This does not mean that when data is entered by a customer on a web form that the customer is the data owner, but that the responsibility of the data owner is where the information first touches the organisation. In this case the owner of the application or database that first receives the customer information.

The data owner will often define the format of the data, the access to the data, and will exist as the primary port of call for those who wish to ask queries of the data. If there are any issues with the use of the data the owner will be involved. The data owner will have a business-level responsibility that is relevant to the data. For example, the head of the contact centre may be data owner for customer information that is generated by a contact centre. In terms of data quality, the data owner is ultimately responsible for "getting it right first time".

47.5.4 Data Stewards

There are many different definitions for data steward in existence; the most common is that data stewards look after the data whilst it is under their control. A data steward is responsible for any transformations to the data after receipt. A typical data steward might be the functional lead of a business area, who will inherit information from, for example, a contact centre, and then pass it on to a reporting team. An example using product data is shown below for clarity.

The marketing team as data owner creates product characteristics

⬇

The contact centre creates customer records and loan records (Data Owner) – but is a data steward for the product details.

⬇

The arrears department contains a data steward for the customer and loan and product records, but a data owner for the delinquency records.

⬇

The arrears reporting department will contain a data steward for all the records above, but owns (creates) no data of its own.

From a data quality perspective the data stewards are the "eyes and ears on the ground". They are the local face of data governance, and will look to identify where data management tasks – such as data quality – are failing in their job. Where they see data quality issues they would be expected to raise this with local management (or the project if they are a project data steward) and track whether it is addressed. It is worth mentioning that data stewards may not be tied to data, but may be tied to systems (as in a data warehouse) or even themes (for example data quality). It is perfectly possible to have a matrix of data stewards in an organisation. As such, the consideration of poor product data quality in the data warehouse may involve a meeting of a number of individuals who can each bring their area of specialism to the discussion.

47.5.5 Business Data Users

A data user is someone (or a department) who purely uses data that others provide, creates none of their own, and is not responsible for its safekeeping. This does not mean, for example, that these individuals will be junior, only that they do not themselves create data. The data users are important stakeholders in the quest for data quality – it is they who are most likely to identify issues with the data quality, and they need to have a mechanism for highlighting data quality issues to the data quality management framework in such a way as the issues are addressed.

47.5.6 Business Data Creators

Business data creators have been mentioned a number of times in this book. These are the people who actually type the data into information systems, often with a customer on the other end of a phone or across the other side of a desk, or trying to transcribe a poorly written scrawl on a form. It should of course be noted that the actual contact centre agents will directly create the data that the rest of the business uses. They need to be aware of this responsibility and its importance. As has been repeatedly stated, it is far, far, easier to get data creation right the first time than to remediate the data at a later date. These people are rarely, if ever, encouraged to put data quality at the forefront of their work but are more often encouraged to prioritise factors which actively make quality more difficult, primarily speed.

There needs to be a sea change in the way in which organisations value staff to ensure that the importance of their work is acknowledged. If the organisation defines these people as "business data creators" it not only makes the importance of their work obvious, but may actually allow the people concerned to see the importance of their role, and hopefully for their managers to see the importance of their role too.

47.6 Governance: the role of Information Technology

It has been repeatedly stressed throughout this book that Information Technology (as a department) is the enabler, and not the definer or user of data quality. It is however essential for the IT department to be fully on-side with the elements of data quality that need to be addressed by those of greater technical background. In fact, it can be said that data quality, and the achievement thereof, is very much a partnership between business and IT.

Designated individuals within the IT department should be assigned as "IT Representatives" to the various committees which govern data within an organisation. It would be ideal to have several IT representatives, one from each part of the technology space, for example application, databases and networks.

Each can bring their own specialist knowledge to bear. It should be stressed that they should be working together with the business to achieve the businesses aims, and informing on the effort required or difficultly inherent in achieving those aims, not defining the aims or simply being there to represent the interests of the IT department.

An example

An organisation may wish to migrate data from one poorly designed, controlled and organised database to a new database which only allows numerical entries in phone number fields. It may be found that a high number of data items are in the wrong format (e.g. "(0126) 12345 except in evenings when ring (07658 213432)). There are a number of various possibilities:

- Letting the migration take place, in which case it is extremely likely that a message such as "800,000 records migrated, 85,763 set to null due to type conversion failure" will be seen. Translating the techspeak, what it actually means is that the organisation has just lost 10% of its customer phone records. Permanently, irrevocably, and with a cost of re-instatement many, many times greater than the cost of employment of the person who has just pressed "enter".
- The person can look at the data, realise it won't transfer, and reset the characteristics of the new, shiny, database to match those of the old, poorly designed and organised database. In this case all the data will transfer, but the organisation will end up with simply a new, poorly designed, controlled and organised database.
- The person could look at the data, and escalate to a local data steward that a large amount of data is in the wrong format and needs remediation before any bulk transfer takes place. A remediation project can be designed and the data corrected.

Of the three possibilities, (1) is by far the least onerous in terms of the IT department but you can hear the business scream (2) would cause the IT department to twitch but keep the business happy, and (3) is by far the correct thing to do.

47.7 Implementation of Data Governance

Many data governance frameworks are a paper exercise implemented at a high level which do not end up having much real meaning or effectiveness. An executive waving some consultant-written papers does not create a workable governance framework. In this section I will outline a variety of ways of implementing governance. Data Governance is a people and process function, and the most important part of implementation is to gain buy-in from key stakeholders across the organisation, and to put in place a framework that will work with the individual organisation and can be sustained. Personally I always promote governance as a positive force for change in the organisation, empowering individuals who work with data on a daily basis, and reducing the wasted time these people have to spend in cleansing bad data and chasing good data.

This is why one of the easiest ways of implementing data governance is using what already exists in the organisation. In reality, a large number of the individuals within any organisation are already performing data governance roles, they are just not formally designated in that way, probably don't have the tools or the time to do the job well, and are frustrated because they don't have the authority to solve the problems that plague their everyday working life. One of the cheapest and most effective methods of implementing data governance is to use these people, and give them what they need, being the tools, time and authority to perform a data governance role.

An example may be that an individual receives a data file from an upstream department. It is late, of poor quality, and they spend time processing it, making it fit for purpose and then using it.

The individual in the upstream department may prepare a file for a downstream department. They may have no idea of the quality that is expected by the downstream department and prepare what is the easiest for them, or sometimes they will try and be helpful and create what they think would be useful for the downstream department. In reality, both of these individuals are in data governance roles and data silos. The easiest way to implement data governance is to call one a data owner (the creator of the data) the other a data steward, and give them the time to talk to each other and solve the data problems. This – fitting existing roles to data governance tags – will be welcomed by the individuals themselves – and is seen by employees as empowering them rather than imposing another governance structure from the top. In the same way, there are likely to be many existing committees that in reality have some form of data governance remit. Hijacking these, or giving them an additional responsibility for data governance may not be the purest way of implementing data governance but it is the easiest.

An alternative is to start small and build. One of the most effective implementations I have seen was an organisation who started with the finance function and implemented data governance in this area. It then rolled this out to the rest of the organisation once the policies and procedures had been tried and tested.

As stated earlier, there are a number of excellent books that go into the implementation of data governance in detail, and some I list at the end of this chapter.

47.8   Measurement of Data Governance

One of the areas that tend to stump organisations is how to measure data governance. "Governance" is a euphemistic term, and defining metrics may appear counter-intuitive. However, like any area of the organisation, how do you measure success if you cannot measure anything? The trick here is to measure the effects of governance, and the buy-in to governance. For example:

- It is possible to measure the buy-in to governance by measuring the amount of people that turn up to meetings. An attendee may score 5 for turning up in person, 3 for sending a delegate, and 0 for neither. A minimum score for the year can then be set.
- It is possible to measure the coverage of data definitions within the organisation. If the core reporting data covers 500 fields, it is possible to measure how many of these have an agreed definition.
- It is possible to gain feedback on data governance from a questionnaire, or from training. "How many people have completed their governance questionnaire this year with a score of 90% or higher?"
- It is possible to measure the coverage of data lineage, the "auditability" of data or the degree to which the varying components of data management are meetings standards.
- I have on occasion designed a project assessment framework for data governance, where each project was scored against the DAMA framework. Hence each project would have to demonstrate – for example – how it defined data quality metrics.

The summary here is that it is perfectly possible to measure data governance given a bit of lateral thinking and ingenuity.

47.9 Data Governance: Technology to the rescue

> "One aspect of tools to understand at this point is that you should not feel compelled to buy data governance tools just because you are doing data governance. By definition, a tool exists to improve something you are already doing. If you are not doing formal data governance yet, or if you are doing it poorly, then casting about for a tool to help you deploy DG is a waste of time. This flies in the face of typical IT philosophy, where the tool is usually acquired first. This is a notoriously silly thing to do."
> **"Data Governance"**, John Ladley, Esevier, 2012

There are a number of vendors that look to promote a technological solution to data governance. This is worth discussing as data governance is not a technological challenge and therefore can only partially be facilitated by technology. Where these "data governance" tools are able to help is facilitating many elements of data management. These tools are generally focused on the maintenance of data lineage and data definitions. A typical example might allow data lineage to be imported from Extract-Transform-Load tools, or may enable data definitions to be proposed and then approved by relevant individuals in the organisation. Whilst having all lineage and meaning in one place is most certainly a considerable boon for data management of the organisation, it is not a one-stop solution for governance.

47.10 Data Management

We have looked at data governance, which is the orchestration of the activities that are included within data management. The next stage is therefore to look at data management and see what those activities are and how they relate to data quality. Within this chapter I have used the DAMA framework as a basis, as it is industry standard and I find it is a useful checklist for data management activities, and whilst it doesn't cover everything, and may need some tweaking for each individual organisation, it is a good start. The DAMA framework lists the following as activities within the data management space.

- Data architecture management
- Data development
- Data operations management
- Metadata management
- Data warehouse and BI management
- Data quality management
- Document and content management
- Data security management
- Reference data management

It might be an easy assumption to make that the only elements of this overall framework associated with data quality are those within quality management, but all aspects of data management contribute to data quality. For example, we have already discussed at length how the data architecture of the organisation will affect the ability of the organisation to achieve its data quality aims. In the interest of brevity, however, this chapter will focus on the data quality management element of the DAMA framework. DAMA states that the components of data quality management are:

- Develop and promote data quality awareness
- Define data quality requirements

- Profile, analyses and assess data quality
- Define data quality metrics
- Define data quality business rules
- Test and validate data quality requirements
- Set and evaluate data quality service levels
- Continuously monitor and measure data quality
- Manage data quality issues
- Clean and correct data quality defects
- Design and implement operational data quality measurement procedures
- Monitor operational data quality measurement procedures
- Audit data quality management

The reader at this point can clearly see that the content of this book has covered all but the last of the above. Audit is outside scope, being part of the governance solution of the organisation and not specific to data quality. As the elements have already been covered, there is no value in simply repeating large sections of the book text here, so in the table below I have merely noted where in this book these elements are discussed.

Data Quality Management Topic	Covered in The Data Quality Blueprint
Develop and promote data quality awareness	See communication (under "hearts and minds" in initiation stage)
Define data quality requirements	See data quality requirements (under direction stage)
Profile, analyses and assess data quality	See discovery and data quality reporting
Define data quality metrics	See data quality metrics (under direction section)
Define data quality business rules	See data quality requirements (under direction stage)
Test and validate data quality requirements	See data quality requirements (under direction stage)
Set and evaluate data quality service levels	See data quality requirements (under direction stage)
Continuously monitor and measure data quality	See data quality reporting (under direction Stage)
Manage data quality issues	See governance and data quality reporting
Clean and correct data quality defects	See remediation
Design and implement operational data quality measurement procedures	See data quality metrics (under direction section)
Monitor operational data quality measurement procedures	See data quality reporting (under direction Stage)
Audit data quality management	Not covered in this book

The above table also demonstrates that The Data Quality Blueprint is entirely in accordance with and supports the DAMA framework.

47.11 Third Party Data

A special case for data management is third party data, as using data supplied by third parties exposes the organisation to risk. This risk will include, but is not limited to:

- Supply of incorrect data, resulting in poor decision making, time spent on data cleansing or poor customer experience.
- Supply of correct data in a wrong format, resulting in poor decision making, time spent on data cleansing or poor customer experience.
- Supply of data with a different meaning to that which the organisation expects (poor understanding of requirements) resulting in poor decision making, time spent on data cleansing or poor customer experience.
- Inappropriate access to organisation customer data.
- Loss of data due to poor backup and recovery systems.
- Legal or regulatory breach or loss of reputation due to any of the above.

It is critical that the organisation is as diligent in its control of data that is received from third parties as it is with internally sourced data. Data that is received from third parties needs to conform – in exactly the same way – to the data principles, and hence the data governance and data management activities that the organisation mandates.

47.12 Further reading

I have clearly stated throughout this book that I am covering topics at a high level and with a focus on data quality. In this data governance is no exception. However it is fully appreciated that a reader may wish to delve into subjects more thoroughly, and in the case of data governance if the reader would like to learn more about this topic then the list below contains a number of publications that I would recommend for further reading.

- *Data Governance*, John Ladley, Morgan Kaufman, 2012.
- *Data Governance Tools,* Sunil Soares, MC Press, 2014.
- *Data Stewardship.* David Plotkin, Morgan Kaufman, 2014.
- *Non-Invasive Data Governance,* Robert Seiner, Technics Publications, 2014.
- *Performing Information Governance,* Giordano, IBM Press, 2015.
- *Master Data Management and Data Governance,* Berson & Dubov, McGraw Hill, 2011.
- *COBIT 5*, **Information Systems and Control Association**, 2013.
- *Data Management Body of Knowledge, DAMA-BOK,* Mosely et Al, Data Management Association, 2010.

47.13 Summary

In this chapter I have discussed the way in which data governance can be used to embed data quality within the organisation. I have taken time to define the meaning of data governance and how it is different from both data management and also data quality. I have outlined a typical data governance framework, and explained how the actors within that framework can work together to promote data quality in the organisation. I have discussed briefly the measurement and implementation of data governance and finally have demonstrated how the approach recommended in The Data Quality Blueprint covers the data management activities that are outlined by DAMA.

I hope that the end of the chapter the reader can clearly explain data governance and how it can be implemented in an organisation, what a data governance framework is and, importantly, how it is directly relevant to data quality.

In the next chapter I will discuss training, one of the topics most relevant and important to data quality.

SECTION 5.7 EMBEDDING: KEEPING THE DATA GOOD

CHAPTER 48 TRAINING

48.1 Structure

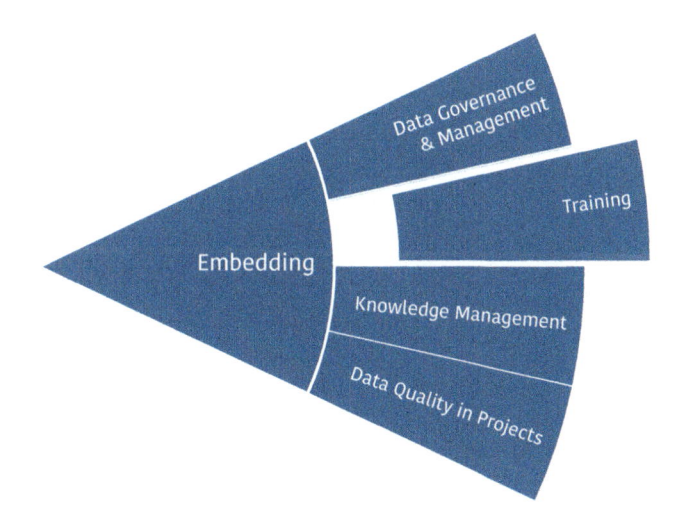

This stage of The Data Quality Blueprint includes the following topics:

1. Data Governance & Management
2. Training
3. Knowledge management
4. Data quality in projects

This chapter covers the second of these topics.

48.2 Overview

INPUTS
- All artefacts created and utilised by the project to date
- Existing training collateral

OUTPUTS
- Data quality assessment of existing training
- New training plans
- Course notes
- Delivered courses

DEPENDENCIES
- Buy-in from HR
- Access to key stakeholders

TASKS
- Scope and Objectives
  - Identify scope of training for data quality
  - Define training goals
  - Agree with sponsor
  - Document and upload to project repository
- Information Gathering
  - Obtain existing training documentation
  - Attend induction and refresher training
  - Interview selection of critical staff (e.g. contact centre agents)
  - Interview key stakeholders
  - Create and circulate awareness questionnaire
  - Discuss training approach for data quality with training team
  - Collate responses
- Assess Existing Training
  - Assess training against data quality
  - Understand training gaps
  - Assess messaging
  - Draft training assessment
  - Agree with training team
  - Agree with sponsor and key stakeholders
  - Upload to project repository
- Design New Training
  - Create training strategy
  - Identify training KPI
  - Draft new induction training
  - Draft new refresher training
  - Draft new remediation training
  - Draft awareness training
  - Draft executive orientation
  - Define success criteria
  - Agree with training team
  - Agree with sponsor and key stakeholders
  - Upload to project repository
- Pilot and quick wins
  - Training
    - Agree initial groups with training department and key stakeholders
    - Run pilot training
    - Measure success criteria
    - Obtain feedback and update training material
    - Receive written signoff
    - Baseline and upload into project document repository
  - Awareness
    - Discuss approach to awareness with key stakeholder group
    - Define awareness KPI
    - Prepare awareness training roadmap

- Implement pilot
- Measure awareness after pilot
- Document
- Baseline and upload into project document repository
- Rollout
  - Rollout new training schedule
  - Measure KPI and compare with success criteria
  - Report on overall strategy
  - Update training as required

NHS Report outlines cause of poor data quality
"The causes of poor data quality can vary for the individual data set and organisation submitting the data," the NHS Information Centre's report found. "However ... there are a number of consistent areas which lead to poor quality of data across all activities, sectors and data sets."

These are the absence of standards and guidance to measure data quality; poor training and awareness of data quality issues; badly configured or integrated systems and organisational change."
Information Age, July 2012.

One of the most overlooked areas in relation to data quality is training the staff of the organisation. Training is fundamental. It is probably the number one defence against poor data quality, and it is rarely done at all, let alone done well. In this chapter I will answer the questions:

- Who to train?
- How to train?
- What to train?
- When to train?
- How to ensure training is effective?

I am not going to try and replicate the excellent bodies of knowledge that exist and cover the ways and means of creating training manuals, or even running a training course. This chapter is a light touch discussion of training. I will look to explain the importance of training and how data quality can (and should) be included in the overall training strategy.

48.3 Who to train

48.3.1 Executive

The executive need to know what is expected of them, they need to set the tone for data quality in the organisation, and they need to know the effects of data quality. A common challenge with executives is helping them to understand the complexity of fixing data quality issues – a view I have come across is that "IT should do it" or "can we buy some software that will solve the problem?"

Obviously a reader of this book knows that neither is the case, but education of the executive is most definitely part of the script. For the executive the message is as follows:

- Poor data quality costs you money.
- There isn't an "easy" fix.
- Software or IT isn't a possible solution.
- If you want to solve this problem we need the executive to sponsor it, fund it and support it.

The executive have to be bought in to the data quality process – and understand that they have to be bought in to the data quality process.

A one hour training session with the executive can save many days of frustration later in the process.

48.3.2 Business managers and staff

The business managers and staff need to understand the complexity of the IT landscape, and the way in which information flows through the business. For business staff the message is as follows:

- The information is your information.
- Its quality is your responsibility.
- It is much easier to stop problems occurring then solve them later.
- There is no easy solution – IT cannot just "wave a magic wand".
- Poor processes and procedure create bad data.
- There is an inverse relationship between speed and quality.

Business managers and staff need to understand it is their problem to own the data and to both stop the problems occurring in the first place and also to address the problems – with the help of IT.

48.3.3 IT Staff

IT will know that data is not an IT problem, but often hold the view that the business are IT-illiterate and do not know what they want out of the information systems. For IT the message is as follows:

- The business owns the data.
- The business needs good quality data.
- The definitions of good data are not necessarily IT's view of good data.
- Just because the business doesn't understand IT does not mean they don't understand the information they need.
- All data is valuable.

A key point here is that IT needs to help the business solve the data quality problem. Washing their hands of it and stating that it is the business' problem to solve does not improve the relationships between business and IT, nor does it actually help the problem get solved any faster.

48.3.4 Primary data entry staff

These people need to be treated as the gold dust they are and given training to ensure that they understand the importance of data quality and act on data quality issues. The main consideration is that they need to understand the importance of getting it right first time. More than that, they need to understand the effect on the organisation, they need to buy into the need for data quality, and they need to be sufficiently bought in that they feel confident to challenge the manager who tells them to speed up at the cost of quality. As such, these staff not only need to cover the data quality elements of the training, but also need to cover the reporting and governance element of the data quality framework. For the primary data entry staff the message is as follows:

- Poor data quality costs the company money.
- You are at the forefront of the data quality of the organisation.
- If you get it wrong everyone else has to clear up your mess.
- This is being measured.
- Taking care over data quality is being a good corporate citizen.
- If anyone tries to degrade your data quality then this is the way you address that.

A key point here is that primary data entry staff are highly valued, and that it is OK to take time to get data entry right, and that there is an escalation process if pressure is applied to promote throughput over accuracy. In this section I have started with the top of the organisation (the executive) and worked down. However, in terms of overall effect on data quality, those at the bottom are arguably the most important.

48.4 How to train?

"Quality is not an act. It is a habit."
Aristotle

Quality of data is integral for the decision making process for the organisation. Without data that is captured accurately, effectively and efficiently the decisions made based on this data are flawed. These may be operational decisions – whether to lend a customer a certain amount of money, managerial – whether a certain member of staff is performing well or not, strategic – whether the organisation is meetings its strategic targets in terms of market penetration, or visionary, whether the organisation is well placed to become what it needs to in 10 years time.

It is essential that staff are well aware of the effect of poor quality information. Often it is the case that staff are either told to "get it done as quickly as possible" – with the commensurate effect on quality, are not incentivised on quality, or simply are not considered important enough to be trained as to the effect poor quality has on the organisation. In addition, the organisation, by undertaking data quality training, is promoting a data quality culture where all staff with a responsibility for data capture, analysis and reporting are aware of the impact this role has on others. The next question to ask is "how to train". There are several main approaches to training, and I will now discuss some of the main types and their advantages and disadvantages.

48.4.1 On-line and computer-based Training

Probably the most common way that training is delivered in large organisations – in terms of volume of training at least – is via on-line training. The training material is available on the corporate intranet and downloaded – in whole, in part, or streamed – onto an employee's PC. There are many advantages of this kind of training:

- The delivery cost is low.
- It can be created at low cost.
- It can be easily tracked via the system that is used to deliver it.
- The training material can be updated easily.
- The employee can proceed at their own pace.

The disadvantage is that it is not good at transferring information into the head of an employee. Unfortunately it is often delivered via a scenario where the employee is given no specific time to do the training, but is expected to get it done during their working hours. Since most employees don't have spare time lying around for training, it naturally follows that they will try and complete the training in as short a time as possible. Also unfortunately, most online training facilitates this. Even those that track progress and do not let the employee move onto the next page until a training video has completed are vulnerable to an employee simply fast-forwarding the video. The best kind of training is the kind that makes it clear at the outset that there will be an exam at the end of the "course", and the best only give a limited number of attempts for the exam. This will get a much better engagement. However, if this is going to be the strategy, then the employees need to be given time to complete the training – expecting them to do it in their normal working hours is simply going to cause resentment and lack of engagement – exactly the behaviours that the trainer is trying to avoid.

48.4.2 Classroom training

Classroom training is traditional training, and has the advantage that it is one of the best ways of ensuring engagement with the training material. In addition, it is possible to build in simulations, case studies and role-play (of which more later) which can increase the level of engagement. The challenge is that it is expensive in terms of time. An instructor (who is likely a senior individual) and a group of attendees are taken out of their working environment. There must be senior commitment to allow this to happen, especially when a low-cost alternative – on-line training that will be completed in the employee's own time – is on offer. A strong business case needs to be made to justify the mass training of many people in a classroom environment. There are other challenges with classroom training

- The level of interactivity can vary with this kind of training. A simple "lecture" where an individual at the front drones on, and participants either doze off or play with their phones will be an extremely inefficient way of transferring information. On the other hand, training where the participants are forced to interact can be much more effective in terms of engagement, but then time is lost in efficiency.

- Classroom training is often at the mercy of the quality of the individual whi is running the training.
- Scheduling classroom sessions for large numbers of trainees can be difficult – especially when trainees are at multiple locations.
- Often training has to go at the pace of the slowest or accept that they will be left behind.

On the other hand, classroom training does have advantages:

- Engagement is better than other types of training. The instructor can see if the class are flagging or disinterested and a good lecturer can either change the pace or tone, or will have a range of techniques at their disposal to bring back the disinterested or energise the environment.
- Everyone gets the same information at the same time – in theory at least.
- It can be given to many people at the same time. In reality large class sizes do not work.
- Those people who are flagging or not keeping up can be given individual coaching to make sure that everyone reaches the end of the course successfully.
- Those who progress faster than the rest can be given extra questions or material to keep their interest.

48.5 Specific Techniques

48.5.1 Case Studies

Case studies can be powerful training aids – especially for data quality – as they are a real life situation giving an example of where it has gone wrong before. In the case of case studies the participants can be asked to give their opinions on:

- What went wrong?
- Why did it go wrong?
- What could have stopped it going wrong?
- Whose fault was it?
- What processes and controls could have been effective?

This engages the participants in the problem, as well as seeing how small mistakes can have large consequences.

To take an example
Earlier in the book I described a situation where a company made a significant cash loss overnight due to poor data quality in one of their systems. A scenario can be constructed around this example as follows.

In a bank, the bank may source funds overnight to fund the mortgages that it has sold during the day. The amount of mortgages sold was passed through from one system to another via a look-up table, and the values looked up were typed into one system by an operator. The operator mistyped one of the codes for mortgages, resulting in a whole section of foreign currency mortgages being missed and not included in the funding that was negotiated overnight.

As a result it had to be funded extremely quickly in the morning, but a significantly higher exchange rate was paid. The difference in the amount paid at the emergency rate and the amount that would have been paid if it had been included in the overnight rate was well into the millions of pounds.

It can be easily seen how this particular example can be woven into a case study, with participants suggesting changes that could have been made to avoid the problem.

48.5.2   Role Play

A role-play takes a specific situation and walks through it with the training participants playing the part of one (or more, in rotation) actors within the situation. The advantage of a role play done well is that the individual participant will understand the pressures and drivers behind the behaviour that is evidenced by the role, and hence – when coming to the same situation in real life – will better understand the ways in which a specific situation can be handled. One of the specific situations where role-play can be utilised to good effect is the scenario of a manager trying to tell an employee to speed up and ignore the data quality rules, because of a huge backlog. This could include an instruction to enter everything as default values, or to simply enter "anything" in critical fields. This – in real life – is:

- Likely to come up
- Going to be challenging for the employee to deal with

Giving some practice to deal with this kind of challenging situation should pay considerable dividends in the long term data quality of the organisation. Another technique is to run a mock round-table discussion with a group of participants who are given the scenario of a data quality problem that has caused a major issue in an organisation, and the organisation has brought all key players into a workshop to address it. The actors may be:

- The managing director – who has just had to explain to a regulator why there are major data quality problems in the submitted data.
- A primary data entry staff member, who is under pressure to complete forms quickly
- Their manager, who needs to demonstrate throughput and is under fire because of long customer wait times to an contact centre – you can add in recent staff cuts by the managing director due to a desire to increase profitability if you like.
- The reporting department, who have to cleanse the poor data when it comes to them because of poor data entry
- IT who are being criticised for the data quality when actually it is not their fault

As with all role-plays the quality of the learning that comes out of this will be directly proportional to the quality of the scenarios and the back-story that are given to the participants.

48.5.3 Forum Theatre

There is also another version of role play called Forum Theatre. This is similar to role-play but utilises actors with scripts and characters to facilitate the discussion, and then employees can comment and engage with the subject matter and the actors. This is really useful for those employees who have previously had difficulty in engagement with role-play scenarios.

48.5.4 Blended Learning

An answer when it comes to the kind of training to implement is that a little bit of everything works best, an approach that is normally termed as "blended learning". This may consist of an initial e-learning package with a quiz and limited number of attempts, and then a shorter classroom discussion which recaps the key points and then gives the opportunity for role-play or case study. This can then be followed up by additional e-learning and questionnaire feedback.

48.6 When to train?

48.6.1 Induction

The data quality strategy and data quality policy must be an integral part of the induction process for any staff dealing with information, in exactly the same way that data security policies often are part of the induction process. Induction packs should include references to the data strategy/information strategy as well as transparent information as to why data quality matters to the organisation. It should be made clear that concentration by managers on throughput at the expense of quality is not acceptable, and to give intranet/website links and contact details for staff who feel that they are not being given enough time to perform their duties to a required quality standard for guidance and potential escalation. A typical induction pack should cover:

- Why data quality is important to the organisation
- How data quality supports the vision and strategy of the organisation
- How responsibility for data quality is delegated to data owners and stewards
- The data quality framework within the organisation
- How any queries in relation to data quality can be escalated
- How data quality is relevant to the role which the individual has been employed to do

Some staff may of course indicate that they are not being given enough time when in reality they are being given plenty. Here the issues lie with the staff rather than the manager, but that is for the management to manage, as they would any other similar performance related issue.

48.6.2 Awareness

The organisation has a responsibility to ensure that all staff are aware of the vital importance of data quality. Whilst an initial steer in this direction can be given by induction packs, a pragmatic approach would recognise that new starters have a lot to comprehend and ingest in a short period of time, and regular refresher sessions would be required. For existing staff, it is necessary to ensure that they are aware of the importance of data quality, and this can be especially difficult if the focus has not been on data quality to date. The organisation should instil a data quality culture where data quality is at the centre of processes and practices within the organisation. To embed a proactive approach and data quality culture will be to add context to the data issues and identify the impact in organisational terms and the effect this has on financial results and customer care.

48.6.3 Application Training

All staff with a responsibility for collecting and managing information should be required to successfully complete training specific to the systems they will operate. This should include training in relation to maintaining the quality of the information within those systems, how the information quality within those systems will impact on the wider organisation, and the common pitfalls in relation to data quality. For example:

- Duplicate entries resulting in a poor customer experience and poor ability to cross sell.
- Customer annoyance at incorrect static data.
- Time-to-cleanse being used as an example of why good quality data is important.
- Understanding that speed is not actually everything and remediation negates any advantage that initial speed may bring.

Access to systems should be controlled by the individual line manager and only allocated once the individual has completed quality training and is accredited to by the ICT Training Team to use the system.

48.6.4 Appraisals and reward systems

In an effort to reinforce the importance of data quality and install a positive data quality culture data quality leads (owners or stewards) should ensure staff receive feedback regarding their data quality responsibilities and review this as part of the staff appraisal process. Individuals will work to what is measured and by what they are rewarded for – if data quality is not part of this process then it is unlikely that data quality will form part of their everyday work. Lines of escalation should be clear, and any individual who may have concerns about data quality must report those concerns to the relevant line manager, data quality lead and in turn the data quality manager.

48.7 Define training success factors

48.7.1 Metrics

The most effective way of understanding whether training has been effective is to record data quality metrics before and after the training has taken place. However in most organisations this may be problematic as a rolling programme may make it difficult to isolate the effects of the training in terms of overall quality. Many areas will contribute to the data quality at any point in the information flow. In the specific case of primary data entry it is possible to record the quality of entered data before and after training. For other areas, more indirect methods have to be used. Examples are:

- Feedback from the training
- Questionnaires in relation to the way in which staff approach data quality issues, immediately after the training, and then at monthly intervals
- Feedback from downstream recipients of the data
- Questionnaires on how much time is taken by downstream recipients in cleansing data

48.7.2 Train the trainer

Another good way of ensuring that training is effective is training people who are then able to train others. It is often said that one of the most effective ways of finding out whether you have learned a particular subject is to then explain that subject to someone else, and this applies to data quality as well. In addition, training a trainer, who then goes on to train others is an efficient way of cascading information throughout the organisation.

48.8 Further Reading

- *How to Design and Deliver Great Training,* Alan Matthews, CreateSpace Independent Publishing Platform, 2012
- *How to Run a Great Workshop:* **The Complete Guide to Designing and Running Brilliant Workshops and Meetings,** Nikki Highmore SImms, Pearson Business, 2006
- *The Trainer's Toolkit: Bringing brain-friendly learning to life,* Kimberly Hare, Crown House Publishing, 2005
- *The Accelerated Learning Handbook: A Creative Guide to Designing and Delivering Faster, More Effective Training Programs,* Dave Meier, McGraw-Hill Professional, 2000
- *Training for Dummies,* Elaine Biech, For Dummies, 2005
- *Games Trainers Play: Experimental Learning Exercises,* Scannell and Newstrom, McGraw-Hill Professional, 1980.

48.9 Summary

Within this chapter I have explained to the reader how training is an integral part of the effort to embed data quality within the organisation so a large remediation project does not have to be undertaken again in the future. As in the nature of other chapters within the book, this is not meant to be any more than a high level introduction to the subject, and many texts exist on the subject of effective training which cover the subject in far more detail than I have here. However, that said, I have endeavoured to cover, at a high level, the answers to the following questions:

- Who to train?
- How to train?
- What to train?
- When to train?
- How to ensure training is effective?

I have outlined the people that need training, and what are the key points that need to be surfaced for each group. I have covered the various types of training, and their appropriateness to the overall data quality effort, and concluded by looking at when to train. The next chapter will take the concept of training further and look at the sharing of knowledge in a wide context, specifically knowledge management.

SECTION 5.7 EMBEDDING: KEEPING THE DATA GOOD

CHAPTER 49 KNOWLEDGE MANAGEMENT

49.1 Structure

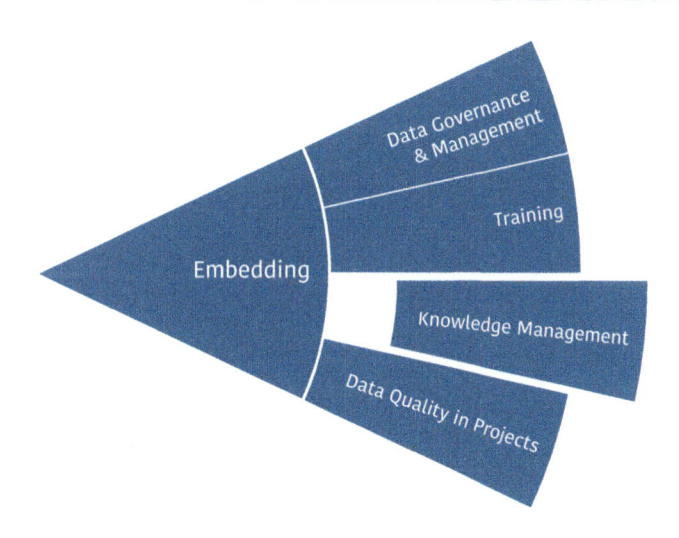

This stage of The Data Quality Blueprint includes the following topics:

1. Data Governance & Management
2. Training
3. Knowledge management
4. Data quality in projects

This chapter covers the third of these topics.

49.2　Overview

INPUTS	TASKS
■ All project artefacts ■ All project personnel	■ Scope and Objectives 　- Identify scope of knowledge management 　- Define knowledge management goals 　- Agree with sponsor 　- Document and upload to project repository ■ Information Gathering 　- Obtain existing knowledge management strategy 　- Define existing knowledge sources 　- Connect to and investigate existing KM sources 　- Interview critical personnel ■ Assessment of existing Knowledge Management 　- Analyse existing knowledge management in relationship to data quality 　- Create knowledge management assessment 　- Discuss with knowledge management team 　- Discuss with sponsor and key stakeholders 　- Finalise and upload to project repository ■ Design future plan for Knowledge Management 　- Define information 　- Assess sources of information 　- Define who needs the information 　- Define how they need to access this information 　- Define information that needs to be documented 　- Create knowledge management strategy 　- Create knowledge management plan ■ Pilot and quick wins 　- Define scope of pilot and/or quick wins 　- Define target audience 　- Define knowledge and sources of knowledge 　- Define method of sharing 　- Implement pilot 　- Measure success ■ Rollout 　- Rollout knowledge management 　- Measure success 　- Report on overall strategy 　- Receive written signoff 　- Baseline and upload into project document repository
OUTPUTS	
■ Catalogs ■ Data stores ■ Knowledge fairs ■ Knowledge maps ■ Training ■ Focus groups ■ After action reviews	
DEPENDENCIES	
■ Training ■ Knowledge champions ■ Knowledge management professionals ■ Facilitators	

"Everything not saved will be lost"
Wii quit screen

Unfortunately, knowledge management is not so much done badly in organisations, but not done at all. However over the period of the data quality project the organisation has gained an enviable understanding of the way in which information flows through it. This will include:
　■ Knowledge of the data

- Knowledge of the way in which various feeds and extracts work
- Knowledge of ETL and the transforms within
- Knowledge of what data is needed where in the organisation
- Knowledge of quality requirements for all data in the organisation
- Knowledge of data lineage

Clearly the organisation does not wish to repeat the project, and the organisation should act to manage that knowledge so it is not lost. In addition, the organisation should act to ensure that the information remains current and is easily accessible by those who wish to use it. This knowledge store will provide information to trainers as well as IT, business staff, and in fact anyone who uses data in the organisation

As data quality is embedded in the organisation and fades from an ever-present active project, recording this information and making sure that it stays current is key to keeping the data quality good.

This chapter looks at the various considerations of data quality knowledge management, and how information can be retained. I will start by looking at the various areas of knowledge management, and how knowledge can be retained for future use and then managed so that the organisation can gain the most use. The questions that need to be answered are:

- How is the information retained after the project is finished or when project members leave the organisation?
- How is the information that has been gained by the project and the project members then shared?
- How does an individual seeking after knowledge on any element that is touched by the data quality project most easily find it?

I stress that knowledge management is much more than simply creating an intranet site where information can be uploaded to moulder away in peace, where no-one uses it for years and it becomes stale and out of date. Knowledge management should be a means of sharing and using and – most importantly – gaining value from the knowledge on a day by day basis.

A popular misconception is that KM focuses on rendering that which is tacit into more explicit or tangible forms, then storing or archiving these forms somewhere, usually some form of intranet or knowledge portal. The "build it and they will come" expectation typifies this approach: Organizations take an exhaustive inventory of tangible knowledge (i.e., documents, digital records) and make them accessible to all employees. Senior management is then mystified as to why employees are not using this wonderful new resource. [63]

As with other areas of this book, this chapter merely scratches the surface of a vast, multi-disciplinary subject, and many publications, books, blogs, articles and papers have been written on a subject that has really blossomed – especially in the last decade. If you wish to learn more – and I urge you to do so as knowledge management is both a fascinating subject and also something in which many organisations fall short – then I have created a list of useful publications at the end of

---

63. *The Introduction to Knowledge Management*, MIT Press.

this chapter. As an aside I would say that knowledge management in most organisations I have been involved with is more or less non-existent. In the same way that I believe data quality is probably ten years behind data security in terms of maturity within the average organisation, knowledge management is probably another ten years behind that.

However, this is a digression, and the first steps towards an effective knowledge management strategy are to answer some key questions:

- What is the information?
- Where is the information?
- Who wants the information?
- How do people try and find knowledge?
- How do we move the information into the people?

You will note how different the above is from the common approach used by most organisations implementing a technological knowledge management solution.

49.3   What is the Information?

Knowledge management that comes out of a data quality project covers a number of areas.

- Knowledge of data quality and remediation. This is the people knowledge of approaches to data quality, the project itself, and how to do it.
- Knowledge of the data (structures, databases, ETL)
- Knowledge of data processes
- Knowledge of data architecture
- Knowledge of data process management
- Knowledge of data architecture management
- Knowledge of data quality management
- Knowledge of techniques such as process mapping, process remediation, process simulation.
- Knowledge of change management techniques
- Knowledge of who shares and uses data within the organisation.

All of these "knowledges" have been created by the project process. The final act of the project should be to make sure that they are not lost.

49.4   Where is the Information

The first stage to consider in knowledge management is where the information is located. The information will be in two places, either in people's brains, or written down. In the case of the written down, these will be either formal deliverables, or rough notes, unfinished documents, drafts, explanatory notes, emails and similar that never made it into a formal deliverable.

Knowledge that is written down is explicit knowledge. Explicit knowledge is stored in documents, or via electronic media such as emails, presentations, databases and servers. Explicit knowledge is that knowledge that most organisations think of when they think about knowledge sharing.

Knowledge that is in people's heads is referred to as tacit knowledge – this is knowledge that the individual has amassed through study, experience and interaction with others. It is context specific, in that it relates to that individual's own experiences – both the subject matter and the individuals they are working with and, on occasion, the timeframe when it occurred. Tacit knowledge is also subjective, and that subjectivity is not necessarily obvious. Sharing of tacit knowledge is dependent on getting the time with the relevant individual to extract the knowledge from them.

Most organisations are fairly bad at the management of explicit knowledge, and don't try and manage tacit knowledge at all. However they both represent a great and largely untapped resource in most organisations.

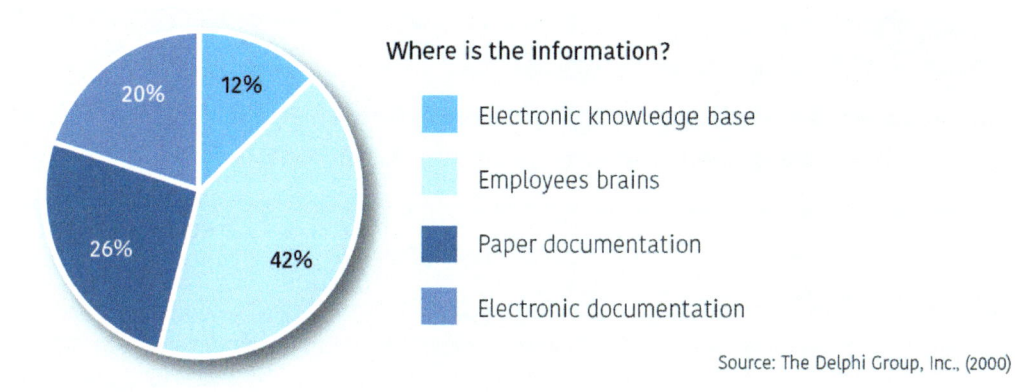

Where is the information?

- Electronic knowledge base — 12%
- Employees brains — 42%
- Paper documentation — 26%
- Electronic documentation — 20%

Source: The Delphi Group, Inc., (2000)

In the case of a data quality project, the knowledge is both tacit and explicit, and in neither case does the organisation wish to lose it. However the first stage is to look from the other angle, which considers what and how people look for knowledge. This recognises that if knowledge currently within people's heads and within project documents can be placed in an environment where people will seek for it, there is some possibility that it might be found. As a result, knowledge management can be divided into two main areas, which split into collecting information and connecting people.

49.5   Who needs the Information

The problem of the "build it and they will come" approach to knowledge management has been touched on above, and the main problem is that it ignores who actually wants the information. The organisation must understand who needs the information generated from a data quality project. Largely, I would submit that the answer to that question is:

- Business units that are within scope
- Reporting that is within scope
- Any user of the data that is within scope

Hence pretty much anyone internal to the organisation.

49.6   How do People try and find Knowledge?

Ignored by builders of knowledge bases worldwide is that people, as a preference, turn to other people to find knowledge, rather than look on the server or in a knowledge base. A survey undertaken by IBM as far back as 2000 proved that knowledge bases ranked fourth after people, prior material, and the web.

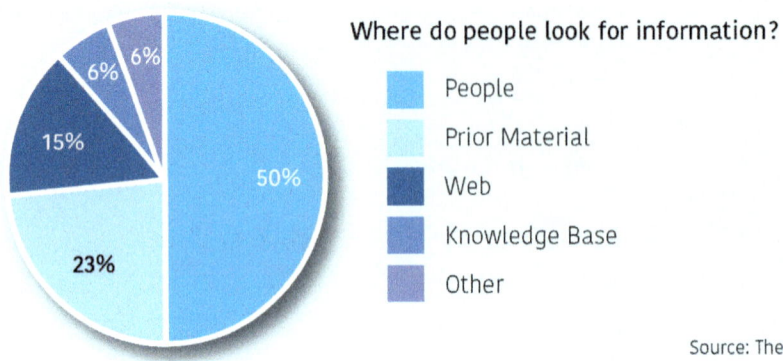

Where do people look for information?

- People: 50%
- Prior Material: 23%
- Web: 15%
- Knowledge Base: 6%
- Other: 6%

Source: The Delphi Group, Inc., (2000)

The desire for people to first turn to people may be an indication of a basic human propensity, or may be an indication of the poor quality of the other options. Certainly this survey was reasonably historical, whilst the web was in its relative infancy. I would suspect that the web is now much larger as a proportion of the total; however I doubt knowledge bases improved their position.

> "Other people are the preferred source of information for a number of reasons. One is of course that it is often faster, but this is not the only reason. When we turn to another person, we not only end up with the information we were looking for but we also learn where it is to be found, how to reformulate our question or query, whether we were on the right track, and where we strayed. Last but not least, the information is coming to us from a known and usually trusted, credible source." [64]

There is limited value in spending vast amounts of money creating and maintaining a knowledge base, and there is no point in creating and maintaining a knowledge base that does not accept the fundamental truism that people will want to talk to people.

Anecdote

I recall an organisation which had spent millions on a technological knowledge base. No-one used it. It was style-rich and information-poor, and finding anything in it was impossible. To the point where "I might as well look on the knowledge base" was informal staff shorthand for a pointless, unproductive quest.

Unfortunately I have read knowledge management books where this particular knowledge base at this particular organisation was touted as one of the best examples of a technological solution.

---

64. *Knowledge Management in Theory and Practice*, Kimiz Dalkir

49.7   So what is the Strategy?

Based on the above, it should be clear that technology is not going to be a solution for knowledge management. We have to accept that people are going to want to gain knowledge from other people, and work around that as a base assumption. Otherwise good money is certainly going to be thrown away. The strategy for managing the knowledge that has been created as part of the data quality project has to have people at its centre.

Step one is to identify what people know. One of the greater problem in large organisations is that people are multidisciplinary items, who may have a primary specialism (which may or may not be the area in which they are employed), several secondary specialisms, and knowledge and ability that continues all the way to down to knowledge of how they tie their shoelaces. Any typical individual will have a range of skills.

In most organisations the "total" knowledge – or lack thereof – is not relevant. John Parkinson's inability to recognise a weed from a prized flower is utterly irrelevant to his employer, but highly important to his wife. However most organisations make choices about where they will place individuals based on a single specialism, and the result is that other relevant abilities of the individual are lost. What makes knowledge special is its use to the organisation and its rarity. A high proportion of individuals in developed countries have the ability to drive, and hence this is rarely noted as a skill. However in many large cities mass transit infrastructure is so good – and the traffic jams so bad – that there is a growing proportion of non-drivers. In a national organisation the ability to drive is then important. Part of the character of knowledge management is to bring out the hidden knowledge and to identify where knowledge is held in the organisation regardless of where it may be.

49.8   Focus Groups

Focus groups are a directed way of taking information from the heads of the project team, and disseminating this information into the heads of the business as usual teams. A focus group is simply a collection of individuals who work on a particular subject; these can be effectively used for knowledge sharing.

A focus group is a meeting or series of meetings that connect those with the knowledge (the project team) with those who do not. The objective is to share the knowledge gained during the lifetime of the project and to understand the issues with the data. Focus groups can be run for more or less every subject within the project. The project will touch on data, process, and especially architecture, but will also contain much information on project management and other subject areas. Focus groups are a way of transferring that knowledge in a face to face environment to as to disseminate the information to the people in the organisation who can best benefit from it.

To take an example:
The project team is likely to have a large amount of knowledge that has been created to look at the existing data – results from profiling, for example.

This information is likely to be of great interest to the business users of that information, managers who rely on information from reporting, risk managers who need to understand the problems with their data, and IT departments who want to understand the varying different formats of the data that they are working with.

49.9 Project Blogs

An interesting way of sharing knowledge – especially a project that is going to affect large parts of the organisation – is by the use of a project blog. This can be a regular update on the status of the project, and depending on the level of openness within the organisation can be a "warts and all" dissemination of the project, what is going well and what is going badly, through to a relatively well-managed dissemination from the project leadership of the current status.

The interesting point about blogs of this nature is that they are a way of allowing individuals outside the project to look in and understand what is going on within the project boundary. It allows them to ask about areas that they wish to know more about, or think will affect them, and also allows them to volunteer to contribute to the project as a whole. A project blog is a way of sharing knowledge about the project as it happens but also is a way of sharing what is going on in the data quality space to the wider organisation. The advantage of a blog is that it can be written relatively quickly by members of the project team in turn, and hence is an efficient way of sharing knowledge. Stakeholders can "tune in" as much or as little as they like.

49.10 After Project Review

The after project review – in some taxonomies the "lessons learned review" – brings together the project team, their customer and suppliers, and other interested parties who have touched the project over its lifecycle. It is extremely important that the after project review does not become a blame game, otherwise participants with valuable contributions to share will not engage and the operation will become a contractual slanging match. The process should be facilitated, with clear ground rules, and anyone who starts introducing a negative atmosphere re-aligned accordingly.

The after project review should be somewhere where people can be honest about the project, where everyone is comfortable to contribute, and where individuals can understand how they can continue with the elements they did well and how they can learn to get better in others.

49.11 Create a Data Governance function

It may appear a somewhat strange approach, but many of the abilities that have been created within the scope of the project are ideally suited to the ongoing data governance of the organisation. An interesting approach is transitioning these people into data stewards, as they will have the knowledge of where the data has come from and, if there are any problems, what is likely to have caused them. If they don't know then they are likely to know the person who does. Each of these people now, post project, represents a "node" of information that relates to their area of working within the business. Unlike most business personnel, where knowledge is restricted to process, these people will have a holistic-at-a-point understanding of information flows around them, probably from top to bottom of the technical spectrum and upstream and downstream of their own point. They present a network within the organisation of data quality specialists, and maintaining this network is one of the goals of knowledge management.

49.12   Embed the Information within the Business Areas

All of the information that has been created within the data quality project will relate to a business area. This information will include:

- Data lineage relating to that business area
- Possibly data meaning and definitions relating to that business area
- Process documentation relating to that business area.

Documentation is the key here. Not only what to do, but why to do it the way it is documented (a common failure of much procedural documentation). Procedures should document not only how a process should be done but the effect on data quality of doing it badly.

49.13   Knowledge Bases (SharePoint or Intranet Sites)

Every organisation has an intranet or SharePoint site that acts as a knowledge repository for the organisation. The problem with many of these sites in many of the organisations that I have worked with is that they are not very good at knowledge management. Typical characteristics include:

- Difficult to search or search terms return irrelevant links.
- Populated with out of date material.
- Access restrictions everywhere.
- High level information only (intranet sites).
- There is no way to find out what is in a document before opening it.

My personal view is that simply creating a SharePoint site and populating it with information artefacts generated as part of the data quality project is a useful way of storing the information, but not a good way of either keeping it current, or getting people to read it. As said, people connect with people, so a more effective strategy is to have the repository, but assume that individuals will as a preference connect with other people to find out the location of the knowledge. Another problem with SharePoint (or any other repository) is that too often people are told to "find it on the SharePoint", which is not helpful if the SharePoint runs to thousands of sections with tens of thousands of documents. The command of "find it on the SharePoint" is efficient for the person doing the telling but massively inefficient for the person doing the finding, who will then spend many hours trawling useless information. They may not try again.

49.14   Knowledge Map or Community Yellow Pages

Knowledge mapping is a technique for showing where knowledge can be found, as opposed to actually containing the knowledge itself. It is vastly faster to create a knowledge map than a knowledge repository, and people are easier to interlink than documents. An example of a knowledge map might be as shown below.

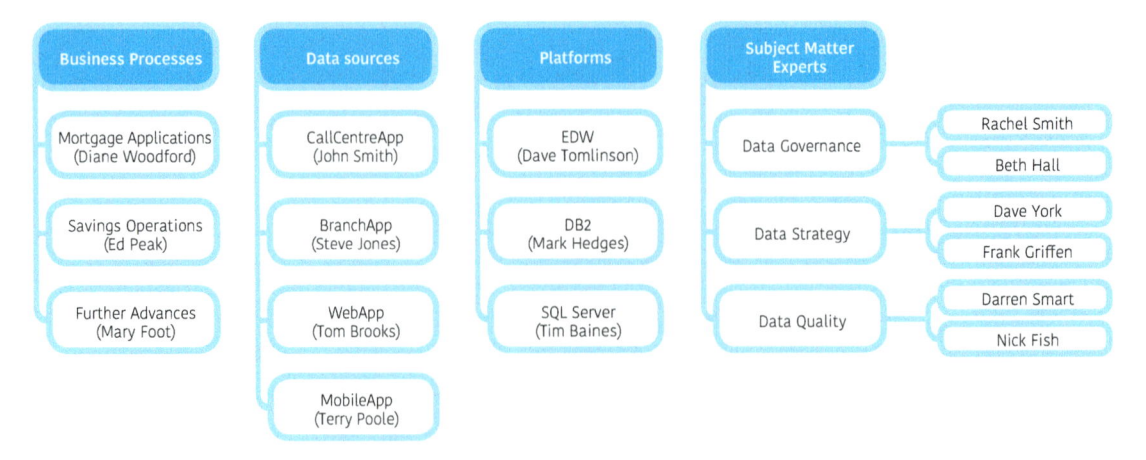

Business Processes	Data sources	Platforms	Subject Matter Experts	
Mortgage Applications (Diane Woodford)	CallCentreApp (John Smith)	EDW (Dave Tomlinson)	Data Governance	Rachel Smith / Beth Hall
Savings Operations (Ed Peak)	BranchApp (Steve Jones)	DB2 (Mark Hedges)	Data Strategy	Dave York / Frank Griffen
Further Advances (Mary Foot)	WebApp (Tom Brooks)	SQL Server (Tim Baines)	Data Quality	Darren Smart / Nick Fish
	MobileApp (Terry Poole)			

The objective of the knowledge map is to show where knowledge can be found in the organisation. This may be in terms of people but it would be relatively easy to add information as to where information can be found on a company network. The problem is that information on a network moves over time and is often out of date. However, people retain their knowledge, or at the least will know where to go. Also, finding a broken link on a network is frustrating as there is no way of finding the right link, whereas finding an individual may simply require referring to the organisation's directory. If they have left the organisation their department is likely to have a substitute available.

One of the most basic ways of sharing knowledge is the community yellow pages, often known as expertise location systems. In a similar way to a knowledge map, this concentrates on linking the searcher and their problem with those who are able to solve it. In a data quality context this may be the data consumer who is finding an error in the data and doesn't know where to find it, or the individual who wants to know whether anyone is using this database before they instigate the procedures to turn it off. A yellow pages will list areas of expertise and those individuals who have that expertise. It is as simple as that.

A yellow pages can be reasonably easy to set up as well – just email everyone asking for their three specialist areas and collate and publish the results. From a data quality view, if a yellow pages exists, then it may be as simple as adding the information that certain individuals have data quality knowledge to the overall knowledge repository. I have created an effective knowledge map from scratch in a week for a national organisation. Most "knowledge bases" take six months or more to even start to be effective.

49.15 Knowledge Cluster/Centre for Excellence/Community of Practice

Knowledge clusters are ways of connecting people, and a community of practice is simply a less formal knowledge cluster. The knowledge cluster is a virtual team of like minded people who work to further their specialist area. In this case a perfect example of a knowledge cluster might be a team with data quality knowledge who work together to keep the data quality fire burning after the project is finished. The people can create content, monitor performance, and be the go-to people for data quality in the organisation. The advantage here is that the knowledge is kept in a group, and there is a commitment to keeping the knowledge going over time after the project completes.

Often, one of the great disappointments of project work is that the individuals involved in the project return to their day jobs and rarely coincide again. Creating a knowledge cluster enables an ongoing relationship, and also enables other individuals who were not involved in the initial project to become involved with a group who have a considerable amount of knowledge regarding the organisation and how it works. A knowledge cluster or community of practice may include:

- Email distribution lists
- Regular meetings or conference calls
- Once-a-year away days

All of these foster a practice of sharing information.

49.16 Knowledge Fair

A knowledge fair is where those individuals who have the information relevant to the organisation invite a wider group to attend an event for the purpose of knowledge sharing. The advantage of this kind of event is that it enables a multi-faceted approach to the sharing of information. Those who attend the fair can interact at every level from merely browsing posters to actively interacting with "stallholders" and talking to them about the problems they are facing and how the knowledge held by "stallholders" can help. Take-away handouts can provide a physical means of transmitting information, and the ability to sign up to mailing lists or focus groups provides a way of creating an ongoing interest and participation.

Knowledge fairs that I have been involved with have not only produced an excellent learning experience from the attendees (one senior stakeholder said to me "you make me realise that this is just common sense!"), but also offers a fantastic opportunity for the practitioner to understand the problems within the organisation. In the best case scenario the practitioner and the delegate will work together in the future to share knowledge and solve the problems faced in the delegate's area of the organisation. For a knowledge fair after a data quality project, the "booths" could include:

- A stall on the data architecture of the organisation – how the data flows through the organisation.
- Where does your data come from?
- The effects of poor data quality.
- What the regulator needs.

The other point about a knowledge fair is that the delegates will choose what interests them, rather than being subject to a presentation on a subject that may or may not interest them. The mere fact of them choosing to interact shows interest. In most organisations individuals are interested in areas outside their immediate work, and a knowledge fair is a way of facilitating the expression of this interest.

49.17 Bringing it all together

I have mentioned a number of tools and techniques for knowledge management, but how does this all come together? As a starting point the proposed approach should consider some (or all) of the below.

- Perform an after project review and document as much information as you can.
- Retain the people as a group. This may be as part of a governance function, as a virtual group, or as a department, but keep them talking and keep the project team as a unit.
- Treat this group as a centre of excellence on data quality.
- Given them custody of the artefacts created as part of the project. However make sure the artefacts are in some form of knowledge base that is accessible to all.
- Make sure everyone knows how to find the group. Publicise them widely; place their names in the community yellow pages or knowledge maps.
- Use them to train the departments to which the artefacts and knowledge relate. This may involve focus groups, and use these focus groups to embed the knowledge in the business areas.
- Use the focus groups, and the newly trained individuals, to roll out training to the rest of the organisation on the benefits of data quality.
- Create a community of practice of those who have a concern about data quality within the organisation. These people will be the data users and producers of the organisation.
- Run periodic knowledge fairs to distribute the knowledge around the organisation.

The above will not guarantee that the knowledge will not leave the organisation – the entire project team can walk out the door on the last day (or – worse – are allowed to leave on the basis of "oh, well, their contract's finished, we don't need them any more"). However, it will give the organisation a better chance of retaining and using the knowledge than simply letting the artefacts created moulder in peace and the people disperse.

49.18 Further reading

As stated at the beginning of this chapter, knowledge management is a fascinating subject of great complexity which is poorly served by its treatment in the hands of many organisations. If you have further interest in the subject, the below is a selection of further reading that I would recommend.

- *Knowledge Management Toolkit,* Swiss Agency for Development and Co-operation, SDC 2009.
- *Knowledge Management in Theory and Practice,* Kimiz Dalkir, Elsvier, 2005.
- *Introduction to Knowledge Management,* Filemon A Uriarte Jr, ASEAN Foundation, 2008.
- *Knowledge Management Strategy,* World Health Organisation, 2005.
- *Knowledge Management Tools and Techniques Manual,* Dr Ronald Yound, APO 2010.
- *Knowledge Management Tools and Techniques,* Leask et Al, IDEA, 2008
- *Case Studies in Knowledge Management,* Murray Jennex, IDEA 2005
- *The Knowledge Management Toolkit: Practical Techniques for Building a Knowledge Manage-*

ment System, Second Edition, Pearson Education 2002.
- *Learning to Fly,* Collison and Parcell, Capstone 2004.

49.19 Summary

In this chapter I introduced the concept of knowledge management. I have shown that this is much more than a simple technology solution, but equally can have a considerable upside when performed well. I have taken the reader thorough some of the ways in which knowledge can be successfully shared within the organisation, and given a brief outline of each technique. These include:

- Knowledge network or community yellow pages
- Knowledge cluster/ Centre for excellence/ Community of practice
- After project review
- Project blogs
- Knowledge fairs
- SharePoint or Intranet sites

I have also looked to show the way in which the problem of information being "lost" can be avoided, and how time taken in knowledge management can replay the investment many times over. After this chapter the reader should have a much better understanding of the management of knowledge, and will understand that simply creating a document repository is not an effective way of sharing knowledge.

In the final chapter before the wrap-up I will discuss how data quality should be managed in projects separate from a specific data quality project. This is a very common scenario, and addresses the situation where a project faces data quality issues but is not sure how to management them. This final chapter shows how this can be done.

SECTION 5.7 EMBEDDING: KEEPING THE DATA GOOD

CHAPTER 50 DATA QUALITY IN PROJECTS

50.1 Structure

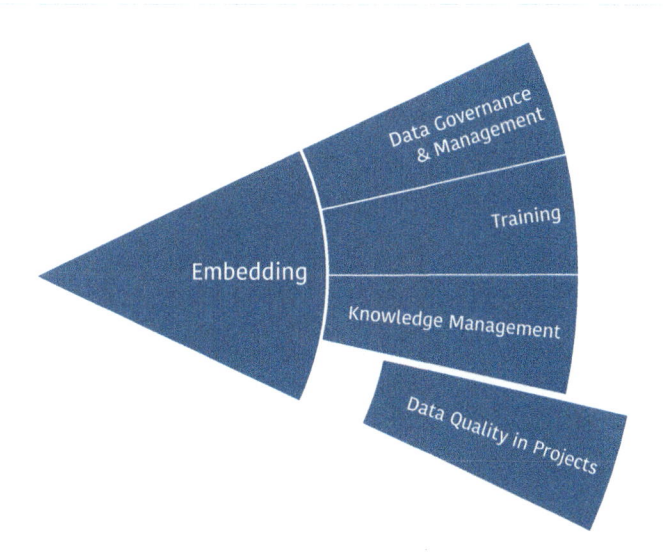

This stage of The Data Quality Blueprint includes the following topics:

1. Data Governance & Management
2. Training
3. Knowledge management
4. Data quality in projects

This chapter covers the last of these topics.

50.2 Overview

One of the questions that I am often asked relates to the consideration of data quality within a project environment. There are two facets to this:

- Projects undertaken after a data quality project has completed, where the new project does not wish to undo the good work already undertaken by the data quality project.

- Projects operating in an environment where there is no overall data quality strategy or where the organisation may be quite immature in terms of its overall approach to data quality. Here either the organisation may wish to improve its maturity, or has employed an enlightened project manager who understands that data quality may be fundamental to project success.

These subjects are (as always) other books in themselves. However, I wanted within this chapter to give a flavour for the considerations that should be made in these circumstances.

Where the approach is a smaller version of the overall framework, I will pass over these areas lightly,. assuming that the reader can mentally scale down the effort in, for example, considering "all" the data sources to "just those relevant to the project". Where specific elements relating to the project are not covered elsewhere I will use more detail. This chapter would be relevant to any project that deals with or changes the data landscape within an organisation and will face data quality issues.

Particular projects that are likely to suffer badly if they do not consider data quality within the overall project scope would be data migration projects, data warehouse projects, and business intelligence projects.

It should be noted that "consideration" of data quality issues does not necessarily mean "solve" the data quality issues. It means understand the impact of them, understand how they are going to affect the project, and what will be required to mitigate or communicate the effect of the data quality issues to the end user. Data quality in projects can be loosely divided into the following topics which I will cover in order:

- Why is addressing data quality in projects important?
- The project environment – data and project governance
- How can a project manage its data? – project data forums & data quality processes
- Managing the data coming in – understand your sources & understand your data
- Project communications

50.3 Why is this Important?

It is important for a project to consider data quality as a project may expose previously hidden data issues, and the project may then be blamed for the poor data quality. Alternatively, a project may go vastly over budget because of data quality issues that were not known at the time the budget was prepared.

These problems unfortunately become visible at a level of the organisation that is well placed to make a lot of noise about the poor performance of the project. Poor quality data materialises especially in the management layer, primarily in poor quality data in reports and extracts. If a project does not manage the data quality understanding of this group of vocal individuals there is a high probability that they will look at the new reports, data, extracts or information and opine to all and sundry that the project has messed up their data. They are unlikely to consider the state of the data before the project started, as it is likely that poor quality issues were not visible, so no-one worried about them. The irate management are much more likely to blame the project for the scenario rather than admit that their reports had been wrong for years and they had not noticed.

The project can – and will – explain that there has been no degradation in the quality of the data, but that will not stop the perception of the project as a failure, the perception of the people within the project being incompetent, and the perception that the project has caused a problem that it will take years to fix. It is absolutely essential that the project acts to guard against this situation occurring.

50.4   Use of Embedded Data Governance and Project Governance

In a well governed data environment, there will be multiple ways in which the organisational decision making and risk mitigation governance engages with the project. These may include:

- Business decisions board
- Projects decisions board
- Project management office
- Architecture decisions boards
- Data governance forums
- Data stewards

All of the above represent an opportunity for the project to highlight data quality issues in the data that is being used or transformed within the project. They also represent an opportunity for the project to gain help in addressing data quality problems, setting dependencies in relation to data quality problems, or gaining additional resources to help understand and deal with data quality problems. The overall governance of the organisation and the project landscape needs to understand the effort required and the effect that poor data quality will have on the individual project.

Important Note
It is imperative that the project lets the governance of the organisation know that it is facing data quality issues, and does not accept brush-offs like: "Oh, we'll just address the data problems later", "Just ignore data quality issues and transfer the data as-is", and especially the "we will put through a change request to bring data quality in your scope"

50.5   Project Data Forums

Within any major project that deals with data, a senior board should be set up and empowered to make decisions on the data issues within the project and to communicate these to the stakeholders. There are many names that can be used for this – data decisions board, data forum, technical data board, data decisions committee, etc. I will use the former.

The data decisions board brings data governance into the project, and is a formal forum for consideration and authorisation of changes to data, and for the consideration of the impact of any data quality issues. It should liaise with any overall project or data governance within the organisation, so that the project can ensure that the project data decisions are aligned with the risk appetite and principles of the organisation.

A data decisions board has the responsibility to:

- Review and approve referred data decisions
- Support swift resolution of referred data issues
- Drive alignment to corporate, business, IT and data strategies
- Promote and foster adherence to good data requirements and practices

The data decisions board has the principle objective of managing all data design decisions (business and technical), that cannot be resolved within the project. An example may be a compromise to the defined data requirements or usage of data that has implications within the project or even outside the project. Responsibilities for a data decisions board would cover:

- Definition and maintenance of project data requirements and practices.
- Provision of business expertise and approval of business data requirements for input to the detailed designs.
- Creation and maintenance of detailed designs, including: data models, data mappings and escalation of any data related issues.
- Resolution of referred data issues.
- Review of detailed data products or data specific content in detailed designs to ensure their adherence to defined data requirements.
- Assurance of consistency of approach for data design and data deliverables across the project.
- Ensuring that all data tasks are appropriately delegated and defined in the project plan.
- Highlighting of any external dependencies and level of impact.
- Evaluation of data issues and endorsement of any resultant resolution/change before they are presented to the data governance board.

It would not cover:

- Producing the detailed design; this is completed by the project in association with the solution architect.
- Running a solution workshop; project analysts/architects should present issues with proposed resolutions for ratification.

- Reworking of detailed documentation as a result of decisions taken.
- Approving budget or planning change; any decisions that have budget or planning implications will still need to be assessed and approved by the relevant authority.
- Management of data quality in production systems (new or legacy systems), other than where there is a direct impact on the project data design.
- Data governance or management for any production systems.
- Master data management, other than data lineage required for the project solution.

Representation is generally required from Data Architecture, Solution Architecture, Business Analysis, Business, and Data Steward/Data Governance.

50.6 Data Quality Processes

If data quality issues are identified during projects, especially large projects and especially those relating to movement or mapping of data (for example data migrations), it is necessary to create a process to escalate these issues and to respond to them in a timely basis. An example of such an issue may be a discovery within the data profiling that a data field will not load into the target system due to poor data quality in the field. The processes run as follows:

> After issue identification, the issue is defined as either a business or an IT issue. If identified as an IT issue further analysis is undertaken to identify to which system the issue relates. Based on this identification it is then assigned to a system owner.

> If it is identified as a business issue, further analysis enables it to be identified as relating to specific departments and then again assigned to a department owner.

> The system or business owner will then triage the issue and assign it to an issue owner for action.

Issues can then be tracked through the project, and a clear visibility of the status of the issues in flight understood. This will involve a workflow management system, but can be as simple as a spreadsheet. Alternatively there are open source workflow tools available. Finally, the use of a workflow enables the service levels for responding to queries to be tracked effectively.

50.7 Understand your Sources

The next element to consider in a project environment is understanding of data sources. The project needs to understand where the data is coming from and how it moves inside the project boundary. This may cause a number of surprises, as it is often the case that information does not come from where the organisation thinks it comes from. Don't take people's word for it, prove it. If you don't know then this will build up problems for a later stage of the project.

One example from my own experience is where it took two years to identify where one dataset was coming from. Admittedly this is unusual, but data not being sourced from the location originally assumed is common.

Also, stating the obvious, don't forget to document this. You may find that you are bringing in a large number of source systems, but it is much better to understand the number of sources at this point, early on in the project, rather than finding out at a later date that unknown data is going to impact the project in unknown ways.

50.8   Understand your Data

After identification of the sources the next stage is to understand the information that is held within them. This will involved two processes; profiling the data and understanding the meaning. Everything that was said in the data discovery chapter applies here in terms of profiling. Profiling is a standard step in data understanding in many types of projects, not just data quality projects. Data migration projects, for example, should always start with an exercise to understand the data that needs to be moved from the source systems. The profiling exercise needs to cover all the data that is relevant for the project.

The stage of understanding meaning may take at least as long as the profiling and finding out the various sources. Meaning will be likely hidden in data transformations and system extract code, and the users of information may not be aware of what it actually represents. Those that think they understand the meaning and contents of data may be mistaken. In one organisation 17 different calculations were discovered within source systems for one verbal description. Of those 17 only 5 were actually calculated how the users thought.

Example
One organisation I am aware of had a problem with the gross outstanding mortgage balance. Specifically, two departments had differing views of what the number was. This number is (a) large and (b) material to the functioning of the banks and (c) is a number reported to the regulator.

As it turned out, one set of figures was the capital balance at the beginning of the month, and the other was the capital balance plus accrued (but not paid) interest on that balance. The calculation of both numbers was hidden in the source systems and both were technically correct, it depended on the meaning.

50.9 Communications

It might appear an obvious statement, but the most successful way of getting the key stakeholders to see it your way is to communicate with them. My belief is that the best chance of avoiding a painful and embarrassing expose of the poor quality of the data at the end of the project is to have it considerably earlier. Messaging can then be managed.

Stage 1:	We really want to make sure that we provide you with the right data for your reports and extracts, so whilst we know that you have given us requirements ("us" being the project), we want to work through the project stages with you. This is better than us receiving requirements, then going away and building them, then you receiving the product at the end and not being happy. We want to work with you throughout the project, and let you have early sight of the data and the reports, so we know we are on the right track. [this is good practice anyway]
Stage 2:	We are seeing some issues with the data. Can you come and walk us through what might have happened here. We've done a like-for like comparison with the old reports and everything appears ok, but we are getting some strange results.
Stage 3:	We've tried to amend the data to solve some of the bigger data problems, but there are many issues. What do you think we should do?
Stage 4:	OK, we'll do our best to provide you with the reports you need but with the data in this state it is going to be difficult. Let's sit down and see what we can give you that will achieve what you need. Also, can we set up a process for all these data quality queries so that we can both track them?
Stage 5:	We don't think we are going to be able to give you the reports you asked for without doing quite a major job to remediate the data. Obviously we can do this, but it's going to have to be taken to the steering group as we would need a decision for the additional spend. If we cannot have the additional spend then let's work together to see what we can do under the existing budget and with the current data quality.

You get the idea. Stakeholders are updated at multiple points in the project on the state of the data and the effect it is having on the project, and are, as far as possible, brought on board. This means that when the project is finalised, not only are they well aware of the data quality issues, but are equally responsible for the decisions taken to provide the eventual solution.

Projects that change data can also uncover issues with the data. Users are consequentially likely to be extremely unhappy that data they have relied on for many years has been incorrect. An important point that is mentioned earlier in the book and is equally applicable to projects is the importance of understating the impact of any changes to data, especially historical data. Historical data has been used in presentations, pamphlets, brochures and not least, accounts. Any change to this data needs to be carefully considered as history is potentially being changed. In cases like this the affected parties need to be consulted. These affected parties may include:

- Those responsible for year-on year comparisons
- The regulator, who suddenly needs to know that much of the information they have been supplied with may be incorrect.
- The board – who will have to understand that the soundbites they have been giving out to press, regulator and staff will now have to be restructured.
- Managers, who need to understand that prior year comparatives will change, which will change their performance this year if their performance is based on a year on year uplift.
- Business intelligence, who may have to change the way in which their analysis occurs, and what filters are applied.

Most parts of the organisation need to understand that if data changes then they also need to change. It is at this point that the average project will look to ensure that things don't change, because the view is that if today is the same as yesterday, then people are happy, even if yesterday was wrong. The project needs to broadcast the message that improvement is a good thing, and remaining in ignorance of poor data quality or – worse – using poor data and not caring about the quality because it is more convenient and avoids awkward questions – is not acceptable.

50.10   Summary

Within this chapter I have briefly looked at the ways in which data quality can be brought into the project environment in the absence of any enterprise-wide framework that would naturally cover all the projects within an organisation.

I have considered the way in which the project can use pre-existing governance structures and whether they exist or not, I have argued for the establishment of a data decisions board that will address data quality issues that occur within the project. I have touched on a number of elements that will keep the project honest in terms of data. I have outlined the way in which data quality processes can be designed, and also the importance of the project understanding the data that it uses. Finally, I have looked at the way communications management can help reduce the risk of a poor perception of the project.

SECTION 6 — LAST WORDS

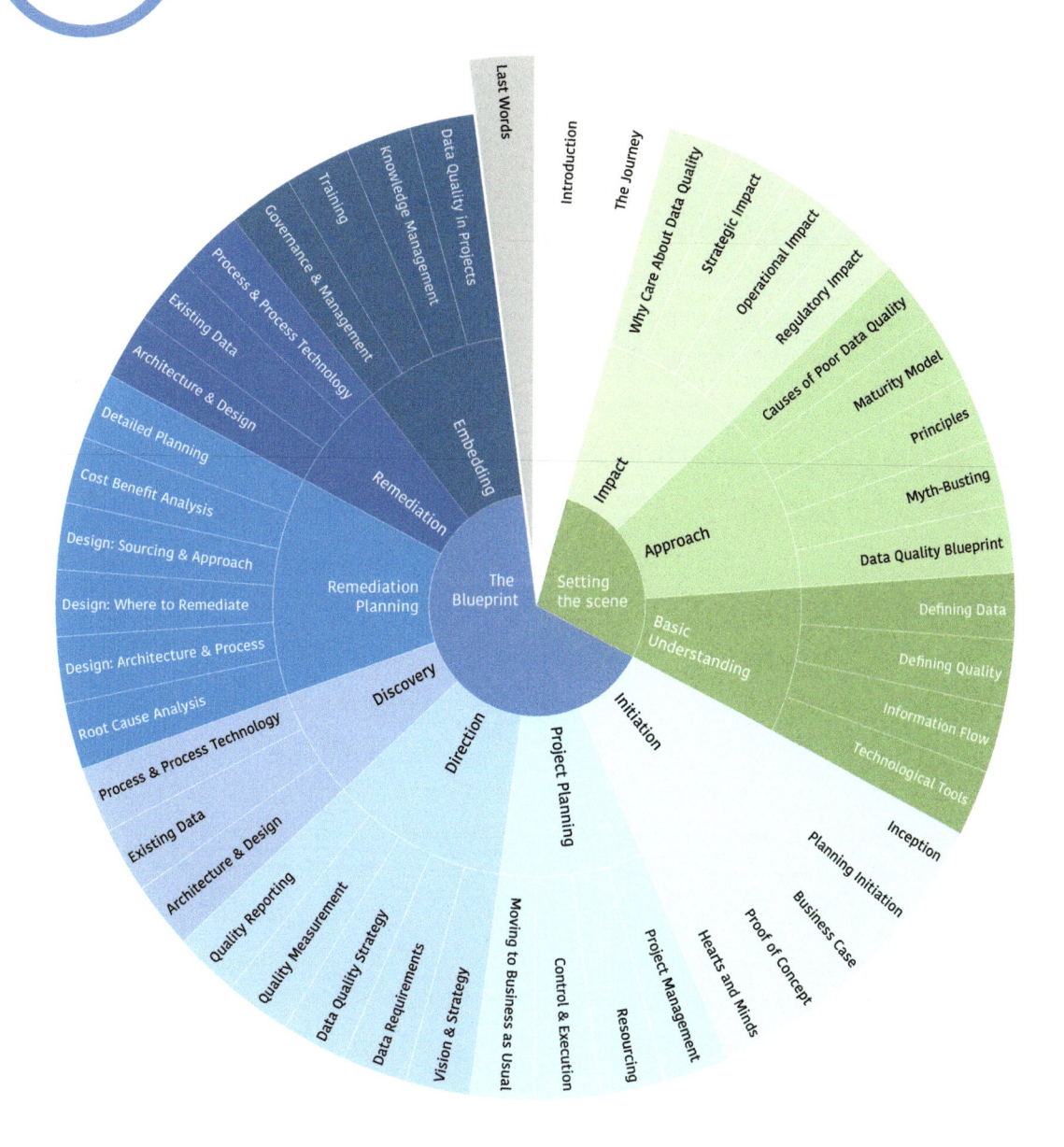

SECTION 6: LAST WORDS

CHAPTER 51: WRAP UP

51.1 Future Data

Before the final wrap-up, I would like to talk briefly about future data. The objective is to ensure that whatever the nature of the data that the organisation encounters in the future, that its quality will not compromise the data that the organisation has just spent time and resources making good. The problem with future data is that you don't know what it will be and how it will integrate into your organisation. However, this does not mean that you cannot prepare for it. Within the first stage of the data quality project, you will have defined a data strategy for the organisation, and this will include principles that can be applied against all data sources, whether they currently exist or not. Also within the strategy there will be an understanding of what data will be used to manage and grow the organisation. Within process and architecture the organisation now has a robust system for managing data, and the governance and training that has been put in place will put the organisation in a good place to manage the data that is over the horizon as well.

But what will be the nature of that data? I would submit that where data is going in the near future is reasonably foreseeable, and the nature of data further in the future is guessable in terms of its characteristics.

Near future data is data that you know will be available for exploitation within the next few years. Publications, news articles and industry information will inform an organisation of both the information that may be available, and also the way in which it may be used. Sometimes this is not necessarily data that does not exist yet, but data that does exist, but you either do not have access, or do not use it. Many financial organisations have access to the contents of a customer's current account. It is relatively trivial to see what the individual is paying for their mortgage, insurance, mobile phone, etc from that information, and only a step further to see what shops they visit, which ATM's they use and hence where their location is likely to be at any given moment of any day with some degree of reliability. This can (and probably will) be used in the future, if nothing else than as a guard against fraud. A prudent business that is considering using such data would think about that data and what are the consequences of poor quality.

Looking further in the future it would appear likely that location information on individuals is likely to be available – in fact it can already be bought from mobile phone companies. This would have appeared utterly inconceivable in the relatively recent past – it would not have been expected that individuals would give third parties the ability to track their every movement, and for no other reason than to map their running workouts.

It is not in the scope of this book to speculate wildly, however I would imagine that biometric technology will be available fairly soon. Mobile phone apps that monitor health, such as heart rate, skin temperature, and so on already exist in some sectors. Add this to location and some interesting information can be drawn out about how individuals react to their environment. Add this to a record of where an individual is looking and the possibilities are endless. Just in advertising, having access to the medical information of an individual when they look at your advert would be useful indeed.

So, how will future data differ?

I believe volume will be the main thing. Whereas the number of data points that may be available for an individual may be currently limited, location data will provide thousands of data points per day. If we use the example above and factor in not only where an individual is located but what they are looking at this could scale to millions of data points and terabytes of data per person per day. An organisation needs to think about where they want to be in this future, utopia or dystopia depending on your perspective, and how this information will be utilised by the organisation looking for competitive advantage. Most importantly, how do they make sure that the information they receive and process is accurate, how they will ensure their decisions are based on quality information, and what happens if the information, and hence their decisions, are wrong?

51.2   The Last Word

So the journey is over and the book is (almost) closed. In this book, I have tried to outline my own blueprint for an approach to data quality. This holistic approach is the way the organisation needs to approach data quality if it wishes to create a solution that is lasting and effective. So what are the key messages?

- Poor data quality is a business problem which impacts the enterprise in many ways.
- Poor data quality is costly, and worth remediating.
- Actually addressing data quality in a holistic manner requires more than just remediating data.
- Remediating data quality requires looking at the organisation as a whole. It means looking at the organisational design and its processes as well as its data.
- This is an exercise which you do not wish to do more than once.
- That most of it is common sense. It helps to have a guide from those of us who have gone before, but really anyone and any organisation can do this.

Many disciplines come together within a data quality project. Data quality is not a discipline on its own, but an amalgamation of many others. The data quality practitioner should have knowledge in many areas:

- Business Analysis
- Data Analysis/Mining
- Process Mapping
- Business Process Management
- Data Architecture
- Data Profiling
- Business Process Analysis
- Business Process Engineering
- Enterprise Architecture
- Data Governance

- Data Management
- Data Integration
- Knowledge Management
- Data Strategy
- Database Administration
- Training

The effect of the wide ranging nature of both data quality itself and also the various disciplines that are required to remediate it is that this book has been written at a high level. If I covered each area in detail I would probably triple the size of the book, and there was already much that I had to remove on space grounds. Whilst the comprehensive book (or books) may be something that I would like to write some day, at present outlining the varying approaches to data quality at a high level is a start.

If this book deflects an organisation from spending millions on an ineffective IT solution but enables them to sit back and create the most appropriate remedy for their data quality problem, resulting in a long term and effective solution, then the cost of this book has been worthwhile. Remember again the principle is to do as little work as necessary.

I hope that you, as a reader, have enjoyed the book and found it informative. I hope that it encourages you to think about "data" problems more holistically, and I hope this blueprint enables different parts of an organisation to work together for the greater good.

Lastly, I would like to thank you, the reader, for buying and reading the book.

John Parkinson,
2016

SECTION 7: APPENDICES

SECTION 7: Index

CHAPTER 52: Bibliography — 559

CHAPTER 53: Data Quality Artefacts — 561
- 53.1 Introduction — 561
- 53.2 Project Setup – Artefacts — 561
- 53.3 Initiate Artefacts — 561
- 53.4 Project Planning Artefacts — 561
- 53.5 Direction Artefacts — 561
- 53.6 Discovery Artefacts — 562
- 53.7 Remediation Planning Artefacts — 562
- 53.8 Remediation Artefacts — 563
- 53.9 Governance Artefacts — 563
- 53.10 Training Artefacts — 564
- 53.11 Knowledge Management Artefacts — 564

CHAPTER 54: Sample Interview Questions — 565
- 54.1 Introduction — 565
- 54.2 Basic Questions — 565
- 54.3 Culture and Strategy — 566
- 54.4 Defined Responsibility and Governance — 566
- 54.5 Continuously Measure and Monitor Data Quality — 567
- 54.6 Audit and Audit Reports — 568
- 54.7 Define Data Quality Requirements — 568
- 54.8 Define Data Quality Metrics — 568
- 54.9 Define Data Quality Business Rules — 568
- 54.10 Test and Validate Data Quality Requirements — 569

54.11	Set and Evaluate Data Quality Service levels	569
54.12	Manage Data Quality Issues	569
54.13	Clean and Correct Data Quality Defects	569
54.14	Design and Implement Operational DQM Procedures	570
54.15	Monitor Operational DQM Procedures and Performance	570
54.16	Process Design	570
54.17	Profile, Analyse and Assess Data Quality	570
54.18	Quality and Management tools	571
54.19	Data Architecture	571
54.20	Projects	571
54.21	Data Quality Challenges	571
54.22	Business Intelligence	572

CHAPTER 55: Sample Data Strategy — 573

55.1	Introduction	573
55.2	Scope	573
55.3	Purpose of the Strategy	573
55.4	Information Needs of the Organisation	574
55.5	Key Principles	574
55.6	Data Acquisition	575
55.7	Information Governance	576
55.8	Data Management	577
55.9	Information Policy and Practice	577
55.10	Information Management Lifecycle	577
55.11	Knowledge Sharing and Collaboration	578
55.12	Learning and Development	578

CHAPTER 56: Sample Data Quality Strategy — 579

56.1	Introduction	579
56.2	References	579
56.3	Scope	579
56.4	Exemptions	580
56.5	Purpose of the Strategy	580
56.6	Data Quality Principles	580
56.7	Why Data Quality Matters	581
56.8	Strategic Aims for Data Quality	581
56.9	Analytical Requirements	582
56.10	Operational Aims for Data Quality	582
56.11	Benefits of the Strategy	583
56.12	Data Quality Governance Framework	584
56.13	Monitoring and Review	585
56.14	Systems, Process and Procedures	585
56.15	Risks and Risk Management	587
56.16	Emerging Data	587

56.17	Data Supplied by Third Parties	588
56.18	Data Quality Process Framework	588
56.19	Risk Appetite	588
56.20	Urgent Issues or Breaches	589
56.21	Policy Waiver	589

CHAPTER 57: Data Governance Terms of Reference — 591

57.1	Information Governance Steering Group	591
57.2	Information Governance Board	592
57.3	Data Quality Board	592
57.4	Data Owners	593
57.5	Data Stewards	593
57.6	Data Creators	594
57.7	Data Consumers/users	594

CHAPTER 58: Sample Project Plan — 595

58.1	Introduction	595
58.2	Level 1 Plan	596
58.3	Level 2 Plan	597
58.4	Level 3 and below Project Tasks	597

SECTION 7: APPENDICES

CHAPTER 52: BIBLIOGRAPHY

Poor Quality Cost, Harrington, ASQC Quality Press, 1987.
Men at Arms, Terry Prachett, Corgi, 1993.
Data Governance, John Ladley, Morgan Kaufman, 2012.
Data Governance Tools, Sunil Soares, MC Press, 2014.
Data Stewardship, David Plotkin, Morgan Kaufman, 2014.
Non-Invasive Data Governance, Robert Seiner, Technics Publications, 2014.
Performing Information Governance, Giordano, IBM Press, 2015.
Master Data Management and Data Governance, Berson & Dubov, McGraw Hill, 2011.
Selling Information Governance to the Business, Sunil Soares, MC Press, 2011.
The IBM Data Governance Unified Process, Soares, MC Press, 2011
COBIT 5, Information Systems and Control Association (ISACA), 2013.
Data Management Body of Knowledge, DAMA-BOK, Mosely et Al, Data Management Association, 2010.
Data Warehouse Design, Modern Principles and Methodologies, Golfarelli et al, 2009, McGraw-Hill
Data Integration Blueprint and Modeling, Giordano, IBM Press, 2011
The Corporate Information Factory, Inmon et al, Wiley, 1999
The Ultimate Guide to Business Process Management, Panagacos, 2012.
Business Process Change, Paul Harmon, Morgan Kaufman, 2007
Business Process Analysis, Geoffrey Darnton, Requirements Analytics, 2012
The Basics of Process Mapping, Robert Damelio, CRC Press, 2011
Practical Data Migration, Johny Morris, BCS Learning and Development, 2012
Knowledge Management Toolkit, Swiss Agency for Development and Co-operation, SDC, 2009.
Knowledge Management in Theory and Practice, Kimiz Dalkir, Elsvier, 2005.
Introduction to Knowledge Management, Filemon A Uriarte Jr, ASEAN Foundation, 2008.
Knowledge Management Strategy, World Health Organisation, 2005.
Knowledge Management Tools and Techniques Manual, Dr Ronald Yound, APO 2010.
Knowledge Management Tools and Techniques, Leask et Al, IDEA, 2008
Case Studies in Knowledge Management, Murray Jennex, IDEA 2005
The Knowledge Management Toolkit: Practical Techniques for Building a Knowledge Management System, Second Edition, Pearson Education 2002.
Learning to Fly, Collison and Parcell, Capstone 2004.
Managing Successful Projects with PRINCE 2, TSO 2009
Credit Risk Management, Gestel and Baesens, Oxford University Press, 2009.

Practitioner's Guide to Data Quality Improvement, David Loshin, Morgan Kaufman, 2011
Information Quality Applied, Larry English, Wiley, 2009
Improving Data Warehouse and Business Information Quality, Larry English, Wiley, 1999
Measuring Data Quality for Ongoing Improvement, Laura Sebastian-Coleman, Morgan Kaufman, 2013
Business Analysis, Third Edition, Paul, Cadle & Yeates, BCS, 2014
The Business Analysts' Handbook, Podeswa, Course Technology, 2009
Master Data Management in Practice, Cervo & Allen, Wiley, 2011
Master Data Management, David Loshin, Morgan Kaufman, 2009
The Multidimensional Manager, Connelly, McNeil and Mosiman, Cognos, 1999
Business Intelligence Strategy, Boyer et al, MC Press, 2010
The Performance Manager, Connelly, McNeil & Mosimann, Cognos, 2007

SECTION 7: APPENDICES

CHAPTER 53: DATA QUALITY ARTEFACTS

53.1 Introduction

During the course of the data quality project a large number of artefacts will be created. I have listed these artefacts separately within this chapter to facilitate product based planning, creation of a work breakdown structure, or simply to facilitate a list of project deliverables, and to make is clear what the project has to produce over its lifetime.

53.2 Project Setup – Artefacts

- Initial problem statement
- Initial scope
- Initial objectives
- Meeting minutes
- Daily log
- Query log
- Issue log
- Holiday tracker
- Draft onboarding document
- Initial task list
- List of key stakeholders
- Draft stakeholder map
- Interview schedule
- Interview material
- Meeting notes
- Initial problem statement for interviews
- Draft list of pain points
- Data domains in scope
- System domains in scope
- Process domains in scope
- Requirements for the project
- Expectations for the project
- Draft high level project objective
- Draft low level (detail) objectives for the project
- Project definition
- Project approach document
- Draft work breakdown structure
- Technical and licensing requirements
- Project roles and responsibilities
- High level project plan
- Resourcing plan
- Draft communications plan
- Draft detail initiate plan
- Initial RAID Log
- Initial business case
- Project brief

53.3 Initiate Artefacts

- Updated initiate plan
- External RACI
- Draft full project plan
- Updated daily log
- Updated risk log
- Updated assumptions log
- Updated issues log
- Updated dependencies
- Updated query log
- Draft terms of reference
- Meeting schedule
- Detailed scope
- Cost of poor quality for the organisation
- Terms of reference for project and/or governance
- Issues, impacts, and costs for remediation
- Workshop and interview responses
- Cost of remediation
- Feedback from staff members involved in PoC
- Initial list of options for remediation
- Questionnaire
- Scope in each area

- High level CRUD matrix
- Pain points
- Cost benefit analysis of project
- Workshop materials
- Rules of engagement
- Pain points to be addressed
- Initial business case
- Objectives in each area
- POC implementation plan
- Other areas of the business that will experience costs/benefits
- Mission statement for the project
- Stakeholder assessment template
- Elevator pitch
- PoC costs and benefits
- Posters
- Interest/influence matrix
- Updated key stakeholder list
- Updated stakeholder assessment
- Strategy template
- Draft communications plan
- Vision statement for the project
- Draft initial list of issues
- "Day in the life"

53.4 Project Planning Artefacts

- Updated definition of domains in scope if necessary based on initiation stage
- Updated definition of processes in scope if necessary based on initiation stage
- Updated definition of systems in scope
- Detailed description of deliverables
- Required skill sets per project stage
- Initial list of organisational (as opposed to project) personnel required
- Change capacity assessment
- Mock-up of deliverables
- Change template
- Project modules
- Change mitigation strategy
- Risk assessment template
- Updated work breakdown structure
- Overall risk assessment
- Template with deliverables and requirements
- Reporting strategy
- First draft of task list
- Reporting template
- Basic workflow
- Reporting template
- Approach for KPI reporting
- Project initiation document
- Change management strategy
- Change management template
- Updated dependencies
- Updated risks
- Updated assumptions
- Resource profile over the project lifecycle
- Risk appetite of the organisation
- Software required during project lifecycle
- Updated issues
- Project plan and add resourcing
- Internal RACI
- Updated project plan
- Staff availability
- Draft deliverables list
- Updated requirements

53.5 Direction Artefacts

- Template for the data quality strategy
- Data impacts of corporate strategy
- Data requirements needed to support the vision
- Mapping of corporate vision to data vision
- Data quality governance framework
- Template for data strategy
- Timescale for the definition of requirements
- Proof of concept mock-up of reporting
- Data requirements
- Data quality requirements
- Data strategy
- Corporate vision
- Draft reporting suite
- "Basket" of metrics
- Data quality strategy
- Template for requirements
- Data quality process framework

53.6 Discovery Artefacts

53.6.1 Architecture

- Validate scope
- Draft reporting template
- Documentation of timescales
- Key personnel to interview
- Define architectural notation
- Approach document
- Impact resulting from each of the issues
- Exception process document
- Architecture documentation
- Issues raised from documentation assessment
- Documentation of pain points
- Documentation of issues
- Architecture assessment

53.6.2 Data

- Updated dependencies, assumptions and risks
- Fields to be profiled (and not profiled)
- Profiling planning document
- Dependencies
- Team identification and allocation to system or domain
- Extract and/or data source requirements
- Exception process
- Existing data assessment
- Exception process document
- Profiling task list
- Updated plan
- Profiling deliverable

53.6.3 Process

- Known list of processes
- Interactions between processes
- CRUD Matrix
- Holistic process map
- Team identification and allocation to system or domain
- KPIs
- Processes not to be assessed and why
- Documentation of walk through process
- Sampling criteria (if sampling used) and expected output
- Assessment approach
- Issues with current process
- Process assessment deliverable
- Process assessment task list
- Exception process
- Assessment planning document
- Dependencies
- Type of assessment per process

53.7 Remediation Planning Artefacts

- Key architecture concerns
- Impact analysis of architecture issues
- Define the replacement data required
- Common root causes
- Final root cause list
- Updated plan
- Cost of each root cause
- Root cause analysis document
- Process roadmap
- Architectural roadmap
- Transition states
- Options costing
- Document process roadmap
- Resource requirements
- Data roadmap
- Perform best source analysis on replacement data
- Options benefits
- Option appraisal
- Impact/effort grid
- Quick wins
- Final task list
- Dependencies (external and internal)
- List of document and physical deliverables
- High level roadmap for remediation stage
- Updated business case
- Detailed plan for remediation
- Best source analysis
- Success criteria
- Data quality roadmap
- Fishbone analysis

53.8 Remediation Artefacts

53.8.1 Architecture

- Data issues changed or altered by the changes to architecture
- Architectural issues to be addressed
- Architecture changes to be implemented
- Transition states
- Implementation plan
- Initial and end KPI
- Process issues to be changed by architecture
- Lessons learned
- Ratify that changes meet plan including KPI
- Updated workflow
- Change assessment
- Documented updated architecture

53.8.2 Existing Data

- Implementation plan
- Final task plan
- Integration plan
- Working database
- Document results and update plan for POC learning
- Extract of existing and target data into working database
- Environment approach

- Success criteria
- New source of data
- Remediation approach
- Documentation of updated data including reference data & valid values
- Document final plan
- Initial and end KPI

53.8.3 Process

- Remediation approach
- Processes in scope
- KPI
- Success criteria
- Future process options
- Final preferred option
- Implementation Plan for pilot
- Pilot results
- Initial and updated KPI
- Updated process documentation
- Updated implementation plan for lessons learned from pilot

53.9 Governance Artefacts

- Data governance processes and procedures
- Information needs of the organisation
- High level data governance implementation plan
- Pain points
- Initial cost estimates
- Governance questionnaire
- Risks/assumptions & dependencies
- Gaps in governance or management
- Vision and mission statement for data governance
- Risk assessment updated RAID
- Areas or poor management or quality
- Cost impact of pain points
- Stakeholder assessment
- Change capacity assessment
- Draft governance assessment
- Initial business case
- Rollout and sustainability plan
- Governance principles
- Elevator pitch
- Framework design
- Forum design
- RACI
- Process design
- Forum terms of reference
- Data management and governance taxonomy
- Mapping of governance to data quality pain points
- Draft process for identification of owners and stewards
- Sustainability plan
- Governance impact analysis
- Data governance intranet information
- Change management plan
- Communications strategy for governance
- Process for identification of owners and stewards
- Data steward training
- Scope for initial stand-up
- Issue reporting forms
- Project assessment framework
- Governance metrics
- Data governance deliverables
- Data owner training
- Drivers for data governance
- Information management assessment
- Documentation of data lineage
- Data dictionary
- Data standards
- Data governance scorecard
- Data governance goals

53.10 Training Artefacts

- Scope of training
- Training goals
- Awareness questionnaire
- Training assessment
- Training strategy
- New induction training
- New refresher training
- New remediation training
- Awareness training
- Executive orientation
- Success criteria
- Measure success criteria
- Report on pilot
- Awareness training roadmap
- Pilot implementation plan
- KPI before and after

53.11 Knowledge Management Artefacts

- Scope of knowledge management
- Knowledge management strategy
- Scope of pilot and/or quick wins
- Knowledge management assessment
- Knowledge & sources of knowledge
- Information definition
- Knowledge management plan
- Knowledge management goals
- Existing knowledge sources
- Source assessment
- Method of information sharing
- Target audience for pilot
- Pilot assessment
- Pilot plan
- Report on overall strategy

SECTION 7: APPENDICES

CHAPTER 54: SAMPLE INTERVIEW QUESTIONS

54.1 Introduction

I have conducted many stakeholder and fact-finding interviews over the last twenty years, and whilst I do not have a set question bank personally – I tend to make it up as I go along based on a rough idea of subject areas put together prior to the interview – this is a technique that I have refined over many years, so to a degree I am relying on my own mental question bank. In order to help others in the process of creating this book I have brainstormed a list of questions that can be drawn on by the practitioner in order to gain information from – or give information to – a stakeholder, process owner, data owner, data steward, call centre agent, and so on.

The questions below are by necessity generic, and I would encourage the practitioner to use them as a base and source for inspiration rather than copy them verbatim, as targeted questions specific to the organisation will always result in better information than generic questions fired at random.

54.2 Basic Questions

1. What is your name?
2. What is your department?
3. How long have you worked at the organisation?
4. What departments have you worked in?
5. What is your position/role?
6. Could you describe how you use data?
7. How long have you been in your current role?
8. Do you have any data-related responsibilities?
9. How does your area of the organisation utilise data?
10. Are you aware that we are looking at a project to improve data quality?
11. How do you think such a project could help your day to day work?
12. How would you like to be involved in the project?
13. Do you have any concerns about the project you would like to highlight?
14. Is there anyone that you think would be particularly good for us to speak to?

54.3 Culture and Strategy

15. Do you know if there is a defined data strategy for the organisation?
16. Do you know what areas of the organisation it covers?
17. Do you know how old is it/when it was produced?
18. Is it shared with the organisation?
19. Is there a long term data vision for the organisation?
20. Do you know whether it is linked in to the strategy?
21. Do you know whether it contains any provision for data quality?
22. Do you know whether there is an information management strategy?
23. Do you know what it covers?
24. Is it shared with the organisation as a whole?
25. Is it possible for us to have copies of any of the above?
26. Do you know if there is a data quality strategy?
27. If so, when was it produced?
28. Is the data quality strategy updated for the current data architecture?
29. Is the data quality strategy aligned with the data vision?
30. Is the data quality strategy aligned with the data strategy?
31. What does the data quality strategy cover??
32. Do you feel that is it restricted in terms of domain or department?
33. Is the data quality strategy freely available?
34. Has the data quality strategy been reviewed or guided by the regulator?
35. Is the data quality strategy regularly updated for changes in architecture, the overall strategy, or data quality events?
36. How is the data quality strategy being implemented ?
37. How is the data quality strategy being communicated?
38. Who are the individuals responsible for implementing the data quality strategy?
39. Do you feel that there is a culture that promotes quality in the organisation?
40. Why do you think this about the culture?
41. How do you think this culture, and the effect on data quality, could be improved?
42. Is there pressure to compromise quality for greater speed or reduced cost?
43. Is data quality awareness promoted in the organisation by senior management?
44. If so, how is it promoted?
45. Are awareness campaigns used to promote the case for data quality?
46. Is the importance of data quality included in induction training?
47. How is this done?
48. Is there mandatory training (e.g. annual) on the importance of data quality?
49. Do you know how compliance with completion of this training is monitored?
50. If so, do you know what is the compliance rate?
51. Are executives trained on data quality, covering the impact of data quality, and how they can positively affect the culture of quality in the organisation?
52. If they are trained, how are executives trained on data quality?
53. How is the overall approach to data quality training managed?
54. How would you describe your organization's information management culture?
55. How do you think it could be improved?
56. How do you think your information management culture compares with your competitors?
57. Do you think that the organisation has enough information to enable it to manage itself effectively?
58. Why do you think this?

54.4 Defined Responsibility and Governance

59. Who is responsible for the quality of information in the organisation?
60. Is there a CDO (Chief Data Officer)?

61. What are their specific responsibilities around data?
62. Is the CDO responsible for data strategy – if not who creates the data strategy?
63. Do you know if the board considers information quality?
64. Could you give me an example of an executive decision concerning information in the last year?
65. Is your industry regulated, and by who?
66. Are you aware of the specific regulations around data, data governance and data quality?
67. Is there a data governance function in your organisation?
68. Is there a data governance framework?
69. What is the involvement of the CRO, Internal Audit, or Compliance?
70. Are there defined data owners and data stewards?
71. Is there a data governance forum?
72. Are there data policies (not just data security policies)?
73. Are there data standards?
74. How does data governance interact with other areas of governance (e.g. IT governance, Corporate Governance, Project Governance)?
75. Are any applications used to facilitate data governance?
76. How is data quality aligned to overall data governance?
77. Does any kind of forum exist specifically to further data quality in the organisation?
78. How are data quality issues raised by staff members?
79. Can you give me an example of a data quality issue that has been raised recently?
80. What was the outcome?
81. What is the importance given to data quality issues?
82. If a data quality issue is not addressed in a timely manner, what is the escalation path for data quality issues?
83. What feedback do you get if you raise a data quality issue? Are you kept aware of progress, is feedback on data quality issues welcomed?
84. Who chases resolution of data quality issues – is it the person who initially raised the issue or a senior forum?
85. How is data quality managed?
86. Do you feel that information is treated as an asset?
87. Is there an information asset register?
88. What information governance is performed in your area?
89. Who is responsible for information governance in your area?
90. How do they interact with the wider data governance framework?
91. How do they interact with local staff members who no specific responsibility for data governance?
92. Is there a data dictionary/business glossary in the organisation?
93. How is the data dictionary maintained?
94. Who is the data dictionary maintained by?
95. Is the data dictionary up to date?
96. How is the data dictionary used?

54.5 Continuously Measure and Monitor Data Quality

97. How is data quality monitored in the organisation?
98. Is the measurement of data quality continuous or ad hoc?
99. If ad hoc, how often does this occur?
100. What areas of data quality are measured?
101. What are the components of data quality?
102. What is the nature of the output?
103. Are there specific data quality metrics?
104. Is there a service level agreement for data quality?
105. If a data quality issue is identified, who is responsible for the resolution?
106. Is there a data quality dashboard?
107. Who sees this dashboard?

108. Can you give an example of a question asked in the last year as a result of reported data quality metrics?
109. Do you think that any data quality metrics are missing?

54.6 Audit and Audit Reports

110. Does internal audit specifically cover data quality?
111. Does external audit specifically cover data quality?
112. How does it cover data quality?
113. Have any audit reports specifically mentioned data quality as an issue?
114. What was that issue and how was it resolved?
115. What was the priority given to that issue?

54.7 Define Data Quality Requirements

116. Does the organisation have a defined list of data requirements?
117. Are these requirements organisation-wide, or are they specific to a department (e.g. finance)?
118. Do the requirements cover only a specific part of the data landscape (for example, customer data)?
119. How are data requirements defined?
120. How are they aligned to business requirements?
121. Who defines the data requirements?
122. Are data requirements ever changed, and by whom?
123. Is there a central repository for data requirements?
124. Is this repository freely accessible?
125. Does the organisation define quality requirements for each of its data items?
126. Are data quality requirements set organisation-wide?
127. Do they cover all data items, or are they restricted to a specific department or type of data (e.g. finance data)?
128. How are they aligned to business requirements?
129. Are they realistic or do they state that all data must be perfect?
130. Have the data quality requirements been created in full awareness of the monetary impact to the organisation if they are not met?
131. Are data quality requirements recorded in a central repository?
132. Are the accessible to all staff?
133. Are there any data quality requirements with which you would disagree?

54.8 Define Data Quality Metrics

134. Does the organisation have defined data quality metrics?
135. How are they defined?
136. In terms of the definition of data quality metrics, are some business units better than others?
137. How are data quality metrics defined in your area?
138. Are there any challenges with the definitions of data quality metrics?

54.9 Define Data Quality Business Rules

139. Does the organisation define data quality business rules?
140. How are data quality business rules created?
141. Are data quality business rules stored in one place?
142. Who creates the data quality business rules?
143. Who can modify the data quality business rules?
144. Who can sign off the data quality business rules?
145. Do data quality business rules change over time?

146. What are they used for?
147. Are they held in an application?
148. Are there any challenges with creation and maintenance of data quality business rules?
149. Can we have a copy of the ruleset?

54.10 Test and Validate Data Quality Requirements

150. How are data quality requirements tested?
151. What does this testing consist of?
152. How are the requirements validated?
153. Who performs the testing, and to what criteria?
154. Do you consider this testing to be rigorous?
155. What happens when the testing fails?
156. Who signs off the testing and/or validation?

54.11 Set and Evaluate Data Quality Service levels

157. Does the organisation set data quality service levels?
158. How are data quality service levels set?
159. Who sets data quality service levels?
160. How are they related to business requirements?
161. How are service levels evaluated?
162. Do you face any challenges in this area?
163. How do you feel these challenges can be addressed?
164. Do you feel the service levels are too high or low?
165. Do service levels exist throughout the organisation?
166. Do service levels cover all domains (e.g. finance, customer data, etc)?
167. Do you believe that service levels cover enough data items?
168. Is performance against service levels published?

54.12 Manage Data Quality Issues

169. How are data quality issues managed in the organisation?
170. Is there a central log of data quality issues?
171. How are data quality issues recorded?
172. Is this publically available?
173. Is there a service level agreement for resolution of data quality issues?
174. What is the reaction if you raise a data quality issue?
175. Have you raised a data quality issue in the last year?
176. If so what was the issue, and what was the result?
177. What do you feel are the challenges in managing data quality issues?
178. Can you give an example of an issue that was not managed well?
179. Do you know how many data quality issues are currently outstanding?
180. Can we have a list of current data quality issues?

54.13 Clean and Correct Data Quality Defects

181. Does the organisation actively clean data quality defects?
182. How do you know?
183. Can you give an example of recent cleansing of data quality defects?
184. Does the organisation deduplicate customer data?
185. If so, how often is this performed?
186. What are the rules for merging customers?
187. Are reports run on the results of the deduplication?

188. Is any root cause analysis performed on the causes for data quality defects?
189. Are processes amended to stop poor quality data being created or is the effort primarily "back end", to cleanse the data?
190. When cleaning data what best source analysis is performed?
191. How are the success criteria set for cleansing of data?
192. Are cleansing operations measured against data quality requirements?
193. If success criteria are not met, what occurs?
194. What challenges exist in correcting data quality defects?

54.14 Design and Implement Operational DQM Procedures

195. Do Data Quality Management procedures exist in the organisation?
196. Are DQM procedures defined?
197. Who defines DQM procedures?
198. Are DQM procedures reviewed on a regular basis?
199. What do the DQM procedures cover – are they domain specific or department specific?
200. Are DQM procedures freely available to staff?
201. Who designs DQM procedures?
202. Who signs DQM procedures off?

54.15 Monitor Operational DQM Procedures and Performance

203. How does the organisation ensure that DQM Procedures are being followed?
204. What is the review process for DQM procedures?
205. How often is a review done?
206. How is this reported?
207. How are any failings (i.e. staff not following DQM procedures) addressed?
208. If a DQM procedure is determined to not be effective, how is it amended?

54.16 Process Design

209. Is there a central department covering process design?
210. Is data quality taken into account during process design?
211. How is it taken into account?
212 Are processes benchmarked for the data quality that they produce?
213. Do processes have data quality targets?
214. How are processes measured against these targets?
215. Are processes amended if they do not meet data quality targets?

54.17 Profile, Analyse and Assess Data Quality

216. Is any data quality profiling done?
217. What systems does the data quality profiling cover? Is it specific to domain or department?
218. How often is profiling undertaken?
219. Is there a standard template for data quality profiling?
220. What data quality attributes does it cover?
221. How is data quality reported?
222. Do profiling activities result in data quality defects being raised?
223. Can you give me an example of where profiling has resulted in a data quality defect?
224. How was this defect addressed?
225. Was any consideration given to the business impact of the defect?
226. Would it be possible to have a copy of recent data profiling results?
227. What challenges does the organisation have in data quality discovery?

54.18 Quality and Management tools

228. Are any applications or tools used to profile data quality?
229. Are any applications or tools used to manage data quality?
230. How effective are these tools?
231. Are there any challenges in utilising these tools?
232. What are the advantages of using these tools?
233. If the organisation does not use a data quality tool, are there any plans to implement one?
234. Have you undertaken any vendor presentations recently?
235. If you are looking for a toolset, what attributes do you consider important?

54.19 Data Architecture

236. Is there a data architecture function in the organisation?
237. Does it cover all aspects of architecture (Business/Application/Data/Infrastructure)?
238. Is there a defined enterprise architect?
239. Does their role include responsibility for data quality?
240. Is there a defined approach to architecture in the organisation (E.g. TPGAF, Zachman)?
241. How is data lineage defined?
242. How is data lineage managed?
243. Are there specific architectural issues within the organisation that are causing poor data quality?
244. Are there multiple copies of data?
245. Are there any plans to merge multiple copies of data?
246. Is there any intention to create a single customer view?
247. Is there any intention to implement master data management?
248. Is there an organisational data model?
249. What areas does the data model cover – does it cover all domains and lines of business?
250. How is it maintained?
251. Where is it stored?
252. How do people needing to utilise the data model gain access to it, and what advice do they get
253. on data modelling?

54.20 Projects

254. How do projects consider data quality?
255. How are projects measured on data quality?
256. If a project is facing a data quality problem, how is this addressed?
257. If a project is making data quality worse, how is this addressed?
258. How does a project ensure that it is maintaining the integrity of data assets?

54.21 Data Quality Challenges

258. How good is information quality in your organisation?
259. How would you rate the quality of information in your area?
260. In your area, can you list the top three data quality pain points?
261. Why are these particularly bad?
262. What has been done to try and address these data quality problems?
263. How often do you use information to make evidence-based decisions?
264. What are the top three reports that you do not receive that would make your decision making better?
265. What other areas of the organisation have data problems?
266. What are the top things that can be done to improve information quality?
267. How does Data Quality affect your confidence in reporting?

268. What questions cannot be answered with the information you have?
269. What do you feel are the critical problems in getting the data you need?
270. Is significant time taken cleansing data before it can be used?
271. What is used to do this cleansing?
272. How long does this take, and how often is the cleansing performed?
273. Would you see significant cost and time savings if you did not have to cleans the data?
274. Does everyone in your area face the same problems?
275. Could you tell me about a data quality problem you faced recently?
276. How did it affect the department?
277. How did the data quality problem affect the business?
278. Was the business affect enumerated?
279. How was the data quality problem addressed?
280. What was the end result?
281. Do you have any known long term data quality issues?
282. If so, what are they, and have there been any initiatives to address them?
283. If they did not succeed, why do you think that was the case?
284. Could you give an example of where not having access to the right information is causing you problems?
285. What are these problems and how do you think they can be addressed?
286. What would be the effect if it was addressed?

54.22 Business Intelligence

287. Are there any data quality issues that are specific to reporting?
288. How are these addressed?
289. Is there any functionality in the BI tool to cleanse data?
290. Do you feel that poor data quality affects the decision-making process?
291. Can you give me an example of where this has occurred?
292. Does poor data quality slow up decisions whilst data is checked?
293. Have there been any past projects to increase data quality for business intelligence?
294. How successful were they?
295. If they did not succeed what do you think was the reason?
296. Do you think the business intelligence function delivers the information users need?
297. Have you had feedback in respect of business intelligence information?
298. How do you think that analysis can be improved?
299. How do you think the information you can access compares with your competitors?
300. How do you ensure that business intelligence is aligned with business needs?

SECTION 7: APPENDICES

CHAPTER 55: SAMPLE DATA STRATEGY

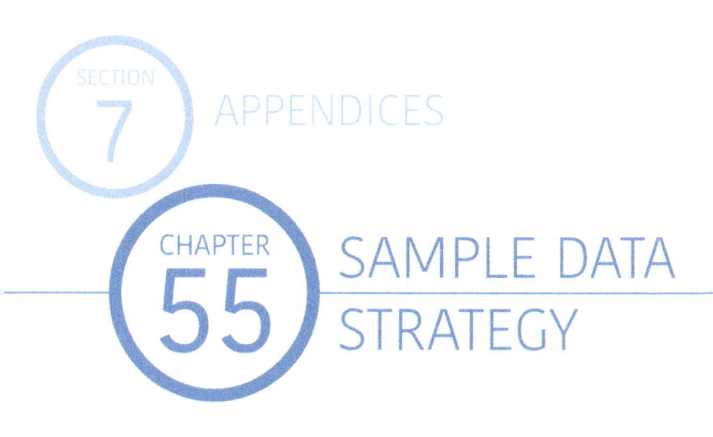

55.1 Introduction

This strategy sets out the approach for the organisation to manage and control its data over the next five years. The strategy will be reviewed on a yearly basis by the Chief Financial Officer of the organisation and the Chief Data Officer of the organisation.

This strategy sets out the aspirations of the organisation to be a market leader in its sector in respect of information governance, management, quality and exploitation.

55.2 Scope

The scope of the data strategy is all data in the organisation, regardless of the media on which it is held. It also includes data that is held outside the organisation but is supplied to the organisation for its use by third parties, or data that is created and maintained outside the organisation – for example on the internet – but is used by the organisation [65].

55.3 Purpose of the Strategy

The purpose of the data strategy is to outline and codify the approach of the organisation to information. The data strategy will also inform the:

- Data Quality Strategy
- Data Requirements Document
- Data Quality Performance Metrics
- Data Quality Policy

The data strategy is aligned to the data vision and the corporate strategy, and also acts to align with the risk appetite of the organisation and the regulatory environment in which the organisation resides.

It should be noted that the data strategy is owned by the business, not information technology.

---

65. For example interest rate data or house price data.

55.4 Information Needs of the Organisation

The information needs of the organisation will be set by the business. Information needs will include:

Data Category	Explanation
Visionary	The organisation must understand what information will be available in the future that will be necessary to effectively run the business. This information may not yet be in existence, it may exist but not be accessible, or it may simply not be used.
Strategic	The organisation needs to understand and define what information is required to support its strategic aims and to enable the organisation's executive to make effective strategic decisions.
Regulatory	Some data is primarily used by – and often defined by – the regulator. In the case of this organisation this will be the Bank of England and the Prudential Regulatory Authority. These regulators will have information needs in order for them to effectively regulate the industry and the organisation.
Managerial	The organisation needs to understand and define the information that is required to manage itself. This will consist of mainly high level summary information covering all areas of the organisation.
Operational	Operational data is data that is required for the day to day operation of the organisation.

In order to set the data strategy, the organisation will define its requirements for each of the above. It is understood that some data may fall into more than one category.

55.5 Key Principles

The following comprise the key data principles of the organisation. Every data initiative or decision should refer to these principles as a guide to the overall desired direction of information within the organisation.

No.	Principle	Explanation
1	Business Need	▪ The use and collection of data should support the needs of the organisation. ▪ There is no reason to capture and store information if it does not support the needs of the organisation ▪ Data that already exists that does not support the existing or future information needs of the organisation should be deleted
2	Capture	▪ Data should be captured once, and correctly
3	Uniqueness	▪ For any element of information there should be a single version of the truth
4	Classification	▪ Information should be classified into types for the purpose of security and retention

5	Security	■ Data should be held securely
6	Accuracy	■ Data should reflect the real life measure to which it corresponds
7	Appropriateness	■ Data should be appropriate for the use to which it is put
8	Sharing	■ Knowledge is shared within the organisation
9	Recording of Information	■ Data stores are recorded

Any data decisions that are not supportive of these principles must be escalated to the CDO or CFO of the organisation. Projects and business units should be aware that they may be required to demonstrate their compliance with the data principles.

55.6   Data Acquisition

Data will be acquired from a number of disparate sources in order to fulfil the organisations information needs. The primary sources of this information are listed below.

Source	Explanation
Customer	The customer will provide information on themselves via contact centres (relating to information received via phone or post), branches and via the internet. The customer may also use other forms of communication such as text messages and emails.
Partners	Partners will supply data to the organisation via all means including but not limited to: EDI, data dumps, electronic transfer, secure physical means and FTP.
Suppliers	Suppliers will supply data to the organisation via all means including but not limited to: EDI, data dumps, electronic transfer, secure physical means and FTP.
Staff	Staff may supply data to the organisation in the normal course of business via the same methods as customers, but also will have direct access to the organisations systems. The manner in which staff add information to the information systems must be carefully considered.
Web	It is possible that data may be acquired directly from the internet in the case of the download of information from authoritative sources such as the Bank of England or the Halifax House Price Index.
Third Parties	Third Parties will supply data to the organisation via all means including but not limited to: EDI, data dumps, electronic transfer, secure physical means, and FTP.

The organisation must consider each of the above sources of data, and define how each source of data will be managed and used.

55.7 Information Governance

55.7.1 Definition of Information Governance

Information governance is an integral part of Corporate Governance. As such it will support the organisation in the same way as Risk Governance, Regulatory Governance and IT Governance. The organisation will implement an information governance and management framework, with appropriate roles and responsibilities. The definition of information governance will be:

"The formal execution and enforcement of authority over data management and thereby the alignment of data management with the strategy and risk appetite of the organisation."
The role of information governance is not to manage data assets, it is to ensure that such management is performed, and performed effectively.

55.7.2 Information Governance Framework, Roles and Responsibilities

The organisation will implement a robust information management framework. This will include:

- Information Governance Steering Group: To ensure that the creation, management and utilisation of data (operational, financial and customer) in the organisation is effective, compliant and aligned with risk appetite. The Information Governance Steering Group is the owner of the data strategy, the data quality strategy, and, aside from the executive, is the most senior group within the organisation in respect of data.
- Information Governance Board: The Information Governance Board is the operational governance of the organisation. Its objective is to create, maintain, implement, and monitor policies, processes, and standards to ensure data reliability and sustainability.
- Chief Data Officer: The Chief Data Officer is a board position with responsibility for organisational data. The CDO is the final decision point for data decisions, and is responsible to the executive board and the shareholders. The Chief Data Officer will head up the Information Governance Steering Group.
- Head of Data Governance: The Head of Data Governance is the operational head of data within the organisation. Reporting to the Chief Data Officer, the Head of Data Governance will head the Information Governance Board and be a member of the Information Governance Steering Group.
- Data Owners: The operational owners of data; they are responsible for the definition of organisation data and operational rules and enforcement of related data policies and standards.
- Data Stewards: Data Stewards are the caretakers of the organisation data assets. The data stewards ensure that data is understood, used and shared effectively, and meets quality and integrity standards.
- All users. All information users within the organisation have a responsibility to use data effectively and to highlight to the relevant group where data issues occur.

55.8   Data Management

The data management of the organisation will follow the DAMA framework and will hence cover the following areas:

- Data Architecture Management
- Data Operations Management
- Data Quality Management
- Data security management
- Data warehouse and BI management
- Data Development
- Metadata Management
- Document and content management
- Reference data management

The DAMA framework will be considered the authority for data management. Decisions in respect of data management will be taken with reference to the DAMA Data Management Body of Knowledge. Where it is necessary for the principles of the organisation to diverge from the framework this will be documented in full, with the reasons why such a divergence is required.

55.9   Information Policy and Practice

The organisation will develop a data policy that will cover the expectations of the organisation of its staff in respect of information. Adherence to this policy will be the responsibility of all staff in the organisation and will be part of the annual appraisal cycle. Adherence to the data policy will be written into the staff roles and responsibilities. The information policy will support and elaborate on the data principles that are listed in the data strategy.

55.10   Information Management Lifecycle

The organisation will actively manage information at all stages of the information lifecycle. The information lifecycle is described below.

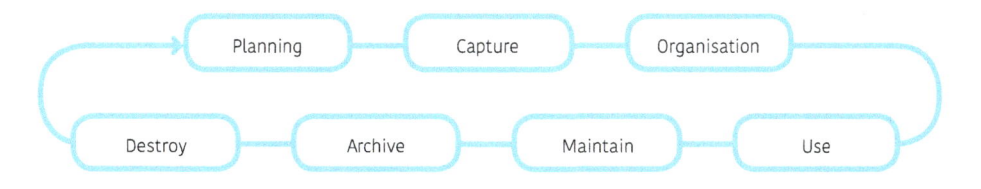

Planning → Capture → Organisation → Use → Maintain → Archive → Destroy → (back to Planning)

Lifecycle Stage	Description
Planning	The organisation will plan for the data that it requires, will plan how it will capture this data, and how it will operate with this data in each part of the information management lifecycle.
Data Capture	The organisation understands that data capture is a critical stage of the information lifecycle and it is imperative that the organisation captures information in an effective and accurate manner. The organisation will look to measure the effectiveness of its information capture and understand why and how failures occur, and act to rectify them in a timely manner.

Organise	The organisation will understand that information is not useful unless it is organised and hence will develop a corporate data model. This will be based on the information requirements of the organisation. The data model will govern how data is organised. A reference architecture will be developed and this will be implemented at each of the organisation's sites.
Use	The organisation will look to use information in an effective manner. Information that is used will be appropriate for the purpose and information use will in all respects look to follow the data principles of the organisation. Data use will follow the relevant legislation in respect of data privacy for our customers and suppliers. Data will be protected as a valuable asset.
Maintain	The organisation will act to invest in its data assets to ensure that their value is retained by keeping them current. The organisation will, where necessary, act to improve the quality of the data that it holds. Where information is out of date then remedial action will be taken.
Archive	Where information is not currently utilised by the organisation, but has not yet reached the due date for destruction, the organisation will look to improve the efficiency of its data storage by archiving data into a higher latency and lower cost solution.
Destroy	The organisation will destroy data when it is no longer of use to the organisation, when a customer legitimately requests us to do so, or when legally required. Unless any of the three instances occur, the organisation will hold data for a minimum of seven years.

10.11 Knowledge Sharing and Collaboration

Key to the effective exploitation of data within the organisation is sharing of knowledge between departments and across divisions. Private or departmental stores of information are not permitted unless the information is only of use to that particular department or there is a legal or privacy issue with not doing so (e.g. security of HR data). In general, data stores should be shared across the organisation and the location and contents of such stores entered into the data store catalogue.

10.12 Learning and Development

Key to the effective governance, management, quality and exploitation of the data in the organisation is training on the correct and effective use of data.

All individuals employed by the organisation, of whatever grade, will be required to attend a minimum amount of training per annum to update them on current data issues and make them aware of their obligations as data users in the wider governance and management framework of the organisation.

Individuals in critical positions will be required to undertake significant additional training on information governance, management, quality or use, appropriate to their role.

SECTION 7 APPENDICES

CHAPTER 56 SAMPLE DATA QUALITY STRATEGY

56.1 Introduction

This strategy sets out the approach for the organisation to manage and control its data quality over the next five years. This strategy will be reviewed on a yearly basis by the Chief Financial Officer of the organisation and the Chief Data Officer of the organisation.

56.2 References

This Data Quality Strategy references the Corporate Vision, the Corporate Strategy, the Organisation Data Strategy, and the Organisation Data Requirements.

No	Name	Reference	Date
1	Corporate Vision	V1.0	
2	Corporate Strategy	V1.0	
3	Data Strategy	V1.0	
4	Data Requirements	V1.0	

56.3 Scope

The scope of this Data Quality Strategy is all data within the organisation that supports:

- Financial reporting
- Regulatory reporting
- Operational reporting

The referenced Data Quality Requirements are mandatory and apply throughout the entire data life-cycle; creation, storage, transmittal, usage and destruction of data.

Where data does not fall into the above categories then the data is still subject to the data strategy that covers all data in the organisation. There are no exceptions to the data principles except as described in the data strategy.

56.4 Exemptions

There are no exemptions to this strategy provided data is within the overall scope.

56.5 Purpose of the Strategy

The purpose of the strategy is to outline the strategy and framework for the maintenance and continued adherence to data quality requirements. It is also to define the direction and allocation of resources at high level to pursue this strategy. In order to determine the strategy for the data quality of the organisation, it is necessary to consider:

- What is the current data quality?
- What are the data quality requirements?
- How will the transition from current data quality to good data quality be implemented?
- How will the organisation measure success?
- How will the continuous maintenance of good data quality be ensured?

The intention is to support and promote:

- The executive board in their commitment to producing transparent and high quality information available for customers, the public, staff and regulators.
- The importance of high quality data to provide a quality service; drive performance improvement; make robust decisions and support accurate predictions.

This document is subsidiary to the Corporate Strategy and Information Governance Strategy and ranks above the Data Quality Policy. It should be read in conjunction with the Data Quality Requirements.

56.6 Data Quality Principles

The data quality principles underlie all parts of the data quality strategy. They are:

- Data is captured once, and correctly.
- Data quality issues, once raised, are taken seriously.
- The goal of the organisation is minimum data rework.
- All staff are aware of the way in which data quality underpins everything the organization does.
- There should be no doubt as to whether information is poor quality.

As in the case of the data principles, any data decisions that are not supportive of these principles must be escalated to the CDO or CFO of the organisation. Projects and business units should be aware that they may be required to demonstrate their compliance with the data quality principles.

56.7 Why Data Quality Matters

A proactive data quality program is a critical factor in the organisation's ability to direct its operations. The issue of data quality therefore pervades all aspects of the delivery of customer care, operational reporting, strategic decision-making and reporting to the regulator. Data is one of the key assets for the organisation and as such must be viewed as an essential enabler to the organisation achieving its strategic objectives. Data quality is critical to:

- Effective and high quality delivery of customer services
- Effective performance monitoring and planning
- Compliance with current legislation
- Accurate and timely reporting to the regulator
- The ability to manage financial, operational, credit and information risk

As part of this requirement, the organisation will need to:

- Identify and track customer and product
- Report to the regulator on the organisation's operations
- Effectively manage the organisation's operations
- Promote the organisation externally
- Identify and track customer satisfaction
- Apply transactions to the customer accounts accurately

It should be noted that in the current marketplace, data quality failings that result in customer dissatisfaction may easily result in reputational damage for the organisation.

Data quality also affects:

- Employee efficiency: Staff having to re-work tasks, taking a longer time to complete a process and dealing with unhappy customers who have cause for complaint due to poor data
- System, Process and Governance efficiency: Processes requiring work-arounds (for example data cleansing) wasting valuable resources
- Incorrect financial data impedes reputation resulting in lost business.
- Compliance with the Data Protection Act and other legislation.
- The organisation's ability to be regulatory compliant.

It can be seen that good data quality is essential to the future health of the organisation and its role in delivering customer service.

56.8 Strategic Aims for Data Quality

The strategic aims are primarily to support the corporate vision and mission statement. The key attributes of which are:

- The customer should be at the heart of everything we do.

- Quality of customer information is not optional; it should be an expected right.
- Data quality needs to facilitate the ability of the organisation to make the right decision, first time.
- The data quality of the organisation needs to support its vision and strategy.
- The organisation needs to understand its customers. Data quality is key to this understanding.
- The organisation needs to understand its marketplace. Data quality is key to this understanding.
- The organisation needs to work with the regulator to ensure positive outcomes for the sector. Data quality is key to regulatory satisfaction.

It is clear that good data quality is necessary in order to enable the overall corporate strategy.

56.9 Analytical Requirements

Performance reports and performance monitoring reflect historic activity and information. The reporting is after the fact. A key challenge for performance reporting is to look at future propensity to perform in light of historical trends on the basis of analysis. The organisation can then benefit from historical analysis to predict the future. None of this is possible if the historic data is of poor quality.

56.10 Operational Aims for Data Quality

The organisation needs to enable data quality reporting for key operational measures, and ensure that staff are aware that data quality reporting is in place and that data quality issues will be reported on an ongoing basis and followed up as necessary.

56.10.1 Capture

Data needs to be captured, transported, transformed and used in accordance with sound principles. The organisation aims to adhere to the regulator's principles of good data quality. The components of data quality in this organisation are defined below:

- Validity – all data maintained by the organisation must comply with business rules.
- Completeness – all necessary items must be collected.
- Existence – data should not be populated when it is not correct to do so.
- Consistency – all data must be collected and recorded in a consistent way to enable comparison and analysis.
- Coverage – data collection will reflect all products sold by the organisation.
- Accuracy – all recorded customer data must be correct the first time it is input.
- Timeliness – all data will be recorded in a timely manner in accordance with agreed deadlines.

56.10.2 Compliance

- That the organisation will be able to respond to regulatory requests on a timely basis and with a high quality of data
- That the organisation will, as far as is possible, be able to anticipate regulatory needs
- That the organisation will be able to supply data quality metrics on any data item that is used for compliance or regulatory reporting

56.10.3 Monitoring

It is essential that regular reporting is carried out to measure the current data quality. The reporting should include:

- "State of the Nation" – The quality of the data landscape.
- Effectiveness of remediation.
- Trend analysis.
- Early warning of issues.
- Problem escalation and resolution.

56.10.4 Enhancing

The organisation will look to enhance its existing data. This will be performed by:

- Selective replacement of data where the existing data quality is of too poor a quality to be cleansed.
- Cleaning of existing data based on in-house knowledge.
- It is understood and anticipated that some data cleaning will require going back to the customer to validate data.

56.11 Benefits of the Strategy

It is intended that implementation of this strategy will lead to:

- Improved customer satisfaction.
- Improved information capture at source to support efficient and effective analysis.
- Enhanced management information for internal use to drive service delivery and analysis of customer satisfaction.
- Enhanced information for external use by regulators.
- Demonstration of board ownership for good data quality.
- Increased ownership of data quality with organisational staff.
- Clarity within the organisation in respect of data quality.
- Raising awareness on the principles of good data quality.
- Ensuring that systems conform to operational and management data quality needs.
- A definition of the governance framework within which data is captured, managed, monitored and reported.

- Clear definitions of responsibilities and accountabilities, including appropriate reporting mechanisms for providing feedback
- The setting out of a risk based approach to the assurance over data
- Creating a framework within which data quality issues can inform the needs of education and training projects
- Identifying the organisation's policies and procedures supporting data quality
- Allocation of responsibilities for reviewing, updating and amending documentation, with established timescales for monitoring systems and ensuring compliance with policies and procedures

56.12 Data Quality Governance Framework

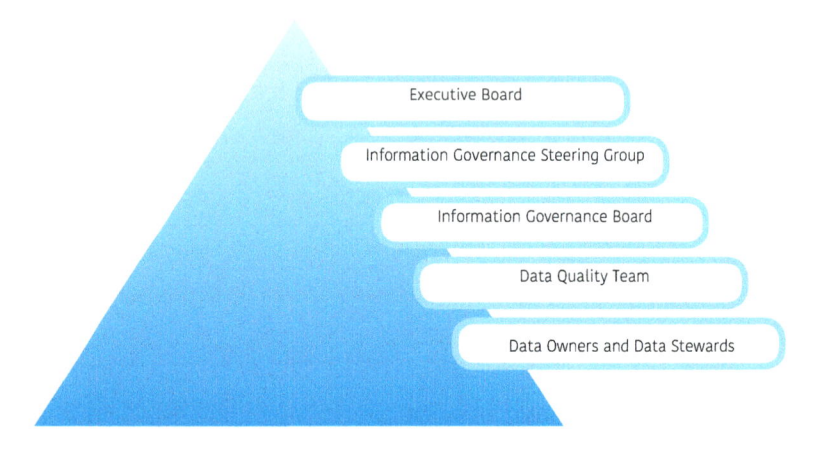

Executive Board
Information Governance Steering Group
Information Governance Board
Data Quality Team
Data Owners and Data Stewards

People	Function/Forum and Responsibility	
Executive Board		- Ultimately responsible for data governance, data management and data quality
Business Leaders	Information Governance Steering Group	- Set data quality strategy - Set data strategy - Escalation of issues not resolved at IGB - Escalation of funding requests not resolved at IGB
Function Leaders	Information Governance Board	- Escalated issues from DQT - Resolution of intra-department disagreement on data quality - Escalation of data quality issues to IGSG
Data Quality Specialists	Data Quality Team	- Logging of data quality Issues - Management of data quality - Reporting on data quality - Monitoring of data quality - Raising and escalating data quality issues - Provision of a centre of excellence for data quality

Operational Leaders	Data Owners and Data Stewards	■ "Eyes and ears" of data quality ■ Operationalisation of data quality ■ Escalation of issues
Data Quality Champions	Local team members	■ Provide support to data stewards ■ Operate in local data quality training ■ Provide a local reference point

Further details are included in the Data Governance Framework within the Information Governance Strategy.

56.13   Monitoring and Review

56.13.1   Data Quality Team

The data quality team will be a central department responsible for monitoring of the data quality within the organisation. It will report to the Information Governance Board. Its role is to monitor data quality throughout the organisation. This will cover:

- Data input into source data systems (i.e. primary data capture process).
- Data within source systems.
- Data within warehousing environments.
- Data in MI.
- Data in board and regulatory reporting.
- Operational data.

The data quality team will meet on a monthly basis. The data quality team will liaise with data stewards and data owners throughout the organisation to determine the reasons for data quality issues and to agree and monitor the resolution of these issues. It should be noted that it is not the responsibility of the data quality team to remediate data issues themselves, but to act as a instigator and monitor of the remediation of data quality issues.

The data quality team will be responsible for the instigation and monitoring of training on data quality. In a similar way to the above, they will not be responsible for performing the training, but ensuring that the training occurs.

56.14   Systems, Process and Procedures

The executive has ultimate responsibility for all systems that operate within the organisation. This includes the systems, the data they hold, and the proper performance of the processes that capture, transform, transport and use information.

56.14.1 Systems and process support for data quality

All parts of the organisation systems, processes and procedures should be designed with consideration for data quality. Often, it is the case that data quality issues arise where systems and interfaces between systems are complex or overly manual (e.g. re-keying data from one system to another). As far as is possible systems, processes and procedures should be implemented to allow adherence to data quality best practice to be as easy as possible.

56.14.2 Systems and process controls

Systems, processes and procedures should contain embedded controls to pick up data quality errors before the data is finalised. This may include:

- Format and edit checks.
- Re-keying critical data.
- Sign-off by peer or superior.
- Associative checks within the system, for example that title matches gender matches forename.
- Automatic reconciliation checks.

Whilst it is fully understood that data checks of this nature may increase initial overhead, it is much easier to prevent data quality issues entering the system than try and correct them afterwards, where typically considerably more effort will be required.

56.14.3 Interface controls

Especial consideration should be made to interfaces between systems. Systems designed by different manufacturers, or at different times, may not process or hold information in the same way. When data is transferred from one system to another data quality issues may arise, in some cases information may be lost.

When interfaces are designed and implemented consideration of data quality issues should be undertaken and appropriate controls, or reconciliations, embedded within the system to prevent and detect errors.

56.14.4 Data Owners

Each of the information systems operated within the organisation should have a named individual responsible for the quality of information held within the system. In accordance with this data quality strategy, the individually named officer will be responsible for:

- Ensuring policies and procedures are kept up to date in line with changes to the systems.
- Ensuring compliance with policies and procedures via spot checks and a rolling programme of audit.

- Ensuring staff receive adequate training in the use of the systems and are appropriately accredited to do so before use.
- Monitoring error rates and investigating the recurring problems in order to instigate corrective actions.

The responsibilities of the named individual should be explicitly identified in their job description, and will also form part of the post holder's appraisal process. The data owner should have input into control and processes within the relevant system to enable them to raise issues where the systems and processes do not support data quality aspirations.

56.14.5 Data Quality Leads

The Data Quality Strategy endorses the formation of an Information Governance Board which will have representation from across the organisation at a business operational and Information Technology level. The executive for each division will be responsible for nomination of data quality leads within their area of responsibility and to ensure attendance and engagement.

The responsibilities of the data quality leads should be explicitly identified in their job description, and will also form part of the post holder's appraisal process.

56.14.6 Operational Staff

This data quality strategy aims to ensure that operational staff have access to high quality information that is essential for the provision of the best possible customer service. In order to support the data quality strategy the organisation has appointed customer and product data quality champions to support the work. The responsibilities of customer and product data quality champions should be explicitly identified in the job description for these posts, and should form part of the post holder's appraisal process.

56.15 Risks and Risk Management

Data quality risks and risk management will be the overall responsibility of the Information Governance Steering Group, through may be delegated to the Information Governance Board. The Information Governance Steering Group is accountable for the co-ordination of the data quality strategy with the overall risk appetite and governance of the organisation.

56.16 Emerging Data

The strategy needs to consider not only the data quality of data used now but also the data quality required for future data needs. The organisation needs to build a framework that will support the integration of future data when it is available. This framework may not be able to specify the data concerned, but it can cover the governance, management framework and documentation that will need to be applied to future data.

The data quality strategy needs to reflect the methods used for data capture. The technology advances in respect of data capture need to be recognised within the strategy, together with an appreciation of the inpact that such future developments could have.

56.17　Data Supplied by Third Parties

The organisation may rely on data that is supplied by third parties. In this case it will be the responsibility of the organisation to put in place service level agreements that will govern the quality of the data that is supplied.

Where this is not possible (for example, house price data), data quality requirements should be put in place and the data should be monitored against these requirements on receipt. The responsibility for development of the data quality requirements will be the receiving system owner, and they will be expected to develop these requirements with the assistance of the receiving business unit or units and the data quality team.

56.18　Data Quality Process Framework

Stakeholders in the data quality framework are any individual or organisation who may raise a data quality issue, process or remediate such an issue, or be affected by such an issue. There are few individuals within the organisation who do not fall into one or other of these categories. The process framework will follow a five stage process, as shown below.

CONTACT	INITIATE	ASSESS	IMPLEMENT	ESCALATE
▪ A member of the organisation notices a data quality issue ▪ They escalate the issue to a responsible individual within the organisation ▪ This may be the data quality unit, or a data steward.	▪ The issue is oficially logged ▪ The issue is assigned to an individual for investigation ▪ A service level is agreed for the issue	▪ The data quality issue is assessed for criticality, cost of rectification, cost to the organisation ▪ The data quality issue is then listed for remediaiton	▪ The strategy for remediation of the issue is agreed ▪ The process for implemention is agreed ▪ The remediaiton of the issue is implemented	▪ Where the issue is not resolved or where it is not possible to gain agreement as to the correct treatment the issue is escalated to the data quality unity or the informaiton governance teams

56.19　Risk Appetite

The organisation will define a data quality risk appetite. This is the appetite of the organisation to take risks with data quality. This will be department-specific. For example, it would be anticipated that if the marketing department send an email to the incorrect individual as part of a product launch this is embarrassing, however not as serious as a statement sent to the wrong address.

56.20 Urgent Issues or Breaches

Urgent issues or breaches may need to be addressed in a different manner to the usual process. However they should still be logged within the information governance framework before going to assessment. It should be noted that regardless of urgency no changes should be made to the live system without being tested in advance, whatever the urgency, or the seniority of the complainant.

56.20 Policy Waiver

Policy waivers need to be applied for in writing to the Information Governance Board.

SECTION 7: APPENDICES

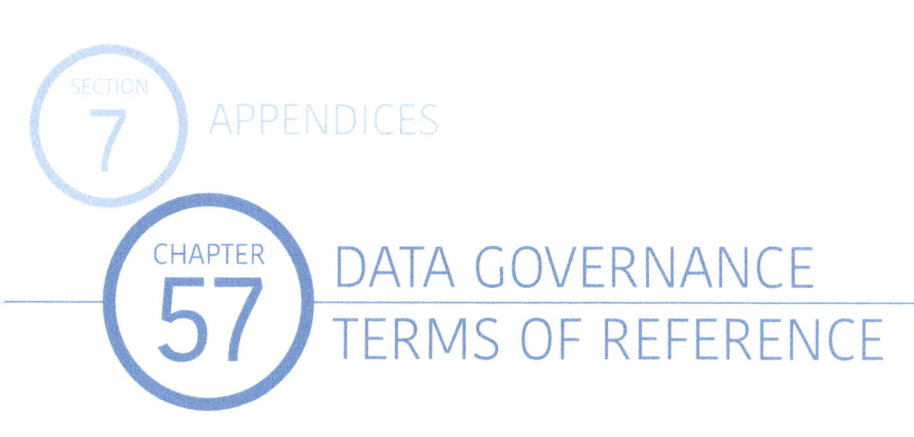

CHAPTER 57: DATA GOVERNANCE TERMS OF REFERENCE

57.1 Information Governance Steering Group

- Executive
- Information Governance Steering Group
- Information Governance Board
- Data Owners, Stewards and Creators
- Data Consumers

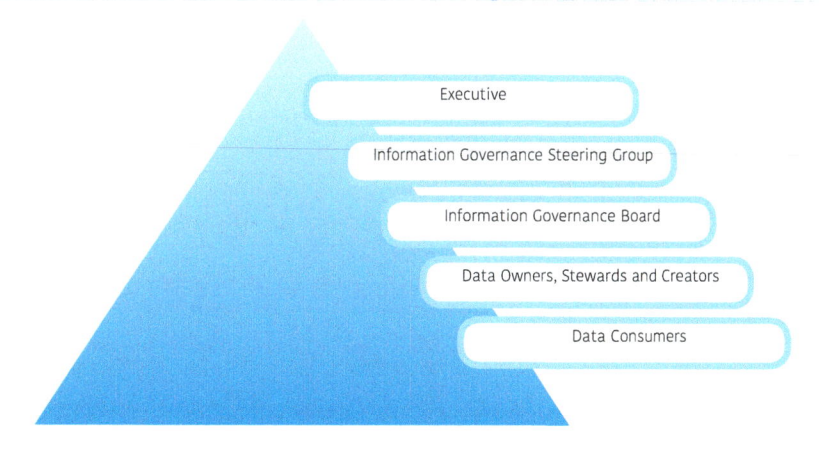

Objective: To ensure that the creation, management and utilisation of data in the organisation are effective, compliant and aligned with risk appetite.

Key responsibilities:

- Creation and maintenance of the Information Governance Strategy.
- Data-related operational and compliance issues are appropriately resolved.
- Data-related risks are adequately mitigated.
- Escalating data management and quality issues to the Executive Board where appropriate.
- Ensuring that significant changes to data-related policy, procedures and practice are implemented successfully.
- Ensuring that transformation and significant change projects delivering direct improvements to the organisation data quality and management have appropriate data governance representation at delivery stream, project & programme level.
- Ensuring that transformation and significant change projects impacting on the organisation data (or its management or utilisation) are meeting agreed quality and timing requirements

in as far as they impact on the organisation data quality, governance standards and risk profile.
- Ensuring that data-related incidents are appropriately managed and lessons are learned to avoid repetition.
- Ensuring that all parts of the organisation (BAU or project/change related) adhere to the policies and standards as outlined and controlled by the Data Governance Board.
- Approval of requests for specific exceptions to data management or data governance strategy, policy and practice.
- Approval of formal data-related reports to the organisation executive.

57.2   Information Governance Board

Objectives: To create, maintain, implement, and monitor policies, processes, and standards to ensure effective data governance and management of data within the organisation. To be an initial arbitrator. To act as a centre of excellence to review and advise on the implementation of Data Governance.

Key responsibilities:

- Oversight of data governance throughout the organisation and escalation to the Information Governance Steering Group as appropriate.
- Management of the data steward network, reviewing data issues brought to its attention by any individual inside or outside the organisation.
- Guidance for other areas of the organisation in respect of activities relating to data governance and data management.
- Ownership of the data governance and data management risk and issue log.
- Training of data stewards
- Reviewing all changes to data governance and data management.
- Ensuring that projects act in accordance with the data governance and data management framework
- Ensuring that the operational organisation acts in accordance with the data governance and data management framework

57.3   Data Quality Board

NOTE: The activities below may be subsumed as part of the responsibilities of the Information Governance Board, or may be the subject of a separate forum.

Objective: To create, maintain, implement, and monitor policies, processes, and standards to ensure data quality, reliability and sustainability.

Key responsibilities:

- Oversight of data quality throughout the organisation and escalation to the Information Governance Steering Group as appropriate.

- Oversight of tasks relating to the remediation of data quality to meet the defined data requirements.
- Monitoring of data quality through KPIs & metrics.
- Oversight and monitoring of compliance with data quality requirements.
- Review of all changes to process framework components.
- Identifying and oversight of approved process improvement opportunities.
- Advising on the data quality impacts of projects.

57.4   Data Owners

The operational owners of the data in the organisation; they are responsible for the management of organisation data and operational rules and enforcement of related data policies and standards.

Key responsibilities:

- Accountable for organisation (shared) operational data.
- Definition of organisation data requirements.
- Definition of the level of quality required to satisfy operational needs across the organisation.
- Definition of data processes and procedures (create, update, transform, read, archive, delete).
- Accountability for compliance with data policies and standards.
- Creation of organisation data definitions and/or business glossaries.
- Working with data stewards to identify and address data interdependencies across businesses and functions

57.5   Data Stewards

Data Stewards are the caretakers of the organisation data assets. The data stewards ensure that data is understood, used and shared effectively, and meets quality and integrity standards.

Key responsibilities:

- To be an advocate for effective application and usage of data within the organisation
- To act between departments and individuals to resolve data-related conflicts
- To identify opportunities for improvement in the management or use of data
- To assist with the implementation of data processes and procedures
- To assist with the implementation of data policies and standards
- To asset in the establishment of data and operational governance for new systems
- To help gather and report data quality and wider data management metrics
- To work with data creators and data consumers to ensure owners have a practical understanding of front line data challenges, and how data governance can help address these challenges

57.6 Data Creators

A specific description of data creators is not necessarily expected by the typical data governance framework; however I have mentioned a number of times in the book that these are special individuals and should be treated as such. Creating a role description for them is not too much of a stretch if one is looking to create a quality culture. The description below is an example.

Data Creators are responsible for either the creation of the data or are the touch point where data enters the organisation. They need to act as gatekeepers to ensure that poor quality data does not enter the organisation, as it is much harder and costs more to remediate data after it is created than to create it correctly in the first place.

Key responsibilities:

- To input data accurately
- Where data cannot be input accurately (e.g. unreadable content) to highlight this to the local data steward.
- To highlight where there are faults in received data to the local data steward
- Where part of the role, to create appropriate metadata to describe the data they create.
- Where part of the role, to store such metadata in a manner that promotes reuse.
- To engage with downstream data users and understand their requirements.
- Where applicable, ensure external agencies are aware of the governance, management and quality requirements of the organisation.
- To act to get data right, first time.

57.7 Data Consumers/users

Another role that is rarely described is that of the data user. The utility in describing this role is again when the practitioner is looking to establish a quality culture at the organisation. By explicitly stating the role of a data user, and their ability to use well, or badly, it is possible to write this role into the profile of all in the organisation.

In reality data consumers are all employees that use data. Their actions have the ability to actively help the data governance and data management of the organisation. Any data consumer has responsibility to act to safeguard data, in terms of its quality, integrity, and management, through compliance with data governance and data management policies.

Key responsibilities:

- Adhere to the data principles of the organisation.
- Support the data governance and data management of the organisation.
- Highlight issues with data to the appropriate authority.
- Adhere to the data polices of the organisation.
- Use data legally and responsibly.

SECTION 7: APPENDICES

CHAPTER 58: SAMPLE PROJECT PLAN

58.1 Introduction

The intention of this appendix is to answer the question "OK, so you have spent several hundred pages detailing the reason why data quality is important, how to assess it, how to remediate it, but how is a data quality project going to look, really?" It's going to look a bit like this.

The below is only an example. Large elements are drawn from real-life projects. I have tried to create something that can be used as a basis for creating a data quality project plan in reality. As part of pulling together this plan I have made some assumptions about size and scale, and also about the approach to planning. The main assumption is that the organisation wants to do a decent job, but also wants to get the work done as soon as possible. This has a number of effects:

- Corners have not been cut with the fundamentals
- Everything is clearly controlled and documented
- Where a section of work can start ahead of the end of the previous stage/phase, then I have allowed it to do so
- On the other hand, I have not gone to extremes to bring every task forward to the earliest point where it can be started. That's a job for a project manager whose project is "Red" and who has an unhappy client shouting at them. Hence the logical integrity of the overall approach is retained.
- I have assumed the plan starts on 1/1/2018. The sole reason for this is that 1/1/2018 is a Monday
- I have based duration on my own experience. For example, at the beginning of the project I have assumed it takes a week to set up a meeting with an executive. This is because – in my experience – getting time in an exec's diary is difficult. That time drops over the period of the project (as do sign-off times) as my assumption is that the exec and senior stakeholders will become increasingly bought-in
- Profiling times are based on my experience and assume manual or semi-manual profiling, on the basis that an expensive tool cannot be guaranteed
- I've not resource-leveled this plan – it's tasks only. I am aware that without resource constraints how do you know that you can profile a system in 10 days? Here I've assumed the other way – that resources will be available to perform the work in the timescales noted. The timescales are reasonable based on the resources discussed in the project chapter.

- The Data Quality Blueprint describes, by its nature and design, a modular project. Bits can be swapped around. "What can be done when" can and will change depending on the organisation. This plan is not mandatory, but a guide.
- Hygiene points. This is a fairly big plan, at over 1,500 tasks. I have done my best to avoid errors and it has been checked and double checked and triple checked. However if any errors have crept in, apologies.

Lastly, this plan was created in MSProject. I'm not a MSProject Guru, I'm passable user. If there are tips and tricks that I've not used then my apologies to the MSProject gurus out there.

58.2 Level 1 Plan

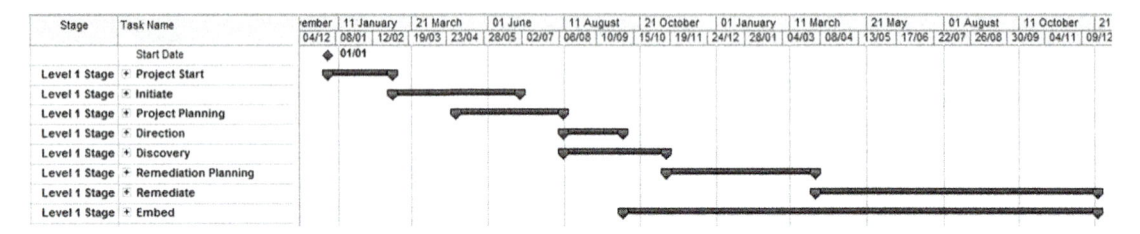

Stage	Task Name	Start Date
Level 1 Stage	+ Project Start	01/01
Level 1 Stage	+ Initiate	
Level 1 Stage	+ Project Planning	
Level 1 Stage	+ Direction	
Level 1 Stage	+ Discovery	
Level 1 Stage	+ Remediation Planning	
Level 1 Stage	+ Remediate	
Level 1 Stage	+ Embed	

This level 1 plan shows the overall approach. Points to note:

- After Planning has been completed, Direction and Discovery start at the same time. It is not essential to finish the remediation before starting to implement governance, for example.
- One could, in theory, run Embedding alongside the whole remediation project in parallel. However the knowledge management element of embedding is dependent on the completion of the remediation project, so this aspect would have to wait, but Governance and Training could in theory start from day 1.
- "Planning" as a stage starts immediately after the "Business Case" and hence overlaps with "Proof of Concept" and "Hearts and Minds".
- Overall duration is around 18 months to 2 years, with 6 months of up-front planning. This approach is planning-heavy, for the good reasons explained elsewhere in the book.

58.3 Level 2 Plan

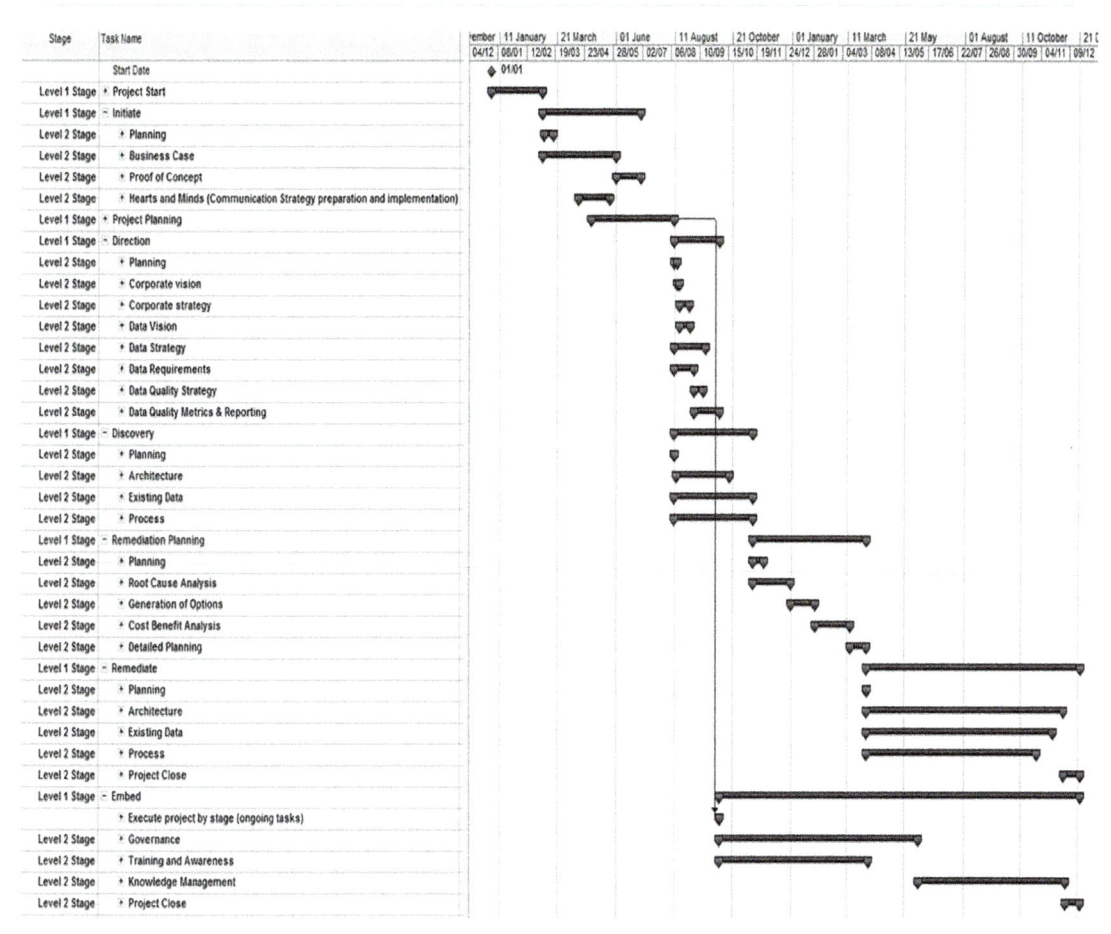

Stage	Task Name
	Start Date
Level 1 Stage	+ Project Start
Level 1 Stage	− Initiate
Level 2 Stage	+ Planning
Level 2 Stage	+ Business Case
Level 2 Stage	+ Proof of Concept
Level 2 Stage	+ Hearts and Minds (Communication Strategy preparation and implementation)
Level 1 Stage	+ Project Planning
Level 1 Stage	− Direction
Level 2 Stage	+ Planning
Level 2 Stage	+ Corporate vision
Level 2 Stage	+ Corporate strategy
Level 2 Stage	+ Data Vision
Level 2 Stage	+ Data Strategy
Level 2 Stage	+ Data Requirements
Level 2 Stage	+ Data Quality Strategy
Level 2 Stage	+ Data Quality Metrics & Reporting
Level 1 Stage	− Discovery
Level 2 Stage	+ Planning
Level 2 Stage	+ Architecture
Level 2 Stage	+ Existing Data
Level 2 Stage	+ Process
Level 1 Stage	− Remediation Planning
Level 2 Stage	+ Planning
Level 2 Stage	+ Root Cause Analysis
Level 2 Stage	+ Generation of Options
Level 2 Stage	+ Cost Benefit Analysis
Level 2 Stage	+ Detailed Planning
Level 1 Stage	− Remediate
Level 2 Stage	+ Planning
Level 2 Stage	+ Architecture
Level 2 Stage	+ Existing Data
Level 2 Stage	+ Process
Level 2 Stage	+ Project Close
Level 1 Stage	− Embed
	+ Execute project by stage (ongoing tasks)
Level 2 Stage	+ Governance
Level 2 Stage	+ Training and Awareness
Level 2 Stage	+ Knowledge Management
Level 2 Stage	+ Project Close

This is now starting to show the detail, and it is possible to directly relate each element of the plan to the book sections. Points to note:

- The start of the project is largely waterfall
- Requirements are triggered by the planning stage
- Discovery of Architecture, Data and Process start at the same time, as do their remediation
- Governance and Training starts after Direction, and Knowledge Management does not start until after Discovery

At this point, breakout to further detail and including a Gantt chart would be impossible, so for Level 3 and below I will just list tasks.

58.4 Level 3 and below Project Tasks

Note: "D" marks project deliverables.

Line No	D	Stage	Task
1			Start Date
2		Level 1 Stage	Project Start
3		Level 2 Stage	Initial set-up
4		Level 3 Stage	Initial meeting with sponsor
5			Arrange and attend meeting
6			Identify key stakeholders
7	D		Define initial problem statement
8	D		Draft initial scope
9	D		Draft initial objectives
10	D		Document meeting
11			Agree communications frequency
12			Agree next steps
13			Set up follow-up meeting
14			Confirm actions to project sponsor
15		Level 3 Stage	Logistics
16	D		Create daily log
17	D		Create query log
18	D		Create issue log
19			Identify project team
20			Determine availability
21	D		Create holiday tracker
22	D		Initial draft onboarding document
23			Create project repository
24	D		Create initial task list
25			Assign task list to project team
26		Level 3 Stage	Organisational Understanding
27			Research background to organisation
28			Discover internal roles and responsibilities
29			Obtain details of organisational systems
30			Obtain details of organisational domains
31			Obtain details of organisational structure
32	D		Update list of key stakeholders
33			Upload documentation into project repository
34		Level 3 Stage	Initial Stakeholder Interviews (30 min - 1 hour max each)
35			Identify stakeholders to interview
36	D		Draft stakeholder map
37			Request interviews
38	D		Prepare interview schedule
39	D		Prepare interview material
40			Perform Interviews
41	D		Document and confirm meeting notes with individual stakeholders
42			Upload interview notes into project repository
43		Level 3 Stage	Problem Statement
44	D		Update initial problem statement for interviews
45	D		Draft list of pain points
46			Agree with project sponsor and key stakeholders
47			Update as required
48			Upload into project repository
49		Level 2 Stage	Project Approach
50		Level 3 Stage	Scope
51	D		Define data domains in scope

52	D		Define system domains in scope
53	D		Define process domains in scope
54			Agree with project sponsor and key stakeholders
55			Obtain written signoff
56			Upload to project repository
57		Level 3 Stage	Objectives
58	D		Define requirements for the project
59	D		Define expectations for the project
60			Link requirements and expectations to problem statement
61	D		Draft high level project objective
62			Agree with project sponsor and key stakeholders
63			Obtain written signoff
64			Upload to project repository
65	D		Draft low level (detail) objectives for the project
66			Agree with project sponsor and key stakeholders
67			Obtain written signoff
68			Upload to project repository
69		Level 3 Stage	Project Definition
70	D		Create project definition
71			Agree with project sponsor and key stakeholders
72			Obtain written signoff
73			Upload to project repository
74		Level 3 Stage	Approach
75			Define overall methodology to be used
76			Draft high level approach
77			Estimate timescales
78			Define project tasks at a high level
79	D		Create the project approach document
80			Upload to project repository
81		Level 3 Stage	Work Breakdown Structure
82	D		Draft work breakdown structure
83			Agree with team
84			Upload to project repository
85		Level 3 Stage	Technical and Licensing
86	D		Draft technical and licensing requirements
87			Agree with IT stakeholders
88			Upload to project repository
89		Level 3 Stage	Resourcing
90			Define skill sets required
91			Define training needs
92			Confirm availability
93	D		Draft project roles and responsibilities
94			Upload to project repository
95		Level 2 Stage	Initial planning
96		Level 3 Stage	Project Plan
97	D		Create high level project plan
98	D		Create resourcing plan
99	D		Draft communications plan
100	D		Create draft detail initiate plan
101			Agree with project sponsor and key stakeholders as required
102			Upload to project repository
103		Level 3 Stage	RAID Log
104			Brainstorm initial risks with team and/or key stakeholders
105			Brainstorm initial dependencies with team and/or key stakeholders
106			Brainstorm initial assumptions with team and/or key stakeholders
107			Brainstorm initial issues with team and/or key stakeholders
108	D		Document initial RAID Log

The Data Quality Blueprint

109			Agree with key stakeholders
110			Upload to project repository
111		Level 3 Stage	Draft Business Case
112			Create estimates of the cost of poor quality to the business
113			Create benefit estimates of the project
114			Socialise with key stakeholders if required
115	D		Draft initial business case
116		Level 3 Stage	Project Brief/SOW
117			Inputs
118			Background
119			Problem statement
120			Scope
121			Objectives
122			Requirements
123			Expectations
124			Project definition
125			Approach
126			Work breakdown structure
127			High level plan
128			Resource plan
129			Team structure
130			Draft business case
131			High level risks
132			High level assumptions
133			High level dependencies
134			Creation and agreement
135	D		Create project brief
136	D		Presentation of project brief to sponsor
137			Obtain agreement and signoff for initiate stage
138			Present project brief to board
139			Obtain go decision and funding for initiate
140			Baseline and upload into project document repository
141		Level 1 Stage	Initiate
142		Level 2 Stage	Planning
143		Level 3 Stage	Plan
144	D		Update initiate plan
145			Confirm resourcing
146			Confirm skillets required from resources
147			Confirm availability of resources
148			Create internal RACI
149			Create external RACI
150			Define training needs for resources
151			Deliver training if required
152			Confirm draft timescales of project
153	D		Complete initiate project plan
154			Agree with project sponsor and key stakeholders
155			Baseline and upload into project document repository
156			Draft full project plan
157	D		Create draft full project plan
158			Socialise with team members
159			Update for feedback as required
160			Upload to project repository
161		Level 3 Stage	Initial Artefacts
162	D		Update daily log
163	D		Update risk log
164	D		Update assumptions log
165	D		Update issues log

166	D		Update dependencies
167	D		Update query log
168			Upload to project repository
169		Level 3 Stage	Forums
170			Steering Committee
171			Identify members
172	D		Draft terms of reference
173			Agree with key stakeholders
174			Brief members on purpose of meetings
175	D		Create meeting schedule
176			Upload to project repository
177			Data Design Authority
178			Identify members
179	D		Draft terms of reference
180			Agree with key stakeholders
181			Brief members on purpose of meetings
182	D		Create meeting schedule
183			Upload to project repository
184			Governance
185			Agree relationship with organisational governance
186	D		Agree terms of reference for project and/or governance
187	D		Agree relationship with project management office
188	D		Agree terms of reference
189			Agree appointment of project data steward
190			Brief members on purpose of meetings
191	D		Create rules of engagement
192			Agree with key sponsors
193			Upload to project repository
194		Level 3 Stage	Logistics
195			Agree hotel rates
196			Book hotels
197			Agree travel rates
198			Update on-boarding pack
199			Upload to project repository
200		Level 2 Stage	Business Case
201		Level 3 Stage	Information Gathering
202			From initial scope identify the architectural, data and process items in scope
203	D		Document detailed scope
204			Agree with sponsor and key stakeholders
205			Identify key stakeholders across architecture, data, process
206	D		Draft communications plan
207			Agree with key sponsor and stakeholders
208			Where stakeholders are to be interviewed, arrange interviews
209	D		Where a questionnaire is to be used, prepare questionnaire
210	D		Where a workshop is to be used, prepare workshop
211			Send out questionnaire
212			Distribute briefing information for workshops
213			Distribute preparation material for interviews
214			Perform interviews
215			Run workshops
216	D		Collate and document responses
217	D		Collate and document pain points
218			Upload to project repository
219		Level 3 Stage	Initial Architecture Assessment
220			From project brief identify domains in scope
221			From project brief identify systems in scope
222			From project brief identify processes in scope

223			Document architectural scope
224			Identify key architectural documents
225			Obtain key architectural documents
226	D		Draft initial list of issues using documentation and output from interviews, workshops and questionnaires
227			Estimate impact of issues
228	D		Draft initial list of options for remediation
229			Estimate cost of remediation
230	D		Document issues, impacts, and costs for remediation
231			Upload to project repository
232		Level 3 Stage	Initial Data Assessment
233	D		From project brief identify domains in scope
234	D		From project brief identify systems in scope
235	D		Document data scope
236			Identify key data documents
237			Obtain key data documents
238	D		Draft initial list of issues using documentation and output from interviews, workshops and questionnaires
239			Estimate impact of issues
240	D		Draft initial list of options for remediation
241			Estimate cost of remediation
242	D		Document issues, impacts, and costs for remediation
243			Upload to project repository
244		Level 3 Stage	Initial Process Assessment
245			From project brief identify domains in scope
246			From project brief identify processes in scope
247	D		Document scope
248			Identify key process documents
249			Obtain key process documents
250	D		Create high level CRUD matrix
251	D		Draft initial list of issues using documentation and output from interviews, workshops and questionnaires
252			Estimate impact of issues
253	D		Draft initial list of options for remediation
254			Estimate cost of remediation
255	D		Document issues, impacts, and costs for remediation
256			Upload to project repository
257		Level 3 Stage	Objectives
258			Collate issues from the initial assessment
259			Discuss with sponsor and key stakeholders
260			Update the objectives for the project
261	D		Document objectives in each area
262			Upload to project repository
263		Level 3 Stage	Scope
264			Update scope based on objectives
265			Based on objectives and pain points define scope in terms of business areas
266			Define scope in terms of architecture
267			Define scope in terms of process and systems
268			Discuss and agree with sponsor and key stakeholders
269	D		Document scope in each area
270			Upload to project repository
271			Risks, assumptions and dependencies
272			Document high level risks, assumptions and dependencies using the RAID log as source
273		Level 3 Stage	Analysis of Poor Quality Cost
274			Collate details of pain points
275			Estimate financial impact of pain points
276	D		Draft the overall cost of poor quality for the organisation

277			Agree with key sponsor and stakeholders
278			Update as required
279		Level 3 Stage	Option Appraisal
280			Collate options for remediation
281			Estimate cost of options
282	D		Document cost of remediation
283			Agree with key sponsor and stakeholders
284		Level 3 Stage	Cost Benefit Analysis
285	D		Document cost benefit analysis of project
286			Agree with key sponsor and stakeholders
287			Upload to project repository
288		Level 3 Stage	Prepare Business Case
289			Draft template and agree with key sponsor
290			Add project definition
291			Add project approach
292			Add cost benefit analysis
293			Add risk assessment and management strategy
294			Add change assessment and management strategy
295			Add data, process and architecture assessment
296			Add pain points
297	D		Finalise initial business case
298			Agree with key sponsor
299			Socialise with key stakeholders
300	D		Prepare presentation pack for board
301			Present to board
302			Obtain signoff
303			Upload to project repository
304		Level 2 Stage	Proof of Concept
305		Level 3 Stage	Planning Proof of Concept
306			Determine if proof of concept required
307			Identify elements of the organisation where a PoC will show fast benefit
308	D		Identify pain point to be addressed
309	D		Determine current cost of poor data quality
310			Interview business and system owners of the area under consideration
311			Discuss implementation of a data quality proof of concept
312	D		Identify how the effectiveness of the PoC will be measured
313	D		Identify expected positive effects of PoC
314	D		Identify expected negative effects of PoC
315			Agree an implementation plan with the business and system owner
316	D		Document the implementation plan
317			Discuss and agree Implementation plan with sponsor
318			Upload to project repository
319		Level 3 Stage	Implementing Proof of Concept
320			Remediate either data or process
321			Measure the positive and negative effects
322			Determine overall positive negative benefit
323	D		Obtain feedback from staff members involved
			(this is critical to identifying other benefits like improved customer engagement)
324			Obtain feedback from business owner
325	D		Identify other areas of the business that will experience costs/benefits
326			Interview (if required) downstream business owners to identify benefits
327	D		Quantify costs and benefits
328			Extrapolate the effect of rollout across the business
329	D		Write up implementation
330			Present results to sponsor
331	D		Finalise the implementation documentation
332			Upload to project repository

333		Level 2 Stage	Hearts and Minds (Communication Strategy preparation and implementation)
334		Level 3 Stage	Information Gathering
335			Validate domains in scope
336			Validate business units in scope
337			Validate systems in scope
338	D		Update key stakeholder list
339			Input stakeholder information for all interviews, workshops and questionnaires created to date
340			Input organisation chart
341			Input business unit /organisation chart
342			Identify key system owners
343			Identify key process owners
344			Identify key data owners
345			Identify data stewards
346			Identify key influential personnel
347			Upload to project repository
348		Level 3 Stage	Stakeholder Assessment
349	D		Agree stakeholder assessment template
350	D		Create interest/influence matrix
351	D		Update external RACI
352			Identify information gaps
353			Schedule interviews to fill information gaps
354	D		Update stakeholder assessment
355			Agree with key sponsor
356			Upload to project repository
357		Level 3 Stage	Communications Strategy and Implementation plan
358	D		Agree strategy template
359			Define communications options
360			Define communication frequency
361	D		Draft implementation plan
362			Agree with sponsor and key stakeholders
363			Upload to project repository
364		Level 3 Stage	Initial Communications
365			Vision
366	D		Create vision statement for the project
367			Upload to project repository
368			Mission
369	D		Create mission statement for the project
370			Upload to project repository
371			Elevator Pitch
372	D		Create elevator pitch
373			Upload to project repository
374			Day in the life
375	D		Create "day in the life"
376			Upload to project repository
377			Interviews
378			Define approach from communications strategy
379			Define interviewees
380	D		Prepare briefing material and distribute
381			Arrange and conduct interviews
382			Obtain feedback and apply to next interview
383			Questionnaires
384			Define approach from communications strategy
385			Define recipients
386	D		Prepare questionnaire
387			Send out questionnaires
388			Obtain feedback and update approach as required

389			Workshops
390			Define approach from communications strategy
391			Define delegates
392	D		Prepare briefing material and distribute
393			Deliver workshop
394			Obtain feedback and update approach as required
395			Presentations
396			Define approach from communications strategy
397			Define delegates
398	D		Prepare briefing material and distribute
399			Deliver presentation
400			Obtain feedback and update approach as required
401			Posters
402			Define approach from communications strategy
403			Define locations
404	D		Design posters
405			Mount posters
406			Obtain feedback and update approach as required
407		Level 3 Stage	Ongoing Communications
408			Frequency
409			Agree frequency and update as required
410			Interviews
411	D		Hold interviews
412			Obtain feedback and update approach as required
413			Questionnaires
414	D		Deliver questionnaires
415			Obtain feedback and update approach as required
416			Workshops
417	D		Deliver workshops
418			Obtain feedback and update approach as required
419			Presentations
420	D		Deliver presentations
421			Obtain feedback and update approach as required
422			Posters
423	D		Deliver poster campaign
424			Obtain feedback and update approach as required
425	D		Other methods (e.g. website, blog, etc)
426		Level 1 Stage	Project Planning
427		Level 2 Stage	Scope & Objectives
428		Level 3 Stage	Requirements, Expectations, Scope
429	D		Update expectations as necessary based on initiation stage
430	D		Update requirements as necessary based on initiation stage
431	D		Update definition of systems in scope if necessary based on initiation stage
432	D		Update definition of domains in scope if necessary based on initiation stage
433	D		Update definition of processes in scope if necessary based on initiation stage
434			Agree with sponsor and key stakeholders if required
435			Document and upload to project repository
436		Level 2 Stage	Deliverables
437	D		Create draft deliverables list
438			Discuss and agree with sponsor and key stakeholders
439	D		Create detailed description of deliverables
440	D		Ideally create mock-up of deliverables
441			Discuss and agree with sponsor and key stakeholders
442			Upload to project repository
443		Level 2 Stage	Change Capacity Assessment and Management Strategy
444	D		Create and agree change assessment template
445			From interviews, workshops and questionnaires assess capacity for change

446			Identify change issues
447			Discuss with key sponsor and, if required, key stakeholders
448			Estimate impact of issues
449	D		Document change capacity assessment
450			Identify mitigating actions
451			Identify residual risk to change
452	D		Prepare change mitigation strategy
453			Agree with key sponsor
454			Upload to project repository
455		Level 2 Stage	Risk Assessment and Management Strategy
456	D		Create and agree risk assessment template
457			From interviews, workshops and questionnaires assess risks
458	D		Define the risk appetite of the organisation
459			Query whether data quality risk has been differentiated between departments
460			Identify risks of pursuing a data quality project
461			Identify impacts of individual risks
462			Identify the risks of NOT pursuing a data quality project
463			Identify impacts of individual risks
464	D		Create overall risk assessment
465			Identify treatment of risks (e.g. mitigate/ignore/etc)
466			Create risk management strategy
467		Level 2 Stage	Detailed Approach
468		Level 3 Stage	Modules
469			Define project modules with go/no go decision points
470			Discuss and agree with sponsor and key stakeholders
471	D		Document modules
472			Upload to project repository
473		Level 3 Stage	Work Breakdown Structure
474	D		Update work breakdown structure
475			Discuss with relevant project resources
476			Update as required
477			Upload to project repository
478		Level 3 Stage	Task list
479	D		Create first draft of task list
480			Discuss with relevant project resources
481			Update task list
482			Discuss and agree with sponsor and key stakeholders
483			Upload to project repository
484		Level 2 Stage	Control Strategy
485		Level 3 Stage	Reporting
486			Discuss reporting strategy with sponsor and key stakeholders
487	D		Draft reporting template
488	D		Document reporting strategy
489			Agree with sponsor and key stakeholders
490			Upload to project repository
491		Level 3 Stage	KPI
492			Discuss project KPI with sponsor and key stakeholders
493	D		Draft reporting template
494			Define source for KPI
495	D		Document approach for KPI reporting
496			Agree with sponsor and key stakeholders
497			Upload to project repository
498		Level 3 Stage	Workflow
499			Agree use of workflow with the engagement team
500			Source workflow tools as required
501	D		Set up basic workflow
502			Agree roles and responsibilities (e.g. review/perform)

503			Document roles and responsibilities
504			Upload to project repository
505		Level 3 Stage	Change management
506			Discuss change management strategy with sponsor and key stakeholders
507	D		Draft change management strategy
508			Discuss with engagement team and steering group
509	D		Draft change management template
510			Agree with sponsor and key stakeholders
511			Upload to project repository
512		Level 3 Stage	Traceability matrix
513			Create template
514	D		Populate template with deliverables and requirements
515			Note updating the traceability matrix will be an ongoing task throughout the project
516		Level 3 Stage	RAID
517	D		Update risks
518	D		Update assumptions
519	D		Update dependencies
520	D		Update issues
521		Level 2 Stage	Resource Plan
522		Level 3 Stage	Required skills
523	D		Determine required skill sets per project stage
524	D		Determine resource profile over the project lifecycle
525			Identify available skills and hence skill gaps
526			Requisition relevant resources
527			Interview and onboard new team members
528			Verify final list of team members
529			Verify training needs of team members
530		Level 3 Stage	Availability
531			Discuss project with proposed team members
532			Verify availability
533			Verify holiday plans
534			Agree with team members start and end dates
535		Level 3 Stage	Plan
536	D		Take project plan and add resourcing
537			Allocate tasks to individuals
538	D		Create internal RACI
539			Perform resource levelling
540			Socialise resource plan with team members
541			Obtain feedback
542			Update plan as required
543		Level 3 Stage	Organisational resourcing requirements
544	D		Create initial list of organisational (as opposed to project) personnel required
545			Distribute to departments concerned
546	D		Agree and document availability
547			Verify this fits in with plan dates
548			Update plan as required
549		Level 3 Stage	Software and licensing
550	D		Define and agree software required during project lifecycle
551			Agree licensing and delivery schedule
552			Agree environment access
553			Agree purchase responsibility
554			Agree installation responsibility
555			Agree installation timescale
556			Document, obtain signoff, and upload to repository
557		Level 2 Stage	Project Plan
558	D		Create draft project plan
559			Socialise with engagement team

560			Update as required
561			Socialise with key sponsor
562			Update as required
563			Socialise with key stakeholders
564			Update as required
565			Socialise with steering group and/or board
566			Update as required
567			Obtain written signoff
568			Upload to project repository
569		Level 2 Stage	Project Initiation Document
570			Update project brief into a full initiation document
571			Update problem statement
572			Update project definition
573			Update scope and objectives
574			Update RAID
575			Update business case
576			Update team and roles
577			Update resource plan
578			Update risk management strategy
579			Add change management strategy
580			Add results from POC
581			Add communication management strategy
582			Update project plan
583	D		Finalise project initiation document
584			Agree with executive sponsor
585			Agree with board (if required)
586			Receive written signoff
587			Upload to project repository
588		Level 1 Stage	Direction
589		Level 2 Stage	Planning
590			Validate plan still on track
591			Validate resource availability for stage
592			Execute project by stage (ongoing tasks)
593			Plan and update workflow as work items are completed
594			Allocate and manage resources, both in-project resources and also subject matter experts.
595			Update plan for new information and as work items are completed
596			Update product and task lists as required.
597			Create and deliver weekly reporting
598			Create and deliver monthly reporting
599			Create and deliver stage reporting
600			Manage deliverables
601			Update risk assessment for new risks and changes to risks and risk profile
602			Update assumptions
603			Update dependency log and manage dependencies
604			Update issue log and report and manage issues
605			Update daily log as required
606		Level 2 Stage	Corporate Vision
607			Discuss corporate vision with sponsor and key stakeholders
608	D		Obtain or document the corporate vision
609			Upload to project repository
610		Level 2 Stage	Corporate Strategy
611			Discuss corporate strategy with sponsor and key stakeholders
612			Obtain the corporate strategy
613			Assess corporate strategy for data elements
614	D		Document data impacts of corporate strategy
615			Present to key sponsor
616			Upload to project repository

617		Level 2 Stage	Data Vision
618			Obtain data vision if it already exists
619			Determine vision for each functional area
620	D		Determine the data requirements needed to support the vision
621	D		Map corporate vision to data vision
622			Assess for data impact on current landscape
623			Present to key sponsor
624			Upload to project repository
625		Level 2 Stage	Data Strategy
626			Obtain data strategy if it already exists
627	D		Agree template for data strategy with sponsor
628			Input data and corporate vision
629		Level 3 Stage	Create data strategy
630			Scope
631			Purpose
632			Define information requirements of the organisation
633			Key principles
634			Information acquisition
635			Information governance
636			Management framework, roles and responsibilities
637			Information policy and practice
638			Information management lifecycle
639			Data classification
640			Information protection
641			Knowledge sharing and collaboration
642			Delivery and communications
643			Technical implications
644			Analyse strengths and weaknesses of organisation
645			Analyse strengths and weaknesses of competitors
646			Analyse strengths and weaknesses of the market
647	D		Draft data strategy
648			Present to sponsor and other critical individuals and gain feedback
649			Finalise data strategy
650			Receive written signoff
651			Baseline and upload into project document repository
652		Level 2 Stage	Data Requirements
653			Template and timescale
654	D		Define template for requirements
655	D		Define timescale for the definition of requirements
656		Level 3 Stage	Regulatory
657			Discuss regulatory reporting requirements with regulatory reporting manager
658			Identify regulatory reports required
659			For each report define fields needed and meaning (often available via regulator's website)
660	D		Collate into regulatory data requirements
661			Note and add any quality requirements
662		Level 3 Stage	Board
663			Obtain existing board reports
664			Obtain existing financial accounts
665			Discuss with key sponsor or board and identify missing information
666			Define data required to support the vision and strategy
667			For each report define fields needed and meaning of these fields
668	D		Collate into data requirements
669			Note and add any quality requirements
670		Level 3 Stage	Managerial
671			Obtain existing management reporting
672			Discuss with users what information is missing or required
673			Potentially use workshops to define requirements

674			For each report define fields needed and meaning of these fields
675	D		Collate into data requirements
676			Note and add any quality requirements
677		Level 3 Stage	Operational
678			Obtain application forms and customer reports
679			Discuss with users their information needs
680			For each report define fields needed and meaning
681	D		Collate into data requirements
682			Note and add any quality requirements
683		Level 3 Stage	All areas
684			Collate and rationalise requirements
685	D		Document requirements and circulate for review
686			Update as required
687			Discuss and agree with sponsor and key stakeholders
688			Upload to project repository
689		Level 2 Stage	Data Quality Strategy
690			Relate data quality strategy to data strategy
691			Determine how data quality relates to and supports the corporate vision
692			Determine how data quality relates to and supports the corporate strategy
693	D		Agree template for the data quality strategy with sponsor
694		Level 3 Stage	Create data quality strategy
695			Scope
696			Exemptions
697			Purpose
698			Objectives
699			Benefits
700	D		Data quality governance
701	D		Data quality process framework
702			Risk appetite
703			How to deal with breaches and urgent issues
704			Data archiving
705			Data remediation
706			Data reconciliation and control
707			Draft data quality strategy
708			Present to sponsor and other critical individuals and gain feedback
709	D		Finalise data quality strategy
710			Receive written signoff
711			Baseline and upload into project document repository
712		Level 2 Stage	Data Quality Metrics & Reporting
713	D		Collate data requirements and quality requirements
714			For each requirement identify critical data items
715	D		For each critical data item define metrics
716			Map requirements and metrics to each business process
717	D		Create "basket" of metrics
718			Discuss and agree with sponsor and key stakeholders
719	D		Draft reporting suite
720			Update as required
721			Draft approach for capture of metrics
722	D		Create proof of concept mock-up of reporting
723			Discuss and agree with sponsor and key stakeholders
724			Update as required
725		Level 1 Stage	Discovery
726		Level 2 Stage	Planning
727			Validate plan still on track
728			Validate resource availability for stage
729			Execute project by stage (ongoing tasks)
730			Plan and update workflow as work items are completed

731			Allocate and manage resources, both in-project resources and also subject matter experts.
732			Update plan for new information and as work items are completed
733			Update product and task lists as required.
734			Create and deliver weekly reporting
735			Create and deliver monthly reporting
736			Create and deliver stage reporting
737			Manage deliverables
738			Update risk assessment for new risks and changes to risks and risk profile
739			Update assumptions
740			Update dependency log and manage dependencies
741			Update issue log and report and manage issues
742			Update daily log as required
743		Level 2 Stage	Architecture
744		Level 3 Stage	Scope
745			Confirm domains in scope
746			Confirm systems in scope
747			Confirm business units in scope
748	D		Validate scope against pain points, objectives and requirements
749		Level 3 Stage	Plan approach
750	D		Draft reporting template
751			Divide architecture into functional areas
752			Divide architecture into information flows
753			Divide architecture into business processes
754			Allocate specialists to separate areas
755	D		Define and document timescales
756	D		Identify key personnel to interview
757			Understand data requirements of the organisation
758	D		Define architectural notation
759	D		Create approach document
760			Upload to project repository
761		Level 3 Stage	Exception Process
762	D		Document exception process
763			Determine escalation points/people
764			Determine required timescales for exception turnaround
765			Discuss exception process with process and business owner
766			Obtain buy-in to exception process
767			Agree SLA for exception process
768	D		Deliver exception process document
769			Upload to project repository
770		Level 3 Stage	Documentation Review
771			Collate existing architecture documentation
772	D		Where documentation does not exist create documentation
773			Identify areas where architecture looks to be inadequate
774			Identify areas where (from previous interviews) there are data quality issues
775	D		Document issues
776			Upload to project repository
777		Level 3 Stage	Architecture review
778			Arrange and perform interviews
779			Identify pain points
780	D		Document pain points
781			Confirm architectural issues with key personnel
782	D		Document issues
783			Upload to project repository
784		Level 3 Stage	Architecture Assessment
785	D		Collate pain points
786	D		Collate issues raised from documentation assessment
787			Assess the architecture in relation to its effect on data quality

788	D		Assess the impact resulting from each of the issues
789			Document the impact
790			Estimate the cost of the impact
791			Agree with key stakeholders
792	D		Create architecture assessment
793			Upload to project repository
794		Level 2 Stage	Existing Data
795		Level 3 Stage	Scope
796			Identify domains in scope
797			Identify systems in scope
798			Validate scope against pain points, objectives and requirements
799		Level 3 Stage	Approach
800			Plan Approach
801			Obtain existing system documentation
802			Obtain conceptual model of system(s)
803			Discuss conceptual model with system and business subject matter experts
804			Input pain points from initial interviews/workshops/questionnaires
805	D		Create profiling task list (fields to be profiled)
806	D		Agree fields to be profiled (and not profiled) with business
807			Agree profiling approach including reporting template and milestones
808	D		Deliver profiling planning document
809			Agree with business stakeholders
810			Update assumptions and risks
811	D		Update dependencies and constraints
812	D		Determine and document extract and/or data source requirements
813	D		Team identification and allocation to system or domain
814			Team training
815			Exception process
816	D		Design and document exception process
817			Determine escalation points/people
818			Determine required timescales for exception turnaround
819			Discuss exception process with system and business owner
820			Obtain buy-in to exception process
821			Agree SLA for exception process
822	D		Deliver exception process document
823			Source system access
824			Request access to source systems
825			Enquire about level and nature of masking and determine if it will cause an issue with profiling
826			Agree schedule for availability of data (if extract) or access to systems and data (if direct access)
827	D		Document schedule and include within plan
828			Obtain extract or access
829			Profiling tool
830			Determine if profiling tool required
831			Identify and source profiling tool if required
832			Determine appropriateness for organisation (i.e. whether it meets requirements)
833	D		Install profiling tool and ensure it can access data. (this may take a long time - I've seen two months)
834			Perform training on profiling tool if required
835		Level 3 Stage	Profile
836			Agree template with key stakeholders
837	D		perform profiling work - System 1
838	D		Perform profiling work - System 2
839	D		Perform profiling work - System 3
840	D		Perform profiling work - System 4
841	D		Perform profiling work - System 5

842	D		Create profiling results
843			Upload to project repository
844		Level 3 Stage	Existing Data Assessment
845			Perform initial investigation of cause
846			Identify "headline issues"
847	D		Collate into stakeholder groupings (e.g. all the issues that need to be presented to each stakeholder)
848			Present back to business and IT (and exec) stakeholders
849			Document business feedback and revisit causes
850	D		Create profiling deliverable
851	D		Create existing data assessment
852			Socialise deliverable with stakeholders
853			Upload to project repository
854		Level 2 Stage	Process
855		Level 3 Stage	Scope
856			Identify domains in scope
857			Identify processes in scope
858			Validate scope against pain points, objectives and requirements
859		Level 3 Stage	Approach
860			Plan Approach
861			For each domain identify a domain owner
862			Discuss with the domain owner the processes that lead to data creation or change
863			Discuss with users and process owners the processes that lead to data creation or change
864	D		Create and document known list of processes
865	D		Document interactions between processes
866	D		Create CRUD Matrix
867	D		Create holistic process map
868			Replay to domain owners
869			Obtain process documentation
870	D		Create process assessment task list
871	D		Note processes not to be assessed and why
872	D		Define type of assessment per process
873	D		Define sampling criteria (if sampling used) and expected output
874	D		Define assessment approach including reporting template and milestones
875	D		Create assessment planning document
876			Upload to project repository
877	D		Define dependencies
878			Baseline and upload into project document repository
879			Determine if tool required
880			Source and install toolset
881	D		Team identification and allocation to system or domain
882			Team training
883			Design exception process
884	D		Design and document exception process
885			Determine escalation points/people
886			Determine required timescales for exception turnaround
887			Discuss exception process with process and business owner
888			Obtain buy-in to exception process
889			Agree SLA for exception process
890			Deliver exception process document
891			Upload to project repository
892		Level 3 Stage	Fact-finding
893	D		Interview process users and walk through process - Domain 1
894	D		Interview process users and walk through process - Domain 2
895	D		Interview process users and walk through process - Domain 3
896	D		Interview process users and walk through process - Domain 4
897	D		Interview process users and walk through process - Domain 5

898	D		Document process interactions
899			Identify and document elements that affect data and data quality
900			Model current processes (if necessary)
901	D		Identify and document KPIs
902			Benchmark current process
903			Agree documented process and issues with user and domain owner
904	D		Document issues with current process
905			Upload to project repository
906		Level 3 Stage	Process Assessment
907			Perform initial assessment of issues with current processes in respect of data quality
908			Identify headline issues
909			Identify potential process improvements
910			Collate into stakeholder groups (i.e. all issues relating to each stakeholder)
911			Present back to business stakeholders
912			Document feedback and revisit as required
913	D		Create process assessment deliverable
914			Socialise deliverable with stakeholders
915			Upload to project repository
916		Level 1 Stage	Remediation Planning
917		Level 2 Stage	Planning
918		Level 3 Stage	Plan Validation
919			Validate plan still on track
920			Validate resource availability for stage
921			Validate scope against pain points, objectives and requirements
922			Execute project by stage (ongoing tasks)
923			Plan and update workflow as work items are completed
924			Allocate and manage resources, both in-project resources and also subject matter experts.
925			Update plan for new information and as work items are completed
926			Update product and task lists as required.
927			Create and deliver weekly reporting
928			Create and deliver monthly reporting
929			Create and deliver stage reporting
930			Manage deliverables
931			Update risk assessment for new risks and changes to risks and risk profile
932			Update assumptions
933			Update dependency log and manage dependencies
934			Update issue log and report and manage issues
935			Update daily log as required
936		Level 3 Stage	Information Gathering
937			Input issues from architecture assessment
938			Input issues from data assessment
939			Input issues from process assessment
940			Input architectural documentation
941			Input process documentation
942			Input data documentation
943			Input stakeholder assessment
944			Input change capacity assessment
945			Input risk assessment
946		Level 3 Stage	Consider Architectural Issues
947			Assess architectural issues for major items
948			Determine impact of these issues on the rest of the project
949			Decide if they are important enough to be addressed first or will have significant impact on the project
950	D		Document key concerns
951			Discuss with sponsor and key stakeholders
952	D		Prepare impact analysis of either doing or not doing them first

953			Based on impact analysis present recommendation to sponsor and key stakeholder, together with impact on the project
954			Feed decision into remediation planning
955		Level 2 Stage	Root Cause Analysis
956		Level 3 Stage	Identification of Root Cause
957			Input issues from architecture assessment
958			Input issues from data assessment
959			Input issues from process assessment
960			Define approach and method to be used for root cause analysis
961			For each issue track back to root cause
962	D		Document root cause analysis
963			Socialise with key stakeholders
964			Update for feedback
965			Upload to project repository
966		Level 3 Stage	Collate results
967			Collate root causes
968			Assign to architecture/process/data/direction/etc
969			Group root causes
970	D		Identify common root causes
971			Discuss with stakeholders
972			Update for feedback
973			Upload to project repository
974		Level 3 Stage	Link root causes across organisation
975			Create organisation-wide root cause list
976			Identify key root causes
977			Analyse interaction of root causes
978	D		Create final root cause list
979			Upload to project repository
980		Level 3 Stage	Assign degree of responsibility
981	D		For each issue allocate responsibility to a root cause
982			Collate results
983			Discuss with stakeholders
984			Update for feedback
985			Upload to project repository
986		Level 3 Stage	Assign cost
987			Input business case
988			For each root cause assign the poor quality cost for which it is responsible
989	D		Document the cost of each root cause
990			Present to key stakeholders
991			Update for feedback
992			Upload to project repository
993		Level 3 Stage	Complete root cause analysis
994	D		Prepare final root cause analysis document
995			Present to key stakeholders
996			Update for feedback
997			Upload to project repository
998		Level 2 Stage	Generation of Options
999		Level 3 Stage	Architectural Design
1000			Understand architectural scope
1001			Engage organisations architectural function
1002			For each architectural root cause understand issue
1003			For each architectural root cause consider options
1004			Discuss with architecture function
1005	D		Determine and document most appropriate options
1006			Ensure alignment with long term architectural roadmap
1007	D		Document architectural roadmap
1008	D		Define transition states (if required)

The Data Quality Blueprint

1009			Present to key stakeholders
1010			Update for feedback
1011			Upload to project repository
1012		Level 3 Stage	Process Design
1013			Understand process scope
1014			Engage process owners
1015			For each process root cause understand issue
1016			Ensure process correctly documented
1017			For each process root cause consider options
1018			Discuss with process owners
1019			Generate process design
1020	D		Determine and document most appropriate options
1021			Ensure alignment with future process roadmap
1022	D		Document process roadmap
1023	D		Define transition states (if required)
1024			Present to key stakeholders
1025			Update for feedback
1026			Upload to project repository
1027		Level 3 Stage	Data Design
1028			Understand data scope
1029			Engage data owners, data governance and data management
1030			For each data root cause understand issue
1031			For each data cause consider options
1032			Discuss with data owners, data governance and data management
1033			Generate options
1034			Determine approach for remediation
1035	D		Define the replacement data required
1036			Source replacement data
1037	D		Perform best source analysis on replacement data
1038	D		Document data roadmap
1039	D		Determine and document most appropriate options
1040			Present to key stakeholders
1041			Update for feedback
1042			Upload to project repository
1043		Level 2 Stage	Cost Benefit Analysis
1044		Level 3 Stage	Option Costing
1045			Input options from design process for architecture, data and process
1046			For each option cost solution
1047			Agree cost with key stakeholders
1048	D		Document options costing
1049			Upload to project repository
1050		Level 3 Stage	Benefit valuation
1051			For each option determine whether it will solve problem and to what degree
1052			Assign benefits to each option (% of problem solved)
1053			Agree benefit valuation with key stakeholders
1054	D		Document benefits
1055			Upload to project repository
1056		Level 3 Stage	Option appraisal
1057			For each option group the issues
1058			Identify options to treat each root cause
1059			Identify synergies where applicable
1060			Identify dependencies where applicable
1061			Analyse whether the identified options will create an effective solution
1062			Identify transition states (if any)
1063			Prepare estimation of cost for each option
1064	D		Document costs and benefits (i.e. perform an option appraisal)
1065			Agree option appraisal with key stakeholders

1066			Upload to project repository
1067		Level 3 Stage	Option baskets
1068			Collate options into baskets
1069			Calculate resulting financial impact
1070	D		Draft impact/effort grid
1071	D		Identify quick wins
1072			Create priorities for baskets
1073	D		Create final draft list of work for remediation
1074			Discuss with sponsor and key stakeholders
1075			Update for feedback
1076			Upload to project repository
1077		Level 3 Stage	Review Business Case
1078			Review business case in light of current information
1079			Discuss any changes to the business case with key stakeholders
1080			Obtain additional approvals if necessary
1081	D		Document changes to business case
1082			Obtain signoff
1083			Upload to project repository
1084			Create task list
1085	D		Create final task list for remediation
1086		Level 2 Stage	Detailed Planning
1087		Level 3 Stage	Roadmap
1088	D		Create high level roadmap for remediation stage
1089			Validate with team members and subject matter experts
1090			Validate with business and IT owners
1091			Upload to project repository
1092		Level 3 Stage	Detailed planning
1093			From initial planning and remediation roadmap create draft detailed plan
1094	D		Identify dependencies (external and internal)
1095	D		List document and physical deliverables and agree with stakeholders
1096			Update RAID log
1097			Socialise proposed remediation plan with business users
1098			Agree resources with business users (e.g. subject matter experts)
1099			Agree resources with IT (e.g. environments, databases)
1100			Agree dependencies with providers
1101			Resource level plan
1102	D		Finalise detailed plan for remediation
1103			Discuss with sponsor and key stakeholders
1104			Update for feedback
1105			Upload to project repository
1106		Level 1 Stage	Remediation
1107		Level 2 Stage	Planning
1108			Validate plan still on track
1109			Validate resource availability for stage
1110			Validate scope against pain points, objectives and requirements
1111			Execute project by stage (ongoing tasks)
1112			Plan and update workflow as work items are completed
1113			Allocate and manage resources, both in-project resources and also subject matter experts.
1114			Update plan for new information and as work items are completed
1115			Update product and task lists as required.
1116			Create and deliver weekly reporting
1117			Create and deliver monthly reporting
1118			Create and deliver stage reporting
1119			Manage deliverables
1120			Update risk assessment for new risks and changes to risks and risk profile
1121			Update assumptions
1122			Update dependency log and manage dependencies

1123			Update issue log and report and manage issues
1124			Update daily log as required
1125		Level 2 Stage	Architecture
1126		Level 3 Stage	Architecture-specific final planning
1127			Discuss and define methodology in consultation with key sponsor
1128			Document process issues changed or altered by the changes to architecture
1129	D		Document data issues changed or altered by the changes to architecture
1130	D		Define architectural issues to be addressed
1131	D		Define architecture changes using the remediation plan for architecture
1132	D		Define transition states from remediation plan
1133	D		Refine and complete implementation plan
1134			Agree with sponsor and key stakeholders
1135			Upload to project repository
1136		Level 3 Stage	Start transition #1
1137			Start governance
1138	D		Measure KPI
1139			Update architecture (note in reality all tasks below will interact and whilst can be considered separately the implementation will need to be carefully planned and orchestrated between them)
1140			Update business architecture
1141			Update process architecture
1142			Update data architecture
1143			Update application architecture
1144			Update infrastructure architecture
1145	D		Ratify that changes meet plan including KPI
1146	D		Document lessons learned
1147	D		Update implementation plan for next transition based on lessons learned
1148			Agree with key sponsors and obtain decision to proceed to next transition
1149		Level 3 Stage	Start transition #2
1150			Start governance
1151	D		Measure KPI
1152			Update architecture (note in reality all tasks below will interact and whilst can be considered separately the implementation will need to be carefully planned and orchestrated between them)
1153			Update business architecture
1154			Update process architecture
1155			Update data architecture
1156			Update application architecture
1157			Update infrastructure architecture
1158	D		Ratify that changes meet plan including KPI
1159	D		Document lessons learned
1160	D		Update implementation plan for next transition based on lessons learned
1161			Agree with key sponsors and obtain decision to proceed to next transition
1162		Level 3 Stage	Start final transition
1163			Start governance
1164	D		Measure KPI
1165			Update architecture (note in reality all tasks below will interact and whilst can be considered separately the implementation will need to be carefully planned and orchestrated between them)
1166			Update business architecture
1167			Update process architecture
1168			Update data architecture
1169			Update application architecture
1170			Update infrastructure architecture
1171	D		Ratify that changes meet plan including KPI
1172	D		Document lessons learned and changes to architecture
1173			Agree with key sponsors and obtain signoff

1174			Complete architecture remediation
1175		Level 2 Stage	Existing Data
1176			Planning
1177			Validate plan still on track
1178			Validate resource availability for stage
1179			Validate scope against pain points, objectives and requirements
1180		Level 3 Stage	Data specific final planning
1181			Discuss approach with key sponsors utilising data remediation plan
1182			Define approach for each data set (manual/automatic)
1183			Manual
1184			Planning
1185			Identify teams to perform remediation (set up teams if necessary)
1186			Determine team locations (if a dedicated team look to co-locate)
1187			Identify toolsets required for team
1188			Identify access required for team
1189			Discuss toolsets and access with IT
1190			Agree timescales for implementation of infrastructure
1191			Identify training needs and deliver training
1192			Identify any need for process documentation
1193	D		Create process documentation
1194			Implement and initiate workflow
1195	D		Create final task plan
1196			Agree and signoff with stakeholders
1197			Data Issues Block M1
1198			Identify data (likely on production systems)
1199			Calculate initial data quality KPI
1200	D		Define success criteria
1201			Identify new source of data
1202			Allocate data remediation tasks to teams
1203			Perform remediation
1204			Prove updated data quality KPI
1205			Determine whether success criteria is met
1206			Update workflow
1207			Confirm data quality KPI
1208	D		Document results
1209	D		Obtain signoff of remediated data
1210			Data issues block M2
1211			Data issues block M3
1212			Data issues block M4
1213			Data issues block M5
1214			Automatic
1215			Planning
1216	D		Define and agree approach for environments (i.e. where is data remediated)
1217			Implement and initiate workflow
1218			Test environment access
1219	D		Create working database in relevant environment
1220			Test access to target data
1221			Test access to source data
1222	D		Upload source data sets if required
1223			Test any toolsets
1224	D		Create integration plan
1225			Agree and signoff with stakeholders and IT
1226		Level 3 Stage	Data Issues Block A1
1227			Preparation for remediation
1228			Identify data
1229	D		Extract cut of target data into working database
1230			Validate data cut

The Data Quality Blueprint

1231			Calculate initial data quality KPI
1232	D		Define success criteria
1233	D		Define new source data
1234			Take new source data into database
1235	D		Define means of remediation
1236	D		Document final plan
1237			Update workflow
1238			Proof of Concept
1239			Use subset of data to prove remediation works
1240			Prove updated data quality KPI
1241			Determine whether success criteria is met
1242			Update workflow
1243	D		Document results and update plan for POC learning
1244	D		Obtain written signoff and agreement for scale update
1245			Implementation
1246			Perform remediation
1247			Prove updated data quality KPI
1248			Determine whether success criteria is met
1249			Upload cleansed data into cleansed repository
1250	D		Document results
1251	D		Receive written signoff and agreement for integration
1252			Integration
1253			Prepare for integration/replacement of original data
1254			Integrate new data into original source (if required)
1255			Validate integration
1256	D		Confirm data quality KPI
1257			Obtain signoff of remediated data
1258			Documentation
1259	D		Baseline and upload into project document repository
1260			Complete data issues block A1
1261		Level 3 Stage	Data issues block A2
1262		Level 3 Stage	Data issues block A3
1263		Level 3 Stage	Data issues block A4
1264		Level 3 Stage	Data issues block A5
1265		Level 2 Stage	Process
1266			Planning
1267			Validate plan still on track
1268			Validate resource availability for stage
1269			Validate scope against pain points, objectives and requirements
1270		Level 3 Stage	Process-specific final planning
1271			Discuss issues with key sponsors utilising process remediation plan
1272			Source documentation for processes in scope
1273	D		Define and agree approach for remediation
1274			Implement and initiate workflow
1275			Test any technology required
1276		Level 3 Stage	Process Issues Block 1
1277			Preparation for Remediation
1278	D		Define processes in scope
1279			Collate process maps for processes in scope
1280			Collate issues/pain points for processes in scope
1281	D		Define KPI if not already done
1282			Calculate data quality KPI on existing process
1283	D		Define success criteria from remediation plan
1284	D		Determine future process options
1285			Evaluate and benchmark options
1286	D		Determine final preferred option and agree with process owner
1287			Update workflow

1288	D		Plan implementation of pilot
1289			Obtain signoff and agreement for pilot
1290			Proof of Concept/Simulation/Pilot
1291			Implement pilot
1292			Create updated data quality KPI
1293			Determine if success criteria met
1294			Update workflow
1295	D		Document results
1296	D		Update implementation plan for lessons learned from pilot
1297			Obtain signoff and agreement for full implementation
1298			Implementation
1299			Plan roll-out
1300			Implement roll-out
1301			Update workflow
1302	D		Document results
1303			Receive written signoff
1304			Baseline and upload into project document repository
1305			Complete process issues block 1
1306		Level 3 Stage	Process issues block 2
1307		Level 3 Stage	Process issues block 3
1308		Level 3 Stage	Process issues block 4
1309		Level 3 Stage	Process issues block 5
1310		Level 3 Stage	Set up KPI, Measurement and reporting
1311			Define measurement criteria
1312			Define source data for reporting
1313			Define timing and frequency of reporting
1314			Design dashboards
1315			Agree approach with users and sponsor
1316			Create POC (mock-up, not functional)
1317			Obtain feedback and update
1318			Determine mechanism for obtaining source data
1319			Define data integration approach
1320			Define data quality data model
1321			Define data quality metadata
1322			Design target database (if applicable)
1323			Implement extraction and transformation of data
1324			Implement dashboarding tool
1325			Implement dashboards
1326		Level 2 Stage	Project Close
1327			End Project Report
1328			Data quality assessment
1329			Budget assessment
1330			Timescale assessment
1331			Benefits review plan
1332			Lessons learned
1333			Outstanding issues
1334	D		Create end project report
1335			Agree with sponsor and key stakeholders
1336			Obtain written signoff
1337			Baseline and upload into project document repository
1338		Level 1 Stage	Embed
1339			Execute project by stage (ongoing tasks)
1340			Plan and update workflow as work items are completed
1341			Allocate and manage resources, both in-project resources and also subject matter experts.
1342			Update plan for new information and as work items are completed
1343			Update product and task lists as required.
1344			Create and deliver weekly reporting

1345			Create and deliver monthly reporting
1346			Create and deliver stage reporting
1347			Manage deliverables
1348			Update risk assessment for new risks and changes to risks and risk profile
1349			Update assumptions
1350			Update dependency log and manage dependencies
1351			Update issue log and report and manage issues
1352			Update daily log as required
1353		Level 2 Stage	Governance
1354		Level 3 Stage	Scope and objectives
1355			Identify scope of data governance for this project
1356	D		Define drivers for data governance
1357	D		Define data governance goals
1358			Agree with sponsor
1359			Document and upload to project repository
1360		Level 3 Stage	Initial Plan
1361	D		Draft high level data governance implementation plan
1362			Identify team members and training needs (if any)
1363			Create resource plan and team organisation
1364	D		Draft risks/assumptions & dependencies
1365	D		Create initial cost estimates
1366			Agree with sponsor
1367			Document and upload to project repository
1368		Level 3 Stage	Information Gathering
1369			Identify key stakeholders (if not already done)
1370			Obtain existing governance documentation (if any)
1371			Obtain terms of reference for existing forums
1372			Obtain lists of existing data owners/stewards
1373			Attend forum meeting
1374			Interview key stakeholders
1375	D		Create and circulate governance questionnaire
1376	D		Identify information needs of the organisation (if not already done)
1377			Obtain existing lists of issues/resolutions
1378			Hold information-gathering workshops
1379	D		Create stakeholder assessment (if not already done)
1380	D		Perform change capacity assessment if not already done
1381	D		Perform risk assessment and update RAID
1382		Level 3 Stage	Assess existing governance (if any)
1383			Assess existing governance against best practice
1384	D		Identify pain points from interviews/questionnaires
1385	D		Identify cost impact of pain points
1386	D		Identify areas or poor management or quality
1387	D		Identify gaps in governance or management
1388	D		Draft governance assessment
1389	D		Draft initial business case
1390			Agree with sponsor and key stakeholders
1391			Finalise and upload to project repository
1392		Level 3 Stage	Design future governance structure
1393	D		Draft vision and mission statement for data governance
1394	D		Create governance principles from the data principles in the data strategy
1395			Socialise with sponsor and key stakeholder for agreement
1396	D		Create elevator pitch
1397	D		Draft framework design
1398	D		Draft forum design
1399	D		Draft RACI
1400	D		Draft process design
1401	D		Draft terms of reference

Chapter 58: Sample Project Plan

1402	D		Draft data management and governance taxonomy
1403	D		Map the effects of governance to data quality pain points
1404			Identify any need for data governance toolsets
1405	D		Draft process for identification of owners and stewards
1406			Socialise all of the above with key stakeholders and update for feedback
1407			Upload to project repository
1408		Level 3 Stage	Rollout and Sustainability plan
1409			Update initial implementation plan
1410	D		Create sustainability plan
1411	D		Create communications strategy for governance
1412	D		Create change management plan
1413	D		Update costs and benefits
1414	D		Create rollout and sustainability plan
1415			Agree with sponsor and key stakeholders
1416			Upload to project repository
1417		Level 3 Stage	Roles and responsibilities
1418			Identify data owners and discuss roles with them
1419	D		Write data owner training
1420			Identify data stewards and discuss roles with them
1421	D		Write data steward training
1422			Finalise data steward network
1423		Level 3 Stage	Initial stand up and quick wins
1424	D		Define scope for initial stand-up
1425	D		Identify owners and stewards
1426			Train owners and stewards
1427			Convene initial forum meetings
1428			Present to key stakeholders
1429	D		Create project assessment
1430			Identify and implement quick wins
1431	D		Identify governance metrics
1432	D		Document data governance deliverables
1433	D		Create governance impact analysis
1434	D		Draft process for identification of owners and stewards
1435			Present to sponsor and key stakeholders
1436	D		Design issue reporting forms
1437	D		Start documentation of data lineage
1438	D		Start documentation of data dictionary
1439	D		Start creation of data standards
1440		Level 3 Stage	Implementation
1441			Identify immediate priority tasks and complete
1442	D		Create data governance scorecard
1443			Start project assessment
1444	D		Create data governance processes and procedures
1445			Agree with key stakeholders
1446	D		Start information management assessment
1447			Continue project assessment
1448	D		Include data governance in intranet information
1449			Implement data governance scorecard
1450			Implement data governance toolsets
1451		Level 2 Stage	Training and Awareness
1452		Level 3 Stage	Scope and Objectives
1453	D		Identify scope of training for data quality
1454	D		Define training goals
1455			Agree with sponsor
1456			Document and upload to project repository
1457		Level 3 Stage	Information Gathering
1458			Obtain existing training documentation

The Data Quality Blueprint

1459			Attend induction and refresher training
1460			Interview selection of critical staff (e.g. contact centre agents)
1461			Interview key stakeholders
1462	D		Create and circulate awareness questionnaire
1463			Discuss training approach for data quality with training team
1464			Collate responses
1465		Level 3 Stage	Assess Existing Training
1466			Assess training against data quality
1467			Understand training gaps
1468			Assess messaging
1469	D		Draft training assessment
1470			Agree with training team
1471			Agree with sponsor and key stakeholders
1472			Upload to project repository
1473		Level 3 Stage	Design New Training
1474	D		Create training strategy
1475			Identify training KPI
1476	D		Draft new induction training
1477	D		Draft new refresher training
1478	D		Draft new remediation training
1479	D		Draft awareness training
1480	D		Draft executive orientation
1481	D		Define success criteria
1482			Agree with training team
1483			Agree with sponsor and key stakeholders
1484			Upload to project repository
1485		Level 3 Stage	Pilot and quick wins
1486			Training
1487			Agree initial groups with training department and key stakeholders
1488			Run pilot training
1489	D		Measure success criteria
1490	D		Obtain feedback and update training material
1491			Receive written signoff
1492			Baseline and upload into project document repository
1493			Awareness
1494			Discuss approach to awareness with key stakeholder group
1495			Define awareness KPI
1496	D		Prepare awareness training roadmap
1497			Implement pilot
1498			Measure awareness after pilot
1499	D		Document
1500			Baseline and upload into project document repository
1501		Level 3 Stage	Rollout
1502			Rollout new training schedule
1503	D		Measure KPI and compare with success criteria
1504			Report on overall strategy
1505			Update training as required
1506		Level 2 Stage	Knowledge Management
1507		Level 3 Stage	Scope and Objectives
1508	D		Identify scope of knowledge management
1509	D		Define knowledge management goals
1510			Agree with sponsor
1511			Document and upload to project repository
1512		Level 3 Stage	Information Gathering
1513			Obtain existing knowledge management strategy
1514	D		Define existing knowledge sources
1515			Connect to and investigate existing KM sources

Chapter 58: Sample Project Plan

1516			Interview critical personnel
1517			Assessment of existing Knowledge Management
1518			Analyse existing knowledge management in relationship to data quality
1519	D		Create knowledge management assessment
1520			Discuss with knowledge management team
1521			Discuss with sponsor and key stakeholders
1522			Finalise and upload to project repository
1523		Level 3 Stage	Design future plan for Knowledge Management
1524	D		Define information
1525	D		Assess sources of information
1526	D		Define who needs the information
1527	D		Define how they need to access this information
1528			Define information that needs to be documented
1529	D		Create knowledge management strategy
1530	D		Create knowledge management plan
1531		Level 3 Stage	Pilot and quick wins
1532	D		Define scope of pilot and/or quick wins
1533	D		Define target audience
1534	D		Define knowledge and sources of knowledge
1535	D		Define method of sharing
1536			Implement pilot
1537			Measure success
1538		Level 3 Stage	Rollout
1539			Rollout knowledge management
1540			Measure success
1541	D		Report on overall strategy
1542			Receive written signoff
1543			Baseline and upload into project document repository
1544		Level 2 Stage	Project Close
1545	D		Finalise risk assessment taking account of all project risks. Include risks to BAU that have been identified
1546	D		Finalise dependency log, indicate any remaining dependencies and their stage
1547	D		Finalise assumptions log
1548	D		Finalise issues log including any unresolved issues
1549	D		Document lessons learned and feed into knowledge management framework
1550	D		Document any unfinished work
1551	D		Perform team appraisals and give feedback
1552	D		Finalise workflow and note where items are not closed
1553	D		Document tasks remaining or required to complete work
1554	D		Complete final project costs, and compare with budget.
1555			Create end project report. This covers the performance of the project against objectives, key data quality KPIs before and after remediation, project costs and time measured against budget.
1556			End Project Report
1557			Data quality assessment
1558			Budget assessment
1559			Timescale assessment
1560			Benefits review plan
1561			Lessons learned
1562			Outstanding issues
1563	D		Create end project report
1564			Agree with sponsor and key stakeholders
1565			Obtain written signoff
1566			Baseline and upload into project document repository
1567			Agree ongoing communications with project team and key stakeholders.
1568			Agree ongoing knowledge management with team and key stakeholders.

CHAPTER 59 INDEX

Appendices, 555
Architecture
    Alignment with enterprise architecture, 405
    Application architecture, 87
    Architectural Change Frameworks, 460
    Architectural Design, 393
    Architectural issues, 302
    Assessment, 339
    Business architecture, 87
    Capability and redundancy, 403
    Centralisation, 394
    Choke Points, 343
    Collapse of the clones, 405
    Data architecture, 87
    Data Lakes, 396
    Data Model Changes, 400
    Data Quality Layer, 397
    Detail Investigation and description, 339
    Discovery Deliverable, 346
    Encapsulation, 397
    Engage the existing architecture function, 337
    Example of architectural change, 463
    Federalisation, 395
    Generation of options, 393
    Globalisation, 401
    Governance of architectural change, 462
    High level definition and scope, 338
    Historical Systems/Applications, 340
    How does it affect data quality?, 88
    How to approach architectural change, 456
    MDM, 397
    Multitudinous Feeds, 341
    No reference architecture, 345
    Plan, 338
    Removing blockers, 401
    Reversing the pipes, 396
    Siloed business processes, 342
    Siloed Data, 340
    Simplification, 398
    Supplementation, 395
    Technology architecture, 88
    The half-finished project, 344
    The new acquisition, 343
    The rapidly growing or cool division, 344
    The secret data factory, 342
    The shiny kit, 345
    The tactical solution, 345
    Timing, 403
    Too many applications, 341
    Unification, 404
    Virtualisation, 402
    Where to start, 455
Basic Understanding, 123
Bibliography, 559
Business Case
    Building the Business Case, 187
    Business Options, 199
    Objectives, 196
    Pain points, 193
    Pain points, objectives and scope, 192
    Reasons for undertaking the project, 191
    Risks, assumptions, and dependencies, 201
    Scope, 197
    Timescale, 201
Causes
    No defined direction, 84
    No governance or management, 85
    People, 89
    Poor architecture, 86
    Poor process and resultant poor data, 89
Causes of Poor Data Quality, 81
Communication, 209
    Communication Planning, 223
    Communications strategy, 215
    Further reading, 230
    Get the message at the right level, 214
    Liaison with existing functions, 215
    Principles, 216
    Propaganda - The Elevator Pitch and day in the life., 216
    Stakeholder Analysis, 220
    Sustaining/Keep Happy, 229
    Targeting and Execution, 227
    The regulator, 229
    Timing of the message and repeating the message, 213

Controls
  Interface controls, 586
  Systems and process controls, 586
Corporate Vision & Strategy, 283
Cost Benefit Analysis, 200, 435
  Baskets of options, 440
  Benefit valuation, 467
  Option Appraisal & Assessment, 438
  Option costing, 437
  Reviewing the business case, 441
  Task List, 442
Data Acquisition, 575
Data Classification, 290
Data Creation, 362
Data Governance, 112, 497, 576
  Activities of Data Governance, 501
  Actors, 505
  Data Consumers/users, 594
  Data Creators, 594
  Data governance and management tools, 164
  Data Management, 510, 577
  Data Owners, 586, 583
  Data Quality Board, 592
  Data Quality Governance Framework, 584
  Data Stewards, 593
  Framework, 502
  Further reading, 512
  Implementation of Data Governance, 508
  Information Governance, 289
  Information Governance Board, 592
  Information Governance Framework, roles and responsibilities, 576
  Measurement of Data Governance, 509
  Technology to the rescue, 510
  Terms of Reference, 591
  The role of Information Technology, 507
  Third Party Data, 512
Data Lakes, 149
Data Lineage, 151
Data modelling, 152
Data Profiling, 354
Data Quality Attributes
  Accuracy, 138
  Appropriate, 139
  Completeness, 137
  Consistency, 139
  Ease of use, 141
  Existence, 138
  Presentation, 141
  Timely, 139
  Trust, 141
  Uniformity, 140
  Uniqueness, 141

Validity, 133
Data Quality Blueprint, 115
  Direction, 118
  Discovery, 119
  Embedding, 120
  High Level Methodology, 116
  Initiate, 117
  Project Planning, 117
  Remediation, 120
  Remediation planning, 119
  The Approach to Data Quality, 77
Data Quality Blueprint, 13
Data Quality implementation plan, 310
Data Quality in Projects, 541
Data Quality Leads, 587
Data Quality Management, 308
Data Quality Maturity Model, 91
Data Quality Operational Staff, 587
Data Quality Policy, 300
Data Quality Process Framework, 309, 588
Data Quality Requirements, 301
Data Quality stakeholders, 308
Data Quality Strategy, 303
  Operational aims for Data Quality, 587
  Overview, 304
  Purpose of the Strategy, 580
  Scope, 304, 579
  Strategic Aims for Data Quality, 581
Data Quality Team, 585
Data reconciliation and control, 310
Data Requirements, 293
  How to approach Data Requirements, 300
  What are data requirements, 295
  What should data requirements include?, 297
Data Sourcing and approach, 421
Data Strategy
  Data Acquisition, 288
  Data Strategy Overview, 284
  Information needs of the organisation, 286
  Key components of a data strategy, 285
  Management framework, roles and responsibilities, 289
  Objectives of the strategy, 286
Data Vision, 284
Define
  Data, 127
  Quality, 135
Direction, 277
Discovery, 331
  Architecture & Design, 335
  Artefacts, 562
  Existing Data, 347
  Process & Process Technology, 359

Embedding: Keeping the data good, 491
Existing Data
    Discovery Assessment, 357
    Discovery Deliverable, 357
    Dynamic Data, 355
    Engagement of the existing data function, 349
    High level definition and scope, 350
    Plan, 352
    Streaming Data, 357
Future Data, 551, 587
Impacts, 25
    Business Intelligence, 42
    Cost of Project Failure, 48
    Data Migration, 57
    IT Costs, 52
    Lack of trust of data, 40
    Mailing Overspend, 53
    Missed opportunities, 41
    Missed sales opportunities, 49
    Operational Impacts of Poor Data Quality, 45
    Poor Customer Relations & Customer Retention, 51
    Poor decisions, 94
    Poor relations between IT and the business, 39
    Profitability, 58
    Regulatory Impacts of Poor Data Quality, 61
    Reputational impact, 43
    Risk and capital management, 36
    Strategic Impacts of Poor Data Quality, 33
    Time cost of repeatedly reworking of existing data, 46
    Transactional failures, 56
Information Flow, 143
    Channel Applications, 145
    Channels, 144
    Data Marts, 146
    Data Warehouse, 146
    End User Computing, 148
    ETL, 145
    Extracts and Reports, 147
    Putting it all Together, 149
Information Management Lifecycle, 290, 577
Information needs of the organisation, 574
Information Policy and Practice, 290, 577
Information Protection, 290
Initiation
    Artefacts, 561
    Creating the plan, 185
    How long will the initiation stage take, 184
    Initiation plan, 185
    Obtaining Buy-in, 171
    Resources for initiation, 184
Knowledge Management, 527
    After Project Review, 534
    Bringing it all together, 538
    Create a Data Governance function, 534
    Embed the information within the business areas, 535
    Focus Groups, 533
    Further reading, 538
    How do people try and find knowledge, 532
    Knowledge Bases (SharePoint or intranet sites, 535
    Knowledge Cluster/Centre for Excellence/community of practice, 536
    Knowledge Fair, 537
    Knowledge Map or Community yellow pages, 535
    Knowledge sharing and collaboration, 291
    Project Blogs, 534
    Strategy, 533
    What is the information, 530
    Where is the information, 530
    Who needs the information, 531
Knowledge Strategy, 578
Laying the foundations: Inception, 175
Learning and Development, 158
Maturity
    Analysis, 96
    Aware, 93
    Engaged, 93
    Ideal/Optimising, 95
    Managed, 94
    Self-Defeating, 92
MDM, 111
Myths, 105
    Any data is better than no data, 108
    IT will solve it, it's their data!, 107
    Technology to the rescue, 106
    The data quality department, 110
    The Internal Audit Solution, 106
Operational aims for data quality, 307
Overview, 1
Principles, 99, 306
    Data Quality Principles, 580
    Data Strategy, 287, 574
    Do as little work as possible, 202
    Do it once, do it well, 100
    Embed data quality in the organisation, 102
    People are the key, 101
    The business is in the driving seat, 99
    Treat data as an asset, 101
    We're all in this together, 100
Process
    Common Problems, 369
    Considerations for process change, 483
    Data Create/Update, 407
    Data Focused Assessment, 367
    Data read/use, 364, 408

- Data transform (update/delete), 363
- Data Transformation, 408
- Data Transport, 363, 407
- Design, 406
- Engagement of existing process functions, 362
- Implementation, 487
- Plan, 364
- Process Discovery - Deliverable, 369
- Process Documentation, 365
- Process Focused Assessment, 366
- Testing, 488
- Workflow, 489

Process Control, 408
- Corrective, 411
- Detective, 410
- Non-technical preventative controls, 409
- Preventative, 409
- Technical Preventative Controls, 410

Project End, 271
- Approach, 273
- End project assessment, 275
- Problems to be faced, 274
- Transitioning the project team, 273

Project Planning, 233
- Assumptions and Constraints, 241
- Business case, 240
- Change capacity assessment, 241
- Communications, 546
- Control & Execution, 263
- Data Quality as a modular project, 237
- Data Quality processes, 545
- Deliverables, 243
- Dependencies, 242
- Dependencies & Deliverables, 448
- Detailed Planning, 443, 447
- Further reading, 268
- Issues, 242
- Key roles, 253
- Level 1 Plan, 246, 596
- Level 2 Plan, 247, 579
- Level 3 and below project tasks, 598
- Mapping project stages to IT architecture, 248
- Objectives and success, 239
- Organisation, 255
- Planning the Initiation Stage, 181
- Planning the rest of the project, 238
- Project Data Forums, 544
- Project Initiation Document (PID), 248
- Project Management, 264
- Project Plan, 246, 595
- Questions that the plan needs to answer, 445
- Resource profile of the project, 261
- Responsibility and Resourcing, 448

- Risk Assessment, 240
- Roadmap, 445
- Task List, 446
- Understand your data, 546
- Understand your sources, 545
- Use of embedded data governance and project governance, 543
- Work breakdown structure, 243
- Workflow, 267

Project Planning, 231

Proof of Concept, 208, 203
- After the Proof of Concept, 206
- Approach to a Proof of Concept, 207
- Business pound value based approach, 206
- Challenges of Proof of Concept, 225
- Data approach, 207
- Process-based approach, 206

Quality Measurement, 313
- Customer complaints, 321
- How to get the metrics, 318
- Introduction of Metrics, 314
- Types of Metrics, 306

Quality Reporting, 323

Question Bank, 565
- Audit and Audit reports, 568
- Basic Questions, 565
- Business Intelligence, 572
- Clean and Correct Data Quality Defects, 596
- Continuously Measure and Monitor Data Quality, 567
- Culture and Strategy, 566
- Data Architecture, 571
- Data Quality Challenges, 571
- Define
  - Data Quality Business Rules, 568
  - Data Quality Metrics, 568
  - Data Quality Requirements, 568
  - Responsibility and Governance, 566
- Design and Implement Operational DQM Procedures, 570
- Manage Data Quality Issues, 569
- Monitor Operational DQM Procedures and performance, 570
- Process Design, 570
- Profile, Analyse and Assess Data Quality, 570
- Projects, 571
- Quality and management tools, 571
- Set and Evaluate Data Quality Service levels, 569
- Test and Validate Data Quality Requirements, 569

Regulation
- How can poor data quality impede compliance?, 65
- How the regulator is enforcing its wishes, 73
- ISO 8000, 75
- What does the regulator require?, 63

Remediation, 449
    Architecture & Design, 453
    Best Source Analysis, 432
    Data, 465
    Manual remediation (BAU), 468
    Manual Remediation (dedicated back office), 469
    Process and Process Technology, 479
    Remediation by or with IT (Bulk update), 470
    Remediation by use of specialist remediation toolsets, 475
    Remediation design for Architecture and Process, 391
    Replace or Remediate: Replace, 423
    Replace or Remediate: Remediate, 424
    Sources of Good Data, 425
    Types of remediation, 468
    Where do we stop?, 470
    Workflow, 476
Remediation Planning, 371
    Artefacts, 563
Remediation Tools
    Combo tools, 163
    Integrated Stacks, 165
    Profiling and/or remediation with reference data, 159
    Profiling Tools, 157
    Profiling with business rules, 158
    Remediation with business rules, 161
    Technology Tools for Data Quality, 155
    The technological marketplace, 156
    Workflow toolsets, 162
Reporting
    Reporting on specific business-relevant data, 325
    Reporting the data quality in existing reports (data reliability reports), 326
    Reporting the effect of poor data, 326
    Reporting tools, 327
    Technical data quality reports, 325
    Timing of reports, 326
    Types of Dashboards, 327
    What should reporting include, 324
    When should dashboards be created, 328
Resourcing
    Direction, 257
    Discovery, 258
    Embedding, 261
    Initiation, 256
    Laying the foundations, 265
    Remediation, 260
    Remediation Planning, 259
Resourcing, 251
Risk Appetite, 588
Root Cause Analysis, 379
    Asking Why, 383
    Assign degree of responsibility to root causes, 387
    Assigning cost to root causes, 388
    Collation of results, 385
    Fishbone analysis, 384
    Identification of root causes, 383
    Link root causes across the organisation, 386
Sample Data Quality Strategy, 579
Sample Data Strategy, 573
Strategic Aims for Data Quality, 387
Third Party Data, 588
Training, 515
    Define training success factors, 525
    Further Reading, 525
    How to train, 519
    Specific Techniques, 521
    When to train, 523
    Who to train, 517
Visual map, 13
Where to Remediate, 413
    After the presentation layer, 418
    At source, 415
    In Data Warehouse & Data marts, 417
    In the lake (if applicable), 417
    In the presentation & reporting layer, 418
    Where is best and why, 419
    Within ETL, 415
Why Data Quality Matters, 306, 581
    Why care about Data Quality, 27
    Why is nothing done, 28
Why did data quality become such a major issue?, 6
Why is this book required?, 5
Wrap-Up, 519

Lightning Source UK Ltd.
Milton Keynes UK
UKOW07n1352091217
314175UK00002B/6/P